THE HARVARD ORIENTAL SERIES

VOLUME THIRTY-TWO

HARVARD ORIENTAL SERIES

EDITED

WITH THE COÖPERATION OF VARIOUS SCHOLARS

BY

CHARLES ROCKWELL LANMAN

Professor at Harvard University; Honorary Fellow of the Asiatic Society of Bengal, of France, of England, and of Germany; Corresponding Member of the Society of Sciences at Göttingen, the Russian Academy of Sciences, and the Académie des Inscriptions et Belles-Lettres of the Institute of France

Volume Thirty-two

(*AUTHORISED REPRINT*)

THE RELIGION AND PHILOSOPHY OF THE VEDA AND UPANISHADS

BY

ARTHUR BERRIEDALE KEITH

D.C.L., D.LITT.

Of the Inner Temple, Barrister-at-Law, and of the Scottish Bar; Regius Professor of Sanskrit and Comparative Philology at the University of Edinburgh; formerly of the Colonial Office

The second half, Chapters 20–29
Page 313 to page 683

MOTILAL BANARSIDASS PUBLISHERS
PRIVATE LIMITED
DELHI

First Edition : 1925
Reprinted : 1970, 1976, 1989

ISBN: 81-208-0646-8

Also available at :

MOTILAL BANARSIDASS
Bungalow Road, Jawahar Nagar, Delhi 110007
Chowk, Varanasi 221 001
Ashok Rajpath, Patna 800 004
24 Race Course Road, Bangalore 560 001
120 Royapettah High Road, Mylapore, Madras 600 004

By arrangement with Harvard University Press

PRINTED IN INDIA
BY JAINENDRA PRAKASH JAIN AT SHRI JAINENDRA PRESS, A-45 NARAINA INDUSTRIAL AREA, PHASE I, NEW DELHI 110 028 AND PUBLISHED BY NARENDRA PRAKASH JAIN FOR MOTILAL BANARSIDASS PUBLISHERS PVT. LTD., BUNGALOW ROAD, JAWAHAR NAGAR, DELHI 110 007

CONTENTS OF VOLUME 32

CONTENTS OF PART IV.—THE SPIRITS OF THE DEAD

CONTENTS OF PART V.—THE PHILOSOPHY OF THE VEDA

APPENDIX

CHAPTER 20

THE SACRIFICES OF THE ÇRAUTA RITUAL

§ 1. *General Characteristics*

THE rites of the Çrauta ritual have much essentially in common, in addition to the necessity of the use of the three or one at least of the three fires in place of the domestic fire. They necessitate the presence of priests numbering from one up to sixteen, or with the Kauṣītakins seventeen,[1] to whom should be added the actual performers of some of the minor actions in the more complicated forms of the ritual, whose number is not defined, and whose menial functions rendered them of no consequence in the eyes of the priests of the higher rank. It is obvious, for instance, that in the slaughtering of the victims there must often have been need for other aid than that of the Adhvaryu and his assistants proper, and the Çamitṛs are occasionally referred to as charged with the actual slaying : more often a general term like servant is used to apply to such helpers.

As a result of the constant development of the ritual, the festivals of the Çrauta type are full of details which are of no consequence with regard to the meaning of the sacrifice : practically in no case is an important rite addressed to one god only : the effort on the contrary was clearly to find as much room as possible for as many gods as possible. We find, too, many variations among the details of the rites, of which but a few can be reduced to any simple principle. Thus we know that some families like the Jamadagnis and the Bhṛgus made five divisions or layers of the offerings, while other families[2] made but four, whence the former are called *pañcāvattins*, and the latter *caturavattins*. Another distinction which has more religious value is the differences between families based on the distinction of the use of Tanūnapāt or Narāçaṅsa, as one of the deities invoked at the Āprī litanies of the animal sacrifice,[3] while the difference of dressing the hair is also of interest from the point of view of social usages,[4] having many parallels in other lands.

In the Sūtras the principle is laid down that the sacrifices are to be distinguished as Prakṛtis and Vikṛtis, the former being the base on which the later are built up ; thus the new- and full-moon sacrifices are the model for other sacrifices of the type known as Iṣṭi, and for the animal sacrifice, in its form as an offering to Agni and Soma, on which further animal offerings are based. The Agniṣṭoma again is the fundamental form of the Soma sacrifice :

[1] See Keith, *Rig-Veda Brāhmaṇas*, pp. 48, 498, n. 1.

[2] KÇS. i. 9. 3 ; Eggeling, SBE. xii. 192.

[3] Weber, *Ind. Stud.* x. 89 ff.

[4] Zimmer, *Altind. Leben*, p. 264 ; Hillebrandt, *Rituallitteratur*, pp. 7, 8.

on it are based other performances up to the Dvādaçāha inclusive, while on the latter are based the Sattras. Each sacrifice is divided into Pradhānas, the characteristics which mark it out as a special offering, and Añgas, the auxiliary parts which are common to many sacrifices, and which build the framework, Tantra, which serves to maintain the sacrifice. The distinction between the Yajatayas and the Juhotayas, the latter managed by the Adhvaryu alone and accompanied by the mere utterance of the word Svāhā, 'hail',[1] has already been noted.

In the Soma offering there is added the complications of the recitation of the Sāmans. The rule is that the Sāman is a melody, which is performed on a verse of the Rigveda, and the verses can be sung to different melodies, for which purpose they have to be eked out by the addition of letters, or even of whole syllables, which have themselves no meaning, and of which as many as fifteen are enumerated.[2] The nature of the tunes must have been varied in the extreme, to judge from the many names recorded, of which the Bṛhat and the Rathantara are the most notorious, but the nature of Indian music is an unsolved problem, and perhaps insoluble.[3] Seven notes are mentioned, but their significance is much disputed. Each Sāman is divided into parts, the most usual being that into Prastāva, introduced by the word *hum* (*huñkāra*), sung by the Prastotṛ, the Udgītha, introduced by *om*, sung by the Udgātṛ, the Pratihāra, introduced by *hum*, sung by the Pratihartṛ, and the Nidhana, or finale, sung by all together. In some cases the Pratihāra is divided into two parts, the latter, the Upadrava, being sung by the Udgātṛ, or the Hiñkāra is made into a separate element. Moreover there are Upagātṛs, three in number, who accompany the song with the word *ho*. The contempt which through the Indian literature is more or less clearly shown for Sāman singers is justified by the extraordinary stupidity of the position assigned to them.

The singing of more than one verse on a tune is a Stotra, which usually is made up of a triplet or a Pragātha, a double verse, which is made into three for recitation purposes. From the Stotras are built up the Stomas, or forms of chanting Stotras. Of these there are many varieties. The simplest in some ways is the Trivṛt, which is the first used in the Agniṣṭoma: it consists of nine verses, which can be variously arranged in sets of three, either as *adg*, *beh*, *cfi*, which is the Udyatī form, or *abc*, *def*, *ghi*, the Parivartinī, and *abc*, *efd*, *igh*, the Kulāyinī. On the other hand the other Stomas, the Pañcadaça, Saptadaça, Ekaviñça, which with the Trivṛt are the main Stomas of the Agniṣṭoma, and others such as the Pañcaviñça, Triṇava, Trayastriñça, Caturviñça, Catuçcatvāriñça, and Aṣṭācatvāriñça, are all based on three verses or a Pragātha made into three. The numbers of the Stomas are derived from the number of verses which are used: thus the Pañcadaça in one form is made up of *aaabc*, *abbbc*,

[1] Hillebrandt, *Rituallitteratur*, p. 100.

[2] Cf. Felber, *Die indische Musik der vedischen und der klassischen Zeit* (1912); A. H. Fox Strangways, *The Music of Hindostan* (1914); Caland and Henry, *L'Agniṣṭoma*, pp. 461–7; Oldenberg, GN. 1915, pp. 522 ff. For the metre see H. Weller, ZII. i. 115–84.

and *abccc*, the Hiṅkāra being said before each set of three similar verses. Further complications will be noted later on.

Before the Stotras can be performed the singers must obtain the approval of the Brahman and the Maitrāvaruṇa, who give it with the words *oṁ stuta*, the Brahman saying also one of the Stomabhāgas, certain formulae provided for the purpose. The Stotra is followed by a Çastra, a recitation of the Hotṛ or his fellows, the signal for it being given by the performer of the Stotra saying *eṣā*, 'this is the last verse.' The Hotṛ asks the Adhvaryu if he is to recite, the latter agrees. But at the morning litany in front of this dialogue are placed certain syllables, and a muttered prayer to Mātariçvan and the Kavis. This is followed by the silent praise, Tūṣṇīṁjapa, and by the Puroruc, 'that which shines before', but in the midday and evening Çastras the place of the Puroruc is taken by Nivids, which are inserted in the hymns of the Çastra. The Nivids are introduced by the procedure of asking the Adhvaryu's authority to recite, but this formality is omitted in the case of the Puroruc at the first Çastra in the morning: at the second Çastra, on the other hand, we find seven Purorucs preceded by the dialogue of Hotṛ and Adhvaryu, and followed by a triplet. In the case of the midday Çastras there are further complications. In the first Çastra of the midday and the evening pressings there are found sets of three verses called Pratipad and Anucara, which are preceded by the usual dialogue; then comes in the case of the midday Çastra, the Māruta Çastra, a Pragātha addressed to Indra, which is recited as three verses, the last part of each verse being repeated with the first of the next: thus the Pragātha, which consists of a Bṛhati[1] and Satobṛhatī[2] or Kakubh[3] and Satobṛhatī, is made into a Bṛhatī and two Kakubh verses. This is followed by a Pragātha for Bṛhaspati, Dhāyyās, supplementary verses, a Pragātha for the Maruts, the hymn in which the Nivid is inserted, the Ukthavīrya formula, and then as in the other Çastras come the offering verse and the libation. In the case of the second Çastra of the midday and evening pressings, and all the Çastras of the assistants of the Hotṛ, the Hotrakas, the same sort of beginning is prescribed, but the verses are called Stotriya and Anurūpa, names which refer to the fact that they follow the strophe and antistrophe of the corresponding Stotra of the Sāman singers, which obey the rule that the Anurūpa, 'corresponding verse', should follow the Stotriya in metre, number of syllables, and deity. As usual the rule is obeyed that the two verses of the Stotriya are made into three in recitation, and so with the Anurūpa. Then in the second Çastra of the midday pressing, the Niṣkevalya, come Dhāyyās, a Sāmapragātha, the hymn with the Nivid, the Ukthavīrya and the offering verse with the libation.

In the first Çastra of the evening pressing, the Vaiçvadeva, the Pratipad and Anucara are followed by a hymn with a Nivid, then a verse for Vāyu, then a hymn with a Nivid to sky and earth, a hymn with a Nivid for the

[1] A verse of 4 lines (8+8+12+8 syllables).
[2] 12+8+12+8 syllables.
[3] 8+12+8 syllables.

Ṛbhus, three isolated verses, and a hymn with a Nivid to the All-gods. The second, the Āgnimāruta, is composed of a hymn with a Nivid to Vaiçvānara, a Dhāyyā, a hymn with a Nivid to the Maruts, the Stotriya and Anurūpa made from Pragāthas, a hymn with a Nivid to Jātavedas, and a mass of miscellaneous stanzas addressed to the waters, &c. The other Çastras are less important: the specimens given indicate the confusion and elaboration of ideas.

In other cases there takes place an elaborate process of intermingling both verses and parts of verses of different strophes with one another. This is the rule with the recitation of the Vālakhilya hymns, which may be treated in two different but both complicated ways,[1] with the Mahānāmnī verses,[2] with the verse for the Āpyāyana or swelling out of the dry Soma stems, and so forth. It is only worth noting that as early as the Rigveda these puerilities seem to have been in vogue.

The most important division of the sacrifices is that between the Soma offerings and the offerings which are sometimes classed as Haviryajñas, and which differ essentially from the Soma sacrifice as they do not employ the Sāman singers. With the latter may be classed the animal sacrifice, but it also forms an integral and important part of the Soma offering.

§ 2. *The Establishment and Re-establishment of the Fires*

The ritual texts lay down various periods as appropriate for the setting up of the sacred fires,[3] the spring is the season for a Brahman, the summer for a Kṣatriya, the rainy season for a Rathakāra, and the autumn for a Vaiçya, or the cool season is suited for all castes. They also suggest that the proper time is the new moon, especially in conjunction with certain asterisms, but the full moon is also permissible. The essential part of the rite which takes two days is the setting up of the fires: on the first day are set up two sheds, the one for the Gārhapatya, the other for the Āhavanīya fire: the actual altar of the first is round, that of the second square: the Dakṣiṇa fire is south of the Gārhapatya and is shaped like a half moon. The fire is obtained for the Gārhapatya either by friction, or by being borrowed from the house of a wealthy man or distinguished sacrificer. The night of the first day is spent by the sacrificer and his wife in wakefulness to the noise of lutes and flutes. Early in the morning the new fire for the hearths is produced by friction, and a horse is brought to watch and further the process by its presence, doubtless as a symbol of the fire or the sun. Moreover, while the fire is being produced by friction from the wood,[4] Sāmans may be sung. As soon as the fire appears the sacrificer breathes upon it and inhales it. It is placed on the Gārhapatya and

[1] Cf. Oldenberg, *Prolegomena*, pp. 212 ff., 494 ff., 514 ff.; GGA. 1907, pp. 230 ff.; Scheftelowitz, *Die Apokryphen des Ṛgveda*, pp. 36 ff., 89 ff.

[2] Cf. Oldenberg, GN. 1915, p. 377.

[3] ApÇS. v. 1 ff.; BÇS. ii; MÇS. i. 5; 6. 5; KÇS. iv. 7–10; AÇS. ii. 1. 9 ff.; ÇÇS. ii. 1; LÇS. iv. 9. 10 ff.; 12. 6 ff.

[4] Roth, ZDMG. xliii. 590–5; Schwab, *Altind. Thieropfer*, pp. 77 ff.

wood placed upon the fire: it is addressed with words which recall the ancestors of the offerer: thus an Āñgirasa refers to Añgiras, a Bhārgava to the Bhṛgus, a Rājanya to Indra, a Kṣatriya to Varuṇa, a Vaiçya to Manu Grāmaṇī, the typical village headman, and a Rathakṛt to the Ṛbhus, the famous chariot makers among the gods. At the same time Sāmans may be sung, not by the Sāman singers, but, as in the Vājapeya and the Sautrāmaṇī rites, by the Brahman or alternatively by the Adhvaryu himself. Then a brand is taken from the Gārhapatya and borne to the Āhavanīya, the horse preceding it, and the sacrificer following it so that the smoke reaches him: it is carried at first knee high, then navel high, and then the height of the face. The Dakṣiṇa fire is then in one version lighted in the same way; according to others it precedes the setting up of the Āhavanīya: it may also be made from the fire which on the preceding day was placed on the Gārhapatya for cooking the porridge for the priest: at any rate it afterwards can be used for cooking any offerings save meat offerings.

After the Āhavanīya is set up follows, in the case of a Kṣatriya only it seems, the setting up of a Sabhya fire, one doubtless in the Sabhā, the meeting hall of the community. The ceremony for that is accompanied by the dicing for a cow as a prize by the priests perhaps or by Kṣatriyas: the game is as usual unintelligible: it seems to have amounted to a test of the power to produce even numbers.[1] In the normal case this ceremony is not performed, and the establishment of the fires ends with a full offering of butter to Agni, after which the Agnihotra can be duly performed with the fires. Twelve days afterwards, the fires being carefully maintained in the interval, may be performed the Tanūhavis offerings which are offerings to Agni in three forms, Pavamāna, Pavāka, and Çuci. As soon as the performance of the establishment is over, the sacrificer is bound to observe chastity for 3 to 12 days, maintain the fire, offer the Agnihotra, and sleep on the ground near the fire. After that he must for all his days avoid untruth, place no bad wood on the fire, eat nothing cooked by a covered fire, drink no water from a ship, and so on. If he is prosperous he must keep up the fires all his life.

The ceremony of re-establishment [2] is prescribed in cases where the fires bring the sacrificer no luck. The old fires are allowed to go out, and, after a break of three days to a year, new fires are established in much the same way as before, but the fire is nourished when produced with Kuça grass, not with wood. In the fore- and after-offerings which are part of the rite the use of different forms, Vibhakti, of the word Agni is expressly enjoined, doubtless to secure the special attention of the god to the new fires. The fees for the priest contain references to the character of the rite; so for instance a mended garment and repaired chariot are given. Traces of a periodic re-establishment of outworn fires cannot be proved: the mere fact that the re-establishment,

[1] Macdonell and Keith, *Vedic Index*, i. 2 ff.; Lüders, *Das Würfelspiel im alten Indien* (1907).

[2] ApÇS. v. 26; BÇS. iii. 1–3; KÇS. iv. 11; AÇS. ii. 8. 6 ff.; ÇÇS. ii. 5. 1; Vait. viii. 3.

if necessary, is placed at the period of the rains as well as at other times is inadequate evidence on which to found any theory.[1]

§ 3. *The Fire-God Oblation or Agnihotra*

It is the duty of the man who has established his fires, as of the man who has no fires, to offer daily, morning and evening, the Agnihotra:[2] the precise time of offering, whether just before or just after the rising of the sun in the morning, and whether after sunset or after the appearance of the first star in the evening, is a subject of much discussion in the Brāhmaṇas and Sūtras. If the fires were kept perpetually alight, then they required only to be brightened up for each occasion: if not, then the fire must be taken from the Gārhapatya, either only every evening, it being used also for the morning, or each time: the Dakṣiṇa might be kept perpetually alight, or taken out daily, or only on the new- and full-moon days, on which according to some authorities the sacrificer must himself perform the ritual. The main offering was milk, milked by an Aryan into a pail made by an Aryan: the milk was heated and mixed with water on the Gārhapatya, and offered in the Āhavanīya and Gārhapatya. At the end the sacrificer eats and offers four water libations to the gods, the Fathers, the seven seers, and Agni on the earth, or to other deities also. The Dakṣiṇa fire received no special honour.

With the Agnihotra might be performed the ceremony of homage to the fires, Agnyupasthāna, usually carried out at the night service only. The Āhavanīya is honoured first, then the cow from which the milk was taken, then the Gārhapatya, and then the cow, or its calf might be substituted for the cow. At the end the sacrificer names the name of his dear son who is to succeed him in the duty. The same close connexion of the offering and the home is seen in the fact that, on going on a journey, the householder takes leave of the fires, and on return approaches them with wood and words of welcome. If he goes away from the old house for good, he offers a libation to Vāstoṣpati, the lord of the abode, while his cart has one horse, the right-hand one, spanned, and the other not yoked. The obligation to offer the Agnihotra ends only when one becomes a wandering mendicant.

There can be little doubt that even as early as the Rigveda there was present the idea that the Agnihotra, with its brightening up of the fires, was a spell to aid the rising of the sun, a view which was doubtless the ground of the opinion of those who pressed for the performance of the ceremony before sunrise.[3]

[1] Hillebrandt, *Ved. Myth.* ii. 77 ff.

[2] ApÇS. vi; BÇS. iii. 4–9; MÇS. i. 6; KÇS. iv. 12–15; AÇS. ii. 2–5; ÇÇS. iii. 7–12; Vait. vii.

[3] Weber, *Ind. Stud.* x. 329. Cf. the worship of Hestia in Greece and Vesta in Rome, and the holy fire of the Lithuanian tradition, as well as the still greater development of the fire cult in Iran. The view of Feist (*Kultur der Indogermanen*, p. 345) that the fire worship takes its origin in respect to the spirits of the dead who congregate at the hearth is untenable; cf. Wissowa, *Archiv f. Religionswissenschaft*, vii. 45 ff. For Germany, see Caesar, *B. G.* i. 50; Helm, *Altgerm. Rel.* i. 258. See also below, Appendix E.

But we must not decide from this that the origin of the rite was a mere spell: it is clearly the tendance of the god in the house, the family fire in a developed form in the Çrauta, in a simple form in the domestic ritual.

§ 4. *The New-moon and Full-moon Sacrifices*

These sacrifices [1] are of special value as they form the model for all sacrifices of the type called Iṣṭi, which include an enormous number of offerings for special ends; in all these cases the sacrifice is assumed to be performed precisely as in the new- and full-moon offerings, but with the distinction that some special rite is inserted in the place of the essential features of these offerings, which are at the full-moon offering a cake for Agni and Soma, and at the new-moon offering a cake for Agni and Indra. Moreover, at the latter offering some authorities allowed a milk mess made of sweet and sour milk for Indra or Mahendra, while others restricted this offering to one who offered the Soma sacrifice. The new and full moon themselves received no offerings, except in the view of certain authorities who prescribed offerings to the Parvans: the times served only to fix the dates of the offerings, and there was, it is clear, difficulty in deciding exactly when the offerings should be made. Two days were required at new moon, but one might suffice at the full moon. On the first day the ceremonies were in the main preparatory, the making ready of the fires, and the taking of a vow by the sacrificer, which involved abstinence from meat, sleeping on the ground, the cutting of hair and beard, and so on. If the milk mess were to be offered on this day, a twig of Palāça or Çamī wood was cut to drive away the calves from the cows, for the milking of the latter, a rite which is paralleled in western Europe.[2] The ceremonies of the second day consisted in the preparation of the rice, its pounding and husking, the cooking of the cakes, the preparation of the altar, the girding of the wife of the sacrificer, the looking at a pot of butter, the covering of the altar with the grass, and the setting up of the partitioning sticks which were intended to keep off evil spirits. At the end of these preliminaries the real sacrifice begins; first come fifteen Sāmidhenī verses accompanying the laying on of kindling wood. The verses are joined into a single whole by the device of pausing after the first half verse of each. Then come two libations of the butter, doubtless in part at least necessary to make the fire burn brightly; between them comes the Pravara, the enumeration of the seers who were claimed as ancestors by the sacrificer—or if he were not a Brahman by his Purohita—and the invitation of the gods, whom Agni is invoked to bring to the offering in the order in which they were to be honoured. After the second of these Āghāras comes the formal choosing of the Hotṛ by the Adhvaryu on the authority of

[1] ApÇS. i–iii; BÇS. i; MÇS. i. 1–3; KÇS. ii–iv. 5; AÇS. i. 1, 4–13; ÇÇS. i. 4–15; Vait. i–iv; Hillebrandt, *Neu- und Vollmondsopfer* (Jena, 1880); Weber, *Ind. Stud.* x. 329 ff. Even magic sacrifices are normally based on this principle; see below, Chap. 22, § 8. Cf. Keith, *Taittirīya Saṁhitā*, i. p. cv.

[2] Kuhn, *Herabkunft des Feuers*², p. 159.

the Āgnīdhra, in which the ancestors of the sacrificer are again named. The Hotṛ then touches the Adhvaryu and Āgnīdhra, in order doubtless to establish a community between them. Then come the fore-offerings of butter to the kindling sticks, the god Tānūnapāt or Narāçaṅsa, the sacrificial food (*iḍā*), the gods who have been invited to the offering and are now honoured. Then come the Ājya offerings of butter for Agni and Soma, which at the new moon must be accompanied by verses containing the word *vṛdh*, 'grow', and at the full moon by verses referring to the slaying of Vṛtra. There follows a cake for Agni, a butter offering made in a low tone for Agni and Soma, and then the offering, to Agni and Soma at the full moon, to Agni and Indra, with or without a milk mess for Indra, at the new moon. The close of the offering is marked by an offering to Agni Sviṣṭakṛt, 'the maker of the sacrifice correct', in which all the gods are invoked. Then comes the tasting of the offering by the priest, the Brahman has a special portion, the Prāçitra, the Āgnīdhra another, the Ṣaḍavatta, and all the priests invoke the Iḍā, which is taken from all the offerings, and, while doing so, they touch the sacrificer. Then the cakes are given to them, and thereafter each has a part of the Iḍā. The Fathers are invoked to take part, and the fees are given, in this case the Anvāhārya mess cooked in the Dakṣiṇa fire, perhaps merely because of the name. The distribution of the fees is followed by the Anuyājas, to the strew, Narāçaṅsa, and Agni Sviṣṭakṛt, and the Sūktavāka, which concludes with an invocation of prosperity for the sacrificer and a prayer; at the end of this prayer the Prastara, or bundle of grass which is supposed to represent the sacrificer, is put in the fire. Then comes the Çaṁyuvāka, an invocation of prosperity, accompanied by the burning of the enclosing sticks. The remains are offered to the All-gods, then follow four Patnīsaṁyājas, offerings to the gods with the wives of the gods, to Soma, Tvaṣṭṛ, the wives of the gods, and Agni Gṛhapati: the third is offered under a covering while the wife of the sacrificer touches the Adhvaryu: the offerings are of butter, and made in the Gārhapatya fire. Then come minor rites to accompany the burning of the strew, and to make good defects, the Rakṣases are given the fragments which have been produced in the husking of the rice, the wife's girdle is loosened and laid down, the sacrificer in imitation of and assimilation to Viṣṇu strides three steps from the south hip of the altar ground, which is made to be like the shape of a woman, to the east, pays reverence to the Āhavanīya and Gārhapatya, and then lays aside his vow.

The rite is to be performed all one's life, or for thirty years, or for fifteen only, in which case the two offerings are to be conjoined: in the Dākṣāyaṇa form[1] it is celebrated every day for a year only, both forms being used. In the case of the first offering of the new- and full-moon sacrifice, the Anvāram-

[1] ÇB. ii. 4. 4. 1–6, where is given the history of the transmission of the rite from Prajāpati through Pratīdarça Çvaikna, Suplan Sārñjaya, Devabhāga Çrautarṣa, and Dakṣa Pārvati to the royal Dākṣāyaṇa line. Similarly a list of the handers down of the drink for the king at the royal consecration is given in AB. vii. 34.

bhaṇīyā Iṣṭi is offered, which consists of a cake on eleven potsherds for Viṣṇu, a pap for Sarasvatī, and a cake on twelve potsherds for Sarasvant. It is offered as an independent rite on the first full-moon day after the Agnyādhāna and Agnihotra. Each new- and full-moon sacrifice can be followed by an offering to Aditi and to Indra Vaimṛdha, and the sacrifice can be carried out with Soma if desired and so also the other Haviryajñas.[1]

The position of Agni and Soma in the ritual is peculiar in view of the rarity of the conjunction of these gods in the Rigveda, and it is a legitimate and probable conjecture of Oldenberg's [2] that the place they obtained was only gradually won by them, in consequence in some degree at least of the tendency to see the moon in Soma.

§ 5. *The Four-month or Seasonal Sacrifices*

The three four-month offerings [3] are connected intimately with the seasons of the year, the Vaiçvadeva being offered in spring, the Varuṇapraghāsas in the rains, and the Sākamedhas in the autumn, at the beginning of each season. The connexion with the seasons is shown by the formulae, the names of the months which are connected with certain libations, and the formal cutting of the hair which is connected with certain of the rites. The man who first performs them must begin with an Iṣṭi to Agni Vaiçvānara and Parjanya or an Anvārambhaṇīyā Iṣṭi. In each case the sacrifice is introduced by five libations to Agni, Soma, Savitṛ, Sarasvatī, and Pūṣan. In the first follow offerings to the Maruts, to the All-gods, and to heaven and earth, the first and last of cakes, the second of a milk mess. The season is indicated by the use of a tree with budding branches for the wood for the fire, while the strew is made from plants which are shooting.

The second offering, the Varuṇapraghāsas, is more important. One point in it is the preparation of two animals, a ram and sheep, from barley, which the sacrificer and his wife cover with wool and equip with the marks of sex made prominent; the Adharyu makes the one, the Pratiprasthātṛ the other: there are two Vedis, and the south one is assigned to the latter priest, who there performs a mimicry of the action of the Adhvaryu. There are offerings to Indra and Agni, to Varuṇa, to the Maruts and to Ka: the ram and the ewe are offered in the milk messes presented to Varuṇa and the Maruts respectively, the remainder being eaten. A further important point is the ceremony already referred to,[4] by which the wife of the sacrificer is called upon to admit what lovers she has and to offer in the Dakṣiṇa fire the plates of Karambha, 'porridge', which number one more than the members of the family. The two figures Hubert and Mauss (*Année sociol.* ii. 111) adopt the view that they represent the spirit of barley as fertilizing and fertilized, which is eaten in the rite, and that the ram is 'Varuṇa visible', but this is quite impossible, or a mere mistranslation of ÇB. ii. 5. 2. 16.

[1] ÇÇS. xiv. 2 ff.; LÇS. iv. 9 ff.

[2] *Rel. des Veda*[2], p. 439, n. 2.

[3] ApÇS. viii; BÇS. v; MÇS. i. 7; KÇS. v; AÇS. ii. 15–20; ÇÇS. iii. 13–18; Vait. viii. 8 ff.; Weber, *Ind. Stud.* x. 337.

[4] Above, Part III, Chap. 18, § 3. For the

husband and wife then share a bath, washing each other in it. The two elements of the rite are clearly enough the aim to secure the abundance of the flocks, and the sin offering to Varuṇa, whose presence in the rite may be due either to his deep and undeniable connexion with water, or merely be accounted for by the sin offering and the concluding bath, which are clearly in great measure merely pieces of magic to which a religious connexion has been attached.

The third festival is the Sākamedhas: the number of offerings in it, especially for the Maruts, is considerable, but the most important element is a feast for the dead, the Pitṛyajña, or Mahāpitṛyajña, where the Fathers are honoured as Somavantas, 'connected with Soma', sitting on the strew, and as 'burnt by Agni'. The rite follows the rules for offerings to the dead: it takes place in a hut south of the Dakṣiṇa fire, in which a Vedi is made and the fire there placed: the offerings are made with the term Svadhā [1] in place of Svāhā. Still more important is an offering to Tryambaka,[2] which is an offering to Rudra, everything therefore being done in the north, the region of that god. At a cross-way a fire is made and cakes offered in it, at least four, but properly one more than the number of the members of the family. One, however, is thrown upon an ant-heap in the north with the words, 'This is thy portion: the mole is thine animal, O Rudra'. On returning the priests engaged and the sacrificer all say, 'We supplicate Rudra away from us, away the god Tryambaka'. As in the offering to the Fathers, they go round the fire thrice from right to left, smiting the left thigh, then thrice in the opposite and normal way, smiting the right thigh, and the same form is followed by the unmarried women of the family, in verses which show that they hoped thus to secure marriage and avoid death. The remains of the cakes the sacrificer throws up in the air and catches as they fall: the cakes are then tied up in two baskets, tied to a bamboo, and placed on a tree [3] or some similar object so high that an ox cannot reach them. Rudra is then asked to go away beyond the Mūjavants, after which the breath is held and the sacrificers return from the place without looking back,[4] and touch water. The fee is a white horse,

[1] This term is of ambiguous sense, but refers perhaps to the self-disposal or volition of the dread spirits. This according to Oldenberg (*Rel. des Veda*[2], p. 531, n. 3) is due to their partaking of the food for the dead. *Contra*, Colinet, *Mélanges Lévi*, pp. 159 ff.

[2] Arbman, *Rudra*, pp. 48-64; Hillebrandt, *Ved. Myth.* ii. 186 ff.

[3] So also in the Bauḍhyavihāra rite in HÇS. ii. 9. 1. Rudra thus stands out in ritual as associated with a primitive mode of offering. Cf. above, Chap. 9, § 10.

[4] This common rite in connexion with chthonic powers Weber (*Rājasūya*, p. 11, n. 4) ingeniously but most implausibly conjectures to be due to a desire to show the complete confidence of safety produced in the mind of the performer by his devotion. The placing of gifts on a tree is a rite with many parallels; Meyer (*Gesch. d. Alt.*[3] I. ii. p. 722) holds that the idea is to bring the offering (e.g. in Ilion and Bambyke live animals) into immediate contact with the divinity temporarily resident in the tree. Cook (*Zeus*, i. 533) holds that the fertilizing animal is placed on the tree to secure its life. We are reduced to

or a bull, white or with white marks. The festival is followed by an offering to Çunāsīrau, which is evidently an agricultural rite for ploughing, addressed to two parts or deities of the plough. The features of it are a cake on twelve potsherds for Çunāsīrau or Indra Çunāsīrīya, fresh milk or barley gruel for Vāyu, and a cake on one potsherd for Sūrya : the fee is a six or twelve span plough or two plough beasts, while for the offering to Sūrya a white horse or sheep is the fee. A curious way of celebrating the whole of the offering together, in five days from the 11th day of the light half of Phālguna to the full moon, is recorded as practised by the Kaṭhas. The offerings can also be connected with the Soma and the animal offering in such a way that the six days of the three make up a Pṛṣṭhya Ṣaḍaha.

§ 6. *First-fruit Sacrifice (Āgrayaṇa Iṣṭi) and others*

Before partaking of any of the fruits of the fields it is necessary for a man who has established the fires to make offerings.[1] The normal offerings are those of rice in autumn, and barley in spring : alternatives are bamboo seeds in summer, and millet in autumn or the rains : in these two cases Soma is the god to whom the offerings are made : in the other case Indra and Agni receive a cake of the new fruits, and the All-gods and heaven and earth also have offerings. In the first case the fee is a garment or a repaired car, in the second the firstborn of the calves cast that year. In place, however, of the ordinary Iṣṭi the new- and full-moon sacrifices may be performed, or the Agnihotra made night and morning with the new fruits. Or, again, the rice or barley may be given to a cow to eat, and then the Agnihotra offered with the milk of that cow. In that case the motive of the offering may be taken as merely a desire to secure that the first-fruits shall, in the first place, be used by some one other than man; but it is more probable that we have nothing more here than the not rare practice of giving animals food in place of the deities, or yet more probably that the offering is merely a variety of the normal offering, milk being used instead of the actual first-fruits, a simple explanation, and one perfectly reasonable in itself. The offering of first-fruits then remains a perfectly natural offering to the gods, rather however as the formulae show an offering to secure the safe use of the fruits, than the expression of gratitude to the gods for their gift. That it was felt to be in any way sacramental, or even as inducing a special sense of community, is not to be seen in the Vedic evidence.

Of other Iṣṭis there are innumerable varieties, but they are all based on the model of the new- and full-moon offerings, and differ only in the presence of

mere conjecture. Helm (*Altgerm. Rel.* i. 244 f.) ascribes the German rite (Tac. *Ann.* i. 67) either to an offering to wind and air demons or to tree spirits.

[1] ApÇS. vi. 29. 2 ff. ; BÇS. iii. 12 ; MÇS. i. 6. 4 ; v ; KÇS. iv. 6 ; AÇS. iii. 9 ; ÇÇS. iii. 12 ; Vait. viii. 4 ; Lindner, *Festgruss an Böhtlingk*, pp. 79 ff. In Mexico the eating of maize had to be preceded by a human sacrifice ; Sahagun, trans. by Jourdanet and Siméon, pp. 126, 135 ; Hubert and Mauss, *Année sociol.* ii. 95, 97.

certain new offerings. Thus, there are Iṣṭis for one who desires a son, for various purifications, for making people subject to the sacrificer, and so on. One of the most interesting is the Kārīrīṣṭi, which is obviously a dressed up rain spell. A black horse is placed in the east facing west; the sacrificer robes it with a black garment and makes it neigh, and from the sounds which it makes and its actions he can foretell rain.[1] The new- and full-moon offerings themselves can be applied to fulfil wishes, and forms of these offerings are mentioned such as the Munyayana, Turāyaṇa, and Vasiṣṭhayajña, which may extend to a year in duration.

§ 7. *The Animal Sacrifice*

According to the Sūtras we must distinguish between the animal sacrifice as an independent offering and the sacrifice as connected with the Soma sacrifice: the offering of a goat to Agni and Soma in that offering is often treated as the Prakṛti of all animal sacrifices, but in some cases the independent animal offering which is called the Nirūḍhapaçubandha [2] takes the place of the Agnīṣomīya. The rite is to be performed by any man who establishes the fires, before he eats meat, and then yearly or half yearly, in which case the beginning of the bright course of the sun and the end of that period are prescribed by some authorities. The form of the offering is that of the new-moon sacrifice, the victim taking the place of the milk offered to Indra or Mahendra, but there is present another priest, the Maitrāvaruṇa, whose duty it is to give directions to the Hotṛ to say his Yājyā verses. For Indra and Agni, or Sūrya, or Prajāpati, a goat is the victim; it must be perfect, free from blemish, such as the loss of a horn or an eye; but in other offerings than the Nirūḍhapaçubandha are found many other animals, including normally oxen and sheep; and exceptionally, as at the piling of the fire, at the horse sacrifice and at human sacrifices, large numbers of victims are alleged to be offered, mainly if not entirely in theory. For Nirṛti the dove, owl, and hare are offered,[3] to the Rakṣases the black dog, the ass with lop ears, and the unknown *tarakṣu*.[4] Some animals appear as unfit for ordinary sacrifice, the dog, the *durvarāha*, 'bad boar', and *eḍaka*, 'vicious ram'. The normal rite occupies two days, of which the former is filled by preliminary rites, the second being the day of the actual sacrifice. The two days however may be compressed into one.

An essential feature of the rite is the use of a post, to which the victim is

[1] HGS. xxii. 13.

[2] ApÇS. vii; BÇS. iv.; KÇS. vi; MÇS. i. 8; AÇS. iii. 1–8; iv. 11, 12; ÇÇS. v. 15 ff.; vi. 18 ff.; Vait. x; Schwab, *Das altindische Thieropfer* (Erlangen, 1886); Haug, *Aitareya Brāhmaṇa*, ii. 72 ff.; Weber *Ind. Stud.* x. 344 ff.; Hubert and Mauss, *Année sociol.* ii. 62 ff. (with many parallels from Jewish and Greek records); Keith, *Rig-Veda Brāhmaṇas*, pp. 134 ff., 403 ff.

[3] MS. iii. 14. 19.

[4] MS. iii. 14. 21. For the dog offering cf. that of a dog to Robigus in the Roman religion; Warde Fowler, *Religious Experience of the Roman People*, p. 197. The motive in both cases was presumably propitiation; the choice of an abnormal victim being due to the abnormal character of the recipient.

tied : in the greater rites as many as eleven are used : the tree is solemnly cut down with protestations that it is not being injured, and, when a splinter is struck out of it in the cutting, that is kept and placed ultimately in the pit in which the post is inserted. The stump is treated with respect, and receives a libation, accompanied by a prayer that it shall spring up with a hundred shoots. The post is placed in a hole which is half within, half without the altar. Round the post a band is placed at the height of the navel; if the sacrificer wishes little or much rain he places it lower or higher. For the sacrifice the altar is placed west of the fire, and in the east third of it another altar, Uttaravedi, is provided as at the Varuṇapraghāsas, and a fire placed there, which takes the place of the normal Āhavanīya, while that serves as the Gārhapatya. There are required also special implements, the spit for the heart, and the utensils by which the omentum is cooked. When the preparations are over, the victim is bathed, and brought up, and tied to the post by a string, which is fastened to the left forefoot, round the back, and over the left horn : it is then sprinkled and given a drink.[1] Then the kindling verses are said, the butter oblations are offered, the victim is anointed with the butter,[2] and the usual procedure of the new- and full-moon sacrifices followed down to the fore-offerings, which number eleven and to which the Āprī litanies provide the Yājyā verses. After the tenth of the fore-offerings, the splinter of the tree, and the one edge of the two-edged knife, are dipped in the butter : the actual slaying must be done with the unconsecrated side by the slaughterer or Çamitṛ, the other being used by the Adhvaryu to cut off portions for offering. The Āgnīdhra thrice carries a brand round the victim, the Apāvya libations are performed, the Adhvaryu gives through the Maitrāvaruṇa the order to the Hotṛ to recite the old litany [3] for the slaying of the victim ; from the Gārhapatya fire flame is placed on the Çāmitra fire, the victim is then taken over to that fire, preceded by the Āgnīdhra with his firebrand, followed by the Pratiprasthātṛ, touching it with the spit, the Adhvaryu holding on to him and the sacrificer to the Adhvaryu, thus keeping in close contact with the holy power in the victim. Then the victim, with its head facing west, its feet north, is by the Çamitṛs strangled or pierced without sound,[4] while the rest of those present turn their heads away. Then a libation is made, and the wife of the sacrificer brought up. The Adhvaryu or the wife pours water over the members of the victim and washes them. The omentum

[1] Perhaps originally to secure a free flow of blood ; cf. Eitrem, *Opferritus und Voropfer der Griechen und Römer*, p. 435 ; Keith, JHS. xxxvi. 109. Doubtless it may have been felt in time as purificatory (cf. the sacrificer's rinsing of his own mouth), as taken by Hubert and Mauss (*op. cit.* 65, n. 1).

[2] Cf. the Roman *mola salsa*, the Greek *οὐλαί* (JHS. xxxvi. 108).

[3] Roth, *Nir.*, pp. xxxviii ff. ; AB. ii. 6 ; KB. x. 4 ; cf. Warde Fowler, *Religious Experience of the Roman People*, p. 180.

[4] For this requirement cf. the solemn display of the corn at Eleusis ; probably in silence the corn was cut and displayed likewise in silence ; cf. Reinach, *Revue des Études Grecques*, xvi. 342 ff. ; E.S., JHS. xxxvi. 105 ; Farnell, *Cults of the Greek States*, iii. 183 f.

is taken out and placed on a spit: in the first blood a grass blade is dipped, and thrown north-west or south-west as a spell to devote the enemy to the deepest darkness. It is cooked on the Çāmitra fire, and then placed on the Uttaravedi, where it is covered with butter. Then come the eleventh fore-offering, the two butter portions, and then the offering of the whole of the omentum, which is covered with pieces of gold and butter. The spits are then cast into the fire, and the fees distributed, three barren or three milch cows. Then come the making of the rice cake and the cutting up of the victim: of these eighteen portions are made, of which the first eight count as *daivatāni*: the heart is cooked separately on a spit, the rest of the pieces are cooked in a pot, while the excrement, blood, and stomach are offered to the Rakṣases, in a pit west of the Çāmitra fire outside the altar-ground. The various parts of the animal are then offered, the priests have shares both of the Iḍā as usual and of the meat. Then come the 11 after-offerings, offerings to the strew, the divine doors, &c. With each of the after-offerings a supplementary offering is connected in which the Pratiprasthātṛ offers pieces of the intestines which are left over. The splinter, the staff, of which the Maitrāvaruṇa never lets go, and the Prastara, 'bundle of grass', are put into the fire. The offering to the wives of the gods is performed with the tail of the victim, the heart spit is buried, with a verse imploring Varuṇa to forgive sin, in the presence of the sacrificer, his wife, and all the priests.[1] As they go back they each pick up three dry twigs, and place them on the Uttaravedi.

The animal sacrifice can be used for many special purposes, in which cases some variation is made to adapt it to the special end in view.

In all its essential features the offering must be regarded as a gift only: the presence of the divine essence in the victim is clearly proved by abundant evidence, and the priests all taste of it. But there is not the slightest sign in the elaborate ritual, nor in the formulae which are recorded in full, that there was any idea that the death of the victim was the ritual death of one of the gods, or that the ceremony was a sacrament, in which worshippers renewed or strengthened their union with the god by a common meal.[2]

§ 8. *The Soma Sacrifice*

The model form of the Soma sacrifice may be said to be the Agniṣṭoma,[3] which is the simplest form of the one-day Soma sacrifice, that is an offering on which the Soma is offered on one day only, in the morning, at midday, and

[1] Above, Part III, Chap. 18, § 6.

[2] *Ibid.*, § 5. Hubert and Mauss (*Année sociol.* ii. 81, 82) indeed compare the invocation and consumption of the Iḍā to the Mass and transubstantiation; but this is clearly a grave exaggeration. The Iḍā is the divine power present in the food when eaten: there is no question of the death and eating of a divinity.

[3] ApÇS. x–xiii; xiv. 8–12; BÇS. vi–viii; MÇS. ii; KÇS. vii–xi. 1; AÇS. iv, v, vi. 11–14; ÇÇS. v–viii; LÇS. i, ii, v. 5 ff.; Vait. xi–xxii; Caland and Henry, *L'Agniṣṭoma* (Paris, 1906); Keith, *Taittirīya Saṁhitā*, i. pp. cxv ff.; *Rig-Veda Brāhmaṇas*, pp. 53 ff.

in the evening. The name Agniṣṭoma appears to be due to the fact that the last of the Sāmans used on the day is addressed to Agni. Its time of performance is left vague by the texts : the evidence that it was a spring festival, celebrated at the new- or full-moon, which marked the beginning of the year, at which the nectar of the gods was offered to them in the shape of King Soma, as is held by Hillebrandt, is clearly inadequate even to make probable this thesis.

In the Soma sacrifice the animal sacrifice plays an important part. In the first place, on the last of the Upasad days, which precede the day of pressing, there is an offering of a goat for Agni and Soma : secondly, there is a victim which is offered throughout the day of pressing, and which is sacrificed to Agni in the Agniṣṭoma, but in the Ukthya form of the Soma sacrifice to Indra and Agni, in the Ṣoḍaçin to Indra, and in the Atirātra to Sarasvatī : the more prevalent view, however, adds the extra victim to each different form, so that the Atirātra form has all four. Thirdly, after the final bath and before the concluding Iṣṭi there is a barren cow for Mitra and Varuṇa, or three for Mitra and Varuṇa, the All-gods, and Bṛhaspati.

The offering is preceded by the choice of the priests, who are invited to come by a herald announcing the offering, and the obtaining of a place of sacrifice which the sacrificer asks from the prince, and which the latter must give on pain of the grave displeasure of the priest. Before or after this act, the consecration of the sacrificer takes place in the manner above [1] described. The length of the consecration may last anything from one, three, or four days up to a year : he sends out people to obtain food for him in this time, and his name is absolutely taboo. Then comes the purchase of the Soma, in which takes place a pretended buying by a cow, but it is taken away from the seller : there is a clear mimicry in some measure of the winning of the divine drink from the hands of the Gandharvas. The Soma is then brought forward on a cart, and the Subrahmaṇya utters the formula, whence he derives his name, and which invites Indra to the drinking of the Soma. The guest-offering is then given to the Soma, and the priests and the sacrificer, by touching together butter taken from the guest-offering, conclude a close alliance not to prove false to one another in the rite. The Āgnīdhra brings the Madantī waters which all touch, and the sacrificer undertakes the Avāntaradīkṣā, ' intermediate consecration ', in which he draws tighter his girdle, clasps more firmly his fist, and only drinks warm milk. Then comes the Pravargya rite, which will be described below, and three days of Upasads, in which offerings are made before and after midday with reference to the iron, silver, and golden forms of Agni. The term refers to sieges, but it is impossible to accept the suggestion of Hillebrandt [2] that the rites of besieging cities have been here interpolated : the siege is a mythical one. The second Upasad day is the time

[1] Part III, Chap. 19, § 1.

[2] *Rituallitteratur*, p. 127 ; *Ved. Myth.* i. 300. Hauer (*Die Anfänge der Yogapraxis im alten Indien*, p. 35) suggests that Upasad means fasting.

for the construction of the Mahāvedi, 'great altar'. The carts, which have the Soma, are placed in it, and three paces east from its west end is the Sadas, 'seat', which is a hut covered over, in which ceremony the Udgātṛ helps the Adhvaryu as in other parts of the service. In front of the axle of the right-hand cart four sounding holes are made, which are used as an earth drum to increase the sound of the pressing of the Soma with the stones. Over the holes, which at the foot are not separated, are placed the pressing-boards, and over them again the skin on which the stones are placed. The earth thrown up from the pit serves to make six fire hearths or Dhiṣṇyas, which extend from south to north, and are appropriated to the Maitrāvaruṇa, Hotṛ, Brāhmaṇācchaṅsin, Potṛ, Neṣṭṛ and Achāvāka. Outside the Sadas, on the right side of the Vedi, is the Mārjālīya hearth, used for cleansing the utensils, and opposite it the hut for the Āgnīdhrīya fire.

The offering of the victim to Agni and Soma is the occasion of an interesting rite: the sons, grandsons, and relatives of the sacrificer are invited to assist in it: the Adhvaryu takes hold of the sacrificer, the wife of the Adhvaryu, of her the sons, of them the grandchildren, and of them the relatives, thus presenting a picture of family ritual, which is the more noteworthy in that it is not connected as usual with the worship of the dead. The whole body set themselves in procession to the Āgnīdhrīya and the Āhavanīya to the recitation of verses for the bringing forward of Agni and Soma. Before the offering is actually made, the Avāntaradīkṣā comes to an end. The sacrificer unloosens his girdle, lets go his fist, and gives up the restrictions hitherto imposed on him. The victim is then offered, and the waters for use are drawn in some place shadowed from the sun, while the cows are milked, and the sacrificer spends the night awake and guarding the Soma.

The early dawn of the next day sees the service commenced by the performance of the Prātaranuvāka, 'morning litany', addressed to Agni, the Dawn, and the Açvins: the rule according to some texts is that the recitation is to be kept up from very early in the morning to the break of day. At the same time cakes are made ready for offerings to Indra Harivant, Indra and Pūṣan, Sarasvatī, Bhāratī, Indra, and Mitra and Varuṇa. Then comes the ceremony of fetching waters for use in the mixing of the Soma.

The pressing of the Soma may be preceded by the offering of cups of curds, butter, or Soma, in which case a few stalks only are pressed: in the Vājapeya and the Rājasūya there are also the Aṅçu and Adābhya cups, the first of sour milk merely touched with Soma stalks, the latter of Soma. The great pressing is preceded by the Upāṅçusavana which provides Soma for the Upāṅçu cup. The pressing takes place in three rounds: the Adhvaryu, Pratiprasthātṛ, and Unnetṛ are the performers: the juice is poured into the Ādhavanīya vessel, which is filled with water, and is then passed through a sieve to the wooden tub. The Unnetṛ draws Soma from the Ādhavanīya with a vessel, and pours it into the Hotṛ's cup, and the sacrificer then pours from it an unbroken stream on the sieve from which the next cups are drawn for offering, the Antaryāma, Aindravāyava, Maitrāvaruṇa, Çukra, Manthin, Āgrayaṇa, Ukthya, and Dhruva, which, therefore, are called Dhārāgrahas, as opposed to the other cups, which are made full from the wooden tub with the vessel called Pariplavā. The rest of the Soma is placed in the Pūtabhṛt vessel, except a part needed to fill the goblets, Camasas, of the priests. After libations to atone for loss of drops of Soma, the Bahiṣpavamāna Stotra is performed by the priests to accompany the purifying of the Soma: it is repeated outside the Sadas. The priests creep to the performance of this Stotra, each holding the previous one,[1] and the Adhvaryu starts the performance by handing to the Prastotṛ a handful of Darbha grass, which the latter hands to the Udgātṛ, asking the Brahman's authority to begin. The song is duly sung, the Āçvina cup is offered, and the victims sacrificed, and a cake offering is made in accordance with the preparation of the early morning. The cups for the double deities, Indra and Vāyu, Mitra and Varuṇa, and the Açvins, are then offered; then are filled the goblets of the priests, and offerings of the Çukra and Manthin cups made for the strange figures of Çaṇḍa and Marka. The oblations are made from the cups of the priests by the Adhvaryu, and the priests partake of the remainder. The emptied cups are now filled again and placed under the back part of the southern Soma cart, receiving the name Nārāçaṅsa and being allotted to the Fathers as Avamas, Ūrvas, and Kāvyas. The Achāvāka hereupon makes his appearance, and, if the Hotṛ consents to allow this late innovation among the priests to have a share in the rite, he is given a portion of the cake; then follow 12 or 14 season offerings and then the Hotṛ recites his Ājya Çastra, the contents of which have already been given.[2] The end of the Çastra is marked by the offering and partaking of the cup of Soma and the Nārāçaṅsa cups are also partaken of, but not offered. From them is taken a cup for the All-gods, and then follows the second Stotra, followed by the Praüga Çastra of the Hotṛ; the cup is offered and partaken of with the Nārāçaṅsas as before. Then a third of the Ukthya is taken for each of Mitra and Varuṇa, Indra, and Indra and Agni respectively, and used as the libations for the Stotras and Çastras, three in number, which end the pressing: the Çastras are recited by the Maitrāvaruṇa, Brāhmaṇāc-chaṅsin, and Achāvāka.

The midday pressing follows mainly the form of that of the morning: the season cups and those for two deities are omitted, and a new priest appears in the shape of the Grāvastut, 'praiser of the stones', whose business it is to say the verses addressed to the pressing stones, and who during his work keeps his head covered in a cloth lent to him by the sacrificer.[3] The Çukra and Manthin, the Āgrayaṇa, the two Marutvatīyas, and the Ukthya before or between them form the cups for the midday pressing. The Bahiṣpavamāna is represented by

[1] A very good parallel to this rite is the Mexican water ritual referred to by Usener, *Archiv f. Religionswissenschaft*, vii. 285.

[2] Part III, Chap. 20, § 1.

[3] This is a rare feature in Vedic ritual, but recurs in the covered head of the Roman sacrificer. Cf. below, § 9.

the Mādhyandinapavamāna Stotra. At the end of it there is the place of the preparation of the drink of hot sour milk, the Dadhigharma, which is proved to have existed even in the time of the Rigveda. Then come the cake offering, the filling of the goblets, the offering of the Çukra and Manthin cups, and the further ceremonies down to the depositing of the Nārāçaṅsa cups, after which the fees should be given, consisting of 7, 21, 60 to 1,000 cattle, or all the sacrificer's goods save his eldest son. In case of these two highest numbers he must also give a mule, for some uncertain cause. The sacrificer divides his largesse, cattle, sheep, horses, elephants, servants, clothes, in four heaps, the Adhvaryu has one share, out of which portions are obtained by the Pratiprasthātṛ, the Neṣṭṛ and Unnetṛ, of a half, a third, and fourth respectively of the Adhvaryu's share, and so with the other priests. An Ātreya is given a gold gift in addition: Kaṇvas, Kaçyapas, and ignorant Brahmans get nothing: even a daughter may be given in the form of marriage known as *daiva*, 'divine'.[1] After the fees are received two Marutvatīya cups are offered, and then a third which is the occasion of the Marutvatīya Çastra of the Hotṛ. Then a libation is made to Mahendra, which is accompanied by the first Pṛṣṭha Stotra of the Sāman singers, and the Niṣkevalya Çastra of the Hotṛ. Three Atigrāhyas are offered at the same time, for Agni, Indra, and Sūrya. Then follows as in the morning three Ukthya cups with the second to fourth Pṛṣṭha Stotras and the three Çastras of the Maitrāvaruṇa, Brāhmaṇācchaṅsin, and Achāvāka.

The evening pressing is intended by an Āditya cup, which is the means of producing magic effects according as it is prepared. It is made out of the remains of the cups for two deities, and is made ready, when both doors of the hut of the Soma carts are closed. The main pressing is much as in the morning, but the old Soma shoots are used as well as new. The Āgrayaṇa is performed with four streams, not three as at midday, or two as at the morning. The Ārbhavapavamāna Stotra is followed by the proceeding with the unfinished animal offering, then the cake offering takes place, and the rest goes on as at midday until the Nārāçaṅsa cups are disposed of. There follows a libation in which the Fathers are referred to. After that the Sāvitra cup is offered, and thereafter the Vaiçvadeva cup which gives rise to the Vaiçvadeva Çastra. Now a pap is offered: and the Udgātṛs look at themselves in butter. Then a Pātnīvata cup is offered, in connexion with which the Agnīdh sits on the lap of the Neṣṭṛ, who fetches thereafter the wife of the sacrificer. The Adhvaryu starts the Yajñāyajñīya Sāman, the sacrificer repeats the formula called Saptahotṛ, the Neṣṭṛ causes the wife to be looked at by the Udgātṛ, and she pours along her thigh water. Then follows the Āgnimāruta Çastra. With this the rite is drawing to a close: the main sacrifice is completed, the Hāriyojana cup is offered, and finally there is the Avabhṛtha in which many of the utensils are thrown into the water; the sacrificer and his wife have a bath, and put on new clothes. There still, however, have to be performed an Udayanīyā

[1] On Vedic marriage cf. Macdonell and Keith, *Vedic Index*, ii. 479 ff.

offering, the sacrifice of a barren cow to Mitra and Varuṇa, for which the Bahvṛcas substitute a mere milk offering, an offering to the minor deities, or in the case of a king to the divine impellers, and the burning of the strew and other minor rites, and at last an Udavasānīyā offering.

There can be no doubt whatever as to the great part played by Indra in the Soma offering: the midday pressing is almost entirely his, the Maruts appearing only in his company, though at the evening pressing his place is comparatively slight. In the morning we find in the Praüga Çastra, which is certainly to be traced to the Rigveda, invocations of seven sets of gods, first Vāyu, then Indra and Vāyu, Mitra and Varuṇa, the Açvins, Indra, the All-gods, and Sarasvatī, while the three litanies of the assistants of the Hotṛ are devoted to Mitra and Varuṇa, Indra, and Indra and Agni. In the evening the ritual finds places for the Ādityas, Savitṛ, the All-gods, Agni with the wives of the gods, and Indra with the bay steeds. The Ṛbhus thus play a very minor part, though they have verses and though their old importance, which is asserted in the Rigveda, may be traced in the name of the Ārbhavapavamāna Stotra. In the case of the Ādityas we have evidence in the Rigveda of their having a share in the offering, and so also in the case of Agni and the Maruts, but so comparatively seldom as to show that the position of these gods was distinctly far from assured as regards their share in the Soma sacrifice. The wives of the gods are also mentioned in the Rigveda as having a part, but never Savitṛ, a fact which is doubtless fair evidence that the Rigveda did not know him as having a place in the rite, and that he was later brought in, perhaps because of his growing importance, perhaps as an Āditya. The position of Agni also in the rite is a proof that he was not at first one of the great Soma drinkers: he appears in it in the main as connected with Indra, or as one of many other gods. On the other hand, the evidence of the Rigveda forbids the adoption of the view that the Soma offering was originally given to Indra alone: if that were the case it lies in times beyond our possibility of knowledge. The exclusion of Rudra, which seems, however, to be post-Rigvedic, though it is marked in the ritual, is the obvious result of his hostile nature.[1]

In some places it is clear enough that the Soma sacrifice was considered as a rain spell:[2] the pressing of the juice from the plant, and the pouring of the water and the juice through the sieve, are sufficient in themselves to import a rain spell of the normal Vedic type, and there can be no doubt that this view explains the fact that Soma is often regarded as a rain bringer, though doubtless in part that idea may be merely an extension of the practice of applying to any great god all the powers, which are important to man. But to go so far as to suggest, as Hillebrandt[3] does, that the essence of the sacrifice was a piece of magic, the moon's rays being full of nectar and being represented by the shoots of the Soma plant, so that the manipulations of the priests are

[1] RV. i. 122. 1 recognizes his share and his dual nature increases in force in the later development.

[2] Oldenberg, *Rel. des Veda*², p. 456; Henry, *L'Agniṣṭoma*, p. 486.

[3] *Ved. Myth.* ii. 217 ff.

adequate to supply the gods with the nectar drink which they love, is to misunderstand the nature of the sacrifice completely, and further the whole idea is vitiated by the assumption which the author has never proved nor even made plausible that Soma in the Rigveda is the moon. Nor, as we have seen, is there any real possibility of proving that the Soma offering has any totemistic flavour: it can be shown to be nothing but the offering to the god of the intoxicating drink, which in itself, on the other hand, creates the conception of the god Soma, who later and only among the Brahmans in the first instance is by the exercise of creative fancy equated with the moon.[1]

An ingenious but implausible suggestion is that of von Schroeder,[2] who, accepting as primitive the connexion of Soma with the moon, holds that the purpose of the rite was to enable the sacrificer to assimilate in the form of a symbol of the moon the strength of the moon itself, just as in the Pravargya ceremony[3] we may see the sacrificer acquiring the strength of the sun by drinking the hot milk, which is as naturally offered to the sun as is Soma to the moon. There is, however, clearly no positive evidence to support these suggestions as representing primitive views of either offering.

§ 9. *The Pravargya or Hot-milk Sacrifice*

In the Soma sacrifice the Pravargya[4] is inserted by the ritual text-books as an element which is to be performed twice a day in the course of the Upasad days, giving, with the normal three Upasads, six performances. But there is great doubt as to whether the rite is necessary, or whether it should be performed also at the first Agniṣṭoma, or not until after one has been performed. The discrepancy of opinion suggests that the rite was originally a separate sacrifice altogether, and this is borne out by the Rigveda, where it seems to have been an offering made in the morning only. From clay chosen from a pit east of the Āhavanīya fire, to which a horse leads the way, a Mahāvīra pot is made, a span high, two spare pots, and various other utensils. A stool of Muñja grass is also made as a throne for the pot. The pot is heated, the milk of a cow and a goat is poured in. Finally, the hot drink is offered to the Açvins, and two Rauhiṇa cakes are also offered in the morning to the day, in the evening to the night. At the outset of the ceremony the wife of the sacrificer is made to cover her head, but she joins with the rest at the close in the finale of the Sāman which is sung. At the end the offering utensils are arranged so as to make up the semblance of a man, the three Mahāvīra

[1] Keith, *Taittirīya Saṁhitā*, i. pp. cxx ff. Hubert and Mauss (*Année sociol.* ii. 129, 130) see in the rite the birth and death of the god, but in this case as usual they read into the rite much more than even what the Brāhmaṇas see as a pure speculation: we have no right whatever to regard this view as primitive or popular.

[2] *Arische Religion*, ii. 388, 390, and cf. *Die Wurzeln der Sage vom heiligen Gral* (1911).

[3] See below, § 9.

[4] ApÇS. xi. 2. 5 ff.; BÇS. ix; MÇS. iv; KÇS. xxvi; AÇS. iv. 6, 7; ÇÇS. v. 9 ff.; LÇS. i. 6; Vait. xiii; Garbe, ZDMG. xxxiv. 319 ff.; Weber, *Ind. Stud.* ix. 218 ff. For possible Greek parallels cf. Cook, *Zeus*, i. 676.

vessels marking the head, and so on. There are as usual prescriptions for the various accidents which may happen in the course of the rite, and, when it is performed, the sacrificer for a year eats no food, has intercourse with no woman of a certain class, and drinks from no earthen vessel. Moreover, for a year before the offering the same taboos should be observed and the rite studied in advance.

The rite is explained by the Aitareya Brāhmaṇa [1] as a mystic union of the gods which provides a new body for the sacrificer, and this theory is accepted by Geldner,[2] who regards it as an allegory of sexual union generally. This is not an attractive explanation: the explanation of the Mahāvīra pot as a symbol of the Liñga is wholly unsupported by a single word in the formulae, and the explanations of the Brāhmaṇas are always to be taken with the utmost care. On the other hand, we have clear suggestions in other passages that the rite, which is one of a specially dangerous, that is, sacred type,[3] was understood as a sun spell, and this is directly indicated by the formulae used at the rite. The pot is covered with a golden plate, which can be nothing else than a symbol of fire or the sun, the pot glows, the milk, which in its whiteness is a sun symbol, boils with heat. The sacrificer by drinking as usual a share of the milk thus gains power at the same time as the sun is strengthened. Nor is there any objection to the fact that the offering is made to the Açvins: the turning of magic into prayer and sacrifice is a constant feature of the Vedic ritual, parallel to the turning of prayer and sacrifice into magic, and, once the rite existed, the idea of presenting the milk to the Açvins, the harbingers of morning, was almost inevitable.[4]

Mystically the rite seems in the Çatapatha Brāhmaṇa [5] to have been interpreted in the sense that the pot was the sun, the milk the divine flood of life and light which falls to the sacrificer: as the sun is the head of the universe, so the pot is the head of the sacrificer: the rite provides the sacrificer and the universe alike with a head. Hence the deep reverence paid to the pot, and its optional character in the rite, since the Soma sacrifice by itself would confer the same blessings. The Aitareya Brāhmaṇa holds that it must not be performed until after a Soma sacrifice, a view which is explained by the Kauṣītaki Brāhmaṇa which requires that the body of the sacrificer should be first completed by the Soma sacrifice, and so made able to receive a head.

§ 10. *The Aikādaçina Animal Offering*

This is a special form [6] of the animal sacrifice which takes the place of the simpler ritual observed in the Agniṣṭoma, when it is preferred to use eleven

[1] i. 22. 14; KB. viii. 3–7.

[2] *Ved. Stud.* ii. 135.

[3] Cf. ÇB. xiv. 2. 2. 45; 3. 1. 14; TA. v. 3. 7; 6. 12. Hence the treatment of the rite in TA. iv and v; Oldenberg, GN. 1915, p. 387.

[4] Oldenberg, *Rel. des Veda*[2], pp. 448 ff.; Hillebrandt, *Ved. Myth.* ii. 217 ff.

[5] Keith, *Taittirīya Saṁhitā*, i. pp. cxxiii–v; Eggeling, SBE. xliv. pp. xlvi–l.

[6] ApÇS. xiv. 5–7; BÇS. xvii. 11–16; KÇS. viii. 8. 6 ff.; xii. 6. 11 ff.; ÇÇS. vi. 9. 3, 4; 10, 11; Vait. xxii. 20; Keith, *Taittirīya Saṁhitā*, i. p. 466, n. 11.

for the one victim there prescribed. In that case the ceremony is lengthened by the performance for each of the victims of the formal rite of the slaying, &c.: the general parts, such as the fore-offerings, are not repeated for each. Thirteen posts are used in place of one : the twelfth, the Upaçaya, is not set up, and the thirteenth is reserved under the name of Pātnīvata for an offering at the end of the ceremony. The middlemost post is placed near the fire, then one on either side, the rule being that the height increases from north to south : the Upaçaya is bound round with two cords, and placed at the southern post with maledictions on an enemy. To the centre post is tied the victim for Agni, north to it the sheep for Sarasvatī, south the goat for Soma, and so on, ending with the victim for Varuṇa on the south : mentally a beast of the wild, such as a mole, is attributed to the Upaçaya. After the offering of the omentum of the Anubandhyā cow, preparations are made for an offering of a victim to Tvaṣṭṛ at the Pātnīvata post, but the victim, which must be reddish brown, after the carrying round of fire is allowed to go free, being replaced by butter, with the offering of which the rite ends, unless it is stopped sooner at the carrying round of the fire.

§ 11. *Other Forms of Jyotiṣṭoma*

The ritual texts rank the Agniṣṭoma as the first form of the series of Soma sacrifices which bear the generic title of Jyotiṣṭoma. The list is in their view the Atyagniṣṭoma, the Ukthya, the Ṣoḍaçin, the Vājapeya, Atirātra, and Aptoryāma or Āptoryāma. The number of the series is seven, and it is most probable that the number is simply the sacred seven, and not a trace of an original view. The Atyagniṣṭoma, the Vājapeya, and the Aptoryāma have not the place of forms of the Jyotiṣṭoma in the older Saṁhitās, and probably were added to make up the number to seven.[1]

The essential distinction of the Ukthya from the Agniṣṭoma lies in the fact, that at the third pressing of the Soma the number of Çastras and of Stotras is brought up to five each by the addition of three others, so as to correspond with the five of each which are found in the other two pressings. The Stotras and Çastras accompany the rounds of goblets at the other pressings. Further, the Çastras bear the name Uktha or Ukthya of the Ukthya cups which are given to Indra and Varuṇa, Indra and Bṛhaspati, and Indra and Viṣṇu, and not to the same deities as at the morning and afternoon pressings. The name of the sacrifice is of obscure origin : the more probable view is that it was so called, because there was a discussion as to whether the Ukthya cup in its three portions was to be used at the third pressing : the question would then be a disputed one and the sacrifice, in which they were used, would be called that with the Ukthya or more shortly Ukthya.[2] The Sāmans of the extra

[1] ApÇS. xiv. 1–4 ; BÇS. xvii. 1–10 ; KÇS. x. 9. 28 ff. ; xii. 5. 1–6. 10 ; AÇS. vi. 1–7 ; xi. 1, 2 ; ix. 11 ; ÇÇS. ix. 1–21 ; LÇS. ii. 5. 23 ff. ; iii. 1 ff. ; v. 4. 24 ff. ; Vait. xxv ff. ; Eggeling, SBE. xli. pp. xiv ff. ; Keith, *Taittirīya Saṁhitā*, i. pp. cxv ff. ; *Rig-Veda Brāhmaṇas*, pp. 54 ff.

[2] Eggeling, SBE. xli. p. xv.

Stotras seem to have been the Sākamaçva, Saubhara, and Nārmedha. A further difference lies in the fact that there is a change of Sāmans at the Pṛṣṭha Stotras of the mid-day pressing : in the first and the third of these the Bṛhat and Çyaita replace the Rathantara and Naudhasa, while the second and the fourth retain the old Sāmans, Vāmadevya and Kāleya. There is also a second victim, a he-goat for Indra and Agni, for the day of the pressing.

The Ṣoḍaçin [1] differs from the preceding rite by the addition of a ram for Indra, and by the possession of a sixteenth cup, which is offered at the morning pressing or at all three, as the last of the Dhārāgrahas. It is accompanied by a special Stotra and Çastra making the number up to sixteen, with the fifteen of the Ukthya, and, in accordance with this increase, there are also four sets of goblets in place of three as at the Ukthya. The Soma cow has to be of very small stature and have red ears. The Ṣoḍaçin cup is treated with special care : it is placed in a square vessel of Khadira wood, addressed as soon as it is put on the Vedi, and, in giving the signal for the commencement of the Stotra when the sun is half set, a gold piece is handed to the Udgātṛ in place of the usual piece of grass. The sacrificial fee is a reddish brown horse or a female mule.

The Atyagniṣṭoma is closely connected with the Ṣoḍaçin, though in the view of the ritual texts it is treated as if it were simply an Agniṣṭoma with an extra Stotra and Çastra. It is really a Ṣoḍaçin in which the three Stotras and Çastras of the Ukthya, and of course the corresponding goblets and Ukthya cup, are omitted. Its real place in the ritual is not as a separate sacrifice at all, but as the form of service on the tenth day of a Daçarātra, a period of ten days, which with an Atirātra before and after it makes up the common form of a Dvādaçāha rite : it must in all probability be treated as a variant form, produced by those theologians who did not approve the addition of the three Stotras and Çastras at the Ukthya rite.

The Atirātra attains the number of twenty-nine Stotras and Çastras by adding a series of twelve of both, which are used to accompany three rounds, Paryāyas, each of four sets of goblets, which in turn are led off by that of the Hotṛ, Maitrāvaruṇa, Brāhmaṇācchaṅsin, and Achāvāka. The offerings are made during this nocturnal carouse, which gives the name to the rite, to Indra Apiçarvara. When the cups have been duly offered and the priests have drunk, then the Sandhi Stotra is performed, while a cake is made ready for the Açvins, the name of the Stotra being derived from the twilight, which is about to break. It has nine verses and is sung to the Rathantara tune. Then follows the Prātaranuvāka to the Açvins, which must contain a thousand verses or more, or a thousand Bṛhatī verses, made up artificially from other metres : [2] the last verse is to be said after sunrise. Then the Adhvaryu takes the cup of the Hotṛ, the other assistants of the Adhvaryu the rest, and with the Soma

[1] Hillebrandt (*Ved. Myth.* iii. 217 ff.) sees in it a rite to strengthen the sun at the winter solstice ; cf. AB. iii. 41 ; KB. xvii. 1.

[2] Cf. Keith, *Aitareya Āraṇyaka*, pp. 29, 214 ; Eggeling, SBE. xliii. 111.

from the previous night, a cup is offered to the Açvins, while the Pratiprasthātṛ offers the cake. There is also a fourth animal victim, a he-goat for Sarasvatī.

The Atirātra might, it is clear, be performed without the Ṣoḍaçin cup and the corresponding Stotra and Çastra, but this is not the prevailing view. It lasted with its nocturnal continuation over the night, and so can be considered as the tail of the sacrifice, which laps over from the end of the month into the next month.[1]

The Aptoryāma is classed sometimes with the Atirātra as an Ahīna, that is a rite lasting more than a day, instead of as an Ekāha like the other forms of the Jyotiṣṭoma. It is marked out from the Atirātra by the addition after the Sandhi Stotra and the Āçvina Çastra of four more Stotras and Çastras, accompanying four sets of goblets for the priests which are drawn for Agni, Indra, the All-gods, and Viṣṇu, or according to others for the deities of the Sandhi goblets. As an independent rite, it is practically unknown: it is, however, occasionally mentioned with other forms of one day ceremonies.

The last form of the Jyotiṣṭoma is the Vājapeya, which is of special nature and will be treated below.

§ 12. *Other Soma Sacrifices of One Day's Duration.*

The Agniṣṭoma is the model on which innumerable[2] other kinds of sacrifice can be formed, in order to bring about certain desires. The Viçvajit[3] is occasionally mentioned: in it a man gives all his goods as the fee, or at least a thousand cattle and hundred horses. In the former case he first hands over to his eldest son his share in the property. After the offering he spends twelve nights in different places, three where an Udumbara is, eating fruits and roots only, three among Niṣādas, without eating the grains cultivated by them, three with folk, and three with folk like himself, or according to another view either Vaiçyas or Rājanyas. The symbolic nature of the rite is obvious.

The six Sādyaḥkras[4] are offerings which in one day include all the rites, including the Dīkṣā from the beginning to the end of a Soma sacrifice. The first serves as a model of the rest: the priests, Hotṛ, Udgātṛ, Adhvaryu, and Brahman, are stationed in the four quarters at considerable distances: the altar is a sown field, or field full of ripe barley or rice: the Uttaravedi a threshing-floor. Milk is churned into butter in a skin by the primitive mode of shaking it. The offering is supposed to bring the attainment of heaven, of cattle, and of the defeat of a rival. The second removes disease, and brings strength and food. The fourth is the Viçvajit Çilpa, at which one should give as many fees as possible; the fifth is the Çyena, which is employed for

[1] Keith, *Taittirīya Saṁhitā*, i. p. cxvii.

[2] See e. g. the list in BÇS. xviii.

[3] KÇS. xxii. 1. 9 ff.; LÇS. viii. 1. 28; 2. 1 f. PB. xvi. 6; JB. ii. 183 f.; KB. xxv. 15; ApÇS. xvii. 26. 14–18.

[4] Cf. the Ādityas' and Añgirases' strife to win heaven first; JB. iii. 187 f.; ii. 115–17; AB. vi. 34 f.; KB. xxx. 6; PB. xvi. 12. 1; BÇS. xviii. 22 f.

exorcism, and the fee in this case consists of one-eyed lame cattle without horns or tails, mixed with diseased ones.[1]

Of special importance are the four Vrātya Stomas,[2] which are rites apparently intended for the admission into the Brahmanical community of persons who though Aryans have been living outside that community. It is in the ritual said to be intended for the case of persons who have lost their position as twice born by various reasons, including living among non-twice-born people. Of such people it is said that they do not study, do not practise agriculture or trade; they call good words bad, perhaps a reference to differences of dialect, they punish the guiltless with blows, presumably an allusion to difference of law, and, though unconsecrated, speak the speech of the consecrated. According to the views of Kātyāyana, the first offering is for Vrātyas, who, skilled in dance, song, and music, are capable of teaching these arts to a company of Vrātyas, the second for eunuchs, the third for those of little account, and the fourth for old impotent men. The dress of the Vrātyas is described as including a special kind of turban (*uṣṇīṣa*), white garments with black fringes, and a curious kind of bow without a string (*jyāhroḍa*): at the rite also is used a special sort of cart (*vipatha*), and a silver ornament as worn by Vrātyas. The Gṛhapati, who is to be chosen from the leader of the Vrātyas to be converted, carries two skins, one white, one black, and a pair of shoes, black and shaped like ears, or provided with ears. All these articles are to be given as a fee at the proper time to an unworthy Brahman from Magadha, a sign that Magadha was not regarded as strictly Brahmanical, or to Vrātyas who have not yet been converted, and who are thus made scapegoats. When the ceremony is over, the Vrātyas cease to have that characteristic: they become admitted to full membership of the Brahmanical society, and can engage in the pursuit of sacred learning.

The rites are specially interesting, as they mention several words which are not easily explicable, and evidently were not well understood at a very early date: they may be borrowed from the speech of the eastern tribes, and together with the mention of the Brahman from Magadha suggest, but do not prove, that the Vrātyas came from the east rather than from the west, though we know that the western tribes were by no means fully Brahmanized,[3]

[1] KÇS. xxii. 3. 26 ff.; BÇS. xvii. 20 ff.

[2] PB. xvii. 1–4 (a later view in JB. ii. 222); BÇS. xvii. 24–6; KÇS. xxii. 4; LÇS. viii. 6; Weber, *Ind. Stud.* x. 101 ff.; Macdonell and Keith, *Vedic Index*, ii. 341–5; Keith, JRAS. 1913, pp. 155 ff. Vrātyas may have been non-Aryan, but this is not probable; cf. Weber, *Ind. Lit.*, p. 73; Hopkins, *Rel. of India*, p. 179; Hillebrandt, *Rituallitteratur*, p. 140; Bloomfield, *Atharvaveda*, p. 94. In some cases Aryans who have fallen from grace may have been so reinstated. Cf. below, Chap. 22, § 9.

[3] A rash hypothesis (cf. above, Chap. 1), based on late linguistic facts, and supported by worthless ethnological material, claims that the Vedic Indians were Aryans who entered their homes from Chitral and Gilgit and not directly connected with the Punjab (see e.g. Risley, *People of India*, pp. 55 ff.). The theory contradicts the evidence of the Rigveda, and the Chitral route, as Holdich (*The Gates of India*) insists, is impracticable for a people's migration.

and it has been suggested that the Vrātyas represented one or other of the many Aryan tribes which were in motion in the period 1500–1000 B.C. There are clear traces that the Udgātṛs were specially active in the business of bringing in these outlying members of the Brahmanical society : possibly this may stand in some relation to the fact that the Chandogas were never held in the highest repute among the Vedic Indians.[1] The suggestion of Charpentier [2] that we are to see in these Vrātyas adherents of Rudra-Çiva must be regarded as impossible. It is, however, of interest to note that already in the Atharvaveda [3] the Vrātya is a well-known figure, and by the curious ideas of that Veda is turned into an expression of the supreme deity.

Of other rites of this class the Upahavya [4] is interesting, as it is born of strife between the gods and the Asuras, and in it the names of the gods are carefully changed to avoid mentioning them aloud : thus the name of Indra is Çakra, of Soma Indu, and likewise the *hotā deva* is changed to *hotā yakṣe*, and so on, even the simple word *sarva*, all, becoming the old *viçva*. There is a rite, the Sarvasvāra,[5] for one who wishes to die : the sacrificer in it is completely covered over and sits facing south on a dark skin. In the Bṛhaspatisava,[6] on the other hand, which is offered by one who wishes such rank as a Purohitaship, the sacrificer must be treated with respect, be greeted by others without returning the salutation, and be styled Sthapati, 'lord', all these things by sympathetic magic working the desired end. If the Apacitis [7] are offered to bring a man honour, he must pay dearly in Dakṣiṇās in proportion to what he aspires to attain, and so in all these offerings the greed of the priest for fees shows itself.

The Gosava is of special interest, because it involves incest with one's mother, sister, and a woman of one's own Gotra, that is with whom marriage is forbidden. The Jaiminīya Brāhmaṇa [8] records that Janaka of Videha declined to undertake it, though it would have secured him the world of the Ox, doubtless Prajāpati as in the Atharvaveda,[9] but a Çibi king did perform it, carrying out literally the rule of acting according to nature.

[1] Burnell, *Devatādhyāya Brāhmaṇa*, p. ix ; Muir, *Sansk. Texts*, iii. 26 ; Hillebrandt, *Sonnwendfeste*, p. 34.

[2] VOJ. xxv. 355–88 ; see Keith, JRAS. 1913, pp. 155–60. Caland (JB., p. 184) amazingly argues that the fact that in JB. Īçāna is hostile to the Vrātyas supports the theory.

[3] xv. This shows some trace of the influence of Rudra worship. It is clearly late.

[4] LÇS. viii. 9 ; comm. on PB. xviii. 1. 3 ; BÇS. xviii. 28 has a different version.

[5] KÇS. xxii. 5. 31 ; 6. 1 ff.

[6] BÇS. xviii. 1, 2 ; cf. § 13. Other rites dwelt on in the JB. are Çada, Upaçada, Punastoma, Valabhid, Udbhid, Durāça, Tīvrasoma, Ṛtapeya, &c.

[7] KÇS. xxii. 10. 13 ; LÇS. ix. 4. 13 ; BÇS. xviii. 39 ; ApÇS. xxii. 12. 4 f. ; JB. ii. 100 ff. ; PB. xix. 8.

[8] ii. 113 ; ApÇS. xxii. 13. 1–3.

[9] iv. 11.

§ 13. *The Vājapeya or Drink-of-Strength*

The Vājapeya[1] is of especial interest in that it preserves, despite the formalism imposed upon it by its inclusion in the Soma ritual, many traces of very popular origin. It is said by many authorities to be a festival of the autumn, and it is also allowed either to perform it independently, or as the sixth day of a Sarvamedha or universal sacrifice. It consists of one pressing day and at least 13 days of consecration and three Upasad days, so that it takes up at least 17 days and may be spun out to a year. It adds to the ordinary Ṣoḍaçin form a seventeenth Stotra and Çastra, and the number seventeen is also introduced into the Bahiṣpavamāna and Mādhyandinapavamāna Stotras in place of the Trivṛt and Pañcadaça Stomas there normally used. The number of cups in the ordinary rite is increased by the addition of the Añçu and Adābhya, and also five Vājapeya or Aindra cups; there are added a dappled barren cow for the Maruts, and seventeen goats for Prajāpati, hornless but capable of procreation. The sacrificer, his wife, and the priest all wear garlands of gold, which form the fees. The special features of the rite begin with the midday pressing, at which a warrior with seventeen arrows measures out a course for a race, marking the place where the last falls with a twig of Udumbara. Then three horses of the sacrificer are yoked to his chariot, sixteen others are yoked with four horses each, and the sacrificer is victorious in a formal race, during which 17 drums are beaten, and the Brahman climbs up a post, on which is fastened a wheel of Udumbara wood, to sing the Sāman of the strong steeds, while the wheel is turned to the right. The horses are given, before and after the race, the offering to Bṛhaspati to smell, to gain its strength. In the second place, along with the cups of Soma there are offered by the Neṣṭṛ alternatively cups of Surā, which are purchased from a long-haired man and placed in a special place. Mention is also made of a cup of honey, which is not used for any offering, but is placed in the hand of a Kṣatriya or Vaiçya competitor, and seems to be an unintelligible remainder of an older rite. In the third place, the sacrificer for himself and his wife solemnly mounts to the sun by climbing with the aid of a ladder to the top of the sacrificial post which is decorated by placing on it a wheel-shaped garland of meal, in which position he is touched by the priest or others with salt in Açvattha leaves. He then descends and sits on a throne, and is sprinkled with a mixture of water, milk, and seventeen other substances, or so many as can be thought of, with the exception of one of which he never again eats. The rest of the mixture is used for certain libations called Vājaprasavīya, and the festival closes with seventeen Ujjitis, 'benedictions', which can be accompanied by libations.

[1] ApÇS. xviii; BÇS. xi; KÇS. xiv; AÇS. ix. 9; ÇÇS. xv. 1 ff.; xvi. 17. 1 ff.; LÇS. v. 12. 8–25; viii. 11, 12; Vait. xxvii; Hillebrandt, *Ved. Myth.* i. 247 ff.; Weber, *Über den Vājapeya* (SBA. 1892, pp. 765 ff.); Eggeling, SBE. xli. pp. xxiii ff. For parallels see von Schroeder, *Arische Religion*, ii. 191, 395, 650, cf. 349 ff.; 379. Cf. N. N. Law, *Ancient Indian Polity*, pp. 160 f., 177 ff.; Keith, *Taittirīya Saṁhitā*, i. pp. cviii ff.

The name of the offering is explained by tradition as 'food and drink', by Oldenberg [1] as 'the drink of strength', and by Weber as 'the protection of strength'. The last rendering is clearly to be rejected: the drink which Weber denies to be seen in the offering is the Soma, and we cannot assume that the name is older than the use of Soma in the rite. It is important to note that the rite could, it is clear from scattered notices, be used by a Vaiçya and not merely by a Brahman or a Kṣatriya, but it is also clear that the offering was connected with the attainment of high prosperity, and it may well be that it was intended to be offered only by one who was in the technical sense a *gataçrī*, 'who had attained prosperity', and so could aspire to highest things. Moreover, this is indicated by the fact that the person who performs this offering is not expected to take notice of persons who have not done so, go behind them, or share a bed with them. The nature of the rites is clearly on the one hand that of the attainment of victory and power by the symbolic acts of winning, of being hailed as victor, and anointing: references to fertility are obvious also, and the sun spell of the wheel is noteworthy. It is accordingly impossible to lay down precisely the original character of the rite: [2] it was not merely the feast of victory of the winner in a chariot race, such as might be paralleled in Greek ritual, nor was it solely an agricultural rite: it has been blended by a mixture of many elements to form a general offering available for any successful person.

This curious position of the Vājapeya clearly led to confusion: some texts place it above the Rājasūya, and say that by the latter mere kingship is conferred, by the former paramount lordship. But other texts make the Vājapeya appropriate for a paramount lord, and the Rājasūya for a universal monarch like Varuṇa.[3] The simplest solution is that which makes the Vājapeya a rite which is performed by the king before the Rājasūya and by the Brahman before the Bṛhaspatisava.[4] The essential priestly character of the rite as it stands is shown by the prominence of Bṛhaspati and the part played by Prajāpati.

Other special forms of sacrifices for obtaining a special rank are the Sūta, Grāmaṇī, Sthapati, and Go-Savas.[5]

§ 14. *The Royal Consecration*

The royal consecration [6] is a Soma sacrifice having the usual Dīkṣā and Upasad days and preceded by a long series of preparatory rites. It is mythically connected with the consecration of Varuṇa or with Indra, and it

[1] *Rel. des Veda*², p. 470.

[2] Keith, *Taittirīya Saṁhitā*, i. pp. cviii–cxi. For the sun-wheel see Cook, *Zeus*, i. 197 ff.

[3] TB. ii. 7. 6. 1; ÇB. v. 1. 1. 13. See Macdonell and Keith, *Vedic Index*, ii. 256.

[4] AÇS. ix. 9. 19. For the Bṛhaspatisava, see JB. ii. 128–30 (used by both Brahman and Kṣatriya); PB. xvii. 11; TB. ii. 7. 1; KS. xxxvii. 7; BÇS. xviii. 1.

[5] BÇS. xviii. 3 ff.; comm. on TB. ii. 7.

[6] ApÇS. xviii; BÇS. xii; KÇS. xv; AÇS. ix. 3, 4; ÇÇS. xv. 12–27; xvi. 18; LÇS. ix. 1–3; Vait. xxxvi; Weber,

displays many popular elements in its character, as was inevitable from its nature. The great nobles and office bearers of the court play an important part, the Purohita performs many of the priestly functions, the people are at least present to hear the announcement of the consecration of the sovereign. It connects itself with Vedic history: the tribes who are mentioned are the Bharatas or their successors in blood and tradition, the Kuru-Pañcālas. The preliminary ceremonies begin with the first day of Dīkṣā on the 1st Phālguna, followed by offerings to Anumati and to Nirṛti, who receives the fallen portions of the grain on a salt piece of ground in the south. With the 15th of the month commence the observances for a year of the four-month offerings, the periods between the new- and full-moon days being filled up either by the new- and full-moon offerings or offerings to the sun and the moon. These offerings cease with the Çunāsīrīya offering on the 1st Phālguna of the following year, and on that and the next two days offerings are made to the deities of the quarters, and others, and then on the 4th to the 15th offerings called the Ratninām̐ Havīn̐ṣi, which are offered in the houses of the 'jewels' of the king,[1] his wives and high officers, the deities chosen being the appropriate gods for the persons in whose houses the offerings are made, as for Aditi in that of the chief queen, for Nirṛti in that of the discarded lady. After these follow various libations, and on the 1st of Caitra comes the day of anointing, which is performed as an Ukthya rite. There are offered on it eight offerings to the divine instigators, who are to pay heed to the crowning of the prince in the rite. The actual anointing takes place after the Marutvatīya cups: seventeen kinds of waters, brought from the Sarasvatī, drawn against the current of the stream, or with it, &c., are used: they are sieved after mixing and poured into four vessels, of Palāça, Udumbara, Nyagrodha, and Açvattha. The sacrificer clad in splendid raiment takes from the Adhvaryu a bow with three arrows, and is proclaimed with the Āvid formulae which he repeats announcing his anointment. The evil spirits are appeased by the gift of copper placed in the mouth of a long-haired man. The sacrificer then strides to the various quarters, and steps on a tiger-skin, beneath which is a piece of lead, on which he tramps as on the head of Namuci. With gold under his feet and a gold fillet over his head, he is anointed by the Adhvaryu in front, and also by a kinsman, a Rājanya, and a Vaiçya, representing the whole people. After this are performed six Pārtha libations which are offered to correspond with six before the anointing;[2] the king steps on the skin the steps of Viṣṇu and puts in the

Über die Königsweihe (APAW. 1893), who is exhaustive, but had not then available ApÇS. and BÇS.; Eggeling, SBE. xli. pp. xxiv ff.; xliv. pp. xv ff. The term of the ÇB. and the Black Yajurveda is Rājasūya, the Abhiṣecanīya denoting the actual aspersion of the king in the course of the whole rite. Cf. TS. i. 8; TB. i. 6–8; PB. xviii. 8–11; AB. vii. 13; viii; ÇB. v. 2. 3–5. 5; N. N. Law, *Ancient Indian Polity*, pp. 161 ff.; Keith, *Taittirīya Sam̐hitā*, i. pp. cxi ff.; *Rig-Veda Brāhmaṇas*, pp. 61 ff.

[1] See Macdonell and Keith, *Vedic Index*, ii. 200.

[2] At this point or later is recited by the Hotṛ the legend of Çunaḥçepa, in which

Palāça dish the remains of the mixture, which he hands to his eldest son, that he may continue his work and strength. An offering is also made in which the names of the father and son are first confused, then rightly said. A mimic expedition for booty is performed : the king in his chariot goes out against cattle of his kinsfolk : at the time of the fees he plunders them and they surrender their belongings : a third of their goods goes to the priest, a third to the drinkers of the Daçapeya, and the owners are allowed to have a third back. But they also receive villages, and are called Rājanyas, but unworthy of anointing.[1] In another account,[2] which does not in this interesting way bring out the conception of the pretenders to the royal throne and their defeat, the king mounts his horse and advances to the quarters, a parallel to which is quoted from the ceremony of coronation of the King of Hungary. Before descending from the chariot which he mounts for the fray, the king puts on sandals of boar's hide, and prays neither to injure the earth, nor be injured by it, a clear allusion to his high sanctity. After the later Keçavapanīya rite he never stands with bare feet on the ground. He then sits on a throne placed over the tiger-hide, and takes five dice from the Adhvaryu : the priest gently beats him from behind with sticks of pure trees, doubtless to expel any taint of ill.[3] Before the dicing begins the Purohita hands the king a wooden sword, which he passes on to his brother, and through him it is taken by a man who marks out the place for dicing, where a hut is erected. After the dicing, which is merely formal and which deliberately was so carried out as to make the king a victor, the sacrifice progresses to the normal end, but the bath is followed by an offering to Indra and Viṣṇu of a special nature. Then comes the preparation for the Daçapeya offering, for which the Dīkṣā consists in ten Saṁsṛpāṁ Havīṅṣi. The offering itself seems to have been in origin an independent offering : it is performed on the 7th of Caitra : the performers must have ten generations of Soma drinkers : from ten cups ten drink together at each : it is uncertain if the relatives of the king may drink or not, but he certainly has a goblet. After this, according to some authorities, the king, the people save the Brahmans, and the steeds may not have their hair cut for a year. There are also a number of minor offerings to propitiate the quarters, to

has been seen a trace of an old human sacrifice ; above, Part III, Chap. 18, § 2. See also Keith, *Taittirīya Saṁhitā*, i. pp. cxi–cxiii. Wellhausen (*Archiv f. Religionswissenschaft*, vii. 33–9) argues that the touching is the essential and primitive feature of the Hebrew royal anointment.

[1] LÇS. ix. 1. 14 ff.

[2] Hillebrandt, *Rituallitteratur*, p. 146. The Buddhist legend preserves this feature in the account of the movements of the Buddha on birth ; see Windisch, *Buddha's Geburt*, pp. 130 ff.

[3] KÇS. xv. 7. 4. There is no Mantra for this in any Saṁhitā. Weber (p. 63) compares the occasional beating of the bridegroom in the marriage ceremony (*Ind. Stud.* v. 300), but erroneously thinks that the rite is a symbol of priestly power. Reinach (*Cultes, Mythes et Religions*, i. 173 ff.) finds totemism in ritual flogging ; Mannhardt (*Myth. Forsch.*, p. 72), much more plausibly, mere fertilization, as obviously in the Lupercalia (Warde Fowler, *Religious Experience of the Roman People*, pp. 54, 479). Cf. JRS. iii. 162 ff.

win the seasons, for Aditi or the Ādityas, and the Maruts or the All-gods. In Jyaiṣṭha follows in the next year the ceremony of the cutting of the hair, the Keçavapanīya, which may be followed by two Vyuṣṭi offerings a fortnight later, and the Kṣatradhṛti, a month later, a rite interesting as it is connected with the ruin of the Kurus.[1] The fees are exaggerated beyond measure, even 240,000 cows being given.

The rite is full of magic and symbolism : its nature is obvious and has innumerable parallels : it is worth noting that the king is expected to rub in the substance of the anointing mixture with the horn of a black antelope : it is thus clear that the holy strength is actually in the mixture, and must be made to impregnate the system ; the keeping of the long hair, like the Frankish kings, is to preserve for a time this holiness. The position and prominence of the game of dice [2] are interesting : it is possible to see in it a connexion with the foretelling of prosperity, but it must have been made the more natural in that the king was interested, we may believe even at this period, in the revenue to be derived from dicing, which was carried on in the Sabhā, 'house of assembly', and which in later times was assuredly a valuable monopoly, and probably so in earlier days.

Different forms of consecration are referred to : the Aitareya Brāhmaṇa [3] distinguishes the great consecration, Abhiṣeka, of Indra from the renewed consecration of a consecrated king, and its account of the consecration, which deals only with the anointing, differs very greatly from that of the Yajurveda, which it possibly presupposes. Great stress is laid on the fact that the king is only given a curious mixture to drink, being absolutely denied the use of Soma, a fact explained by a long mythological story.

§ 15. *The Horse Sacrifice*

The horse sacrifice [4] is in the ritual reckoned an Ahīna, that is a rite with more than one day on which the Soma is pressed, in this case three. It is an old and famous rite, which kings alone can bring, to increase their realms : we have lists of the great kings of old [5] who were consecrated and who performed the horse sacrifice. The horse chosen must be swift, in front black, behind white, and with a dark mark. The offering begins on the 8th or 9th of Phālguna or in summer. On that day a mess of rice is cooked for the priests, and the king, his four wives, and their four hundred maidens of different ranks

[1] According to ÇÇS. xv. 16. 11.

[2] Lüders, *Das Würfelspiel im alten Indien* (1907) ; cf. Keith, JRAS. 1908, pp. 823 ff. ; *Vedic Index*, i. 2 ff.

[3] viii. 5, 12. Kauç. xvii has the consecrating of a subordinate prince and a sovereign ruler respectively : the dicing plays an important part in either case ; in the latter the king goes to his queens, a symbol of his royal status ; a tiger-skin is used in the latter, a bull-hide in the former case ; cf. Henry, *La magie dans l'Inde antique*, pp. 146–8.

[4] ApÇS. xx ; BÇS. xv ; KÇS. xx ; AÇS. x. 6 ff. ; ÇÇS. xvi. 1 ff. ; 18. 10 ff. ; LÇS. ix. 9–11 ; Vait. xxxvi. 14–xxxvii. 8 ; N. N. Law, *Ancient Indian Polity*, pp. 181 ff. ; Keith, *Taittirīya Saṁhitā*, i. pp. cxxxii ff.

[5] AB. viii. 21–3 ; ÇB. xiii. 5. 4.

assemble, the king spending the night at the Gārhapatya fire. Next morning the horse is bound, and sprinkled in standing water: a man of low class kills with a club of Sidhraka wood a four-eyed dog, and lets it float on a mat under the horse. The sacrificer says, 'He who will kill the horse attacks Varuṇa: away the man, away the horse!'[1] The horse is then led back to the fire, and offerings are made of cakes to Savitṛ in various forms for three days. The horse is then set free to wander with a hundred old horses, and guarded by four hundred youths of the same relative rank as the ladies of the queen, who are armed with armour, with swords, arrows, or sticks according to their rank, as princes, warriors, sons of heralds and headmen, and sons of attendants and charioteers. They must guard the horse from any danger, including bathing and intercourse with mares, doubtless acts calculated to reduce its sanctity of power. The princes among them are promised the royal consecration as the reward for success. If any ill fall upon the horse, it must be atoned for: if it dies, a new horse is found and some ceremonies repeated. During the period of its absence the priests and the sacrificer sit on golden thrones: the Hotṛ begins the telling of the cyclic[2] narrative, Pariplava Ākhyāna, the telling of tales, Ākhyānas, of ancient kings, which last by series of ten days for the whole year. At the end of the performance the Adhvaryu offers in the Dakṣiṇa fire libations for the movements of the steed, and in the Āhavanīya, after sunset, the Dhṛti libations to secure the success of the rite: at his bidding a lute player, a Rājanya, sings to the lute three Gāthās, verses, made by himself which refer to victories in battle connected with the sacrificer. All the performances repeat themselves daily for a year, or six months, or even for half a month, if the period is reduced. When the horse returns, the king, who has been celebrated hitherto with the kings of the past, is from the Dīkṣā day of the new sacrifice hailed as with the gods, and on the three pressing days proper with Prajāpati. The first pressing day[3] falls on the full moon of Vaiçākha: there are 21 posts and 21 victims for Agni and Soma: on the days of pressing the victims are two sets of eleven each. The second pressing day is the most important. The Stotra is started at the neighing of a horse in the morning: after the Çastra of the Hotṛ, three other horses are yoked with the sacrificial horse, and are driven to bathe. On the return of the horses the victim is anointed by the chief of the queens, and 101 gold pieces placed in its mane and tail. It is given the remains of an offering made the previous night; but, if it will not eat them, they are cast into water. Then take place curious riddles between the Brahman and the Hotṛ, the Brahmodya.[4] Then the victims are bound to the posts, in all 327 or 349 tame animals and a large number of wild animals from the elephant to the bee,

[1] AÇS. x. 6. 10; ÇB. xiii. 4. 3. 5.

[2] There is nothing of sequence in the several narratives.

[3] The forms of the rites on these days are subject to much dispute, e.g. KÇS. xx. 4. 22; 5. 1; 8. 12, 13; AÇS. x. 8. 2; 9. 8.

[4] Bloomfield, *Religion of the Veda*, pp. 216 ff. Cf. for a specimen of this sort, JB. i. 258.

making 609 in one version. The large numbers, especially of the wild animals, which were, however, to be let go after the fire had been carried round them, are suspicious : the best defence [1] to be made is that there was need of large numbers for the festival to follow the sacrifice. The horse is covered with a garment and slain : the queens go round it from left to right thrice, and thrice *vice versa* : the chief queen goes near the horse : both are covered with a garment, and the queen unites with it : meanwhile the priest and the maidens and the other wives indulge in ribald dialogue. Then the horse and the other victims are cut up. The blood is cooked, the omentum offering of the ordinary ritual prepared : before it another Brahmodya between Hotṛ and Adhvaryu, Brahman and Udgātṛ, sacrificer and Adhvaryu, takes place. The rest of the horse is cooked, the blood offered at the end of the Sviṣṭakṛt offering and also on other occasions. Before the Sviṣṭakṛt offering the cooked flesh is offered to Prajāpati, and at the end of the second day offerings are made, through the night, of various plants.

The offerings of the third day are followed by the final bath, in which is performed the curious rite of an offering on the head of a man already referred to.[2] The fees are given in various forms : the conquered land is to be divided : even the wives of the sacrificer are sometimes demanded : the Adhvaryu apparently obtains a daughter in wedlock, and also the fourth wife.

The Rigveda [3] clearly knows this greatest of all Vedic sacrifices, though it is certain that the holocaust of victims was not then usual; only a goat appears to lead the way for the horse, and, though this is not conclusive, still it makes it doubtful whether the early ritual had the large number of victims offered. The victims too seem to be led round the fire, not *vice versa*. But it is clear that the offering was already a Soma sacrifice, and that in essence the rite was known : reference is also made to the use of gold and the cloths for decking the steed.

The meaning of the sacrifice is in the former view of Oldenberg [4] the offering to Indra, the god of the warriors, of a swift strong steed from which the sacrificer would thus derive magic power, whether directly or indirectly through the fact that Indra would thus be made strong to aid him. The slaying of the dog he thinks intended as the destruction of hostile powers, or perhaps in origin as providing the horse with a guardian; such a function is sometimes given to a four-eyed dog in the Avesta. The relation of the queen and the horse is clearly a fertility spell, while the obscene language, he thinks, might be explained in the same sense, or as an amusement of the gods, or a

[1] Hillebrandt, *Rituallitteratur*, p. 152. Açoka records the large numbers of animals killed in his time (Pillar Edict V; Vincent Smith, *Asoka*, p. 204).

[2] Part III, Chap. 18, § 3.

[3] i. 162 and 163.

[4] *Rel. des Veda*[1], pp. 306, 356, 473–5. His later view (pp. 473 f.) makes the rite magic; the horse embodies royalty, and by its consecration is made especially sacred so that its slaughter gives strength to the sacrificer. He observes, however, that in RV. x. 56 a horse sacrifice to the dead occurs, which may be the imitation of the horse sacrifice or its prototype.

mere relic of the plain speech of the crowd. In the view of Eggeling [1] the horse, the next animal to man in the scale, is the appropriate offering on great occasions : at the sacrifice the steed can be identified with Prajāpati, and so Prajāpati comes properly into the ritual. On the other hand he points out that the horse is connected with Varuṇa, in that the horse is the sun horse which traverses the heaven, which is Varuṇa and is conceived as a sea of waters, so that the horse is sprung from the waters. Varuṇa may, therefore, have been the earlier deity of the offering.

The original force of the rite is somewhat obscure. The possibility of comparison with the October horse at Rome [2] is obvious, and the eating of the horse, the fertility rite in which it appears, and the obscenity of the conversation, point to a vegetation ritual, but the absence of any suggestion that the horse was a vegetation spirit, or that its body was in part used for a direct vegetation magic, is against that theory. In the view of von Negelein,[3] the offering was one made to the sun conceived as a steed, in order to strengthen him for his course in the heaven. As Indra with his steed defeats the Asuras, so the earthly king by the horse sacrifice, uniting himself mysteriously with the sacrificial horse and its magic power, defeats the Asuras. Indra's horse is the thunderbolt which slays Vṛtra, and so the human horse aids the king to defeat his enemies. Varuṇa then, and later Prajāpati, were given by tradition the ownership of the horse, first connected with Indra. The difficulty of this theory is to see exactly why the horse is connected with Indra. He is not the sun in Vedic and probably not even in pre-Vedic myth. On the other hand Varuṇa is the god of the waters *par excellence* : the waters in many lands are conceived as horses, both sea and fresh waters being so regarded : to rivers and the sea horses are offered as in Greece : Indra would then not be the primary figure in the myth as von Negelein holds, but a natural intruder in the rite. The most attractive alternative to this view is undoubtedly the acceptance of the sun as the sun horse,[4] offered originally to the sun as a spell to strengthen it, and the chief difficulty in that view is merely the fact that the sun is not the recipient of the offering, in any measure. If he were actually offered to, it

[1] SBE. xliv. pp. xviii–xxiv. For the four-eyed dog, cf. Moulton, *Early Zoroastrianism*, p. 333, whose suggestion as to aboriginal Magoi connected with Indian aborigines I do not share (JRAS. 1915, pp. 790–9). The dogs of Yama and Yudhiṣṭhira's faithful hound may be recalled.

[2] Festus, p. 178 ; Mannhardt, *Myth. Forsch.*, pp. 156–201 ; Warde Fowler, *Roman Festivals*, pp. 242–50 ; MacCulloch, *Rel. of Anc. Celts*, pp. 213–15.

[3] *Das Pferd im arischen Altertum*, p. 97 ; for offerings of the horse to the sun in Greece and Illyria, see Cook, *Zeus*, i. 180, 181 ; Keith, JRAS. 1916, pp. 548, 549. Cf. E. Lehmann (de la Saussaye, *Lehrb. der Religionsgesch.*[3] ii. 37), who takes the rite as one to present the sun with a new horse for his team, but of this the texts show no trace, though a votive offering of this kind is natural (cf. Helm, *Altgerm. Rel.* i. 178 f.).

[4] Keith, *Taittirīya Saṁhitā*, i. pp. cxxxiv ff., where all the older views are discussed. Needless to say, while Frazer makes it a corn spirit, Reinach (*Cultes, Mythes et Religions*, iii. 124–40) sees totemism, like E. Monseur, RHR. li. 16 ; for a refutation see A. van Gennep, *L'état actuel du problème totémique*, pp. 291 f.

would be easy to understand the place of Indra : that Indra should have completely superseded him is odd, but on the whole the explanation of the horse as the sun steed seems the most plausible. It is at least certain that in the Vājasaneyi Saṁhitā the steed was regarded in the rite as identical with Dadhikrāvan whose sun character is not to be doubted.[1] Perhaps the true solution lies in the view that two rites are confused, the offering of a horse to the sun and of a horse to Varuṇa as god of the waters. Prajāpati must in any case be deemed to be a later addition to the rite. It is of course possible that the position of Varuṇa was not won until after he had become prominent in the ritual of the final bath, and that then he appropriated in part the sacrifice of the steed.

§ 16. *The Human Sacrifice*

The human sacrifice as prescribed in two of the ritual texts [2] is based closely on the horse sacrifice ; while there the chief victims are the horse, a Gomṛga, and a hornless goat, here a man is added, a Brahman or Kṣatriya bought at the price of a thousand cows and a hundred cattle, and he is permitted like the horse a year of freedom, in which he can do as he wishes, save that he must remain chaste. The offering is to be performed by a Brahman or a Kṣatriya who is not successful. When slain, the chief queen must lie beside the victim as beside the horse : the attempt to find a reference to this practice in the Rigveda [3] is a failure. On the other hand the nominal offering of large numbers of other men, 166 at 11 posts, is mentioned by the Çatapatha Brāhmaṇa,[4] but we have every reason to assume that this is mere priestly imagination, unless, as is possible, the conceptions of the priest were occasionally made real by a king. It is laid down [5] that a king may on this occasion give up his goods and enter into the life of the wandering mendicant, but this seems merely to have been a facultative rule. It must, however, be noted that the rite of an actual slaying of man is not described in the Brāhmaṇas at all : there is in the Çatapatha and the Taittirīya and their Sūtras merely the symbolic offering of men, who are let free like the wild animals at the horse sacrifice, and therefore the actual offering rests merely on Sūtra evidence, the Vaitāna and Çāñkhāyana, and not even on the early Sūtras. It is not credible that the Brāhmaṇas should have passed over the rite if they had actually known of it ; its mention in the later Sūtras is consistent only with the invention of it, as a reasonable complement to the theory of sacrifice which saw an anomaly in the omission of man from the victims.[6]

[1] Cf. Henry, *Album-Kern*, pp. 10 ff. ; *contra*, Oldenberg, *Archiv f. Religionswissenschaft*, vii. 212–14.

[2] ÇÇS. xvi. 10 f. ; Vait. xxxvii. 10 ff. ; Weber, ZDMG. xviii. 262 ff. ; *Episches im vedischen Ritual*, pp. 9 ff. ; *Rājasūya*, pp. 47, 52 ; Hillebrandt, *Rituallitteratur*, p. 153 ; Keith, *Taittirīya Saṁhitā*, i. pp. cxxxv, cxxxvii, cxl.

[3] x. 18. 8 ; 85. 21, 22 ; Hillebrandt, ZDMG. xl. 708–11 ; *Ved. Myth.* ii. 109. See Oldenberg, GGA. 1907, p. 218, n. 1.

[4] ÇB. xiii. 6 ; KÇS. xxi. 1 ; TB. iii. 4. 1–19 ; ApÇS. xx ; HÇS. xiv. 6.

[5] ÇB. xiii. 6. 2. 20 ; KÇS. xxi. 1. 17.

[6] Oldenberg, *Rel. des Veda*², p. 363 ; Keith, *Taittirīya Saṁhitā*, i. pp. cxxxvii-cxl ; Eggeling, SBE. xliv. pp. xl ff. Hopkins

No other trace of human sacrifice exists in the Vedic literature apart from the quite different case of the use of a man and four other victims as an offering at the piling of the great fire altar.[1] This usage is not actually laid down for the contemporary time by any Brāhmaṇa : the most contemplated is the use of the head of a man who has been slain by lightning or by an arrow shot, not a victim killed for the purpose, and normally the head of a goat seems to have sufficed. But it is clearly no real sacrifice at all. The legend of Çunaḥçepa, which has been thought to embody an old legend of human sacrifice which was later abolished, and for which the recitation of the story suffices when recited to the king at the royal consecration, has been noted above ; its essential feature of the horror of the proposed offering, whether the victim is the son of the king or merely a priest, and the view thus taken is quite incompatible with the idea that the actual human sacrifice was performed in Vedic India.[2]

§ 17. *Other Ahīna Rites*

While the human sacrifice occupies five pressing days, the universal sacrifice, Sarvamedha,[3] takes ten, and it is modelled on the offering made of himself by Brahman Svayambhu, in the beginning of things. Its relation to the human sacrifice is held to be the perfection of the former : at the human sacrifice, according to Çāñkhāyana, the offerer gives away the kingdom with the people : at this he gives the earth away also, and in Hillebrandt's [4] view the rite marked the act by which the king left the royal life for the ascetic, as the Buddha afterwards did. It is, however, difficult to take the offering seriously : it is based on myth, and seems no more than a purely priestly fiction : this is borne out by the fact that it is mentioned only in the latest Sūtras, though it figures in the legend of Naciketas.

There are many other forms of the Ahīna rite, with more than one and not more than twelve pressing days, making up at most with the Upasads, &c., not over a month. The number of variations is very large indeed, and the different forms are given names, according to the families or individuals who invented or practised them. Of their make-up the most important rule is that they must end with an Atirātra rite, and in all the days of the Abhiplava and Pṛṣṭhya Ṣaḍahas are usually brought into account : of these further particulars will be given below.

Apart, however, from mere priestly inventions, there are clear traces of popular rites : the most interesting is the Çabalīhoma,[5] performed in spring to increase the herds. The sacrificer cuts hair and beard, puts on an unused

(*Rel. of India*, pp. 198–200), however, accepts it.

[1] Hubert and Mauss, *Année sociol.* ii. 104.

[2] Punishment of crime occasionally takes the form of a sacrifice (ApDS. i. 9. 25. 12 ; VasDS. xx. 25 f.), but this is isolated and abnormal ; Oldenberg, *Rel. des Veda*², p. 363, n. 1.

[3] KÇS. xxi. 2 ; HÇS. xiv ; ÇÇS. xvi. 15, 16 ; Vait. xxxviii. 10 ff.

[4] *Rituallitteratur*, p. 154.

[5] PB. xxi. 3 ; LÇS. ix. 8. 1 ff. ; Weber, *Ind. Stud.* v. 437–47.

garment, lies twelve nights on an uncovered elevated spot, and drinks hot milk. The fire in his house must be kept burning: no one, save a friend to give him the directions to perform his functions, must accompany him: he must say little and keep close. On the morning of the twelfth day he offers a libation of honey and sour milk with a formula addressed to Çabalī. Before the voices of beings are heard, he goes from the village to a wood where he can hear none of the sounds of the village animals, takes a bunch of grass and cries thrice with loud voice 'Çabalī': if any animal other than a dog or an ass replies, his sacrifice will be successful. If no answer comes he repeats the performance a year later; if, however, at the third time there is no reply, or an ass or dog answers his first appeal, he will have no success. In the view of Henry,[1] Çabalī is the personified cloud, of varied hue, whose purpose can be expressed by the cow rich in milk. Originally a rain spell, the rite was developed for more general purposes. The Pañcaviñça Brāhmaṇa,[2] however, treats Çabalī, the wonder cow, as representing Vāc, speech.

§ 18. *The Sattras or Sacrificial Sessions*

The rite of twelve days, Dvādaçāha,[3] may be performed either as an Ahīna or a Sattra, and all rites with more than twelve pressing days are Sattras: the number of years they may be continued extends to thirty-six or more up to 1,000. The Sattras all differ from other forms of the Soma sacrifice, because all the performers must be consecrated and must be Brahmans: there is therefore no separate sacrificer: all share in the benefits of the offering: each bears the burden of his own errors, whereas at the ordinary sacrifice the sacrificer receives the benefit and the evil results of errors alike. Moreover, they should usually be Brahmans who perform the same kinds of rites, and have the same deity, Tanūnapāt or Narāçaṅsa, at the Āprī invocation; if not, the deity of the majority is adopted. During the Sattra all other sacrifices cease to be performed by the priests taking part in the rite: any sexual intercourse is forbidden, as are swift movements, laughing without holding the hand before the mouth, untruth, connexions with non-Aryans, and so forth. One of them plays the part of sacrificer: the others hold on to him when he does those acts which only one man can perform. The Adhvaryu consecrates the sacrificer, and so on until a student consecrates the Unnetṛ. The wives of the priests are also consecrated each with her husband. There are no fees: instead the priests go south saying as they shake black skins, 'What here from my life departeth, that, O Agada, I bring to thee as a fee,' evidently a device to secure long life. The aims of the Sattras are most

[1] *La magie dans l'Inde antique*, pp. 70, 71.

[2] xxi. 1. 5; *Trans. Conn. Acad.* xv. 27, n. 2. For the wish-cow idea, cf. JB. i. 181; ii. 83 f.; iii. 146 (wish-cows in the world to come).

[3] ApÇS. xxi; BÇS. xvi; KÇS. i. 6. 13; xii; AÇS. x. 5; ÇCS. x–xii; LÇS. x. 1. 11 ff.; Vait. xlii. 14 ff., Hillebrandt, *Rituallitteratur*, pp. 153–6; Keith, *Rig-Veda Brāhmaṇas*, pp. 55 ff.

various: the obtaining of wealth, of cattle, of offspring, of prosperous marriage, and many other things. Much as they are, it is clear, elaborated by the priest, they reflect here and there primitive conceptions of sacrifice.

The model of all Sattras is the Dvādaçāha, which is made up of a Prāyaṇīya and an Udayanīya, which, as in all Sattras as opposed to Ahīnas, must both be Atirātra days, as the beginning and concluding rites respectively of a Pṛṣṭhya Ṣaḍaha, and of either 4 Chandomas or 3 Chandomas and an Avivākya day as the tenth. The name Pṛṣṭhya is based on the different treatment of the Pṛṣṭha Stotra of each day corresponding to the Çastra of the Hotṛ: on the first it is in the Rathantara tune, on the second the Bṛhat, the third the Vairūpa, the fourth the Vairāja, the fifth the Çākvara, the sixth the Raivata. Of these days the first and fourth are Agniṣṭomas, the others Ukthyas. The Chandomas are Ukthyas, the tenth is an Atyagniṣṭoma: it is called Avivākya, because on that day no dispute about errors in the ceremony is allowed.[1] A further variation is possible: on the fourth and ninth days the Āgrayaṇa cup may be drawn first, on the six and seventh the Çukra, in which case the Stotras and the Çastras must also be transposed, or they may be transposed without change in the order of the cups: this makes the period of ten days bear the term *vyūḍhachandas*. The Soma is daily watched by one priest, the rest may study the Veda, fetch wood, and eat. The tenth day is marked by interesting rites, the singing of the Sāman called the success of the Sattra, and the performance of a Brahmodya like that at the horse offering or regarding the unqualified Prajāpati.

Rules are given for building up the Dvādaçāha to longer Sattras; the simplest addition is that of a Mahāvrata day after the period of ten days: other additions are inserted before that period, the shorter before the longer. But these rules are very much varied in practice. Of the various forms by far the most interesting is the Gavām Ayana, 'the way of the cows', which is a Sattra of one year's duration.

The beginning of this Sattra [2] is variously prescribed, at the full moon of Phālguna or Caitra, or four days before the full moon of these months or of Māgha. The middle day, the Viṣuvant, divides it into two halves, of which the latter is in many respects intended to be the reverse of the former. The scheme of the offering is a Prāyaṇīya Atirātra, a Caturviṅça day on which the twenty-four-fold Stoma is used, the form being either an Agniṣṭoma or an Ukthya; five months each of four Abhiplava Ṣaḍahas and one Pṛṣṭhya; a sixth one of one Pṛṣṭhya, three Abhiplavas, one Abhijit, an Agniṣṭoma rite, and three Svarasāman days making up 28, to which the first two days are added to complete the month. Then comes the Viṣuvant. The second half-year has as the seventh month three Svarasāmans, one Viçvajit, one Pṛṣṭhya, and three Abhiplavas; then months 8 to 11 have one Pṛṣṭhya and four

[1] Cf. Eggeling, SBE. xli. p. xvii; Keith, *Rig-Veda Brāhmaṇas*, p. 247.

[2] ApÇS. xxii, xxiii; BÇS. xvi; KÇS. xiii; xxiv. 4, 5; AÇS. xi. 7; xii; ÇÇS. xiii. 19; LÇS. iii. 5–iv. 5; Vait. xxxi. 6–34; Eggeling, SBE. xliv. 140 ff.

Abhiplavas each, and the last has three Abhiplavas, one Āyus day, one Go day, one Daçarātra, and the Mahāvrata and Udayanīya days.

The Abhiplava Ṣaḍaha, which is often used in Sattras of all kinds and also in Ahīnas, differs in certain respects from the Pṛṣṭhya. In the first place in it the Pṛṣṭha Stotra is alternatively Rathantara and Bṛhat only. In the second place the days of the Abhiplava are differentiated as Jyotis, Go, and Āyus according to the Stomas used for the different Stotras. The Jyotis form, which is an Agniṣṭoma, having twelve Stotras only, employs for 1–6 the Pañcadaça, for 7–11 the Saptadaça, and for 12 the Ekaviñça. The other two are Ukthyas and have fifteen Stotras: for 1 the Go uses the Pañcadaça, for 2–5 the Trivṛt, for 6–10 the Saptadaça, for 11–15 the Ekaviñça. The Āyus has for 1 Trivṛt, for 2–5 Pañcadaça, for 6–10 Saptadaça, and 11–15 Ekaviñça.

At the Viṣuvant the sun is honoured with offerings, but the Mahāvrata [1] is much more fully known to us. The rite is according to the ritual allowed to be performed variously as a one-day rite, an Ahīna, or in a Sattra, and the latter is its natural place. It is clearly an old festival of the winter solstice, and not even originally, as Hillebrandt holds, of the summer solstice, when the strengthening of the sun was an essential duty. There is beaten an earth drum, doubtless to scare away the demons who might attempt to overthrow the power of the sun; the Hotṛ sits on a swing and is swung to and fro, to represent the path of the sun in the sky, and strengthen its power to perform it; ritual abuse is exchanged for fertility purposes, between a student or, in a later usage, a Māgadha, and a hetaira; there is actually carried out sexual intercourse; the consecrated persons are alternately praised and reviled; there is a mimic fight between an Aryan and a Çūdra for the possession of a white round skin which is declared to be a symbol of the sun; [2] the skin of an unfruitful cow is hung up or stretched out and warriors pierce through it with arrows, perhaps as a rain spell.[3] Women celebrate to the sound of the lute in the south the patrons of the ceremony: maids dance round the fire with water pitchers, while the Stotra is being performed: they pour the water on the fire, and their song shows that they desire richness in milk with water for the cows. The desire of heat and rain seems clearly united: the position of the sun nearest earth is indicated by the priest, who touches the board of the

[1] Hillebrandt, *Sonnwendfeste* (*Roman. Forsch.* v. 299 ff.); Keith, *Çāñkhāyana Āraṇyaka*, pp. 79 ff.; Eggeling, SBE. xliii. pp. xxv ff.; Max Müller, SBE. i. pp. xcii ff.; von Schroeder, *Arische Religion*, ii. 137 ff., 210 f., 243 f., 317 ff., 599, 631 ff., adducing parallels. See TS. vii. 5. 9 f.; KS. xxxiv. 5; PB. vi. 5. 13–21; 6. 11–15; JB. ii. 404–10, which negatives performance on the Viṣuvant.

[2] Keith, *Taittirīya Saṁhitā*, i. p. cxxxi. For ritual swinging see Frazer, *The Dying God*, pp. 277–85; Warde Fowler, *Religious Experience of the Roman People*, pp. 61–7.

[3] Brunnhofer (*Arische Urzeit*, p. 304) interprets RV. viii. 20. 8 as the shooting of arrows by the Sobharis against the Maruts' car to bring down the honey-dew, and cites the practice of the Mapongas to shoot arrows to bring down rain. The skin may represent the clouds, as the Aegis brings the thunderstorm (*Il.* xvii. 593 ff.; *Aen.* viii. 352 ff.).

swing and the earth with one hand, and says, ' The God hath united with the goddess '.[1]

From the point of view of the priest, most important elements of the Mahāvrata are the Mahāvrata Stotra or the Pṛṣṭha Stotra, corresponding to the Mahaduktha of the Hotṛ : it is noteworthy for the fact that it is intended to reproduce the form of the fire, the five Sāmans, the Gāyatra, Rathantara, Bṛhat, Bhadra, and Rājana, are equated to the head, right and left wing, tail and body, and accompanied by the Stomas from Trivṛt to Pañcaviṅça in order. The later ritual of the Çāñkhāyana Çrauta Sūtra identifies the Stotra with the body of a man, showing the influence of the mystic speculations of the priests who performed the Agnicayana, ' piling of the fire ', and who saw in this act the making up of the universal father, the creator god Prajāpati, identified with the primeval giant who in the Puruṣasūkta is conceived as having, when sacrificed, provided the material for the whole world.[2]

Of other Sattras an interesting one is that performed on the Dṛṣadvatī,[3] a specially sacred river, and still more that on the Sarasvatī, which is marked by many special rites. The sacrifice is performed as the sacrificer moves along the bank from the place where the Sarasvatī disappears in the desert, across the confluence with the Dṛṣadvatī, at the crossing of which an offering is made to Apāṁ Napāt, to the place where the stream arises, the Plakṣa Prāsravaṇa,[4] where an offering is made to Agni as Kāma, ' desire '. The sacrifice is accompanied by the driving of a hundred young calves along with a bull into the wood, and is terminated when these have reached the number of a thousand, or the sacrificer dies, or the cows disappear. At the end of the whole sacrifice, a mare and a woman are given as a present to the worthiest of those who have taken part in the performance. The final bath is taken at Kāravapacava on the Yamunā. This and the Dṛṣadvatī offering are important for the fact that they mention several places of the Kuru land, such as Parīṇah,[5] and indicate the boundaries of that country, the chief home of Brahmanism.

§ 19. *The Sautrāmaṇī*

The Sautrāmaṇī [6] is not a Soma sacrifice, but is classified by the Sūtras as a Haviryajña, though its chief characteristic in its form as recorded is the offering of Surā. It has two distinct forms, the Kaukilī, which is an independent offering, the other the Carakā, an offering which forms part of another

[1] This is clearly the wedding of sun and earth, a form of that of sky and earth ; cf. Brunnhofer, *Arische Urzeit*, pp. 325–7 ; Cook, *Zeus*, i. 526 ff., 604, 672, 709, 733.

[2] Other Ayanas (e. g. Utsargiṇām Ayana, JB. iii. 393–7 ; TS. vii. 5. 6 f. ; KS. xxx. 7 ; PB. v. 10) are given in the Brāhmaṇas and Sūtras.

[3] PB. xxv. 13. 1 ff. ; LÇS. x. 18. 12 ff. ; KÇS. xxiv. 6. 32 ff. ; ÇÇS. xiii. 29. 27 ff.

[4] See Macdonell and Keith, *Vedic Index*, ii. 65.

[5] *Ibid.* i. 170 ; JB. ii. 300.

[6] BÇS. xvii. 31–8 ; MÇS. v. 2. 4, 11 ; ApÇS. xix ; HÇS. xiii. 24 ; KÇS. xv. 9. 27 ff. ; xix ; AÇS. iii. 9 ; ÇÇS. xv. 15 ; LÇS. v 4. 11 ff. ; Vait. xxx.

offering, as the Rājasūya and the Agnicayana. It is prescribed for various occasions, but the characteristic ones are the rites for a man who is vomiting Soma, or from whose nose, ears, &c., Soma flows as a result of over-indulgence in the drink. The Carakā form seems clearly a reference to the school of the Black Yajurveda, which is often so named: the view of Hillebrandt [1] that it alludes to the medical teacher Caraka, in whose school Surā was used as medicine, is improbable and unsupported by any evidence. The differences between the two forms are of detail: thus the Kaukilī is marked by the singing by the Brahman of certain Sāmans. The use of the Surā is accompanied by offerings of animals, to Indra a bull, to Sarasvatī a sheep, and to the Açvins a goat. These are offered on the fourth day of the rite, which is modelled on the fourth-day Soma sacrifice, along with oblations of milk, of Surā, and of animal fat. The goat for Agni and Soma, which in the Soma sacrifice precedes the pressing day, is replaced by a bull for Agni, and the barren cow at the end of the Soma rite is replaced by a bull for Indra Vayodhas. In the Surā, which is prepared from various kinds of herbs in a wonderful way, are mixed hairs [2] of a lion, a tiger, and a wolf, to confer corresponding characteristics on the partakers of the cups of Surā. The Fathers also receive an offering of the Surā. After the libation to Vanaspati in the animal offering, a throne of Muñja grass is set down between the two Vedis, which, as at the Varuṇapraghāsas, are used in this rite, and on this the sacrificer sits down with silver under his left and gold under his right foot: the offerings, thirty-two in number, of fat are then made, while the remainder is used to sprinkle the sacrificer, so that it flows from his mouth. The Adhvaryu then touches the sacrificer, who calls on his servants with their ritual names, and they lift him up first knee high, then navel high, and then as high as the mouth. He then steps on to a tiger-skin as establishing himself in the lordship: the thirty-third cup of fat is offered, a Sāman is sung, and all join in the finale. A milk offering to Mitra and Varuṇa, and a bull for Indra Vayodhas conclude the rite.

It is conjectured by Hillebrandt [3] that the rite was taken over by the Indians from a non-Brahmanical tribe, and then remodelled on the basis of the Soma ritual: he thinks that the Surā was once a drink akin to the Madhu, and offered to the Açvins. The Açvins are not prominent as Soma-drinkers, but they certainly are connected with the Madhu, and the Surā seems from the evidence of the Avesta to have been once a sacred and honoured drink. The Madhu or Surā cult, he thinks, may have flourished on the banks of the Sarasvatī, where the Vasiṣṭhas show little anxiety about the Soma cult, and may not originally have practised it, but have learned it from later intruders. The

[1] *Rituallitteratur*, p. 159. Windisch (*Buddha's Geburt*, pp. 51, 52) thinks that the medical school has its name from the Vedic school in which, he thinks, medicine was much studied. Of this, however, there is not the slightest proof. Cf. also Keith, ZDMG. lxii. 135 ff.; *Taittirīya Saṁhitā*, i. p. cxxii. The two kinds in MÇS. are Kaukilī and Aiṣṭikī.

[2] Cf. the use of hairs of a bull in feeding the newly born child; below, Chap. 21, § 3.

[3] *Ved. Myth.* i. 250 ff. On the Avestan Hurā see Geiger, *Ostiran. Kultur*, p. 233.

hypothesis, however, is not supported by any evidence of value,[1] and there are clear traces that the rite was based on myth, that of the effects on Indra of over-indulgence in Soma and the resulting illness which was cured by the efforts of the Açvins and Sarasvatī, a fact alluded to in the Rigveda.

§ 20. *The Piling of the Fire*

The piling of the fire altar[2] is a rite which is regarded as being always available for performance along with the Soma sacrifice, but which is declared to be obligatory only in certain cases, including the Mahāvrata, and even that view is far from being universally prescribed. There can be no doubt that it was by no means a normal or frequent rite: its elaboration is such that no ordinary sacrificer would trouble himself with it, and it must have been only occasionally used. The main authority for it in the Çatapatha Brāhmaṇa is a different authority from the chief source of rules on the rest of the sacrificial ritual including the Soma sacrifice, Yājñavalkya: it is attributed to Çāṇḍilya, and others mentioned in connexion with it are Tura Kāvaṣeya,[3] who performed it on the Kārotī, and Nagnajit Gāndhāra, names which have been held with some force to point to the North-West, where in conjunction with the fire cult there may have been special activity, perhaps in consequence of contact with Iran.

The beginning of the sacrifice is the offering of victims, including a man: the heads are to be built into the altar and the bodies are placed in the water whence the clay for the fire-pan and the bricks of the altar are derived. The clay is solemnly collected with the aid of a horse, an ass, and a goat, a procession being formed to the place which the horse is supposed to determine, and the clay being brought formally back. Then the wife of the sacrificer makes the Aṣāḍhā brick, and the sacrificer makes the fire-pan and the three Viçvajyotis bricks. The fire-pan is kept filled with fire, from the time of the consecration, which takes place fourteen days after the animal offering, and for a year the sacrificer carries it about, and performs various rites, striding the Viṣṇu steps and adoring the fire in the pan. Then comes the actual ceremony of the building of the altar, which is made in five layers, of which the first[4] has 1,950 and the whole together 10,800 bricks, which are given diverse names; the length of time used in the rite differs greatly: the first four layers may occupy eight months and the last four, or a few days may suffice. Noteworthy features of the building are the placing in the lowest layer of a golden figure of a man, which seems to be meant as symbolic

[1] Bloomfield, JAOS. xv. 193 ff.; Keith, *Taittirīya Saṁhitā*, i. pp. cxxii ff.

[2] ApÇS. xvi ff.; BÇS. x; KÇS. xvi–xviii; AÇS. iv. 1. 21 ff.; ÇÇS. ix. 22; LÇS. i. 5. 5 ff.; Vait. xxviii f.; Weber, *Ind. Stud.* xiii. 217–92; Eggeling, SBE. xli. pp. xxvi ff.; xliii. pp. xiii ff.; Oldenberg, GN. 1917, pp. 9 ff.; Keith, *Taittirīya Saṁhitā*, i. pp. cxxv ff.

[3] Macdonell and Keith, *Vedic Index*, i. 314.

[4] In the White Yajurveda ritual there are considerable differences in detail from the rules of the Black Yajurveda, but the points are of no real consequence; cf. Weber, *Ind. Stud.* xiii. 325 ff.; Eggeling, SBE. xliii. 357 ff.

of Agni, who is thus as it were put bodily in the altar, while a tortoise is also immured alive,[1] and addressed as a mystic being. After the altar has been erected, there are 425 libations for the Rudras, made of all sorts of wild plants. The mode of cooling the altar is also noteworthy: the Adhvaryu draws lines on the altar with a reed to which a flag, a twig of Vetaça, and an Avakā plant, all things closely connected with the waters, are tied. The formal placing of fire on the altar is carried out with much ceremony: the priest and the sacrificer step upon the altar: milk of a black cow with a white calf is offered on the last-deposited naturally perforated brick, the fire-brand is deposited on it, and special wood is used to kindle it. Then come a number of libations, for Vaiçvānara, for the forty-nine winds, which are to be as helpful to the sacrificer as they were formerly for Indra, the shower of wealth libations, 372 libations for Agni, thirteen for the names of the months, sixteen again for Agni, the Pārtha offering, one introduced by the mythical king Pṛthi Vainya [2] at his royal consecration, and fourteen Vājaprasavīyas, whose remnants mixed with milk and water serve to anoint the sacrificer, who, according as he touches the altar or stands or sits, uses a black antelope-skin as a carpet, or a goat-skin, has certain wishes fulfilled. After the anointing, follow six further Pārtha oblations, twelve Rāṣṭrabhṛts, and three oblations to the winds, which are offered in the place of the horses of the chariot, and treated as if they were horses. The first pressing day of the rite is marked by the yoking of the fire before the Prātaranuvāka, and by its releasing with appropriate formulae at night. To the ordinary rites of the Soma sacrifice are added offerings to the minor deities, Anumati, Kuhū, Rākā, Sinīvālī, and for Dhātṛ at the Udayanīyā Iṣṭi, and at the very end of the final libations an offering of milk for Mitra and Varuṇa. The performer of the piling is subjected to certain taboos: he may not go out in the rain, nor eat the flesh of a bird, the altar being deemed to be of bird or human form, nor have relations with any save a wife of the same caste: after a second offering of the Agnicayana, which is permissible if the first has not good results, he may only have relations with his own wife, and after a third not even with her. In these cases the obvious meaning is that the sacrificer is to avoid wasting in any way the sacred power of the fire, which is within him, and which might be dispersed uselessly, while he must not eat the bird which is the symbol of the fire.

There can be little doubt that this vast ceremonial is not a simple or primitive rite: it is a definite attempt of the priest to embody in the ritual the conception already found in the Rigveda [3] of the creation of the universe from the dismemberment of the primeval giant, which requires as its complement the process of building up the fire altar, which is a symbol of the universe, and of the cosmic sacrifice which is eternally repeated. It falls, therefore, to be considered below as an important expression of the theory of sacrifice of

[1] This practice may clearly be connected with the recorded discovery of toads living inside rocks, &c.

[2] Macdonell and Keith, *Vedic Index*, ii. 16.

[3] x. 90.

the Brahmans: much as there is of magic and many offerings as there are in the ritual, it is essentially in conception the embodiment of philosophic theory, a fact which explains its loose connexion with any real sacrifices.[1]

§ 21. *The Hotṛ Formulae*

The ritual requires in many places the use of the Hotṛ formulae, which are formulae in which the priests are mentioned as being identical with deities and other objects, the formulae being distinguished according to the number of priests so mentioned as Caturhotṛ, Pañcahotṛ, and so on. They are termed offerings, because they represent various sacrifices from the Agnihotra to the Soma offering inclusive. They are often used in the course of important rites, in which case they are normally assigned to the sacrificer, but also they can be employed independently, either by themselves or with the accompaniment of cups of some offering and the cry Svāhā. Thus a man, who wishes cattle, must for twelve nights drink hot water, put on a fresh garment and sleep on the ground. Early next morning he goes east, says the Daçahotṛ, and offers the Caturhotṛ with butter. They can even be used as spells, in which case an offering is made on salt ground, or a break in the earth, and in place of the ordinary Vaṣaṭ-call harsh words like *khaṭ* or *phaṭ* are used. This use is clearly an abuse: the formulae are of the nature of Upaniṣads, and must be treated as representing the desire to substitute mental processes for the tediousness of the sacrifice. But it was inevitable that even they should sink to magic uses.[2]

§ 22. *The Expiations*

In the intolerable complications of the Vedic sacrifice, coupled with the tendency to inaccuracy of the Indian mind of the Vedic period, may be found ample excuse for the number of prescriptions which are laid down for the purpose of expiating errors in the sacrifice.[3] In some cases the expiations are elaborate in the extreme: in most they are fairly simple. Of the former the most notorious case is that of the Kuṣmāṇḍa,[4] which serves as a means of purification from grave sins, and which is dealt with in detail in the Taittirīya Āraṇyaka, whereas most of the other expiations are confined to the Sūtras or to the later portions of the Brāhmaṇas.

Of these expiations the most interesting are given in the Kauçika Sūtra,[5] which details magic ceremonies intended to remove the evil results of the violation of certain taboos. One of these is the primitive dread of disturbing

[1] Eggeling, SBE. xliii. pp. xv ff.; Keith, *Taittirīya Saṁhitā*, i. pp. cxxv ff.

[2] TA. iii. 2 ff.; AB. v. 25; ÇÇS. x. 14–18; for use in magic rites, ApÇS. xiv. 13–15; MÇS. v. 2. 14. See Weber, *Ind. Stud.* x. 139, 140.

[3] ApÇS. ix; xiv. 16 ff.; MÇS. iv; KÇS. xxv; AÇS. iii. 10–14; vi. 6–10; ÇÇS. iii. 19–21; xiii. 2–12; Atharva Prāyaçcitta (von Negelein, JAOS. xxxiii. 71–144).

[4] TA. ii. 7, 8.

[5] Henry, *La magie dans l'Inde antique*, pp. 211–19.

the earth, for which a natural explanation can be found in the deadly character of the work of commencing agricultural operations in a tropical climate: the earth must be consoled for the wound on her by the operation of opening her body.[1] An expiation is equally required for the eating of food which has been buried in the ground: it takes the homoeopathic form of offering in the fire grains which have been so buried.[2] In domestic life the sin of marrying before an elder brother must be expiated and two hymns are provided for this express purpose.[3] Expiations are also provided against Agni as Kravyād, the term which applies to the fire by which the body of the dead is burned, but which denotes also a definite aspect of Agni which he may assume without the actual contact with the dead.[4] But the list of expiations is endless: there is hardly any sphere in which errors cannot be committed and expiations required, and the Brahman is the author *par excellence* of these rites.

[1] Kauç. xlvi. 51, 52; AV. xii. 1. 35, 61.
[2] Kauç. xlvi. 33–5.
[3] Kauç. xlvi. 28, 29; AV. vi. 112, 113.
[4] Kauç. xliii. 16–21; AV. iii. 21.

CHAPTER 21

THE DOMESTIC RITUAL

§ 1. *The General Character of the Domestic Sacrifices*

THE householder of the Vedic period was expected to maintain a fire normally in his dwelling, sometimes, however, in a special place outside the actual house. The establishment of such a fire was normal on marriage, on the division of the property of a family, the return of a student from his studentship, or the death of the head of the family, when his eldest son was expected to kindle a new fire. The fire might be produced by friction, but normally it was obtained from the house of a wealthy man, or from one who made many sacrifices. It was the duty of the householder, his son, wife, daughter, or pupil to keep it alive: if it was allowed to go out, it had to be rekindled by friction or reborrowed. If its existence had been interrupted for twelve days, a completely new establishment was prescribed. From it on going a journey the householder took leave and greeted it on his return, kissing his eldest son thereafter to the accompaniment of formulae, while daughters were kissed on the head, not the lips, in silence.

The sacrifices of the domestic ritual were expected to be performed normally by the householder; his wife, however, might act for him as at the morning and evening libations, and at the evening Bali:[1] a Brahman might be used in nearly every case, though at the Pāka offerings and one or two others the householder was required to act himself, according to some authorities at least; a Brahman was required for the offerings to Dhanvantari and the spit-ox offering.[2] If the householder wished to perform the function of the Brahman, he placed a sunshade and a garment, or straw puppet, on the seat in the south which a Brahman would occupy, if employed. The Brahmans claimed that at a marriage the formulae for the bridegroom must be said by them unless he were a Brahman himself, evidently an effort to extend their field of employment.[3] The sacrificer wore a thread under the left armpit and over the right shoulder at offerings to the Fathers, but in the reverse way for offerings to the gods.[4]

The divisions of the domestic offerings are very differently and confusingly given by the different authorities:[5] clearly the matter was not one of

[1] GGS. i. 3. 15; 4. 19; 4. 29; 9. 8, 9; BhGS. iii. 12.

[2] AGS. i. 3. 6.

[3] GGPar. ii. 24. Women are authorities for supplementary rites at marriage, ApGS. ii. 15, though in general not approved, viii. 3; they share in agricultural rites, PGS. ii. 17. 18. The idea that these limited functions are due to priestly influence (Arbman, *Rudra*, p. 103) is implausible.

[4] TA. ii. 1; GGS. i. 2. 1 ff.; JGS. i. 1.

[5] Weber, *Ind. Stud.* x. 326; Oldenberg, SBE. xxx. p. xxiii.

agreement: one division [1] distinguishes seven species of Pāka offerings, where Pāka probably denotes cooked food, another [2] distinguishes what is offered in fire, what is exposed merely, offerings to the Manes, and offerings which are given to a Brahman to eat. The material included milk, barley gruel, porridge, curds, melted butter, rice, barley, sesame, and, but very rarely, animal victims. The butter offering—various kinds of butter [3] are distinguished—is of a fairly simple character: a ladle called Darvī, or a Sruva, is used; also blades of grass for purifying purposes, water to cleanse the grass blades, and kindling sticks, while enclosing sticks are laid around the fire. The Pāka offerings [4] differ from the Çrauta in having no fore- or after-offerings, no invocation of the Iḍā, and no kindling verses or instruction formulae, known as Nigadas. At the end of some at least of the rites, a ceremony called the Yajñavāstu is performed: of the grass of the sacrifice a handful is taken, dipped in the butter, with a request to the birds to lick it, sprinkled in water, and offered to Rudra as lord of the beasts.[5]

The animal victim is prescribed for a guest reception, for offerings to the Fathers, and at marriage: there is also a special spit-ox offering. The cow is the normal victim, but a goat is allowed to take its place. The ceremony of the offering was clearly akin to that of the Çrauta ritual; there is the same touching of the victim, the setting up of a Çāmitra fire, which is derived from the fire-brand thrice carried round it, the taking out first of the omentum and its separate offering, and the cutting of pieces of flesh. The feast was in effect an opportunity, doubtless readily appreciated, for a meal of flesh.[6]

§ 2. *The Various Offerings*

The daily offerings of the householder include offerings at night and morning to Agni and Prajāpati, and Sūrya and Prajāpati respectively: [7] there is, however, great divergence as to the nature of the offerings, usually rice or barley, and the exact deities and times of offering. Further, there are five great offerings to be performed; [8] the first is the Devayajña, that for the gods made in the fire morning and evening, when the meal is ready. The second, that called Bhūtayajña or Bali,[9] is offered on the ground for all manner of beings; in the version of Gobhila, the first is for earth, the second for Vāyu, the third for the All-gods, the fourth for Prajāpati, then the fifth is offered in the water-holder for the god of the waters, the sixth at the middle posts for plants and

[1] ÇGS. i. 1. 15.

[2] ÇGS. i. 5. 1.

[3] AB. i. 3. 5, with comm.; Macdonell and Keith, *Vedic Index*, i. 250, 437; ii. 20.

[4] See Arbman, *Rudra*, pp. 64 ff.

[5] GGS. i. 7 ff.; AGS. i. 10. 6 ff.

[6] Macdonell and Keith, *Vedic Index*, ii. 145–7.

[7] GGS. i. 3. 16; MGS. ii. 3. 1, 2; JGS. i. 23. The cow, however, may be let go; cf. BhGS. ii. 25 f.; VārGS. xii; BGS. i. 2, where great stress is laid on the use of a ram or goat in lieu, or flesh of a wild beast, and in default only is cereal allowed.

[8] GGS. i. 4. 1 ff.; PGS. ii. 9. 3 ff.; AGS. i. 2. 4 ff.; ÇGS. ii. 14; Kauç. lxxiv. 2; BGS. ii. 9; BhGS. iii. 14; VārGS., p. 22.

[9] Cf. Chap. 12, § 5; Arbman, *Rudra*, pp. 189 ff.

trees, and the seventh at the house-door for the ether; an eighth in the bed for Kāma, and finally one in the dustbin for the Rakṣases. But many other names are also given, including offerings to hosts of serpents. The third great offering, the Pitṛyajña, is the throwing of the rest of the Bali sprinkled with water to the Fathers. The fourth, the Brahmayajña, is the repetition of some part of the Veda, usually reduced within narrow limits, and the fifth, the Manuṣyayajña, is the feeding of Brahmans, guests, and beggars.

In the version of Çāñkhāyana,[1] Vaiçvadeva offerings are made in the fire evening and morning to Agni, Soma, Indra and Agni, Viṣṇu, Bharadvāja Dhanvantari, Viçve Devās, Prajāpati, Aditi, Anumati, and Agni Sviṣṭakṛt. Then come the actual Balis offered in the centre of the floor for the same deities, followed by Balis for Brahman and the Brahmans and Vāstoṣpati. Balis are then distributed through the different quarters of the horizon in due order to the presiding deities, Indra, Yama, Varuṇa, Soma, and Bṛhaspati, each with those connected with him. Then turning towards the disk of the sun offerings are made to Aditi and the Ādityas, the Nakṣatras, seasons, months, half-months, days and nights, and years. On the thresholds offerings are made to Pūṣan as maker of ways, Dhātṛ, Vidhātṛ, and the Maruts; on the grindstone to Viṣṇu, on the mortar to the tree; in the place where the herbs are kept to the herbs; near the water-pot to Parjanya and the waters; at the head and the foot of the bed respectively to Çrī and Bhadrakālī; in the privy to Sarvānnabhūti; in the air in the evening to the night-walkers, in the morning to the day-walkers; in the north to the unknown gods and Dhanapati, the lord of wealth. Finally the remnants are poured out in the south for the Fathers, and then a Brahman or student and women are formally fed, as well as boys and the old. In this version we have a duplication which shows the fire ritual encroaching on the ordinary Bali ritual, which involves merely the placing on the ground of the offering for the use of the divinities. There is no doubt of the substantial antiquity of the latter rite, which is attested for Iran by the express and clear assertions of Herodotos,[2] and has also parallels in the usage of the Slavs, Lithuanians, and Germans.[3] It is further clear from Çāñkhāyana that we have in this elaborate rite the development of something far more simple and primitive, the purpose of which is hinted at in the further directions which are given that one should eat nothing without having cut off and offered a portion thereof as a Bali, nor should one eat alone or before others. Not merely the eating of firstfruits is a dangerous thing, rendering a preliminary offering to the gods and the Fathers desirable to break any taboo, but in every case of a meal it is well to propitiate by sharing the food which is enjoyed.[4] Hence Çāñkhāyana recommends, though

[1] ii. 14; Arbman (*Rudra*, p. 191) omits Brahman and Varuṇa, doubtless *per incuriam*.

[2] i. 132.

[3] Carnoy, *Les Indo-Européens*, p. 232.

[4] Cf. GGS. i. 4. 20; Manu, iii. 117 f.; RV. x. 117. 6; MGS. i. 9. 13; at the Madhuparka, AGS. i. 24. 15 ff.; ÇGS. iv. 21. 7 ff.; PGS. i. 3. 18 f. See also the Prāçitra legends, TS. ii. 6. 8. 3; ÇB. i. 7. 4. 1. Arbman (*Rudra*, pp. 204 ff.) compares modern Tibetan (JRAS.

not as part of the formal rite, the giving of food to the dogs, the dog-butchers, and the birds, and Manu [1] formally includes in the Bhūtayajña dogs, outcastes, diseased persons, birds, and insects. In the Kauçika Sūtra [2] we find abstract deities, Dharma, Adharma, hope, faith, wisdom, prosperity, modesty, and knowledge, along with the Vedic gods and snake deities such as Vāsuki, Citrasena, Citraratha, Takṣa, and Upatakṣa.

In this generosity we may take it gods, Fathers, and men shared with all manner of beings, and the term Bali applied to all the offerings. Bhūtayajña may well have been a synonym, whence first were differentiated by regard to the recipients of the offerings the Fathers and men, Pitṛyajña and Manuṣyayajña. All these offerings were precisely of the same kind, made in the same way, without the use of fire, but the domestic ritual suffered expansion by the priests [3] through the introduction of the fire ritual, and we have the spectacle of the Devayajña introduced making up with the Brahmayajña, Vedic study,[4] a set of five sacrifices. The Devayajña, it is plain, is later than the Bhūtayajña in this connexion, and this renders the effort [5] to interpret Bhūta in the light of the existence of the Devayajña out of the question. It is significant of its later character that the deities of the Devayajña differ greatly and are largely priestly; thus Gobhila[6] make them to be the late figure of Prajāpati and the technical one of Agni Sviṣṭakṛt, who is far removed from popular rites. The absence of fire is found also, as we have seen, in parts of the Çrauta ritual, as in the hanging of offerings for Rudra on trees, a usage familiar from Germanic ritual, and it is common in the ritual of offerings to the dead which are frequently placed in pits.

The new and full moon offerings [7] of the domestic ritual agree closely in the deity and other details with those of the Çrauta, but for cakes are substituted paps as offerings, and the offerings to Indra or Mahendra entirely disappear. Other deities are, however, sometimes substituted. At the end the wife of the sacrificer makes an offering to the man, the woman, the age—or the bird, the white, the black toothed, the lord of bad women and others, who are difficult fully to explain. The sacrificer and his wife should spend the night before the offering in telling each other stories, and the sacrificer should follow some at least of the other rules applicable to the sacrificer with the Çrauta ritual. A spring festival in the month Caitra [8] is recorded by one Sūtra only, figures of

1894, pp. 265 ff.) and Indian usages, as well as Greek and Roman and other parallels. Cf. Hubert and Mauss, *Mélanges*, pp. 74 ff.; Hopkins, *Origin of Religion*, pp. 155, 171.

[1] iii. 92.

[2] lxxiv. 2 ff.

[3] Cf. ÇB. xi. 5. 6. 1, which has the five; ApDS. i. 12. 13 (*brāhmaṇokta*).

[4] This is patently late; cf. ApDS. i. 13. 1; Manu, iii. 80 f.

[5] Arbman, *Rudra*, pp. 189 ff., who fails to realize the complex and artificial character of the series of five, and the essential unity of the meal in which all share, gods generically, Fathers, and men.

[6] i. 4. 3.

[7] GGS. i. 5; 8. 22; AGS. i. 10. 5; ApGS. vii. 17.

[8] ÇGS. iv. 19. Cf. MGS. ii. 7. 6–8 (the *talpa* is addressed).

pairs of beasts are made from meal, which suggest a vegetation magic as at the Varuṇapraghāsas of the Çrauta ritual.

At the month Çrāvaṇa,[1] when the rains begin and snakes become very dangerous, an offering is made to appease them in the southern fire by the keeper of the fires, in the house fire by the ordinary householder, or a fresh fire may be lighted. In that offerings are made to many deities, including the earth spirit, Bhauma, the rains, Çravaṇa, as well as Agni, Sūrya, Vāyu and Viṣṇu; Çveta, a genius which is with its foot to drive away the snakes is also invoked. The second part of the sacrifice is one addressed directly to the snakes, who are given water to wash themselves in, a comb to comb themselves with, unguents, and so forth. Finally a Bali is offered to the snakes of the three regions: it is made of groats or roasted barley. This performance goes on daily, until the time when the beds of the sacrificer and his wife, which have been raised up since the beginning of the rains, are replaced on the ground with the advent of drier weather. A stream of water is poured round the house to keep the snakes at the desired distance from it.

On the full moon of Prauṣṭhapada [2] an offering is prescribed by one Sūtra for Indra, Indrāṇī, the one-footed goat, the serpent of the deep, and the Prauṣṭhapadas, and a Bali at the end to the Maruts, the other receiving butter libations. The mention of the two rare deities is clearly due to the presence of the twin Nakṣatra, Prauṣṭhapadas.

On the full moon of Açvinī [3] is prescribed an offering to Paçupati, Çiva, Çaṅkara, and Pṛṣātaka; it consists of the sacrifice of a mixture of milk with butter. The deities, however, differ greatly, and it is not clear that the ceremony is intended for the welfare of the herds. The priest and the sacrificer partake of the Pṛṣātaka, and put on amulets, and later the cows are allowed to have a share of it, and eventually the calves and the cows are shut in together.

The Āgrahāyaṇī festival [4] is celebrated at the full-moon day of the month Mārgaçīrṣa: it is, as the name denotes, the festival of the beginning of a new year, and is characterized by a thorough cleaning of the house, followed by a smoking of it parallel to German rites observed at the new year, in which the house is smoked. The offerer also pours water into a water-jug set on a firm stone, which constitutes the consecration of the water-holder, in which daily Balis are offered. The use of six or nine kinds of plants in this ceremony is paralleled by the use of nine in Germany. At this time, the danger from snakes being over, the beds come back to the ground: the ceremony is

[1] GGS. iii. 7. 3; AGS. ii. 1. 15; ÇGS. iv. 15; PGS. ii. 14. 9; ApGS. xviii. 5–xix. 2; HGS. ii. 16; MGS. ii. 16; BGS. iii. 10; BhGS. ii. 1.

[2] PGS. ii. 15.

[3] AGS. ii. 2. 1; ÇGS. iv. 16; PGS. ii. 16; GGS. iii. 8. 1–8; KhGS. iii. 3. 1. Pṛṣātaka is really the name of the offering, and it is characteristic that Āçvalāyana turns it into a deity which none of the others do, and adds Çiva and Çaṅkara as forms of Paçupati. In MGS. ii. 3. 4–8 Pṛṣātaka and cows are both revered.

[4] GGS. iii. 9; AGS. ii. 3; ÇGS. iv. 17; PGS. iii. 2; ApGS. xix. 3; HGS. ii. 17; MGS. ii. 7. 1–5; BhGS. ii. 2; Weber, *Naxatra*, ii. 332.

carried out in due form, the householder sitting on a strew west of the fire with the rest of the family beside him in order of age, and then his wife and children, and those of the other members of the family: the earth is entreated to be friendly to them all. The snakes also receive offerings. A special form of snake offering [1] is commenced in Bhādrapada for one injured by a snake: a five-headed snake of wood or clay is made and revered for a whole year.

Of the occasional offerings the most interesting is the Arghya,[2] the paying of honour to special guests, namely the teacher, the priest, a Snātaka, if he come as a wooer or on the day when he completes his studies by the bath, whence his name is derived, a connexion by marriage, or a friend. Only once a year apparently should the full ceremony be paid, but constantly to a priest invited to sacrifice. The gifts are six, one or two stools to sit on, water to wash the feet, Argha water, a portion of which is poured over the guest's hands, water to cleanse the mouth, the Madhuparka, a mixture of curds, honey and ghee, with or without water and barley groats. The guest may eat all, or give a portion to a son or pupil or other person: the king merely accepts *pro forma* and gives them to his Purohita. Finally the cow is offered and slain, unless the guest politely declines the offer, when other flesh may be used in its place. The deity varies in the cases of the different guests, Agni, Bṛhaspati, Indra and Agni, Prajāpati, Indra and Mitra, being given as the appropriate gods, for obvious reasons in most cases.

The directions as to the building of the house [3] are numerous and complicated. Of interest is the fact that the presence of certain plants and certain trees on the chosen place, or in its vicinity, is forbidden: the Açvattha is connected with the Açvins and causes the danger from fire, Yama's Palāça danger of death, Varuṇa's Nyagrodha danger of fighting, and Prajāpati's Udumbara bad eyes. The chosen place is thrice surrounded by a thin stream of water. The food chamber should be where water runs away, the parlour looking north, but opinions vary: the door should be in the west: it is also desirable that the householder should be ensured privacy at his meal and ritual. When the posts are driven into the earth, an Avakā plant is put in the hole to prevent fire. When the middle post is put in, Kuça grass is strewn, water, rice, and barley are poured on it, and homage paid to the earth spirit. An anointed stone is also buried, to which a parallel exists in the burying of stones in Buddhist temples in Siam. When the house is complete, an offering is made to Vāstoṣpati, which is repeated yearly according to some authorities. Brahmans are fed, and expected to wish good luck for the place. Even a black cow or a white goat may be offered: the former in its colour is similar to the black cock killed at the foundation of a new house in Greece.[4] Ten Balis

[1] AGPar. iii. 16. For magic rites against snake-poison, see Henry, *La magie dans l'Inde antique*, pp. 108 ff., 198 ff.

[2] GGS. iv. 10; AGS. i. 24; ÇGS. ii. 15; PGS. i. 3; ApGS. xiii. 20; HGS. i. 13; MGS. i. 9. 1; BhGS. ii. 23–6; BGS. i. 2.

[3] GGS. iv. 7; AGS. ii. 7, 8; HGS. i. 27; MGS. ii. 11; AV. iii. 12; vii. 41; Bloomfield, JAOS. xvi. 12 ff.

[4] Winternitz, *Mitth. Anthrop. Ges. Wien*, 1887, xvii. 37 ff.

are also offered to the quarters. Of human sacrifice there is no trace in the ritual, which is meant in special of ordinary houses: such a practice is only recorded of the much more important Agnicayana. But there are traces of such a practice later [1] in legends and in history, perhaps coming from a period when the simple buildings of Vedic India had been superseded by large buildings of stone, which, like the brick altars, were supposed to need special measures to make them secure.

The new house is entered when complete formally by the householder with his eldest son and his wife: they carry with them food, and partake of honey and butter to secure prosperity in it. On leaving and returning to it formulae of good luck are said.[2]

Other acts of consecration are those of a grove or a tank of water: the offerings in the latter case include one to Varuṇa, as god of the waters.[3]

The agricultural festivals are not unimportant, and are numerous. Formulae are regularly used for the driving out and the return to their stalls of the cattle.[4] Many curious performances [5] are recorded as devices to secure the multiplying of the herds: the marking of a pair of calves male and female is one: in another a pap is offered to Agni, Pūṣan, Indra and Īçvara, and honour is paid to the bull, whose neck and horns are ornamented and who is fed. In the case of a horse, Yama and Varuṇa are included in the offering, and the same respect is paid to the horse. A cow which has two calves should be given away. The spit-ox [6] sacrifice brings wealth and is of a special character: an ox is offered in spring or autumn to Rudra. The offering is made away from the village after midnight, or at least after sunset: Rudra's twelve names are invoked. The omentum is offered with a leaf or a wooden instrument, not with the Juhū ladle. Balis are offered also in all four quarters to appease the troops of Rudra.[7] The tail, skin, &c., are thrown into the fire, the blood is poured out on Kuça or Darbha grass for the snakes, to whom formulae are addressed. None of the victims may be brought into the village, since the god is fain to hurt men, no connexion of the sacrificer may be near the place of sacrifice, and he himself shall not eat the flesh save for a very special instruction, in which case, however, he will prosper greatly. In another version of the offering, place is found for the wives of Rudra, Rudrāṇī, Çarvāṇī, Bhavānī, and for Indrāṇī: the blood-covered entrails are burned or cast into the fire. In another quite different form [8] the offerings take the place of three messes of rice, which are offered to three animals, a bull, a cow, and a calf, which are styled the Çūlagava or Īçāna, the bountiful one, and the victor respectively: when the offerings are given, Rudra is hailed by all his

[1] Haberlandt, *ibid.* 42 ff.

[2] AGS. ii. 10. 2; ÇGS. iii. 4. 9. For magic rites as to houses see Henry, *La magie dans l'Inde antique*, pp. 96–9. Cf. BGS. i. 5; BhGS. ii. 4–6.

[3] ÇGS. v. 3; AGPar. iv. 9, 10.

[4] GGS. iii. 6. 9.

[5] GGS. iii. 6; KhGS. iii. 1; HGS. i. 18.

[6] AGS. iv. 8; PGS. iii. 8; not in GGS.; very briefly in MGS. ii. 5. Cf. BhGS. ii. 8–10; BGS. ii. 7.

[7] Arbman, *Rudra*, pp. 156 ff.

[8] HGS. ii. 8; ApGS. xix. 13 ff.; see above, Chap. 18, § 4.

names, the second offering is made to the wife of Rudra, the third to Jayanta. The cows are placed round the fire so as to smell the burnt offering, and all go round it from left to right, while verses are addressed to the Çūlagava. It is perfectly clear [1] that here the bull and the cow are fetishes for the god and his wife, but the position of Jayanta is less obvious : possibly a child of the two is deemed to be represented by him. At the same time it must be realized that the beasts are so treated merely as a substitute for the other rite of slaughter ; the rite has every appearance of being a later elaboration.

Another rite,[2] the Bauḍhyavihāra, a curious name of dubious origin, for the propitiation of Rudra and his hordes, is the making of a basket of Palāça leaves, the placing in it of rice and butter, and hanging it on a tree as an offering to the god as wearer of the quiver : the offerer also spreads leaves about and touches the cattle with a number of things, with sandal, salve, Surā, water, cow-dung, and a cow's tail to secure luck. Further, an offering is made to Kṣetrapati,[3] who is represented by a bull as at the Çūlagava rite.

Mention is also made, as appropriate to be performed on the new moon after full moon in Phālguna, of the marking of the cattle, which is accompanied by the expression of the hope that the work will be more in the following year.[4] The ceremony of letting loose a bull [5] is performed at the full moon of Kārttika : it is performed by lighting a fire among the cows, offering six libations of butter and a pap for Pūṣan, and with a verse addressed to Rudra the bull is set free, after being ornamented. The Brahmans receive a meal for the preparation of which milk from all the cows has been used.

Of agricultural rites proper there are several of importance. The ceremony of ploughing is formally accomplished after the plough has been yoked.[6] On the east side of the field an offering is made before the plough to sky and earth. Among the deities to whom offerings are also made are Indra, Parjanya, the Açvins, the Maruts, Udalākāçyapa, Svātikārī, Sītā and Anumati, and others : the bulls receive honey and butter. Other rites of the same kind are those to the furrow, the offering on the threshing-floor, at sowing, at harvest and at threshing, and here may be mentioned the offering made to avert danger from the moles or mice to the king of the moles or mice : a similar practice may be the explanation of the connexion of the mouse with Apollo in which totemism has been so often seen.[7]

The offering to the furrow is described at some length in one Sūtra.[8]

[1] Haradatta's effort to ignore this is quite indefensible.

[2] HGS. ii. 9. 7 ; ApGS. xix. 20.

[3] HGS. *l. c.* ; ApGS. xx. 13 ff.

[4] ÇGS. iii. 10 ; cf. MGS. ii. 10. 1 ff. : the women are not to eat of one offering (a *tundila* (?) for Agni).

[5] PGS. iii. 9 ; Kauç. xxiv. 22. For other magic rites for cattle see Henry, *La magie dans l'Inde antique*, pp. 102–6 ; for agriculture, pp. 106–111. See also AV. vi. 141 ; Delbrück, *Gurupūjākaumudī*, p. 48. AV. ii. 32 is directed against worms in cattle.

[6] ÇGS. iv. 13 ; GGS. iv. 4. 27 ff. ; PGS. ii. 13 ; Kauç. xv.

[7] Cf. Lang, *Custom and Myth*, pp. 103 ff. ; Farnell, *Cults of the Greek States*, iv. 164, 265, who lays stress on the probability that the connexion is rooted in pre-Hellenic custom.

[8] PGS. ii. 17 ; cf. MGS. ii. 10. 7.

East or north of the field on a place which is pure, and has been ploughed without injury to fruits, or in the village, a fire is kindled, and Darbha grass mixed with rice or barley, according to the season, is strewed round it : then offerings of butter are made to Indra, Sītā, the furrow, and Urvarā, the ploughfield, and from the food cooked in a pot to Sītā, Yajā, the personified sacrifice, Çamā, 'energy', and Bhūti, 'prosperity'. On the Kuça grass remaining from the strewing an offering is made to the guardians of the furrow, who sit in the east with bows and quivers, in the south to those with mail, in the west to the mighty Bhūti, Bhūmi, Pārṣṇi, and Çunaṁkuri, and in the north to the terrible ones. The women should also make offerings.

In a period lying outside the Vedic period proper we are carried by the Caitya offering which is recorded in one Sūtra :[1] it is interesting, as it seems clearly to refer to the offering of homage to the memorials erected to the memory of some teacher or other distinguished personage. The procedure contemplates that the Caitya cannot be visited in person : therefore the sacrificer prepares two bales of food, and gives them to a messenger real or symbolical, to take to the destination, providing the messenger with a weapon and boat, if the journey is a long one. The offering to Dhanvantari, which is mentioned with emphasis as needing the co-operation of priests, is not explained in the texts.

The offerings of firstfruits belong to the domestic as well as to the Çrauta ritual ; as in it there are offerings of rice, barley, and millet at different periods, and at these offerings Indra, Brahman, and Vāsuki are to receive libations. Another similar offering is the Āsasyabali, to be performed by the householder alone, of barley up to the rice harvest, and of rice up to the barley harvest.[2]

§ 3. *Birth Ceremonies and others*

As is natural the domestic ritual devotes much space to the minute description of large number of rites, mainly magical in essence, which accompany the child from even before birth to its death. In the third or fourth month or even later after pregnancy takes place the rite for quickening a male child, Puṁsavana,[3] the essence of which consists in the placing in the nostril of the wife by her husband of a Nyagrodha shoot, which he purchases in due form and which is pounded, either by a young girl, or a student or a wife who is keeping a vow, or a Brahmabandhu, a term which is perhaps best taken as a Brahman

[1] AGS. i. 12 ; Oldenberg, SBE. xxix. 178. Similar late offerings are those to Ṣaṣṭhī (MGS. ii. 13), who is giver of wealth and is called Çrī ; to the Vināyakas (*ib.* 14 ; Yājñ. i. 274 ff.) ; to Nejameṣa (*ib.* 18. 4). The Soma text gives remedies for evil omens from a pigeon (ii. 17) and evil dreams (ii. 15).

[2] GGS. iv. 7. 43 ; i. 4. 30 ; ÇGS. iii. 8. 1 ; PGS. iii. 1. 1 ; ApGS. xix. 6.

[3] GGS. ii. 6 ; ÇGS. i. 20 ; HGS. ii. 2 ; MGS. i. 16 ; BGS. i. 9 ; BhGS. i. 22 ; JGS. i. 5 ; AV. iii. 23 ; vi. 11 ; vii. 17, 19. Magic rites for love purposes are rare outside Atharvan texts, e. g. RV. x. 145, 159, 162, 183 ; TS. ii. 3. 9. 1 ; MS. ii. 3. 2 ; TB. ii. 3. 10 ; BAU. vi. 4 ; ApGS. ix. 4 ; xxiii. 3 ; see Bloomfield, *Atharvaveda*, pp. 69 ff.

by birth only, not by learning. A further rite is that to prevent an abortion, or more generally to secure the safety of the embryo, which is accomplished by offering a cooked mess, and rubbing butter on the limbs of the wife.[1] The ceremony of the parting of the hair [2] is performed once only for the first pregnancy, and is not repeated : it is celebrated in the fourth month or later. The wife sits west of the fire, her husband puts round her neck an Udumbara branch with an even number of unripe fruits, he parts her hair from the front backwards with Darbha grass,[3] Vīratara (' very male ') wood, a full spindle, and a porcupine's quill; he also makes her look at the mess of rice, sesame, and ghee, and asks her to see in it offspring. Some authorities allow two lute players to sing the king, or him that is higher than the king, that is Soma. One special Gāthā is prescribed which should end with the name of the stream on which the people dwell, and one or two such verses have been preserved to us. Other authorities provide for Brahman women sitting beside her, and uttering phrases indicating that she is to be the mother of living children. Old Brahman women are said also to be the authorities for the acts to be done in these cases. The wife should keep silence after the rite until the stars appear, when she should touch a calf, say the Vyāhṛtis, Bhūḥ, Bhuvaḥ, Svar, and then speak. There are also ceremonies for the actual birth : the place is anointed against the Rakṣases : a Brahman loosens all the knots in the house, as in Germany all doors and locks are opened ; water and the Tūryantī plant are placed before the mother.[4] If the child dies in birth, special rites are ordered. When the child is born alive, a fire [5] is lit in the house to warm utensils and be used for the smoking of the child,[6] which is performed by throwing into the fire grains of corn and hemp, with formulae to drive away demons of various kinds. For ten days the offering of sesame and rice grains is prescribed. On the twelfth day the special fire disappears, the old household fire comes out into use, the purification of the wife and child having been performed.

Immediately on birth are performed the ceremonies for securing long life, the Āyuṣya, and the production of intellect, Medhājanana : in the case of girls these ceremonies may be performed, but then without the accompanying formulae. The father breathes thrice upon the new-born child, and gives it to eat a mixture of butter, honey, and sour milk, to which others add rice and barley, and even whitish black and red hairs of a black bull. The child is fed with a golden instrument. In some authorities five Brahmans are expected to invoke its possession of the breaths of life, or the father makes up for this

[1] ÇGS. i. 21 ; HGS. ii. 2. 7. Cf. also Kauç. xxxiv. 3–11.

[2] GGS. ii. 7 ; ÇGS. i. 22 ; PGS. i. 15. 3 ; ApGS. xiv ; HGS. ii. 2 ; MGS. i. 15 ; cf. Kauç. xxxv. 20 with Keçava's comment ; BhGS. i. 21 ; BGS. i. 10 ; JGS. i. 7.

[3] For the later practice of putting on a red mark, to frighten demons, see Hopkins, *Origin of Religion*, p. 119, and cf. VārGS. xvi.

[4] ApGS. xiv. 14 ; HGS. ii. 2. 8 ; Henry, *La magie dans l'Inde antique*, p. 143.

[5] ÇGS. i. 25. 4 ; PGS. i. 16. 23 ; JGS. i. 8.

[6] The Greek ritual substitutes an Amphidromia in which the child is carried swiftly round the fire to acquire strength and speed. The fire here too purifies.

by going about the child in the several quarters. The child is asked to become a stone and an axe, and in some cases these instruments are actually present at the rite. At this point the smoking of the child may take place. Intellect is given by repeating a prayer in the ear of the babe, asking Savitṛ or Mitra and Varuṇa to give it intelligence: with the fourth gold-covered finger butter and honey are given to the infant to eat. Thereafter the navel string is cut, and the child is washed and given the breast. After that a water jug is placed on the head of the mother, and she is commended to the protection of the water.[1]

The child has two names,[2] one secret for the knowledge of father and mother alone, and apparently given immediately on birth at the life-giving ceremony. This name from its close connexion with the life of the child is not allowed to be known in order to prevent injury through the use of the name by enemies. The second normal name is given on the tenth day in agreement with the Brahmans, or on the twelfth or even a year later. It should be of an even number of syllables, different merits being connected with the diverse numbers, begin with a soft letter, contain a semi-vowel, and end in *s* or a long vowel; for a Brahman it should be a compound [3] in *çarman*, 'protection', for a Kṣatriya in *varman*, 'armour', and for a Vaiçya in *gupta*, 'protected'. A girl's name should have an uneven number of syllables. The giving of the name is accompanied by offerings to Prajāpati, the day of birth, the Nakṣatra of that day, and the god of the Nakṣatra. Another name is the Nakṣatra name derived from a lunar mansion such as Rauhiṇa: the notices regarding it are confused with that of the name by which the boy is to designate himself when he becomes a student and announces his name in greeting others, and one or both of these names seem to be made out to be the secret name. A Soma sacrificer may have yet another name in due course. Birthday offerings to Agni, Indra, heaven and earth, the All-gods, the day and constellation of birth, and the deities of both, are prescribed every year.

On the tenth or twelfth day after birth the father and mother and the child are washed, the house purified, and offerings made to the day of birth and three constellations, to Agni and Soma. The special fire is now extinguished, and the old household fire resumes its functions. The child is now named and enters thus into the full life of every day, just as in the Salic law, at the end of nine days,[4] it received its name and became a subject of wergeld.

[1] GGS. ii. 7; AGS. i. 15; ÇGS. i. 24; PGS. i. 16; ApGS. xv; MGS. i. 17; HGS. ii. 3; BGS. ii. 1; BhGS. i. 24–6.

[2] GGS. ii. 7. 15 ff.; AGS. i. 15. 4 ff.; ÇGS. i. 25; PGS. i. 17; ApGS. xv. 8; MGS. i. 18; HGS. ii. 4; Weber, *Naxatra*, ii. 317 ff.; BGS. ii. 1; BhGS. i. 26; JGS. i. 9.

[3] This is the normal Indo-European mode of name formation; cf. Feist, *Kultur der Indogermanen*, pp. 302 ff.

[4] The variation in India from 9, which is a common number in these cases, is probably due as regards 10 (ÇGS. i. 25. 1; GDS. xiv. 16; VDS. iv. 21) to inclusive reckoning and the fondness for a unit like 10, and in the case of 12 to the frequent use of that number (= that of the months) in the ritual as a period of time.

On the third day of the third month the moon is revered by the father, and the mother is newly washed, the child being first handed by the mother to the father and then given back to her by him. In the fourth month the first going out takes place, when the child is made to look at the sun. In the sixth month the first solid food is given: its kind is dependent on what qualities are desired, quickness is due to fish eating, holy brilliance to the partridge, glory to rice and butter, oratory to Bhāradvājī flesh, and so on.[1] By one Sūtra an offering to speech and strength is prescribed.

The ceremony of the tonsure [2] is usually performed in the third year, or the fifth and seventh for a Kṣatriya and a Vaiçya respectively: the essence of the ceremony is the formal wetting of the child's hair, the putting of bunches of Darbha on it, the cutting of the right and then the back and then the left side with a razor, which is not to injure the child, and which is addressed as an axe. The hair with the Darbha is thrown away in the cow-stall, near water, or in a pool of water or elsewhere. For three days after, the barber, it seems, must not use the razor: as often, in the case of girls the formulae used for boys are omitted. The hair is then arranged in the peculiar mode of the family, or in a number of tufts according to the number of seers hailed as belonging to the family tree in the Pravara ceremony. The barber receives as his fee rice and butter, or another gift: the family teacher a cow. In the sixteenth year, or the 22nd and 24th for the Kṣatriya and Vaiçya, follows the shaving of the beard based on the same model, but the cutting is extended to hair, beard, hair of the body, and nails. The fee to the priest is a pair of cattle, to the barber a goat. The shorn youth should for a year, or at least three days, observe chastity, and not cut his hair again.[3] The piercing of the ears in the third or fourth year is a rite which is only recorded in one late text.[4]

§ 4. *Studentship*

A Brahman child in the eighth year from conception or birth, a Kṣatriya in the eleventh, a Vaiçya in the twelfth, should be received as a student by a teacher:[5] the period can be increased to 16, 22, and 24 years respectively, but after that a youth has lost the right to say the Sāvitrī verse, and should not be associated with, taken as a pupil, permitted to sacrifice, or accepted as a son-in-law: if the Sāvitrī is lost for three generations, the right of the sacraments is lost, and can only be regained by the performance of the Çrauta rite called the Vrātya Stomas. The ceremony of the reception is performed with much form before a fire newly lighted by friction or taken from the household fire: north of it are laid the necessary utensils, a stone, a fresh garment, a skin,

[1] AGS. i. 16; ÇGS. i. 27; PGS. i. 19. 2; MGS. i. 20; BGS. ii. 3; BhGS. i. 27.

[2] GGS. ii. 9; AGS. i. 17; ÇGS. i. 28; PGS. ii. 1; ApGS. xvi; BGS. ii. 4; BhGS. i. 28; HGS. ii. 6; MGS. i. 21. The AV. (vi. 21, 136, 137) has spells to make hair grow.

[3] GGS. iii. 1, 2; AGS. i. 18; ÇGS. i. 28. 19.

[4] Speijer, *Jātakarman*, p. 21.

[5] GGS. ii. 10; AGS. i. 19; ÇGS. ii. 1; PGS. ii. 2; BGS. ii. 5; BhGS. i. 1–10; ApGS. xi; HGS. i. 1; JGS. i. 12, 13; MGS. i. 21 ff.; Glaser, ZDMG. lxvi. 1 ff.

a girdle, a staff, and twenty-one pieces of wood. The Sūtras give innumerable details of the garments, the skin, and the staff: the materials and colour differ for each caste: thus the skin is of a black antelope for a Brahman, of a Ruru deer for a Kṣatriya, of a goat or of a sheep for a Vaiçya, their girdles of Muñja, of a bowstring, or wool, and so on, but the differences are endless; the garment should be woven on that day. The teacher makes the pupil stand on the stone to secure firmness, he puts on his new garment and girdle and the sacred cord, and then the skin; the boy is fed and a water libation offered.[1] Then comes the formal taking of the student as a pupil by the teacher, effected by a dialogue of request and acceptance under the auspices of Savitṛ, and with reference to the seer ancestry of teacher and pupil. They both wash. Then follow rites to bring the two into close contact: the teacher takes the pupil by the shoulders and grasps his right hand with suitable formulae, and says to him, 'On the instigation of Savitṛ, be the pupil of Bṛhaspati: taste water, lay wood on the fire, do thy work, sleep not by day'. Then the teacher touches the pupil's heart with a magic formula to unite their hearts, touches his navel, then whispers formulae in his ear and prays for wisdom for the child: finally he commends him to the care of gods and demons, or gods only.

The teacher may then or later teach the pupil the Sāvitrī: the two sit opposite to each other, the pupil takes the teacher's right foot or both feet in his right hand, and begs to be taught the verse: the teacher repeats it by quarter, by half verses, and then as a whole. Different verses are prescribed for the different classes. The pupil then puts kindling wood on the fire for the first time, and the staff is now usually given, after which the teacher receives a gift which may be whatever the pupil can afford, and the pupil pays reverence to the sun. For three days the fire continues to burn, the pupil must eat no salt or spiced food. At the end of three days the Brahmans are fed, and bestow benedictions.

The first duty of the pupil is to secure wood from the forest, without destroying living trees, for the fire which he tends morning and night: some authorities require also that he should with prayers revere the morning and evening twilights in the woods, wearing the sacred cord and performing the usual ablutions. The making of sectarian marks on the body with ashes from the fire is not recognized in any save an interpolated text.[2] In the second place, he must beg food for his teacher and himself, in the first instance from his mother or other friends: twice a day this is done, and two meals, one after the first expedition and one after sunset, are prescribed. Thirdly, he must sleep on the ground, and he is also enjoined to eat no spiced or salt food, to avoid resorting to women, not to sit on a high seat, &c. He is, fourthly, to be obedient to his teacher, to rise when he is spoken to, and answer at once.

The mode of study was simple: the two sat down north of the fire, the

[1] For the initiation as a rebirth, cf. Hauer, *Die Anfänge der Yogapraxis im alten Indien*, pp. 79 ff.

[2] ÇGS. ii. 10. 1.

teacher as usual facing east, the pupil west, and the teacher at the request of the pupil recited the verse he was to learn, giving the seer, deity, and metre of each: in the case of the Rigveda the pupil might learn all the hymns of each seer, or of each of the eighty-five Anuvākas, or so much as the teacher wished to teach him, or the first and last hymns of each seer or Anuvāka, or a verse at the beginning of each hymn. Doubtless there were differences in the extent of the teaching, according to the desire of the pupil and his caste: explanations of the texts and of the rites which they were to accompany must clearly have been given. At the end of each lesson Kuça grass balls were taken by the teacher, a pit of cow dung made at their roots, and water poured on. A mistake on the part of the pupil required for atonement a twenty-four hours' fast at least.

During his period of studentship the pupil may have several vows [1] to perform, each of which requires an initiation ceremony, and at the end the removal of the initiation. They are the Çukriya vow, which precedes the study of the Rigveda, the Çākvara before that of the Mahānāmnī verses, the Vrātika before the Mahāvrata, and the Aupaniṣada before the Upaniṣads. The first may last from three days to a year, the last three each a year. The last three cannot be undertaken until the Rigveda has been completely studied: they contain the secret texts. For them a preparation is necessary of three days or a night only: the teacher envelopes the head of the pupil in a garment,[2] and bids him, while ceasing to observe the rule of laying wood on the fire, begging, &c., to spend the time in a wood, or temple,[2] or place where the Agnihotra is offered: the teacher himself abstains from flesh and sexual intercourse, and then at the end of the period of probation instructs him in the forest in the secret texts, the pupil wearing a turban: in the case of the Mahānāmnī verses the instruction is as usual; in the other cases the pupil listens only. He gives the teacher as fees a turban, a vessel, and a cow. Other vows are prescribed for learners of the Jyeṣṭha Sāman, who must not eat bird flesh, and must avoid contact with Çūdra women. The Çakvarī vow must have been popular, as a mother is represented as wishing for her infant that he may perform it. The three verses of the Stotra which make up the Sāman are revealed at the end of the three portions of the vow. The pupil must fast, and shut his eyes to receive them, a clear reference to their dazzling power.

The beginning of each term of study is marked by a festival under the Nakṣatra Hasta or Çravaṇa, but there are traces of different openings of the year; roughly the rainy season may be said to have been the popular time, when other forms of activity were hampered. The ceremony was performed

[1] GGS. iii. 1, 2; ÇGS. ii. 11, 12; JGS. i. 16–18; MGS. i. 23 ff.; BhGS. iii. 4, 5; BGS. iii. 2; Oldenberg, *Ind. Stud.* xv. 139, 140. Cf. VārGS. vi.

[2] Cf. the covering of the head of the Grāvastut priest in the Soma sacrifice.

[3] The Upākaraṇa; GGS. iii. 3; AGS. iv. 5; ÇGS. iv. 5; BhGS. iii. 8–11; MGS. i. 4. 1–5; PGS. ii. 10; HGS. ii. 18; Bühler, *Ind. Ant.* xxiii. 238 ff., whose conclusions as to the antiquity of Vedic practices are not to be accepted (above, Part I, Chap. 1).

by means of offerings of grains with ghee and milk, and with the repetition of either the whole of the Rigveda or the first verses of sections and many offerings : the deities vary from each Veda, and it is only of interest to note that they include abstractions such as Medhā, 'intelligence', Dhāraṇā, 'fixing in memory', Çraddhā, Anumati, 'favour', and Sadasaspati and other deities : the divisions of the texts were sometimes ascribed to deities, and the seers are duly honoured. The ceremony was followed by three days' break of study, and similarly a break occurred at the end : breaks are also prescribed after the Aṣṭakās, when offerings were made to the Fathers, and on many other days, full- or new-moon days, while deaths and other things such as Çrāddhas, the sight of unholy persons, dogs, asses, or jackals, the noise of a Sāman, the cries in distress of men and so forth, prevent learning ; the aim of the Sūtras seems to have been to interrupt study as often as possible. Thunder, lightning, rain, earthquakes, meteors, and other prodigies more reasonably interrupt study.[1]

The term comes to an end in Māgha or Taiṣa, after from 5½ to 6½ or occasionally even only four months' duration : it is marked by the Utsarga,[2] 'dismissal' festival, where offerings are made to gods, seers, &c., and a bath is taken by teacher and pupils, of whom the number to be taken by any one teacher is in no wise limited. After this an old rite of offering to the Fathers is described by Hiraṇyakeçin in full detail. Even, however, after this Utsarga, which normally brought work to an end for the year, some might resume their studies and continue working throughout the year. The total length of the study might extend to forty-eight years, or twelve for each Veda, or such time as was necessary to learn each : clearly the matter was not in the slightest degree fixed. The end of the period of learning is marked by the final bath,[3] which is best taken when the student has completed his instruction and performed all his vows, but may be taken if either is complete. With the bath, the exact time for which is variously stated, are combined shaving, hair cutting, nail paring, and teeth washing. The hair is thrown away in a cow stall, beside an Udumbara or Darbha grass. The whole of the pupil's outfit is cast into the water, and the Snātaka, 'one who has bathed', puts on a new suit, shoes, sunshade, staff, garland, powder, salve for hands and lips, eye-salve and turban, and the teacher does likewise ; or the teacher alone can adopt this gay clothing. The student has also ear-rings and a mirror. All day he must keep from the sunlight and remain silent till the stars appear : then he goes east or north, pays reverence to the quarters, and to the stars and the moon, converses with his friends and goes to where he expects to receive the Argha gift, which is appropriate for a Snātaka immediately after the bath. For the first days after his completion of his study, he should eat no flesh, not

[1] ÇGS. iv. 7 gives many cases ; AGS. iv. 4. 17 ff. ; GGS. iii. 3. 24 ff. ; PGS. ii. 11. 7 ff. ; MGS. i. 4. 6.

[2] GGS. iii. 3. 14 ; ÇGS. iv. 6 ; AGS. iii. 5 ; PGS. ii. 12 ; MGS. i. 4. 7–9 ; HGS. ii. 18. 8 ; BGS. ii. 6 ; JGS. i. 19.

[3] GGS. iii. 5. 21 ff. ; PGS. ii. 5. 31.

drink from a clay vessel, neither speak to nor see women, Çūdras, corpses, cows, dogs, &c.[1] By gleaning ears of corn, by gifts given without asking, or begged from the pious, or by assisting in sacrifices he may live, but the last mode of livelihood is the worst.[2] He is also forbidden to look in a well, and many other taboos are imposed on him ; on the other hand he is also not to speak of what he has not seen or heard as if he had, to avoid whatever hinders study, and to guard himself like a vessel of oil.[3] Curious is the rule that he is to avoid mentioning undesirable things, which are more or less taboo to him, by their own names; a pregnant woman he is to call 'without children'; a Nakula, 'ichneumon', Sakula ; a Kapāla, 'skull', Bhagāla ; and so on.[4]

§ 5. *Marriage*

The duty of the Vedic Indian to marry is assumed by all the texts, and the domestic ritual gives precise rules for the performance of the legitimate and honourable form of marriage,[5] ignoring as a rule the irregular forms based upon capture, violence, or mere mutual love without parental approval, which are recognized by the law books in various forms, Gāndharva, Āsura, Paiçāca, and Rākṣasa, as well as the romantic form of nominal self-choice by the bride of a suitor, the Svayaṁvara which bears traces of a test of skill of suitors by the king or other parent of high rank similar to that of Kleisthenes. The youth should obtain permission from his parents or his teacher to marry : only one Sūtra [6] prescribes the numbers of brides, three for the Brahman, two for the Kṣatriya, and one for the Vaiçya, and in one view a Çūdra for each : this refers clearly to a rule by which each caste could have a wife of its own and one of each inferior caste. The later texts prescribe that the maiden must be of the same caste and land, but not of the same Gotra as the father or a *sapiṇḍā* on the mother's side, rules which are difficult to define with precision.[7] Maidens with names of stars, rivers, or trees are to be avoided, as are those with names with *r* or *l* as the penultimate consonant. The physical marks are most important, but, as it is difficult to be sure of them, the maiden may be given eight or nine lumps of earth chosen from different places, and, as she choses, her disposition can be gauged.[8] The bridegroom should be of good family and character, have good bodily signs, be healthy and learned. As considerations in marriage family ranks above intelligence, beauty, and wealth.[9]

[1] PGS. ii. 8.
[2] ÇGS. iv. 11, 13.
[3] GGS. iii. 5. 24.
[4] GGS. iii. 5. 20 ; cf. Frazer, *Taboo*, pp. 392–418.
[5] GGS. iii. 4 ; ii. 1 ff. ; AGS. i. 6 ff. ; ÇGS. i. 11 ff. ; MGS. i. 7–12 ; BhGS. i. 11–20 ; BGS. i. 1 ff. ; JGS. i. 20 ff. ; PGS. i. 4 ff. ; ApGS. v ff. ; HGS. xix ff. ; Haas and Weber, *Ind. Stud.* v. 177 ff. ; Winternitz, *Altind. Hochzeitsrituell* ; von Schroeder, *Die Hochzeitsgebräuche der Esten* ; Hillebrandt, *Rituallitteratur*, pp. 63–8 ; Zachariae, VOJ. xvii. 135 ff., 211 ff.
[6] PGS. i. 4. 8–11.
[7] Macdonell and Keith, *Vedic Index*, ii. 258–260.
[8] GGS. ii. 1. 3–9 ; Kauç. xxxvii. 7–12.
[9] BhGS. i. 11 ; Keith, JRAS. 1914, pp. 1081 f., confirmed by VārGS. x.

The first formal step in the procedure, which doubtless was often carried out only after the marriage had been duly arranged beforehand by the parents with the advice of the Brahmans, was for the bridegroom to send wooers, usually his own father and the Ācārya of the house, to the father of the other family: the new-comers announced themselves, and set out the Gotra names —doubtless to show that the relationship was not a forbidden one—and if the other side agreed, all touched a pot filled with grains, fruits, flowers, &c., pronounced a formulae expressing agreement and assurance, and then the teacher of the bride's family placed the pot on her head. When the girl is to be taken to her new home, she is first formally washed by women of the same caste, and she names her husband in a verse addressed to Kāma, 'love'. She puts on a red or uncoloured garment and sits behind the fire, and holds on to the priest as he offers to Indra and Indrāṇī: the bridegroom offers similarly to Vaiçravaṇa[1] and Īçāna. Thereafter four or eight women dance in the house of the bride, and receive food, and the Brahmans are also fed. The appropriate time for the wedding ceremony is the northern course of the sun and the increasing half of the month, but some authorities allow any time almost to be used: the two months of the cool season and the last hot month are by some excluded. The bridegroom is led to the house of the bride by gay young women, not widows, to whom he must behave with complaisance. On his arrival, he should, according to some authorities, be received with the Argha offering of a cow, but by others this is postponed until the actual consummation of the marriage: a second cow is also later slain in the bridegroom's own house in honour of his father, teacher, and others. The bridegroom, with the permission of the maidens, gives the bride a new garment, anoints her, puts in her right hand a porcupine quill, perhaps for the ceremony of hair-parting, which takes place after pregnancy, and in the left a mirror. Her relatives then put on her a reddish black cord of wool or hemp with three amulets, and place Madhuka flowers on the bridegroom.

Other preparations have been made for the wedding. A fire is lit outside the house, water is procured by Brahmans, roast grains and a stone are in readiness. The maiden is formally handed over by the father to the bridegroom, but the place of this rite, the Kanyāpradāna, differs in the various authorities. The bride and bridegroom sit down on a mat behind the fire, and then butter oblations are offered, and also an oblation by the father or brother of the bride on the head of the bride, with a sword point or a ladle, in order to secure her pre-eminence in the house of her stepfather. Then comes the pouring into the joined hands of the bride of grains by her brother or mother; she is made to stand on a stone, when she receives the grains, and her husband invokes her to be firm as the stone: she offers the grains and her husband leads her round the fire, keeping her right side turned to it: this is all done thrice, the offerings being to Varuṇa, Aryaman, and Pūṣan respectively.

[1] I. e. Kubera (AV. viii. 10. 28; ÇB. xiii. 4. 3. 10; ṢB. v. 6; TA. i. 31. 6; Kauç. xxv. 34, &c.).

Then the bride takes seven steps in the north-east direction, the quarter of victory, the bridegroom takes her by the shoulders, and touches heart and navel as at the ceremony of the initiation of a student, and water is sprinkled on her. Then the bridegroom, in the version of Gobhila, takes the hand of the bride as she sits facing east and he stands facing west: this rite is placed differently by other authorities: the manner of seizing the hand depends on what is wished: if he desires sons only the thumb, if daughters the fingers, if both the whole hand. Then gifts are made: the Ācārya receives a cow from a Brahman, a village from a royal personage, a horse from a Vaiçya. If he has a daughter, he receives a hundred cows and a car, unless, as is much more probable, the provision really refers to the old practice of purchasing a wife.[1] The bridal garment is also given to the knower of the Sūryā hymn, which is used for the rites, and is apparently hung up on a post.[2] The bride is now taken to her new home by a car, horse, or elephant, and formulae are provided for all eventualities, when she cries,[3] when there is a breakdown *en route*, and so on. If they cross a stream, she is not to look at the crew. Fire is carried with them so that, if the car breaks, it can be mended, and then be sprinkled with butter left over from the offering made. This fire serves also to be the fire used by the householder at the sacrifices which his marriage imposes upon him. Some authorities prescribe the spending of the first night of marriage in the house of an old Brahman woman, whose husband and children are still alive, in which case the bride sits in silence on a red skin, hair upwards, until the stars appear: when this happens her husband offers six butter libations, pours the remains over her head, and shows her the stars Arundhatī and the pole star [4] as symbols of constancy. When they arrive at the home of the husband, he unyokes first the right, then the left animal, and Brahman women, with living husbands and children, help her down. She must enter the house without touching the threshold, and sit down on a skin, hair up, but she may be lifted over it and so put down by a strong man. On her lap a male child is placed, fruits are put in her hands, and Brahmans wish her prosperity. Then, if not before, the ceremony of looking at Arundhatī and the pole star may take place.

The marriage is not consummated for three nights after it: for that time the newly married couple must lie on the ground, avoid spiced or salted food, and, if they refrain from consummation for a year, the birth of a seer son is predicted for them. Between them in this period at night a staff is placed which is clad in a garment: it is clear that it is a symbol of the Gandharva

[1] Hillebrandt (*Rituallitteratur*, p. 67) prefers to take the words as referring to the priest, but sale is quite a recognized Brahmanical form of marriage: Macdonell and Keith, *Vedic Index*, i. 484 ff.

[2] Kauç. lxxix. 22.

[3] In which—absurdly—a trace of marriage by robbery has been seen.

[4] Cf. Macdonell and Keith, *op. cit.* i. 405, 406. For the use of a strew of Ulapa grass over which the pair walk from the chariot to the house, cf. Caland, ZDMG. li. 133; Zachariae, VOJ. xvii. 151; von Schroeder, *Arische Religion*, ii. 308; for the hand grasping, von Negelein, *Weltanschauung*, pp. 157 ff.

Viçvāvasu, who is addressed when on the fourth night it is cast away. The exact force of the practice is uncertain: the desire by refraining from consummation to deceive evil demons and cause them to depart is a possible motive. Viçvāvasu as a Gandharva [1] seems to claim his rights of connexion with women even after the marriage, and must at first be appeased and then formally be banished.[2] But the obvious connexion of the rite with other similar rites over the world down to the *ius trium noctium* is a warning against any feeling of security in the interpretation of the customs, which are of immemorial antiquity and based on feelings which are perhaps to us no longer psychologically even possible. The Vedic marriage does not contain any hint that by a previous rite of any sort the danger of interference with virginity [3] was removed, and, therefore, the first three nights may have seemed a time of too great danger to allow of immediate consummation of the marriage. In that case there may have arisen the idea that the Gandharva Viçvāvasu possessed these three nights, and the idea may be due to the rite, not a cause of it.

The removal of the period of continence is marked by an offering in the fire to Agni, Vāyu, Sūrya, Aryaman, Pūṣan, Varuṇa, and Prajāpati, with Sviṣṭakṛt as the eighth. To this list others add Candra and Gandharva.[4] The root of the Adhyāṇḍā plant is pounded, and some of it placed in the nostrils of the wife at the time of the menses, as a rite to secure conception.[5] Before and after the first period of intercourse, formulae must be recited at great length: they are clearly love spells to secure affection and offspring. On the fourth day of the marriage finds place a ceremony mentioned by one Sūtra alone: the husband and wife have their hair and nails cut and then go out of the village to pay honour to an Udumbara tree, and to pray for good fortune on their marriage. Fish also are caught in a fresh cloth and offered as a Bali to the water birds.[6]

The rite, which is of course paralleled in innumerable details by the practices of Greeks, Romans, Germans, and many other peoples Aryan and non-Aryan, is on the whole but loosely connected with religion. The Vedic ritual prescribes many verses and offerings, but the great wedding hymn,[7] which

[1] This position of the Gandharva is clearly a relic of more primitive thought than that which makes, as a result of the belief in transmigration, the Gandharva the being which at conception enters the womb, and it is to this popular and ancient belief that we must look in the main for the choice of this name rather than (as does Windisch, *Buddha's Geburt*, pp. 13 ff.) to transmigration into a Gandharva.

[2] Oldenberg, *Rel. des Veda*², pp. 88, n. 2; 249, n. 2.

[3] Crawley, *The Mystic Rose*; Farnell, *Archiv f. Religionswissenschaft*, vii. 88; *Greece and Babylon*, pp. 277–81; Hartland, *Anthropological Essays presented to E. B. Tylor*, pp. 190 ff.; J. J. Meyer, *Das Weib im altindischen Epos*, pp. 235 f.; Fehrle, *Kultische Keuschheit*, p. 40. Cf. BhGS. i. 20; Keith, JRAS. 1914, p. 1088.

[4] ÇGS. i. 18. 2 ff.; PGS. iii. 1.

[5] Winternitz, *op. cit.*, p. 101.

[6] BGS. i. 13; Zachariae, VOJ. xviii. 299 ff.; xx. 291.

[7] RV. x. 85; 109. 2 (AV. v. 17. 2).

makes the wedding of Sūryā, the sun maiden, and Soma, the mysterious god known by the Brahmans, doubtless the moon, the prototype of the human wedding, is clearly a late production, and the outcome of much priestly elaboration. Agni alone is the real object of much feeling, and it is as the living fire on the hearth that he is really worshipped.[1]

As in the case of the wedding ceremony, it is easy to find parallels for many of the rites of the Vedic domestic life, nor is it in the slightest degree doubtful that the formulae, which are used in the Vedic texts, were in the main invented or transferred, very often very badly, from other rites for use with practices which came into being and developed without any assistance from priestly influence. In many cases, of course, the formulae are merely redactions of the actual words which often must have accompanied these rites in the first instance : in others, as in the wedding service, much new matter was introduced. But in these cases the essential point of interest is rather the alteration by the Brahmans than the primitive rites, which are common to civilized Indians and much more savage tribes, and some of which persist among the highest civilizations of the earth. The case of the initiation of the boys of the people is the most striking instance of the peculiar character given to a rite by the influence of the priests. It is clear that, already by the period of Indo-Iranian unity, the ceremony has assumed a good deal of its present shape, and that a spirit of civilization had been introduced into barbaric rites. The conception of Vedic India saw in the initiation a species of second birth : by it the boy became fully a twice-born person, and failure to undergo initiation as we have seen might lead to inconvenient results for the person so failing. Certain taboos applied to the youth, but most of them had been reduced to reasonable limits, and could be supported by primitive ideas of what foods were suitable, as for example in the case of the interdiction of the use of flesh and honey for a growing boy who was in his studentship. Moreover, the relation of pupil and teacher has clearly been in some degree remodelled on the analogy of human marriage, in order to make it an expres sion of spiritual union.

In other lands and among other peoples strange puberty or initiation rites have been recorded, many of them accompanied by violent physical tortures and applied both to boys and to girls, of which Sparta in historical times still preserved relics, and which are still practised widely among modern savages. The idea of a second birth has often been connected in the minds of the performers of these rites with the practices which they follow and carried to the logical extreme of requiring the newly born people to start life at the infant stage,[2] to pretend that they have forgotten how to speak, or to feed themselves. Severe scourgings, the knocking out of teeth, circum-

[1] Babylonian religion—which hardly has a hearth deity—has almost no religion in its marriage ceremony; Farnell, *Greece and Babylon*, p. 134. For the Cretan marriage of sun and moon, see Cook, *Zeus*, i. 2 ff.

[2] Cf. the Vedic Dīkṣā, above, Chap. 19, § 1.

cision, the pouring over the initiated of kindred blood and other agreeable absurdities are recorded of such tribes, and it is natural of course to see in the Vedic rite a deliberate and reasoning reduction of these practices to sensible limits. There must be a certain amount of truth in this, but it is essential to note that we have no evidence to what extent the more violent of these customs ever prevailed among the ancestors of the Indo-Europeans.[1] The customs in question agree in the main only in their infinite variety, and it would be impossible to establish any form for initiation. In some cases doubtless the practices often were changed and assumed new forms: the drastic treatment of the Spartan boys may have been seriously intensified with a definite view to discipline character, though the origin may have been merely the driving away of evil influences at a critical time of youth, the appearance of puberty: in the case of girls, the Vedic Indians, in accordance with their usual practice as regards women, ignored entirely their claim to be initiated, and therefore prescribed no form of ritual at all for them.

The motive [2] for the doctrine of initiation is not alluded to in the Indian rite: beyond the obvious possibility of it being a mere expulsion of dangerous influences, and an effort by the fiction of a new birth to deceive the demons, there is no suggestion of much cogency. In the view of Sir J. Frazer the whole of these rites and the origin of totemism may be due to the wish to deposit permanently at a dangerous time of life the external soul in some safe object, but the suggestion lacks both external proof and internal cogency.[3]

Of the other domestic rites, that of the parting of the hair raises many problems. Various motives [4] may be assigned: the alteration of the mode of wearing the hair at marriage is known among other peoples than the Vedic Indians.[5] It is possible that it must be reckoned as a piece of deception magic, to deceive demons at a time when a woman is certainly exposed to much danger: possibly the idea may be to render more easy the entry of the child desired into the woman, if we ascribe to the period [6] the doctrine that a child enters *ab extra*.

[1] Rome had reduced them to very slight traces; cf. Warde Fowler, *Religious Experience of the Roman People*, p. 42.

[2] Oldenberg, *Rel. des Veda*[2], pp. 466 ff.

[3] Keith, JRAS. 1916, pp. 548, 549; Reinach's view is of course totemism pure and simple.

[4] Oldenberg, *op. cit.*, p. 463, n. 3; Hopkins, *Origin of Religion*, p. 119.

[5] Kauç. lxxix. 14.

[6] It is clearly the later, Buddhistic and general Indian, view (Windisch, *Buddha's Geburt*, pp. 9 ff.). It is the Arunta belief, and that of palaeolithic Europe if we believe Reinach (*Cultes, Mythes et Religions*, iv. 361 ff.), but cf. Cook, *Zeus*, i. 703.

CHAPTER 22

MAGIC IN THE RITUAL

§ 1. *The Relations of Magic to Religion*

THE theory that all religion is later than magic has already been discussed, and its fundamental weakness pointed out,[1] and it is therefore possible to consider the question of the relation of these two factors apart from any preconceived doctrine of the priority of magic. The position in the literature of Vedic India is a simple one : with very few exceptions the Rigveda is a book in which magic is not dealt with : a few late hymns are indeed found there, but these stand out as exceptions in a religious milieu. The Atharvaveda is a book of magic, mingled with some theosophy : that it is priestly magic, and not popular magic uninfluenced by the priests is clear : the priests have constantly altered, and changed much of what they dealt with, but the book itself is conclusive proof that the priests of that time were keenly concerned with magic rites. The position is further made clear by the Brāhmaṇas, which show beyond possibility of doubt that the whole of the sacrifice was penetrated by conceptions of magic. Scarcely any rite but can be so adapted as to produce magic ends : the rites are often varied in detail for this very purpose, the mode in which the post is covered with the cord will determine the amount of rain which will fall, the priest can bring to nothing the kingdom if he varies by manipulations the offering ; he is constantly told how to alter the words, when he dislikes the sacrificer, or when he seeks to obtain for him such special blessings as a male child.

The Atharvaveda and the Brāhmaṇas prove, therefore, that the India of their period was one in which magic and religion were inextricably blended : the same conclusion is suggested by the Rigveda itself : the man who is pure complains that he is called a magician and a companion of evil spirits,[2] and doubtless many among the priests who composed the songs of the Rigveda were not devoted to magic or specially interested in it. The exaltation which saw in the poetry of the Rigveda the highest form of honour which the gods could receive, would scarcely trouble itself about the lower field of magic. But we cannot believe [3] that there was ever a time when the Vedic sacrifice was not filled with magic elements,[4] and all that we can say with certainty is

[1] Cf. also Jevons, *Idea of God* (1910).

[2] RV. vii. 104. 16.

[3] Magic and sacrifice represent two different aspects of man's efforts to accomplish his desires. They are essentially distinct and are felt to be so in the higher faiths. But in primitive religions the elements lie side by side in no strongly felt differentiation.

[4] So the Babylonian and in less degree the Greek ; Farnell, *Greece and Babylon*, pp. 158, 176–9, 291–301 ; Fossey, *La magie assyrienne* ; R. C. Thompson, *Semitic Magic* (1908). For Vedic magic,

that the desire to see magic in everything was one which was growing in the period of the Brāhmaṇas, which degrade the sacrifice from the position of an appeal to the bounty of heaven to the position of the greatest power on earth, which controls the gods and produces whatever is desired by the priests. Magic thus won a powerful support from theosophy, and we cannot in the Vedic literature say that magic was regarded as a wicked thing, except when it was practised by others against a man. If he could, he would himself use magic to confound his enemies.[1] The code of Manu [2] in effect well sums up the point of view of its own, and also of the earlier Vedic period, in the doctrine that, while witchcraft is a bad thing, the Brahman who is wronged need not seek redress tamely by civil process through the intervention of the royal authority, but should assert his own power by his magic arts. The position is natural enough; all religions have to contend with magic, and, while the higher religions cast much aside, they cannot be successful in removing all. The Vedic religion had, however, developed no such moral or religious basis as would render it possible to demand the disappearance of magic rites, and thus magic flourished under its aegis in almost a disconcerting degree. Nothing shows how much the idea of the magic power of the sacrifice and its importance superseded moral considerations in the minds of the priests than the offerings prescribed by one text [3] to enable a man to break faith at pleasure without punishment by Varuṇa.

§ 2. *The Nature of Vedic Magic*

In the sphere of Vedic magic we have to do both with personal and with impersonal substances. The conception of all sorts of demons as threatening man is one which is supplemented by the more impersonal view of substances or potencies, which dwell in things, and which are often, therefore, of value in magic rites. It is possible that the earlier view is that which conceives these potencies either animatistically as actually alive, or animistically as spirits, but in the Vedic literature the two views, personal and impersonal, are both clearly found, and, like everything in the Veda, they are never clearly kept apart. Such powers [4] are the power of error in the sacrifice which clings to the sacrificial post, and therefore may pass to the sacrificers,[5] if care is not taken to render it harmless, the nature in woman, which causes her to slay her husband or to bear no children to him, and to bring death and disease among his cattle.[6]

see V. Henry, *La magie dans l'Inde antique*, and Caland, *Altindisches Zauberritual*; Macdonell, ERE. viii. 311–21. For the Roman attitude to magic, see Warde Fowler's *Religious Experience of the Roman People*.

[1] AV. vii. 70. 2.

[2] xi. 32, 33. Cf. Henry, *op. cit.*, p. 253; Jevons, *Idea of God*, pp. 8 ff.

[3] TS. ii. 2. 6. 2.

[4] One term for these is *tanū*, body, e.g. used of hunger and thirst in TA. iv. 22; Oldenberg, *Rel. des Veda*², p. 478. The instances given show that this is not by any means the same as *mana* as defined by Marett (*The Threshold of Religion*).

[5] Kauç. cii. 2; HGS. i. 16. 16.

[6] ÇGS. i. 18. 3.

It is not vitally to be distinguished from the strength of the tiger, which is found in its hair and its skin, and which makes these things suited for use in many magic performances, by which man seeks to attain for himself strength and kingship over men, such as the tiger exercises over animals. The frog and the Avakā plants can be used for cooling, for they have in them the nature of the water, a fact which shows clearly how real the presence of the deity in a symbol was to the Vedic conception. The banished king uses a clod of earth from his home in his desire to regain his kingdom : the lightning [1] leaves its strength in the tree which it blasts, the boar in the earth which it kicks up : [2] the name, the image, the hair, the very footprints [3] of man, are so connected with him as to be suitable modes of injury. Hence we can understand such legends as the theory that in laughing Makha [4] allowed his brilliance to depart from him, that the gods placed it in the plants, and thus was millet produced. Or again the white Vālakhilyas [5] practised asceticism : half of it with the resulting power Tārkṣya drank, and thus created the bird Garuḍa. The same idea displays itself in the constant fear of being affected by the mouth, which is one of the motives, no doubt, of the fasting recommended often by the Veda ; of being affected by mere inhalation, whence often the holding of the breath is laid down ; or of being affected by sight, whence often the eyes must be shut, or the sacrificer must at least not look round. The constant play of fancy between the real substance and the spirit is seen in the treatment of such ideas as Pāpman,[6] impersonal evil, or the spirit of a thousand eyes, or of Takman, the actual fever disease,[7] which seizes the patient, and makes him shiver, and the spirit which brings this about.

Of the means, which we may describe as magic in opposition to the rule of petition and offering which is religion, much of course is based on actual observation of fact, and much is based on mistaken fancies : magic, indeed, is doubtless in some sense and in fact the forerunner of science,[8] and like science is slow in clearing away misconceptions of all kinds. At times it is desirable to attract substances or spirits, at times urgently necessary to drive away such things : another branch of the subject is divination, which rests on the same foundation of contiguity or similarity, upon which rest the other laws of magic. The means are various : the word is of great importance, and so again are figures or representations of things which may be used as substitutes for or in addition to articles connected with the things or persons, who form the subjects of the conjuration. The time again is of importance : many things should be done at night, but others at special times of the day or the year, and

[1] Kauç. xlviii. 37.

[2] Kauç. xv. 2.

[3] Kauç. xlvii. 25.

[4] TA. v. 1. 3.

[5] Suparṇādhyāya, 2.

[6] AV. xi. 8. 19 ; vi. 26.

[7] Grohmann, *Ind. Stud.* ix. 383 ; cf. Jambha, ‘convulsions’, AV. vii. 10. Kaṇva, a disease demon (AV. ii. 25), may be a case of a soul of the dead as a demon.

[8] Cf. Henry, *La magie dans l'Inde antique*, pp. 241–60 ; Frazer, *The Magic Art.* Both, however, have unsatisfactory views of the relation of magic and religion. See also L. Thorndike, *The History of Magic* (1923).

various places are specially favourable, such as cross-roads, or graveyards, where spirits do mostly congregate, and where are the evil birds of prey and the jackals. But in special circumstances almost any place is suited specially for the rite.

It is natural, that, representing as it does a part of the primitive science of man, magic should be found in similar forms all the world over. There is little that is of special character in Indian magic, and the variety of its rites is enormous : fortunately or unfortunately for our opinion of the intelligence of the Vedic Indian not only has the Atharvaveda come down to us, but the Kauçika Sūtra contains (vii–lii) in the fullest detail, often however unintelligible to us, the nature of the rites which were used with the texts of that Veda. Other details occur in the Pariçiṣṭas of the Atharvaveda, in the Sāmavidhāna Brāhmaṇa, in the Ṛgvidhāna and minor texts. The antiquity of these works is by no means very great : the age of most of the practices may be indefinitely remote. The only practices of which we can say definitely that they are innovations are those, not at all few in number, in which priestly ingenuity has used mythical ideas, in order to found on them a magic practice. Thus in one rite laid down in the Kauçika Sūtra [1] we find that as a means of driving away evil spirits the use of a food is prescribed, which has been cooked with wood of a tree in which birds nest : this is due merely to the fact that in accompanying verses Indra, the averter of evil spirits, is invited to come as a bird to a tree.

§ 3. *The Removal of Hostile Influences*

In a modified degree the principle is adopted in Vedic ritual that hostile powers should be propitiated. Thus the Rakṣases are given the portions that fall away from the grain, when it is pounded for the offerings : the blood, the entrails, the excrement of the animal victim, are made over to them or the snakes. Diseases treated as demons are propitiated and shown reverence in the hope, which is expressed, that they will depart, being satisfied with what is done for them. The disease Takman is entreated to depart, and addressed as a god, just as among the Esths down to modern times the same procedure of paying homage was adopted to make a disease depart.[2] What is more interesting is that both methods might be tried in close conjunction : the jackal might be addressed with formulae of reverence at the one time, and at the same time a fire brand be thrown at it.[3] The ants receive an offering, but, if that fails, a poisonous mixture is made for them, and the aid of the gods in their utter extirpation is invoked.[4] Snakes are simultaneously treated with reverence, and their extinction invoked : in the snake offering itself, while the snakes are fed, the sacrificer draws round the house a line of water to keep them away from it. But as a rule the attitude of the Vedic Indian to

[1] xxix. 27. Based on AV. vi. 2. 2 ; Oldenberg, *Rel. des Veda*², p. 480, n. 3.

[2] Grohmann, *Ind. Stud.* ix. 413 ; cf. AV. i. 12, 13 ; v. 7 ; vi. 13, 20 ; PGS. i. 16. 24 ; HGS. ii. 7. 2 ; BDS. ii. 1. 32.

[3] HGS. i. 16. 20 ff.

[4] Kauç. cxvi.

the hostile powers is the desire to banish them far from his life, to deceive and cheat them in every way: hence such actions as fasting to forbid them entrance, refraining from breathing, from intercourse, from looking round and so on. The same idea is also to be seen in the fact that on certain occasions disguises are adopted, and that the hair which is cut from the child or youth is carefully buried. In this last instance, however, in many cases the hair is prescribed to be buried in such a place as a cow stall, and in that instance it may be that the burying was rather to bring prosperity to the cows [1] than as a piece of prophylactic magic, or the two ideas may have been merged into one. The difficulties of realizing the precise sense of magic rites is far greater than that of interpreting religious ceremonies. Other modes of avoidance are mentioned, in addition to not looking round at any dread sight, or not coming into physical contact with what is dangerous: thus the mother is impure for ten or twelve days after birth and is avoided, and the bricks for Nirṛti at the setting up of the fire altar are put in place without actual contact. Steps are taken to efface the footsteps of the priest, who carries the fire of the sacrifice, just as a clog is bound to the foot of the dead to wipe out the tracks. Similarly the use of different doors from the normal may be prescribed: the child attacked by the doggie demon cough is taken into the assembly hall, where the spell to exercise the demon is to be performed, through a hole made in the thatch.[2] When the sacrificer dies, and the fire hitherto maintained by him becomes the place of resort of powers of death, it is removed, but not by the door. Or, again, something may be interposed to shut out the demons: water they cannot cross,[3] and the use of water prevents the evil influence of the bricks for Nirṛti [4] or the funeral rite exercising its power. Similar cases of the interposition of obstacles are presented by the use of a stone to sever the living from the dead, the mat [5] employed for the same purpose, and at the sacrifice the enclosing sticks placed round the fire in order to keep off the demons.

The use of water for actual washing away different forms of evil is extremely common, as in the final bath: the place where a pigeon has alighted is washed clean: the bride is washed to rid her of all evil influences: after dealings with Rudra, demons, or the Fathers, it is necessary to purify oneself by touching water, but not rain water, which is deemed to have some degree of impurity and to spoil offerings on which it falls. The face is wiped after an evil dream.[6] Lead and wool are used also for cleansing purposes.[7] The urine of a cow has as in Iran and in modern India great properties of cleansing.[8] The new-born child is washed, and also the breast of the mother: but smoke is also used to purify the child, while fire is a constant source of protection. The sickle with which is cut the grass for the sacrifice is made glowing by means of fire, thus driving off the Rakṣases.

[1] Cf. Frazer, *The Magic Art*, i. 28 ff.
[2] HGS. ii. 7. 2.
[3] MS. iv. 8. 5.
[4] Weber, *Ind. Stud.* iii. 243.
[5] Kauç. lxxxvi. 14.
[6] HGS. i. 16. 5.
[7] Kauç. lxxi. 16, 17.
[8] KÇS. xxv. 11. 16.

The use of noise to drive away demons is common: the drums at the Mahāvrata rite are paralleled by the sounds made by the Soma stones at the pressing, which are made doubly resonant by the device of putting under them sounding holes. The noise of the Sāman is also powerful to drive away evil, if the critics of the Sāman singers also make it a ground for the breaking off of the holy study for the day on which it is heard. Pots are beaten at burial. When a gong is beaten, it is expected that the demon which has a child in its grip will be driven away.[1] The fragrant bdellion also serves to drive away demons, while the Apāmārga plant is famed for this service, which, as its name denotes, it derives from its power to wipe off the influences of such powers. The ritual use of beating is not unknown: it occurs during the royal consecration, when the priests gently beat the prince,[2] and it may perhaps be recognized in the beating of their thighs by the maidens who dance round the fire at the Mahāvrata, bearing on their heads the water pitchers.[3]

The use of a staff is of special interest: the student is given a staff, and is forbidden ever to let anything intervene between his body and it. When his studentship is over, it is thrown in the water with the rest of his outfit, but he obtains a new staff, and this is expressly stated to be of use not merely for protection against human foes but also from Rakṣases and Piçācas.[4] The Soma offerer has a staff, which he receives from the priest to guard him, and which he ought never to let go.[5] The Maitrāvaruṇa priest stands through the service with staff in hand, slightly bending forward, in the attitude of readiness to smite the demons.[6] A specially consecrated staff brings fortune wherever one goes: if a circle is drawn with it and one thinks of a place, then no enemy can enter that place.[7] The wooden sword of the sacrificer is used to cut up the earth on the altar place, and it is thrown into the dust heap, being treated as the enemy, Araru, who is destroyed.[8] After an offering to the Fathers the sword is drawn over the altar to send away the demons. Small staves are shot in the air at the wedding ceremony to destroy the sight of the Rakṣases.

Yet another form is that of shaking: the black antelope skin used at a sacrifice is shaken out with the view of removing any evil that may have crept there: the corner of the garment of him who offers to the Fathers is similarly shaken to remove any evil spirit. Remains of Surā were thrown away on an ant heap. Akin to these rites is the use of a comb to purify the hair of the bride from dangerous influences of any sort, and also the passing of people through narrow holes, of which the classical example is that of Apālā in the Rigveda,[9] whom Indra dragged through the hole of the chariot, of the cart,

[1] Kauç. lxxxvi. 15; HGS. ii. 7. 2.

[2] KÇS. xv. 7. 6; Weber, *Rājasūya*, p. 63.

[3] Cf. PB. ix. 8. 9; Vait. xxxiv. 9, 10.

[4] GGS. iii. 1. 14, 27; iv. 9. 17; AGS. iii. 8. 20; ÇGS. ii. 13. 1, 2, 8; PGS. ii. 6. 31, &c.

[5] ÇB. iii. 2. 1. 32.

[6] TS. vi. 1. 4. 2; AÇS. iii. 1. 20; KÇS. vi. 4. 6.

[7] SVB. ii. 4. 1, 2.

[8] VS. i. 29 ff.; ÇÇS. iv. 4. 2.

[9] Cf. Kauç. xv. 4; lxxii. 16; RV. viii. 91. 7; von Schroeder (VOJ. xxii. 223 ff.) has a fanciful explanation of the legend; cf. Oldenberg, *Ṛgveda-Noten*, ii. 142, 143; Zachariae, *Zeitsch. des Vereins f. Volksk.* xx. 154 ff.

and of the yoke, and so healed of a skin disease, and which is to be seen also in the marriage ritual, when the hole of the yoke of a car is placed on the bride.[1] The aim of this rite is probably also to be seen in the making of a hole in the roof of the assembly hall for the introduction of the boy who is ill: the narrowness was probably a feature of the rite. The question which arises in this case, as in the case of the passing of an army under the yoke in the Roman usage,[2] is whether the guilt of blood or the disease is considered to be wiped away by the contact with the sides of the hole, or whether it is to be classed as one of the devices by which an enemy is deceived and the angry demons or spirits of the dead are baulked of their prey.

In many other cases the plan is adopted of the transfer of the evil to some other person or thing. The principle is at work in the case of the scapegoat, of which the classic example is to be found at the final bath of the horse sacrifice. The bride's garment after marriage is hung up on a tree or post, so that the evil influence in it may be disposed of. Similarly the cloth with which she is wiped is given to the guardian of the maiden, who puts it in a cow-stall or hangs it up in the wood.[3] The Vrātyas at the end of the festival, by which they are admitted to the Brahmanical community, hand their apparel and utensils to other Vrātyas, or an inferior Brahman of Magadha, who bears away the defects inherent in them. A cow which is unfit for a fee is given to an enemy. After a miscarriage the woman is taken to three different huts: she is made to stand on lead and washed, her dark garment is taken off, and the hut burned.[4] The sufferer from a headache goes out with a turban on and scatters grains: when an attack comes on, he deposits the turban, the winnowing fan which he has used, and a bowstring: apparently the demon is to come out of the head into the turban and to make for the grains, when he will be attacked by the bow.[5] To avert a bad omen a hook is tied to the foot of a black bird, a cake attached, and it is sent away to hang on to the enemy as the hook hangs to it. Sleeplessness is banished to Trita Āptya or to an enemy. An offering is prescribed, by which it is possible to prevent two enemies transferring to a third person their mutual hatred. For a person who is possessed of an evil spirit various devices are combined: fragrant substances are mixed together and burned, the person concerned stands against the water of a stream, and water is poured over him, an offering is hung up on a bird-frequented tree, in each case to take away the evil.[6] Fever is banished to the distant people of Gandhāra and the Mūjavants. A ceremony is prescribed by which when a man is thirsty in illness he transfers the thirst to another man.[7] The disease jaundice is transferred to birds of appropriate hue, like the

[1] Winternitz, *Hochzeitsrituell*, pp. 43 ff.

[2] Warde Fowler, *Religious Experience of the Roman People*, pp. 267, 268; Frazer, *Balder the Beautiful*, ii. 192; Caland, *Altindisches Zauberritual*, p. 31; Henry, *La magie dans l'Inde antique*, p. 133.

[3] Kauç. lxxvi. 1; lxxix. 24; AV. xiv. 2. 48–50.

[4] Kauç. xxxiv. 3.

[5] Kauç. xxvi. 2. Cf., however, Henry, *La magie dans l'Inde antique*, pp. 206, 207.

[6] Kauç. xxvi. 29 ff.

[7] Kauç. xxvii. 9 ff.

thrush or parrot. Fever is transferred to a frog by pouring water over the patient and putting a frog under the bed ;[1] the connexion of the frog with the disease may be very old. An interesting means of finding out the presence in a house of a demon like a Piçāca is to hang up in the house kindling wood, and the strew for the sacrifice : if they are moved, the presence of the spirit is certain.[2]

Diseases are specially often the subjects of exorcism in one form or another : a woman suffering from lung disease must be rubbed by a chaste man with balls of fresh lotus leaves, limb by limb, and thereafter the leaves are thrown to the west.[3] He who suffers from an inherited disease is deluged with water and a plough is held, apparently a mixture of washing and contact.[4] Diarrhœa is dealt with by tying a string round a bunch of Muñja grass, and giving the patient to eat earth from a field and from an ant-heap.[5] Sick cows are made to drink salt water.[6]

§ 4. *The Attraction of Beneficial Substances and Powers*

The sacrificer must avail himself of the same means to attack his enemies as they use to attack him : if the enemy assail, the skilled priest can send against them the demon Apvā which seems to be the diarrhœa caused by terror, and to symbolize in emphatic fashion the fear produced by panic in battle : this performance is already recorded in the Rigveda.[7] So also it is perfectly in keeping with the ideas of magic that terror and fear would be conveyed to the enemy by the process of sending a white-footed one, presumably a sheep, against the opposing host.[8] In such a case Apvā is indeed a dreadful thing, but it is in the control of the priest and therefore useful to him. In other cases he has more direct control : he can use one substance for washing himself, another he can drink or eat, another use as an amulet ; with yet another he can rub or anoint himself.[9] The avoidance of the touch of anything dangerous is one side of a practice, of which the other is the touching of things which are beneficial. The touching of the victim has two sides : it may convey the death to which the victim is being led, but it may also convey—and this is the view which Brahman logic[10] finally adopts—the power and strength of the divine essence. Hence we have an enormous number of rites, the standing on a tiger-skin to obtain royal power, the use of an antelope-skin, the placing of the wife on a bull's hide, the placing of her and of the student upon a stone to attain firmness, the depositing at the fire-piling and other offerings on the place of the fire altar of a piece of earth

[1] Kauç. xxvi. 18 ff. ; xxxii. 17 ; cf. Hubert and Mauss, *Année sociol.* ii. 92 ; Bloomfield, JAOS. xvii. 173.
[2] Kauç. xxv. 34.
[3] ApGS. ix. 10.
[4] Kauç. xxvii. 1 ; Henry, *op. cit.*, p. 204.
[5] Bloomfield, *Seven Hymns of AV.*, p. 3.
[6] Kauç. xix. 1. Other rites in TA. iv. 36 ; KhGS. iv. 3. 13.
[7] RV. x. 103. 12 ; Kauç. xiv. 21.
[8] Weber, *Ind. Stud.* xvii. 269 ; Kauç. xiv. 22, 23. Caland, however, thinks that an arrow with white feathers is meant.
[9] AV. xix. 45. 5.
[10] ÇB. iii. 8. 1. 10.

from an ant-heap, since the ants as finders of waters give richness : the same ants *per contra* are often used to destroy dangerous substances like the remnants of offerings.

Various strange messes are prescribed for eating : the least unpleasant may be the mixture of milk, of cow-dung, of bdellion, and salt which is taken at an agricultural offering : the burying of a similar mess could, however, produce equal results.[1] The wife must eat a barley-corn with two beans attached to secure a male [2] and a strong infant. A peculiarly unpleasant drink, in which the members of a cow form an element, will secure all desires. The common eating of the king and the priest [3] and of the bride and bridegroom show that unity of essence was thus produced : it may be conjectured [4] that the Tānūnaptra ceremony was originally of this kind, though the common eating has disappeared. The idea would then be that he who injured any of those united to him by the common meal would injure himself. The use of anointing is often recorded : an enemy might be injured by anointing sweat on reed arrow-points and offering them.[5] The king and the sacrificer at the royal consecration and the Sautrāmaṇī were formally anointed and so on. Other means are breathing, as upon the new-born child to give it life, and the putting of substances in the nose to produce offspring.[6]

The eyes should not see many things, such as the taboos imposed on the Snātaka and his teacher, but, on the other hand, the eye may have purifying influence, and hence with the eye of Mitra the guest may look on what is given to him.[7] But the glance of a snake is deadly,[8] and so may the glance of the bride be : therefore her husband places salve on her eyes to secure his safety.[9]

In a number of interesting cases effective results are produced by using in the rite things connected with the object to be attained. Thus for a prince in exile it is well in the rite to use, for the kindling wood to cook a magic drink, wood from a stump of a tree which has grown again, or to place on the fire altar earth from his old realm. To defeat the ants when troublesome the use of a ladle of Bādhaka wood is valuable, as Bādhaka means ' repelling '. If victory in battle is the object, earth which a boar has torn up may be placed on the altar, and thus give the rite the strength of the boar.

In other cases burying things produces good results, as in the burying above referred to of a curious mixture for the prosperity of the herds : so too the burying of hair and other objects such as nails. On the other hand, it is necessary to provide rites to dig up objects, such as one's own hair and nails, which an enemy has buried : a special ceremony for this is mentioned in the Taittirīya Saṁhitā.[10]

[1] Kauç. xx. 25 ; xix. 9.
[2] HGS. ii. 2. 2, 3 ; AGS. i. 13. 2.
[3] Weber, *Rājasūya*, p. 140 ; Kauç. xvii ; Kauç. xii. 7 has a ceremony of eating in common to procure harmony.
[4] Oldenberg, *Rel. des Veda*[1], p. 502, n. 4 ; cf. below, § 7.
[5] Kauç. xlvii. 44.
[6] ÇGS. i. 24. 2.
[7] VS. v. 34.
[8] AB. vi. 1 ; KB. xxix. 1.
[9] RV. x. 85. 44 ; ÇGS. i. 16. 5. On the evil eye see Caland, *Zauberritual*, p. 79, n. 27.
[10] v. 2. 11 ; ÇB. iii. 5. 4.

For the purpose of protection the use of amulets is very common indeed: it is not indeed quite clear exactly what idea was conceived to be embodied in the use of these amulets. In the opinion of Oldenberg,[1] the view taken of the amulet was, in the first instance, that there was in it a spirit which took its abode therein, but in the period of the Vedic belief the view had been altered by a process of development, so that the effect of the amulet is produced by a substance resident therein.[2] It is, however, a little difficult to accept this view of the development of ideas. The view that the first element is spirit, and that the belief in the utility of the amulet is due to the view that a spirit is living in it, is unnecessarily refined: the fact, admitted by Oldenberg, that the amulet is not rarely addressed and treated as having an actual spirit in it, is most naturally of all explained by the fact of animatism: the amulet is conceived to be a living substance: only by a natural development of thought is there any element of a non-spiritual substance found. Animism in the strict sense of the word, therefore, need hardly come into operation, in so far as it postulates the belief in a mere detachable spirit.

The potency of nakedness as a magic rite is seldom mentioned save for rain spells: the Kauçika [3], however, tells how to expiate a day of ill omen by sitting naked and rubbing the forehead, and in its collection of spells for inducing slumber in women it prescribes nakedness in the performer of a rite, consisting in the besprinkling of the place where she is from a vessel full of water and the remains of an offering.

§ 5. *Mimetic Magic*

In one special class of cases the effect which it is desired by magic means to produce in nature is brought about by the simple plan of representing in sensible form, within the means available to man, the operations which it is desired should take place. Thus when an enemy is to be defeated [4] it is useful to break in two a piece of grass which is thrown towards the opposing host: the breaking of the grass symbolizes the breaking in two of the armed foemen. Or the rite can be made more effective in quite a simple way: as a daughter-in-law by an old taboo is expected to shrink away from her father-in-law, so by taking the hostile enemy as the daughter-in-law, and by

[1] *Rel. des Veda*[2], pp. 512, 513. Cf. AV. x. 6. 5 for a clear case of the amulet as living. Henry (*La magie dans l'Inde antique*, pp. 89–92) suggests that the *srāktya* amulet owes its name to its form, which was like that of the Semitic 'seal of Solomon' amulet and was borrowed from Semites, but this is needless; cf. AV. ii. 11; viii. 5; Bloomfield, SBE. xlii. 675. For comparison of Teutonic use of amulets see SBE. xlii. 409.

[2] Cf. ERE. ii. 392 ff.; Helm, *Altgerm. Rel.* i. 22 f.

[3] xxxviii. 4 and xxxvi. According to Henry (*op. cit.*, p. 109) nudity has this value because it brings man back to his primitive dress; cf. Zachariae, *Kl. Sch.*, pp. 238 f.; Samter, *Geburt, Hochzeit und Tod*, pp. 112 ff.; Hopkins, *Origin of Religion*, p. 188. For nudity in rain ritual cf. Mitra, JRAS. 1897, pp. 471–84; Frazer, *Golden Bough*[3], i. 283 ff.

[4] Kauç. lvi. 10; xiv. 19–22 gives other devices, noted above.

addressing to it the remark that the father-in-law is looking at it, the hostile army will then break up in utter confusion.[1] More elaborate instances of the same thing are of course the ceremonies of the Mahāvrata where the water thrown on the fire produces rain, and the winning of the white round skin which represents the sun is a spell representing the recovery of the sun from the hostile powers affecting it. In the royal consecration the victory of the king over his rival is graphically depicted in mimic form: his success in dicing[2] is a picture of his success in the position of king on earth. The fertility of the earth and of the crops is produced by the mimicry of sexual relationships at the Soma sacrifice, at the horse sacrifice, and by the actual performance of ritual intercourse at the Mahāvrata offering. At the Vājapeya the chariot race is a magic performance to secure the pre-eminence of the sacrificer, just as in the rite he is made to be the victor in the race in question.[3] The Sautrāmaṇī offering is a clear imitation of the story of the healing of Indra from his intoxication with Soma after the slaying of the demon Namuci:[4] it is used to secure the sacrificer the success for which he is anxious in whatever sphere of life he may live. This sort of magic is particularly common in rain magic:[5] herbs are often dipped in water, black garments assumed, black victims offered. One rite is of interest: the heads of a dog and a ram, hairs, and old shoes are fastened to the end of a bamboo, and passes are made in the air as if in combat with a demon: the animals may be intended to aid in the breaking open of the sky, just as at the Mahāvrata the shooting of arrows through, but not so as to penetrate, a skin, is presumably intended to let the waters of the skies flow down on the earth.

The death of a man can be, as in all lands, compassed thus in many ways: an image of him may be made of wax and melted or it may be pierced to the heart, or again his shadow, which is in some degree the man, may be likewise treated: again a chameleon may be killed and formally burned in mimicry of the rite of the burning of the dead man.[6] The footmark of a maiden can be used as a means of winning her love:[7] the footmark of a beleaguered king is scattered to the winds.[8] Worms are generally to be banished by the crushing and the burning of twenty-one selected Uçīra worms.[9] The running away of a slave or some other persons may be prevented by the idiotic rite of pouring round the person affected the urine of the performer from the horn of a living animal, a symbol of strength: the urine represents the person to whom the slave belongs, and thus the person in living presence is in the vicinity and prevents the slave from running away.[10] The destruction of misfortune of any kind often takes the shape of the burning or throwing away in water of old

[1] AB. iii. 22. 7; Liebich, VOJ. xxvii. 474–7.

[2] ApÇS. v. 19. 2 ff.; 20. 1 ff.; Weber, *Rājasūya*, pp. 69 ff.

[3] Weber, *Vājapeya*, pp. 27 ff.

[4] Oldenberg, GN. 1893, pp. 342 ff.

[5] For these rites cf. Henry, *La magie dans l'Inde antique*, p. 110; Caland, *Altindisches Zauberritual*, p. 141.

[6] Kauç. xlvii. 54 ff.; 39 ff.; Caland, *op. cit.*, pp. 164, 166.

[7] SVB. ii. 6. 8; Caland, *op. cit.*, p. 163.

[8] MS. ii. 2. 1; cf. Caland, *l.c.*

[9] Kauç. xxix. 24.

[10] HGS. i. 14; PGS. iii. 7.

things such as garments, sunshades or shoes.[1] To destroy the borer insect which is damaging crops, one of the species is buried, head downwards, the mouth closed with thread, to prevent further depredations.[2] When the Soma is being pressed, he who desires to destroy a foe should think of him as he pounds with the pressing stone: the pounding will directly affect the foe. More amusing is the device to be adopted to secure the transfer of a stream from one course to another: the new bed desired is watered, plants like the Avakā are put along it, and a frog is also put there. The stream will therefore follow the path thus laid down.[3] The same principle is at work in the rule by which objects to be attained are often expressed in a speech as so won. Thus when the wife is given an offering to look at in the ceremony of the parting of the hair and is asked, 'What dost thou say ?' she replies, 'Offspring.' Similarly in the rite to attain male offspring her answer as to what she drinks, in the magic drink given to her, is the producing of a son. The husband and wife on the fifth day after the wedding ask a young Brahman what he sees, to which he replies, 'Sons and cattle.'[4] So in the rite of the animal offering the question, 'Is it ready ?' has always the answer that it is; in the plough festival[5] the question of the wife whether the ploughing has been accomplished receives an affirmative reply; and such cases are to be found in every important rite. A mode of divination can be made a mode of conveying good fortune in this way: thus a merchant, going on a journey, places balls of dung on the limbs of a friendly Brahman and asks what sort of day it is, to which the latter replies that it is good and lucky.[6]

§ 6. *Divination and Ordeal*

The principle of divination is in large measure directly due to the doctrine of mimetic magic:[7] if the use of a representation of things can produce them, it is also legitimate, if less easy, to deduce the future of events from the behaviour of things, which are supposed to be an imitation of the events. This, however, is no doubt not the whole ground of the belief in the power to read the future, and, moreover, the fact that the future was uncertain must have induced many people to resort to the gods for aid in unravelling it. In these cases the performances are indeed much the same as in an ordinary species of divination, but the belief is different: it is the view that the future is revealed by the god, through the means employed: magic here is supplemented as often by religious conceptions.

[1] Kauç. xviii. 9 ff.; cf. Henry, *op. cit.*, p. 163.

[2] Kauç. xi. 19; AV. vi. 50. 1.

[3] Kauç. xl. 1–9; Henry, *op. cit.*, p. 101 Weber, *Ind. Stud.* xvii. 243.

[4] GGS. ii. 7. 10; AGS. i. 13. 3; Winternitz, *Hochzeitsrituell*, p. 101.

[5] Kauç. xx. 16 ff.

[6] Kauç. l. 15; Henry, *op. cit.*, p. 70; Bloomfield, SBE. xlii. 532 ff.

[7] Oldenberg, *Rel. des Veda*², pp. 484, 507 ff.; Henry, *op. cit.*, pp. 59–62. Divination from the entrails of the victim, which is specially Babylonian (Farnell, *Greece and Babylon*, pp. 248, 249), is not Vedic. For Babylon, cf. Meyer, *Gesch. d. Alt.*³ I. ii. pp. 585–7; for Greece, W. R. Halliday, *Greek Divination* (1913).

The use of means is very varied : the fire of the sacrifice and the victim at the sacrifice are specially suited to give knowledge by their magic connexion with the gods as well as religious conceptions : more clearly connected with the activity of divine powers in Vedic belief is the drawing of omens from the flight and the movements of animals, which are specially clearly connected with birds or beasts, with gods or spirits of the dead or demons. When a ceremony is performed to win for a maiden a husband, the side from which crows first appear is that from which her wooer will come.[1] The movement of the cow at a particular moment in the Soma sacrifice shows the fortune of the sacrificer.[2] The clear flaming of the fire at a sacrifice brings with it the prospect of twelve villages for the sacrificer; if it smokes, of at least three.[3] More interesting is the rule that, when the body of the dead is being burned, the soul will go to the heaven, atmosphere, or the earth according as the eastern, western, or southern fire first reaches it.[4] The owl is invoked to fly round the village and give signs for the future : it is a bird which flies to the dwellings of the gods, and the Rigveda already knows birds of omen.[5] The hyena's howl is uttered either of its own will, or on the prompting of other powers.[6] The battle's result can be judged by the lighting of a special fire on a suitable place and observing the movements of the fire, or it can be forecasted by taking three bowstrings, and placing them on a fire : the movements of the three, of which the middle one is treated as death, will show the event : that which keeps clear from it will represent the victorious army, that which comes into contact with it the army which is to be ruined.[7] The character of the bride can be judged by the choice by her of balls of earth chosen from very various places : [8] the sex of the future child by the fact whether the member of the body of the prospective mother which a Brahman boy touches has a masculine or feminine name.[9]

The meanings of dreams is an interesting part of Vedic magic and is dealt with in various passages, including an Atharvan Pariçiṣṭa. The Rigveda [10] already regards as ominous the making of a garland or neckband in a dream. Ten dreams which forebode death are recorded in the Aitareya Āraṇyaka : [11] when one sees in a dream a black man with black teeth who kills him, when a boar kills him, when a wild cat springs on him, when one eats and then spits out gold, when one eats honey and lotus roots, when one goes to a village with asses or boars, or when one drives south a black cow with a black calf, wearing

[1] Kauç. xxxiv. 24.
[2] ÇB. iv. 5. 8. 11.
[3] GGS. iv. 8. 15.
[4] AGS. iv. 4. 2 ff.
[5] HGS. i. 17. 3 ; RV. ii. 42 and 43.
[6] HGS. i. 17. 1.
[7] Kauç. xiv. 31 ; xv. 15.
[8] GGS. ii. 1. 3 ff.
[9] Kauç. xxxiii. 19. For other modes see Henry, *op. cit.*, p. 67.
[10] viii. 47. 15 ; Oldenberg's note to x. 164.
[11] iii. 2. 4. For an evil dream one should turn over on the other side, saying AV. vii. 100, and for expiating the dream of eating in sleep should say AV. vii. 101 (cf. Caland, *Altindisches Zauberritual*, p. 151 ; Pischel, *Album-Kern*, pp. 115 ff.) ; Kauç. xlvi. See also J. von Negelein, *Der Traumschlüssel des Jagaddeva* (1912), p. 378.

a garland of nard. If one has a dream, one should, as we have seen, wash one's mouth. The view is also held that certain stars are unlucky, especially Mūla.[1] Moreover, many sights forebode evil: the sun seeming as the moon, the heaven red like madder, when one's shadow appears upside down in a mirror or water, or when one's head smells like a crow's nest.[2] Evil is further portended by meteors and lightning. Of ominous birds the main classes are those which are black or whose appearance or utterance is horrible: the pigeon, the owl, the vulture, the Dīrghamukhī, &c., but the bird is also called generally the mouth of Dissolution. Birds,[3] too, are said to go about in the semblance of the Fathers, other animals are seldom mentioned in this regard; the fact that a horse on several occasions is used to forecast prosperity, or other results, is rather due to its connexion with the offering than to its intrinsic nature as ominous, though fortune in popular superstition can be inferred from the neighing of a horse.[4] Other prodigies are the appearance of an ant-heap in the house, the making of honey there by the bees, the scream of a jackal, the drinking of one cow from another, the cows giving blood for milk, and so on.[5]

The existence of men skilled in the interpretation of omens is natural and is also recorded, as for instance in the case of the men who could tell the marks which led to luck or otherwise in the choice of a wife. We hear also of a prophet who made his prophecies on the basis of the smoke of dung, the Çakadhūma of the Atharvaveda, whose business it was, it is clear, to forecast the weather.[6] We learn also of men who by the means of plants such as the Sadaṁpuṣpā[7] were able to behold sorcerers male and female, whether they went in the sky or on the earth: the same idea of the power of socerers to assume various forms is found in the Rigveda[8] where it asks for the destruction of the demons, who in form of birds fly about the village at night. Necromancy, however, is not apparently known,[9] nor the inspection, on a system, of the entrails of the victims, in order to read the future.

The ordeal is nothing more than a form of divination in one of its aspects: the idea in it is not that the deity would actually punish an accused person so much as that it should by its treatment of him show whether or not he is innocent of the charge made against him. But the analogy of the ordeal to the oath in which the swearer invokes a penalty on himself, if he is telling untruth, shows that the separation of the ideas of punishment and discrimination cannot be assumed to have been present to the Vedic mind:[10] the form

[1] Kauç. xlvi. 25 ff. Cf. Bloomfield, *Atharvaveda*, pp. 83, 85.

[2] AA. iii. 2. 4; cf. LÇS. iii. 3. 6 ff.; ApÇS. ix. 20. 10. The sight of the dead presages death to the seer; JUB. iii. 29.

[3] AB. ii. 15. 4; BDS. ii. 8. 14. 9, 10.

[4] Grimm, *Deutsche Myth.*[4] iii. 442.

[5] ÇGS. v. 11. 10; HGS. i. 16. 19; 17. 6; Kauç. cxii.

[6] Bloomfield, *Atharvaveda*, p. 81; Henry, *op. cit.*, pp. 68 ff.

[7] Kauç. xxviii. 7; AV. iv. 20.

[8] vii. 104. 18.

[9] Oldenberg, *Rel. des Veda*[2], p. 569, n. 2.

[10] *Ibid.*, p. 508; Jolly, ZDMG. xliv. 346; Macdonell and Keith, *Vedic Index*, i. 364, 365, 392; Glotz, *L'ordalie* (1904);

of ordeals recorded for early Vedic times shows the prevalence of punishment at the same time as the test of fact: the Rigveda has not any certain example of the ordeal: the only Brāhmaṇa cases are those in which Vatsa asserts his purity of Brahmanical origin by walking through the fire without harm affecting him,[1] Triçoka's assertion of superior Vedic knowledge by a fire ordeal and the successful crossing of a stream, and the glowing axe which is brought up for the purpose of testing the accused thief.[2] The fire as a sentient power by failing to burn or by burning shows innocence or guilt: but it punishes at the same time, and this is roughly speaking true of some of even the later ordeals, such as the poison and water ordeals.[3] A procedure to prevent the burning of the hand in the ordeal of plunging the hand into boiling oil to extract a piece of gold is prescribed in the Kauçika.[4]

§ 7. *The Magic Spell*

The power of the word is very marked in all systems of magic and naturally not least in India. The magic spell is sometimes in prose, in the style of the formulae used by the Adhvaryus at the sacrifice, more often in verse, sometimes newly made for the purpose, sometimes, and indeed very often, chosen without any appropriateness from the vast body of existing sacred literature. Of this latter tendency two examples may be given: the number available is legion. The finest hymn to Varuṇa in the Vedic literature is found in the Atharvaveda where it has been preserved in a charm.[5] The great hymn of the Rigveda, which celebrates the god Prajāpati in the form of questions, has the second verse used in a spell for preventing the miscarriage of a cow, doubtless for no better reason than that the idiotic system on which names of authors were assigned to every hymn of the collection resulted in postulating an author Hiraṇyagarbha, 'he of the golden womb', really an epithet of the supreme god, and the fact that the deity was Prajāpati.[6]

Of the spell one characteristic is the regularity with which many gods are invoked: it is absurd to suppose that in these enumerations there was normally any sense of the different deities invoked: all that was desired was to strengthen the spell by the utterance of as many names of deities as possible: in some cases the mention of individuals is dropped and merely the numbers are given, 99 or 88 or 77 and so on: the fondness for such numbers

Keith, ERE. *s.v.* Ordeal; Hopkins, *Origin of Religion*, p. 256.

[1] PB. xiv. 6. 8; JB. iii. 233 ff.

[2] CU. vi. 16. Cf. the use of fires to discriminate after death, ÇB. i. 9. 3. 2; below, Chap. 28, § 10.

[3] As weighing ordeal, without punishment directly, is hinted at n ÇB. xi. 2. 7. 33, where a man's fate after death is determined by weighing his good and evil deeds.

[4] lii. 8, 9; Henry, *La magie dans l'Inde antique*, p. 100.

[5] iv. 16. It is not clear if the spell is against an enemy who curses or is cursed: *çapyantam* may (*pace* Caland on Kauç. xlviii. 7) be an irregularity (cf. *badhya*, BD. v. 134; vi. 14). See Weber, *Ind. Stud.* xviii. 66; Henry, *op. cit.*, pp. 235–9.

[6] Kauç. xliv. 5; RV. x. 121. 2.

is a feature of many forms of magic.[1] Analogous to this feature is the fact that when anything is to be dealt with every conceivable place where it may be is enumerated: a disease is banished, not merely from the place where it is paining the person afflicted, but from all his members. On the other hand, where possible the exact name and origin of the thing dealt with must be given: if one can name father and mother so much the better: the drum[2] is described as coming from the lord of the forest and strung by the cows. Sometimes names of, to us, inexplicable and perhaps esoteric character are given, such as *hrūḍu* applied in the Atharvaveda[3] to fever, in accordance with the well-known rule that in magic a mysterious name is the most potent of all.[4]

A second characteristic of the spells is the stress laid on the recital of comparisons which have magic effect in producing the results desired. The kidneys are made to settle themselves firmly by comparison with the mountains which abide for ever, or the bird which is at rest in its nest, or the cows which have come back to the stall.[5] The amulet is made effective by the fact that it was the one bound by the Dākṣāyaṇas on Çatānīka.[6] The dying round the Brahman, which is prescribed in the Aitareya Brāhmaṇa[7] as the spell *par excellence* of the Purohita against the foes of his master, is accompanied by comparison with the mode in which the constellations appear and set again. The birth of the embryo is encouraged by the comparison with the wind which moves the lotus pond on all sides,[8] and so on indefinitely. The use of the word 'grow' is necessary when the Arundhatī plant is addressed in order to heal a broken bone: 'below', 'away', are used when a disease is expelled: if one practises witchcraft, one should use the word 'broken' when offering a cup: in bringing about harmony the word 'in unison' is of value. The importance of the name has already been mentioned: it results in the giving to each child of a secret name. Nor is there missing the rite by which a formula is repeated backwards: if the offering priest is interrupted by the servants of the sacrificer, he should repeat backwards the Daçahotṛ formula, and thus bring the sacrifice to ruin.[9] The use of harsh words like *phaṭ*, &c., is mentioned possibly even as early as the Rigveda.[10]

The word has special force in the form of the curse, which is often recorded in Vedic literature and which as is well known is one of the most common motives in later Indian literature. Fish are killed out of hand by men, because they betrayed to the gods Agni when he fled for shelter to the waters and for that deed Agni cursed them to be slain by men.[11] The trees which

[1] AV. xix. 47. 3 ff.; vi. 25; Kuhn, KZ. xiii. 128 ff. For the motive of such invocations see Henry, *op. cit.*, pp. 12, 19.

[2] AV. v. 20. 1 ff. Cf. Babylonian parallels in Farnell, *Greece and Babylon*, pp. 296–9.

[3] i. 25. 4. Henry's guess (*op. cit.*, p. 184) of a Semitic source of this word is as impossible as Halévy's derivation from Greek.

[4] Legge, *Forerunners and Rivals of Christianity*, ii. 33.

[5] AV. vii. 96. 1.

[6] AV. i. 35.

[7] viii. 28.

[8] RV. v. 78. 7.

[9] ApÇS. xiv. 15. 1.

[10] x. 87. 13.

[11] TS. ii. 6. 6. 1.

caused illness to the gods were cursed by the gods to be destroyed by a handle of the woodman's axe, made from their own bodies.[1] The curse is often mentioned as being invoked to recoil on the curser himself, showing that it was a common form of magic attack. It might also be heightened in effect by a formal offering, in which the rules of the sacrifice are violated and the points of reeds are sacrificed to the accompaniment of formulae declaring that the sacrificer takes from the enemy, who has played him false with his wife, hope and sight, children and cattle, breathing in and breathing out.[2] The curse [3] in the Brāhmaṇas is constantly expressed in a curious form : if a man performs an act in the offering incorrectly, then he places himself in such a position that, if any one were to say of or to him something unpleasant, that would come true. The point is clear : the mistake exposes the man guilty of it to the risk of the effective working of any curse which is invoked upon him.

The Vedic oath is often recorded : the king at the great consecration recorded by the Aitareya Brāhmaṇa must swear to his priest to be true, at the cost otherwise of all his merit in sacrifice and gifts to the priests since the beginning of his life, his good deeds, his offspring, passing from him on the occasion of his falsehood.[4] But a still older form of oath recorded [5] is by cows, or waters, or Varuṇa,[6] and the Indian to this day swears in some cases by Ganges water which he holds in his hand. The legal literature [7] allows oaths for a Brahman by his truth, for a Kṣatriya by his teams and weapons, and for a Vaiçya by his cows, grain and gold, but these are not recorded for the Vedic period, and the first is modern in appearance as compared with the Vedic oaths. Later, too, we find that the touching of oneself in the oath was not rare, as showing the spirits the person to be punished if the oath were not kept : this usage is proved for late Vedic times by the provision that the touch in such a case is, like the offering to Rudra, a ground for purification by means of water.[8] Possibly, too, the curses recorded that a man's head shall fly off, which is paralleled by the Buddhist malediction that the head should split in seven pieces, may be connected with this idea of touching the head.[9] A joint curse is that of the Tānūnaptra rite, which is an oath of fidelity of the priest and the sacrificer in the Soma sacrifice, with a curse on the violator of the oath. There is in the Aitareya Brāhmaṇa [10] an echo of the famous story of the lotus theft, in which the various persons accused of stealing the lotus fibres declared themselves guiltless by the device of invoking the most dreadful

[1] PB. vi. 5. 11.
[2] ÇB. xiv. 9. 4. 11.
[3] ÇB. xii. 4. 1. 4.
[4] AB. viii. 15 ; cf. Kauç. xvii.
[5] TS. i. 3. 11. 1 ; cf. AV. xix. 44. 9; ÇB. iii. 8. 5. 10. For an oath by water, see Rāmāyaṇa, vii. 65. 29 ff.
[6] This form is clearly religious and there is no ground to claim magic as a more primitive source of the oath, both kinds being natural. Cf. von Schroeder, *Arische Religion*, i. 147 ff., 156 ff., 476 ff.
[7] Manu, viii. 113. Cf. TS. ii. 3. 5. 1 and the Pāli Saccakiriya (Burlingame, JRAS. 1917, pp. 429 ff.).
[8] ÇGS. i. 9. 10.
[9] Oldenberg, *Rel. des Veda*^{2}, p. 520.
[10] v. 30 ; Charpentier, ZDMG. lxiv. 65 ff. ; lxvi. 44 ff. ; Geldner, lxv. 306, 307.

misfortunes on the head of the thief, while the true thief, the god himself, revealed his nature by invoking nothing but good. The classical instance of a broken oath is that of Soma, who is punished for failing to keep his promise to dwell with the twenty-seven wives whom he received from Prajāpati, by the disease Rājayakṣma, perhaps consumption.[1]

§ 8. *The Magic Sacrifice*

In many cases the sacrifice itself is degraded to mere magic: this is a precise parallel to the degradation of the formulae to spells which we have already seen, and of which the mystic Hotṛ formulae, originally of a superior type of thought, but later degraded to common magic purposes, are the best example. The actual sacrifice itself may be adapted to magical ends: thus to secure the opposite of the natural results the sorcerer performs it with the arrangement reversed as far as may be: the movements are not from south to north and from left to right, but from north to south, the region of the dead, and from right to left. Or again the offering verse in a sacrifice for Indra may be addressed to the Maruts, and *vice versa* in an offering to the Maruts. The Kauçika Sūtra has full descriptions of black magic, an idea which has never been without votaries and which in the Middle Ages attained great fame.[2] More directly the sacrifice becomes not merely in the theosophy of the Brahmans the great power of the universe: more prosaically it becomes the means by which the sorcerers who practise magic against one can be made to show themselves, by which rival wives can be overcome, by which the monarch in exile can regain his throne.[3] The sacrifice can be adapted to these ends by any manipulations of its component parts or by the precise mode in which the ritual acts are performed.

Slightly different is another method of producing magic results: in this case the nature of the offering chosen differs essentially from the ordinary sacrifice: thus ants are offered poison;[4] for a rival reed-points are sacrificed, the order of sacrifice being also altered;[5] to win cattle,[6] dung of a pair of calves, to win sheep, of a pair of sheep, is offered: long life is aimed at by offering nails of Khadira wood; and from the practice of passing people

[1] TS. ii. 3. 5. 1 ff. Two theories of the effect of a meal combined with an oath may be noted. Oldenberg (*Rel. des Veda*[1], p. 502, n. 4) thinks that the common meal results in creating identity of substance of the partakers, so that he who wrongs another thus wrongs himself. Westermarck (*Anthropological Essays presented to E. B. Tylor*, p. 374) holds that the meal operates a transference of conditional curses to those concerned (and to the god if he is party to the convenant).

[2] Henry, *La magie dans l'Inde antique*, pp. 220 ff. The conjuring up of souls to use them against the living is recorded only late, e.g. SVB. iii. 6. 12; the same text tells (iii. 7. 9) how to bring up demons who give five Kārṣāpaṇas, which never fail to return to their owner, so long as he does not part with all at one time.

[3] AV. i. 8; RV. x. 159. 4; 174.

[4] Kauç. cxvi. See above, Part II, Chap. 11, § 7; Hillebrandt, *Rituallitteratur*, pp. 185, 186.

[5] Kauç. xlvii. 44.

[6] GGS. iv. 9. 13 f.; 8. 11.

through holes to rub off evil or make them invisible to their foes, the use of sacrificing through a hole [1] naturally came into existence.

In one other respect the magician avails himself of the forms of the ordinary sacrifice. One of the most important ingredients in every magic offering is the Saṁpāta, the remnant of the butter offering made at the new and full moon, and the Kauçika Sūtra [2] contains precise instructions for the performance of these offerings, though it would be erroneous to imagine with Caland [3] that every magic ceremony required to be accompanied by such a rite, a rule which would have restricted the workings of magic to a very short period.[4] In the operations of his ceremonies the magician follows closely the ordinary rites of sacrifice : the person in whose interest he sacrifices takes stalks of Darbha grass and touches the priest with them to establish close contact with him, and smells the smoke of the oblations made in the fire by the priest.[5] On the other hand, it is characteristic of the special nature of the rite that it is performed in the north-eastern quarter away from the village,[6] and when it is completed the performers wash themselves in the stream near which the rite has been carried out, and return to the village, never turning round lest they may see the dread presences which they have evoked. The materials of the magic rite, apart from the frequent use of uneatable materials, are in the main the same as those of the ordinary ritual, but the diverse varieties of butter found in that ritual are replaced by the regular use of Ājya alone, while the Iñgiḍa is often mentioned as an ingredient.[7] Special interest attaches to the frequent use of earth from an ant-heap : as we have seen, the ant, doubtless owing to its skill and industry, was regarded as an uncanny animal by the Vedic Indian, and possibly experience may have proved the existence of some value in the earth. An interesting excursion into the realm of sacrifice is made by this belief : in the ceremony of the piling of the fire altar, when the clay for the making of the bricks has been collected, the priest is to gaze at it through an ant-heap, i.e. presumably through a tunnel made in such a heap. The explanation of this rite is obscure : Henry [8] suggests comparison with the German superstition that by wearing a moleskin a man can see sorcerers : possibly the medium of an ant-heap conferred on the priests the faculty of discerning whether any evil influences were affecting his materials. Another curious ingredient is lead, and its three substitutes, iron filings, dried river foam, and a lizard's head.[9] Woods of various kinds play a large part : one list [10] enumerates twenty-two kinds of value, and is not exhaustive as it omits

[1] Kauç. lxxii. 16.

[2] vii. 15.

[3] *Altindisches Zauberritual*, p. vi.

[4] Bloomfield, GGA. 1902, pp. 493 ff.; Henry, *op. cit.*, pp. 39 ff.

[5] Kauç. vii. 21, 28.

[6] Kauç. vii. 13. It is the gate of the heaven (ÇB. vi. 6. 2. 4), because (Henry, *op. cit.*, p. 46) the sun appears there at the summer solstice.

[7] Henry, *op. cit.*, p. 51.

[8] *Op. cit.*, p. 56. Oldenberg (*Rel. des Veda*², p. 499) holds that the richness in water and sustenance of the ants is thus conferred on the sacrificer.

[9] Kauç. viii. 18.

[10] Kauç. viii. 15.

the Açvattha, which is often in fact employed in magic rites. But scarcely anything from an elephant's tooth or hair[1] downwards comes amiss to the sorcerer, who in India as elsewhere is anxious to increase the importance of his action by asserting that his ingredients have been obtained from afar: an antidote against snakes is dug up on the ridges of the mountain with shovels of gold by the little Kirāta maiden,[2] an assertion with which we may, if we will, compare the practice not rarely recorded, under which people of higher culture ascribe to those of lower culture possession of superior magic powers.[3]

In other respects the parallelism between sacrifice and magic ceremony is extremely close: in both cases the operator expects and receives a reward, but the Kauçika Sūtra only rarely gives us an exact measure of the Dakṣiṇā payable: in some cases the materials used may have been the fee,[4] but often these would be too worthless or too valuable and it is reasonable to believe[5] that the fee was usually fixed by agreement. The magic ceremony can serve most of the purposes of the formal sacrifice: just as a main object of the regular offering is long life, so an infinity of charms provide life, and amulets of varied kinds are provided by the magician. There are spells for the house, to guard against fire, to bring rain, to secure increase of cattle, to prevent injury and increase the growth of crops, to secure safety on a journey or trade venture and success in gambling. Spells provide success in the assembly, bring victory in war, restore an exiled king, produce harmony or discord among the several classes of the people just as sacrifices do. Even more than sacrifice are magic ceremonies adapted to secure success in love, the overthrow of rivals, constancy between husband and wife, the birth of a son rather than of a daughter, safety in child-birth, and the protection of the life, always precarious and doubly so in such a climate as that of India, of the infant, and spells as well as sacrifices protect the whole adolescence and life of man. Specially rich in spells is the domain of medicine: remedies are provided in this way against many diseases, including intestinal worms, to which the Vedic Indian attributed many diseases with which they had no concern; fever whose several varieties were already known from their periods of recurrence; wounds and fractures, one formula used having some faint claim to be Indo-European in character;[6] skin affections including even leprosy;[7] the effects of poison; and even perhaps diseases ranked as hereditary.[8] The means employed are often obscure, and, while traces of some medical knowledge are not wanting—the use of the probe[9] has been recognized by Henry[10] and

[1] Kauç. xiii. 2, 3.

[2] AV. x. 4. 14.

[3] Moulton, *Early Zoroastrianism*, pp. 193, 194. His application of this doctrine to the case of the Magoi is not tenable; see JRAS. 1915, pp. 790–9. Henry (*op. cit.*, p. 141) reminds us of the use of obi men made by creoles.

[4] Kauç. viii. 5.

[5] Henry, *op. cit.*, p. 48.

[6] Cf. Feist, *Kultur der Indogermanen*, pp. 349, 350; Bloomfield, *Atharvaveda*, pp. 58, 61; SBE. xlii. 409.

[7] Henry, *op. cit.*, pp. 190, 266; Birdwood, *Sva*, pp. 183 ff.

[8] *kṣetriya*, of uncertain sense; Henry, *op. cit.*, p. 203.

[9] Kauç. xxv. 10–19.

[10] *Op. cit.*, p. 208

Caland [1]—in the main the spell seems to be relied on, together with symbolic acts for banishing, for example, the yellow jaundice to the yellow bird.

A question of some difficulty presents itself as to the performers of these magic rites. Many of them are of such simplicity that it would appear obvious that they could be carried out by each householder for himself, for example, the rites to secure the safety of the cattle against wild beasts while grazing and their safe return at evening.[2] Nor can we reasonably doubt that in the first instance the householder was his own magician as well as sacrificer.[3] But in the Kauçika Sūtra, as is natural, we find it assumed throughout that the performer of the rite is essentially the Brahman priest, whose Veda the Atharvaveda essentially is, and that no rite has any value without his presence. We may, therefore, assume that by the time of the Sūtra, and even earlier, the control of magic had largely fallen into the hands of these priests, and this fact accords well with their clearly increasing importance in the history of the sacrifice proper,[4] in which the services of the Brahman in making good by his presence and his skill defects in the ritual win for him the credit of the performance of half the sacrifice.

Henry,[5] however, goes much further than this and insists that the Brahman was the first of priests, originally a magician, and that the spell is the primitive form whence prayer has emerged, as from the magician the priest has evolved with the growth of religion. Common as this view is, it is clear that it has no support in historical evidence, as in the Rigveda Brahman, both masculine and neuter, means normally priest and prayer, not magician and spell,[6] and as a theory of religion it must be held to be as defective as are all theories which endeavour to develop religion from something essentially not religious.[7]

It is of interest to note that, while in the main the magician is content to use the Vedic pantheon as it appears in the sacrificial ritual, he is also prepared when necessary to fashion fresh figures or to modify those already existing. While Rudra in his forms as Bhava and Çarva is invoked in a hymn [8] against internal disease in terms which are suggestive of the popular favour which was to turn him into Çiva, the great god, Viṣṇu takes an inferior place, though the representation of his three steps can be used to strengthen the magic act.[9] The Apsarases appear in close connexion with dice, possibly as Henry [10] holds in the main because the term *krīḍ*, ' play ', applies to them *par excellence* : such linguistic considerations are of real importance in Vedic

[1] *Altindisches Zauberritual*, p. 69, n. 7.

[2] Kauç. li.

[3] Henry, *op. cit.*, pp. 204, 261 ; Oltramare, *Le rôle du Yajamāna*, p. 34.

[4] So too the Purohita in this period is expected to be an Atharvavedin ; Bloomfield, *Atharvaveda*, pp. 32–4 ; 74–6.

[5] *Op. cit.*, pp. 35–9. Cf. Usener, *Archiv f. Religionswissenschaft*, vii. 16 ff. ; Meyer, *Gesch. d. Alt.*[3] I. ii. pp. 870, 871 ; Marett, *Folk-lore*, 1904.

[6] Bloomfield, *Religion of the Veda*, pp. 205, 273, who criticizes Oldenberg's conception of Brahman as 'Zauberfluidum' (GN. 1916, pp. 715 ff.).

[7] Jevons, *Idea of God*, pp. 122 ff.

[8] AV. xi. 2.

[9] Kauç. xlviii. 35 (cf. AV. vii. 13) ; xlix. 26 (AV. xiii. 1. 56, 57).

[10] AV. iv. 38 ; vii. 109 ; Henry, *La magie dans l'Inde antique*, pp. 113 ff.

thought. In battle charms we find not merely Apvā, the spirit of panic and its physical result, but also Triṣandhi, which is clearly Indra's bolt, Arbudi, and Nyarbudi, who is plainly but a verbal variant of the former.[1] In Henry's view [2] Arbudi himself is a duplicate of Indra, like Namuci, but this view is much less probable than that of Bloomfield,[3] who sees in him an old derivative of Arbuda, the cloud serpent slain by Indra, who comes to be regarded later merely as a serpent divinity and auspicious, like Takṣaka, who also figures in the Atharvaveda.[4] It is characteristic of the Atharvaveda that Asura in independent passages has always an evil sense, that abstract deities like Arāti,[5] illiberality towards priests, and perhaps Nirṛti,[6] dissolution, take a prominent place, and that a faded mythological figure like the mysterious Trita appears, in the form Tṛta,[7] in connexion with a hymn which is interpreted as an expiation for the somewhat venial fault of marrying before an elder brother, a fact on which is based the theory of Max Müller,[8] which Henry inclines to approve, that Tṛta is the departing sun. On the model of Pūṣan is created the god Sūṣan, from *sū*, 'beget', who is invoked to secure safe delivery.[9]

One direct addition to our knowledge of the ordinary sacrificial ritual is made by the Atharvaveda, which in its last, late, book has a section of hymns styled collectively Kuntāpa.[10] The contents of this collection is very varied, but it includes several riddles, in part obscene, as well as a panegyric of a king:[11] doubtless we must assume that these are fragments of popular [12] merriment in connexion with sacrificial rites which have been stereotyped.

In the sacrificial ritual, however, the most interesting of the innovations of the Atharvavedins is the introduction of rites regarding the presentation of the presents claimed by the priests. Instead of mere appendices to the actual offering, these become in themselves offerings of the highest importance and value.[13] The other ritual texts [14] know of Savas as consecrations for various rites of importance, but in the Kauçika [15] the Sava is essentially the ceremony

[1] AV. xi. 9, 10; Kauç. xvi. 21–6.

[2] AV. x–xii, p. 164; on Namuci, *Revue critique*, xxxii. 499.

[3] *Atharvaveda*, p. 75.

[4] Cf. Kauç. xxviii. 1 ff.; Bloomfield, SBE. xlii. 374; Weber, SBA. 1896, p. 684 n.

[5] AV. v. 7; Kauç. xviii. 13–15. Cf. Viçvajit, Trāyamāṇā, Kalyāṇī, Sarvavid (AV. vi. 107).

[6] Henry (*La magie dans l'Inde antique*, pp. 160 ff.), however, prefers, with Speijer, to see in Nirṛti a parallel of Nerthus (cf. Helm, *Altgerm. Rel.* i. 311 ff.) and a goddess of earth.

[7] AV. vi. 113. 1.

[8] Cf. Henry, *op. cit.*, p. 215.

[9] AV. i. 11; Bloomfield, SBE. xlii. 242 ff.

[10] AV. xx. 127–136; see Bloomfield, *Atharvaveda*, pp. 96–101; AB. vi. 32 ff.; KB. xxx. 5 ff.; ÇÇS. xii. 14–16.

[11] Perhaps two: that in praise of Kaurama, King of the Ruçamas (xx. 127. 1–3), is a Nārāçaṅsī clearly, and xx. 127. 7–10, which praise Parikṣit, seem to deal with an earthly king, not merely with Agni. The Nārāçaṅsīs, like the Dānastutis, form one of the germs of the epic; their inaccuracy is recognized in KS. xiv. 15; TB. i. 3. 2. 6.

[12] Possibly a reflex of popular quarrels is the name Kaṇva given to a demon, which devours the embryo in the womb (AV. ii. 25).

[13] Bloomfield, *Atharvaveda*, p. 78. *Per contra*, the simpler and more naïve Dānastutis disappear (save in AV. xx. 127).

[14] e.g. TB. ii. 7.

[15] lx–lxviii.

which centres in the giving of largesse to the priests. The Atharvaveda has many hymns in connexion with these donations, two [1] of which are noteworthy in connecting an ordinary Soma rite with the formal preparation and cooking of porridge for the priests, one preparer boasting that he is the fifteenth of his line who has performed the operation : in other cases animals are the fees, and are extolled in the most exaggerated terms as divine : the goat [2] recalls Aja Ekapād, that faded mythological figure of the Rigveda. In another [3] case a house is taken to pieces and presented to the Brahman. A counterpart to these demands for fees is the stress laid on the sacred character of the Brahman: his wife is inviolable : nay Soma has made over to him his claim to the first mating with every woman.[4] His cow [5] is equally sacrosanct, and on the strength of his own sanctity he can demand, when such a portent as the birth of twin calves takes place, that the erring cow should be made over to him as alone fitted to be its master.[6]

§ 9. *Yoga Practices*

The ritual, as has been seen, both in the case of magic and of the sacrifice, is full of elements which appear systematized in the later Yoga philosophy and practice. But it would be a mistake to exaggerate the degree of correspondence, and in point of fact much that is later characteristic and essential is lacking in the earlier Vedic literature.[7] In special hardly any trace can be found of the importance later attaching to elaborate regulation of the breath, despite the fact that the division of the breaths or vital airs as five is early. The suggestion that the term *çuṣma* is a word with ecstatic implications is wholly implausible. The inducing of perspiration as a part of the Dīkṣā and as a means of exciting ecstasy is clear, but it does not appear as a distinct or important rite as with the Scythians of Herodotos or the aborigines of North America or Australia. Nor do we find any clear reference to the various sitting postures familiar to the later Yoga, for it is absurd to believe that the sense ' altar ', if it ever really belongs to the obscure term Dhiṣaṇā, owes its origin to the fact that by his posture at the place of sacrifice the priest beholds the might (*dhiṣaṇā*) of the gods. The mysterious Uttānapad of the Rigveda [8] as a cosmic power cannot with any plausibility be deemed to yield a proof of the practice of assuming the position of an embryo in the womb as a means of attaining mystic rebirth. That silence and solitude were conducive to ecstasy is, curiously enough, little referred to, and the dirt of both person and garments of the later Yogin is recognized only in a few hints.[9] There is more evidence of fasting, and the hymn of Lopāmudrā and Agastya in the Rigveda [10]

[1] AV. xi. 1 ; xii. 3.

[2] AV. ix. 5 ; a barren cow, x. 10 ; a bull, ix. 4 ; a draught ox, iv. 11.

[3] AV. ix. 3.

[4] AV. v. 17 ; against oppressors are provided v. 18, 19 ; xii. 5.

[5] AV. v. 11 ; xii. 5.

[6] AV. iii. 28 ; cf. Kauç. cix-cxi.

[7] J. W. Hauer (*Die Anfänge der Yogapraxis im alten Indien*, pp. 9–65) adduces all available evidence, but most of it is obviously without value.

[8] x. 72.

[9] RV. x. 136. 2.

[10] i. 179.

appears, despite its obscurity, to express the two kindred ideas of the magic potency engendered by continence on the one hand, and on the other of the cosmic importance of the rite of generation, both doctrines of the later system.[1] The idea of a mystic union between the god and the worshipper, which finds its highest development in the Çakti cults of Bengal, appears wholly unknown to Vedic literature,[2] and dancing as a means of producing ecstasy is never mentioned, though the gods as dancers may be a relic of the conception. The songs, and their musical accompaniments, together with the ritual exclamations which are preserved in the Song-books of the Sāmaveda, may have served a similar purpose; sound may often have accomplished results of spiritual excitement irrespective of the words, and the term Vipra, used of the poet, seems to suggest the trembling or quaking of divine inspiration.[3]

More important than these facts is the striking description of the Muni found in one late Rigveda hymn.[4] He differs entirely from the Brahman student or the man undergoing consecration, for his ecstasy is not connected either with the sacrifice or with any of the rites ancillary to it or to the entry of the youth into the full life of the community. His mortal body men see, but he himself fares on the path of the Apsarases, the Gandharvas, the beasts of the wild, he dwells in the east and the western ocean, the steed of Vāta, the friend of Vāyu, inspired by the gods. He knows secret desires, he is the dearest friend, he supports Agni and both the worlds, he is the heaven and the light, and his ecstasy, it seems, is due to a potent draught which, with Rudra, he drinks from a goblet, perhaps a reference to the use of some poison to produce exhilaration or hypnosis.[5] His hair is long, his soiled garments are of yellow hue.

This description is curiously isolated in the Rigveda and later, not unnaturally, since this aspect of religious life does not fall within the normal outlook of our texts. In the Atharvaveda,[6] however, we find the curious and enigmatical figure of the Vrātya, exalted into a cosmic power, and therefore of obscure origin. It has been suggested that we are to find in him the type of Yogin, produced in the eastern lands under the aegis of the Kṣatriyas, who wandered about the country, received with friendship in the courts, bringing prosperity in his train by reason of his ecstatic practices, in which a part was taken by the hetaera, who is made part of his retinue, and the Māgadha whose loud cries doubtless played a part in his rites. The suggestion is ingenious, but unfortunately it lacks any probative value. The references to the year long standing of the Vrātya and his other actions are too indistinct to enable us to discern with any certainty the outlines of an ancient seeker after ecstatic trances, and the elaboration of his retinue, though it may be paralleled in other lands,[7] is strange to Indian usage.

[1] Haṭhayogapradīpikā, i. 61 ff.; iii. 83 ff.

[2] RV. i. 164. 15 cannot thus be explained.

[3] Cf. Vates; Carnoy, *Les Indo-Européens*, p. 213; Paton, *Spiritism*, pp. 82 ff.

[4] x. 136. Cf. Arbman, *Rudra*, pp. 297 ff.

[5] Cf. AV. ii. 27 (*pāṭā*); 30 (*çamī*); 4. 5 (*çaṇa*, hemp).

[6] xv.

[7] Apuleius, *Metam.* viii. 27 f. is cited by Hauer (*op. cit.*, p. 177).

PART IV. THE SPIRITS OF THE DEAD

CHAPTER 23

THE ABODES OF THE DEAD

§ 1. *The Nature of the Dead*

It is not altogether easy to derive from the Rigveda a precise conception of the nature which was attributed to the spirits of the dead by the mind of the people or of the priest, and it is natural to assume that the ground for this difficulty is to be traced to the variation of both popular and ecclesiastical opinion. The modern view of the spirits and their abode is extremely varied and confused, and it would be ill-judged to assume that it was otherwise in the earlier Vedic religion.

Long before the period of the Rigveda, it is clear that the Indian had realized the difference between life and death and had separated in his imagination the two elements of the man, his body and his spirit,[1] but the distinction must have been vague in the extreme.[2] Of the spirit as distinct from the body we have two expressions which occur frequently enough to let us believe that their meaning was more or less definitely known : of these the first was what we would regard as physical, but what doubtless seemed just as psychical to the Vedic India as any other aspect of the spirit : it is the *asu*,[3] life, which seems clearly to have been based on the conception of the breath of the man, which is the visible sign of life and intellect : later, but not in the Rigveda, the term Ātman, the breath, is the most characteristic term for the self, and the breaths, Prāṇas, are a constant subject of investigation in the Upaniṣads, where often they appear as essentially representing the life and spirit of man. The identification of breath and the *asu* is made formally in the Çatapatha Brāhmaṇa,[4] but this fact is of much less importance than the clear indications of the Rigveda. The other term is, unlike *asu*, which never in later times became an expression of any philosophical importance, one which never loses a place in the thought of India, though it does not achieve the rank of the Ātman. It is Manas, the mind, which in later Indian

[1] Passages like RV. x. 16. 3 ; AB. ii. 6. 13 clearly do not imply ignorance of this fact, which is clearly revealed in many passages, e. g. RV. x. 14. 8 ; 16. 5. The idea of many souls in the individual appears in philosophical form in the doctrines of sheaths of the soul in TU. ii. 4. Cf. Hopkins, *Origin of Religion*, pp. 109 ff.

[2] This is illustrated in detail in Tuxen's *Forestillingen om Sjælen i Rigveda*, but is notorious, see Hopkins, *Origin of Religion*, p. 112.

[3] RV. i. 113. 16 ; 140. 8 ; Oldenberg, *Rel. des Veda*[2], pp. 525, 526 ; for Avestan, *aṅhu*, Geiger, *Ostiran. Kultur*, p. 290.

[4] vi. 6. 2. 6 ; ii. 4. 2. 21.

thought is of importance as the means of knowledge of all internal events,[1] and a necessary link in the knowledge of external events *en route* from the senses. The conception of the Rigveda is seen clearly in the case [2] when the mind of a senseless person is said to have gone away to Yama, the lord of the dead, to sky and earth, to the sea and the mountains, to the sun and the dawn. It is also probable that the conception later prevalent that the mind has its abode in the heart was already developed : [3] the connexion of mind and heart is not rare in the Rigveda. The further view that the mind had the dimensions of a pigmy or a thumb in size, which is found said of the Puruṣa as the principle of life in the Upaniṣads and often later, is not to be proved for the period of the Rigveda.[4]

Naturally enough there is abundant evidence of the simple views which suggest the theory of the spirit : the phenomena of loss of the senses, which is recorded in the Rigveda, is also recorded of the ancient Bhṛgu, who in this condition went to the other world and had experiences of interest there.[5] The view that in the case of a dream the soul might be outside the body and moving about freely at will, which is a common belief of many peoples, is proved by the reference to such a case in the Çatapatha Brāhmaṇa,[6] which warns us of the danger of waking the sleeper too hurriedly, lest the soul should thus fail to find its way back into the body. It appears also that dreams about the dead were deemed to be due to the souls of the dead moving thus about. At least this belief would explain the fact that, on going away from a festival for the dead, the partaker in the rite should rub himself with the Apāmārga plant and ask it to wipe away evil dreams.[7] The danger of the spirit escaping through yawning seems suggested by the rule that in such a case one should say, 'In me be strength and wisdom'.[8] The shadow also is here and there found as being in some way connected with man : if one cannot see his reflection it is an omen of death, and the reflection of one whose mind is gone can be used in a spell to restore his mind to him.[9] All these elements can be supposed to have been steadily at work in Vedic India, and the result is the conception of the spirit as some more or less impalpable substance. It is not *asu* entirely nor mind : it is also breath, and it is very often regarded as

[1] C. Rhys Davids, *Buddhist Manual of Psychological Ethics*², pp. lxxxv ff.; Keith, *Indian Logic and Atomism*, pp. 243–7.

[2] x. 58 ; cf. Feist, *Kultur der Indogermanen*, p. 323.

[3] RV. viii. 100. 5. For the later view see AV. vi. 18. 3 ; AGS. iii. 6. 8 ; Windisch, BSGW. 1891, pp. 163 ff. ; C. Rhys Davids, *Buddhist Manual of Psychological Ethics*², pp. lxxxvi ff.

[4] Oldenberg, *Rel. des Veda*², p. 525 ; cf. BAU. iv. 3. 14 ; Kaṭha Up. iv. 12.

[5] Oertel, JAOS. xv. 234. On the legend of Subandhu's loss of soul and its recovery see JB. iii. 168–70 ; PB. xii. 12. 5 ; Oertel, JAOS. xviii. 41 ; Macdonell and Keith, *Vedic Index*, i. 47 ; RV. x. 57–60.

[6] xiv. 7. 1. 12.

[7] ÇB. xiii. 8. 4. 4.

[8] TS. ii. 5. 2. 4 ; cf. Pease, CP. xi. 429–44.

[9] TS. vi. 6. 7. 2 ; HGS. i. 11. 6. For the shadow see also LÇS. iii. 3. 6 ; AÇS. v. 19. 5 ; ApÇS. xiii. 14. 3 ; AV. xiii. 1. 56 (v. 19. 9 is wrongly so interpreted by Brunnhofer, *Arische Urzeit*, pp. 258 ff.) ; Frazer, *Taboo*, pp. 77 ff. ; von Negclein, *Archiv f. Religionswissenschaft*, v. 18 ff.

asu and mind :[1] or it appears as mind or as *asu*, as in the frequent phrase *asunīti*, '*asu* leading',[2] which is applied both to the process by which the spirits are led from the earth to their home in the sky, and the reverse process by which they are brought back by Agni, as the conveyer of souls, from the heaven in which they live to the offerings made to them on earth. It is, however, of importance that mind is assumed to be with the spirit when it is away from the body : the Fathers of the Vedic creation are thus creatures who are perfectly gifted for intellectual action of all kind, to know, to perceive, to enjoy, and to will. But the view as to exactly what it was which departed at death was never quite clearly settled by the thought of India : the Upaniṣads inclined to regard it as the Ātman, the Buddhist in one view as consciousness, Vijñāna,[3] and later there developed more precise views of the psychic apparatus which transmigrated, but the views of the populace were probably as vague as those of Vedic India itself.

But it would be an error to assume that the body was left for ever at death : this might seem to be the logical view, but it is not the view of the Vedic Indian, as it has not been the view of many different classes of men. The care expressed in the Rigveda [4] itself for the avoidance of injury to the body of the dead, which was to be burned, by a bird or other beast, is confirmed by the express injunction to the dead that he has in the next world to unite himself with his body. The same idea is expressed in the Atharvaveda,[5] which treats as in the next world the body, the *asu*, the mind, the limbs, and the sap all uninjured, and the Fathers are entreated to secure that the bones which have been placed out of order shall all be placed in due arrangement. This unquestionably is the regular view in the Veda : the alternative view once found in the Rigveda,[6] which sends the eye of the dead to the sun, the breath to the wind, bids him go to the heaven and the earth, or if he prefers to the waters, and to dwell among the plants with his members, cannot be treated as more than a mere deviation of no great consequence for the general view of Vedic religion. The connexion of the eye and the sun is also seen in the Puruṣasūkta, where the sacrifice of the primeval giant results in the sun being created from his eye. The concrete character of the entity which is left in the heaven is proved by the fact that the Fathers are always addressed, when mentioned individually, by their own names : there is no such thing as an invocation of the spirit of any individual. He himself continues his life.

[1] AV. viii. 1. 1, 15 ; 2. 26 ; v. 30. 1 ; viii. 1. 7 ; 2. 3.

[2] RV. x. 15. 14 ; 16. 2.

[3] Oldenberg, *Buddha*[6], p. 308. For the Ātman in the Saṁjñāna, see ÇB. xiv. 7. 2. 3 ; BAU. iv. 4. 2. Strictly speaking the aggregate of the Skandhas is the transmigrating element ; Windisch, *Buddha's Geburt*, pp. 37 ff. ; Keith, *Buddhist Philosophy*, pp. 6 ff.

[4] x. 16. 6 ; 14. 8 ; 16. 5. Hauer's reference (*Die Anfänge der Yogapraxis im alten Indien*, pp. 97, 108) of x. 16 to an initiatory ceremony is impossible.

[5] xiv. 2. 24.

[6] x. 16. 3. So of the victim, AB. ii. 6. 13.

§ 2. *The Places of the Dead*

The chief place of the dead in the conception of the Rigveda [1] is unquestionably heaven : the soul leaves the body on death, and by the path of the Fathers it goes to the place where there is eternal light, endowed with lustre like that of the gods.[2] It is said to go as by a car or by wings : [3] more completely the Atharvaveda [4] pictures the dead man as borne up by the Maruts, with gentle breezes fanning him, and cooled by showers until he recovers his complete body, and meets with the Fathers in the highest heaven, where with Yama they dwell. The heaven is called also the home,[5] but the idea can hardly be pressed to the view that the going to heaven is a return home : it is rather that the man reaches in the highest heaven a new and abiding abode. The connexion of this journey of the souls with the actual burning of the body is always a vague one, but the reality of the connexion of soul and body is proved by the emphasis laid in the Brāhmaṇas [6] on the necessity for the due collection of the bones of the dead, and the need of replacing them symbolically in cases where they may happen to be lost.

Another conception of the nature of death is hinted at in the legend of the dogs of Yama,[7] the four-eyed, a term probably derived from the presence of some mark on the dog which gave the appearance of four eyes,[8] brindled, broad-nosed, dogs which wander about and guard the path or sit on it : the spirit is bidden to haste past the dogs, and to join the Fathers with Yama. Delighting in lives, they watch men and serve as messengers of Yama, and are entreated to grant continued enjoyment of life. It is possible that they were conceived as going among men, and taking to the abode of death the souls of the dead. The Avestan parallel is one dog, which four-eyed and yellow-eared watches the head of the Cinvaṭ bridge [9] which reaches from this to the next world, and by his barking scares away the fiends, who would hinder the passing of the souls of the just dead. In the Rigveda there is no clear evidence to any such functions of the dogs as the dividers out of souls as good or bad : the suggestion of Roth [10] and Aufrecht that this was their function is based on interpretations, which are not very probable, and at any rate are uncertain. In the Atharvaveda [11] the messengers of Yama appear already as plural as well as dual. Any possibility of holding that they had duties of discrimination

[1] ix. 113. 7 ff. is the fullest description.

[2] AV. xi. 1. 37.

[3] AV. iv. 34. 4 ; VS. xviii. 52.

[4] xviii. 2. 21–6.

[5] RV. x. 14. 8.

[6] ÇB. xi. 6. 3. 11 ; xiv. 6. 9. 28.

[7] RV. x. 14. 10–12 ; AV. xviii. 2. 12 ; viii. 1. 9 ; JB. i. 6 (Çabala and Çyāma).

[8] Cf. Hommel, *Festschrift Kuhn*, p. 422.

[9] No bridge exists in the RV. (ix. 41. 2 is not a reference to this) nor is there a river (x. 63. 10) : Scherman, *Visionslitteratur*, pp. 110, 111. For the Avesta see Moulton, *Early Zoroastrianism*, pp. 165, 333, n. 4. Later the soul of the bull slain by Mithra is guarded by his hound on its ascent to heaven, with which the dog of the horse sacrifice may be compared.

[10] Based on RV. vii. 55. 2–5 ; Aufrecht, *Ind. Stud.* iv. 341 ; Weber, xviii. 20 ; Oldenberg, *Ṛgveda-Noten*, ii. 42. Bloomfield also (on AV. iv. 5) rejects this view.

[11] viii. 2. 11 ; 8. 11 ; v. 30. 6.

would of course disappear if they were to be regarded as being really the sun and the moon, as is argued by Bloomfield (the day and the night in the Jaiminīya Brāhmaṇa),[1] or the doubles of Yama and Yamī, which was the view of Bergaigne,[2] but it is difficult to go beyond the view that the imagination of the Indo-Iranians and, if the identification—doubtful in the extreme—of Çabala and Kerberos [3] is to be accepted, probably of the Indo-Europeans also, believed that the way to the sky was guarded or infested by a dog or dogs.

The nature of the heaven which is attained by the spirits is described repeatedly in the Rigveda : [4] it is further elaborated in the later Saṁhitās, but all its characteristics are the same : there is light, the sun for the highest waters, every form of happiness, the Svadhā, which is at once [5] the food of the spirits, and the power which they win by it, their self-determination. The spirits are so material as not merely to enjoy the most material things, Soma, milk, honey, Surā, ghee, but also to delight in the joys of love,[6] a fact indicating how corporeal was their nature. The sound of singing and the flute is also among the delights available, and there is a fig-tree where Yama drinks with the gods.[7] There are wish-cows, which yield all desires, and there is perfect harmony and joy unbounded. The picture is singularly simple : it is merely the pleasant things of earth to the priestly imagination, heaped upon one another : the total absence of anything which could be regarded as natural in the heaven of warriors is a striking reminder that the conceptions of Vedic India, in so far as they are within reach of our knowledge, were the ideas of priests and not of the whole community. The idea thus presented prevailed throughout the Vedic periods : even in the Brāhmaṇas among speculations of various sorts, it is often said that men obtain unity with the sun, which clearly means that he goes to dwell in the heaven of the sun where are the Fathers, the gods, and above all Yama.

Yama it is whom, with Varuṇa, the new arrival in the realms of heaven sees. He is closely connected with Agni, and also with Mātariçvan : his is the

[1] JAOS. xv. 163 ff. ; *Cerberus, the dog of Hades* (1905) ; Hillebrandt, *Ved. Myth.*, p. 155.

[2] *Rel. Véd.* i. 93. Arbman (*Rudra*, pp. 258 ff.) makes them refined versions of theriomorphic death demons. Cf. the alleged wolf of death in RV. ii. 29. 6 (Scherman, *Visionslitteratur*, p. 127). See Hopkins, *Origin of Religion*, p. 33, n. 1, and for German wolves who eat the dead, Helm, *Altgerm. Rel.* i. 209 ff.

[3] Rohde, *Psyche*, i. 280.

[4] RV. x. 14–16 ; 27. 21 ; 56. 1 ; 107. 2 ; 154. 5 ; i. 109. 7 ; 125. 6 ; AV. iv. 34. 2–6 ; xi. 4 ; iii. 29. 3 ; vi. 120. 3 ; MS. i. 10. 18 ; ii. 3. 9, &c. ; ÇB. xi. 5. 6. 4 ; xiv. 7. 1. 32, 33 ; Kauṣ. i. 4. It is the highest of the heavens ; RV. x. 14. 8 ; AV. xi. 4. 11 ; ix. 5. 1, 8 ; xviii. 2. 48 ; 4. 3 ; the sun, RV. x. 107. 2 ; 154. 5.

[5] RV. iv. 26. 4 ; Oldenberg, *Rel. des Veda*², p. 531, n. 3.

[6] AV. iv. 34. 2 ; TB. ii. 4. 6. 6 ; ÇB. x. 4. 4. 4 ; Kauṣ. i. 4. Their bodies are freed from all bodily defects ; AV. iii. 28. 5 ; vi. 120. 3.

[7] RV. x. 135. 1 ; cf. AV. v. 4. 3. In Kauṣ. i. 3 it is called the Ilya or Ilpa tree, and we hear of the Vijarā stream, the Sālajya city, the Aparājita palace, &c., in the world of Brahman : cf. CU. viii. 5. 3. It is implausible to see any mythological importance in this tree, which seems merely the reflex of the tree of the Indian village, under which sit the elders. Cf. above, p. 172, n. 2.

third heaven, the other two being Savitṛ's, and his is the highest,[1] the abode of the sun which he gives to men. He does so because he was the first of mortals who died, and who found out the way for many to the realm, where now he reigns rather than rules as king. In the later Saṁhitās [2] his connexion with death, which is his path already on the Rigveda,[3] and with which he may even be identified there, is more and more emphasized: he is connected with Antaka, 'the ender', Mṛtyu, 'death', and Nirṛti, 'dissolution', and Mṛtyu is his messenger as well as his two, or more, dogs. But he is also the father of men with his sister Yamī, who bids him in a dialogue of much interest commit incest with her for the creation of the race, a view which Yama on moral grounds reprobates in the hymn.[4] In the Avesta Yama is the king of a distant paradise on earth, the lord of a golden age where no heat or cold or defects exist. He has, though not in the Avesta, a sister Yimeh from whom with him men are sprung. It is tempting to see in him the king first of a golden age, and then of a realm of the spirits of the heroes of that age, the Ṛṣis mentioned with him as makers of the way to the world to come, as Oldenberg suggests, but the evidence hardly avails to establish this. For India and Iran, however, he is beyond doubt the first of mortals, and therefore also the first to die. The view that he is more than that, a faded divinity, whether Agni as held by Bergaigne,[5] or the sun, as Barth [6] thought, or, as Weber [7] suggested, the parting day, Yamī being then night in whose gloom may be seen sorrow for Yama, or the setting sun and so the lord of the dead, as taken by Max Müller,[8] is not necessary and is not supported by any decisive evidence: still less plausible is the effort of Hillebrandt [9] to find in him the moon as the mortal child of the sun, even if as he holds this conception was indeed Indo-Iranian, but no longer a living belief in Vedic times. The effort [10] to remove Yamī from the tradition and to see in Yama the *alter ego* of the living man, his soul, is clearly contrary to the whole of the Vedic and the Avestan evidence.

Yama, however, and Varuṇa also do not appear as active in the work of controlling the world of the dead: as the great god, Varuṇa's place is there,

[1] RV. i. 35. 6; x. 135. 7; VS. xii. 63.

[2] MS. ii. 5. 6; VS. xxxix. 13; AV. v. 30. 12; xviii. 2. 27; v. 24. 13 (lord of Manes). Arbman (*Rudra*, p. 306, n. 2) seeks to prove that Yama is idealized in the RV. but wrongly; in TS. iii. 3. 8. 3, there is no distinction between hell and heaven, and Yama is lord of earth (TS. iii. 4. 5; v. 2. 3. 1) as first of men. TA. iv. 37 and ÇB. xi. 6. 1. 1 ff. prove nothing for his original nature. His is clearly a case of syncretism of different views of death. Cf. Rhys, *Celtic Heathendom*, pp. 654 ff.

[3] i. 38. 5; 165. 4.

[4] Oldenberg, *Rel. des Veda*², p. 533; cf. Moulton, *Early Zoroastrianism*, pp. 144 ff. To distinguish two Yamas (Hillebrandt, *Ved. Myth.*, p. 155) is quite impossible.

[5] *Rel. Véd.* i. 89.

[6] *Rel. of Ind.*, pp. 22, 23.

[7] *Ved. Beitr.*, 1894, pp. 1 ff. For Yama as a man, see Bloomfield, *Rel. of Veda*, p. 105.

[8] *Anthr. Rel.*, pp. 297, 298; Ehni, *Yama*, p. 8; Carnoy, JAOS. xxxvi. 317.

[9] *Ved. Myth.* i. 394 ff.; (Kl. Ausg.), pp. 151 ff.

[10] *Indog. Myth.* i. 229 ff. See also below, Appendix B.

perhaps too as the god to whom cries proceed for pardon from sin, but neither god is said to punish the dead or judge them for their sins. The idea of judgement of any sort is foreign to the Rigveda as to early Iran, and it is only in the Taittirīya Āraṇyaka [1] that we have the express statement that the truthful and the untruthful are separated before Yama, but his activity in this separation is in no wise indicated, and the idea of the weighing of the deeds of man on his arrival in the other world, which is prominent in the Avesta, is only found in the Çatapatha Brāhmaṇa [2] in a passage of speculative activity. What the dead obtain in heaven is not only long life there by the gift of the mercy of the gods: they obtain the merit of the Iṣṭāpūrta, the sacrifices which they have offered, and the gifts which they have given to the priest,[3] and at the same time they are nourished by the piety of their relatives on earth, as they have nourished in their turn their forefathers. Such nourishment may be either buried with them, when the grains of corn and sesame will become wish-cows and their calves in the heaven, or may be conveyed by the later offerings.[4] It is not a very distant step to the idea of the Buddhists [5] that souls which are miserable can be aided by the gift to monks in their name, and the assignment to them of the merit thus acquired.

The other side of the belief in heaven is the belief in hell. It is of course in itself perfectly possible that the Vedic Indian might not have believed in the existence of hell: the view that annihilation might be the fate of the souls which did not receive the boon of immortal life from the gods is not in itself absurd, but a hell is a natural complement to heaven, and in point of fact the Rigveda [6] itself seems to contain references to a place of punishment, into which Indra and Soma are to hurl the evil doers so that not one can emerge; under the three earths is the place of the enemy and robber, and the demoness is to disappear in endless abysses. There occurs here and in a few other places the idea of the eternal punishment in a place of deep darkness of the evil.[7] The idea of hell is made clear by the Atharvaveda [8] which has the word Naraka Loka in contrast to Svarga, heaven, as the place for female goblins and sorceresses: it is also the place of the murderer,[9] and appears as black,

[1] vi. 5. 13. The references in the RV. are not probable (Scherman, *Visionslitteratur*, pp. 152, 153), despite x. 12. 8. The royal assessors of Yama (AV. iii. 29. 1) are merely transferred from human relations as receivers of tribute from the good deeds of the dead, as kings on earth from their subjects' goods. Yama as the hare in the moon appears in JB. i. 28, but merely because the moon is the abode of the dead.

[2] xi. 2. 7. 33; cf. xii. 9. 1. 1, and for separation by fire, i. 9. 3. 2.

[3] RV. x. 14. 8.

[4] AV. xviii. 4. 32 ff.; iv. 34; Kauç. lxvi. 6.

[5] Cf. B. C. Law, *The Buddhist Conception of Spirits*. Kauṣ. i. 4 recognizes the transfer to relatives and foes respectively of a man's good and evil deeds on death.

[6] Punishment is denied by Roth, JAOS. iii. 329–47; Weber, ZDMG. ix. 238, 239; it is generally accepted now: Scherman, *Visionslitteratur*, pp. 122 ff.; Hopkins, *Rel. of India*, p. 147; Oldenberg, *Rel. des Veda*², pp. 536 ff.; Zimmer, *Altindisches Leben*, p. 417; Macdonell, *Ved. Myth.*, p. 169.

[7] RV. vii. 104. 3, 17, 11; ii. 29. 6; ix. 73. 8, 9; iv. 5. 5.

[8] xii. 4. 36; Whitney, JAOS. xiii. p. civ.

[9] VS. xxx. 5. For Iran cf. Moulton, *Early Zoroastrianism*, pp. 172 ff.

blind or the lowest darkness.[1] There is no trace of the fires of hell, nor of a wolf of hell in the Vedic literature,[2] nor can the view of Geldner[3] that the word Vīci in the Rigveda[4] directly denotes hell be accepted; but there is reason enough to hold that the idea was present in germ. The actual tortures of hell are reserved for later texts in the main, and are dwelt on by Buddhism in a way to make us realize that on the popular mind these horrors had due result. In the Atharvaveda[5] the sinners who injure the Brahman sit in streams of blood eating hair, and in the Çatapatha Brāhmaṇa[6] and the Jaiminīya the proud Bhṛgu goes to the other world, where he sees many horrible things such as men being cut to pieces, and men being eaten, and also the lord of the place as a black man with a staff and yellow eyes beside two maidens, one fair and one, described by an epithet *atikalyāṇī,* as either 'very fair' or 'past her beauty'. The Jaiminīya mentions three hells and three heavens. Another horror is suggested by the Kauṣītaki Brāhmaṇa,[7] which threatens man with being eaten in the next world by the animals which he devoured in this, unless he adopts a certain ritual practice of special potency. The idea of punishment or reward according to one's deeds is constantly expressed in the Çatapatha Brāhmaṇa[8] under diverse forms, but it appears rather as a philosophical doctrine brought out to explain the operation of the universe than as a popular belief. The Vedic view is clearly far other than this: the great majority of men believed themselves to be good and destined to the joys of heaven, but they did not regard these joys as making earth less desirable. The normal attitude of the whole of the Vedic religion, down to the very end of the period of the Brāhmaṇas, is that it is a good thing to behold the light of the sun, and to live a hundred years, for which prayers and spells alike are earnestly resorted to, and that, at the end of the life one attains, there will be another, if different yet analogous, life in the world to come with the same pleasures as on earth, but without the disadvantages of human imperfection.

As compared with the clear conception of the dwelling of the spirit in the highest heaven or in hell, there is little trace in the Vedic literature of the more simple and perhaps more primitive conception[9] which regards the dead as dwelling in the earth, whether actually in the place of burial, or in the under

[1] AV. ii. 14. 8; v. 30. 11; xviii. 3. 3; viii. 2. 24 is like RV. x. 152. 4, dubious.

[2] Oldenberg, *Rel. des Veda*², pp. 539, 540, against Scherman (ii. 29. 6, wolf; iv. 5. 4; vii. 59. 8, fires of hell).

[3] *Festgruss an Weber*, p. 22.

[4] x. 10. 6.

[5] v. 19.

[6] xi. 6. 1; JB. i. 42–44 in JAOS. xv. 234–8. That the man is Yama is unproved; for the *nārakāḥ*, see JB. i. 325.

[7] xi. 3.

[8] vi. 2. 2. 27; x. 6. 3. 1; Weber, ZDMG. ix. 237 ff. Flames or a scale determine their merit, ÇB. i. 9. 3. 2; xi. 2. 7. 33, both apparently speculative doctrines. In JUB. iv. 26 the organs of man are speculatively made ten heavens or hells (*nārakāḥ*). In JUB. i. 5 a deity, perhaps Rudra (above, Chap. 9, § 10), keeps back the evil, but is answered by the assertion that the god saw what he did and really did it, since he else would not have allowed him to act; an interesting, but obscure doctrine.

[9] Cf. Rhys, *Celtic Heathendom*, pp. 657 f.

world. The idea that the dead man's spirit went to the sky is not in the slightest degree essentially bound up with the burning by fire, for the Rigveda[1] expressly places both the Fathers, who have been burnt, and those who have not been burnt, as dwelling in the heaven, and there is no hint of any contrary view in Vedic literature. But undoubtedly here and there the idea is to be seen that the burning by the fires was the moment of the passage of the soul to the sky: of this the best proof is the doctrine of Āçvalāyana[2] that the place attained by the spirit depends on the nature of the fire, which first seizes the corpse when the body is set on the bier within the reach of fires derived from the sacred three fires. But this example in itself is not in the slightest degree a proof that it was the fire which sent the spirit to heaven: it is only a natural, but not primitive, view, as is shown by the mere fact that it depends on the use of the three fires, which the average householder could not dream of maintaining. The real view was doubtless less complicated, and in the same passage Āçvalāyana presents us with a different idea: a pit, knee deep, is to be dug north-east of the Āhavanīya fire, a water plant, Çīpāla, is put there, and with the smoke the soul thence goes to the heaven. This latter view, which looks at the earth as the place of the dead, is also supported by various other considerations. When a man is near to death, a spell is used to bring him from the lower to the upper earth to the protection of Aditi, sun and moon.[3] When a pit is dug, as often in the ritual, it is called the place of the Fathers; what is dug down has the Fathers as its deity;[4] Yama[5] even is lord of the earth; the darkness of the abode of the dead is referred to in passages where we cannot see any reference to the punishments of hell;[6] a spell of the Atharvaveda[7] seeks to send his enemy to the place of Yama; the dead are mentioned as living at the roots of the plants; the dead man in the funeral ritual is spoken of as being laid to rest in mother earth, which is to be kind to him. The path of the gods is often distinguished from the path of the Fathers,[8] the presence of the dogs[9] on the way shows that the road was a special one, and not the peaceful path of the gods; the door of the heaven is in the north-east, that of the world of the Fathers in the south-east,[10] a conception which is clearly due in part at least to opposition to the world of the gods: the relation of the south to the Fathers may be due to the fact[11] that on the shortest day, the time of the spirits *par excellence*, the sun is at the furthest south point in his course. The path too appears to be a different one from that of the gods since it is described as *pravat*, which may denote either a downward path as of a stream, or, at any rate, a path forward to the horizon, rather than one rising erect to the heaven.[12] But, if any doubt existed as to the connexion of the

[1] x. 15. 4; AV. xviii. 2. 34.
[2] AGS. iv. 4.
[3] AV. viii. 2. 15.
[4] TS. i. 3. 6. 1; vi. 3. 4. 2; ÇB. iii. 6. 1. 13; v. 2. 1. 7.
[5] PGS. i. 5. 10.
[6] e. g. RV. x. 132. 4.
[7] ii. 12. 7.
[8] AV. xviii. 4. 62; RV. x. 2. 7; 18. 1.
[9] AV. viii. 1. 9, 10.
[10] ÇB. xiii. 8. 1. 5; xii. 7. 3. 7; vi. 6. 2. 4.
[11] Kern, *Der Buddhismus*, i. 359.
[12] RV. x. 14. 1; AV. vi. 28. 3; xviii. 4. 7; Oldenberg, *Rel. des Veda*², p. 545;

spirits with the earth, it would be removed by the descriptions of the ritual of the dead, which, though not given in detail in the Brāhmaṇas, are set out at length in the Sūtras, and must be of great antiquity in their essence.[1] The gifts for the souls are not sent to them by fire to be conveyed to the sky: they are often laid in pits on the earth or upon the earth, in the neighbourhood of human dwellings which spirits all the world over are ever supposed to haunt: they come to the meal, and sit on the place made ready for them, or they find their way into the water-bottle:[2] they take out the heat of the food, and leave only the outer substance.[3] At the end of the meal they are sent away, politely indeed, with the words, 'The Fathers have satisfied themselves', or, as at the Anthesteria in Athens, more directly with, 'Depart, ye Fathers, Soma-loving, on your ancient deep paths; but return a month later to our house to eat the offering, with wealth in offspring, in heroes.'[4] The shaking out of the garment of the offerer is another proof of the anxiety to be rid of the ghostly guests.[5] But it must not for a moment be supposed that the belief in the presence of the spirits on earth on such occasions was incompatible with the belief in their dwelling in the sky: the two beliefs are inextricably confused in the human mind at the present day, and have been so confused for centuries, probably for thousands of years.

It is perfectly in keeping with the multitude of ideas regarding the nature of the future of the dead which must be produced by our total ignorance of its character, that the idea should be found that the newly departed does not at once join the congregation of the other ancient dead.[6] In the first period, often for a year after death, the monthly Çrāddha offerings are not paid to the newly dead in the usual form of offerings to father, grandfather, and great grandfather: he is offered a separate offering: in this he is not invoked to come, doubtless because he is near at hand; he is not dismissed, but merely bidden be at peace; in place of the prayer that the gifts to the Fathers may be theirs for ever, it is merely asked that they may be present for the dead: the innovation of some schools in which the offerings to the Fathers were supplemented by one to the All-gods, a clear proof that the assimilation of Fathers and gods was in progress,[7] is omitted in the case of the offering to one who has just died. The distinction is made in the later literature and can

reference to a stream in the path is hinted at in AV. xviii. 4. 7; the boat in RV. x. 63. 10, is, however, probably mythological; cf. TA. vi. 7. 2; Scherman, *Visionslitteratur*, p. 112. In Kauṣ. i. 3 it appears as the Vijarā stream of perpetual youth. The later Vaitaraṇī is not mentioned in the Veda, nor does Sarasvatī seem to play this role.

[1] GGS. iv. 2 ff. The authorities are given fully in Caland, *Altindischer Ahnenkult*.

[2] Caland, *Altind. Ahnenkult*, p. 89.

[3] *Ibid.* p. 180.

[4] HGS. ii. 13. 2; Kauç. lxxxviii. 28; Farnell, *Cults*, v. 221 ff.

[5] Kauç. lxxxviii. 27. The mind is similarly recalled when it is conceived as mingling with the souls in the feast, VS. iii. 53 ff.; KÇS. v. 9. 22.

[6] Caland, *op. cit.*, pp. 160 ff., 181.

[7] Ludwig, *Rigveda*, vi. 196; Hillebrandt, *Ved. Myth.* iii. 418.

perhaps be traced right back to Çāñkhāyana [1] by which the recently dead is a Preta, ' departed ' spirit, and is distinguished from the Fathers, Pitaras, *par excellence*. It is, however, clear that the view is not that of the Rigveda,[2] where it is obviously contemplated that the souls join at once the ancient Fathers, but it is not necessary to regard it as a later innovation : it is one of these divergent views, which may be regarded as a sort of compromise between the idea of the soul in heaven and the soul in earth, but which need not have been later than the developed view of the soul as in heaven and which also need not have been ever generally accepted. It must, further, be remembered that the belief in the departure of the soul to the sky cannot be proved to be later than the belief in the soul remaining near the body. But it is natural to assume that in the earliest view the latter was the attitude of mind adopted, before the clear separation of mind and body produced the idea that the mind had no need to remain with the body,[3] and that the soul, at first held to abide on earth near or with the body, was gradually conceived as going to the gods in the highest sky, while the older view lived on, combining in various ways with the new.

It is probable that in the Indo-Iranian period there had already developed the conception of the distinction between the heavenly lot of the blessed dead and the dismal fate in hell of the evil. There is less ground for supposing that such beliefs go back to the Indo-European period ; [4] then it may be that the only idea of the fate of the dead was that of a continued existence in a shadowy and imperfect condition, best represented to us by the Hades of Homer. Of this there may be seen traces in the Vedic conception of the future of the dead ; it is interesting that the vision of Bhṛgu presents us with something of this kind, though evil-doers suffer there, as do even in the Greek Hades certain criminals of conspicuous demerit. As it stands, however, the account is not early, since Varuṇa's heaven appears to be located in the same region as that of the shades.[5]

With the conception of the removal of the spirit to a greater distance is often conjoined with primitive peoples [6] the idea of the final burial of the body which has been provisionally buried. In the Vedic funeral ritual there are different stages of the process of disposal of the dead to be noted, but the ritual does not reveal, as we have it, any trace of this conception of the removal of the Preta to the sphere of the Fathers as connected with the

[1] ÇGS. iv. 2. 7 ; 3. 5, 6. Cf. PGS. iii. 10. 49 ff. The distinction of name and the fact of a Preta becoming a Pitṛ in a year is stated in BGS. iii. 12. 14 ; cf. BhGS. iii. 17.

[2] Oldenberg, *Rel. des Veda*², p. 536. Oltramare (*L'histoire des idées théosophiques*, i. 43) argues that the popular view was essentially that of the dwelling of the soul as a Preta, but this strains the evidence.

[3] Cf. Keith, JHS. xxxvi. 109 ; Helm, *Altgerm. Rel.* i. 135 ff., 147 ff. (development from stone to bronze ages in ideas of future life).

[4] Cf. Carnoy, *Les Indo-Européens*, pp. 222 ff. ; *contra*, L. B. Paton, *Spiritism*, pp. 104 ff.

[5] JB. i. 44.

[6] Wilken, *Rev. Col. Int.* iii. 256 ff. ; ERE. iv. 442 f.

different progress of the burial rites. If the connexion existed, as it may well have done, it is not proved for India by the available authorities.

Even, however, as a Preta there is extremely little trace of the belief of the soul as a ghost which comes to visit men. It is possible, as we have seen, that dreams of the dead were ascribed to visits of their ghosts, though this is not directly recorded; the Rigveda [1] expressly refers to Fathers who sit in the regions of earth or in the dwellings of men; the Taittirīya Saṁhitā [2] declares that the man who draws blood from a Brahman must fail to attain the world of the Fathers for as many years as the blood wets grains of sand. It seems possible that in the case of a dead man, whose soul is to live in the world of earth, because the southern fire first reaches his body, the soul is regarded as remaining away from the world of the Fathers in heaven; reference is made in that view also to the Fathers, who live in the air, and whom we may imagine as ghosts there, but too much faith may not be placed in this conception.[3] We hear of the appearance of Uccaiççravas Kaupayeya to instruct his nephew on a mystery of the Sāman.[4] But the normal view is that men and the Fathers do not appear together,[5] and the Vedic literature hardly shows a trace of the belief in ghosts which abounds in the Buddhist: the idea that evil spirits are caused by men needing proper burial, which is common in modern India, and that ghosts exist everywhere and send disease, is one which is not to be found in the Atharvaveda, which in its innumerable references to demons, Rakṣases, Piçācas, and others, deals with them in such manner as to show that the belief that many of them were merely hostile spirits of the dead was not a living one.[6] The Buddhist view, on the contrary, deals solemnly with ghosts: [7] it treats the stealing of their property on the same footing as stealing the property of beasts, it provides for cases of sexual intercourse with such ghosts; ghosts abide in the lonely woods, on the banks of rivers, in a sugar field. They are often at the cross-roads and they crowd into their old home in eager search for kind friends to give them a little food. But in the main it is clear the ghosts are not normal things: it is not a case of simple belief in the constant presence of the dead among the living which the Çatapatha Brāhmaṇa denies.[8] They are guilty souls suffering punishment, naked or covered barely by their hair, without protection against the heat, which fills them, from water, shade, or wind, hungry and thirsty, for the water even of the Ganges turns to blood in their mouths. A city of ghosts is recorded by the Divyāvadāna [9] of the Buddhists, an island inhabited by ghosts in a Jātaka,[10] and the classical Sanskrit literature contains striking pictures of the ghosts which throng the places of sepulture of the dead. But how far these views

[1] x. 15. 2; cf. AV. xiii. 3. 9; TA. vi. 4. 2.

[2] ii. 6. 10. 2. Cf. Manu, iv. 168; xi. 207.

[3] AGS. iv. 2; cf. RV. x. 15. 1, 2; Hillebrandt, *Ved. Myth.* ii. 91; iii. 417.

[4] JUB. iii. 29.

[5] ÇB. xiii. 8. 4. 12.

[6] Above, Part II, Chap. 5, § 3. On Epic views cf. Hopkins, *Epic Myth.*, pp. 29 ff.

[7] Pārājika, i. 10. 14; ii. 6. 4. See the Petavatthu and B. C. Law, *The Buddhist Conception of Spirits.*

[8] Cf. Lévi, *La doctrine du sacrifice*, pp. 98 ff.

[9] p. 7 (ed. Cowell and Neil).

[10] iv. 2.

were held in the Vedic period it is impossible to say :[1] there is no reasonable doubt that some of the Buddhist ghosts are transmutations of tree and water spirits due to the growing animism which treated the spirit as merely living in, and not having its life in, the tree or the waters. But it is worth noting that in many cases the Buddhist ghosts are to die and go to hell in a certain period :[2] it is natural to see in this the record of the condition before final damnation of the Preta.

§ 3. *The Transmutation of the Dead*

The Rigveda and the Vedic literature of the period of the Saṁhitās and the Brāhmaṇas presents us with no clear proof of the belief in the transmigration of the dead : the scanty evidence which has been adduced to prove the contrary view will be discussed hereafter,[3] but in this place it is important to note certain really popular beliefs of which there are traces in that literature and in that of the Sūtras. The most important piece of evidence is late : it is recorded by Baudhāyana[4] that the birds at the offering to the dead should receive lumps of food, just like the Fathers, on the ground that in the form of birds the Fathers go about. It must, however, be admitted that this is not enough to prove a real popular belief. The idea of the incarnation of men as snakes is clearly to be accepted for the later period,[5] but for the actual Vedic period it is not demonstrated, and it must in all likelihood be deemed to be an idea which entered the religion of the Veda with the advance of aboriginal influences. A more interesting case is recorded in the ritual for the final burial of the bones of the dead ;[6] if they cannot be found, then a garment is spread out, and, if a beast alights on it, it is treated as representing the bones of the dead. But this usage which is recorded for us at a late period cannot be pressed very far. To this scanty evidence may be added such support as can be obtained from such stories as that[7] of a mother, who, dying in the absence of her son, lies in wait for him in the shape of a newly created jackal to warn him of danger. The proof does not come to much, and none of it is of early date.

Of the soul becoming a plant or passing into a plant we have no early evidence save such as may be derived from the solitary address to the dead man in the Rigveda[8] which tells him to go to the plants with his members, and the isolated statement that the Fathers lie about the roots of the plants.[9]

1 Oldenberg, *Rel. des Veda*², pp. 559 ff.

2 Petavatthu, i. 10. 12 ; ii. 7. 12.

3 Part V, Chap. 28.

4 BDS. ii. 14. 9, 10. The Indo-European character of the belief is asserted by Feist, *Kultur der Indogermanen*, pp. 323 ff., but his evidence is not conclusive (Greek religion cannot safely be seen in the Hagia Triada sarkophagos, which is Minoan). Cf. also Johannson, *Solfågeln i Indien*, pp. 20 ff. ; G. Weicker, *Der Seelenvogel in der alten Literatur und Kunst.* That soul birds are referred to in PGS. i. 2. 4 ff., or TS. i. 1. 13, is out of the question (*contra*, Arbman, *Rudra*, pp. 100 f.).

5 Winternitz, *Der Sarpabali*, p. 37 ; *contra*, Paton, *Spiritism*, pp. 96 ff.

6 Kauç. lxxxiii. 22 ff.

7 Jātaka, ii. 388 ; Oldenberg, *Rel. des Veda*², pp. 564, 565.

8 x. 16. 3.

9 ÇB. xiii. 8. 1. 20. Cf. Dieterich, *Mutter Erde*², p. 49 ; Cook, *Zeus*, i. 687, n. 3.

There is much evidence of connexion with stars. This, however, is very different from a normal transmigration: it obviously is connected with the belief in the departure of the souls to the regions of heaven, and on the philosophical side it appears as the doctrine of the identity of the soul with Āditya.[1] The epic notoriously is fond of seeing the souls of the great heroes and priests of the past in the constellations of the heavens. The Çatapatha Brāhmaṇa [2] calls the stars women and the light of those who by their good works have reached the heaven. The same view is found in the Sūtra of Āpastamba.[3] It is possible also that the same idea may be referred to in the Rigveda [4] in the reference to the seers who watch the sun, or those who stand high in heaven through the giving of plenteous largesse to the priest.[5] Perhaps too the name of the Great Bear as the Seven Seers,[6] of one of the Pleiades as Arundhatī, and even the view of the Kṛttikās as wives of the Bears, may be traced to this idea. The view that the moon is the abode of the souls is found also in the later period, but there is no identification with the moon, but merely by a transfer of ideas the change of the resting-place of the souls.[7]

[1] TB. iii. 10. 9. 11; ÇB. ii. 6. 4. 8 ff.

[2] vi. 5. 4. 8; cf. Hillebrandt, *Ved. Myth.* iii. 420–3, who finds planets in most impossible places, e.g. the five Adhvaryus of RV. iii. 7. 7, or perhaps (iii. 321, n. 1) the Pleiades as the Maruts transported to heaven. Cf. above, Chap. 11, § 10.

[3] ApDS. ii. 9. 24. 14.

[4] x. 107. 2; 154. 5; AV. xviii. 2. 47.

[5] Oldenberg, *Rel. des Veda*², p. 566. For the epic see Hopkins, *Epic Myth.*, p. 53.

[6] ÇB. ii. 1. 2. 4; xiii. 8. 1. 9; JUB. iv. 26. 12; HGS. i. 12. 14 ff.; cf. RV. iv. 42. 8.

[7] Kauṣ. i. 2; KÇS. xxv. 6. 11; Hillebrandt, *Ved. Myth.* i. 276, 394 ff.; Scherman, *Visionslitteratur*, p. 29. On shooting stars cf. MS. i. 8. 6; *Ath. Pariçiṣṭa*, lviii b. i. 3 ff.; Hopkins, *Epic Myth.*, p. 34; Haradatta, on ApDS. i. 11. 31. 17. Cf. F. Cumont, *After-Life in Roman Paganism*, pp. 92 ff., 104 ff. It is very dubious if we are to see Chaldean influence, as held by Cumont and E. Pfeiffer, *Studien zum antiken Sternglauben*, pp. 113 ff.

CHAPTER 24

THE DISPOSAL OF THE DEAD

There is nothing in Vedic literature to encourage the view, which has been so energetically contended for in connexion with western civilization, that the custom of burning the dead is one which denotes an essential distinction of race, as contrasted with the practice of burying the dead.[1] The burning of the dead is set over against the burying of the dead in the Rigveda [2] merely as two legitimate alternative methods, and this is the state of affairs throughout the history of India. Burning is normally preferred, the chief exceptions being very holy ascetics and infants under two years of age,[3] but the existence of burial cannot be denied for any period. Moreover it is important to note that the double practice of burial or burning is recorded of many other objects which it is desired to dispose of, owing to their dangerous character. Nor is it to be doubted [4] that the primitive use of fire in this case was that of removing the dread substance, which burial could also effect. The idea that burning was necessary to take the soul to heaven is not Vedic : the Rigveda proves that from the earliest recorded period the unburnt dead went to heaven no less than the burnt.

Other modes of disposal of the dead are referred to in the Rigveda [5] and the Atharvaveda.[6] The dead might be cast away (*paroptāḥ*), or they might be exposed (*uddhitāḥ*). The latter expression seems to mean exposed on trees, a practice which was known in later India, and which is referred to in the Çatapatha Brāhmaṇa,[7] being prescribed as the expiation, in the case in which a cow is slaughtered and found to be in calf, as regards the disposal

[1] Keith, JRAS. 1912, pp. 470–4.

[2] x. 15. 4.

[3] Roth, ZDMG. ix. 471 ; Hopkins, *Rel. of India*, pp. 271 ff. ; Caland, *Todtengebräuche*, pp. 93–5 ; PGS. iii. 10. 5. The placing of the funeral pyre on a ship (as in Teutonic usage) is not proved for India ; the passage cited by Zimmer (*Altindisches Leben*, p. 410) from RV. x. 135 does not naturally bear this sense ; Oldenberg, *Ṛgveda-Noten*, ii. 351.

[4] Cf. Rohde, *Psyche*³, i. 26 ff. ; Helm, *Altgerm. Rel.* i. 152 ; Pfuhl, GGA. 1906, p. 342 ; below, Appendix F.

[5] x. 15. 4 (burnt and not burnt).

[6] xviii. 2. 34. Those cast away may refer to a usage as in Iran of throwing to the beasts to devour (Zimmer, *Altindisches Leben*, p. 402), or merely to depositing dead bodies in cemeteries, as recognized in Buddhist tales ; *Buddhist India*, pp. 78 f. ; below, p. 424, n. 6.

[7] iv. 5. 2. 13. A similar custom is recorded of the Colchians (Ap. Rhod. iii. 200 ff.), who buried women. Cook (*Zeus*, i. 533, 534) conjectured that it was to bestow life on the tree or on the dead ; and elsewhere (p. 687) adopts the view that trees planted round graves were originally homes for the spirits of the dead. Zimmer (*l. c.*) thinks the reference is to persons exposed in old age to death as among the Massagetae and others (*ibid.*, p. 328).

of the embryo. But these ideas are of no importance for Vedic India in general; the rite of burning is the rite which has won approval in the Sūtras, and that of burying the body is there severely restricted.

It is, however, a very different question whether this position is primitive. In one of the funeral hymns in the Rigveda [1] the dead is told to go to mother earth, which is to enclose him, as with a garment a mother her child. It is the view of the ritual texts that these words apply to the later rite by which the burnt bones of the dead are placed in an urn in earth, but the interpretation, though defended by Oldenberg,[2] cannot be treated as natural, and we must admit that it is only reasonable to assume that it is meant for an actual burial. The later ritual which had in the main given up burial for burning naturally had to use the verses somewhere, and the burial of the bones gave an excellent opportunity for this action, but the fact remains that the verses are burial verses, that the Rigveda treats burial and burning as on the same footing, and that it probably represents contemporary fact.[3]

The details of the burning alone can be reconstructed with certainty, but many of them must be assumed to have applied equally to burial.[4] In the moment of death the man was laid on the ground, which is smeared with cow-dung and strewn with grass, near his sacred fire. The dead then was washed and anointed: the hair, the beard, and the nails were closely trimmed: a garland and fresh garment were laid upon him. The women of the house [5] wailed around the place on which he was laid, tearing or loosening their hair, like the mourners at a Roman funeral, smiting their breasts and thighs. The body was borne to the grave or taken there on a car: the tracks of the party—rather than of the dead—were wiped out by means of a bundle of twigs attached to the dead, so as to prevent the recurrence of the spirit of the dead. The mourners accompanied the bier with loosened hair. Perhaps as the procession moved along were repeated verses [6] urging the dead to go on his long way, to unite with the Fathers and with Yama, to leave sin behind, to go home, and to escape the dogs of Yama, while evil spirits were banned. The dead was then laid on the funeral pyre, in the midst of three fires produced by manipulation from the three sacred fires maintained by him, if he did so maintain them. Then the wife of the dead man is placed beside him, but

[1] x. 18; cf. AV. xviii. 2. 50–2.

[2] *Rel. des Veda*[2], pp. 572 ff.; *Ṛgveda-Noten*, ii. 219 ff.; Caland, *Todtengebräuche*, p. 165.

[3] For the Avestan practice, cf. Moulton, *Early Zoroastrianism*, p. 163. See also von Schroeder, VOJ. ix. 112 ff.; Weber, SBA. 1896, p. 255; Hopkins, JAOS. xvi. p. cliii.

[4] ÇB. xi. 5. 2; xiii. 8 for valuable notices; also TS. vi; AÇS. vi. 10; AGS. iv. 1 ff.; ÇGS. iv. 14 ff.; PGS. iii. 10; KÇS. xvi. 3, 4; xvii. 7; Kauç. lxxx. ff.; Oldenberg, *Rel. des Veda*[2], pp. 572 ff.; Caland, *Die altindischen Todten- und Bestattungsgebräuche* (Amsterdam, 1896); and ed. of Baudhāyana, Hiraṇyakeçi, and Āpastamba Pitṛmedhasūtras (1896); Roth, ZDMG. viii. 467 ff.; Zimmer, *Altindisches Leben*, pp. 404 ff.

[5] See Bloomfield, AJP. xi. 336 ff.

[6] RV. x. 14. 7–12. The Sūtras vary; cf. Kauç. lxxx. 35, 42; AGS. iv. 2. 10; ÇGS. iv. 14. 7.

taken away with the words,[1] 'Arise, O woman, to the world of the living; departed is the life of him with whom thou liest; to marriage here hast thou attained with him as husband who graspeth[2] thy hand.' It is clear that the husband's brother or some other—a pupil or aged servant, according to Āçvalāyana—must be meant who takes her in wedlock.[3] The bow[4] is taken from the hand of the dead if a Kṣatriya—in the case of a Brahman[5] a staff, of a Vaiçya an ox-goad, according to the later ritual—with a verse saying that it is taken for attainment of lordly power and strength: the later ritual,[6] however, breaks the bow and leaves it with the dead, as the soldiers of Brennus when they died had their swords broken and laid by them to deceive the learned Polybios and the modern world for two thousand years.[7] Further, in the ritual the offering utensils of the dead are placed on the bier with him, only the stone, metal, or earthen being kept back and given to a Brahman, a practice disapproved by some, or thrown into water, or kept by the son of the dead.[8] This usage is apparently to be seen in the Rigveda[9] as applied to a Soma vessel at least.

The Rigveda[10] expressly refers to the burning of a goat which is the share of Agni, and to the use of the flesh of a cow to protect the body against the flame. In the ritual texts details of the use of the flesh of the cow are given: the omentum is placed over the face, the kidneys in either hand, to satisfy the dogs of Yama—like the honey cake for Kerberos—and the skin is put over the whole. A goat is also tied to the pyre so loosely that it can easily break the cord. The pyre is then lighted or the three fires are directed towards it, and Agni is invoked to take the dead uninjured to the Fathers. Other prayers and offerings seem to have been addressed to Yama, the Añgirases, and Sarasvatī;[11] the sense of the ceremony is shown by the words of the prayer, not recorded in the Rigveda,[12] 'From him thou art born; may he in turn be born from thee.'

The ceremony of the burning of the body is followed by the departure of the mourners who do not turn round: they wash themselves and offer

[1] RV. x. 18. 8; the practice was not in favour with the later feeling; Caland, *Todtengebräuche*, pp. 43–5.

[2] This must be the sense as taken by Oldenberg and Caland. A reference to the dead man is impossible, though taken so by Max Müller and Roth, and TA. vi. 1. 3 clearly negates this sense.

[3] AGS. iv. 2. 18.

[4] RV. x. 18. 9.

[5] AV. xviii. 2. 59; Kauç. lxxx. 48 ff.; *ibid.* 46, and AV. xviii. 4. 56 also prescribe the taking of a piece of gold from his hand. Pieces of gold—failing it, melted butter—are placed on the seven openings in the head of the dead; Caland, *Todtengebräuche*, p. 47; JGS. ii. 4; cf. the Greek and Roman usage.

[6] AGS. iv. 2. 22.

[7] Reinach, *Cultes, Mythes et Religions*, iii. 141. Cf. Helm, *Altgerm. Rel.* i. 140, n. 39; Hopkins, *Origin of Religion*, p. 110.

[8] ÇB. xii. 5. 2. 14; AGS. iv. 3. 18, 19; Kauç. lxxxi. 19; JAOS. xxxiv. 249.

[9] x. 16. 8. Removal of risk for the living may have operated as well as provision for the dead.

[10] x. 16. 4, 7.

[11] Kauç. lxxxi. 34–9; RV. x. 18. 1–6, 13 ff.; 17. 7–9 are used here according to Oldenberg (*Rel. des Veda*², p. 578), but cf. Caland, *Todtengebräuche*, p. 65.

[12] ÇB. xii. 5. 2. 15; TA. vi. 1. 4.

libations of water for the dead: they change their garments: they pass under a yoke[1] of branches of the purifying Parṇa tree, they touch on entering the house purifying things, water, fire, dung, mustard grains, and barley grains, the power of which lies in the name Yava, which is constantly connected in the Vedic mind with *yu*, 'restrain' (demons). Perhaps,[2] too, at this point, and not merely at the putting away of the bones, there takes place the ceremony of removing from the house, and placing in a desolate place, the fire which must not go through the door. It is impossible to believe that this fire was really in the view of the Rigveda kept for the making of offerings to the dead, though the exact meaning of the references to it in the Rigveda is hard to ascertain.[3] Moreover, until the bones are collected, or for three or ten days, the relatives must observe certain restrictions: they must not use their ordinary beds, but sleep on the ground, must observe chastity, cook no food, and live on what they buy, or what others give to them. The nature of these observances is obvious: it is in some way to avoid the risk which death has brought into the vicinity of the relatives: the view that the Preta of the dead is near at hand is clear. The prohibition of cooking is attested by the Avesta also: after death the relatives should cook nothing for three days, and the Parsis observe this rule to the present day.[4] Clearly the death has infected the food and the vicinity in which it was, and to eat it will bring injury. The sleeping on the ground is less easy to explain: it is possibly an effort to avoid the attention of the spirit if it returns: possibly it may be traced to the view that the relative, by contact with the dead, has contaminated himself and must be purified, before the bed can be safely approached, if it is not to be infected for all time to come: or communion with the earth may be desired. The abstinence from intercourse may be explained, as it is explained by Oldenberg,[5] as due to the danger that injury might thus be done to any child which might perchance be born.

The third or tenth day is that of the collecting of the bones of the dead.[6] In the first instance the place of burning is cooled by the use of cooling substances, water plants, one Kiyāmbu with the very name suggesting water, and the inevitable frog.[7] Water and milk are prescribed for the besprinkling of the place of the fire in the later ritual, which also provides for the offering of water and milk for the dead on the night after the death.[8] According to

[1] The Mantras (*Todtengebräuche*, pp. 74, 76) suggest the idea of a barrier between dead and living.

[2] Oldenberg, *Rel. des Veda*², p. 578. The rite seems to follow the putting away of the bones in KÇS. xxi. 4. 28; cf. Kauç. lxix; AGS. iv. 6. RV. x. 16. 9 ff. are used.

[3] Bergaigne, *Rel. Véd.* i. 78.

[4] SBE. v. 382, n. 2. Ethnic parallels in Wilken, *Rev. Col. Int.* iv. 352; Frazer, *Journ. Anthrop. Inst.* xv. 92 f. Cf. Stevenson, *Rites of the Twice-Born*, p. 154.

[5] *Rel. des Veda*², p. 590.

[6] Kaegi (*Die Neunzahl bei den Ostariern*) points to the importance of nine in the funeral rites of Indo-European peoples. In India the periods vary, but ten days is usual; Caland, *Todtengebräuche*, pp. 81–4; Paton, *Spiritism*, pp. 142 ff.

[7] RV. x. 16. 13 ff.; Kauç. lxxxvi. 26, 27; AJP. xi. 342 ff.

[8] PGS. iii. 10. 28.

Āçvalāyana,[1] who places the rite on the tenth day after death, the bones should be put, those of a man in a male urn and those of a woman in a female urn respectively, the reference being to marks on the urns which are treated as like the breasts of a woman.[2] The bones should be picked up by aged persons, in uneven numbers, not men and women together, with the thumb and the fourth finger and deposited without noise, those of the feet coming first, those of the head last. Then the bones are purified with a sieve, and the urn is placed in a pit where waters do not run together from every side, save rain water ; earth is put down upon the urn, and it is covered with a lid. The performers then go away, not turning back, purify themselves, and offer a Çrāddha to the dead. According to the Kauçika Sūtra,[3] a different procedure is adopted, in so far that the bones are deposited at the root of a tree, with a verse of the Atharvaveda,[4] which beseeches the great tree not to press heavily on them ; but it is by no means clear that this is the original sense of the Atharvan verse, which may refer to proper burial.

A still further rite is prescribed by the Çatapatha Brāhmaṇa [5] and mentioned in other texts, the raising of a memorial to the dead. This is to be done a long time after the death ; when even the year is forgotten is a suitable time. The bones are gathered from the hole in the earth or from the tree roots, in which case a verse [6] is used which rather points to the idea of real burial, and may suggest that once the gathering of the bones and the putting away of them in a relic mound were done when the body had decayed after normal burial. If the bones cannot be found, the rite alluded to above takes place : [7] a garment is spread on the water's edge : the dead is called by name, and any beast [8] that alights is treated as representing the bones : in the alternative, dust from the place is used. The night is spent in ceremonies : women beating their thighs with the right hand,[9] with hair loosened, wailing, thrice in the course of the night dance thrice round the bones. Lutes are played, and —doubtless to scare away spirits—a noise made by the beating of an old shoe on an empty pot or in other ways.[10] In the morning the bones are taken to the new place of rest, which must be out of sight from the village, in a place where there is abundance of plants, around whose roots the Fathers are said

[1] AGS. iv. 5. 7–10, using RV. x. 18. 10 ff.

[2] Lanman, *Sanskrit Reader*, p. 404. For the cleansing of the bones, cf. Germanic usage, Helm, *Altgerm. Rel.* i. 154 f. It may be a transfer of the usage of washing the dead body, or an effort to banish the soul entirely from connexion with earth.

[3] lxxxii. 13.

[4] xviii. 2. 25.

[5] xiii. 8. 1 ; KÇS. xxi. 3. 1.

[6] AV. xviii. 3. 70 ; Kauç. lxxxiii. 19. Oldenberg (*Rel. des Veda*², pp. 580, n. 4; 581, n. 4) suggests that the whole rite is a misunderstanding of the verse originally referring to the wood of the pyre, but this is not probable. Original burial is more likely.

[7] Kauç. lxxxiii. 22 ff.

[8] Doubtless normally an insect, which was often regarded in Greek religion as a vehicle of the soul (Cook, *Zeus*, i. 532, n. 12). Cf. the Samoan parallel in *Journ. Anthrop. Inst.* xv. 96, n. 1.

[9] Cf. Eitrem, *Opferritus und Voropfer*, pp. 35, 42.

[10] Kauç. lxxxiv. 9 ; KÇS. xxi. 3. 7.

to creep,[1] but no thorns. A hole is made or furrow ploughed : seeds of all sorts are sowed and the bones deposited. The hole is then covered over with stones and earth to make a memorial mound : in it seeds are sown to feed the dead,[2] and pits are dug in it into which water and milk are poured to please the dead.[3]

The departure from the place of the erection of the memorial is followed by many rites to prevent contamination, the use of fire, of the Apāmārga plant, the obliteration of the footsteps, the crossing of pits filled with water, and so on. The placing of a barrier of some sort between the dead and the living is a rite recorded in the Rigveda[4] itself, whether the object is stone or some piece of earth.

The nature of the mode of disposal of the dead probably showed itself specially valuable in the Indian climate, but apart from this consideration, the influence of the practice of removing evil influences by burning, and of the worship of the fire, and the use of fire as the messenger between men and the gods, must have aided the development of the use of cremation as almost the normal and certainly much the most usual form of disposing of the dead. The belief in the burning of the dead as a suitable mode of disposal may be Indo-European,[5] the evidence for this is merely the practice in early Greece and Germany also—but it may equally have been produced in India, perhaps at first under the influence of the needs of war, where the burial of the dead leaves them exposed to misusage by the enemy. It may be that the belief in burning is older than the belief in the heavenly abode, but that is not susceptible of proof ; the fact that the Rigveda does not require burning in order that the dead may go to heaven may best be explained on the ground that the belief is older than burning of the dead, rather than that it developed and became independent of that burning. Naturally, however, in any case the burning of the dead was regarded as helping the path to the sky, and from another point of view here and there the idea presents itself that the dead man is in a sense[6] an offering to the gods. Such an idea, however, never became of importance, to judge from its rare appearance, and from the fact that the burning of the dead was never decked out with the apparatus of the sacrifice.

1 ÇB. xiii. 8. 1. 20.

2 As at the piling of the fire, Weber, *Ind. Stud.* xiii. 245 ; Caland, *Todtengebräuche*, p. 177, misses the obvious purpose in this case of the rite.

3 For alleged remains at Lauriyā Nandangarh, see CHI. i. 616 ; above, p. 32, n. 1.

4 x. 18. 3 and 4. From the idea of the inability of the soul to cross water is perhaps developed the later idea of the Vaitaraṇī stream and of a mimic boat to cross it (Caland, *Todtengebräuche*, pp. 8, 153). Hillebrandt (*Ved. Myth.* iii. 377) sees the Vaitaraṇī's prototype in the Sarasvatī of RV. x. 17. 7–9, and Roth (JAOS. xvi. p. ccxliii) finds the name in JUB. i. 25. 3.

5 Oldenberg, *Rel. des Veda*², pp. 584 ff. In primitive Greece, as in early Italy and Britain, both modes of disposal are found ; we can hardly believe that in every case an Indo-European rite was superinduced on a non-Indo-European. Cf. Hopkins, *Origin of Religion*, pp. 148 ff. ; for Germany, Helm, *Altgerm. Rel.* i. 152 ff. It was disapproved in Iran.

6 RV. x. 16. 5 ; late Sūtra evidence is given by Caland, *Todtengebräuche*, pp. 178, 179, who seems to overestimate its value.

The exact idea connected with the burning seems to have been that the whole self was burned, soul as well as body, in order to convey it, in a refined form but still unaltered in essence, to the regions of heaven. It is clear from what has been already said that there is no question of the mere sending thither of the soul in the Vedic religion: in the philosophy different ideas appear, but not in the religious faith. Nevertheless at the same time the man is still regarded as being in some measure present in the bones which are left:[1] even if, as is probable, the original force of the verses of the Rigveda and the Atharvaveda, which refer to burial, dealt with real burial, yet when they were adopted for burial of the bones, they must have been felt not to run counter to popular belief.

In the Vedic belief the popular view that the dead must be provided with the same things[2] as they enjoyed in the world of men has been greatly attenuated. It is absurd to suppose that all women were ever burned with the dead:[3] the practice never existed in India at any time which is recorded, and in many cases the result would have been to leave children without proper care. But it is perfectly clear that the wife of a great man might be burned with him, and that the Rigveda[4] shows a stage of opinion in which this rite has been definitely abolished by the Brahmans, and has been replaced by the giving of her to the brother or some other relative of the dead in symbolic, if not necessarily always real, marriage: we may well believe that the marriage might be real only if the dead had left no son alive to perform for him the funeral ceremonies. Similarly the dead was deprived not merely of his bow, but also of a piece of gold, which his eldest son received: it is difficult not to believe that the older practice was as in ancient Greece to allow him to bear with him to his future abode the ornament of gold which he wore in his life on earth.[5] The practice of enveloping the body of the dead in the limbs of the cow is a curious one, and offers possibilities of different explanations. But it is clearly the view of the Rigveda that the heat of the fire is to exhaust its fury on the members of the goat and presumably also of the cow,[6] and it may be that the offering was a sort of substitution for the dead himself, so that evil powers might assail it in place of him. The goat stands in another category: it may be compared to the goat which is slain with the sacrificial horse to show it the way: in the passage to the next

[1] A corporeal resurrection is seen by Jackson in Yasna, xxx. 7; the Persians according to Herodotos (i. 140; cf. vii. 117) buried their dead.

[2] e.g. garments (AV. xviii. 4. 31). No burning of slaves ever occurs, while in Germany it was frequent.

[3] In no country is so universal a custom known.

[4] Cf. AV. xviii. 3. 1 (TA. vi. 1. 3); Macdonell and Keith, *Vedic Index*, i. 488, 489; Feist, *Kultur der Indogermanen*, p. 311; Bergaigne, *Rel. Véd.*, i. 78; Garbe, *Beiträge zur indischen Kulturgeschichte*, pp. 148 ff.

[5] The idea of paying Charon is obviously a misunderstanding. In central Europe the gift is accompanied by the words, 'Thou hast thy due; leave me in peace'; Carnoy, *Les Indo-Européens*, p. 224. Gold possibly was held as a sun symbol to give the dead aid in attaining immortal life.

[6] Oldenberg, *Rel. des Veda*², p. 587.

world the journey may be trackless and the sure-footed goat will find the way.[1]

In addition to the normal rites special forms[2] are prescribed for many cases, such as the death of an Agnihotrin, of a pregnant woman after the saving of the embryo, and a Brahman who has acquired knowledge of the Brahman, the rite in his case being the Brahmamedha.[3] In the case of death in absence the body may be preserved in oil or only the bones brought back for the formal rites. When a man is believed dead the cremation of a figure representing him is allowed, and, if after such a rite has been performed he should return alive, he is subjected to the same form of ritual as a newly born child, including remarriage to his wife.[4] The modern practice by which in the burial of an ascetic his skull is broken open with a coconut to allow the escape of the spirit, though based on a doctrine of the Upaniṣads[5] as to the departure of the soul through the skull on death, is not recorded in any early Vedic text. Though children under two were usually buried or thrown away, they might be cremated if their teeth had grown;[6] burial in the house which is elsewhere often recorded—perhaps as a mode of securing rebirth in the mother—is unknown.

[1] According to AV. xviii. 2. 22, the Maruts are to cool the dead through the goat, perhaps by using up the power of the fire on it.

[2] Caland, *Todtengebräuche*, pp. 85–98.

[3] TA. iii.

[4] Cf. Frazer, *Journ. Anthrop. Inst.* xv. 64.

[5] CU. viii. 6. 6.

[6] So in AB. vii. 14. 4 an animal is fit for sacrifice when its teeth appear. That bodies were often merely dumped on burial grounds is suggested by the Buddhist evidence and that of classical literature, as well as of Vedic evidence (above, p. 417, n. 6). See also Paton, *Spiritism*, pp. 122 ff. The view that Yama's dogs reflect the custom of exposure is implausible; for Hekate and the dog, see Farnell, *Cults*, ii. 510.

CHAPTER 25

THE CULT OF THE DEAD

§ 1. *The Living and the Dead*

THE attitude of the Vedic Indian to his dead is one of distinctive and pronounced individuality. The constant anxiety lest from the dead should come injury to the living is perfectly obvious, but it must be admitted that it does not show any trace of being due to the direct fear of the spirit of the dead : it is the fear of death which marks the attitude of the Indian : the dead has not a hostile nature, but the thing which has affected him is to be feared. It is, therefore, intelligible that the Indian in the Vedic period looks, despite his dread of death, with affection and esteem upon his ancestors, and that much of his existence should be concerned with the means of securing them nourishment.[1] That food is required especially on certain occasions, not less often than once a month and occasionally at other times : in a certain portion of the rainy season the dead are conceived as leaving the abode of heaven and coming to the houses of their kin to seek for food.[2] On the other hand if the men care for their Fathers, it is but natural that these Fathers should be deemed to be anxious to aid and assist them, and the companionship of the blessed dead with the gods encourages the belief that they have power to aid, even as the gods have power.[3] The Fathers generally are often referred to in the Rigveda and the later literature as invoked to confer boons, similar to those which the gods convey, and, though they are distinctly differentiated by a multitude of things, and especially by cult, from the powers of heaven, nevertheless, for the purpose of being a very present help in tribulation, they appear to be ranked as not unworthy of invocation with, or even without, the gods. Like the gods, men pray to them for success, for the defeat of enemies, for the gift of rain, for the bestowal of eloquence, or for abundance of food. Even in battle the Fathers are invoked as warriors.[4] But the energy of the Fathers has one special end, the production of offspring, in which they have the special interest that the rites for the dead can only be kept up by the device of continuing the family. At the offering for the

[1] Caland (*Todtengebräuche*, pp. 171, 172) insists that fear is the only motive even for the feeding of the dead, but this is clearly untenable ; cf. Meyer, *Gesch. d. Alt.*[3] I. i. § 62 ; Warde Fowler, *Roman Ideas of Deity*, pp. 23–6 ; Hopkins, *Origin of Religion*, pp. 74, 78 ff. ; Max Müller, *Egypt. Myth.*, p. 183 ; Helm, *Altgerm. Rel.* i. 136 ff. For modern India, cf. Stevenson, *Rites of the Twice-Born*, pp. 156–92. See also Paton, *Spiritism*, chap. iv.

[2] Caland, *Todtenverehrung*, pp. 43 ff.

[3] Bergaigne, *Rel. Véd.* i. 95 ff. ; AV. iv. 15. 15 ; vii. 12. 1 ; xviii. 2. 30 ; 3. 15 ; ii. 12. 4, &c. ; TA. v. 7, 8 ; AGS. iv. 7. 1.

[4] RV. vi. 75. 9.

dead the great-grandfather, the grandfather, and the father are all invoked to send sons :[1] the wife of the offerer is given a lump of the food made ready for the Fathers with the prayer that they may accord her a son ;[2] the offerer[3] himself, who desires a son, wets his face with the remains of the water poured out for the Fathers. They naturally find a place in the ritual for the marriage ceremony : food is offered to them before the marriage to induce them to give offspring to the bride, and, when the bridal procession starts out, it is thought that the Fathers crowd around to see the bride.[4] But we do not hear in any case that the Fathers were deemed to incorporate themselves in the bride for rebirth, as is one constant view of birth in Australian belief, and as seems in some degree to have been the view taken of the Roman Genius.[5]

In the overwhelming majority of cases the person invoked is not an individual, but the whole body of the Fathers as such : nevertheless in occasional instances an individual ancestor may be invoked, like Kaṇva or Kakṣīvant, or a specific group such as the Vasiṣṭhas.[6] Men too occasionally appear among the gods with divine attributes, such as Kutsa who is invoked along with Indra.[7] Other men may here and there be placed in this position : the name, Udalākāçyapa, of a spirit invoked at the plough festival, does not look very divine or demoniac, but that is a mere speculation.[8]

The attitude of the Fathers to the living is assumed by the latter to be one of friendship : they are invoked to turn the merit acquired by their good deeds to the overthrow of the foe of the living, but to their own they are dangerous only when these sin against them by failing to provide them with due offerings, a fact which seems clearly alluded to as early as the Rigveda.[9] Their power to injure is pre-supposed by the help they are to give in the overthrow of enemies, but very little is said directly about it. In a spell against the Dasyus, who at the offering for the dead mix themselves with the Fathers looking like kinsmen, a torch is employed, but this is hardly any definite evidence that the Fathers *per se* were dangerous.[10] Nor is the mere fact that various objects are buried at cross-roads for the destruction of enemies[11] any proof of their activity in effecting the desired destruction, since many other evil spirits inhabit cross-roads. The souls of unborn children become according to a late piece of evidence blood suckers,[12] and possibly this may explain the special

[1] Kauç. lxxxviii. 28.
[2] Kauç. lxxxix. 6.
[3] AGS. iv. 7. 15.
[4] Kauç. lxxxiv. 12 ; AV. xiv. 2. 73. Cf. RV. x. 40. 10, with Oldenberg's note.
[5] Cf. Reinach, *Cultes, Mythes et Religions*, iv. 361 ff. ; Warde Fowler, *Religious Experience of the Roman People*, pp. 74, 75. In India this view appears only under the influence of transmigration in the Upaniṣad period and in Buddhism ; Windisch, *Buddha's Geburt*, pp. 9 ff. ; cf. Segerstedt, *Le Monde Oriental*, iv. 144 f. ; Oldenberg, *Rel. des Veda*², p. 565, n. 1.
[6] RV. x. 15. 8 ; AV. xviii. 3. 15.
[7] RV. v. 31, 9.
[8] PGS. ii. 13, 2 ; Oldenberg, *Rel. des Veda*², p. 567, n. 3.
[9] x. 15. 6 ; TB. i. 3. 10. 7. Brunnhofer (*Arische Urzeit*, pp. 280–4) cites RV. i. 119. 4 ; vi. 59. 1 in the same sense and refers the idea to phenomena of twilight !
[10] AV. xviii. 2. 28 ; Kauç. lxxxvii. 30.
[11] AV. v. 31. 8 ; x. 1. 8.
[12] Caland, *Altind. Ahnenkult*, p. 32.

objection felt in Vedic religion to the slayer of an embryo, but this explanation is not necessary. The danger from the dead is, as we have seen, fear of death, not of the spirits of the Fathers. Moreover, as we have noted, the Atharvaveda finds for the evils which are practised on men the cause in demons,[1] not in souls of the dead, which is again a strong piece of evidence that the mischievous powers of the dead were not strongly felt in the Vedic period.

As we have seen, ghosts appear very little in the Vedic literature, and similarly the presence of the dead on earth to aid their offspring is practically unknown in Indian literature before the Buddhist era.[2]

§ 2. *The Offerings to the Dead in the Domestic Ritual*

Beside the regular offerings which are prescribed for the Fathers, there are others which are to be performed on special occasions, such as the birth of a son, a marriage, and the giving of the name to the child.[3] In this case the offering or 'Çrāddha', which bears its name[4] of that which is connected with Çraddhā, 'faith', from the fact that the presents to the Brahmans which accompany the offerings to the dead reveal the faith of the offerer in the Brahmans, is to be performed on the waxing half of the month, and before midday: the number of Brahmans chosen is even, not as usual odd: the performances are from left to right, not *vice versa*; barley replaces sesame; the milk meal lumps are mixed with sour milk and roasted grains, and the Fathers are addressed as Nāndīmukha, 'joyful in countenance',[5] in place of 'with tearful countenance', which is elsewhere not rarely used. These rank as the Vṛddhi Çrāddhas, and similar to them are Pūrta Çrāddhas, at the dedication of wells, pools, and so on.

Much more important are the regular monthly Çrāddhas[6] performed on the day of new moon, month by month, and after midday. The important part of the rite is the choice of Brahmans to represent the Fathers, at least three, but often more, and on no account one only at least at the first Çrāddha offered. Moreover, by some authorities, further Brahmans are required to represent the All-gods. Three vessels of metal, stone, and clay are employed: into each water is poured, and in the view of Çaunaka[7] the first vessel is not touched for the whole of the ceremony, as the Fathers would be present in it. Sesame is also put into the vessels. Then the water is offered as Arghya water to the Brahmans, and they are also given garlands, incense, lights, perfumes, and clothes. With the remains of the water the offerer wipes his face, if he

[1] The birth of a Rakṣas from the head of Namuci (ÇB. v. 4. 1. 9) is cited by Oldenberg as showing the close relation of demons and souls, though disguised.

[2] See Mahāvagga, i. 4. 2; Udāna, i. 10, &c.

[3] AGS. ii. 5. 13 ff.; iv. 7. 1; BhGS. iii. 16; BGS. iii. 12. 2–15; GGS. iv. 3. 35 ff.; Caland, *Todtenverehrung*, pp. 39 ff.

[4] Max Müller, *India*, p. 235; see PB. xii. 11. 25; TS. vii. 4. 1. 1; ÇB. xiv. 1. 4. 10; RV. x. 151; Oldenberg, *Rel. des Veda*², p. 566, n. 4; ZDMG. l. 448 ff.

[5] They are clearly not the ancestors beyond the immediate three as has been suggested.

[6] AGS. iv. 7; ÇGS. iv. 1; HGS. ii. 10; BhGS. ii. 11–14.

[7] AGS. iv. 7. 16.

desires a son. Then he asks their permission to offer lumps of food in the fire, and does so or places it in their hands: they are also given other food, which they eat, and the ceremony finishes when they are satisfied.

Distinct from the monthly Pārvaṇa Çrāddha seems to have been another offering, the Māsika,[1] monthly brought on the waning half of the month on an uneven day. The rites for this day are varyingly given, and in some cases the rite seems to have been assimilated to the Aṣṭakā rites. For it Hiraṇyakeçin [2] lays down the rule that the sacrificer up to the age of fifty should offer to the Fathers the seam of his garment, and that otherwise he should offer hair. The first idea is clearly that the dead need garments: the second seems less obvious, and it is possible that it is due to the very different idea of substitution, which becomes the more necessary, since at fifty one is approaching the age when death is claiming a man more and more energetically.[3] But other theories are possible; the giving of hair may be merely a desire for communion, the burial of hair with the dead has been explained by Eitrem [4] as at once due to this desire[5] and to the wish to lay apart that which has been contaminated by death.

The Aṣṭakās [6] are festivals of special importance and difficulty. The rule of Āçvalāyana is that there should be four, on the eighth day of the dark half of the month in the two months of each of the two seasons, winter and the cool season, Mārgaçīrṣa, Pauṣa, Māgha, and Phālguna. But the rule is that the number should be three or less. The normal view seems to be that Taiṣa, Māgha, Phālguna are the months, but the three ceremonies can be reduced to three days, the 7th to 9th of one month, or pressed into the eighth day only. Hiraṇyakeçin allows only one festival, the three-day rite of the Ekāṣṭakā, the eighth day of the dark half of the month Māgha. The deities of the Aṣṭakās are a matter of dispute: Agni, Sūrya, Prajāpati, night, the Nakṣatras, the seasons, and the Fathers have all claims. The nature of the offering is equally disputed: some demand flesh at all three: others cakes at the first, a cow at the second, and vegetables at the third, or the same set but in diverse order. A very odd rite is prescribed by the Mānava school,[7] for the evening before the last Aṣṭakā: at the cross-roads the sacrificer kills a cow, dismembers it, and divides the flesh among the passers-by. The Aṣṭakā is followed by the Anvaṣṭakya, which is allowed to follow all three rites, or the middle one only. The nature of the rite is rather curious: a fire is made, surrounded, and an opening made in the north: an offering strew is laid

[1] AGS. ii. 5. 10.

[2] ii. 10–13; so also at the Piṇḍapitṛyajña, AÇS. ii. 7. 6.

[3] TB. i. 3. 10. 7; Oldenberg, *Rel. des Veda*², pp. 552, 553.

[4] See Keith, JHS. xxxvi. 108.

[5] More plausibly Hopkins (*Origin of Religion*, pp. 118 ff.) holds that the gift of hair, which is endowed with life, is a mode of strengthening the dead, as is the offering of blood (Cumont, *After-Life in Roman Paganism*, pp. 51 f.).

[6] AGS. ii. 4; ÇGS. iii. 12–14; GGS. iii. 10; iv. 1; MGS. ii. 8, 9; BhGS. ii. 15–17; BGS. ii. 11; PGS. iii. 3; HGS. ii. 13; Oldenberg, *Ind. Stud.* xv. 145 ff.; Winternitz, VOJ. iv. 205 ff.

[7] VOJ. iv. 211; MGS. ii. 9. 1–3.

down, and food placed on it, various forms of rice with sesame, milk rice, and mixed messes of meat and sour milk, and of meal and honey. Then he offers to Soma with the Fathers and to Agni Kavyavāhana, and thereafter gives to the Fathers in the east, and their wives in the west, shares of all except the honey drink: the Mothers receive also Surā and the scum of boiled rice. The offering is, according to Gobhila, made with much elaboration in pits which are dug for the offerings. Three lumps of food are made, and salve and sesame oil are also given to the Fathers and the Brahmans: the three lumps at the end are put to varied uses: the middle one his wife eats, if she wishes sons: the others are put in the water, or on a fire, or given to a cow or to a Brahman to eat.[1] The giving to a cow is of interest as it is also provided as a substitute for the offering of a cow at the appropriate Aṣṭakā that a cow should be given food to eat. It is difficult not to feel that this is a case of a very simple desire to save the life of the cow, and of the parallel desire to secure the favour of the cow. Another mode of evading the offering of a cow at the Aṣṭakās was to fire brushwood, an idea which Oldenberg [2] has suggested may be regarded as an effort to strengthen the sun at the period of the winter solstice, in which very roughly the Aṣṭakās tended to fall.

There is clear evidence that, in addition to the three or four Aṣṭakās, another offering was made in the middle of the rains, perhaps in the month of Prauṣṭhapada: it is stated to be intended to be like the Anvaṣṭakya offering or the Pārvaṇa Çrāddha: there is the same dispute as to the nature of the offering: flesh is necessary if at all possible, but one authority calls it out and out a vegetable Aṣṭakā. This provision and the tendency, as we have seen, to make the offerings simple are due doubtless to the fact that they are obligatory offerings, which could not be omitted and which therefore must often be simple.[3]

§ 3. *The Offerings to the Dead in the Çrauta Ritual*

In the Çrauta ritual a leading place in the cult of the dead is taken by the Piṇḍapitṛyajña,[4] which should be offered after midday of the day of new moon. The sacrifice must take place in the southern fire, which is that appropriate to the Fathers, and the regular procedure of such offerings is followed: the sacred cord is to be worn over the right shoulder, not the left; all movements are from right to left, and recitations and acts take place once, not thrice; while in the normal offering movements are from south and west to north and east, in this offering they are in the reverse order, in so far that they must

[1] GGS. iv. 1. 18 ff.; AGS. ii. 4. 8–10. The use of pits is not regularly provided for, but it is clearly old; cf. Homer, *Od.* x. 527 ff.; xi. 23 ff.; Wissowa, *Rel. der Römer*, pp. 234 ff.; Arbman, *Rudra*, pp. 73 ff. (whose German parallel, however, must be corrected; see Helm, *Altgerm. Rel.* i. 244).

[2] *Rel. des Veda*[1], p. 446.

[3] AGS. ii. 5. 9; ÇGS. iii. 3. 13; HGS. ii. 13. 3; PGS. iii. 3. 13 (Çākāṣṭakā).

[4] ĀpÇS. i. 7–10; KÇS. iv. 1; AÇS. ii. 6, 7; ÇÇS. iv. 3–5; Donner, *Piṇḍapitṛyajña* (Berlin, 1870); Caland, *Todtenverehrung*, pp. 3 ff.; *Todtengebräuche*, pp. 172, 173.

begin in the north and end in the south. In the libations the hand has the outer part turned downwards, the space between the thumb and the index finger is the space which serves for the passage of the oblations. Water is touched after each naming of the Fathers, and the offerer looks south, not north.[1] A pit is dug in the earth, south or west of the southern fire, with a formula to drive away the Asuras and the Rakṣases, and a firebrand from that fire is used as an additional mode of causing fear. The offering begins with two libations of boiled grain or butter to Soma with the Fathers and to Agni Kavyavāhana. Then the Fathers are directly approached : at the beginning, middle, and end of the furrow or pit water is poured, and the Fathers are invited to wash themselves.[2] Then Darbha grass is strewn in the pit, and from the remains of the rice pap and butter are made three lumps of food, or according to some authorities four, which are laid down in the pit on the places on which the water was formerly poured. In each case the Fathers are hailed by name if they are known as the father, grandfather, and great-grandfather of the offerer ; if the father of the offerer is still alive, various varieties of procedure are mentioned.[3] The Fathers are invited to delight themselves : the offerer turns his back—doubtless to avoid too close contact, not that they may be unencumbered by his presence,[4] and remains with averted head, until he is breathless or the food is cold : he then turns round to the lumps, says, 'The Fathers have delighted themselves', and pours water on the lumps, adds salve and some pieces of wool—or if over fifty, hair from his arm or breast—and invites the Fathers to wash, anoint, and clothe[5] themselves. He may also smell, if he desires a son, the remains of the pot. The Fathers are then honoured, and the Adhvaryu, looking south-east, and pushing away the lumps, bids them depart, pays reverence to the southern and the Gārhapatya fires, for the removal of all sin against heaven and earth. If the wife of the offerer wishes a son, then she eats the middle lump as in the domestic ritual : the other two may be thrown into fire or water, or eaten by prescribed persons.

The second great Çrauta offering is that of the Pitṛyajña, or Mahāpitṛyajña,

Other distinctions in offerings to the dead are the use of sesame in place of barley, of folded grass instead of straight stalks for the strew, of black not red victims, the use of old worn-out things, and the turning south with hairy side downwards, not east with hair upwards, of skins, doubtless to attract the spirits to take up their place therein.

[2] Cf. Kleidamos in Athenaios, ix. p. 410.

[3] Weber, *Ind. Stud.* x. 82, n. 1.

[4] This is the Indian view ; Caland, *Altind. Ahnenkult*, p. 180.

[5] Possibly the idea of the Fathers clothed only in their hair (Petavatthu, i. 10. 2) may here be present ; Oldenberg (*Rel. des Veda*², p. 552) insists on taking all offerings of hair as redemptions of self. But it is enough to recognize that a hair offering brings the living into close communion with the dead as is shown in many of the usages. Cf. Wilken, *Rev. Col. Int.* iii. 225 ff. ; iv. 345 ff. ; Frazer, *Magic Art*, i. 28 ff. ; Gruppe, *Griech. Myth.*, p. 913 ; Cook, *Zeus*, i. 23, 24 ; Samter, *Geburt, Hochzeit und Tod*, pp. 179 ff. ; ERE. iv. 431 ff. Cf. above, p. 428, n. 5. Disguise is an inadequate motive.

which takes place on the afternoon of the second day of the Sākamedhas, the third of the four-month offerings.[1] The recipients of offerings are the Fathers with Soma, or Soma with the Fathers, the Fathers who sit on the strew, and the Fathers burned by Agni, while some add Yama with or without the Añgirases. The offerings to the three sets of Fathers are a cake, grains, and the offering of meal pap mixed in the milk of the cow, which has lost its own calf, and which has been given another to bring up. The sacrifice is conducted within a hut erected south of the southern fire, in which is made an altar with its orientation based on the intermediate points, on which the southern fire is placed. The technical terms of the offering for the Fathers *oṁ svadhā, astu svadhā, svadhā namaḥ*, replace those used for the gods. An offering for Kavyavāhana is substituted for the usual Sviṣṭakṛt offering at the end of a sacrifice. Washing water is poured out for the Fathers, and lumps are placed at the south-east and west corners of the altar, but the names, not of the latest but of the more distant Fathers, are uttered, the sixth, fifth, and fourth respectively. On the northern side the offerer wipes his hands and says, 'Here, O Fathers, do ye delight yourselves', and then all leave the hut, placing the sacred cord over the left shoulder, and adore the Āhavanīya fire, and then the Gārhapatya. They then return to the hut, altering the position of their cords: the offerer declares that the Fathers have delighted themselves and offers them reverence in the shape of six payings of homage.

The similarity of the domestic and the Çrauta ritual in the case of the offerings to the dead is most marked, indeed more clearly so than in the case of the offerings to the gods, where the presence of the three fires led the Brahmans to constant elaboration of the rites in which they were interested, until they bore but faint similarity to the rites of the householder. In the case of the offerings to the dead, however, the southern fire is the only fire of consequence: the performances of the sacrificer and the priest in the other fires are purely formal, mainly devices to give them something to do, when the Fathers were presumed in spiritual presence to be eating the offerings from which, it is clear, they were deemed to extract the vital heat.

The very clear differences between the form of the worship of the gods and the reverence paid to the dead[2] indicate beyond possibility of doubt that the attitude of the living to the dead differed in a marked degree from their attitude towards the gods, a fact which, so far as it goes, is doubtless evidence against the view that the worship of the gods sprang from the worship of men who had died. It is clear, however, that before the period of the Rigveda the tendance of the dead, the giving of gifts to them to use in the life to come, had developed so as to present the definite view that the dead were possessed

[1] The parallel of the winter All-souls festival of Europe; Caland, *Todtenverehrung*, pp. 78 ff.

[2] Stengel (*Opferbräuche*, pp. 127 ff.) shows in Greek religion the distinction of worship of the dead, and that of even the chthonian gods; see also Farnell's distinction of tendance and worship, *Hibbert Journal*, 1909, p. 417.

of great powers, and were in many respects as important to their descendants from the point of view of conferring boons as the gods themselves. It is a question of great interest, but one which is insoluble by any evidence available, whether we are to assume that in the Indo-European period the conception of the divine dead had been developed : there is no evidence of any value to show that it had: we may safely assume that, as even in palaeolithic times in Europe, the dead were buried with due honour and gifts made to them, but the development of divinity may lie within the period of development of the several nations.[1]

[1] Cf. MacCulloch, *Rel. of Anc. Celts*, pp. 165 ff.; Farnell, *Greece and Babylon*, pp. 208 ff., where stress is laid on the absence of any ancestor worship, so far as yet is known, in Babylonian religion. Hence the cult (assumed as Indo-European by Moulton, *Early Zoroastrianism*, p. 262; Feist, *Kultur der Indogermanen*, pp. 327, 328) cannot safely be postulated. In the Greek area matters are complicated by the existence (as shown in the Hagia Triada sarkophagos) of a pre-Hellenic reverence of ancestors perhaps already as divine. For other evidence of the far from universal character of the belief see Hopkins, *Origin of Religion*, pp. 80–2; Warde Fowler, *Roman Ideas of Deity*, pp. 22 f.; Cumont, *After-Life in Roman Paganism*, pp. 60 ff.

PART V.—THE PHILOSOPHY OF THE VEDA

CHAPTER 26

THE BEGINNINGS OF VEDIC PHILOSOPHY

THE earliest poetry of India already contains many traces of the essential character of the philosophy of India. In nothing indeed does the continuity of Indian life show itself more strikingly than this: the gods of India change, but the alteration of the higher thought is far less marked.

Philosophy in India shows its beginnings as often in the expression of scepticism: the normal belief in the gods here and there seems to have been questioned, and it is not unnatural that the questioning should have arisen in the case of the most human of the gods, him whom the seers most closely fashioned in their own likeness, the vehement Indra. We have not indeed any certain case of a seer who himself doubted the truth of Indra's greatness:[1] no open attack on the god would, we may be sure, have been allowed to come down to us in the Saṁhitā. But we are distinctly told that there were men who asked, 'Who is Indra, who ever saw him?' or asserted that he did not exist at all.[2] There were, we learn, faithless men, who did not believe in the gods of the Brahmans and did not—perhaps a worse thing—give the priests their fees for sacrifice, men who did not believe in Indra, *anindrāḥ*. The pious poets denounce these men and assert in opposition the truth[3] of the greatness of the god, but it is improbable that their hymns had the effect of convincing the impious.

It might, however, have been expected that in the moral law of Varuṇa, which is the counterpart of the physical law recognized by the religion of the Veda as prevailing in the universe, the Ṛta, and in Varuṇa himself as the great guardian of that law, there might have been found a deity in whom the mind of the sceptic might find peace and satisfaction. The case of Iran proves that the nature of the great Asura could easily give rise to the conception of a moral ruler and a deep ethical view of the world. But, whatever the cause,

[1] Radhakrishnan (*Ind. Phil.* i. 87 f.) finds in RV. viii. 96. 13–15 traces of conflict between Indra and Kṛṣṇa, the prototype of the god of the Gītā.

[2] ii. 12. 5; viii. 103. 3. A fetish of Indra alone of gods is mentioned (RV. iv. 24. 10). Hardy (*Ved.-brahm. Periode*, pp. 175, 176) seeks to show a much wider knowledge as probable (e. g. ii. 33. 9; iii. 4. 4; v. 52. 15), but this is untenable, especially as actual references to idols (PGS. iii. 14. 8) or Caityas (AGS. i. 12. 1) are found only at the very close of the Vedic period; cf. pp. 30 f.

[3] Indra's deeds are often declared true; cf. RV. ii. 15. 1; 22. 1–3; i. 84. 17; vi. 27. 1, 2.

it is beyond possibility of doubt that in India from the first philosophy is intellectual, not moral, in interest and outlook. The conception of Varuṇa, which reaches a high level and is majestic enough both in its cosmical and moral aspect, has attained by the time of the Rigveda its highest development: it falls rapidly into unimportance, until the Brāhmaṇa [1] can assert that an ugly deformed man, who is used as a scapegoat at the final bath of the horse sacrifice, is said to be a symbol of Varuṇa. With this decline of the great and noble god goes hand in hand the decline of the interest of Indian philosophy or religion in morality as such: numerous as are the moral precepts which can be found here and there in Vedic literature, it must be admitted that it is quite impossible to find any real or vital principle of ethics.

The tendency to treat Indra as a doubtful personality is paralleled by the somewhat cynical tone which is certainly shown in speaking of him here and there. In one hymn [2] a number of human occupations and desires is mentioned and the refrain is 'O Soma, flow for Indra': the humorous tone of the poem seems obvious, and the refrain alone may have preserved it from oblivion. Another hymn [3] in which Indra expresses his feelings of exhilaration, as the result of the Soma drink, may be considered to be the natural expression of the poet's mind, in describing the splendid results of the glorious drink; it seems to be very doubtful whether the assumption of covert satire is not more natural and probable. The famous frog hymn [4] also presents difficulties; it would be wrong to deny that it is intended as a rain spell,[5] but there is improbability in the attempt to deny that there is some humour intended in the comparison of the frogs to priests: the idea that the hymn is a mere satire on the Brahmans will not do, for such a hymn would not have been preserved if composed, but a hymn may, like those to Indra, be preserved with incidental satire if it contains a religious or magic basis. The Vṛṣākapi hymn [6] which shows Indra and Indrāṇī in dispute over a male ape may be adduced in this connexion, but in the absence of any surety as to its meaning it is difficult to rely upon it.

The positive side of the tendency of the Rigveda to dissatisfaction with the gods of tradition is to be seen in the assertion of the unity of the gods and of the world. When all is said and done this is the one important contribution of the Rigveda to the philosophy of India. It asserts as a norm for the future development of that thought the effort to grasp more concretely and definitely the unity, which it asserts as a fact, but which it does not justify or explain in detail. The assertion is made with emphasis in a hymn [7] attributed to a quite mythical author Dīrghatamas, who develops at much length the riddle of the

[1] ÇB. xiii. 3. 5. 5; TB. iii. 9. 15. 3.
[2] ix. 112.
[3] RV. x. 119.
[4] vii. 103. Cf. Bender, JAOS. xxxvii. 186 ff.
[5] Bloomfield, JAOS. xvii. 173–9; Oldenberg, *Rel. des Veda*², p. 68; but see Deussen, *Gesch. der Phil.* I. i. 101, 102; Hardy *Ved.-brahm. Periode*, p. 146. Cf. von Schroeder, *Mysterium und Mimus*, pp. 396 ff.; Hauer, *Die Anfänge der Yogapraxis*, pp. 68 ff.
[6] x. 86.
[7] i. 164, with Oldenberg's notes and references.

universe. The form of the long hymn of fifty-two verses is remarkable and characteristic. It is a feature of the Vedic sacrifice that at certain points are found Brahmodyas, discussions about the Brahman, the holy power in the universe. Such theosophical riddles are especially common at the horse sacrifice and are often of simple enough kind: the one priest asks, 'What is it that doth move alone? What is ever born again? What is the remedy of cold? and what the great pile?' The answers here are obvious enough, and are given as the sun, the moon, the fire, and the earth respectively.[1] In this long hymn of Dīrghatamas we have a great series of riddles, but there is to be seen in them some degree of cohesion, the influence of the doctrine of the unity of the world. It is frankly expressed as regards the gods in one verse: 'They call it Indra, Varuṇa, Mitra, Agni, and the winged bird (the sun): the one they call by many names, Agni, Yama, and Mātariçvan.' The same idea appears more expressly still in another verse, where the poet asks the wiser to tell him what supported the six regions of the universe, who was the first unborn being. The hymn is of special further value in that it foreshadows one of the most common ideas of the philosophy of the Veda, the identity of the sacrifice and the world: the seven priests of earth are paralleled by seven in the heaven, the speech on earth by that in the heaven; there are also the earthly and the heavenly metres, the earthly Pravargya rite and the rain from heaven, the animal offering and the bull sacrifice of the gods, the altar and the end of the earth, the sacrifice itself and the navel of the world, and the Soma on earth and the sun and rain.

The idea of unity is more fully developed and explained in a hymn,[2] which with all its defects is the most important in the history of the philosophy of India. It is the hymn of creation, and exhibits not merely the putting of the question of the nature of the universe, but an effort to enter into detail, followed by confession of doubt as to the value of the result achieved. The hymn is specially interesting for this latter point: it is true that it may be censured with justice for the fact that its conceptions are full of vagueness, and crudely seek to unite opposites, but the admission of difficulties is a point which must evoke admiration, not so much for the achievement, but for the thinker who had endeavoured to realize, and had failed to satisfy himself. While much of its content is repeated in the later philosophy, its spirit of doubt is wholly alien to the classical philosophical systems of India.

The poem commences with an assertion: in the beginning there was neither being nor not-being:[3] there was no atmosphere nor sky: the question is asked what covering there was, and was there a fathomless abyss of the waters. There was neither death nor immortality, nor night nor day. There was nothing else in the world save the one which breathed, but without wind,

[1] VS. xxiii. 9 and 10. See Haug, *Vedische Räthselfragen und Räthselsprüche* (1875); Ludwig, RV. iii. 390 ff.; Bloomfield, JAOS. xv. 172; JB. ii. 158.

[2] x. 129: the most often translated hymn of the RV. Cf. Whitney, JAOS. xi. p. cxi; ÇB. x. 5. 3. 1; JB. iii. 359 f. That it is a Brahmodya is not probable

[3] So Oldenberg; contrast Geldner, *Zur Kosmogonie des RV.*, p. 16.

of its own power. There was, however, darkness, and a moving ocean without light: through the might of fervour, Tapas, was born a living force enveloped in a shell. Then there developed desire, Kāma, the first seed of mind: the sages found the root of not-being in being, searching for it in the heart. Thus far the first four verses: the fifth is a puzzle: it may be referred to the sages who drove a division through the universe and distinguished the upper and the lower, the world of nature above, the principle of nature below: but this version is wholly problematical. The next two verses end with a deep expression of doubt: the gods are later than the creation and cannot know of its origin: whether the creation was made by itself or not, the overseer of it in the highest space of heaven he knows of it, or perhaps he knows not.

The hymn is clearly difficult to understand: the part of the seers, which appears merely as a statement of what their reflections have arrived at, is even understood by Bloomfield [1] to be a cosmical action, indicating that they took part in the creation of the universe. This seems, however, unnatural and strained, but not more so than the interpretation of verse 5 adopted by Deussen,[2] which would make it into an assertion that the sages were able to discriminate between the thing in itself and the phenomenal world, between *natura naturans* and *natura naturata*. What is clear is that there is conceived as first existing one thing, which is described as breathing without wind,[3] an effort to express a primitive nature different in essence from anything known to the priest, conceived perhaps metaphorically only as a dark ocean or chaos. In this through Tapas, which here must rather be cosmic than refer to the activity of seers or other human powers, by inward fervour, springs up the being enveloped in a shell, which in the later conception is the golden world egg. The next step in development is the appearance of desire, unless that it is to be taken as born of mind, when it is described as the first seed of mind. If so, the mind must be deemed to be an attribute of the one which develops in the shell, whence springs desire: in the alternative the phrase may be taken as the source which produces mind, and desire, unconscious will, may be held to produce conscious will or mind. The latter view, however, is unnatural in point of language and has the additional disadvantage that in the Taittirīya Āraṇyaka [4] we already find that mind is given as prior to desire in a passage which is based on the hymn. Nor can we hold—and this is much more important—that Kāma was conceived as unconscious will: it is rather the natural expression for conscious desire, which would rise from the existence of mind as a substratum. The later philosophy makes the knowledge of desires depend on the existence of mind, and this idea may be

[1] *Rel. of Veda*, p. 237. Cf. the claims of the Druids.

[2] *Gesch. der Phil.* I. i. 124, 125. He compares the Eros of Hesiod (*Theog.* 120) and Parmenides (Aristotle, *Met.* 984 b 25).

[3] To compare (Radhakrishnan, *Ind. Phil.* i. 101) Aristotle's deity, the unmoved mover, is to falsify entirely primitive thought.

[4] i. 23. 1.

foreshadowed here, where mind is made a cosmic *prius* of desire.[1] Beyond this the poet does not go: he ends with the suggestion of a supreme deity as distinct from the gods who are created, and ends with a doubt whether such a deity has power of knowledge, that is, whether it has consciousness at all. We cannot, therefore, really say whether or not the first cause of the world is deemed a conscious entity at all: the assertion that it was not-being, and yet not not-being, which is in words a little inconsistent with the assertion that the sages found the root of being in not-being, searching in the heart, is in effect an assertion that it was a peculiar sort of being, different from ordinary being. The reference to the heart, however, as the place of search reminds us that the heart even in the Rigveda seems the abode of mind,[2] and suggests that in the ultimate issue the final entity might be deemed to be possessed of mind, for consciousness, without an object, is the nature in the Vedānta of the Brahman and even of Puruṣa in the Sāṁkhya.

This hymn is the finest effort of the imagination of the Vedic poet, and nothing else equals it. The conceptions of unity, of fervour as the cause of development, of the power in the shell, of the primeval chaos of waters, are all familiar in the Brāhmaṇas and on the whole degraded in their development. In the Rigveda itself the other efforts to attain the conception of the unity of the universe are directed in the main to setting up personal deities, who are credited with the creation and government of the whole of the universe. Of these the most famous and enduring is Prajāpati.[3] He it is who later at least is the god who is first born, the golden germ, Hiraṇyagarbha, who creates the whole universe, who gives life, whose commands the gods obey, whose shadow is death and immortality, who is lord of man and beast, of the mountain and the sea. Thus in the one god are summed up the duties of creator, of ruler, and preserver of the universe.

In the Brāhmaṇas Prajāpati is eternally identified with the year, the all-creator with the time in which he exercises his eternal process of creation, but this is not stated in the Rigveda, unless in a short hymn[4] we are to find the conception of Prajāpati underlying the year. There fervour, Tapas, is made the starting-point of all: from it come order, Ṛta, and truth, the night, and the primeval ocean: from the ocean was born the year which rules over all, and as creator produces the sun and the moon, the heaven and the earth, the atmosphere and the light of the sun. The parallel to Prajāpati is close, but the identity is not to be certainly established.

Viçvakarman, 'all-maker', is another synonym of Prajāpati, and has two hymns[5] of the tenth book devoted to his honour: they add, however, comparatively little to our appreciation of the beginnings of Vedic thought: but we find here the tendency which is found in Indian conceptions to insist that

[1] In the Sāṁkhya it is from Buddhi 'intellect' that Ahaṁkāra, the principle of individuality which expresses itself in conscious will, springs.

[2] Above, Part IV, Chap. 23, § 1.

[3] x. 121.

[4] RV. x. 190; Deussen, *Gesch. der Phil.* I. i. 134.

[5] RV. x. 81 and 82.

the creator, who is self-created, is not merely the material cause, but also the efficient cause of the world. The process, therefore, by which the world emerges from the unity at its base assumes a decidedly curious aspect: there is first the unity, which may be conceived as a creator god: then, derived from it, the waters or other primeval substance: then the god appears in the waters as a spirit to bring about the development of the universe. This triad of first principle, primitive matter, and the first-born of creation, is carried out mythologically in an interesting hymn to Brahmaṇaspati,[1] in which we learn of Dakṣa as father of Aditi and also her son, an absurdity in which the philosophic basis is clearly that of the conception of the three stages of creation.

Brahmaṇaspati is of interest, since his personality as the god of prayer is closely connected with the mighty power of the prayer to secure the ends of man. This idea finds expression also in the hymn[2] which celebrates Vāc, speech, as the supporter of the world, as the companion of the gods, and the foundation of religious activity and all its advantages: she appears as impelling the father in the beginning of things and again as being born in the waters. The idea which has, of course, long ago been compared by Weber with the Greek Logos, is ingenious: the will of the creator is thus considered as expressed in speech, but the idea is merely a secondary and unimportant one in the Rigveda, and even later is never destined to be developed in much detail, the weight being laid on the Brahman, at once the prayer and the holy power in the universe.

Already in the hymn to Viçvakarman there appears the desire to parallel the creation of the universe with a sacrifice. This idea is carried to its fullest extent in the Puruṣasūkta of the Rigveda,[3] one of its latest hymns, which has often already been mentioned. The first part of the hymn is a strong expression that the Puruṣa is the universe: the whole of this universe is but a quarter of him, three quarters are immortal; he has a thousand heads, eyes, and feet, and extends ten digits beyond the universe. In comparison with the normal gods he represents the whole of the world, and not one fraction only. The idea of the three stages appears here also: the Virāj springs from Puruṣa, and Puruṣa again from the Virāj, which must denote the waters in their cosmic aspect. The next part of the poem insists that the creation of the universe took the form of a sacrifice at which were present the gods, who could not logically have existed: the offering was a holocaust; from the juice of the burning of the offering sprang the speckled ghee, and from it are derived the animals of the air, the house, and the wild; all the Vedas, Ṛc, Sāman, and Yajus, are assigned to his burning, and further the animals with double incisors and those with a single set. Then by change of idea the four castes[4]

[1] RV. x. 72.

[2] RV. x. 125; cf. 71; Weber, *Ind. Stud.* ix. 473–80; Brunnhofer, *Arische Urzeit*, pp. 390–4.

[3] x. 90; Deussen, *Gesch. der Phil.* I. i. 150 ff.

[4] First here mentioned, one of many proofs of the late nature of the hymn; cf. Macdonell and Keith, *Vedic Index*, ii. 248.

are derived from the cutting up of the body, and again by a further change the gods and the parts of the world are derived from him : the eye gives the sun, the breath the wind, the mind the moon, perhaps because of its clear light which might be compared with mind, the head the heaven, the feet the earth, and the navel the regions between. Time is explained as connected with the means of sacrifice : the rains were the butter, the summer the kindling wood, the autumn the gifts to the priests. The idea is crude and rough and so badly suited to the connexion with its context, that it is difficult not to believe that we have here the adaptation to the needs of a pantheistic view of a primitive and rude legend of the primeval giant, whence the world was born, an idea found in a different form in Norse mythology.[1]

[1] Golther, *German. Myth.*, pp. 513 ff. Cf. the construction by Marduk of the universe from Tiāmat's limbs; Farnell, *Greece and Babylon*, p. 182; above, p. 81.

CHAPTER 27

THE THEOSOPHY OF THE BRĀHMAṆAS

§ 1. *The General Character of the Brāhmaṇa Philosophy*

THE value of the Brāhmaṇas as sources of philosophy is difficult to determine with any accuracy. They are works in which the imagination of successive generations of priests has been allowed to run riot: there is no moderation in their conception, and no great Brāhmaṇa is, as far as can be judged, the production of a single mind.[1] The one great merit of Greek philosophy, the appearance of clear-cut ideas expressed in works of individual authorship, is wholly wanting for us in the Brāhmaṇas, and the question constantly obtrudes itself to what extent we can believe that the priests by whom these texts were composed and handed down held the views which they wrote down. In many cases it may be taken that they did not; the works abound in their explanations of rites with all sorts of absurdities, which we need not accuse the priests of being so foolish as not to recognize as absurdities; but the question of the dividing line between profoundity and absurdity presents itself with the greatest frequency.

It is, however, another question whether we can acquiesce in the theory of Deussen [2] that the Brāhmaṇas in various places are conscious of higher philosophical views, which they ignore and turn to ritual purposes. The proofs which he adduces of his theory are far from carrying conviction. In his view the account of the Taittirīya Brāhmaṇa [3] of the origin of the Naciketas fire is really posterior in order of conception to the account in the Kaṭha Upaniṣad. It is there told that Vājaçravasa made an offering, at which he gave to the priests all his goods, retaining, however, his son, Naciketas, as the ritual prescribes; the boy, however, insisted that he should also be given,[4] and his father in just irritation at his persistence gave him to death. The young man goes, in the true spirit of fairy tale, to the house of Yama, who

[1] ÇB. xi. and i. are obviously instances of a later and more comprehensive, and an earlier and more naïve, treatment of the same topic. For the strata in AB. see Keith, HOS. xxv. 40 ff. The Agnicayana rites and speculations are clearly later than most other portions of the ritual discussions; cf. Oldenberg, GN. 1917, p. 16.

[2] *Gesch. der Phil.* I. i. 172–80. Oltramare (*L'histoire des idées théosophiques*, i. 127 ff.) tacitly rejects this view.

[3] iii. 11. 8.

[4] No question of the sacrifice of Naciketas arises; it is all a piece of imagination, parallel to the visit of Bhṛgu to the other world, recounted in the Çatapatha Brāhmaṇa (xi. 6. 1) and the Jaiminīya Brāhmaṇa, i. 42–4 (JAOS. xv. 234 ff.). Barua's view (*Prebuddh. Ind. Phil.*, p. 265), that the Naciketas legend represents the philosophy of the Gotamakas mentioned in the Añguttara, is clearly quite without plausibility.

is away, and who, therefore, for three nights fails in the important duty of the due reception of guests. He must, therefore, on his return make atonement, and he gives the lad three boons. Naciketas chooses the kind reception of him by his father on his return, the imperishableness of his due reward for his sacrifices and gifts to the priests,[1] and the freedom from repeated death—not in this world, in all probability. In the two latter cases the god teaches the boy the way of piling the Naciketas fire. To this Deussen takes exception, and thinks that originally the means to the third wish must have been the knowledge of the eternal redemption from the bonds of death, and he holds, therefore, that in the Brāhmaṇa we have the expression of a polemical attitude to the more philosophical doctrine. The idea appears, however, to be one wholly unjustifiable. The aim of the ritual is simply to assert the value of this fire, and the repetition of the fire as the means of knowledge of the end desired is perfectly natural and simple. That the boy asked for the grant of final release is nowhere hinted at : what he fears, according to the language used, is simply that, as is often threatened in the later Brāhmaṇas, he may fall in due course, even in the next world, under the control of death.

Nor is there any happier result to be seen in the second case adduced by Deussen. It is of course later in the Upaniṣads the doctrine that the whole essence of man is contained in the Ātman, 'self', that the essence of the world is also an Ātman, and that the two are identical. This idea he finds expressed in a sentence of the Taittirīya Brāhmaṇa,[2] where it is said that the various gods, the plants, and trees are in various parts of man, Indra in his strength, Parjanya in his head, the lord, that is Rudra-Çiva, in his anger, the Ātman in his Ātman, the Ātman in his heart, the heart in him, he in the immortal, the immortal in the Brahman. In this passage he thinks that the assertion of the identity of the Ātman is really a reference to the identity of the self of man and of the universe, an assertion of the fundamental view of the Upaniṣads wrapped up with a different view. The answer to this is clearly that the passage cannot be pressed to yield so much : it is possible that it simply has the sense that the body of the world is in the body of man, but it is probably merely a vague identification of self with self, without any profound meaning being either felt, or, though felt, hidden. The conscious identification of the universal spirit and the individual is a very different thing from such a phrase as that in question, and the theory that the phrase indicates a knowledge, but a degradation, of the higher truth, is too far-fetched.

The point is of importance, since the Vedic tradition makes a clear distinction between Brāhmaṇas and Upaniṣads, though it attaches as we have seen the Upaniṣads to Brāhmaṇas. The distinction corresponds, we may fairly say, in the main to a change of time and still more to a change of view. The Upaniṣads hold in some degree at least the doctrine of transmigration, and, though not in a developed condition, the pessimism which follows on it : these views are not those of the Brāhmaṇas, which, taken all in all, know not

[1] Cf. JB. ii. 53 ; KB. vii. 4.

[2] iii. 10. 8.

transmigration, have no conception of pessimism, and therefore seek no release from the toils of life, for which in reality there is no ending. These are fundamental distinctions, and they give an essentially different aspect to the speculations of the Brāhmaṇas as compared with those of the Upaniṣads. A further distinction lies in the fact that the Brāhmaṇas are essentially connected with the doctrine of the sacrifice. The sacrifice clearly occupied the minds of the priests to the practical exclusion of all else, and their theories were in large measure devoted to the consideration of its relation to the universe, to the gods, and to men.[1] In the Upaniṣads this is not the case; the sacrifice is still here and there the subject of speculation, but the speculation is no longer based on the view that the sacrifice is all in all. Hence it is that so little progress can be seen in the Brāhmaṇas towards the development of a real philosophy. The Rigveda carries us nearly as far as anything excogitated in this period.

The conception of order is one which is wholly strange to the Brāhmaṇas, and any treatment of the philosophy implied and contained in them must neglect the divisions of these texts, which in the main follow merely the order of the rites performed in the sacrificial ritual. The most important of these conceptions from the point of view of philosophy are (1) the endeavour to state the nature of the highest principle of the universe, (2) the theory of the sacrifice, and (3) the nature of truth and right. On all of these topics there is available much material, but the sameness of the ideas is obvious through a multitude of detailed differences.

§ 2. *The Highest Principle of the Universe*

In the period of the Brāhmaṇas the god Prajāpati occupies without doubt or question the position of the creator god, the supreme god of the world. The commencement of legend after legend proclaims his creative activity, often figured under the form of the practising of fervour, a reminder of the cosmic heat, whence came forth the power enclosed in the shell according to the view of the hymn of creation.[2] The world egg appears as producing the heaven and the earth from its two parts, and, as Hiraṇyagarbha, it is the form of Prajāpati, in which he proceeds to immediate creation of living beings of all kinds, and the ordering of the universe. These tales, of which there is no end, often tell us that Prajāpati felt at the end of his efforts that he was empty, and had to be filled up again, always by some ritual process. The details of these stupid myths are wholly unimportant: it is enough to note that he is constantly the creator, the ruler, and the preserver of the world and is accepted by every Brāhmaṇa of the period as being the lord of the world: he is, it may be added, without any ethical importance: the conception of him is purely intellectual, that of the unity of the universe, and the choosing

[1] This is the *bandhu* investigated, not the connexion between the rites and the formulae as formerly held by Winternitz (*Gesch. d. ind. Litt.* i. 164, n. 3; see iii. 613). See Oldenberg, *Die Weltanschauung der Brāhmanatexte*, p. 5.

[2] RV. x. 129. Cf. Lévi, *La doctrine du sacrifice*, pp. 18 ff.

of Prajāpati as the symbol of this unity is one of the most striking proofs of the great influence of the Rigveda upon the period of the Brāhmaṇas.

Of Prajāpati's activities the most interesting are his relation as creator to the gods, to the Asuras, whose connexion is with the darkness and cunning, and to men. He is, however, much more than the mere universe: he is the unmeasured, the unexpressed, as opposed to the measured and the expressed in nature: he is the seventeenth beside the sixteen elements of the psychic organs: the thirty-fourth above the thirty-three gods. He is universal peace, the decider of disputes among the gods; he gives Indra his victorious prowess and his crown of victory. He is devoid of sorrow, for there is no sorrow in heaven. He is the lord of the three worlds, he sits above them and sees in himself the seed of creation, and the gods proceed from his mouth, the Asuras from his descending breath, that of nutrition.

It is, however, clear that in Prajāpati the Brāhmaṇas do not find complete satisfaction for their view of the construction of the universe. The Atharvaveda, which in these matters must be ranked with the Brāhmaṇas, in its version of the great hymn of the Rigveda, which, as later expanded,[1] mentions him as all-creator, leaves out the last line giving his name and the Brāhmaṇa of that Veda, which is certainly late, replaces him by the Brahman and Atharvan.[2] In the Brāhmaṇas, therefore, we find efforts made to arise to a principle above and beyond him: in the Rigveda he produced from himself—the idea of world creation is always in the Vedic literature regarded in the light of the sending out of something already there rather than of mere bringing into being—the waters, and then entered them in the form of Hiraṇyagarbha, the golden germ. In the Taittirīya Saṁhitā,[3] we find in the spirit of the hymn of creation the waters treated in two places as the *prius*, and Prajāpati as arising as wind on them, and the Çatapatha Brāhmaṇa[4] goes one step farther in attributing to the waters as Prajāpati's predecessors as first in order the act of fervour, which is primarily his activity in creation. A farther step is taken in the Taittirīya Āraṇyaka,[5] in which the waters come first, then Prajāpati, in whose mind desire arises[6] and who practises fervour; then his body he throws off: from the sap is born the tortoise, who is Puruṣa, who, however, asserts his priority to Prajāpati himself, and from the flesh the seer Aruṇaketu, to whom further creative activity is assigned. Yet another step is reached in the Çatapatha Brāhmaṇa,[7] where the first thing is stated to be not-being, then arises Prajāpati, who is the same as Puruṣa, and then the Brahman, the holy science, the threefold Veda, with which he enters the waters as a creative principle. Thus sprang up the world egg, whence came forth first the

[1] Oldenberg, *Weltanschauung der Brāhmaṇatexte*, p. 28, n. 2, against Oltramare, *L'histoire des idées théosophiques*, i. 25, n. 1.

[2] AV. iv. 2; GB. i. 1, explaining RV. x. 121.

[3] v. 6. 4. 2; vii. 1. 5. 1.

[4] xi. 1. 6. 1; xiv. 8. 6. 1 (BAU. v. 5. 1), where the waters produce the real (*satya*), and it, as the Brahman, Prajāpati, as in xi. 1. 6, the golden egg or the waters produces him.

[5] i. 23.

[6] This is the view here taken of RV. x. 129.4.

[7] ÇB. vi. 1. 1.

Brahman itself, and then Prajāpati in the form of Agni. But in another account [1] the priority of the Brahman over Prajāpati is made absolute, not merely empirical: the first entity is not-being, then springs into life mind, i.e. the Brahman, and then Prajāpati. Later still the Brahman produces Prajāpati, but without face or sight; then it enters him, as breath, and makes him mortal, to arise as a generator of beings.

There is nothing particularly valuable or serious in these attempts, though they merit mention. More interesting are efforts to explain the nature of Prajāpati, and to dispose thus of him. The position of Prajāpati as decider of disputes leads to the view that he intervenes in the great dispute of the mind and speech as to which should be given the higher rank, a dispute settled by Prajāpati in favour of mind.[2] The connexion of speech and mind [3] as elements in Prajāpati himself is expressed by the figure of union between the two within him, and either is occasionally made into the final entity of the world: thus mind is identified with Brahman, with Prajāpati, and even with the first principle, which is neither being nor not-being, of the hymn of creation.[4] Similarly Vāc, 'speech', is identified with Prajāpati, or even placed above Prājapati, identified with Viçvakarman, with the whole world, and with Indra.[5] These identifications are, however, despite their interest, of no importance for Indian philosophy: the will or the intellect as such does not in fact become the essential reality of any Indian orthodox philosophy. Prajāpati is also the sacrifice,[6] and sacrifices himself to the gods, for, as we have seen, the order of the world is constantly compared with the sacrifice, and Puruṣa by being sacrificed creates the universe: he is also the year,[7] or both,[8] and these identifications are of great importance in connexion with the theory of sacrifice to which we shall return.

In the Atharvaveda [9] we find several further efforts to substitute for Prajāpati new names and ideas. In this effort it is certainly difficult to resist the view that the Atharvaveda is out of the main stream of Vedic development: the hymns seem like deliberate efforts to convert into a kind of poetry the philosophical ideas of the Brāhmaṇa period without any real inspiration of any sort. The abstractions Kāla, 'time',[10] and Rohita,[11] 'the ruddy one', probably the sun as the more concrete expression of time, are identified with Prajāpati and praised as all-creating: the ox [12] and the cow, Vaçā,[13] are also identified with the god, and may to some extent be compared with the view of the Brāhmaṇas, that the sacrifice is Prajāpati. But the

[1] TB. ii. 2. 9; JUB. iii. 38. 1 ff.
[2] ÇB. i. 4. 5. 8–11.
[3] ÇB. vi. 1. 2. 7; PB. vii. 6.
[4] TB. ii. 2. 9; KB. xxvi. 3; ÇB. x. 5. 3. 1.
[5] PB. xx. 14. 2; KS. vii. 5; ÇB. v. 1. 3. 11; viii. 1. 2. 9; xi. 1. 6. 18.
[6] ÇB. i. 5. 1. 16; 6. 3. 5, &c.; PB. xiii. 11. 18; vii. 2. 1 f.
[7] ÇB. i. 1. 1. 13; 5. 2. 17, &c.
[8] KB. vi. 15.
[9] Cf. M. Lindenau on ii. 1, ZII. i. 83 ff.
[10] AV. xix. 53, 54.
[11] AV. xiii. 1. 3; TB. ii. 5, 2; Henry, *Les Hymnes Rohitas* (Paris, 1891); Bloomfield, AJP. xii. 430 ff.; Lindenau, ZII. i. 48, n. 2.
[12] AV. iv. 11.
[13] AV. x. 10.

Atharvaveda goes farther and in its pseudo-theosophy exalts many other things to the rank of supreme powers, the ladles, the Darbha grass amulet, the porridge cooked for the priest, the bull offered in the sacrifice, the deity Anumati, and possibly others.[1] In two cases a deeper meaning has been seen by Deussen,[2] who finds in the Skambha hymns [3] an effort to find a principle above Prajāpati which supports the whole universe, and in the Ucchiṣṭa [4] hymn, a glorification of 'what is left over', not, as is normally believed, from the offering, but after all that is empirical has been abstracted from the universe, an idea which he thinks can possibly be reconciled with the normal view by remembrance of the fact that Puruṣa in the sacrifice hymn is said to be only a quarter in the universe, the other three-quarters being beyond it. But it is impossible to take this speculation seriously, and the Skambha hymn has no great claim to be more than a poor piece of theosophical juggling with words, save in so far as it seems to identify Skambha with the Brahman, and as it served as a suggestion for the Muṇḍaka Upaniṣad.[5]

But beside these ideas there is to be found a much more fruitful source of philosophy, the creation of the conception of the Brahman as a cosmic principle. The origin of the meaning of Brahman is uncertain: it is interpreted by the Vedānta school, absurdly, as the absolute from *vṛh*, 'twist', 'tear away'; the view of Max Müller [6] is that it denotes what grows, from *vṛh* in the sense of 'grow', that which expresses itself in speech or in nature as force. The view of Deussen [7] is that it is the human will in its striving to the divine, when the individual in prayer returns to the timeless, spaceless, individualless self of his, which is God. These senses are somewhat elaborate, and render it difficult to think that the word really had any such meaning: neither for the views of Max Müller nor for that of Deussen is there any support in the actual use of the word in the Rigveda. There at any rate the word naturally and normally means prayer, but there are further developments: it can mean spell, for the prayer may be a spell,[8] and not real prayer,

[1] AV. xviii. 4. 5; xix. 32. 9; ix. 4; iv. 35; vii. 20.

[2] *Gesch. der Phil.* I. i. 305 ff.

[3] AV. x. 7, 8. Hauer (*Die Anfänge der Yogapraxis im alten Indien*, pp. 115 f.) sees in this a personification of the ascetic who wins ecstasy by Tapas. For the mystic sense of x. 7. 11, see Lindenau and Geldner, ZII. i. 48 f.

[4] AV. xi. 7.

[5] Hertel's assertion (*Muṇḍaka Upaniṣad*, pp. 45 ff.) that in AV. x. 7. 32 ff. *bráhman* is used as masculine, is not probable, nor is it certain that *bráhman* is the product of Skambha, though that may be the sense of verse 17, as opposed to the identification in 32–4.

[6] *Six Systems of Indian Philosophy*, pp. 68 ff.

[7] *Op. cit.*, pp. 240 ff. For Oldenberg's latest view see GN. 1916, pp. 715 ff.; for connexion with Irish *bricht*, Osthoff, BB. xxiv. 113 ff.; cf. Scandinavian *brag*, Carnoy, *Les Indo-Européens*, p. 236. Hertel's criticism (IF. xli. 205) that the etymology is based on a false interpretation of the sense of Brahman, is itself based on his quite incorrect view of Brahman (see below).

[8] Bloomfield (*Rel. of Veda*, p. 273) insists on the secondary character of this sense and rejects the magic fluid idea of Oldenberg. Oltramare (*L'histoire des idées théosophiques*, i. 12 ff.) sees in it the force passing from men to the

and it often means holy speech and the holy writ, the three-fold Veda. It is not necessary to trace to the original sense of Brahman the fact that the Vedic poet regards himself often as inspired: we cannot really think it probable, and certainly no argument had yet been adduced to show, that the prayer was felt to be the voice of God speaking in the prayer. But in many passages it seems as if Brahman must be taken rather as holy power than as prayer or holy rite: the gods are said to discuss the Brahman, and, when the greatness of the Brahman is celebrated, it is clear that more than the mere word may be intended. But the growth of the idea of Brahman as a suitable expression for the absolute must have been greatly furthered by the extraordinary value attached to the prayer and to the spell. The prayer rapidly passes over to the lower rank: in one late hymn of the Rigveda [1] a prayer is offered that Agni should in union with the Brahman drive away disease. The spell appears repeatedly by itself in the Atharvaveda as a power to destroy evil of all kinds, and the Brahman is actually set over against the three Vedas as a power of equal force.[2] It is a very easy step from the conception of the Brahman as the prayer, which brings into operation the activity of the gods, or as the spell which is the cause of results aimed at by men, and from the conception of the whole body of such spells and prayers, to develop the use of the term to cover the idea of holy power generally, and this rendering is applicable in many passages of the Brāhmaṇas, where the idea of holy writ is too vague and the idea of the absolute is too elaborate.

A further element should doubtless be allowed for in the process of the evolution of the use of the term Brahman. Oldenberg,[3] indeed, has denied that in the Veda there exists either the idea or the word for a supernatural power pervading the universe, akin to that power which in Melanesia is denoted by *mana*, among the Hurons by *orenda*, and variously in other parts of the world.[4] It seems, however, unlikely that no such general idea should have appealed to the intellect of the Indians. If we accept, as we should, the view that individual powers are older in conception than manifestations of a universal power, still it seems natural to suppose that India developed the conception of a power common to the various gods, just as there was admitted the unity of the gods even by the time of certain Rigvedic hymns. This power, we may assume, was naturally denoted by the term Brahman, as a result of the extraordinary importance attached by priests to the prayers and spells which secured them their means of livelihood, and which served to propitiate the gods or to secure ends desired by their patrons or themselves. Other terms such as Māyā, which served in part to denote a power similar to *mana*, failed

gods, or *vice versa*, in religious life; cf. Güntert, *Der arische Weltkönig*, pp. 222 ff.

[1] RV. x. 162.

[2] VS. xi. 2; ÇB. v. 2. 4. 18.

[3] *Weltanschauung der Brāhmaṇatexte*, pp. 49 f.

[4] Cf. Marett, *Archiv für Rel.* xii. 186 ff.; Preuss, *ibid.* xiii. 427 ff.; Söderblom, *ibid.* xvii. 1 ff.; Strauss, *Bṛhaspati im Ṛgveda*, p. 20; Hubert and Mauss, *Année sociol.*, 1902–3, pp. 108 ff.; Söderblom-Stube, *Das Werden des Gottesglaubens*, pp. 54 ff.

to be widely generalized. Asu possibly served the same purpose, if we believe the view of Güntert that Asura denotes primarily and properly the possessor of *mana*.[1]

A very different view of the nature of the Brahman is presented by Hertel,[2] who asserts that the misinterpretation of the term is one of the many fatal errors of Vedic scholarship, shared alike by the Indian and the western interpreters. The essential work of Indian philosophers of the Upaniṣad period was to depersonalize the old gods, and to show that in the macrocosm and the microcosm alike there existed nothing save nature powers and processes, which required no explanation by the assumption of divinities. The Kṣatriyas who were the sources of the doctrine of the Upaniṣads rejected the doctrine of personal deities, and also the theory that man's lot depended on his deeds, and constructed in lieu a materialistic, monistic, science of nature, which was at once morally indifferent and in essence atheistic. The priests decided to render innocuous this doctrine by amalgamating it with their own as an esoteric system. On this view the Brahman is that which fills all beings, stimulates the sense organs, penetrates the whole world, and encircles the universe. Its true nature is revealed in those passages of the Upaniṣads which describe the Brahman as qualified, the unqualified Brahman being manifestly the product of further refinement of speculative thought. Now in certain passages [3] we find that the Brahman is the bodily warmth in man, which is identified with his self, Ātman, and also with the cosmic light or fire (*tejas* or *jyotis*). These passages are to be taken perfectly literally, and this version throws an important light on the Indian ascetic, Tāpasa, who is a very different person from the Christian ascetic. The latter practises chastity and flees from desires, because these are the work of the devil, and he seeks to kill carnal longings. The Tāpasa inflicts even more serious penances on himself and remains celibate, merely to increase the vital fire within him, and fit himself for the abundance of sexual delight which Indian opinion as early as the Atharvaveda [4] and even in the Upaniṣads [5] assures him. The fire, however, which composes the self of the individual, is essentially bound up with the power of thought.[6] The cosmic Brahman, on the other hand, is fire (*jyotis*) in no metaphorical sense;[7] the *brahmaṇaḥ parimaraḥ* of the Aitareya Brāhmaṇa [8] really means that all comes from fire and is resolved into it again. Now the connexion of the individual and the cosmic fire is simple;[9] the rays of the sun bring fire into the heart of the individual, and at death the fire departs from

[1] See *Der arische Weltkönig*, pp. 98 ff., 229 ff.

[2] IF. xli (1923), 185 ff.

[3] BAU. iv. 3. 1 ff.; 4. 1 ff.; CU. iii. 13. 8; Muṇḍ. iii. 1. 5; seed is the concentrated *tejas*, AU. ii. 1.

[4] iv. 34. 2; cf. Lanman, HOS. vii. 206; RV. ix. 113. 11 (cf. TB. ii. 4. 6. 5 f.; Muir, OST. v. 307, n. 462).

[5] Kauṣ. iii. 5 ff.; TU. iii. 6. 1; x. 3.

[6] BAU. iv. 3. 7; CU. iii. 14. 2.

[7] BAU. iv. 4. 16 f.; CU. viii. 3. 4; 4. 2; 12. 2 f.; Muṇḍ. ii. 2. 8; Īçā 8; the sun is the Brahman, CU. iii. 19. 1.

[8] viii. 28; cf. Kauṣ. ii. 12. The interpretation is clearly impossible.

[9] CU. iii. 13. 7 f.; v. 3 (five fire-doctrine); viii. 6. 1 ff.

him back to the sun whence it came, or rather to the heaven of fire, which lies above the earth and of which the sun and the moon are doors pierced in it. The idea of this path of light is older than the Upaniṣads, for it occurs in verses cited in the Bṛhadāraṇyaka Upaniṣad,[1] and the Atharvaveda [2] knows the threads of which life is woven and calls this knowledge the great Brāhmaṇa, that is the great secret of the Brahman. Prior to the Upaniṣads we find the conception in a personal shape, Bṛhaspati, the lord of the heaven of light, the peer of Zeus Pater, of Jupiter, of the German war god, a form of Dyaus himself. It is for this that he appears in the Rigveda as the highest of gods, their father and ruler, guardian of the Ṛta, leader of men, enemy of all that is false, an Indian parallel to Ahura Mazdāh. Significant is his connexion with Narāçaṅsa, for in the Avesta Nairyosaṅha is not merely the envoy of Ahura Mazdāh, but also the fire which burns in the kings and secures them in their power. Bṛhaspati as lord of the heaven is responsible for breaking through its stone boundary to set the sun as a source of the streaming forth of its light; moreover he has placed the stars there, and released through the apertures the waters amid the noise of his thunders.[3] Significant is the assertion that he encompasses or is present in all (*vibhu*), the Rigveda [4] thus saying of the personal deity what the Upaniṣads assert of the depersonalized Brahman.

The obvious question why the term Brahman is so regularly used of prayer in the Rigveda is answered by the theory that the cause is used for the effect, and similarly the use of *ṛc* and *dhī*, *dhīti*, and *dīdhiti* is explained. Moreover a suitable etymology is found in the comparison with the Greek φλέγω and Latin *flagro*, and the Brahmacārin of the Atharvaveda [5] is explained as one who concentrates in himself the fire from which all conditions and actions in the world are derived. The fact that Bṛhaspati appears in the Rigveda already as a moon god, which Hertel accepts from Hillebrandt,[6] is explained as due to the gradual fading out of the idea of the sun and moon as merely doors to heaven and the abode of the Soma, the rain, and the Fathers, and the emergence of the conception of the moon as actually the home of these beings.

Ingenious as is the theory, it is clear that it cannot claim acceptance as probable. The idea that fire pervades and constitutes the essence of the universe is based on the interpretation given to the Brahman; independent evidence is wholly lacking; Hertel cites only an Atharvan [7] passage in which it is stated that fire exists in the earth, the plants, the waters, stones, men, cattle, and horses, and an Avestan reference [8] to six fires which the Pahlavi tradition interprets as the fire in kings, the temple fire, and that of everyday

[1] iv. 4. 8 ff.; cf. CU. viii. 6. 1.
[2] x. 8. 37.
[3] Cf. Part II, Chap. 10, § 2.
[4] ii. 24. 11.
[5] xi. 5. 24; cf. V. Henry, *Les Livres X, XI et XII de l'Atharva-Veda*, pp. viii ff.
[6] *Ved. Myth.* i. 404 ff.; iii. 450.
[7] xii. 1. 19 ff.
[8] Yasna, xvii. 11.

use, the fire in the body of men and beasts, the fire in plants, the fire of lightning, and the fire in the paradise of Ahura Mazdāh. Neither of these passages even suggests that fire is the essential principle of the universe, and the only other proof, the etymology of Brahman, is extremely far from convincing. Not a single passage is adduced in which Brahman normally or naturally denotes fire, and the transfer of meaning alleged is harsh and implausible, for the alleged parallel of *ṛc* and *dhī* is quite unproved. The whole theory in fact rests on the overestimation of the terms light (*tejas* or *jyotis*) applied to the self, individual or cosmic, and insistence on treating them as essentially material. We have to deal with an early stage of intellectual effort, and with the great difficulty of expressing the nature of the self in anything but material terms, as well as with the fact that the Brahman is not an abstraction. It is something which embraces all, and which is manifested in the warmth of the body and in the heat of the sun. But it is manifested also in the breath of man and in the wind, and it is to exaggerate one element out of all proportion to find the fundamental reality in fire, even when that fire is deemed to be endowed with intelligence, and therefore to be much more than merely material.

In the process of evolution of the conception of Brahman an important part is played by the identification of the Brahman and Bṛhaspati, 'the lord of prayer': he is in the later period of the Brāhmaṇas always regarded as the Purohita of the gods, as their Brahman priest in the technical sense of the term and also as the Brahman itself,[1] an idea which is often expressed. Now Bṛhaspati is the depository of great power already in the Rigveda, and this element undoubtedly aided the conception of the Brahman to obtain great prominence. This prominence as usual takes the form of identification with many diverse things, such as speech and truth and holy order, Ṛta,[2] as the wind into which the five deities, sun, moon, fire, lightning and rain all enter and from which they emerge,[3] as the breaths,[4] and often as the sun.[5] In the latter aspect the Brahman appears as the firstborn of the day, and perhaps also as the firstborn of the whole creation, a conception which places it on a lower plane than the final reality. The tendency is, however, more and more to place the Brahman on that plane: as we have seen, Prajāpati, who at first is the superior of and the creator of the Brahman, as the holy writ, became identified with the Brahman, as is often expressly stated in the Brāhmaṇas, and is at last placed below the Brahman as a metaphysical principle. With this view we attain to the conception of Brahman Svayambhu,[6] the Brahman which exists of itself and which is regarded as being the cause of the universe, in which it sacrifices itself in the usual parallelism of the world and the

[1] AB. i. 19. 1; 30. 6; TS. iii. 1. 1. 4; ÇB. iii. 9. 1. 11; xiii. 5. 4. 25.

[2] ÇB. ii. 1. 4. 10; iv. 1. 4. 11.

[3] AB. viii. 28.

[4] ÇB. viii. 4. 1. 3.

[5] ÇB. vii. 4. 1. 14; viii. 5. 3. 7; TS. v. 3. 4. 4; VS. xxiii. 48; KB. viii. 3; TA. x. 63. 15, &c.

[6] TB. ii. 8. 8. 8–10; AV. iv. 1; AB. i. 19. 1; KB. viii. 4; TA. x. 1. 1, &c.; ÇB. xi. 2. 3; xiii. 7. 1. 1.

sacrifice, the ground of the continued existence of the universe, and the source into which on death things return. Hence we meet the idea that by correct sacrifice a man may succeed in obtaining community of life and abode with the Brahman, or by right study of the Veda avoid repeated death and attain identity of essence with the Brahman.[1] The further step is taken to apply to the Brahman the attribute of taking the place of the highest god, Prajāpati or Viçvakarman of the Rigveda, and this is duly done in the Taittirīya Brāhmaṇa.[2] The Atharvaveda [3] in its own peculiar way recognizes the same idea in its explanation of the Brahman and the Brahmacārin, the Brahman student, as the highest of beings.

The final step to be taken in the conception of the Brahman was to identify it with the Ātman,[4] which, from another point of view in the Brāhmaṇas, attains the position of representative of the unity of the world, and this step is partially taken in the Taittirīya Brāhmaṇa,[5] where the Brahman and the omnipresent Ātman are identified, and the self of man, as it seems, is stated to be the mode of finding the Ātman, while knowledge of it frees from contamination by works, and the same idea occurs in the Çatapatha Brāhmaṇa.[6] Both these passages, however, are clearly transitional to the period of the Upaniṣads, and mark the end of the reflections of the Brāhmaṇas before the new views were definitely accepted.

Apart from the most improbable etymology, suggested by Hertel, which has been discussed above, there is, as we have seen, no ground to find more in the word than, in the first place, prayer, and the development which it undergoes is in all probability to be attributed to the growth of the importance of the prayer in the mind of the priest, not in the realization of the subjective nature of prayer as the striving towards the divine, which is in reality the human, will. The Brahman is, therefore, rather a conception of the ritual and of religion, not a psychological principle, and it is in my opinion impossible to accept the view of Deussen,[7] that the Ātman is evolved from the Brahman by developing the conception of the subjective element, which lay in the latter. The conception of the Brahman and the Ātman is late, and has every appearance of being a syncretism [8] due to the fact that the two expressions had by diverse ways come to be regarded as expressions for the same thing, the highest reality and unity of the universe, and the history of the Ātman suggests that it had from the first an independent existence. This view is certainly strengthened by the fact that the opinion of Deussen is based to some degree on a new etymology, which he suggests for that word: in place of the root *an*, 'breathe', *at*, 'move', or *av* (= *vā*), 'blow', and connexion with the Greek ἀτμός, ἀϋτμήν, and Germanic *atum*, *aedhm*, he suggests that

[1] ÇB. xi. 4. 4; 5. 6. 9.
[2] TB. ii. 8. 9. 3–7.
[3] x. 2 and xi. 5.
[4] AV. x. 8. 44, recognizes Ātman as the world soul probably for the first time.
[5] iii. 12. 9; cf. PB. xxv. 18. 5.
[6] x. 6. 3. See also TA. iii. 11. 1; VS. xxxiv. 1–6.
[7] *Gesch. der Phil.* I. i. 284 ff.
[8] Oldenberg, *Buddha*, pp. 30 ff.; *Die Lehre der Upanishaden*, pp. 44 ff.

it is a highly abstract word derived from the roots *a* seen in *aham*, 'I', and *ta*, 'this', so that it denotes 'this I,' the self, which in due course is felt to be the final expression possible for the ultimate fact of existence, arrived by stripping away the various coverings which envelop the ultimate reality, the covering of the body, the covering of the mind, the covering of the intellect. This view he supports, not merely by the undoubted difficulties [1] in the explanation of the form Ātman, and of the corresponding form in the Rigveda, without the *ā*, but also by the suggestion that the development of meaning assumed from 'wind', in which sense it is found only four times in the Rigveda, to 'self' is more difficult than the development of meaning which his own etymology would give. Thus he thinks from 'this I' could easily spring the view of the body in contrast to the outer world, and thence the trunk in contrast to the limbs, and on the other hand the sense of the soul in opposition to the body, and real being in opposition to unessential things. The possibility of such an etymology must, however, be denied: without pretending that the problems of the relation of Ātman and Tman is easy, or that the etymology is certain, the fact remains that the word does mean 'wind' in the Rigveda,[2] that the normal use of it there is 'breath of life', and that the meaning 'wind' is harder to deduce from 'breath', than *vice versa*, and that to deduce either 'wind' or 'breath' from the conception of 'this I' is extremely difficult.

The real history of Ātman seems then to be that from the meaning 'wind' sprang early up that of 'the breath': thence came the meaning 'self', as when it is said of Sūrya that he is the self of that which stands and moves.[3] Then we have the use of the self as a reflexive pronoun, and the use as meaning the body,[4] an idea which is clearly intended when it is contrasted with Prāṇa, 'the breath': the meaning 'trunk',[5] as opposed to limbs, is an easy development from this sense. But the sense 'breath' or 'self' is also capable of being understood in more abstract ways, and we, therefore, find Ātman used to denote the essential nature of a thing: this use is already found in the Rigveda [6] where the nature of the breath, the blood, the self of the earth, is put as a question, and similarly we hear of the self of the disease Yakṣma,[7] of all beings, and the adjective *ātmanvant*, 'possessing existence'.[8] But of much more importance is the development of the use of the word to denote the self of man in direct distinction from the members of his body and his body itself: it must be admitted that the use is far from common in the Vedic literature, but twice in the Atharvaveda [9] the contrast of Ātman with breath and body seems clearly intended, and the same thing must be admitted for two passages in the Çatapatha,[10] in which either one or ten breaths are set over

[1] Bloomfield, AJP. xvi. 421.

[2] vii. 87. 2; i. 34. 7; x. 92. 13; 168. 4.

[3] RV. i. 115. 1; ix. 2. 10; 6. 8, &c.

[4] RV. x. 163. 5, 6; AV. iii. 29. 8; vi. 53. 2; vii. 67. 1, &c.

[5] VS. xix. 93; ÇB. i. 3. 2. 2; vii. 1. 1. 21; viii. 7. 23, &c.

[6] i. 164. 4.

[7] RV. ix. 97. 11; AV. viii. 7. 9, and often.

[8] TB. ii. 1. 6. 1; AV. x. 2. 32; xi. 2. 10.

[9] v. 1. 7; 9. 7.

[10] ÇB. iv. 2. 3. 1; xi. 2. 1. 2.

against the self. Further, it seems that efforts were being made to define the self either as mind or as consciousness, Vijñāna.[1]

The development of the meaning of Ātman was accompanied by the development of the conception of the relation of the Ātman of the universe and the Ātman of the individual. The comparison of the macrocosm and the microcosm had been familiar from the time of the Rigveda,[2] where the cosmic Puruṣa is clearly closely allied to the individual man. In the case of Puruṣa, however, under that name we do not find that the conception of his Ātman was developed : of the individual man we have the question asked, later at least, what is left after his members are dispersed by death ; but, though it might have been expected that this problem would have been posed in the case of Puruṣa, there is no evidence that this was ever done. The reference to the cosmic Ātman seen by Deussen [3] in a passage of the Taittirīya Brāhmaṇa [4] is as shown above too doubtful to found any argument upon : if the cosmic Ātman is really deliberately meant, it is very strange that the series of identifications of macrocosm and microcosm should not end there, but should proceed to the abode of the Ātman in the heart, the heart in the man, the man in the immortal, and the immortal in the Brahman. More important is the recognition of the Ātman as cosmic in the Atharvaveda, as the conclusion of the second Skambha hymn.[5]

In the case of Prajāpati, the development of the conception of the Ātman is very clear : the creator enters, in the view of the Rigveda [6] and of all subsequent texts, into the creation with his spirit, and the terms now used in the late works, the Taittirīya Āraṇyaka [7] and the Tadeva section of the Vājasaneyi Saṁhitā,[8] are that he enters with the self into the self. It is needless to press the exact force of these words : it is sufficient to note that they obviously lend themselves to the view of the identity of the cosmic self with the self of man. The actual expression of this identity is found only occasionally and in late texts such as the Taittirīya Āraṇyaka [9] and the Çivasaṁkalpa section of the Vājasaneyi Saṁhitā,[10] both works which are of the latest period of the Brāhmaṇa epoch and closely analogous to Upaniṣads, while the identification of the Ātman and the Brahman is also, as we have seen, confined to texts of the most developed stratum of Brāhmaṇa philosophy, the Taittirīya Brāhmaṇa [11] and the Çatapatha Brāhmaṇa,[12] in either case in late chapters.

Of other expressions of the inner nature of man, the Puruṣa is of no very serious importance for the philosophy of this epoch : he is indeed mentioned in two sections of the Vājasaneyi Saṁhitā, the Uttaranārāyaṇa and the

[1] ÇB. x. 3. 5. 13 ; cf. iii. 8. 3. 8 (mind).
[2] x. 90. Cf. below, Chap. 29.
[3] *Gesch. der Phil.* I. i. 333.
[4] iii. 10. 8. Cf. above, p. 441.
[5] x. 8. 44.
[6] x. 121. 1.
[7] x. 1. 19.
[8] xxxii. 11.
[9] iii. 11. 1.
[10] xxxiv. 1–6 ; cf. Scheftelowitz, ZDMG. lxxv. 201–12.
[11] iii. 12. 9.
[12] x. 6. 3.

Tadeva, in which he is identified with Prajāpati, and with Brahman, ensouls nature, is before but is also produced by the gods, is the source of time and is without limit in space; moreover the cosmic and the individual self appear to be identified, and we find the doctrine[1] that, as Anquetil du Perron expresses it, 'Quisquis Deum intelligit Deus fit;' the inspired seer can become identical with the deity, entering with his own self into the self.[2] But, though the term Puruṣa is occasionally used as a vague expression for the human personality,[3] it is not destined to become in this period ever a very definite or clear conception. On the other hand the Brāhmaṇas have an important principle of existence to match with the Ātman, and one the prominence of which never disappears entirely in Indian philosophy, though the Sāṁkhya system seeks to diminish its place. This is the conception of the Prāṇa or the Prāṇas, 'breath' or 'vital airs', which achieves an importance denied to the older term Asu.

The importance of the breath is due obviously to its connexion with the life of man or beast, and we find in the Çatapatha Brāhmaṇa[4] the express statement that the victim is the breath, since only while it breathes is it a beast at all, and, when the breath departs, it is a mere inert mass. But the term is naturally enough extended to other forms of the activity of life, the speech, the hearing, the sight, and the mind, and further in the Vedic view between the organ and the activity there was no very clear distinction:[5] the ear is what hears and the hearing, the eye what sees and the sight, and so on. The number of the vital airs is very various: they can be reckoned pretty much at pleasure as two, three, five, seven, nine, twelve, thirteen, and so on. But nine are often mentioned: seven in the head and two below.[6] The seven in the head are the mind, speech, the breath itself, the two eyes and the two ears, and those below the organs of reproduction and evacuation. But the seven can be reduced to five by counting the ears and eyes as one organ each, and from quite different points of view we have six,[7] two eyes, nostrils and ears, or two, Prāṇa and Udāna, or three, Prāna, Udāna, and Apāna.[8] These

1 Cf. AV. ii. 1 as interpreted by Lindenau, ZII. i. 33 ff. His view (p. 37, n. 1) that RV. iv. 26 and 27 refer to the divinity of man is without justification; in neither case is a man the speaker.

2 xxxi. 17–22 (=TA. iii. 13); xxxii. 1–12 (=TA. x. 1. 2–4).

3 Deussen, *Gesch. der Phil.* I. i. 288 ff. Its use in the Sāṁkhya is significant; the one Puruṣa regarded as pure spirit here is split into innumerable entities.

4 iii. 8. 3. 15.

5 An attempt at an analysis of perception occurs in the Buddhist canonical work, the *Dhammasaṁgaṇi*; see C. Rhys Davids, *Buddhist Manual of Psychological Ethics*², pp. lviii ff.; but even there it is quite impossible to say if the conception was not materialistic (as in the Milindapañha, p. 60; Walleser, *Die philosophische Grundlage des älteren Buddhismus*, pp. 113, 114). In truth, the distinction of psychic and physiological elements had not been yet thought out; see below, Chap. 28, § 10.

6 ÇB. vi. 4. 2. 5; ix. 2. 2. 5; x. 1. 3. 4, &c.

7 ÇB. xii. 9. 1. 9.

8 A. H. Ewing, *The Hindu Conception of the Functions of Breath* (1901–3); Caland, ZDMG. lv. 261 ff.; lvi. 556 ff.; Keith, *Aitareya Āraṇyaka*, p. 217, n. 4; Oldenberg, *Weltanschauung der Brāhmaṇatexte*, pp. 65 ff.; G. W. Brown, *Human Body in the Upanishads*, pp. 201 ff.

vital airs are repeatedly called the gods, Devas: they are produced from the ascending airs of Prajāpati with which he created the gods, and the view that these activities are divine is a perfectly natural one from the point of view of Vedic religion, and it is quite unnecessary [1] to attribute the use of the term to the fact that no word for nature powers existed.

The multitude of Prāṇas, however, rest upon a single Prāṇa, which is sometimes, it would seem, sought to be identified with mind, but normally is called the Mukhya Prāṇa, the chief of the breaths. Its position appears clearly in a legend of creation in the Çatapatha Brāhmaṇa.[2] From the not-being arose the seven Prāṇas in the shape of the seven seers: they were kindled up by the Prāṇa in the middle as Indra, whereupon they produced the seven Puruṣas, which again united themselves to one Puruṣa. The same priority of one Prāṇa is elsewhere expressed by the relationship of it to the others as like that of Prajāpati to the gods.[3]

It was of course quite inevitable that the eternal comparison of macrocosm and microcosm should here play its part, and so, in point of fact, we find the relationship of the breath as the principle of life in man, and the cosmic Prāṇa, which is the wind, asserted in the Çatapatha Brāhmaṇa.[4] Nor are there lacking evidences of efforts to make Prāṇa the one reality, as Ātman was so made: Prāṇa is identified with Prajāpati, and also the Ātman, but these views are late and isolated.[5] The theosophy of the Atharvaveda [6] with its cosmopolitanism, however, accepts the Prāṇa readily as an expression of the universal, just as it accepts the Brahman, and as it sees in the Ātman the same essence as the meaning of the universe.

§ 3. *The Theory of the Sacrifice*

Amid an infinity of varied details the Brāhmaṇas present a perfectly definite body of opinion as to the fundamental nature of the sacrifice,[7] and in connexion with the sacrifice of the gods, the Asuras, the seers, and men. This theory is the most characteristic and independent part of the Brāhmaṇas: in the speculations as to the unity of the universe and the god in whom that unity finds expression, the Brāhmaṇas are only inheritors of the speculation of the Rigveda, but in the doctrine of the sacrifice they develop a theory which may have been held in germ at least in the age of the Rigveda, but which is not expressed there and which doubtless in considerable measure is a new creation. This is indicated by one fundamental fact: the sacrifice in the Brāhmaṇas is a piece of magic pure and simple: this is assuredly not the

[1] Hertel, IF. xli. 188.
[2] vi. 1. 1. In vii. 5. 2. 6 it is identified with mind.
[3] ÇB. vii. 5. 1. 21.
[4] ÇB. x. 3. 3. 6.
[5] ÇB. iv. 2. 3. 1; xi. 1. 1. 17. Cf. later JUB. iii. 1 f.; CU. iv. 3; Lüders, SBA. 1916, pp. 278 ff. (the Saṁvargavidyā).
[6] xi. 4; cf. TA. iii. 14.
[7] Practically all the evidence is collected in Lévi, *La doctrine du sacrifice dans les Brāhmaṇas*; the texts (e.g. KS.) not used by him add little of value. Cf. also Oldenberg, *Weltanschauung der Brāhmaṇatexte*, pp. 159–67.

attitude of the average seer of the hymns of the Rigveda. The turning into magic of the sacrifice is, we have seen, a conception which is secondary: the existence of magic as early as the sacrifice is one thing: the converting of what was originally a sacrifice into magic is, like the art of black magic, a subsequent development.

In this theory of the universe there is much that cannot be called in any normal sense philosophical, but taken as a whole it is impossible to deny the name of philosophy to an ordered view of the universe, fully thought out, and within its fundamental limitations logical and complete.

The basis of the whole system is the identification of the sacrifice with Prajāpati, who is the creator *par excellence.* The exhaustion of Prajāpati on creation is the exhaustion of the sacrifice: the work of creation is carried out with the aid of the sacrifices of various kinds: the danger to which the creatures whom he creates are exposed from the jealousy of the gods has to be overcome by new sacrifices invented for them, for Agni, the Maruts, even for Varuṇa. As the sacrifice, Prajāpati is all creative, the gods and the Asuras arise from his upgoing and his descending breaths, from him are sprung men, the beasts, the plants and the trees, the minerals as well as the heaven and the earth and the mountains. But, while he is the all-father, still his nature as the sacrifice presents another relationship: he is father of Agni, but as the sacrifice Agni recomposes him and so is his father:[1] and similarly with the gods as a whole. Moreover he is the creator of the sacrifice as well as the sacrifice: he invents rite after rite to aid the gods in their struggles with the Asuras, and he was the first to invent the words used in the sacrifice and its varied forms. Moreover the sacrifice is not only Prajāpati, but, as he is the first to sacrifice, so he is the first victim to be offered.[2] He gave himself to the gods, and when he did so he created a counterpart of himself in the form of the sacrifice, and thus he redeemed his life from the gods. Yet again, as the first to sacrifice, he is the first to win the reward of sacrifice and to ascend to the sun.[3]

Prajāpati is not merely the creator of beings, but he reduces them to order from their confusion by entering them with form, Rūpa, and name, Nāman.[4] The same feat is accorded to the Brahman by another text, and the form is identified with mind and the name with speech.[5] These two figure in a contest for priority, the mind claiming that speech is but an imitation of it, while speech lays stress on the fact that it gives means of expression and communication. But Prajāpati decides, in favour of the mind, a struggle which is constantly taken up again in the Upaniṣads, and which has a famous parallel in the Roman legend of the contest of the members and the stomach.[6] Speech,

[1] ÇB. vi. 1. 2. 26, 27.

[2] PB. vii. 2. 1; ÇB. xi. 1. 8. 2–4. In RV. x. 121. 2 (*ātmadā*) this sense has been seen, but wrongly (cf. Lindenau, ZII. i. 46, n. 2). See also below, Appendix B.

[3] ÇB. x. 2. 2. 1.

[4] TB. ii. 2. 7. 1.

[5] ÇB. xi. 2. 3. 1–6.

[6] TS. ii. 5. 11. 4; PB. vi. 4. 7; xi. 1. 3; MS. iv. 6. 4; ÇB. i. 4. 5. 8–11; BAU. vi. 3; CU. v. 1. 1; AU. ii. 4; PU. ii. 3; ÇA. ix; Lanman, *Hindu Pantheism*, pp. 18, 19.

however, remains of value and aid to Prajāpati, and encourages him when he is in doubt or is wearied ; he sends her forth to be revealed as the earth, atmosphere, and sky ; she is his bride, to bear creation.[1] She forms, therefore, a ground of contest between the gods and the Asuras : the gods win her by inducing the sacrifice to make overtures to her : [2] again the gods obtain by the offer of her the Soma from the Gandharvas : she brings back the Soma, and the two sides seek to retain her : the Gandharvas recite the Veda, the gods dance and sing and win her foolish heart by these base means. Again she flies from them and enters the wood, but the gods find her and she curses the wood for delivering her up : the trees, however, distributed her in the drum, the lute, and other places.[3] At another time she is wroth with the Añgirases who prefer Sūrya to her as a sacrificial fee, and leaves the gods, remaining in the space between them and the Asuras and becoming a lioness.[4] She is, however, won over. The distinction of speech was accomplished by Indra in return for a fourth part of the Soma : one quarter only is distinct, the other parts are the speeches of the beasts, the birds, and insects.[5] Among men the speech is best in the country of the Kuru-Pañcālas, and the Asuras and barbarians alike talk a bad speech.[6]

To the other gods the sacrifice stands in a slightly different relation : Viṣṇu indeed is often identified with the sacrifice, but this idea, though important, and doubtless an expression of the high standing in the pantheon of that god, is not in all probability much more than a recognition of this importance. Viṣṇu plays no very great part in the theosophy proper. The gods are, like the Asuras, children of Prajāpati, but, though born of the nobler part of the god, are yet in physical strength weaker : they are, however, superior in science, and by their knowledge of the sacrifice they can defeat their rivals. They are essentially in the control of the sacrificer : the seers can even seize and hold them fast, for despite their possession of more than one body they can be present at only one rite at a time. Kutsa holds Indra by cords ; Luça taunts the god who breaks free, but Kutsa with a new Sāman brings him back : a later version of the legend, however, allows of the division of the god into his person and his greatness.[7] The sacrifice or the threefold knowledge, which is the essence of the sacrifice, is the essence of the gods. The gods are lovers of the recondite,[8] compact of truth, but the truth is nothing but exactness in the rites and the formulae of the sacrifice. To the sacrifice they owe the glory and power which is theirs, and, what is far more important, their

[1] PB. x. 2. 1 ; xx. 14. 2 ; KS. xii. 5. In the domestic ritual of the Çabalī rite she appears as a wish-cow ; cf. Hopkins, TCA. xv. 27, n. 2.

[2] ÇB. iii. 2. 1. 18–23.

[3] PB. vi. 5. 10 ; TS. vi. 1. 4. 1 ; MS. iii. 6. 8.

[4] ÇB. iii. 5. 1. 21.

[5] TS. vii. 4. 7. 3 ; MS. iv. 5. 8 ; ÇB. iv. 1. 3. 6.

[6] ÇB. iii. 2. 3. 15 ; 1. 23, 24 ; KB. vii. 6 ; Macdonell and Keith, *Vedic Index*, ii. 279. For speech as a divine gift to the singer, cf. AV. ii. 1. 4.

[7] PB. ix. 2. 22 ; JB. i. 228 in JAOS. xviii. 32 ; cf. PB. ix. 4. 14, &c.

[8] *parokṣakāma*, ÇB. vi. 1. 1. and often ; in AB., TB., GB. as *parokṣapriya*. So Indra = Arjuna, ÇB. ii. 1. 2. 11.

immortality,[1] which they gain by the sacrifice: they are ever represented as being in fear of death, or Yama, or the ender, the year, death, Prajāpati. Over the question of immortality they have desperate struggles with the Asuras, whom the Çatapatha often, and the Pañcavinça once, make their elder brothers: in one case the gods were being steadily killed because Çuṣṇa, the Asura, had in his mouth the ambrosia, which Indra as an eagle stole from him, thus depriving his breath of the power to revive the smitten Asuras.[2] The struggle with the Asuras repeats itself in innumerable forms: in one case Indra metamorphizes himself into a female jackal, and runs thrice round, winning the earth:[3] more famous is the use of Viṣṇu, the sacrifice, as a dwarf to accomplish the winning of the earth from the Asuras,[4] or more directly the three citadels of the Asuras, of iron, silver, and gold in the three worlds, are overthrown by the performance of the Upasad ceremonies.[5] The gods also by the use of the new- and full-moon sacrifices force the Asuras to abandon the half month of waning moon, which they had occupied.[6]

In the struggle the sacrifice plays a constant part: the gods are often aided by advice from Prajāpati, and they apply themselves to severe penances to bring about victory, but the decisive thing in their favour is their knowledge of the correct mode of offering: the Asuras put the bricks in the fire altar with the mark below,[7] in the preliminary rites they shave first the hair, then the beard, then the arm-pits;[8] they offer a white victim born of a black mother,[9] and these errors are fatal. They try magic but without success. The gods on their part cajole the chaplains of the demons, Çaṇḍa, Marka, and Uçanas, and are willing to break faith for victory: they detach the Rakṣases from the Asuras by promise of equal shares of the spoil, and they refuse them any share at all.[10] They defeat the Asuras by the inability of the latter to find a feminine for the word five,[11] but more often they have to fight hard battles. One story shows the Asuras seeking to build a fire altar to reach the heaven: Indra disguises himself, is allowed to put on a brick, and, when it is all but finished, he drags it away with the result that the altar falls.[12] Even, however, within the divine family there are disagreements: the ancient Sādhya gods seem to have vanished from importance,[13] but the Ādityas and the Añgirases are bitter rivals. Here, again, however, the value of knowledge of the sacrifice is the most important thing of all, and the Ādityas are superior by far in this

1 TS. vii. 2. 4. 1; AV. ii. 1. 5; xiii. 1. 7; ÇB. xi. 2. 3. 6; x. 4. 3. 3–8; MS. ii. 2. 2; iii. 4. 7; PB. xxiv. 19. 2, and often. That they, being born, will pass away, is recognized only later (cf. Maitr. i. 4).

2 KS. xxxvii. 14.

3 TS. vi. 2. 4. 3, 4; MS. iii. 8. 3.

4 MS. iii. 8. 3; ÇB. i. 2. 5. 1–7.

5 TS. vi. 2. 3. 1; MS. iii. 8. 1; ÇB. iii. 4. 4, 3–5; KB. viii. 8, &c.

6 ÇB. i. 7. 2. 22–4; TB. i. 5. 6. 3, 4.

7 MS. iii. 2. 7.

8 TB. i. 5. 6. 1.

9 MS. ii. 5. 9.

10 TS. vi. 4. 10. 1; PB. vii. 5. 20; TS. ii. 4. 1. 1; TB. i. 8. 3. 3.

11 ÇB. i. 5. 4. 6–11.

12 TB. i. 1. 2. 4–6; MS. i. 6. 9; KS. viii. 1; ÇB. ii. 1. 2. 13–17.

13 They (like the demons; TS. vi. 2. 5. 3 f.) had two libations only, PB. viii. 3. 6; 4. 9; xxv. 8. 2.

and reach heaven before the Añgirases, who have to serve them in place of being served by them. The same defective knowledge in the Añgirases leads them to require teaching from Nābhānediṣṭha, for which they have to pay dearly, and drives them to compromises with the Fathers.[1]

The sacrifice is, however, the source of disagreement among the gods; the advantages of it are far too great to allow of the gods being content to share equally, and we hear that Viṣṇu, recognized as the first of the gods by reason of his sacrificial skill, makes himself hated for his pride, and the gods induce the ants to gnaw through his bowstring, so that his head is carried away.[2] Even when, at a session in Kurukṣetra, it had been agreed to share the glory of the sacrifice, when it is attained by Soma,[3] he appropriates it, and Indra readily destroys Namuci, when he finds that he can do so by stretching the words of his oath. The several residences of the gods is exclusive; they do not visit one another. They race one another for shares in the offering, and Indra and Vāyu bear off the first places.

The danger from the Asuras drives the gods to close union; they find that they must have mutual confidence, and they make a pact depositing their bodies with Varuṇa, on the understanding that he who violates it shall not be reunited with his forms.[4] They are further compelled to resort to monarchy: they chose Varuṇa, Agni, or Soma, as king, but finally they perform the great consecration of Indra: the All-gods serve as heralds, the water of consecration is poured on by Prajāpati, the Vasus assist at the east, the Rudras in the south, the Ādityas at the west, the All-gods at the north, the Sādhyas and Āptyas in the centre, the Maruts and the Añgirases at the zenith.[5]

Despite the relations of the gods with the sacrifice, the sacrifice is by no means always loyal to them: it flees from them, taking now the form of Viṣṇu, now that of a Suparṇa bird, now that of a horse, or of a black antelope. Nor have the gods ever learned the whole art of sacrifice, even as men have not had it revealed to them: they pick up fragments of it from time to time. They may even have to seek knowledge from the Ṛṣis such as the snake seer, Arbuda Kādraveya.

The place of the seers is in view of their relation to the sacrifice one of great importance: they are the means by which in the normal case men secure the essential knowledge of the ritual, and they are often indebted to the gods for it; Nodhas is taught a Sāman by them in reward for his learning. They even declare that Çiçu Āñgirasa was entitled to call the Fathers 'my children' owing to his knowledge of the ritual, as in the Atharvaveda the seer may by insight win the position of father of his father. The Vaikhānasas, the seers, whom Rahasyu Devamalimluc slew at Munimaraṇa, were revived by Indra, and the same god revived Upagu Sauçravasa, whom his royal master Kutsa

[1] TB. ii. 1. 1. 1.
[2] MS. iv. 5. 9; ÇB. xiv. 1. 1. 1–10; PB. vii. 5. 6.
[3] MS. ii. 1. 4.
[4] TS. vi. 2. 2. 1, 2; MS. iii. 7. 10; ÇB. iii. 4. 2. 4, 5, &c.
[5] AB. viii. 12.

had killed for persisting in the worship of Indra.[1] Atri, on his part, saves the sun from the grip of the Asura Svarbhānu, the darkness disappearing as a succession of variously coloured sheep,[2] and Bharadvāja warns the gods of the presence of the Asuras in the Ukthas, and so saves them.[3] Vasiṣṭha constrains the god Indra to show himself to him in bodily presence, and Indra must agree.[4] Even if the gods seek to keep, as they sometimes do, knowledge from the seers, the latter triumph: they recognize that the gods have put the sacrificial post in upside down, and they find the Nigadas and Praiṣas, which they had at first omitted. The seer also can rely on the gods to enable him to convince men of his seerhood: Kavaṣa Ailūṣa, despised by other priests, is shown to be a seer by the conduct of the Sarasvatī, which pays him reverence by flowing round him:[5] Vatsa walks triumphant through the fire, when his claim is disputed by Medhātithi.[6]

The mode of transmission of the knowledge of the rites explains why the ceremonial can be altered in important detail: the tradition is not established, and the theologians can discuss details even with royal personages, such as Janaka and Açvapati Kaikeya. We are actually told of points on which the great Yājñavalkya held opinions differing from the normal, but which he did not carry into effect.[7]

In its aspect towards men the sacrifice is identical with the sacrificer, and it is identical also with the gods and with Prajāpati. The sacrifice is essentially commensurate with men, and the conclusion is not doubtfully drawn that the sacrifice should be the sacrifice of man himself:[8] he owes debts, to the Fathers to produce a son, to the seers to recite the sacred texts, to men in the shape of hospitality, and to the gods he owes himself, just as Prajāpati offered up himself. The conclusion would, therefore, appear to be that the perfect form of sacrifice should be suicide, but such an idea is not mentioned in the text of the Brāhmaṇas, whether or not it existed then,[9] as it in a sense certainly did in the Buddhist and Jain period. The idea, however, in its less developed form is expressed in various ways: the sap which is the essence of sacrifice is first in man, then it passes on to the other victims, the horse, the ox, the sheep, the goat, and even into the rice, which is thus not in itself worthy of sacrifice, but is still full of the sap of sacrifice.[10] Again the consecration gives man a new and divine life, but it also means the handing over of his old body to the gods as an offering: this offering is not, however, performed: it is redeemed by the offering to the victim to Agni and Soma, which follows, and of that victim one view is that the man should not eat, since it is a

1 PB. xiv. 4. 7; 6. 8.

2 PB. vi. 6. 8; Hopkins, TCA. xv. 35; the gods by noises (PB. iv. 5. 2) accomplish the feat.

3 AB. iii. 49.

4 TS. iii. 5. 2; KS. xxxvii. 17; PB. xv. 5. 24.

5 AB. ii. 19; KB. xii. 3.

6 PB. xiv. 6. 6; cf. the later text, JB. iii. 233–5.

7 ÇB. iv. 2. 1. 7. See also below, § 5.

8 ÇB. xi. 1. 8. 2–5; iii. 6. 2. 16; i. 7. 2. 1–6.

9 Lévi, *La doctrine du sacrifice*, p. 133.

10 MS. iii. 10. 2; ÇB. i. 2. 3. 6; vi. 2. 2. 15; AB. ii. 8.

redemption of his own body.[1] The human sacrifice is also permitted, not as suicide, but as a substitute for oneself, but this is a doctrine which has no direct support in the Brāhmaṇas, and may be a very late conception. The offering of man in the rite of the piling of the fire altar is recorded, but the sense of the redemption of the self is not there pressed, though it receives a classical form in the legend of Çunaḥçepa, who is to serve as a substitute for the offering of the king's son. Here, however, the motive of sacrifice is an ordinary case of the vow of some precious object to a god.

At the same time the sacrifice involves the death of the god in the form of the Soma [2] or the victim. In the former case every effort is made to conceal the fact of death from the god: he is assured that he is being pounded, not for the sake of his death, but to attain the overlordship of the metres: or again one thinks, as one takes up the pressing stone, of one's enemy, and thus kills him and not the innocent Soma.[3] The seller of the Soma is treated with insult and blows as an evil man, and the Soma himself is accorded the guest reception, as he moves to his death in the ritual. These remarks, however, show clearly enough no serious or real feeling for the death of the god: they are products of speculation, not of deep religious conviction.

The sacrifice itself is supposed to undergo a perpetual series of deaths, and of coming again to life: in the etymology of the Brāhmaṇas it is born through movement, hence it is *yañ-ja*, which is as much as *yajña*.[4] The sacrifice is the eater, for it lives on all creatures,[5] but at the same time it is the universal principle of life.[6] The libation offered in the fire is the life of the gods: the eating of the oblation by the priests is the life of men: the placing of the Nārāçaṅsa cups on the oblation holders is the life of the Fathers. Aforetime, indeed, the gods and the men and the Fathers used to enjoy the sacrifice together, and still they do so, but the difference is that the gods and the Fathers are no longer seen by the mortal eyes.[7] The gods depend essentially on the sacrifice: Indra is hungry, and goes and asks for a gift: courtesy is due to them, and, therefore, when they are on the next day to receive the sacrifice, men do not eat but fast, since it would be discourteous to anticipate the feeding of the guests, who have been invited. The gods are so anxious for the offering that they consider eagerly whether they are to receive the sacrifice, or if it is to go to others. They know beforehand the intention of man, for he resolves with his mind, thence the knowledge goes to the breath, thence to the wind, and the wind wafts to the gods the news of the intention.[8]

The gods, despite their close relations to men,[9] and their interest in the

[1] TS. vi. 1. 11. 6; AB. ii. 9; KB. x. 3; ÇB. iii. 3. 4. 21; xi. 7. 1. 3.

[2] TS. vi. 6. 7. 1; MS. iv. 7. 2; ÇB. iii. 9. 4. 2; iv. 3. 4. 1; AB. iii. 32. 2.

[3] ÇB. iii. 3. 2. 6; 9. 4. 17; cf. ii. 2. 2. 1; GB. ii. 3. 9.

[4] ÇB. iii. 9. 4. 23.

[5] ÇB. ix. 4. 1. 11.

[6] ÇB. xiv. 3. 2. 1; iii. 6. 2. 25.

[7] ÇB. iii. 6. 2. 26.

[8] ÇB. iii. 4. 2. 6, 7. The first comer wins Indra, who has favourites, PB. ix. 4. 10 f.

[9] The Brahmans are the gods who do not eat oblations, MS. i. 4. 6; GB. ii. 1. 6.

sacrifice, regard men with some degree of dislike and suspicion: there was even a time when men and gods lived together, but the gods were wearied and disgusted with the demands of men, who used always to ask them for what they wanted *sans phrase*,[1] and therefore departed from the earth. It is the gods who have given men the evils of sleep, sluggishness, anger, hunger, love of dice and of women.[2] The Ṛbhus, admitted indeed into the society of the gods, are disliked because of their human odour.[3] Many are the devices adopted by the gods to prevent men following them into their immortality: they succeed in so far that an agreement with the god of death secures that men shall not attain immortality with their bodies.[4] On the other hand men ever strive to imitate the gods and adopt in the sacrifice the habits of the gods, that especially of preferring the right side for the commencement of all rites as opposed to the left, which men are said to favour: the differences are of absurd detail.[5]

The aim of the sacrifice is the world of heaven: the sacrifice is the ship which bears the sacrificer to that world, and the Bṛhat and Rathantara Sāmans are the two rudders of the ship, which bears the sacrificer to the desired bourne. From another point of view the sacrificer mounts to the heaven: he does this by the special mode of recitation adopted: first he performs the text prescribed, pausing at each quarter verse, thus attaining this world; then by half verses, attaining the atmosphere; then by three-quarter verses, attaining the heaven; and then he says the whole verse, thus winning firmly the sun. If, however, he stops here, then he will definitely lose the world of earth, and the sacrificer is not prepared to enjoy immortality, until he has lived a full life: so he reverses the process, and returns to earth again. The same idea appears in the three steps of Viṣṇu, which the sacrificer steps and thus wins the way to the heaven, but he also must take care to descend again.[6]

For the priest a very important rule must be noted: the sacrifice, as we have seen, dies eternally, and is eternally renewed, but this renewal must be conditioned by the giving of the fees to the priests: the sacrifice goes to heaven, the fee accompanies it, and by holding fast to the fee the sacrificer goes also.[7] The man who sacrifices, without giving fees, is reserved for a dread fate: on him the Āptyas wipe off the sin which was communicated to them, when Indra slew the three-headed son of Tvaṣṭṛ, Viçvarūpa.[8]

It is not only, however, by the sacrifice proper that the sacrificer attains the gods: the consecration is a process by which he is given new birth, and becomes an embryo, his actions and his clothing being based on the comparison

1 ÇB. ii. 3. 4. 4.
2 JB. i. 98; cf. ii. 363.
3 AB. iii. 30. 4.
4 ÇB. x. 4. 3. 9. Ascent to heaven with a body is admitted, PB. xxi. 4. 3.
5 ÇB. i. 2. 2. 9; 7. 2. 9; iii. 2. 2. 16; vii. 2. 2. 6; iii. 1. 2. 4, 5; 3. 14; TS. vi. 1. 1. 5; MS. iii. 6. 3, &c.
6 AB. iv. 22; PB. xviii. 10. 10; ÇB. i. 9. 3. 8–11.
7 ÇB. i. 9. 3. 1; iv. 3. 8, &c.
8 ÇB. ii. 2. 3. 4.

of him with such an embryo. His ordinary body, on the other hand, as we have seen, becomes an offering to the gods or by the gods. He himself is now in a state of extraordinary power, being filled with the sacrifice: if men eat his food, they take a third of any evil in him, those who speak ill of him a third, and the ants who bite him a third.[1]

The motive which induces the sacrificer to sacrifice and to undergo the painful self-torment, which is necessitated by the rite of consecration, is the possession of faith, which the Kauṣītaki Brāhmaṇa [2] declares to be the source of the abiding character of the sacrifice. Now faith is clearly allied to truth, and precision or truth is intimately associated with actual sight, as opposed to mere hearing: the principle of the Brāhmaṇas places sight as the highest source of truth.[3] Faith in the sacrifice by gods and men is attained only by him who sacrifices with faith.[4] Faith is, therefore, necessary in the sacrifice and also in the priest: if Vatsaprī Bhālandana was at first denounced as a thief by the seers, they were confuted by his winning faith through discovering the proper rite.[5] A very odd story tells of the cows: [6] they started a session for the purpose of obtaining horns: they received them after ten months, but some, not satisfied, not showing true faith, insisted on completing the year, where they won rich food, but lost their horns. Bṛhaspati, the priest of the gods, wins their faith by his discovery of the proper ritual.[7] The sacrificer must realize, if he is to prosper, the fixed truth of the rule that the gods receive the offering and he the benediction accompanying it.[8]

The importance of faith is such that it renders the gods of no importance, for the man who has faith realizes that the sacrifice produces its results without need of the gods. Atri is one of those whose deity is faith, Çraddhādeva: when he is in need he does not appeal to heaven, but invents the proper rite and disposes of his disabilities.[9] The first father of men, Manu himself, is the believer in faith *par excellence*: his one aim is the sacrifice: with Iḍā as his daughter [10] he repeoples the world after the deluge, and he continues his long course of sacrifices even down to the point that he is anxious to sacrifice his own wife at the bidding of the demons, Tṛṣṭa and Varutri, and has to be prevented from doing so by Indra, who induces him to let her go, when the fire had already been carried round her as a preliminary to the slaughter. But one version actually attributes to him the performance of the sacrifice at the suggestion of Kilāta and Ākuli, the Asura priests.[11] This faith in the sacrifice

[1] MS. iii. 6. 7; PB. v. 6. 10.
[2] vii. 4.
[3] ÇB. i. 3. 1. 27; MS. iii. 6. 3.
[4] TS. i. 6. 8. 1; MS. i. 4. 10; iv. 1. 4.
[5] MS. iii. 2. 3; PB. xii. 11. 25.
[6] TS. vii. 5. 1 and 2; PB. iv. 1. 1, 2; AB. iv. 17; JB. ii. 374. For curious speculations on its astronomical sense, see A. C. Das, *Rig-Vedic India*, i. 475 ff. Cf. PB. xxv. 3. 6.
[7] TS. vii. 4. 1. 1.
[8] ÇB. ii. 3. 4. 5; cf. TS. ii. 6. 10. 1.
[9] TS. vii. 1. 8. 2.
[10] ÇB. i. 8. 1. 1–10. Güntert (*Der arische Weltkönig*, p. 346) sees in her a relic of the legend of the sacrifice of a bisexual giant (see below, Appendix B).
[11] MS. iv. 1. 6; 8. 1; KS. ii. 30; ÇB. i. 1. 4. 14–17; TS. vi. 6. 1. The ÇB. recognizes the offering.

is encouraged by the long accounts given of the men who flourished by the use, and by the still longer lists of things, which by the sacrifice can be achieved automatically for men by the priests.

The need of faith is the more obvious in that the sacrificer at the sacrifice is hopelessly given up into the hands of the priests. He can by manipulation deprive him of his senses, of his life, of his wealth, of his kingdom; if he thinks of him as he says the Vaṣaṭ call, he hurls upon him the thunderbolt which is contained in that call. The situation is repeatedly developed that the sacrificer may be hated by the priest, and the priest is then instructed how to ruin him: the idea that this is wrong is absolutely derided. But, even if the priest is honest, the sacrifice is a dread thing, a dangerous wild beast, which must be propitiated: the gods themselves suffered terrible mischief by imprudence: Pūṣan's teeth were knocked out, Savitṛ's hands cut off to be replaced with golden ones, and Bhaga lost his eyesight.[1] The priest Bhāllaveya made an error in the sacrifice: he fell and broke his arm.[2] Āṣāḍhi Sauçromateya thought fit to substitute heads picked up anywhere for the five heads of the victims to be slain at the building of the fire altar, and paid for it by his life.[3] The priest is, therefore, a person, who has difficult tasks to perform, and whose services should not be despised: the effect of any offering is definite and precise, and it is idle to seek success in any haphazard manner.

The reward of the sacrificer for his efforts is, in the long run, one in the world to come: he may gain many desired things by the sacrifice and its manipulations in the present life, but these things are incidentals in the main offerings, a point in which they distinguish themselves from the occasional offerings, and from magic performances generally. The sacrifice is reduced in a sense to mere magic by the priests, but it is a performance which, unlike a magic rite or an offering set on foot for some definite object, must be performed regularly, and in it the profit acquired in this life is incidental, while the essential reward lies in the world to come. But this reward of immortality there is not to be construed in the sense that man should seek by an early death to obtain the world to come: on the contrary, in that world his place will be the better, the longer he lives: it is the aim of man not merely to achieve immortality, as eternal life hereafter, but also the full age of a hundred years, which is the allotted span of man. Those who die under twenty years of age by a weird conception attain as their abode the days and the nights, those under forty the half months, those under sixty the months, those under eighty the seasons, those under a hundred the year, and those over a hundred years the boon of immortality.[4] The opposite of immortality is the repeated death,

[1] TS. ii. 6. 8. 3; ÇB. i. 7. 4. 6–8; KB. vi. 13, 14. So Tvaṣṭṛ, by a wrong accent, destroyed his own son in place of Indra, TS. ii. 5. 2. 1; ÇB. i. 6. 3. 10 (*indra-çátru*, 'foe of Indra', mispronounced as *índra-çatru*, 'having Indra for a foe').

[2] ÇB. i. 7. 3. 19.

[3] ÇB. vi. 2. 1. 37.

[4] PB. xxiv. 19. 2; ÇB. x. 1. 5. 4; 2. 6. 8; the amount of eating necessary in the next world depends on the offerings made on earth, ÇB. x. 1. 5. 4.

Punarmṛtyu,[1] of which men are in deep fear. The idea is that the passing once through death is not enough: even after death, when man is in enjoyment of the precious boon of immortality, he may be robbed of it, and have once again to face the terrors of dissolution, of which the Vedic Indian shows himself most deeply afraid. The idea of a second death is, however, that of a second death in the future life, not of rebirth on earth and death in the ordinary sense, and the conception obviously could lend itself to the idea that the death might be not once only, but for numberless occasions: though the idea is actually found in the Çatapatha Brāhmaṇa, where a distinction is made between those born for immortality after death in the world to come, and those born after death only to fall again and again into the power of death,[2] nevertheless the ordinary conception is merely that of a repetition of death. Moreover it must not be forgotten that this idea occurs in the later Brāhmaṇas such as the Kauṣītaki and the Çatapatha.[3]

The dead man, according to the agreement made by the gods with death, is not permitted to enter into immortality with his mortal body, which must be laid aside first. The way to the heaven despite that fact is even then not easy; the Ādityas [4] among others seek to keep back those who aim at heaven, and in addition there are *en route* two fires which try to burn up those whom they should burn, but let pass those whom they ought to let pass.[5] In what manner the discrimination is made nothing is said, and, as we have seen, there is no other trace of the doctrine of a divine judgement in the Vedic literature. Beyond these powers, however, the dead is subject to the power of the sun, which is death: all creatures below it are subject to death, those above are free. The sun owes its position in the heaven to the gods who established it there, and keep it from falling away from its high place. The sun indeed for a time did not appreciate the high honour thus paid: he returned to earth, but found it in the clutches of death: he therefore praised Agni, and won again his home in the heaven.[6] The just men are the rays of the sun, and the constellations are appropriated to those good men who go to the world of heaven.[7]

The dead, however, do not always go to the gods: they may also go to the Fathers, who dwell in the third heaven. The difference of the ways is not explained, and remains as mysterious as the Fathers themselves. Of them diverse accounts are given: they are the children of Prajāpati, born before the gods and after the Asuras; they are the gods, who were slain in the fight with Vṛtra, brought to life as the Fathers.[8] Incorporeal, they are compared to mind,[9] as they cannot be seen. They correspond to the seasons, inter-

[1] ÇP. x. 2. 6. 19; 5. 1. 4; 6. 1. 4; xi. 4. 3. 20; 5. 6. 9; xii. 9. 3. 11, 12. Also in KB. But never in the early part of AB. It is a late idea in the Brāhmaṇas. It cannot be found in RV. x. 14. 14; ix. 113 despite Boyer, JA. 1901, ii. 466; Oldenberg, *Die Lehre der Upanishaden*, p. 27, n. 2.

[2] ÇB. x. 4. 3. 10; cf. ii. 3. 3. 7, 8.

[3] Below, Chap. 28, § 10.

[4] MS. i. 6. 12.

[5] ÇB. i. 9. 3. 2.

[6] ÇB. ii. 3. 3. 7, 8; TS. i. 5. 9. 3; PB. iv. 5. 9–11; TB. i. 2. 4. 2. The idea is clearly suggested by the fire ordeal.

[7] ÇB. vi. 5. 4. 8.

[8] MS. iv. 1. 2; ÇB. ii. 6. 1. 1.

[9] PB. vi. 9. 19, 20.

mediate between the day, which is appropriate to man, and the year of the gods : they correspond to the world of the atmosphere which comes between the earth and the heaven, but their world is not there. With the gods they have been at variance : their chief Yama [1] used to deprive the gods of all that they had, until the intervention of Prajāpati led to the settlement of the dispute. The gods are compelled to share with the Fathers the sacrifice. To their worshippers they are a somewhat dreaded band : [2] they must be appeased by offerings of the fringe of one's garment up to the age of fifty, and thereafter demand the offering of hair : their approach in the later period becomes closer and the need to buy off their demands by the redemption of oneself increases. When they come, it is said the Fathers take a man or they give one.[3] They are also to be honoured by the sacrificer turning away his head, when they come to eat, even as the prince eats without the gaze of the people.[4] They receive offerings for many reasons,[5] to prevent their bringing death with them, to carry out the rule of following the usages of the gods who offered to them, to show benevolence to those whom the gods recalled to life, to elevate the sacrificer's own Fathers to a better world, and to make good the injuries which one inflicts on oneself by misconduct.

Of quite special interest among these speculations is the theory of the piling of the sacred fire, which has peculiarities of its own and deserves, therefore, special consideration.[6] The building of the fire altar, as we have seen, is no ordinary part of the ritual : it is not an essential part perhaps of any sacrifice at all, and it is perfectly clear that the elaboration of the performance meant that it was one to be undertaken only occasionally, and then by a rich noble or prince or Brahman. The essence of the piling is clearly mystic : it has the purpose of carrying out in ritual form the essential act of the reconstruction of Prajāpati, whose sacrifice as Puruṣa has resulted in the creation of the universe in all its parts. This sacrifice cannot be regarded as a single definite act in time : it is rather a constant process, and therefore the dismembered god must ever and again be renewed. The renewal is brought about by the reconstruction of Prajāpati in the shape of the fire altar. The mass of significant members connected in the ritual is noteworthy : the god himself is not merely identified with Puruṣa as is natural, but he is identical with Agni as fire : the identification is carried out in detail : the fire altar is a year in building, and the fire-pan which the sacrificer has is for a year carried about by him. The bricks for the altar are prepared while preparation is made

[1] MS. ii. 5. 3. Oltramare (*L'histoire des idées théosophiques*, i. 47, n. 1) thinks that RV. x. 88. 15 (VS. xix. 47) refers to a hostility of god and mortals on one side and the Fathers on the other. But the passage is hopelessly obscure ; cf. ÇB. xii. 8. 1. 21 ; below, Chap. 28, § 11 ; Oldenberg's note on RV. *l. c.*

[2] The idea that their existence is something dream-like (ÇB. xii. 9. 2. 2, a false explanation of VS. xx. 16 ; cf. KU. vi. 5) is sporadic and unimportant.

[3] TB. i. 3. 10. 7.

[4] TB. i. 3. 10. 6 with comm.

[5] ÇB. ii. 1. 6. 3.

[6] Eggeling, SBE. xliii. pp. xv–xxvii ; Keith, *Taittirīya Saṁhitā*, i, pp. cxxv–cxxviii ; Oldenberg, GN. 1917, pp. 9 ff.

of the fire-pan. The altar is arranged to represent earth, atmosphere, and heaven, and the same arrangement is devised in the fire-pan. The relations between Prajāpati and Agni are not absolutely simple: Prajāpati is the father of Agni, but also the son, since Agni restores him by the sacrifice, and the fire altar is the body of Agni, through which Prajāpati is built up. Agni is also the child of the waters—which in their turn are created by Prajāpati—and in the fire altar there is laid at the bottom a lotus leaf from which Agni is born. The bird shape of the fire altar is also often referred to as well as the mortal shape: the bird shape is clearly connected with the myth of Agni in lightning form bringing down the Soma from the sky: the Soma, moreover, as the sacrifice *par excellence*, is, as was inevitable, identified with Prajāpati. The bird altar has, however, another aspect: the bird is to fly to the sky as the sacrifice, and with the bird the sacrificer who is identified with Prajāpati is to attain the sky.[1] In the piling of the altar the symbolism is carried out in the form of the gold disk, a symbol of the sun, which is placed over the lotus, and over which again is placed the golden image of a man, above whom lie in the first, third, and fifth layers of the pile the three naturally perforated bricks, representing the three worlds, through which the golden man can breathe, and through which the sacrificer must rise to the sun. The symbolism is effective: the ideas of the sun, the god Agni, the all-creator, and the sacrificer, as identical, and the nature of the sacrifice as leading to the world of heaven, are as efficiently produced by the ritual, as can be well conceived.

The ritual as it is seen in the texts of the Black Yajurveda does not seem to go beyond these conceptions, but the Çatapatha Brāhmaṇa in the tenth book,[2] doubtless a later addition to the text, which deals with the secret of the fire, develops the theme more philosophically. Prajāpati is the year, for he is essentially, as the creator, time, and the year is at once the symbol of time, and the period in which the working of nature completes a round, and commences again. The year of the piling of the altar, and the carrying of the fire in the fire-pan by the sacrificer, has been already mentioned: the year is symbolic also of birth: Agni must be borne for a year in the fire-pan before he is brought to life as the fire on the altar itself. In the acts of carrying him in the pan the sacrificer takes Agni into himself and in the fullness of time he brings him forth from himself, in accordance with the doctrine that the father of Agni is Prajāpati, the sacrificer himself. But the fact that Prajāpati is

[1] Oldenberg (*loc. cit.*) takes this as the essence of the rite, but though he justly insists on the non-popular character of the belief, he does not disprove the view of Eggeling, which is strongly supported by the Çatapatha.

[2] x. 3. 3 and 6. 4. The Brāhmaṇas and the Upaniṣads alike have no really philosophic discussion of time which they take for granted; cf. Walleser, *Die philosophische Grundlage d. ält. Buddhismus*, pp. 123–33; below, Chap 28, § 8. A doctrine of time as the absolute (*brahman*) is mentioned, to be rejected, in the Çvetāçvatara Upaniṣad. See also Keith, *Buddhist Philosophy*, pp. 163–8.

time, and that the sacrificer is identical with Prajāpati as time, has another and important side : the effect of time must be that, even if a man attain, as the piling of the altar will aid him to attain, the full life of a hundred years, still he must die, and he dies thus as death itself by his own hands, passing from the realm of material existence and its troubles and limitations to the eternal and abiding happiness of the life to come.[1] But the Brāhmaṇa goes further than this and attributes to Çāṇḍilya the doctrine that the ultimate essence of Prajāpati, of the sacrificer, and therefore of the universe, is mind, from which develop speech, the breath, the eye, the ear, work, fire. The final reality is summed up as the self, made up of intelligence, with a body of spirit, a form of light, and an ethereal nature, which pervades the regions and upholds the universe, though devoid of speech and mental affects. Or, again, it is said that the Puruṣa in the heart is as a grain of rice or granule of millet; like smokeless light, it is greater than the heaven, the atmosphere, and the earth, than all existing things : the self of the spirit is the self of man, and on passing away from life he attains that self. The changed spirit of the speculation in the course of time cannot be better illustrated than by this view, for the Taittirīya Saṁhitā holds closely to the material view that the result of the offering in the next world is to secure the sacrificer his self and his breath therein. The continuance as nearly as possible in the same condition as before of the existence on earth is the ideal of the Saṁhitā : it has been transmuted by the wisdom of Çāṇḍilya [2] into a conception which seeks in its grand manner to solve the question of the existence of the universe and of the individual, by finding in them both the expression of a single spiritual principle. The impression of later growth thus engendered is supported, and made beyond reasonable doubt, not merely by the evidence of language, but by the fact that it is precisely this book of the Çatapatha which gives us the conception of the repetition, not once merely, of death in the world to come.[3] The philosophy of the Brāhmaṇas is merging into that of the Upaniṣads.

[1] This connexion of birth and the year may conceivably be due to the old view—apparently Indo-European—of the year of ten months of gestation, which may be found in the Rigveda as in ancient Rome. Buddhist tradition insists on ten months precisely as the period of his stay in the womb (Windisch, *Buddha's Geburt*, pp. 120 ff.) ; Hopkins (JAOS. xxiv. 19, 392) thinks references to the year are only periods within which, which would prove nothing for a ten months' year. His view that the month is twenty-seven or twenty-eight days in the popular reckoning is counter to the fact that birth is placed in the tenth month, not at the end, so that his month is too short. Probably the thirty-day month is all that is meant. Buddha is clearly a miraculous child.

[2] ÇB. x. 6. 4.

[3] Lindenau's suggestion (ZII. i. 48, n. 2) that AV. xiii. 3. 7 enunciates, as regards Rohita, the doctrine of the necessary mortality of the highest being, so far as involved in the empiric world, rests on a dubious translation.

§ 4. *The Ethics of the Brāhmaṇas*

In the strict sense of the word there is no theory of ethics in the Brāhmaṇa literature: the question of the nature of right action does not seem ever to have in any degree influenced the speculations of the curious spirits which framed the remarkable theory of which the outlines have been sketched above. It was, indeed, natural that the first element of the speculative thought of India should in the main be directed to problems of pure speculation, as was also the case in Greece, but the dominating feature in the philosophy of India is that the question of right conduct never attained the dignity of a subject to be propounded for serious consideration. In the Rigveda, while the hymns of creation and the other efforts to arrive at a philosophical account of the universe have beside them the expression in the hymns to Varuṇa of the prevalence of moral order and the punishment of sin, the latter conception cannot be found in living force any longer in the Brāhmaṇas, a fact which has unwisely been used as a proof that early India was exposed to Semitic influences later not felt.[1]

The contrast here between Indian and Iranian development in religious matters becomes marked. Almost contemporaneously, perhaps, with the development of the thought of the Brāhmaṇas, we find Zoroaster engaged in deepening the meaning of religion for the people of Iran and founding a reasoned ethical system. While Varuṇa was losing ground in India, Zoroaster was developing the figure of Ahura Mazdāh, and depriving him of a rival by degrading Indra, his most serious competitor, as the god of war, to the rank of a demon.[2] At the same time he removed from the character of the god any suspicion of uncertainty or caprice, such as still clings in the Rigveda to Varuṇa, whose noose and whose punishments appear to afflict at times even the innocent, and who is lord of a Māyā, which may be harmful as well as beneficent. Further, to Zoroaster the powers of evil loomed far greater than they had done to the early Aryan mind, which, as in the Rigveda, knows indeed demons in abundance, but has no doubt in the power of the gods to overcome them, nor indeed of its own ability to win the favour of the gods. Vṛtra may be terrible, but he is never victorious, even if it would be unkind to assert that the Vedic demons exist merely for the gods to slay. Zoroaster accepts the impossibility of explaining the evil in the world, if it be assumed that Ahura is all-mighty, and that all has been created by him at his pleasure. On the contrary, the spirit of evil contends against the good, and only after desperate struggles can good be made to prevail. Moreover, in that struggle

[1] Brunnhofer, *Arische Urzeit*, pp. xviii, 89, 90; his etymologies of Vedic words need not seriously be considered; to that of Weber which derives Dulā, one of the Kṛttikās, from a Semitic source no objection in principle is open, but the mere similarity of sound without identity of use is an utterly insufficient ground.

[2] See Güntert, *Der arische Weltkönig*, pp. 211 ff.

each man is free and morally bound to participate; it lies with him to further the conquest of evil; the deeds which he does are not merely personal; they serve to further the constant struggle of good against evil, and have cosmic value. Moreover, by his deeds does a man decide his future fate, in heaven or hell; the intervention of divine favour is excluded;[1] the soul of the dead finds the Cinvaṭ bridge wide or hopelessly narrow, according as his good or evil deeds prevail. Deeds, moreover, are essentially matters of practical utility and activity; prayers and offerings play their part, but the ideal of Zoroaster is the man who founds a family, performs his duties in his tribe, and furthers agriculture, performing useful works, as opposed to the nomad, who is the personification of the lie (*druj*).

It may be that the stern conditions of life in Iran, where cultivation can be maintained only by unceasing toil, and the agriculturist must ever fear the incursions of the nomad, played a definite part in evoking the Zoroastrian outlook, nor, of course, must be ignored the individual character of his teaching, which never was fully assimilated in Iran, but was on the one hand exaggerated and made absurd by the pedantic and cruel pursuit of detail, and on the other hand contaminated by the reintroduction of much of the old nature-worship of Iran.[2] In India under different conditions of climate and life and racial admixture, thought turned to speculation rather than to action, and inclined to see unity, in lieu of regarding life as a struggle between the good and the bad. This contrast interposed for Zoroaster essential difficulties in regarding the world as a single whole, animated by one spirit; in India this was possible, and an absolute came to be recognized in which all was contained, whether good or bad, material or spiritual. Parallel with this movement was necessarily the decline from power of Varuṇa. Indra, as the god of the warrior and the people, remained powerful and popular: recent research, indeed, has shown how much alive, if in humble guise, he is to-day in northern India;[3] first Prajāpati, and then the Brahman absorbed the metaphysical elements of Varuṇa's nature, while the growth in popularity of Yama as king of the dead limited his chthonian functions,[4] so that the god who once was the chief guardian of the Ṛta sank to the function of lord of waters, which was his by right as a sky god, and which no other deity arose to wrest from him. Similarly the conception of the Ṛta passes away before the prevalence of the Brahman.

The development which places the Brahman in the first place is not achieved until the Upaniṣads, but it is in preparation during the period of the Brāhmaṇas, and it is in entire harmony with this spirit that these texts do

[1] For the idea of a future Saviour for the world as a whole, see Güntert, pp. 219, 395 ff.

[2] Cf. Hertel, *Die Zeit Zoroasters*, pp. 9 ff., 48 ff.

[3] See Grierson, ZII. ii. 133 ff.

[4] Cf. Güntert, *Der arische Weltkönig*, pp. 238 f. He (p. 390) lays stress on the folk etymology of Yama as the restrainer (*yam*) as securing his relation as controller of the dead in later thought. Less plausible is his suggestion of Poseidon's history as comparable to that of Varuṇa.

not develop any theory of morality.[1] Indeed they do not normally inculcate morality even on merely empiric grounds. The myths which they recount and invent have this characteristic about them, that they are indifferent to the moral qualities of the acts : the gods are willing to commit sins freely for their own gain : they obtain the aid of the Rakṣases against the Asuras, and then they refuse to carry out their bargain to share equally with the former in the event of victory attending their united efforts. They are not ashamed to purchase the Soma from the Gandharvas by means of Vāc, on the clear agreement arrived at between her and them that she will return to them when invited. They win speech from the Asuras by the low arts of solicitation and of dancing and singing in opposition to the pious recitation of the Veda by their rivals. They are constantly jealous of men, whom they refuse to allow to share with them the happiness of immortality without laying aside the corporeal body in death. But compared with Indra they are comparatively virtuous people: he, however, is quite unashamed: he makes a compact with Namuci and sets about to find a way of violating it, which he does with success : his murder of Viçvarūpa, son of Tvaṣṭṛ, is unmotived and wicked, and brings on him the guilt of slaying a Brahman. His amour with Ahalyā is only accomplished by means of deceiving the lady by adopting the form of her husband,[2] and he gave over to the hyenas certain ascetics, an impure (*amedhya*) act.[3] His adultery [4] is repaid in kind; for his own son, born of his thigh, Kutsa Aurava, takes advantage of his physical likeness, to win the favour of Çacī Paulomnī, his father's wife. But, after all, what could be more degrading than the pictures of him hungry and begging a priest for an offering, and then running about cake in hand, or bound by cords by Kutsa and urged by Luça to break away from this degrading servitude ? [5] Even his own subjects, the Maruts, he plunders, justifying the royal habit of accepting loot plundered from the husbandmen. Prajāpati appears as committing incest, and as adopting in the course of it an animal form, which is slain by the wrath of the gods concentrated in the form of Rudra,[6] and in one rite he is formally reviled. The other gods are constantly jealous of one another ; they have separate dwellings, and are moved by envy of one another rather than by love and friendship. The Vrātyas insult Vāyu and Īçāna, who bar the world of heaven to them, but are shown it by Prajāpati.[7] The gods are essentially selfish ; they give men the six evils of sleep, sloth, anger, hunger, love of dicing and of women.

[1] For an interesting contrast with Confucianism, see M. Weber, *Religionssoziologie*, ii. 136 ff.

[2] Weber, SBA. 1887, p. 903 ; Oertel, JAOS. xix. 120 ; xxvi. 186. For the sins of the gods see PB. i. 6. 10 ; AV. vi. 111. 3 ; x. 1. 12 ; Bloomfield, SBE. xlii. 520. Traces of 'high moral sense and exalted sentiment' (Radhakrishnan, *Ind. Phil.* i. 131) are invisible, and the term Āçrama certainly does not show that it was recognized that all progress involved suffering.

[3] TS. iii. 3. 7. 3 ; PB. xiv. 11. 28 ; xviii. 1. 9.

[4] JB. iii. 199–202.

[5] PB. ix. 2. 22 ; xxi. 1. 1. f.

[6] MS. iv. 2. 12 ; ÇB. i. 7. 4. 1–4 ; vi. 1. 3. 8 ; PB. viii. 2. 10 ; AB. iii. 33 ; ApÇS. xxi. 12. 1 ff.

[7] JB. ii. 222.

It is the case that the gods are said to be essentially true,[1] but the nature of the truth is not vitally moral: it is strictly confined to the precise carrying out of the rites and utterance of the formulae of the sacrificial ritual. Just as man's faith is not in the goodness of the gods, but in the efficacy of the sacrifice, if duly performed, so truth has no real moral content and in intellectual outlook is limited to the sacrifice, which, it must be admitted, is the reality *par excellence* for the Brahmans. But even this truth was not always the possession of the gods: as children of Prajāpati, the gods and the Asuras shared the patrimony of the father, which was Vāc: they then indifferently spoke truth and falsehood: finally the gods abandoned the use of anything but truth, and the Asuras that of anything but falsehood. The gods, however, by saying nothing but the truth became feeble and impoverished, while by the opposite device the Asuras prospered like salt, the Indian equivalent of the green bay tree. But in the end the truth prevailed over the untruth, mainly, it would seem, because by the consecration offering, which they invented, the gods extended truth and made it more effective.[2] The moral apparently, therefore, is that in the long run exactitude in the sacrifice must prevail.

The sense of the importance of exactitude in the rite is seen in the famous ritual of confession which is performed at the Varuṇapraghāsas, when the priest, the Pratiprasthātṛ, asks the wife of the sacrificer with whom she consorts, other than her husband.[3] It is essential that she should confess, since else it will go badly with her kinsfolk, an interesting assertion of the solidarity of the kin. The speaking out of the sin diminishes it, but not, it appears, by anything else than that it brings exactitude again into the order of things: the wife commits an offence against Varuṇa, in that being the wife of one she consorts with another: the statement of the true fact removes the inexactitude, and repairs in so far the defect. It brings truth, i.e. reality, and order into the rite.[4] The position of Varuṇa in this regard is of importance as it indicates in what degree the high conception of the Varuṇa of the Rigveda has been degraded by the passage of time and the growing preference for the sacrifice. He is not regarded in the ritual, as it stands, as more than the power which resents the introduction of irregularity into the facts of the universe.

The position of Varuṇa in this regard is also of interest on another ground: in the Brāhmaṇas Varuṇa is essentially a god of the waters, and this connexion of truth or reality and the waters must be traced to this relation. Hiraṇyadant Baida[5] is quoted as asserting that heaven rests on the atmosphere, the atmosphere on the earth, the earth on the waters, the waters

[1] AB. i. 6. 7; KB. ii. 8; MS. i. 9. 3; ÇB. iii. 4. 2. 8.

[2] ÇB. ix. 5. 1. 12–27.

[3] A painful light is shed on priestly morality by the story of Yavakrī, who was wont to summon to him any woman at pleasure, though intercourse with him meant death. He ultimately was slain by a Gandharva, after an Apsaras had been substituted for the wife of Yajñavacas, and after in madness he had cut off the heads of his cattle.

[4] ÇB. ii. 5. 2. 20.

[5] AB. iii. 6; he appears also in JB. ii. 278.

on truth, truth on the Brahman, and the Brahman on fervour. The waters are, it must be remembered, the primeval elements, they are a fact and they are also based on fact, on truth. The waters are also the conception of law: when the waters come to this earth, then all is in due and lawful order: when there is lack of rain, the stronger oppresses the weaker.[1] The waters are also the reality itself,[2] they are immortality,[3] they are faith,[4] they are the sacrifice.[5] Man must use them to sprinkle himself with water, in order to become ritually pure. The performance of the bath provides even consecration and fervour, for the gods placed consecration in the waters.[6] Moreover, the sap of the sacrifice is in the waters and by it they flow.[7] The impurities of men do not affect the waters themselves, in accordance with the pact they made with the gods. The Darbha grass owes its power to the presence in it of the waters. The waters are as a thunderbolt, and they must be propitiated with suitable words to avoid injury by them. They are extremely powerful to destroy the Rakṣases,[8] and they are, therefore, benevolent if managed well: they form the atonement [9] for every harsh deed in the sacrifice, and on the other hand, when appeased, they confer glory and power on the king at the royal consecration.

But the identification of the waters with truth or reality is not the only identification: the earth is also truth, for it is of all the worlds the most obviously genuine.[10] Gold again is reality; lead, being neither iron nor gold, is a mere appearance.[11] Truth, therefore, is nothing but a species of existence, which the term used, Satya, also properly expresses. But the most important side remains ritual accuracy: the best pair is the union of faith and truth as ritual accuracy.[12] The sacrifice is formally identified with the truth, and so is the threefold Veda, and the Brahman as holy writ, to which conception we must refer the doctrine of Hiraṇyadant Baida that truth rests on the Brahman. More simply, however, the rite is simple fact: the eye is asserted to be truth, because, unlike the mind and speech, it is not prone to give false witness. From this fact, however, there is deduced a doctrine of some value for the guidance of the sacrificer: as in the case of the wife and her lovers, he must see that in the rite he shall duly bring himself into harmony with the truth by the use of true speech.[13] When he is about to undertake a vow, he should realize that he passes from the inaccuracy of ordinary life to the exactitude, which is characteristic in ritual of the god, and, at the end when he lays down the vow, he ceases to be under the bond of accuracy. But in the rite he does not say so openly: [14] he contents himself with the declaration that he is once more as he was—that is one who lives among men, whose nature is inaccuracy.

[1] ÇB. xi. 1. 6. 24.
[2] MS. iv. 1. 4; ÇB. vii. 6. 1. 4.
[3] MS. iv. 1. 9; GB. ii. 1. 3.
[4] TS. i. 6. 8. 1; MS. i. 4. 10; iv. 1. 4.
[5] MS. iii. 6. 2; 6. 9; iv. 1. 4.
[6] TS. vi. 1. 1. 2; MS. iii. 6. 2.
[7] ÇB. iii. 9. 2. 1.
[8] MS. iv. 1. 3.
[9] MS. ii. 1. 5; iv. 5. 4; ÇB. i. 9. 3. 2; AB. viii. 6.
[10] ÇB. vii. 4. 1. 8.
[11] MS. ii. 2. 2; iv. 3. 1.
[12] AB. vii. 10.
[13] ÇB. iv. 3. 4. 16; iii. 4. 2. 8; ii. 2. 2. 19; i. 1. 1. 5; AB. ii. 5–9; TB. i. 1. 4. 1.
[14] ÇB. i. 1. 1. 4–6.

A difficulty, however, arises in practice: if the rule of truth is laid down absolutely as incumbent always on him who has established the sacred fires, what will happen to him? What man can always speak the truth? Aruṇa Aupaveçi, when urged to establish his fires, put the point plainly that he was being condemned by this instruction to silence, as no one could avoid speaking what was false.[1]

In the view of Oldenberg,[2] truth denotes something more than mere accuracy, and it is probable that there is justice in this contention, if it is not pressed too hard. It is characteristic of this period[3] that the terms Satya and Anṛta come to form a formal contrast. As we have seen, in the Rigveda it is impossible to accept the view that Ṛta and Satya, order and truth, are identical,[4] and it would probably be erroneous to assume that the contrast of Satya and Anṛta denoted that in this period the term Anṛta had lost any connexion with the idea of order and righteousness. It may perhaps be said that, while Anṛta tends to be weakened into meaning no more than falsehood, Satya takes on an additional tinge of value[5] and it is certain that Ṛta still means order, though here and there[6] it is tempting, but probably misleading, merely to render it 'truth'.

Varuṇa is the deity who is constantly ready to punish inaccuracies in the ritual: his cords and his knots make him admirably fit for this purpose, and the errors in the offering are at once seized hold of by him. By sacrificing in the southern fire, the sacrificer secures the seizing by Varuṇa of his rival, but the offering if made on the Āhavanīya would entail the same fate for the sacrificer himself.[7] Viṣṇu, on the other hand, repairs the errors of the sacrifice, and does not seize on them as the time for assailing the author of the mistakes.[8] If the rule that a father should not be transgressed against is asserted, and traced to Prajāpati's offspring being punished by Varuṇa for transgress against him, it is at once found that the transgress was a ritual one.[9] In Varuṇa's house when the gods make mutual pledge of loyalty at the Tānūnaptra they deposit their forms: here again the act is a ritual performance.[10]

But the most convincing evidence of all regarding the almost purely ritual character of goodness in the view of the Brāhmaṇas is the fact that their conception of torment in the other world is inextricably bound up with the correct practice, or the failure to follow the correct practice, of the ritual.

1 AB. i. 6. 6; ÇB. ii. 2. 2. 20.

2 GN. 1915, pp. 177 ff.

3 In the RV. Ṛta and Satya come together, usually late, ix. 113. 4; x. 190. 1; cf. vii. 104. 8; *anṛtā́ asatyā́ḥ*, iv. 5. 5; Anṛta regularly is opposed to Ṛta (i. 105. 5; 139. 2; 152. 1, 3; ii. 24. 7; vii. 60. 5; 65. 3; 66. 13; x. 87. 11; 124. 5); to Satya, only vii. 49. 3; x. 55. 6.

4 In KS. xxxvi. 5 and MS. i. 10. 11 Ṛta and Satya are opposed to Anṛta only.

5 Cf. ÇB. i. 1. 1. 4, 5 with KB. ii. 8.

6 e. g. *ṛtám amīṣva*, TS. ii. 3. 5. 1; cf. MS. ii. 2. 7; PB. xxi. 2. 1; cf. Oldenberg, *Rel. des Veda*², p. 519, n. 2.

7 TS. ii. 3. 13. 2; i. 7. 2. 6; ÇB. i. 3. 1. 14–16; xii. 7. 2. 17; iv. 5. 1. 6; PB. xv. 2. 4; TB. i. 6. 5. 4.

8 AB. vii. 4. 4.

9 MS. i. 10. 10.

10 TS. vi. 2. 2. 1, 2, &c.

After death man is weighed in the balance to test the good and the bad, an idea which is evidently not a primitive speculation but a late development,[1] suggested, it may be, by the ordeal of the balance which is known in the later literature: it is, however, at least possible that the idea is no more than one of the passing conceptions of the Brāhmaṇas, possibly a faint echo of the Iranian conception of judgement.[2] But we cannot for a moment assume that the distinction depends on ordinary morality. The real nature of the idea is shown by the story of Bhṛgu, son of Varuṇa, who was so proud that the god for his improvement made him unconscious and sent his spirit to see the world to come. Of the sights seen by Bhṛgu there are two versions preserved in the Çatapatha [3] and the Jaiminīya Brāhmaṇas: [4] according to the latter, he first saw a man devouring another man whom he had cut up in pieces; in the second place he saw a man who was eating another while the latter uttered cries of misery; in the third place he saw a man who was eating another, who, however, kept entire silence; in the fourth place he saw two women guarding a treasure; and in the fifth place two rivers, one of blood guarded by a naked man armed with a mace, and one of butter guarded by men of gold, who with cups of gold draw from it what they desire. Then he saw, last of all, five rivers covered with lotuses blue and white, with waves of honey, where the dance, the song, and the lute resounded, where Apsarases disported themselves, and sweet fragrance was wafted. The Çatapatha version differs in detail: Varuṇa sends Bhṛgu simply on a journey to cure him of pride: he visits the four cardinal points and one of the intermediate spaces. He sees only five instead of six sights, and these five are reduced to four by the fact that the first is really reduplicated, the first being the vision of men who were cutting in pieces and the second of men who were cutting only. The two rivers of blood and of butter, and the five of gold are omitted *in toto*, and the nude man figures in the episode of the two damsels. The explanation of these visions is given to the chastened Bhṛgu by his father Varuṇa: the first exhibits the fate of those men who, without offering the Agnihotra and without true knowledge, cut wood in the world: the trees take thus revenge on them in the world to come; the second is the fate of men who without proper ritual knowledge kill and eat animals; the third applies in the case of eating herbs. The other three visions are faith and lack of faith respectively; the river of blood is the blood of a Brahman, the black man is the sacrifice, the river of butter is formed from the waters used at the offering; the five rivers are the worlds of Varuṇa. If a man performs the due offering, the trees in the world to come do not eat him, nor animals, nor rice and barley: his offerings go neither to faith or lack of faith: he avoids the river of blood, he gains the river of butter. The same idea appears in the Kauṣītaki Brāhmaṇa [5]

[1] ÇB. xi. 2. 7. 33.

[2] Moulton, *Early Zoroastrianism*, pp. 169, 313; Güntert, *Der arische Weltkönig*, p. 218.

[3] xi. 6. 1.

[4] JB. i. 42–4 (JAOS. xv. 234–8).

[5] xi. 3.

also: the animals revenge themselves on man in the next world, unless he adopts the proper form of rite.

A final proof of the brutal morality of the priest can be adduced in the position assigned to women: woman in India has always suffered much from all religions,[1] but by none has she been so thoroughly despised as by the Brahmans of the period of the Brāhmaṇas. The insolence of the question at the Varuṇapraghāsas has been noted: however much it may be explained away, it remains an insult, since it can only be justified on the theory that infidelity in a wife is not surprising; a priest like Yavakrī takes toll of every woman he fancies at pleasure. The wife is the half of man,[2] but this is merely due to the fact that, without her, the man cannot secure the essential off-spring to continue his family, and perform the offerings to him after death. The Maitrāyaṇī Saṁhitā [3] is very outspoken in its view of women: the three things which are connected with Nirṛti, 'Dissolution', are dice, women, and slumber: the reality is the sacrifice, women is lack of truth. Three invitations addressed in a loving tone will overcome the most circumspect women, and their bad taste prefers the dance and song to the recitation of the Veda.[4] Their power of wheedling secrets out of their husband is referred to in contemptuous terms.[5] As compared with men they are always inferior: woman is the inferior part of the sacrifice: she is ritually impure, and must be covered with a girdle.[6] They have been smitten by the gods with the thunderbolt of the butter and hence they are emasculated, they cannot control themselves or an inheritance: [7] even if many women are together and there is but a small boy, he takes precedence of them all.[8] They are inferior even to a bad man,[9] and their inferiority is marked by the ceremony on birth when the child is brought to the father.[10]

On the other hand, it would be wholly unfair to ignore the fact that the Brāhmaṇas do not encourage or contemplate many crimes, which have been committed in other rituals. The exposure of female children which has been asserted to be mentioned in the Brāhmaṇas is a mere error.[11] The Brāhmaṇas, further, never actually prescribe a human sacrifice: the tradition of such an offering in the piling of the fire altar is handed down, and the name of the last sacrificer is given, but, though the Brāhmaṇa [12] does not show any profound horror at the past, and may possibly have regretted the change, it must be remembered that this rite was always a rare and exceptional one. The

[1] Cf., in addition to Winternitz's and Meyer's works, the summary in Frazer, *Indian Thought Past and Present*, pp. 271–306; JB. ii. 269 ff.

[2] ÇB. v. 2. 1. 10.

[3] iii. 6. 3; i. 10. 11, 16; JB. i. 98 f. adds sloth, anger, and hunger.

[4] ÇB. iii. 2. 4. 3–6; TS. vi. 1. 6. 5; MS. iii. 7. 3. Cf. BAU. vi. 4. 12.

[5] KS. xxx. 1; AB. iii. 22.

[6] ÇB. i. 3. 1. 12, 13; the symbolic ritual to secure fertility is slightly refined in PB. viii. 7. 8–13; Hopkins, TCA. xv. 36.

[7] ÇB. iv. 4. 2. 13; TS. vi. 8. 2.

[8] ÇB. i. 3. 1. 9.

[9] TS. vi. 5. 8. 2.

[10] MS. iv. 6. 4.

[11] Macdonell and Keith, *Vedic Index*, i. 395; ii. 115.

[12] ÇB. vi. 2. 1. 39.

slaughter of animals was, of course, prescribed by the rite, but the use of animals for food was the basis of this slaughter, and the doctrine of Ahiṅsā is one which has never even in India received full sanction. The accusation of cruelty in the slaying of the victim, which has often been brought against religious rites, is not specially proved for the Brāhmaṇas: the primitive means of slaying victims available probably caused suffering to the animals, as in the Jewish practice of to-day, but that there was any deliberate lack of humanity is contrary to the desire of the sacrificers to avoid anything unseemly, which might indicate the reluctance of the victim to depart from the world. The Omophagia of the Dionysiac rites is not in the slightest degree hinted at in the Indian sacrifice.

The ritual admittedly contains several rites based on fertility magic, which to modern taste are revolting, and sometimes even horrible, such as the action of the queen at the horse sacrifice. The idea that these rites were invented by the Brahmans, as is suggested even by Victor Henry,[1] must be rejected as an error: the beliefs so expressed are primitive and natural, not priestly, and the only action of the priests in regard to them was doubtless the adoption from the popular belief of these usages and their decoration with the literature of the priests.[2] Even in regard to these usages it is fair to note that there arose among the priests a disinclination to perform the ritual. In the Çāñkhāyana Çrauta Sūtra [3] there is recorded the view that the rite, by which a pair, or pairs, in the course of the Mahāvrata at the winter solstice went through the process of intercourse, ought not to be performed, whether because it was antiquated or too extensive is uncertain. That such a view should have been taken in the face of the prescription of the rite in all the ancient texts [4] is creditable and worthy of notice. It is only to be regretted that it stands almost alone, for the omission in certain texts of the rite of beating the king on the occasion of the royal consecration may be explained otherwise.

Moreover, we must admit that the ritual books show sometimes the most unedifying indifference to morality. The Jaiminīya Brāhmaṇa [5] actually records, without disapproval apparently, a rite, the Gosava, in which the performer pays the ox the compliment of imitating its mode of existence, including incest with mother, sister, and female relative, though it records

[1] *La doctrine du sacrifice*, pp. 107, 108. The Tantras reveal to us a religion—perhaps aboriginal—of sexual orgiastic character, which doubtless in substance is very old and popular; cf. Weber, *Religionssoziologie*, ii. 322 ff.

[2] See, e.g., the rites for sexual intercourse given in BAU. vi. 4, *a priori* an unexpected place, and the speculations of the Garbha Upaniṣad, forerunners of the Kāma Sūtra.

[3] Weber, *Ind. Stud.* x. 125; Keith, ZDMG. lxvi. 729, 730. The term *utsanna* recurs in Samudragupta's record of his sacrifice, raising doubts of its sense; IA. lii. 17.

[4] TS. vii. 5. 9. 4; KS. xxxiv. 5. These texts may be put about 800–700 B.C., the Çrauta Sūtra is dated (Keith, JRAS. 1908, p. 387) about 350 B.C. In JB. ii. 404 f. a Māgadha is given the distasteful duty.

[5] ii. 113; ApÇS. xxii. 13. 1–3.

that Janaka of Videha did not carry out the rite, when he understood its nature, and the Çibi king, who did, concluded that it was a ritual which should be performed in old age only, when the action it prescribed might be more excusable in certain regards. The priestly nature of the rite as it stands is shown by the reward promised, the world of the Ox, a reference to that creature in its Atharvan [1] form as a cosmic equivalent of Prajāpati. Not less brutal is the cynical rite [2] provided when a man desires his wife to have lovers in plenty during his absence from her side.

A more favourable view of the morality of the Brāhmaṇas is taken by Hopkins,[3] who holds that, while in the case of the Pañcavinça the Sāman and the rite make the gist of the Brāhmaṇa's religion, it remains true that there is a real ethical foundation for this religion. The evidence adduced, however, is scanty; untruth is indeed reproved, and the 'hant' follows the slayer, while taking too much is like swallowing poison.[4] But the sacrifice does away with sin automatically; even a sinner by means of wealth gets to the top; goods wrongly accepted can thus be made proper and fit.[5] The conception of sin is mechanical: all slaying, even of demons such as Vṛtra, brings the taint of bloodshed, whether justified or not, the fault of the sacrifice passes to him who blames it, as does a third of the sin of the initiated to any one who speaks ill of them.[6] Evil repute (*açlīlā vāc*) fastens on every killer, irrespective of the nature of his deed. A false accusation makes a man, despite his innocence, avoided by the gods, but the priests can make his sacrifice acceptable to them, and it is wisely said that the false accusers are the real sinners.[7] Untruth is described as a hole in the voice which can be filled by adding a syllable to a verse.[8] We find also the dubious doctrine [9] of 'sins caused by the gods, by the Fathers, by other men or by ourselves', which the commentator explains as evils inflicted by the gods or Fathers in respect of neglect, but not with certain accuracy. Moreover, insistence is laid on the fact that sacrifice increases proportionately man's welfare materially and spiritually.[10]

The Brāhmaṇa, however, contains one doctrine of interest,[11] intended to explain the fact of the grief (*çoka*) which is the lot of the harlot, the eunuch, and the sinner. It adapts the old doctrine of the grief of the earth and sky on parting; Indra removes grief from the earth into the harlot, from the atmosphere, which is the weakest of the worlds,[12] to the eunuch, and from the sky to the sinner; hence their desires are unattainable, and, even if one obtains some part of desire, he attains also a portion of grief.

1 AV. iv. 11.

2 BhGS. ii. 28; ApGS. xxiii. 4; cf. Keith, JRAS. 1914, p. 1088.

3 TCA. xv. 29.

4 PB. xix. 4. 10.

5 PB. xvii. 2. 2; xiii. 7. 12 f.

6 PB. v. 5. 13; 6. 10.

7 PB. xviii. 1. 10–12 (cf. the unholy voice which attaches to a man falsely accused of murder, TS. ii. 1. 10. 2); vi. 10. 7.

8 PB. viii. 6. 13.

9 PB. i. 6. 10; cf. VS. viii. 13; ÇB. iv. 4. 5. 22.

10 Yet 'ill does he who gives all', PB. xvi. 5. 6; 6. 1; 9. 2.

11 PB. viii. i. 9–11.

12 PB. vii. 3. 10; cf. TS. v. 4. 6. 4; PB. xxi. 7. 3; its name is neuter.

The association of purely ritual acts with morality is conspicuous even in the Upaniṣads,[1] and it is not surprising that the Brāhmaṇas remain in hopeless ignorance of the specific character of morality. As in the sphere of the sacrifice, we find confusion of the ideas of divine intervention and magic operation. Thus Varuṇa seizes the doer of evil, and therefore, since the evening is Varuṇa's time, one should then on no account utter falsehood.[2] But, having spoken truth in the evening, it makes no difference how much falsehood one speaks thereafter; the original truth, applied at the proper moment, continues to have, we may say, an abiding and dominant effect.[3] Untruth and impurity can be washed away by water, or wiped away by application of the sacred Darbha grass.[4] The same independence of morality is seen in the new doctrine of the fruit of ritual works, independent of divine action, and the view that man is born into the world hereafter which he has made for himself.[5] The germ of the ideas lies in the gifts and sacrifices (*iṣṭāpūrta*) of the Rigveda with which one is united in the world to come, without any divine intervention. We have here a germ whence later appears the conception of the automatic working of Karman.

One idea of importance, however, can be faintly traced. Impurity, of course, is largely ritual, and a new-born child is ritually impure.[6] On the other hand, we find it definitely asserted that if one perform a certain ceremony of purification one will be left with no more guilt than is in a toothless child, and a similar assertion is made of a child on birth.[7] These assertions clearly admit that sin is not to be ascribed to a being incapable of volition, and in the same strain of thought we have the assertion of the sin which accrued to Soma because he had merely the intention of oppressing the Brahmans.[8] But these are isolated utterances, we have no reason to suppose that there was recognized any general doctrine of the necessity of volition to create responsibility; the opposite clearly appears from the tale of the charioteer who by inadvertence killed a Brahman boy, for the discussion of the incident deals only with the point whether the charioteer, or his master who was riding in the chariot, was to bear the sin of the slaughter.[9]

In the terminology [10] of the Brāhmaṇas, however, appear differentiations

[1] e.g. BAU. iii. 8. 9.

[2] TB. i. 7. 2. 6; i. 5. 3. 3.

[3] KB. ii. 8.

[4] ÇB. iii. 1. 2. 10; 3. 18; AV. x. 5. 22.

[5] KB. xxvi. 3; ÇB. vi. 2. 2. 27. On the imperishableness of the *iṣṭāpūrta* see KB. vii. 4; JB. ii. 53. The idea seems applied to good deeds in TB. iii. 10. 11. 3; Oldenberg, *Die Lehre der Upanishaden*, p. 30.

[6] Cf. TB. iii. 7. 12. 3 f.

[7] ÇB. iv. 4. 5. 23; KS. xxxvi. 5; PB. xviii. 1. 24.

[8] ÇB. iv. 1. 2. 4. The Kali Gandharvas vainly attempt to obtain favour from gods, Fathers, and men by asserting (JB. i. 154 f.) that they had mentally favoured their contest against Asuras, Rakṣases, and Piçācas.

[9] See Sieg, *Die Sagenstoffe des Ṛgveda*, pp. 64 ff.; Macdonell and Keith, *Vedic Index*, ii. 321; JB. iii. 94–6. Intention becomes recognized in Buddhism (Keith, *Buddhist Philosophy*, p. 114). See also Oldenberg, in Mommsen, *Zum ältesten Strafrecht der Kulturvölker*, pp. 76 ff.

[10] Oldenberg, *Weltanschauung der Brāhmaṇatexte*, pp. 186 ff.; GN. 1915, pp. 167 ff.

from the uses of the Rigveda which attest the development of moral conceptions. The conception of Ṛta as righteousness, as has been seen, is less prominent; but the term itself in the negative form, Anṛta, has established itself as the opposite of truth, Satya, which largely supersedes Ṛta. The old conception of law, Dharman, persists, but there appears beside it the later formation Dharma, which the Çatapatha Brāhmaṇa [1] formally personifies. The king now is hailed as the guardian of the Dharma and to him who has the power men resort in matters of Dharma,[2] whence later we have the Dharma Sūtras with their inextricable mixture of ritual, of domestic practices, and of civil and criminal law, all matters which Dharma is wide enough to cover. Vrata in the Rigveda denotes either the will of the god, or the usage of the man who obeys that will, nor does it cease to have this sense in the Brāhmaṇas, for the committer of a breach of the established moral laws can be called one who turns from Vrata (*apavrata*).[3] But it tends to be specialized to denote the course of observance specially undertaken by an individual for some special purpose, and the Brāhmaṇas, like the Upaniṣads and the Sūtras, know of many curious Vratas.

There is development also in the terms for good and evil. The old words Vasu and Çrī [4] continue to denote material prosperity, the earlier sense of the latter term as appropriate to beauty becoming less and less prominent, and the wicked man is still Pāpa. But from its use with terms of motion Sādhu comes to denote what is right,[5] and Puṇya slowly develops, in lieu of its purely unethical sense of 'fortunate' or 'lucky', the implication of goodness,[6] as evinced in prosperity. Both terms are fated to have an important development later, for they are used in those passages of the Upaniṣads which touch on the essential connexion of the position of man in life as affected by the merit or demerit of his deeds in a previous birth.[7]

But though terminology shows a certain advance in view, it remains the case that nothing architectonic arises in the way of conception of good and evil. Truth and falsehood are sometimes set against each other, and once truth, good fortune, and light are opposed to untruth, evil, and darkness. But we miss entirely even what might have been expected, a living effort to combine the opposition of gods and Asuras with the conception of good and evil. Goods remain essentially mundane; the prayers offered are especially for temporal things, prosperity for the crops, the cattle, the boon of children, harmony in the realm, or pre-eminence for the Brahmans, or the restoration of an exiled

[1] xiii. 4. 3. 14.

[2] AB. viii. 12. 5; KS. xvii. 19; ÇB. v. 3. 3. 9.

[3] MS. iv. 2. 12.

[4] Oldenberg, GN. 1918, pp. 35 ff.

[5] ÇB. ii. 6. 3. 8 is dubious, but xi. 2. 7. 33 contrasts *sādhu-kṛtyā* and *pāpa-kṛtyā*; a king, true to his duty (*dhṛtavrata*), speaks and acts *sādhu*, v. 4. 4. 5.

[6] Connexion with *pṝ* or *puṣ* is dubious; for the old sense see RV. ii. 43. 2; vii. 55. 8; TS. i. 6. 11. 4; iii. 3. 8. 5; KS. xiii. 5; xxvii. 10.

[7] *puṇya*, BAU. iii. 2. 13; iv. 3. 15 (against *pāpa*); *sādhu*, *asādhu*, BAU. iv. 4. 22; *sādhu*, *pāpa*, TU. ii. 9; *sādhu*, *puṇya*, *pāpa*, BAU. iv. 4. 5.

king, acuteness of the senses, and rarely the world of heaven.[1] Occasionally the idea appears that all objects of human desire are of minor importance; the chariot of the gods is yoked for the world of heaven, that of men for mere desires. Similarly knowledge is stated to attain a result which neither gifts to the priest nor asceticism can obtain.[2] But this is not the prevailing idea, nor are prayers necessarily moral. Man may sacrifice and pray to be freed from reproach of murder, from persecution by evil spirits, but also to be safe in violating for a year his oath, without meeting punishment from Varuṇa.[3]

It is the conviction of the Brāhmaṇas that life on the earth is on the whole a good thing; for a man to live out his length of days is the ideal, and such traces of discontent as appear are mainly in regard to the doubt that man must feel whether he has even a year more to live.[4] If he must die, then the sacrifice avails to carry him to the world of heaven, but he is never normally anxious to precipitate this result; if a rite carries him to the sky, it ends, none the less, in restoring him to the solid earth. Besides death there are other evils; hunger, dice, women, sleep, cause sin as does untruthfulness; these are of the nature of things, for Prajāpati is untruth and darkness as well as truth and light;[5] but no question is yet raised as to the compatibility of the existence of the creator and evil.[6] Nor is there any effort to evolve a complete code of moral rules; a man owes sacrifice to the gods, Vedic study to the seers, offspring to the Fathers, a triad of obligations, but also hospitality to friends;[7] the duty of truth, as we have seen, is repeatedly asserted. But of the three duties, which in an Upaniṣad[8] are enunciated as the three *da*'s, generosity, self-restraint, and sympathy (*datta, dāmyata, dayadhvam*), only the first is heartily recognized in the Brāhmaṇas. Gifts are a bridge to the heaven, a gift of a cow protects one's life, that of a garment prolongs it; the food destroys him who eats what he should give to others—the priests *par excellence*. It is only in an Āraṇyaka that we have the wise counsel that a man should be able to say 'No' as well as 'Yes' and to give only at the right moment.[9] Self-restraint is asserted in one passage of the gods,[10] but sympathy is a virtue of the Upaniṣad period.

In the undeveloped state of ethical views it would be hopeless to expect any political philosophy, nor have we any. The existence of the castes is taken for granted, and their origin attributed to divine creation whether in the version of the Puruṣa hymn of the Rigveda or in some variant form.[11] The duties and privileges of the castes are often mentioned incidentally, occasionally in more completeness, but there is no effort to develop a theoretic

[1] TS. ii; Caland, *Over de Wenschoffers* (1902).
[2] KS. xxii. 1; ÇB. x. 5. 4. 16.
[3] TS. ii. 2. 6. 2.
[4] ÇB. v. 5. 2. 2; TB. i. 8. 4. 3.
[5] ÇB. x. 6. 5. 1; MS. iii. 6. 3; ÇB. i. 1. 1. 1; v. 1. 2. 10.
[6] A ritual criticism of Prajāpati for creating thieves, flies, &c., is given in ApÇS. xxi. 12. 1 ff.
[7] TS. vi. 3. 10. 5; ÇB. i. 7. 2. 1 f.
[8] BAU. v. 2.
[9] MS. iv. 8. 3; KS. xxviii. 5; TB. ii. 8. 8. 1; AA. ii. 3. 6. Cf. above, p. 477, n. 10.
[10] KB. ix. 1.
[11] e. g. TS. vii. 1. 1. 4; ÇB. xii. 7. 3. 12; BAU. i. 4. 11 f.; PB. vi. 1. 6 ff.; JB. i. 68 f.

version of the matter. The Brahman is required to be of Brahmanical descent, to follow an appropriate course of life, to possess renown for learning, and to be engaged in the spiritual advancement of the people. In return he is entitled to receive honour and presents, and to be exempt from oppression and the death penalty.[1] The Kṣatriyas are to protect the people, and show consideration for Brahmans, while the commonalty in its subjection to these two castes is not very much better off than the Çūdras, children of the Asuras or of non-existence, save in so far as they are sharers in the rites of the twice born. It is assumed[2] that, in the perpetuation of the due subordination of the castes, there is assured prosperity for the people; no attempt is made to demonstrate or render this theory plausible. In the relations of the king and his Purohita there is an element of contract, with which may be compared the effort of the Buddhists to base the existence of caste relations and the state on contractual agreements as well as on creation myths,[3] but the Brahmans insist in the ceremony of the royal consecration that they own no king, for Soma is their overlord, an assertion of the superiority of the priestly to the warrior class doubtless more honoured in theory than in practice, though not without actual importance.

Of the origin of kingship itself we have variant versions, while the condition of anarchy is once vividly described.[4] On one theory[5] Indra owes his kingship among the gods to Prajāpati's favour, who at first made him the most inferior, but later conferred on him his own lustre and made him overlord, of the gods. Another version[6] makes him the chosen of the gods, including Prajāpati, by reason of his eminent qualities of mind and body. Yet another[7] makes the gods choose Soma as their king, because they felt that they owed their defeats at the hands of the Asuras to their lack of a sovereign. Or again they consecrate Varuṇa,[8] their brother, because they see in him the form (*rūpa*) of their father, Prajāpati. Among men the rule of the Rājanya is explained[9] on the ground that he is the representative of Prajāpati, thus being entitled, though one, to rule over many. It is, however, dubious whether this should be regarded as precisely a doctrine of the divine origin of the kingship in any specific sense; at any rate there is no effort to expound a doctrine of hereditary divinity in the Brāhmaṇas, and the ceremony of the Rājasūya, or royal consecration, hints at recollections of an elective kingship by the consent of the people.[10] The inviolability of the king is asserted,[11] and his duty to assert and defend the law,[12] Dharma, but no grounds of a philosophical character for his obligations are alleged.

[1] ÇB. xi. 5. 7. 1; AB. vii. 29; Macdonell and Keith, *Vedic Index*, ii. 82 ff.

[2] Cf. ÇB. v. 4. 4. 19; xiii. 4. 4. 13.

[3] N. N. Law, *Ancient Indian Polity*, pp. 96–8. See also U. Ghoshal, *History of Hindu Political Theories* (1923), pp. 117 ff., 135, 210.

[4] ÇB. xi. 1. 6. 24.

[5] TB. ii. 2. 10. 1 f.

[6] AB. viii. 4. 12.

[7] AB. i. 1. 14.

[8] JB. iii. 152; cf. PB. xiii. 9. 22 f.

[9] ÇB. v. 1. 5. 14.

[10] The view (Ghoshal, *op. cit.*, pp. 38 ff.) of the rise in Vedic times of a nobility of office *versus* birth is not plausible, and the Teutonic parallel is explained by difference of social conditions.

[11] ÇB. v. 4. 4. 7.

[12] ÇB. v. 4. 4. 5; 3. 3. 9. The Dharma Sūtras

§ 5. *Modes of Thought and Categories*

Despite their interminable controversies, of which the Brāhmaṇas contain many hints, there is no evidence of the development of any logical theory. In a late text, the Taittirīya Āraṇyaka,[1] we find, indeed, an enumeration of four means of attaining correct knowledge, tradition (*smṛti*), perception (*pratyakṣa*), communication by one who is expert (*aitihya*), and reasoning (*anumāna*). This occurs in a verse to be used in connexion with the piling of the Āruṇaketuka fire, a late rite, and it has epic parallels,[2] showing that it represents a late popular view. It is obvious that it is unscientific, for tradition and communication obviously are not distinct sources, and what really was meant by reasoning does not appear, nor is the term otherwise defined in the Brāhmaṇas.

The real distinction in the Brāhmaṇas is between what is normally perceived (*pratyakṣa*) and what is beyond mere perception (*parokṣa*), and, as the gods prefer the latter, so men recognize that mere appearances are not the essence of reality. Hence the foundation is laid for the doctrine of forms (*rūpa*) which lie at the basis of the interminable and seemingly absurd identifications of the texts. Philosophically the view has a real importance, for it points to the development of the pantheistic doctrine which asserts the unity of the individual self and the universe; the individual is no more than an aspect of the universal. What is obvious is not what is ultimately true; what is *pratyakṣa* for men is *parokṣa* for the gods; what is *parokṣa* for men, is *pratyakṣa* for the gods.[3] Hence, although the importance of sight as a source of knowledge is asserted, at other times the emphasis is laid on the necessity of thought to penetrate reality, but this stage is not consciously reached until the Upaniṣad period. In the Brāhmaṇas what we find is the assertion of special insight through the power of asceticism, which enables the seers to behold the rising of the metres to the heaven.[4] By asceticism or even without it the seers discover the sacred texts and the rites, for already these are regarded as beyond human creation or invention; they must be seen, learned, or found, not created. Indra himself in visible form reveals the Stomabhāga formulae to Vasiṣṭha, a Sāman converses with Keçin Dālbhya, a voice unseen instructs Devabhāga, a golden bird, a maiden possessed by a Gandharva reveal secret lore. Çrautarṣi Devabhāga discovers the right way to divide the sacrificial victim, but dies without revealing it to any one; a supernatural being tells it to Girija. The great texts trace their revelation to such gods as Āditya, Indra, Prajāpati, or Brahman, though no purposeful action is ascribed in this regard to these deities.

give much information as to royal duties as well as those of other persons, but, apart from their dubious date, they contain nothing of philosophical importance. Cf. Weber, *Religionssoziologie*, ii. 141 ff. The Arthaçāstra is clearly the product of a post-Vedic era.

[1] i. 2. 1; Oldenberg, *Weltanschauung der Brāhmaṇatexte*, pp. 221 ff.

[2] Hopkins, *Great Epic of India*, pp. 145 ff.; Rāmāyaṇa (ed. Gorr.), v. 87. 23.

[3] PB. xxii. 10. 3.

[4] TS. v. 3. 5. 4.

Against tradition of this kind human ingenuity is valueless; Yājñavalkya, always an innovator in spirit, asserts that there are two kinds of created things; the Ṛc verse says three, and its authority is conclusive.[1] Nevertheless human thought must have an outlet, and it expresses itself in the deep consideration of topics, styled Mīmāṅsā, the desiderative form of *man*, 'think', a term so common that it can be omitted, the genitive case alone standing to denote the object of investigation. At other times Mīmāṅsā fares less respectfully; suggestions that a rite should be carried out in other than the established manner may be dismissed as mere speculation. Another term, Vicikitsā, also a desiderative formation, denotes the doubt which prompts inquiry, while the final result is denoted by Sthiti, the station attained.

Unfortunately this consideration does not penetrate to facts, but lives largely in a world of fancy, unrestrained by regard for reality and with extremely slight sense of the limitations of knowledge. If the Taittirīya Saṁhitā[2] in a moment of sanity admits the possibility of doubt whether a man really exists in yonder world or not, that candour is accidental and episodic. The theologians of the Brāhmaṇas are not prepared to admit to ignorance of any sort, and revelation reduces them to interpretation at their pleasure, aided by the fact of the bizarre nature of the revealed texts. If the waters can practise asceticism, it is not surprising that speech can speak standing in the seasons, or that the sacrificial consecration can be pursued by the gods with the aid of the seasons, or that the ascent of the metres to the sky should be visible. The texts operate freely, as already in the later Rigveda, with the conceptions of being or not-being, but they fail to make any serious progress in discovering effective categories. The cardinal points and the year lead very slowly up to more adequate conceptions of space and time, and the two seem endlessly confused even in the Upaniṣads. The conception of causality remains wholly obscure; instances of natural causation are recorded, but equally we have the most fantastic conception of cause and result, and it is significant that neither Kārya, 'result', nor Kāraṇa, 'cause', appears. Other important technical terms are missing; there are no expressions for relation in general or conditions, the expressions Viṣaya, 'object', Viparyaya, 'opposition',[3] Pravṛtti, 'activity', and Nivṛtti, 'cessation from action', are wanting. On the other hand, certain advances are made; the adjective *prākṛta* in the Çatapatha Brāhmaṇa reveals the existence of the conception Prakṛti, 'ground form', later famous in the Sāṁkhya; difference is expressed by Nānātva, though the later Bheda occurs only in the more recent Upaniṣads; the nature of any thing is expressed by a derivative in *tva* or *tā*, and in a late passage in the Taittirīya Āraṇyaka[4] the use, later established, of an abstract in the ablative as giving the ground of some result, is actually found. The terminology of the Brāhmaṇas does not know any

[1] ÇB. ii. 5. 1. 2.

[2] vi. 1. 1. 1.

[3] KU. has Viṣaya and *viparīta*.

[4] i. 7. 6 (*nānāliñgatvāt*). BAU. iv. 3. 23 has *avināçitvāt*, 'by reason of imperishability'.

general expression for sensation or perception, compelling needless repetitions, which the Upaniṣads also adopt, but phrases such as ' In each season there is the form of all the seasons ' show efforts at expressing general conceptions.[1]

When no clear distinction had been made between personal and impersonal, and anything whatever might be conceived as active and living, it was inevitable that little progress could be made with formal definitions. We have instead endless identifications; the sacrifice is man or the year or anything else which may suit the moment, and, if the horse character (*açvatva*) of the horse is explained, it is merely that it came into being from the eye of Prajāpati when it was swollen (*açvayat*). Some of these etymologies were probably recognized as absurd by their makers, but others not, despite the fact that there was already developing itself an acute system of linguistic investigations, which reveals itself in the early appearance of terms for number (*vacana*), case forms (*vibhakti*) and so on, and in investigations as to euphonic combination and phonetical peculiarities.[2] When the priests set to work to define, they normally merely give fanciful identifications, as those of Agni Vaiçvānara, which they propound to Açvapati Kaikeya.[3] Nevertheless, occasionally they reveal more acumen; the vague term Kratu is defined; ' When a man wishes, " May I do that, may I have that," that is Kratu; when he attains it, that is Dakṣa.'[4]

When definition is in so feeble a condition, classification naturally fares no better. The love of numbers already appears as a dominant factor; the term Prāṇa is subdivided into five elements, among other divisions, and these five are obviously incapable of presenting any intelligible picture to the minds of the priests; moreover, under the same title we find not merely varieties of breathing, as is natural, but the quite different set of five, mind, speech, breath, sight and hearing. But other numbers and divisions are also found; we have here signs of that love of numerical enumerations which is seen in its full development in the Aṅguttara Nikāya of the Pāli Canon or the Ekottarāgama of the north, and which on one view has given the Sāṁkhya philosophy its distinctive name.

Reasoning, indeed, we find, but of a peculiar character. Its logical value consists merely in its systematic form, marked by the use of the particles[5] *vai* and *khalu vai*, the former of which marks the general principle asserted as the basis of the reasoning, the latter the identification which renders the general principle apposite. Thus, if it is necessary to explain why during the consecration the person consecrated has milk as his sole food, the principle[6] is asserted, ' By milk indeed (*vai*) embryos wax '; the application follows, ' Now indeed (*khalu vai*) the consecrated person is as it were an embryo ', and the conclusion is arrived at, ' In that he has milk as his food, he causes

[1] ÇB. viii. 7. 1. 3 f.
[2] Cf. PB. xx. 14. 2; AB. v. 4. 3; Wackernagel, *Altind. Gramm.* i. pp. lxii. ff.
[3] ÇB. x. 6. 1.
[4] ÇB. iv. 1. 4. 1.
[5] Delbrück, *Altindische Syntax*, p. 493; cf. Keith, *Rig-Veda Brāhmaṇas*, p. 95.
[6] TS. vi. 2. 5. 3.

himself to wax.' Or again[1] we have, 'By means of the Stoma the gods prosper in this world; the Vātsapra is a counterpart of the Stoma; in that he pays homage with the Vātsapra, so does he win prosperity in this world.' The principles and their application alike rest on mere assertion, and it is seldom that they are self-evident. Naturally, when deductive processes are so feebly represented, there is no effort at induction, which is found only in the Upaniṣads, and even then merely in the form of arguments which exhaust a series of possibilities, assumed, not proved, to be exhaustive, and so assumed tacitly, no expression of the assumption being requisite. There is a further advance in the Pāli canon, but that is of still later date.[2]

With thinking still so undeveloped, it would be impossible to expect any serious advance in the construction of categories to aid in the comprehension of the world. The distinction between what has and what has not life and power of action is not made; the gods, demons, men, plants, beasts of all kinds, are no more alive than the atmosphere, wind, rain, storm, minerals, the sacrifice and its utensils, numbers, metres, qualities or emotions. The holy power and the lordly power are concrete activities, like the strength (*vīrya*) of a man; his greatness (*mahiman*) is even said along with his Ātman to constitute him.[3] The anguish caused to the victim in the slaying adheres to the roasting spit, and if placed on earth will penetrate to the earth; guilt (*enas, āgas*) is a substance which the god can carry with him; a man's good deeds are within the altar, his evil deeds without it.[4] Equally substantial are conceptions such as right, asceticism, evil, death, immortality, truth, falsehood, space and time. These two are normally represented by the cardinal points and the year; gradually we find the development of Ākāça, which denotes the vacancy between objects,[5] such as the Antarikṣa between heaven and earth, but it is also material, as the Upaniṣads frankly recognize, and of Kāla, which primarily means the suitable moment for any thing, but becomes regarded as a cosmic power, similar to the year, in the Atharvaveda.

Even the more imposing conceptions of being and not-being prove to have little profundity. Being does not denote in the Brāhmaṇas the whole of existence as a unity, contrasted with the imperfect plurality of the individual; it is essentially the term to denote that whence the world emerged, and the Vedic thinker proceeds to ask whence it itself came, evolving the answers not-being or something beyond both being and not-being, identified in the usual light-hearted manner in one passage with mind.[6] Not-being naturally as the foundation of all things is subject to similar identifications; it may be said to be the seers, or to practise austerities, or to desire to become being, mere verbal intricacies without trace of serious thought.[7]

Some effort, however, is made to secure order in conceptions, and there can

[1] TS. v. 2. 1. 6 f.

[2] BAU. iv. 5. 6 ff.; Mahāvagga, i. 6. 38 ff.; Oldenberg, *Buddha*[6], pp. 214 ff.

[3] JB. i. 228.

[4] ÇB. iii. 8. 5. 8 f. TS. ii. 5. 1; ÇB. xi. 2. 7. 33.

[5] AB. iii. 42. 1; ÇB. iii. 3. 2. 19; vii. 1. 2. 23.

[6] ÇB. x. 5. 3. 1, 2.

[7] ÇB. vi. 1. 1. 1; TB. ii. 2. 9. 1. See also AV. iv. 19. 6; x. 7. 21.

be traced the gradual formation of the ideas of the five elements and of the five senses, with mind above or beside them, ideas which introduce some degree of system into the conception of the external world and of man's powers, although terminology remains changing and vague. Persistent from the Puruṣasūkta onwards is the effort to distinguish and compare the macrocosm and the microcosm; what is interpreted as regards the gods (*adhidevatam, adhidaivatam*) as earth, atmosphere, and sky, is mind, breath, and speech as regards the self (*adhyātmam*); wind, fire, sun, the quarters, and the moon correspond to breath, speech, eye, ear, and mind. Similarly there is a marked love for arranging things in lists, each with many correspondences; if the creator produces [1] from his mouth the Trivṛt Stoma, it has as correlative the god Agni, the metre Gāyatrī, the Rathantara tune, the Brahman among men, the goat among beasts, and similar series are invented for the other Stomas. Correspondence in any sense is a basis for identification, and affords one of the various rounds of connexion even of the loosest nature which justified a Brahmanical identification.

More interesting is the effort to express aspects of reality by the use of the word Tanū, 'body'. It denotes primarily simply the body of a person or his self regarded as corporeal, as in the reflexive use of the term and in its occasional exchange with Ātman,[2] which denotes the spiritual aspect of the self. But it is specially frequent in the plural to denote what may best be styled aspects; [3] thus Agni has one aspect as bearing the oblations to the gods, another as carrying the offerings for the dead; he has auspicious and dread aspects. The aspects may be mortal or immortal; Prajāpati has five of either, mortal as hair, &c., immortal as mind, &c. Taken together they may make up the whole, or they may be set beside the self, Ātman, as members; or the whole may itself be styled a Tanū.[4] Or the aspects may be in different places; even the Rigveda recognizes that Agni has such aspects. In any case the Tanūs give rise to indefinite possibilities of identification, since in respect of some one or other of them most things can be made similar.

While Tanū is not of enduring importance in Indian thought, Rūpa, 'form', remains a term of high importance. Its primary meaning is visible extension or shape; it is the object of the eye, as sound is that of the ear. Only during life does form exist, being lost in death, a hint of the doctrine of the necessity of the imposition of form on matter to create the concrete individual.[5] Similarly [6] the Brahman is said to enter the world when it is to be made distinct by means of name and form, the name corresponding to the form, and thus—to develop the idea—being the means of expressing the nature of the form, though this conception is far from that of the Brāhmaṇa which treats name and form as two distinct active potencies. Nor can we

[1] TS. vii. 1. 1. 4 ff. Cf. JUB. iii. 1 f.
[2] KS. vii. 6.
[3] KS. xxxvi. 13; vii. 13; ÇB. x. 1. 3. 2, 4.
[4] AB. v. 25. 11; TB. i. 1. 6. 3 f.; KS. xxxiv. 17.
[5] JUB. iii. 32; cf. of animals, ÇB. iv. 3. 4. 14.
[6] ÇB. xi. 2. 3.

venture to attach too much importance to the aspect of Rūpa as form, for even in the Chāndogya Upaniṣad [1] the term denotes not pure form, but a material possessing form; heat, water, food are the results of the creator entering the world with name and form.

Form naturally serves as the basis of identifications, for almost anything can be said to be the form of another, either on solid or on fanciful grounds. Thus the bull can be said to be the form or symbol of Indra, type of male strength, butter and gold of the cow, repaired things of the fire piled after an fruitless effort. Or the firesticks are the hidden form of Agni, while he is the revealed form. If things have any form in common, they can be identified, and though Tanū derives its origin from the corporeal aspect of a thing, and Rūpa comes from the idea of appearance, they tend largely to coincide in force. But, unlike Tanū, Rūpa is regularly associated with name, and the association develops into the expression, name and form, which in Buddhism expresses concrete individuality.

Akin to Rūpa in the view of many scholars is the somewhat vague term Dhāman, especially in cases where we hear of the Dhāmāni of such a god as Soma,[2] or, as often in the Brāhmaṇas and earlier, of the dear Dhāman of a deity, though the sense 'abode' is preferred by Hillebrandt [3] among others. We hear of the butter as the dear Dhāman of Agni, of the mead as that of the Açvins; speech is that of Indra and Agni, salt that of heaven and also of the cattle, the quarters that of Soma.[4] A frequent reward of the man who worships correctly or has the proper knowledge is to attain the Dhāman of the deity, or by the use of the sacrificial strew, which is the Dhāman of cattle, one obtains them.[5] In Oldenberg's view [6] the term denotes what is ordained (*dhā*). Thus in the Rigveda we hear of the ordinances of Mitra and Varuṇa, and with a genitive the term often denotes what is appointed by some power.[7] In other cases, when thus used, the term in the genitive expresses what is ordained, or the substratum, in which the thing ordained has effect; the former may be the meaning in the Rigveda [8] of the phrase the Dhāman of the Ṛta, which is given [9] as the description of the dawn, or the Dhāman of the sacrifice.[10] But, while this explanation has the advantage of being true to the etymology of the term, and is doubtless largely correct, it is clear that the meaning 'abode' early developed, and this sense should probably be recognized much more freely than is admitted by Oldenberg, though he recognizes that the term did develop something approaching this sense.[11]

[1] vi. 2 ff.

[2] So Geldner (*Glossar*, s.v.) as to RV. i. 91. 4, 19, &c. The term occurs frequently in formulae of offering.

[3] *Lieder des Ṛgveda*, p. 66, n. 1.

[4] TS. v. 1. 9. 5; 3. 10. 3; ÇB. xiv. 1. 4. 13; AB. vi. 7. 10; KS. xx. 1; viii. 2; ÇB. iii. 9. 4. 20.

[5] TS. v. 2. 3. 4; KS. viii. 2; MS. iii. 2. 2; cf. RV. ix. 114. 1; Yasna, xlvi. 6.

[6] GN. 1915, pp. 180–90, 401–3. He treats *dāman* in the Avesta similarly.

[7] RV. x. 10. 6; i. 91. 3; 123. 8; x. 81. 5 (Viçvakarman); vi. 21. 3 (Indra).

[8] RV. i. 43. 9; cf. the use of the verb in i. 71. 3; viii. 27. 19.

[9] KS. xxxix. 10.

[10] RV. x. 67. 2 (created by the Añgirases).

[11] ÇB. i. 9. 1. 16; Muṇḍ. iii. 2. 1.

It is significant that contemporaneously we find the science of grammar alone in process of development; the Brāhmaṇas show knowledge of the scientific grouping of the letters,[1] of the distinction of case forms, numbers and so forth, and the elaboration of the system of Pāṇini, as well as the researches of the Prātiçākhyas prove the skill which was being developed in this period. The Nirukta of Yāska which falls in date at the close of the Brāhmaṇa period proves how considerable had been the advances made in regard to questions of etymology, the classification of the parts of speech (of which Yāska reckons four, nouns, verb, prepositions, and particles), and the nature of language.[2] The superiority of Indian achievement in this regard to that of contemporary Greece is manifest, but, on the other hand, there is extremely little evidence of any progress in regard to astronomy or mathematics, for we cannot accept the overestimates of the knowledge involved in the Çulba Sūtras, apart altogether from the doubt as to their date, and the fact of their serving essentially practical ends.[3] Of natural science we know nothing at this period, and both in the Brāhmaṇas and the Upaniṣads the nature of the ideas current is incompatible with any progress in these matters in contemporary thought.[4]

[1] Cf. PB. xx. 14. 2; CU. ii. 22; Wackernagel, *Altind. Gramm.* i. p. lxii; Oldenberg, *Weltanschauung der Brāhmaṇatexte*, p. 233; TU. i. 2; AA. iii. 1 ff.

[2] See Lakshman Sarup's trs. of the Nirukta, Intr. pp. 53 ff.

[3] See Chap. 29.

[4] Regarding Indian medicine, cf. A. F. R. Hoernle, *Studies in the Medicine of Ancient India*, and Keith, ZDMG. lxii. 134 ff. It is impossible to take seriously the Kāma Sūtra tradition which makes Çvetaketu, who figures in the Upaniṣads, an authority on erotics.

CHAPTER 28

THE PHILOSOPHY OF THE UPANIṢADS

§ 1. *The Origin of the Upaniṣads*

NATIVE tradition [1] derives the term Upaniṣad, by means which will not bear scrutiny, from roots which yield as its sense either that which destroys innate ignorance, or that which leads to the Brahman. It is more important to note that from an early period the utmost stress is laid on the secret character of the instruction contained in these works: the rule is that they are the highest mysteries, and that their doctrines should not be imparted to any pupil, other than a son, who has not already studied with the teacher for a year and who does not intend himself to become a teacher. The same view is enforced by the facts recounted in the texts: when the deepest part of the discussions arrives, the two concerned go apart and talk of the new doctrine of action as the source of human fate.

When, therefore, we seek for an origin of the term which will not defy the laws of etymology, it is necessary to find something which will accord with this essential nature of secrecy. The word is derived obviously from the prefixes *upa-ni* and *sad*, 'sit', and the only natural meaning is a session, a sitting down near some person, who naturally is assumed to be the teacher. This accords with the mode of teaching followed in India, which, as we have seen, involved the sitting of the pupil and the teacher facing each other, while the latter repeated the lesson to be learned by the former. The lessons of the teacher to his pupil were not public in the ordinary sense of the word: to be practicable they naturally required quiet, but the ritual texts show us more than that: they bear witness that certain texts of special importance were to be taught to the pupil in the forest, and not in the normal place, the abode of the teacher. With this accords admirably the fact that the Upaniṣads form parts of, or are attached in the case of the most important and old of these works to, texts which tradition gives the names of Āraṇyaka.[2] The name must clearly, as held by Oldenberg, have been derived from the fact that the discussions contained in these works were studied in the forest; the alternative view [3] that the Āraṇyakas were specially intended for study by

[1] Cf. Çañkara on BAU. p. 2; KU. p. 73; TU. p. 9; Muṇḍ. p. 261.

[2] Oldenberg, *Prolegomena*, pp. 291 ff.; GN. 1915, pp. 382 ff. Cf. ÇGS. ii. 12. 11; vi; AÇS. viii. 14.

[3] Deussen, *Sechzig Upanishad's*, p. 7, following the Indian (Āruṇeya Up. 2) tradition of an Āraṇyaka as a Brāhmaṇa for those engaged in the vow of forest life (Sāyaṇa on AA. i. 1; Aufrecht, *Aitareya Brāhmaṇa*, p. iii). The other view is, however, also traditional. Winternitz (*Gesch. d. ind. Lit.* i. 202, n. 1) agreed with Deussen but (iii. 616)

the Vānaprasthas, men who, after serving their apprenticeship as Brahman students and having performed as householders their duties, retire to the forests to study, is clearly a more advanced conception than that obtained in the early Upaniṣads. The later view is an artificial conception, and one which grew up only with the strict division of stages of life enjoined on Brahmans, if not always observed. Naturally, however, the Āraṇyakas, in so far as they are texts of allegorical interpretation of the sacrifice, were studied by such Vānaprasthas more than were the Brāhmaṇas proper, which were rather ritual in their interest, and presumed that the sacrifice was actually being performed. The Āraṇyakas in their more distinctive portions deal with the meaning of the offering, without necessarily assuming that it will be performed : they sometimes suggest modes of performing the sacrifice by meditation and repetition—as of the Hotṛ formulae only. But the distinction of Brāhmaṇa and Āraṇyaka is not an absolute one : in no case have we in the works handed down to us Brāhmaṇas which always suppose the performance of ritual, or Āraṇyakas which assume that it is not to be performed. Nor can we see why the distinction, which was probably the real one between the Brāhmaṇas and the Āraṇyakas, the comparative sanctity of their contents, should have attached itself to precisely the ceremonies to which it did so attach itself. The ritual texts of the different Vedas show us clearly the fact that certain rites and texts were regarded as especially sacred, to be performed outside the village, and these texts are contained not merely in Āraṇyakas but even in the Saṁhitā form.[1] Thus the Pravargya rite is treated in this fashion in the Taittirīya Āraṇyaka iv and v, while the Mantras concerned are also to be found in the later part of the Vājasaneyi Saṁhitā,[2] in which they are followed by other Mantras, containing certain dread names of the Maruts and certain invocations of formidable character used in the horse sacrifice. The Āraṇyagāna of the Sāmaveda and the Āraṇyaka Saṁhitā contain the secret texts of that Veda,[3] and the Aitareya [4] and Çāñkhāyana Āraṇyakas [5] present the secret texts of the Rigveda, of which the most important is that concerning the Mahāvrata, an old and popular rite, while the former contains also the Mahānāmnī verses,[6]

with Oldenberg. Oltramare (*L'histoire des idées théosophiques*, i. 63, n. 1) suggests 'introduction' or 'initiation', hence mystic doctrine.

[1] See Oldenberg, GN. 1915, pp. 382–401.

[2] xxxvi. 1–xxxix. 6 ; 7 ; 8–13. See also TA. i. 32 ; ApÇS. xv. 20. 1 ff. ; BÇS. ix. 19 ; BhGS. iii. 6 ; MÇS. iv. 7. 1 ff. ; KÇS. xviii. 4. 24 ; xx. 8. 5 ; PGS. ii. 15. 6 ; ÇB. xiii. 3. 4. 1 ; xiv. 1. 1. 26 ff. The additional matter in TA. iv. 22–7 is parallel to that in VS. xxxix, while iv. 21 has the Dadhigharma (ApÇS. xv. 18. 17), a rite parallel to the Pravargya at the midday pressing.

[3] GGS. iii. 1. 28 ff.; 2. 1 ff. ; 54; JGS. i. 16 f. The CU. is, of course, treated in this way, and perhaps also the Mantra Brāhmaṇa, which precedes the CU. The Sāmans of this type are especially full of insertions and are longer.

[4] See Keith, *Aitareya Āraṇyaka* (1908).

[5] Trans. Keith (1909). See also JRAS. 1908, pp. 364–87.

[6] Cf. Oldenberg, GN. 1915, pp. 375–81, whose ingenious reconstruction of the original form is, however, not wholly convincing. The verses are known to TS. v. 2. 11. 1 ; MS. iii. 12. 21 ; VS. xxiii. 35 ; AV. xi. 7. 6. Scheftelowitz

which appear in a form strange to the manner of the Ṛigveda and akin to that of the Sāmaveda, in which they are also found. Both texts contain also certain mystic doctrines regarding the Saṁhitā form of the text of the Rigveda, and the Çāñkhāyana deals also with the Mantha. Both also include, like the Taittirīya, philosophical Upaniṣads. The Aitareyins and the Kauṣītakins of the Rigveda placed the Mahāvrata ceremony in the rank of a fit subject for an Āraṇyaka, but the Yajurveda allowed it to appear in the Saṁhitā, and the Sāmaveda treats of it in the Pañcaviñça and Jaiminīya Brāhmaṇas. But we can realize how from their superior sanctity the tendency grew for these treatises to be used as the places of the record of the secret doctrines, which gradually, in the mind of the priests, took the place of the more material performance of the ritual.

As the distinction between Brāhmaṇa and Āraṇyaka is not an absolute one, though the Āraṇyakas tend to contain more advanced doctrines than the Brāhmaṇas, so the distinction between Upaniṣad and Āraṇyakas is also not absolute, tradition actually incorporating the Upaniṣads in some cases in the Āraṇyakas. The most that can be said is that the term Upaniṣad, when applied to a text, normally denotes that it contains speculation mainly on the nature of the universe and of the Ātman or the Brahman. Its use in the Upaniṣad is in one or other of the senses 'secret word' or 'phrase', 'secret text' or 'secret import'. Thus, when the phrase[1] *neti neti*, 'not so, not so', is used as an expression of the highest unity, that is an Upaniṣad; or again the word *jalān* [2] as indicating that in which beings breathe, perish, and are born, or the phrase [3] *satyasya satyam*, 'the truth of the true', or *tadvanam* [4] as the final end is so described. In the texts of the Taittirīya school in special the phrase is used at the end of a section of philosophical teaching as a description of that teaching. Or the word is applied to a special subject of knowledge, such as the meaning of the word Om. In a slightly different way we hear of a man's Upaniṣad, which denotes his secret rule of life, such as that one should not beg.[5] In these senses the term Āraṇyaka is never used, and thus we can perhaps see why the two different words Āraṇyaka and Upaniṣad came into being. The former is a name, denoting the generic character of the texts, as those which from their secret nature must be dealt with in the special manner of being studied in the forest; the latter is a secret text, imparted at such a secret session, and in course of time more and more specifically appropriated to the description of secrets which were of philosophical character. Beyond these generalisms we are hardly likely to be able to penetrate.

Two different theories of the origin of the term have, however, been urged

(ZII. i. 58–68), who inclines to overestimate the age of the verses, as of Rigvedic rank, unfortunately ignores entirely Oldenberg's work.

[1] BAU. ii. 3. 6.

[2] CU. iii. 14. 1.

[3] BAU. ii. 1. 20; 3. 6.

[4] Kena 31 (JUB. iv. 21. 6).

[5] Kauṣ. ii. 1, 2. Cf. the Aupaniṣadika chapters on secret charms of the Arthaçāstra and Kāma Sūtra.

and require some notice. It is the view of Oldenberg [1] that the real sense of Upaniṣad is worship or reverence, that the word expresses the same ideas as Upāsanā,[2] and that it is due to the constant practice of the text to recommend the adoration of the Brahman or the Ātman under the guise of some symbol. There can be no doubt about the fact of the use of symbols in this way, but it is certain that the use of *upa-sad* as a verb in the Upaniṣads is always quite clearly distinguished from the meaning 'worship', and relates only to the going to a teacher, and sitting beside him for instruction: it is admitted that in this sense the normal use is *upa-sad*, not *upa-ni-sad*, but it is also plausible that the choice of the term was dictated by the fact that Upasad has in the ritual a very definite meaning of its own, which rendered the selection of a different word desirable to describe the action intended. In the second place it is clear that the idea of reverence or worship must have passed away at an early date from its original sense, and that, therefore, there is nothing to commend it on the ground of simplicity as an explanation: the Taittirīya Upaniṣad uses the term of the mere knowledge of the combination of letters, and the sense 'rule', as in 'not to beg', cannot be deduced from 'worship' as easily as 'secret instruction' can be deduced from 'session', beside a teacher, as opposed to a gathering for open discussion, Pariṣad or Saṁsad. In the third place, though this is not at all conclusive, the Ātman or the Brahman is not properly the object of reverence at all, since reverence implies the very duality which the Upaniṣads deny, and, if in reality the origin of the word lay in that sense, then it must be admitted that the Upaniṣads bear a name which their essential doctrine transcends. This of course is quite possible in itself: the other two considerations set out make it improbable.

The view of the word taken by Deussen [3] differs from that adopted above, which sees in it a natural counterpart to the term Āraṇyakas, and derives it from the tradition of the Vedic school teaching, in that it assumes a break in the development of the thought of India. For that view it should be observed that there is the advantage of continuity: the Brāhmaṇas shade off imperceptibly into the Āraṇyakas, the Āraṇyakas shade off into the Upaniṣads without violent change of any kind. But on the theory of Deussen we are not to adopt the view that secret import on the subjective, and secret instruction on the objective side, were the meanings developed from the secret teaching in the forest. On the contrary we are to believe that, at this point at a time when the Brahmans were still bent on the study of the ritual, the warrior class developed a new and striking philosophy,[4] which they expressed in secret

[1] ZDMG. l. 457 ff.; liv. 70 ff.; *Die Lehre der Upanishaden*, pp. 37, 348. The epic invests an absurd Niṣad as a form of literature besides Upaniṣad.

[2] Senart (*Florilegium Melchior de Vogüé*, pp. 575 ff.) argues that Upāsanā means 'knowledge', but this is clearly unproved.

[3] *Phil. of Up.*, pp. 16 ff.

[4] *Per contra* Hopkins (JAOS. xxii. 335) conjectures that Yoga practices were grafted on to the Upaniṣad doctrine from the 'royal knowledge'; he gives no ground save that Yoga first appears

formulae like *tajjalān*,[1] called Upaniṣads, because the essence of their character was secret communications, and that these doctrines were accompanied by secret explanations, from which in the course of time arose the first Upaniṣads. We must, it is claimed and has been argued by Garbe [2] with great emphasis, accept the view that it was not to the Brahmans, but to the warriors, to the princes, and the nobles, and to the wisdom of kings that India owed its philosophy.

This argument rests on facts recorded in the texts themselves, in which kings appear as authorities on philosophy. In the Chāndogya Upaniṣad [3] five learned Brahmans desire to learn from Uddālaka Āruṇi the nature of the Ātman Vaiçvānara : he doubts his ability to explain it, and as a result all six betake themselves to the king Açvapati Kaikeya, who gives them instruction, after first demonstrating the inaccuracy of their knowledge. In a narrative which is preserved in the Bṛhadāraṇyaka Upaniṣad [4] and in the Kauṣītaki Upaniṣad [5] a scholar, Gārgya Bālāki, undertakes to set out the nature of the Brahman to the king Ajātaçatru of Kāçí : he propounds twelve views—or in the Kauṣītaki sixteen—which are all defective, and the king then explains the Ātman to him by the principle of deep sleep, prefacing his instruction by the observation that it is a reverse of the rule for a Brahman to betake himself to a Kṣatriya for instruction. Another legend in the Chāndogya [6] shows the Brahmans being instructed in the nature of ether, as the ultimate basis of all things, by the king Pravāhaṇa Jaivali. It is added that Atidhanvan once gave the same knowledge to Udaraçāṇḍilya, and the former name might be that of a prince. Less important is the fact [7] that the Brahman Nārada is represented in the Chāndogya as being the recipient of information from Sanatkumāra, later the god of war, who tells the former that all his Vedic lore is a mere name. The great text regarding the doctrine of transmigration [8] is set out by Pravāhaṇa Jaivali to Āruṇi with the remark that the Brahmans have never before had this information, which so far had remained the monopoly of the Kṣatriyas. In a third version of this account, given in the Kauṣītaki Upaniṣad,[9] the king is Citra Gāñgyāyani.

Now it is always difficult to believe in the sudden evolution of new doctrines, actually associated in the name with the conception of the absolute of the Brahman class, by circles, whose duty was presumably to wield the weapons of war, and who at any rate failed to retain the control of these doctrines : it is absolutely certain that the Upaniṣads, as we have them, are not the work of

in the Upaniṣads of the Yajurveda, the royal Veda, and this is certainly not an argument of any value.

[1] More correctly *jalān*.

[2] *Beitr. zur ind. Kulturgeschichte*, pp. 3 ff. ; Winternitz, *Gesch. d. ind. Lit.* i. 198 ff., modified in iii. 615 f.

[3] v. 11–24. For the plan cf. JB. i. 22–5, where Janaka instructs five Brahmans on the Agnihotra.

[4] ii. 4.

[5] iv.

[6] i. 8 and 9.

[7] CU. vii.

[8] BAU. vi. 2 ; CU. v. 3–10. The rendering of *praçāstṛtvam* as ' rule ' here is clearly wrong, though adopted by Deussen (*Sechzig Upanishad's*, p. 141) and Hertel (*Weisheit der Upanischaden*, p. 77).

[9] i.

warriors, that they were handed down by priests, and that, if the warrior class originated these doctrines, they failed to continue the interest they had shown in them.[1] Stress must also be laid as against the supporters of the theory on the divergent views taken by them of the real work done by the Kṣatriyas. To Garbe they appear to have revolted from the sacrifice, and to have introduced a monist philosophy, centring in the idea of the Brahman—presumably appropriated by them, with a curious sense of humour, from their rivals. The doctrine of Karman is expressly claimed as theirs, so that they must be held, while adopting a monist philosophy, to have insisted on the importance of morality. On the other hand, the Brahmans were forced to adopt this Kṣatriya view by the pressure of public opinion, which compelled them to adopt it into their own system. This, frankly, appears a very curious conception; it is remarkable that the public should insist on a philosophic monism, when we remember that throughout Indian history we find every form of worship pursued with a painful eagerness and precision, and when we remember also how little popular opinion anywhere insists on a strict monism, especially one which empties life of any reality. A further difficulty arises when we find that the Kṣatriyas are credited by Garbe[2] with the creation of the Sāṁkhya philosophy as a revolt against prevailing views; apparently one set of Kṣatriyas operated against another, and, as he accepts Kṣatriya doctrines as the basis of Buddhism, we find that the great schism in Indian views was that of one Kṣatriya view against another. Hertel,[3] again, who accepts the doctrine of the Kṣatriya origin of the philosophy of the Upaniṣads, ignores the fact that the doctrine of Karman is their chief claim, and insists instead that they were rationalists who depersonalized the old gods, substituting in lieu the idea of nature powers—called by them *faute de mieux*, through the poverty of language of the time, deities, and whose philosophy was essentially a monism atheistic, materialistic, and morally indifferent. Judged on this basis it may be doubted if the praise lavished on the Ksatriyas at the expense of the Brahmans would have exactly been acceptable to them.

As has been indicated, stress is naturally laid in support of the theory of Kṣatriya influence on the explicit assertion of the king that the knowledge of transmigration had never belonged to any Brahmans, but the assertion is a very odd one: the king claims that the 'giving of instruction' has been the possession of the warriors because the Brahmans have not studied this doctrine, but even for India such a thought is absurd and meaningless, and reduces the claim of the king to what, it seems, is an idle vaunt. Then again, as it is impossible to deny that the Ātman-Brahman doctrine has a long previous history in the Brāhmaṇas, and is a logical development of the idea of

[1] A further complication is adduced by those who believe that Buddhism was promoted by Kṣatriyas of Mongolian origin (V. Smith, *Oxford History of India*, p. 47); the precise relations of these sets of Kṣatriyas does not appear to be explained by their supporters.

[2] In *Sâṃkhya-Philosophie*[2], p. 13, Garbe shows less assurance than formerly.

[3] IF. xli. 188.

unity of the Rigveda, we must admit that the warrior class must have shared in the intellectual development, which produced that idea, and then started a fresh view—which nevertheless was based on the Brahman, not the Kṣatra—in opposition to the sacrifice, while the priests were deeply engaged in the sacrifice. But the sacrifices were essentially not matters in which the priest acted for himself: he aimed at securing the profit of his patron, and the patrons for the great sacrifices must have been in the main the very warrior class, which we are to assume turned with disgust from the sacrifice.[1] The true solution of the problem is suggested by the obvious difficulties of the position of the maintainers of the theory: we must adopt a solution which explains why the whole Upaniṣad tradition is Brahmanical, and yet why the texts record actions of importance as regards the doctrine by the princes of earth. It is absurd to imagine that these references would have been left to stand had the Brahmans found them derogatory to their dignity: the sense of historical accuracy must have been very strong, incredibly so indeed, which would have induced a priesthood to preserve an exact account of the royal founders of each doctrine, and that they did so is sufficiently disproved by the mere fact that they clearly did not preserve a true account even of the Brahman founders of their doctrines. The prominence of Yājñavalkya can hardly be historical, since he is also the great ritual teacher of the Çatapatha Brāhmaṇa, and the device of assuming more than one man of the same name is absurd in this as in many other cases, since the texts assume that the two are the same: nor again does any one really believe that Sanatkumāra was a human king.

The explanation[2] becomes simple enough when we look at the Brāhmaṇas and the Rigveda: there we find that kings are often mentioned as generous donors: that there are lists of the great kings who performed sacrifices, and who beyond all things gave fees to the priest, just as in historical times great kings, like Puṣyamitra and Samudragupta, boast of their offerings. It was clearly necessary for the priests, who abandoned the doctrine of sacrifice, to live: they, therefore, had to find patrons and they must accordingly, like their predecessors, the sacrificial priests, represent their teachings as worth large sums. As a king must sacrifice to give gifts, so he must at least understand, and take part in discussions, to give gifts, and the position of the kings might easily be wholly deduced from the needs of the priest. But it would be unnecessary, and, it may be added, perhaps unjust to hold this view: the thought of the Upaniṣads with all its demerits is a far nobler thing than the thought of the Brāhmaṇas: as later among the Buddhists, the minds which could rise from the mere sacrifice to the consideration of the self were quite capable of accepting help from other minds: of low origin, Satyakāma,

[1] Actually we find Janaka instructing Yājñavalkya regarding the Agnihotra, and as a boon becoming a Brahman. See ÇB. xi. 6. 2, and see JB. i. 22–5.

[2] Keith, JRAS. 1908, pp. 468–73; Bloomfield, *Rel. of Veda*, pp. 220 ff.; Oldenberg, *Buddha*[5], p. 73, n. 1; *Die Lehre der Upanishaden*, pp. 166 ff.; Oltramare, *L'histoire des idées théosophiques*, i. 64 ff.; Weber, *Religionssoziologie*, ii. 155 ff.; Dahlmann, *Der Idealismus der ind. Rel.*, pp. 126 ff.

whose mother was a mere slave girl Jabālā, who ran about with men and who could not tell his father, was taken as a pupil by Hāridrumata and attained the complete knowledge :[1] even the epic, in one of its juster moments, allows a learned Çūdra honour and permits a merchant to instruct a Brahman.[2] In modern India saints of the highest rank have been other than Brahmans in caste. The princes were now and then seers, like Divodāsa, son of Vadhryaçva,[3] and they may for their part have now and then wearied of the sacrifice, and sought a higher truth, just as, inversely, we hear of seers who sought kingly rank for their offspring,[4] and there may be that degree of accuracy in the figure played by them in the legends.[5] But that the philosophy of the Brāhmaṇas as seen in the Upaniṣads is essentially the development of the philosophy of the Brāhmaṇas cannot reasonably be doubted. Nor is there any ground for thinking that the philosophy had its chief home anywhere save in the holy ground of the Brahmans, the land of Kurukṣetra, which seems to have been in this period as in the earlier epoch the place of Brahmanical culture *par excellence*.[6] The culture was not absolutely restricted to that area : the mention of Açvapati Kaikeya carries us further to the north-west, while we hear of Brahmans who dwelt in Magadha,[7] though that was rare. The Kauṣītaki Upaniṣad [8] preserves for us in the movements of Gārgya Bālāki the traces of the extent of the activity of the new movement : he went among the Kurus, the Pañcālas, the two folks then being joined, the Kāçis and Videhas, and the Vaças and Matsyas, and among the Uçīnaras. All this accords with the extent of the land in which the sacrifice was prevalent, and the addition of the Kosalas would complete the list : doubtless their omission here is mere chance. Other allusions to countries do not show any substantial extension of the geographical horizon of the authors : the Vindhya mountains are, it seems, known to the Kauṣītaki Upaniṣad, and this is perhaps a proof that the Vedic civilization was extending southwards [9] in greater degree than in the preceding period. The references to the Indus region, whence came salt and noble horses, suggest that it was afar off, but against this is to be set the mention of Gandhāra as not at all a distant country in the Chāndogya Upaniṣad.[10] But culture was not in any event rigidly confined to the middle country : scholars in their wanderings penetrated as far as the Madras, on the Hyphasis.[11]

Inevitably the question arises, how far in this period thought was affected by the growing intermixture of the people with the aborigines or earlier

[1] CU. iv. 4.
[2] MBh. iii. 216. 13 f.
[3] JB. i. 222 ; PB. ix. 2. 8.
[4] Cf. Viçvāmitra (JB. ii. 221) and Aṣṭaka ; Keith, *Rig-Veda Brāhmaṇas*, p. 67.
[5] That Raikva (CU. iv. 1) was a Çūdra (Hertel, IF. xli. 189) is certainly wrong.
[6] Macdonell and Keith, *Vedic Index*, ii. 125, 126 ; often in JB.
[7] ÇA. vii. 13 ; cf. Oldenberg, *Buddha* (ET.), p. 400, n. There is no doubt in the Sūtra period of the contempt felt for Magadha and its Brahmans ; a Māgadha is prescribed for an undignified rite in JB. ii. 404, and in the Vrātyastoma.
[8] iv. 1 ; Keith, JRAS. 1908, p. 367.
[9] Cf. Keith, *Aitareya Āraṇyaka*, p. 200.
[10] CU. vi. 14. 1.
[11] BAU. iii. 3. 1.

inhabitants, Dravidians or others. It has frequently been suggested that the philosophy of the Upaniṣads is essentially Dravidian rather than Aryan, and plausible grounds can be adduced in this sense.[1] Thus, we may be fairly certain that, as time went on, Dravidian blood came more and more to prevail over Aryan, though in candour we should admit that the evidence on this head is purely speculative in the absence of any real knowledge of the Aryan physical type which entered India. In the second place the changes in language may be due to Dravidian influence ; [2] here again the evidence is scanty enough, in the absence of independent evidence of the Dravidian languages for the period of the Brāhmaṇas and Upaniṣads, and the difficulty of tracing to them any definite influence on the language ; the use of cerebral or domal letters, and forms like the second future (*kartāsmi*) or perfect participle used verbally (*kṛtavān*), or the development of constructions with the indeclinable gerund, may have been encouraged by tendencies among the Dravidians ; but this cannot be definitely established. That Rudra-Çiva is mainly aboriginal is rather a guess based on the belief that the name denotes 'red' than an ascertained fact, and we have no assurance on the strength of which we could claim that the use of trance and asceticism or caste were Dravidian elements appropriated by the Aryans. The pantheism of the Upaniṣads may be deemed to be a philosophical development from the animistic views which Jainism and in a sense Buddhism presents, and which may be contrasted with the anthropomorphic nature gods of the Aryans, and a contrast may be drawn between Iranian religion and Indian,[3] suggesting that the former presents us a picture of the practical Aryan mind as opposed to the more mystic Indian intelligence. These contentions, we may admit, do not lead to any assured results in the sense of establishing the Dravidian [4] claim. What they indicate is the unquestionable fact that the Upaniṣads, as in some degree all earlier thought in India, represent the outcome of the reflections of a people whose blood was mixed. We may, if we desire, call the Upaniṣads the product of Aryo-Dravidian thought ; but, if we do so, we must remember that the effect of the intermixture must be regarded in the light of chemical fusion, in which both elements are transformed.

§ 2. *The Extant Upaniṣads*

The texts which have come down to us are certainly not the beginning of the intellectual activity of the time : they bear every trace in their manner and matter of representing the result of many discussions, and deviations of opinion among the priestly schools. The doctrines have been handled and

[1] A. E. Gough in his *Philosophy of the Upanishads* explains their demerits as due to racial intermixture. For a recent claim for the Dravidians, see G. W. Brown, *Studies in honor of Bloomfield*, pp. 75 ff. Frazer (ERE. *s.v.*) states the case for intermingling happily. See below, Appendix G.

[2] Konow, *Linguistic Survey*, iv. 278 ff.

[3] Cf. above, Chap. 27, § 4.

[4] It may be noted that Dravidian religion, as we know it, shows no special affinity to Sumerian as described, e.g. in *Camb. Anc. Hist.* i. 371, 384, 441 ff.

rehandled, and the names to which they are ascribed cannot be taken *au pied de la lettre*: as in the case of Yājñavalkya, we cannot assume that they really prove or indicate activity in philosophical research on the part of the men who are mentioned. It is also important to note that the texts, such as they are, are, in the case of the more important at any rate, not the productions of a single hand: they are redactions, perhaps made at more than one time,[1] of varying philosophic arguments, and they therefore contain very various doctrines, which are not often consistent.

It is perfectly possible to arrive at a rough estimate of the relative periods of the Upaniṣads. The first place must probably be accorded to the Aitareya Āraṇyaka [2] in its philosophic portion, that is the first three sections of the second book, and probably the Aitareya Upaniṣad, which fills the remaining three sections of the second book, is not to be dated later than any of the other Upaniṣads: the only evidence of later date alleged by Deussen [3] in the case of the Upaniṣad cannot be taken as sufficient to prove his view. After these works must certainly come the Bṛhadāraṇyaka Upaniṣad in its main portion, books i–iv, and the Chāndogya Upaniṣad. The Chāndogya is in almost every case, as far as one can judge, secondary in its versions of matter which it shares with the Bṛhadāraṇyaka Upaniṣad. But at any rate it is certain that the Taittirīya Upaniṣad, which forms books vii–ix of the Taittirīya Āraṇyaka, is later than the two last-mentioned: it exhibits the doctrine of five [4] as opposed to three elements,[5] and that in a way which renders the simple view that the distinction is unimportant most improbable. This is a matter of real consequence in the progress of thought,[6] and the argument is of quite different weight than that derived by Deussen from the fact that the Aitareya Upaniṣad [7] knows of four classes of living beings to three of the Chāndogya: [8] the classification is merely mentioned *en passant*, and is of no moment in other Upaniṣads. The Kauṣītaki is much later than the others, except the Taittirīya, but is probably earlier than it. Its version [9] of transmigration is a new edition of that in the two great Upaniṣads, the Bṛhadāraṇyaka [10] and the Chāndogya,[11] and its account [12] of Gārgya is a more developed one than

[1] BAU. consists of three parts (i–ii, iii–iv, v–vi); ii. 4 is repeated in a secondary form in iv. 5. The 8 books of the Chāndogya seem each distinct. AA. consists of three parts, ii. 1–3; ii. 4–6; iii. 1–2. See especially Deussen's analyses in *Sechzig Upanishad's des Veda.* Full bibliographies, translations, and a valuable intr. are found in R. E. Hume's *Thirteen Principal Upanishads* (1921).

[2] Keith, *Aitareya Āraṇyaka,* pp. 43 ff.; Winternitz, *Gesch. d. ind. Lit.* iii. 616 f.

[3] *Phil. of Up.*, pp. 23, 24.

[4] ii. 1.

[5] CU. vi. 2. So TU. ii. 8 is obviously later than BAU. iv. 3. 33.

[6] An advanced and profound doctrine may be early in appearance, as Yājñavalkya's view in BAU., for philosophy does not present any orderly advance of ideas, and Yājñavalkya was evidently too subtle for his age, which, however, was strongly influenced by views which it could not wholly adopt.

[7] iii. 3.

[8] vi. 3. 1.

[9] i.

[10] vi. 2.

[11] v. 3–10.

[12] iv.

that in the Bṛhadāraṇyaka,[1] while in another section [2] it is clearly later than the Aitareya.[3] Finally the Kena, which is in part metrical and is in itself a part of much longer Upaniṣad, the Jaiminīya Upaniṣad Brāhmaṇa, is no doubt to be ranked as the last of the older Upaniṣads. The Jaiminīya Upaniṣad Brāhmaṇa itself is of the nature of an Āraṇyaka rather than a mere Upaniṣad : that it does not bear the title Āraṇyaka is perhaps an idiosyncrasy of the Sāman schools, none of which actually call any text of theirs an Āraṇyaka. As an Āraṇyaka it has no claim to any very early date : it seems in fact to be certainly later than the Aitareya. The Taittirīya Āraṇyaka,[4] on the other hand, apart from the Upaniṣad section (vii–ix and x), is of most miscellaneous content and various date. The Bṛhadāraṇyaka Upaniṣad forms part of the last book of the Çatapatha Brāhmaṇa,[5] and the title shows the close relation of Āraṇyaka and Upaniṣad. In the case of the Chāndogya, the first two sections of the work are of the Āraṇyaka type, but as with texts attached to the Sāmaveda generally do not bear that name. The Kauṣītaki, like the Aitareya, is part of a longer Āraṇyaka.[6]

The next group of Upaniṣads is marked by the fact that it is composed of texts in metre, with very slight exceptions. It contains the Kaṭha, the Īçā, the Çvetāçvatara, Muṇḍaka and Mahānārāyaṇa,[7] that is the last book (x) of the Taittirīya Āraṇyaka. The texts are distinguished from the previous group, not merely by their form, but by their contents. The old discussions with their tentative and confused efforts to reach definite results are replaced by a definite phraseology, in which the results of speculation have been summed up in brief dogmas, expressed often with an obvious desire for the paradoxical and the bizarre. The allegories, not rarely found in the Upaniṣads of the older class, which share them with the Āraṇyakas, disappear altogether. More marked still is the relation of the texts to the other collections : the Kaṭha bears the name of a famous school of the Black Yajurveda whose Saṁhitā is still preserved for us, but its nature is that it is really a rewriting, from a philosophical as opposed to a ritual point of view, of the story, found in the Taittirīya Brāhmaṇa, of Naciketas and the winning of boons from Death by him. The Mahānārāyaṇa is reckoned in some authorities as the tenth book of the Āraṇyaka of the Taittirīya school, but the Āraṇyaka is a body of very various and confused contents, and between it and the Upaniṣad there is no inherent connexion at all, such as always exists in the previous group. Similarly the Īçā Upaniṣad has succeeded in obtaining entry as a book (xl) of the Vājasaneyi Saṁhitā, with which it has nothing really to do, and which

1 ii. 1.

2 iii.

3 iii. 3.

4 See Keith, *Taittirīya Saṁhitā*, i. pp. lxxviii ff.

5 It is preserved in two recensions ; the later probably is the Mādhyandina, the earlier the Kāṇva, which places ÇB. x. 6. 4, 5, before the rest of the text. ÇB. xiv. 1–3 ranks as the Āraṇyaka, 4–9 as the Upaniṣad in the Mādhyandina recension. Cf. Liebich, *Pāṇini*, pp. 62 ff.

6 Keith, JRAS. 1908, pp. 363 ff. ; *Çāñkhāyana Āraṇyaka*, pp. v ff.

7 Cf. R. Zimmermann, *Quellen d. Mahānārāyaṇa-Upaniṣad* (Leipzig, 1913) ; IA. xliv. 130 ff., 177 ff.

has been much added to in the course of time, parts of its contents in books xxxi, xxxii, and xxxiv [1] belonging in conception to the period of the Brāhmaṇas. The Çvetāçvatara and the Muṇḍaka have not even a nominal effective connexion with any extant text, beyond the fact that the Muṇḍaka uses the Atharvaveda (x. 7), and we need not suppose that they ever had any such connexion.

In this group it is quite clear that the Kaṭha takes the first rank : its style is suggested already by the metrical part of the Kena and by verses found in the Bṛhadāraṇyaka in a later addition.[2] The Īçā is clearly dependent on the Kaṭha,[3] and the Çvetāçvatara is certainly [4] well aware of the Kaṭha, and is probably a good deal later even than the Īçā, which is free from the sectarian spirit of the Çvetāçvatara in which the philosophy leads up to the glorification of Rudra as the god *par excellence*. The Muṇḍaka uses apparently the Çvetāçvatara,[5] and it again is probably presumed by the Mahānārāyaṇa.[6]

The last group of important Upaniṣads consists of the Praçna, the Maitrāyaṇīya, and the Māṇḍūkya. They are in prose, but they differ essentially in every respect from the older prose Upaniṣads : the diction is in style much more elaborate than the early prose, and in the case of the Maitrāyaṇīya, which Max Müller wrongly believed early in date, the language is obviously closely allied to classical Sanskrit, which it follows in the introduction of greater development and complexity of style. The order of the Upaniṣads in this group is certain as regards the Praçna and Maitrāyaṇīya,[7] and probable as regards the Māṇḍūkya.[8] In philosophy they show their wide knowledge of the earlier texts, which they freely use. The Praçna is proved to be later than the Muṇḍaka by the fact that it presupposes it and quotes it.[9]

With these the list of important Upaniṣads closes : but the manufacture of these works went on indefinitely down even to modern times. The later Upaniṣads claimed connexion with the Atharvaveda, and it is probable that the Muṇḍaka and the Praçna were really so connected : the others had no real bond of union, but were pleased to assume one for their own purposes. These Upaniṣads fall into four classes, according as they (1) merely develop doctrines already found in the older Upaniṣads ; or (2) devote themselves to

[1] For its several parts see Scheftelowitz, ZDMG. lxxv. 201–12.

[2] iv. 4. 8–21.

[3] Īçā 8 compared with KU. v. 13. With Īçā 9–11, cf. Kena 3.

[4] Deussen, *Sechzig Upanishad's*², p. 289. The irregular form *brahmam* (i. 9, 12) suggests that its author was far from a Çiṣṭa, but there is nothing to show that this group of Upaniṣads comes from another *milieu* than the older texts as Jacobi (*Die Entwicklung der Gottesidee*, p. 20, n. 1) suggests.

[5] Cf. iv. 6 f. with iii. 1. 1 f. That Īçā answers the Muṇḍaka is implausible, despite Barua, *Prebuddh. Ind. Phil.*, pp. 259 f., 424.

[6] Cf. x. 2 f. with ii. 1. 8 f.

[7] vi. 5 quotes PU. v. 2.

[8] Cf. Māṇḍ. 3 with Maitr. vi. 4.

[9] iii. 5. Both texts show the use of *tha* in the 2nd plural Imperative as in Pāli and Buddhist Sanskrit, but we cannot say if this is more than an error of tradition, and it would be rash to accept on the strength of such evidence Buddhist influence, *via* Çaiva sects, as suggested by Hume (*Upanishads*, p. 7). For other errors in the Muṇḍaka, see below, p. 504, n. 2.

the glorification of the Yoga practices, by which religious ecstasy was produced; or (3) deal with the condition of the Sannyāsin; or (4) finally give themselves up to the glorification of Rudra-Çiva.

The history of the text of the Upaniṣads is of interest, but not of importance for philosophy: the Atharvan Upaniṣads seem the first to have been collected into one set: we know of collections [1] of 34 or 52,[2] in which case others from the older type were added. A later collection, which arose in South India, has 108 Upaniṣads, including all the great Upaniṣads of the older type. A collection of 50 Upaniṣads was made at some unknown date and was translated into Persian in 1656 for Dara Shukoh: a literal Latin translation from the Persian made by Anquetil du Perron in 1801–2 was the means of bringing the Upaniṣads to the notice of Schopenhauer,[3] and winning for them that place in the history of philosophy which they have never lost. The collection includes in 12 Upaniṣads the older texts, 26 Atharvan Upaniṣads and 8 others, and makes up the total by adding four chapters of the Vājasaneyi Saṁhitā.[4] Of the dates of the making of these collections we have no proof: it is, however, possible that by the time of Çañkara (9th cent. A.D.) the Praçna and Muṇḍaka were already studied together. It is certain that he made use of all the Upaniṣads included in the three great groups, save the Maitrāyaṇīya and the Māṇḍūkya, which he perhaps did not regard as an Upaniṣad at all. To him also are ascribed, though with doubtful justice in all cases, commentaries on these Upaniṣads, except the Kauṣītaki and the Maitrāyaṇīya, and also a commentary on the Māṇḍūkya, which however is probably the work of a different Çañkara.[5] The Upaniṣads used by Rāmānuja include all those of the great groups, save the Māṇḍūkya (though the Kārikā of Gauḍapāda is cited), the Subāla and Cūlikā, and once even the Garbha, Jābāla, and Mahā. The Jābāla and Paiñgi as well as the Kārikā are mentioned by Çañkara.

The question of absolute dates for the Upaniṣads is one far more difficult than that of the relative order of the texts, and admits of no decisive solution. The one argument of weight is the fact, really undeniable, that the doctrines of the Upaniṣads are presupposed by the doctrine of the Buddha, and that, accordingly, if we accept the view that the opinions of the Buddha can be gathered with approximate accuracy from the older texts of the Pāli Canon, it is probable that the older Upaniṣads are, substantially at least, older than say 500 B.C.[6] The argument is not by any means perfect: it may be criticized

[1] Weber, *Berlin-Handschriften*, ii. 88.

[2] The lists of Nārāyaṇa and Colebrooke; see Deussen, *Sechzig Upanishad's*², p. 537. For various MSS. collections see Eggeling, *I. O. Catal.* i. 104 ff.; Keith, *ibid.* ii. 205 ff.

[3] *Parerga*, 2, § 185 (*Werke*, vi. 427).

[4] xvi, xxxi, xxxii, xxxiv.

[5] Jacobi, JAOS. xxxiii. 52, n. 2; Walleser, *Der ältere Vedānta*, p. 55. This fact invalidates much of Deussen's argument (*Phil. of Up.*, pp. 30 ff.). For this date of Çañkara cf. references in JRAS. 1916, pp. 151 ff.; Garbe, *Sâṃkhya-hilosophie*², p. 157, n. 2.

[6] e. g. Rhys Davids, *Dial. of the Buddha*, i. pp. ix ff.; Walleser, *Die philosophische Grundlage des älteren Buddhismus*,

on the ground that even now the date of the Buddha is only established by very conjectural means, and still more so by the fact that the date of the Buddhist Canon rests on mere tradition, which is demonstrably in many respects defective, so that the frequently repeated assertion that the Nikāyas represent approximately a period shortly after the death of the Buddha is wholly unproved and almost certainly quite untrue. A more serious argument is afforded by the really antique character of the metre of the metrical Upaniṣads,[1] such as the Kaṭha, Kena, and Īçā, but here again no absolute date is arrived at, since the only standard of comparison is either the epic, which is of very uncertain date and being not *in pari materia* not an absolutely safe criterion, or Pāli texts, which, apart from their own uncertainty of date, are written in a different speech, and, therefore, certainly not cogently to be adduced as evidence.[2] Perhaps more secure is comparison with the metre of the Bṛhaddevatā,[3] which is with much plausibility assigned to the fourth century B.C., and this certainly suggests that the metre of these texts is older.

More positive evidence cannot be found: the view that the Kaṭha Upaniṣad is older than Buddhism, because the legend resembles in some degree the legend of the Buddhist Māra,[4] ignores the fact that the story is already found in the Taittirīya Brāhmaṇa. The suggestion of Walleser[5] that in the Tevijja Sutta we are to find a reference to the Aitareya, Chāndogya, and Taittirīya Upaniṣads is quite impossible,[6] and the definite use of any particular Upaniṣad by any Buddhist Sutta has still to be proved. The similarity[7] of the language of the early Upaniṣads to that of Pāṇini is decidedly against a very early dating. Certainly it is wholly impossible to make out any case for dating the oldest even of the extant Upaniṣads beyond the sixth century B.C., and the acceptance of an earlier date must rest merely on individual fancy.

In the case of the later Upaniṣads any dating must be still more vague. Hopkins[8] indeed suggests the fourth century for such works as the Kaṭha, Maitrāyaṇīya, and the Çvetāçvatara, but this appears to be as regards the Maitrāyaṇīya much too early a date: style and content alike suggest that this is one of the most recent of the important Upaniṣads. In the case of the Çvetāçvatara, the date selected by Hopkins appears high in view of the fact

Part 1; *contra*, Keith, *Buddhist Philosophy*, chap. i; de la Vallée Poussin, *Muséon*, 1905, pp. 213 ff.; *Bouddhisme*, pp. 29 ff.; ERE. iv. 179 ff.; Lévi, *Les Saintes Écritures du Bouddhisme* (1909); Franke, JPTS. 1908, pp. 1 ff.

[1] Cf. Oldenberg, GN. 1909, pp. 219 ff., and his reff.; Zimmermann, IA. xliv. 130 ff., 177 ff.; Oldenberg, GN. 1915, pp. 490 ff.

[2] Jacobi, *Rāmāyaṇa*, p. 93.

[3] Keith, JRAS. 1906, pp. 1 ff. Evidence of Pāli influence on the Karman of BAU. iii. 2. 13, or the BAU. iv. 3. 2 (*palyayate*), seen by Hume (*Upanishads*, p. 6), is negligible.

[4] Oldenberg, *Die Literatur des alten Indien*, p. 83.

[5] *Die philosophische Grundlage des älteren Buddhismus*, p. 67.

[6] Cf. Rhys Davids, *op. cit.*, p. 303.

[7] Cf. Liebich, *Pāṇini*, pp. 28 ff.; A. Fürst, *Der Sprachgebrauch d. älteren Upaniṣads*; W. Kirfel, *Nominalkomposition in den U.*; O. Wecker, BB. xxx. 1 ff., 177 ff.

[8] JAOS. xxii. 336, n. 1.

that he is convinced that this Upaniṣad is later than the orthodox atheistic Sāṁkhya, and than the theistic Sāṁkhya-Yoga, and marks the appearance of the illusion doctrine foreign to the early Upaniṣads. But this view of his can hardly be accepted for reasons which will later be given, and there is, accordingly, no strong objection to the suggested date beyond the fact that there is no cogent evidence for it. A very different view of the date of the Çvetāçvatara, the Muṇḍaka, and the Māṇḍūkya Upaniṣads is suggested by Walleser,[1] who holds that the illusion theory is posterior to, and derived from, the nihilistic school of Buddhist thought, and that in particular the Māṇḍūkya is not necessarily anterior to the Kārikā of Gauḍapāda—taken by him as a designation of a Bengal school, not of an individual—which expounds the illusionist form of Vedānta for the first time, and which was in being by A.D. 550, but not necessarily very much earlier. This view, however, is without any sound foundation, and of these Upaniṣads no assured date can even be suggested.

The investigation of J. Hertel [2] as to the age of the Muṇḍaka Upaniṣad yields little that is positive. Its comparatively late date is assured, apart from its imitations of the Kaṭha among others, by the fact that it mentions for the first time, except perhaps for the Taittirīya Āraṇyaka,[3] the seven worlds by name, that it has a list of Vedic sciences which includes the six Vedāñgas, though that term is not used,[4] and the Atharvaveda by that title, and uses the term Vedānta of the doctrine of the Upaniṣads. It knows in all probability the personal Brahman.[5] In certain points Hertel indicates similarities with Jain views ; thus, as the title indicates, the work seems to belong to an Atharvavedin sect which practised the habit of shaving the head or pulling out the hair,[6] a Jain practice. The Puruṣa in the Upaniṣad is described by comparing his various members to the fire and other cosmic powers ; the Jains, unlike Buddhists and Brahmans, are wont to represent the universe in human shape in their cosmographical fancies. The Upaniṣad approves asceticism, as does Jainism, and treats release as attained by one who has gained the Brahmaloka, and it is from that world that the man who is freed [7] attains his final abode in the Jain system, and a parallel can be drawn between the terms in

1 *Der ältere Vedānta*, pp. 5 ff. His date for the Kārikā is contrary to the tradition which makes him the spiritual grandfather of Çañkara ; Deussen, *Sechzig Upanishad's*², p. 574.

2 *Muṇḍaka Upaniṣad* (1924), pp. 64 ff.

3 x. 27, 28 ; Kirfel, *Kosmographie*, p. 24*. The TA. x. is probably later than the Muṇḍaka.

4 As it occurs in RV. Prātiçākhya (xiv. 30) and the Nirukta (i. 20), it is impossible to deduce any late date from the mere knowledge of the Vedāñgas, but their appearance is new in the Upaniṣads as a definite group, excluding the other miscellaneous texts found in BAU. and CU.

5 See i. 1. 1 f. and 2. 5.

6 Çañkara (on iii. 2. 10) takes it as a putting of fire on one's head, but this severity is probably not Vedic, though in keeping with Hindu and even Buddhist practices.

7 But in Jainism freedom does not mean extinction of individual existence, as in Brahmanism ; cf. von Glasenapp, *Die Lehre vom Karman*, p. 105.

which the Upaniṣad and the Jain texts describe the ascent. Certain of the terms of the Upaniṣad have Jain currency (*cyu, nirveda, rāga, vītarāga, samyagjñāna, granthi*). It is, however, clear that in all these cases there is no reason to assume Jain priority. Nor do metrical tests do more than show what is otherwise certain, the priority of the Kaṭha.[1] Grammatical forms [2] of pronounced inaccuracy suggest careless composition rather than assure any definite date.

Another possible source of evidence is the date of Īçvarakṛṣṇa, the author of the Sāṁkhya Kārikā. It is perfectly clear that the Sāṁkhya system was substantially older than he in its substance and even in detail, so that a considerable age must be assumed for it, if Īçvarakṛṣṇa is to be assigned to the first century A.D. or even the first half of the second century A.D. Unfortunately the evidence as to Īçvarakṛṣṇa is by no means satisfactory. It seems, however, clear that he was either an older contemporary, if he is identified with Vindhyavāsa, of Vasubandhu, or still older, but this clearly, accepting the earlier date of Vasubandhu, which terminates his existence about A.D. 350, does not lead us further back than about A.D. 300, or half a century earlier.[3] A further argument, however, has been adduced by S. K. Belvalkar,[4] who holds that the commentary on the Kārikā, which was rendered into Chinese by Paramārtha about A.D. 560, was the work of Māṭhara, and is to be dated about A.D. 400. Now as the Māṭhara-Vṛtti frequently calls Īçvarakṛṣṇa Bhagavant, a term which would not readily be applied to a recent author, we may assume the date of the first century A.D. or shortly after for Īçvarakṛṣṇa.

Unfortunately the evidence for these conclusions is peculiarly unsatisfactory. The work for which the title of Māṭhara-Vṛtti is claimed bears this title on the strength of a single colophon only in a MS. apparently of A. D. 1400, which is a very slender piece of evidence. The careful analysis of Belvalkar himself shows that it contains up to 3 per cent. of what he regards as contaminations with Gauḍapāda, and 20 per cent. of students' additions, including a reference to the Hastāmalaka attributed to Çaṅkara, while it gives apparently an extra Kārikā, which certainly has no real claim to be original. In these circumstances, instead of claiming that we have the Māṭhara-Vṛtti established as the source of Paramārtha and Gauḍapāda, the natural conclusion seems to be that this is a compilation derived from the original commentary, now lost, to which the style of Māṭhara-Vṛtti has been given without authority in the lighthearted manner of scribes and owners of MSS. Practically fatal to the theory of Māṭhara as the author of the original com-

[1] They do not, it may be observed, really aid in dividing the text into an original and an interpolator's hand, for the one point made by Hertel (p. 52) is clearly invalid.

[2] e. g. *bhavate, parimucyanti* (pass.), *ādadāyan* (= *ādadat*), *çraddhayantaḥ, pravedayanti* (in sense of simple verb), *viddhi* (from *vyadh*), *jānatha, ācaratha* (imperative), *atharvāya* (dative), *yoṣitāyām*; *vibhum* (nom. neut.) is doubtless a mere misprint; *adreçyam* is uncertain; the use of *pravadeta* for imperfect is the chief sign of later date; the irregularities have epic parallels.

[3] See Keith, *Sāṁkhya System*[2], pp. 79 f.

[4] *Māṭhara-Vṛtti* (*Ann. of Bhandarkar Institute*, 1924, pp. 133 ff.).

ment is the fact that the translator nowhere gives or hints at this name, which is also ignored by Gauḍapāda. What we really do know of an early Māṭhara is that Jain texts [1] which refer to the Saṭṭhitanta add to it the Māḍhara, which means probably that Māṭhara wrote on the Ṣaṣṭitantra, with which agrees precisely the assertion of Guṇaratna Sūri in his commentary on the Ṣaḍdarçanasamuccaya that Māṭhara's Bhāṣya was Ṣaṣṭitantroddhāra-rūpa. Otherwise, the silence regarding Māṭhara as a commentator of the Kārikā is complete. We are, therefore, left without any evidence of the real authorship of the original commentary, which, if not by Īçvarakṛṣṇa himself, need not go back earlier than A.D. 500.

Mention should perhaps be made of the argument deduced by Jacobi [2] from the Kauṭilīya Arthaçāstra from which he infers that the Sāṁkhya and Yoga systems were in existence as well as the Pūrva Mīmāṅsā and the materialist system of the Lokāyata by the fourth century B.C. Unhappily the evidence adduced for this is not satisfactory, as the date of the Arthaçāstra must probably [3] be placed some centuries after the date of the minister of Candragupta under whose name it passes.

From a literary point of view the Upaniṣads command interest by their introduction of new forms. The dialogue appears beside the simpler dogmatic exposition of the Brāhmaṇas, expanded and developed from the brief discussions in this form of ritual problems which the Brāhmaṇas occasionally present. The individual character of the new teaching, which was a mystery, naturally furthered this mode of treatment, and dialogues are recorded between very strange interlocutors as well as between teacher and pupil. Interesting is the fact of competitions in which the speakers contend against one another, in order to win favour and the prize offered by a rich prince. Or two Brahmans are enjoying the meal offered by admirers; one comes to them and wins food by setting a clever riddle. A son returns to his father to report that he has been questioned, and has found himself unable to return a reply; his father assures him that he has told him all he knows, and goes with him to seek instruction. The wise can be induced by strange causes to give of their wisdom. The geese sing the praises of Raikva; he is found under a cart, scratching himself; offers of cows he haughtily refuses, but, when Jānaçruti presents his daughter, he taunts him with not realizing that this was the boon with which he should have sought his favour.[4] Janaka of Videha is the king who appears as the greatest of patrons, and Yājñavalkya the wisest of Brahmans; in one contest of wits alone he vanquishes nine opponents;

[1] Nandī and Anuyogadvāra Sūtras in Weber, *Ind. Stud.* xvii. 9; *Berlin Catal.* ii. 697.

[2] SBA. 1911, pp. 732 ff.; Oldenberg, *Die Kultur der Gegenwart*², I. v. 32–4.

[3] Keith, JRAS. 1916, pp. 130–7; 1920, p. 628; Jolly, ZDMG. lxviii. 355–9 and pref. to ed. (Lahore, 1923); Winternitz, *Gesch. d. ind. Lit.* iii. 518; O. Stein, *Megasthenes und Kauṭilya* (SWA. 1921). Jacobi's defence of his thesis (ZDMG. lxxiv. 254; *Die Entwicklung der Gottesidee bei den Indern*, p. 41, n. 1) is ineffective. Use of Yājñavalkya is shown by T. Gaṇapati Śāstrī in his ed. (Trivandrum, 1924), pp. 8 ff.

[4] CU. iv. 2.

the head of the last, Çākalya, splits open as the result of his failure, while robbers steal his bones.[1] Women are not excluded from contests, a maiden seized by a Gandharva or even one of Yājñavalkya's wives shows herself an adept in these questions. The gods appear; Prajāpati instructs the intelligent pupil Indra and the stupid demon Virocana.[2] Animals lend their quota of tuition; the pupil, who watches his master's kine increase, receives instruction from the bull of the herd, from the fire, from a gander, and from a Madgu bird.[3] It would, of course, be rash to trust to the historicity of the dialogues; they are attached readily to famous names, as in the Kaṭha Naciketas and Yama carry on a dialogue in the later form of verse.

There is, of course, much that contrasts strangely with the Platonic dialogue. An element of grave risk enters into such discussions, as we have seen in the case of the rivals of Yājñavalkya; to hold a wrong view often involves risk of death in an age when the curse is believed to have power to work its own end.[4] Again of real dialectic there is hardly any; the inquirer is ignorant and makes wrong guesses, the teacher dogmatically expounds the truth, with little or no leading up to it, and with still less reasoning for its support; curiously enough, it is in the discussions between Indra and Prajāpati [5] that we find more of the expression of uncertainty leading to a final illumination than usual. There are, however, especially in the dialogues of Yājñavalkya, signs of planning; the outcome is attained by a process of rejection of inferior views, arranged in something like a series of lower to higher.[6]

No serious advance in logic is made over the Brāhmaṇas, though faint traces of induction by simple enumeration may be traced.[7] On the other hand, there is a certain gain in literary form; the description of the unity of the universe produces passages of much higher feeling than was possible when dealing with the sacrifice,[8] and distinct power is shown in the invention of such designations of the Ātman as 'Not so, not so,' which excludes all particularization, while the phrase 'That thou art' not unworthily sums up the mystery of the identity of the self and the universe. In other cases we have empty mysticism as in the unintelligible *jalān* [9] or *tadvanam* [10] as expressions of the absolute. One distinctive feature of value is the use of similes, often of complexity and interest; they are treated as conclusive arguments, though often only fanciful analogies, and though as always, if these are pressed, they tend to confuse the precise meaning of the text, and have afforded cause for doubt both to ancient and to modern interpreters.[11] Riddles,

[1] BAU. iii. 1; cf. ÇB. xi. 6. 3.
[2] BAU. ii. 4; iv. 5; CU. viii. 7 ff.
[3] CU. iv. 4 ff.
[4] JUB. iii. 8. Cf. ÇB. xi. 4. 1; GB. i. 3. 6.
[5] CU. viii. 7 ff.
[6] BAU. iii. 1 ff.; iv. 3. 23 ff.; CU. v. 12 ff.
[7] CU. vi. 1. 4–6; above, Chap. 27, § 5.
[8] CU. iii. 14; ÇB. x. 6. 3.
[9] Böhtlingk, BSGW. 1896, pp. 159 f.; 1897, p. 83.
[10] Kena 31; Hopkins, JAOS. xxii. 362.
[11] e.g. BAU. ii. 4. 7 ff.; Oldenberg, *Die Lehre der Upanishaden*, p. 183, n. 1. The idea that the late Muṇḍaka (iii. 2. 4) has Liṅga in the technical logical sense (Radhakrishnan, *Ind.*

inherited from the sacrificial tradition, are curiously rare, though not unknown, and in the earlier Upaniṣads the employment of verse is restricted, though it occurs here and there in the Bṛhadāraṇyaka and the Chāndogya. Interesting as presaging the manner of the Pāli texts is the constant repetition of the same idea in slightly different forms; thus whatever is said of one sense is normally repeated verbatim, with only the essential changes, for another; the generic terms which would have spared the tedium have not yet been invented or even felt to be necessary and appropriate.[1]

§ 3. *The Interpretation of the Upaniṣads*

It was attempted by the great philosopher Çañkara to find in the Upaniṣads the expression of a single simple doctrine, carried out consistently through all, and in his commentary on the Vedānta as set out in the Brahma Sūtra of Bādarāyaṇa it is his object to interpret that Sūtra and to bring out at the same time the doctrines of the Upaniṣads, the whole forming a great system of philosophy in which no contradictions should exist.[2] The plan adopted by the philosopher for this purpose was simple: he found in the Upaniṣads the principle that knowledge was of two kinds, wholly different. On the one hand the higher knowledge recognized the existence of absolutely nothing save the Brahman or the Ātman, the one unity, which was at once real, thought, and bliss. The force of these terms must be understood in a special sense: reality is not something outside the Brahman: no predication is possible of the Brahman, for predication involves diversity and in the Brahman there is no diversity. Thought or consciousness, which is not an attribute of, but the essence of the Brahman, does not mean actual activity, the νοῦς νοήσεως of Aristotle on the most probable view of that famous doctrine:[3] it is consciousness without any object or subject, and therefore differs so entirely from the very nature of consciousness as not in our view to deserve the name at all. The bliss also is that of being which has no consciousness of any kind and no feeling, and therefore is merely a metaphorical expression. This single thing is all that the world really is, the one Brahman which is the Ātman. All the multiplicity of phenomena is unreal: the saving truth which redeems the individual from the constant stream of births is the recognition of this fact, that he himself is really the one Ātman, not related as part to it, but solely and absolutely it. In the expression 'That thou art',[4] which is enunciated in the Upaniṣads, is set out the fundamental fact of all existence, the indivisible unity.

Phil. i. 263) is implausible. Similarly Vyaṣṭi and Samaṣṭi in BAU. iii. 3. 2 can hardly denote distinction and generality, or distributive and collective aggregates, or Siddhi, in KU. iii. 3, proof.

[1] Cf. the Canonical Buddhist style; Oldenberg, GN. 1912, pp. 123 ff.

[2] See e.g. his comment on the Sūtra, iii. 3. 1. The best defence of this theory is in A. E. Gough, *Philosophy of the Upanishads.*

[3] For an attack on Aristotle's view see Gomperz, *Greek Thinkers*, iv. 211 ff.

[4] CU. vi. 8. 7; cf. 'I am Brahman', BAU. i. 4. 10.

The apparent multiplicity of the universe and the empirical knowledge of man is not in the view of Çañkara to be denied for a moment. Çañkara wages war both against the idealistic school of Buddhism, which denies that there is any real distinction between dreams and waking reality, and the nihilistic school, which asserts that all is mere void. Existence is not momentary at all: it has a substantiality and is real, but only from the point of view of the lower knowledge.[1] The Ātman in itself has allied with it a power, Māyā, illusion, which limits it: the limitation is not indeed real, for that would hopelessly violate the essential doctrine of Çañkara which denies any dualism whatever; but from the point of view of the lower knowledge that illusion exists, and through that illusion exists all that there is in the universe as known to us. Thus, there is room for a great god, the Hiraṇyagarbha of the Veda, who occupies the position of a demiourgos, inasmuch as he is the Ātman, when it is obscured by illusion, and there is afforded an explanation for the seeming multiplicity of souls, for the unending stream of life, for the world of living creatures and inanimate nature. All indeed is an illusion, but it has within that fundamental fact all the appearance of reality.[2]

It will be seen at once that in this doctrine Çañkara has a powerful weapon, with which to explain the whole of the system of the Upaniṣads as the product of a single philosophical impulse. Nevertheless, the attempt is undoubtedly merely a clever *tour de force* without final validity, and its ingenuity is as great but no greater than its improbability. That this is the case could be easily proved by the examination of the Upaniṣads in detail, but it is sufficient to state that the Brahma Sūtra itself did not take the view adopted by Çañkara: it is now certain, thanks to the efforts of Thibaut,[3] Sukhtankar,[4] and Jacobi,[5] among others, that the real view taken by Bādarāyaṇa was more akin to, though not identical with, that taken by the commentary of Rāmānuja,[6] whose work dates some two centuries after Çañkara. The view of that scholar was that the explanation of the world and of the individual souls as mere products of illusion, enveloping the nature of the Brahman, was wholly wrong: on the contrary the two elements, the world and the individual souls, had a definite entity of their own, which was perfectly real, even if they were only parts of, and, therefore, much inferior in order of rank to, the Brahman, who is conceived no longer as mere impersonality but as personal being. The views of Rāmānuja are in many points difficult to formulate

[1] For a modern defence of Çañkara, see Max Müller, *The Silesian Horseherd* (1903); a good criticism is given by Dahlmann, *Die Sāṁkhya-Philosophie*, pp. 236–55; cf. also Walleser, *Der ältere Vedānta* (1910).

[2] Cf. de la Vallée Poussin, JRAS. 1910, pp. 128 ff.

[3] SBE. xxxiv and xlviii.

[4] VOJ. xxii. 120 ff.

[5] JAOS. xxxi. 1 ff.; xxxiii. 52–4; in *Festschrift E. Windisch*, pp. 153–7, he traces in Çabarasvāmin on Mīmāṅsā Darçana, i. 5, the view that BAU. iii. 9. 26; iv. 5. 12, recognize a multiplicity of souls *contra* Çañkara's view (Brahma Sūtra, iii. 3. 53); cf. also de la Vallée Poussin, *Le Brahmanisme*, pp. 73 ff.

[6] See Keith, ERE. *s. v.*; Bhandarkar, *Vaiṣṇavism, Śaivism, and Minor Religious Systems*, pp. 50 ff. See also Kokileswar Sastri, *Adwaita Philosophy*.

with precision: there is vagueness regarding the position of the individual soul, the world and the divinity, which is probably unavoidable, but certainly undeniable. But at any rate the system of pure idealism of the most abstract kind, which Çaṅkara put forward, is confronted with a system which is pantheistic, for the individual souls and the world are in some sense part of the deity, but which has also a strong theistic element in the fact that the individual souls, even when they become free from transmigration through the influence of their devotion to the lord and his compassion for them, are deemed still to retain a separate existence and not to be merged in the deity. As in the case of all Indian thinkers, the tendency of Rāmānuja is to be hazy regarding the nature of the deity, and the part played in that nature by consciousness, which, as we have seen, for Çaṅkara disappears into a meaningless abstraction, but the individual soul seems, contrary to the clear tendency of the Upaniṣads, and of the epic Sāṁkhya-Yoga,[1] to retain in its final form of existence some kind of consciousness which is consistent with its enjoyment of the most perfect bliss.

Rāmānuja quotes the Upaniṣads as agreeing with his doctrine, but he has not made any such determined and deliberate effort to bring the Upaniṣads into one definite scheme as has Çaṅkara: he relies rather on the Sūtra than on the Upaniṣads, but still he offers an alternative view which suits admirably many of the Upaniṣad passages, which he cites. He has, of course, the obvious advantage that the distinction of two kinds of knowledge is one which is artificial, and which has no direct sanction from the Upaniṣads themselves, so that Çaṅkara is forced in effect to postulate a distinction of knowledge, which is not asserted in his sources.

Of modern interpreters of the Upaniṣads, the most important, Deussen,[2] as before him Gough[3] also, has endeavoured to show that the view of Çaṅkara is the best key to the secrets of the Upaniṣads: Deussen insists that in his view, which is that of the Yājñavalkya of the Bṛhadāraṇyaka Upaniṣad, Çaṅkara formulates the essential doctrine of the distinction between the empirical reality and the thing in itself, which was first made perfectly distinct by Kant, and which reaches its complement in the Christian and Schopenhauerian doctrine of the primacy of the will over the intellect. Deussen holds that this form of idealism is the main doctrine of the Upaniṣads in the sense that it was definitely formulated and laid down, and that other doctrines are really deviations from it, caused by the inability of man to remain on the high level of thought postulated in the distinction, and by the constant effort to apply empirical categories to the thing in itself. From the tendency to regard

[1] This doctrine is definitely pantheistic; the Brahman realizes itself in the individual selves through the operation of Buddhi, 'intellect', and Ahaṁkāra, the principle of individuation, and recognition of the unity of the individual and the Brahman is the release aimed at; see Dahlmann, *Nirvāṇa* and *Die Sāṁkhya-Philosophie*, who contends that this is the primitive Sāṁkhya as a logical (*ānvīkṣikī*) science of the Brahman; see below, § 7.

[2] *Phil. of Up.*, pp. 39 ff.

[3] *Philosophy of the Upanishads.*

the universe, however, as actually real and an absolute thing, there grows up the view that the Ātman is the universe which we know, that is a system of pantheism. Even Yājñavalkya, like Parmenides in Greece,[1] could not resist this tendency, and falls into the error when he describes the Ātman as the internal ruler, or as supporting the sun and moon, heaven and earth, and the whole universe, or as expanding into the whole external universe. But this standpoint was also liable to difficulties : the identity was difficult to hold fast, and gave way to the simpler empirical conception of causality : the Ātman produces the universe, and he enters into it with his self, an idea which of course had abundant parallels in the Brāhmaṇas, when applied to personal deities such as Prajāpati. This doctrine is found, he thinks, nowhere in the Bṛhadāraṇyaka, but in the Chāndogya, the Taittirīya, the Aitareya, and later. The Ātman, however, still remains the same in the world as in itself : it does not create other spirits, but enters in as itself. The pantheism thus passes into cosmogonism, and from this point of view or from the former can be explained the insistence on the identity of the spirit in the heart with the infinitely great outside. The next stage of thought produces theism : the relation of the Ātman to the soul in man is conceived as no longer one of identity, but as one of some degree of contrast and independence : the Ātman of the individual is set over against the Ātman in its highest aspect, tentatively even in some old passages, then definitely and openly in the Kaṭha Upaniṣad, and still more markedly with the presentation of the Ātman as the god Rudra in the Çvetāçvatara Upaniṣad. The road was now open for the disappearance of the deity, since the individual souls were now independent entities, and could explain the universe if taken in conjunction with the principle of the world other than souls, Prakṛti, the primeval nature. The idea of god, therefore, disappears in the Sāṁkhya faith, and later the Yoga, which in deference to the demands of the popular movement of the day asked for a god, introduces the divinity *ab extra* with an obvious inconsequence, which makes him of no real importance in the philosophy of the theory.

This is a brilliant and attractive theory, and it, of course, affords a far more rational ground for the historical comprehension of the Upaniṣads than does that of Çañkara with its contrast of the two kinds of knowledge, and its wholly incredible suggestion[2] that the authors of the views found in the Upaniṣads really were making this distinction between the higher and the lower forms of knowledge, when it is plain to the reader that they are simply doing their best to express their philosophic beliefs for what they were worth. Nevertheless, the idea that the different stages of view are related in the form given by Deussen is one impossible to accept : the obvious history of the Upaniṣads,[3] if we are not led astray by the belief in the opening up of new

[1] What was Parmenides' real view in the second part of his poem is doubtful in the extreme, and Deussen's assertion is far from being certainly correct.

[2] Cf. Speyer, *Indische Theosophie*, p. 307.

[3] Edgerton (JAOS. xxxvi. 197–204; *Studies in honor of Maurice Bloomfield*, pp. 117–35) very justly emphasizes the con-

ideas by the warrior class, would suggest that the cosmogonic is the oldest form of the doctrine of the Brahman or Ātman. The Vedic cosmogonism is the natural standpoint: we have there the first principle, the first creation or emanation of that principle, and the entry of that principle into the creation. The tendency of the Veda is throughout to treat creation, not as something which is developed by the mere will of the creator, but as something lying in his nature *ab initio*: creation is rather development than the bringing into being of something hitherto not existing in any way. Hence the way is paved for the doctrine of identity in the Ātman:[1] the principle is manifested in the whole world, as in the myth Puruṣa by his sacrifice becomes the whole world, and the further step of identifying the spiritual principle in each man with the spiritual principle which is the *prius* of the world, is an obvious and easy one. The pantheism of the Brāhmaṇas is thus inseparably connected with their cosmogonism: it would be unwise to seek to establish for the Upaniṣads any real distinction between these ideas.

The tendency of the Brāhmaṇas is certainly to diminish the personal aspect of the deity, but the influence of the popular religion must be borne in mind, as explaining the nature of the development of the philosophy of the Upaniṣads. The worship of Rudra was, it is perfectly clear from the Brāhmaṇas themselves, a very important thing indeed for the Brahmans and the people alike, and the inevitable tendency of this vivid belief in powerful and real gods, not an abstraction, was to make the character of the universal change. Prajāpati had been in some measure a god of the ritual: his name helped to make him more than mere priestly fiction, but he could not be expected to have that vivid nature, which is the characteristic of the form of Rudra. The effect of this personal adoration of great gods with the sense of dependence on them and trust in them, which is a real element in the religion of India,[2] shows itself in philosophy in the theism which begins to be clearly marked in the Kaṭha Upaniṣad and which is expressed in the doctrine of predestination there enunciated, in the form that the saving knowledge is not a matter of learning, but is revealed to the fortunate man by the highest power itself. It is only a step hence to the sectarianism of the Çvetāçvatara Upaniṣad, a work which has often wrongly been deemed of much more modern date than it really is, because of the belief that the spirit of devotion to god was a product of the introduction of Christian influences. The theism of the Upaniṣads is, then, we may believe, a later stage than their pantheism and cosmogonism, and is due to the influence of the personal element in the religion of the priest and Brahmans alike.

tinuity of the Vedic tradition; the philosophic hymns of the AV. have relations with the Upaniṣads.

[1] Hopkins (JAOS. xxii. 380, 381) insists that Ātmanism without illusion is the essential side of the Upaniṣads and that illusion is late, but this again is overstraining the position to some slight extent at least.

[2] Bhandarkar, *Vaiṣṇavism, Śaivism, and Minor Religious Systems* (Strassburg, 1913); Keith, JRAS. 1907, pp. 490–3; 1915, pp. 833 ff.; Grierson, 1908, p. 361; Nicol Macnicol, *Indian Theism* (1915); Weber, *Religionssoziologie*, ii. 319 ff.

There is, however, undoubtedly another side of the absolute, which must be set off against the theistic development which in the time of Rāmānuja was used to place on a philosophic basis the worship of Viṣṇu, as in the Çvetāçvatara Upaniṣad it had been made the base of the worship of Rudra. We know of its existence from two independent sources of the highest value, the Buddhist and the Sāṁkhya systems of philosophy, which reveal to us such despair of and disbelief in the one Ātman and the absolute as to present us with nothing but individual souls in the Sāṁkhya, and even to deny, though in a foolish and superficial way, the existence of souls in the Buddhist faith. It is certainly not easy to see how the pantheism and cosmogonism or the theism of the Upaniṣads could have produced this outlook on the world, and it suggests that there must have been in existence a view of the Ātman as absolute which emptied it of much significance, and made it therefore tempting for those, who desired to rise superior to the mere fictions of the popular religion, to find true reality in something nearer hand, the existence of the individual and of the external universe. The theory which postulated an Ātman of no real content was indeed to be found, and that was the theory of Yājñavalkya. It is true that the teaching in question is not consistently carried out, as Deussen admits, but it is plain that it lays stress on the three propositions that (1) the Ātman is the knowing self, is the subject of cognition; (2) that as such it can never be an object of knowledge of any sort; and (3) that beyond the Ātman there is no reality at all, as it is the sole reality. These propositions form the basis of the views of Çañkara, and it would be a complete error to suppose that the position of Çañkara was really due[1] to the effect of the teaching of the nihilist and idealist schools of Buddhism, the Mādhyamikas and the Vijñānavādins. That Çañkara was deeply influenced by their doctrines is doubtless true enough, but at the same time it seems beyond doubt that the doctrine which he maintained was originally the property of a school of Aupaniṣadas, and that, therefore, it was descended from an interpretation of the Upaniṣads, whose accuracy is confirmed by the actual texts of the Upaniṣads in so far as they bear out the meaning of Yājñavalkya's own doctrine: the distinction of the two forms of knowledge, and the effort to show that other views in the Upaniṣads can be reconciled with Yājñavalkya's on this basis, are of course the work of the predecessors of Çañkara.

The view of Yājñavalkya cannot, save by paradox, be deemed the earliest view or the dominating view expressed in the Upaniṣads: it must be taken as one view of considerable importance, which has received expression in portions of two of the oldest Upaniṣads, the Bṛhadāraṇyaka and the Chāndogya, but most of all in the first. Independent and older are the cosmogonic and pantheistic views which appear in the Aitareya Āraṇyaka[2] and in the

[1] As held by Gañgānātha Jhā, *Khaṇḍanakhaṇḍakhādya*, i. p. xii; cf. Keith, JRAS. 1916, pp. 379–81. The same view appears in Walleser, *Der ältere Vedānta* (1910), but it is incredible that, as he held, it is really first in Gauḍapāda's Kārikā on the Māṇḍūkya Upaniṣad that the real Vedānta appears.

[2] Keith, *Aitareya Āraṇyaka*, pp. 41 ff.; JRAS. 1906, pp. 490 ff.

Brāhmaṇas, and the dominating influence of the view of Yājñavalkya ascribed to it by Deussen cannot be established. Its interest for us is not lessened by that fact: it is the most characteristically individual of the doctrines of the Upaniṣads, and in some ways of the greatest philosophic value. It is, moreover, the chief matter in which an advance on the views of the Brāhmaṇas can be recognized.

If we are to seek a more plausible theory of stages of development, we may assume that the fundamental question of finding a unity in the world was attacked from two points of view, already foreshadowed in the Brāhmaṇas. On the one hand the conception of the Brahman was developed to include the whole of the universe; the holy power which controls things becomes expanded in idea into that which contains and accounts for all. On the other hand the psychic element is also developed, in part doubtless through the study of the stages of the spirit in waking and sleep; the unity here is imagined first as breath, Prāṇa, then it becomes conceived as intellect, Prajñā, and finally in the more abstract form of the self, Ātman, a term which has the advantage of including the conception of breath, and also of intelligence, while transcending both. A decisive advance occurs when, in lieu of inadequate efforts to express the nature of the Brahman, we have the pregnant assertion of the identity of the individual Ātman with the Brahman regarded as a cosmic Ātman. But this assertion leaves us with unsolved difficulties; on the one hand it leads to suggestions such as those implied or made by Yājñavalkya which indicate the illusory character of the world of appearances, asserting the unity of Ātman, broken in life by the duality induced by individuality, which is merged temporarily in deep sleep, finally in death; on the other we have efforts, as in the Kaṭha, to accept as real, and deduce from the Brahman, the whole of the spiritual and non-spiritual world, efforts which lead to antinomies regarding the relation of the absolute and individual souls and end in the abolition of the absolute in the Sāṁkhya, and of both absolute and individual in Buddhism.

§ 4. *The Problem and Conditions of Knowledge*

It is an essential feature of the Upaniṣads that, though they make, as we have seen, little or no advance in logical doctrine, they do tentatively raise and deal in some measure with the question of the source of knowledge of the Brahman or Ātman. The view of the Brāhmaṇas, of course, is that knowledge is to be found in the Vedas, and the authority of the Vedic texts is not discussed. In the Upaniṣads, however, we find that the question of the means of knowledge is definitely raised: the three Vedas or the four, which are sometimes recognized, are not always recognized as the sources of complete knowledge: Çvetaketu, despite much Vedic learning, cannot solve the question of transmigration, Nārada admits to Sanatkumāra his incompetence to understand the Ātman. The Taittirīya Upaniṣad [1] expressly reduces the knowledge

[1] ii. 3.

of the Vedas to an inferior position by assigning them to the stage of the mind-made Ātman, which has to be surmounted before reaching the final truth. But these views were gradually and naturally supplemented by another, which makes the Upaniṣads an essential part, the secret instruction, of the Veda: hence the term Vedānta which first occurs in the Çvetāçvatara Upaniṣad [1] and denotes the Upaniṣads, as the end of the Veda in which its deepest secret is disclosed.

The Brāhmaṇas had recognized, beside study of the Veda, the duty of sacrifice, and the importance of asceticism, and on both these points the thinkers of the Upaniṣads were bound to take a clear stand. The sacrifice is least reputed in the Bṛhadāraṇyaka Upaniṣad [2] where, with a certain insolence, the worship of anything except the self is derided, and the relation of the ordinary worshipper to his gods is compared with that of housedogs. Again Yama is said to have his abode in the sacrifice, and the sacrifice in the fees. The Chāndogya [3] also seems in part to recognize the demerits of the sacrifice. But it would be an error to think that the general depreciation of the sacrifice is characteristic of the Brahmans; it is clear that a few enlightened minds had a poor opinion of the whole apparatus, but the normal view of the Upaniṣads is quite removed from that of opposition to sacrifice, which is often believed to mark them out. The sacrifice, however, is expressly relegated to an inferior place: the faithful performance of offerings takes a man but to the world of the Fathers, whence he will return to earth again in due course,[4] and not thus can final liberation be won. On the other hand the actual performance of the sacrifice is rendered needless by the substitute for the ritual acts of allegorical acts: the three periods of life supersede the three Soma offerings,[5] inhalation and speech the Agnihotra,[6] the organs of the self the four priests, and so on. The tendency, however, to restore the sacrifice to honour steadily grows: the Kaṭha [7] recognizes it as of value, the Çvetāçvatara [8] recommends recourse to it, the Maitrāyaṇīya [9] asserts that without the study of the Veda, the observance of caste duties, and the following of the orders of life, through the stage of student householder, forest hermit, and wandering ascetic, the reunion of the individual and the personal self is impossible. Doubtless in this we can recognize the growing aversion of the Brahmans to the Buddhist and the Jain tenets.

The part of asceticism in the pursuit of knowledge is similar to that of the sacrifice. The Bṛhadāraṇyaka [10] is not inclined towards it, recognizing in it as in sacrifice at most a way to the lower bliss of the world of the Fathers,[11]

1 vi. 22; Muṇḍ. iii. 2. 6. Cf. Kena 33.

2 iii. 9. 6, 21.

3 i. 10–12; iv. 1–3.

4 BAU. i. 5. 16; vi. 2. 16; CU. v. 10. 3; PU. i. 9; Muṇḍ. i. 2. 10.

5 CU. iii. 16.

6 AA. iii. 2. 6.

7 i. 17; iii. 2. Cf. also Īçā 11.

8 ii. 6, 7.

9 i. 1; iv. 1 ff.

10 iii. 8. 10; iv. 4. 22.

11 vi. 2. 18; in view of this passage we may perhaps hold that in CU. v. 10. 1 the qualification for full enlightenment is not faith and Tapas (as in PU. i. 10; Muṇḍ. i. 2. 11; Windisch, *Buddha's Geburt*, p. 73, n. 1) but faith as Tapas, as the words *çraddhā tapa ity upāsate* normally mean; see below, § 10.

the Chāndogya [1] substitutes the faith of the forest dweller for penance. The Taittirīya Upaniṣad,[2] on the other hand, places value on Vedic study and asceticism, and even insists on the supreme value of the latter: the Mahānārāyaṇa [3] sets renunciation, Nyāsa, above even asceticism: and from the Kena[4] onwards the value of asceticism for the obtaining of the knowledge of the Brahman is absolutely recognized and sometimes insisted upon. In this, as in regard to Vedic study and sacrifice, the process is one of steady accommodation to the popular view, which was at the same time the profitable view to the priests. It is needless, however, to see in this the fact of the borrowing of the theory of the Ātman from an external source: the facts accord perfectly with a reform within the Brahmanical fold: the reformers gradually sink back into the main body, while their doctrine in some degree at least is adopted by the main body of the priests.

Nor in the oldest stratum of the Upaniṣads do we find the necessity of instruction by a teacher laid down: Yājñavalkya [5] on several occasions teaches persons such as his wife, Maitreyī, informally and without initiation, and Açvapati [6] teaches the Brahmans who come to him freely. The rule of taking a teacher is absolute in the Kaṭha,[7] and is approved in the Chāndogya,[8] where the teacher is regarded as being as essential as the removal of a bandage to a blindfolded man, who wishes to find his way home to Gandhāra. In these texts the vague requirements also occur that a man should be endowed with self-restraint, renunciation, tranquillity, patience, and collectedness.

But beyond these minor matters, which are none of them recognized as essential in the oldest Upaniṣads, a further question arises, how far there can be real knowledge at all of the Ātman. The natural desire of the philosopher is to know the Ātman: the Upaniṣads are in very real sense the search for that knowledge, but the conviction is clearly early felt that there were serious difficulties in assuming the possibility of empiric means giving the desired result. The Rigveda [9] already contained the idea that the first principle in some degree disguised itself, and the world of name and form becomes in the Bṛhadāraṇyaka [10] the immortal concealed in truth, or reality, and as the reality of reality is seen the self. The only normal sense which can be given to these passages is that suggested by the description of the whole universe in the Chāndogya [11] as a matter of words, a mere name. The reality of the world is empiric, the true reality is the Ātman, which the empiric reality conceals. It follows, therefore, that all so-called knowledge is really ignorance, Avidyā, and that in death in casting off the body the soul throws aside ignorance.[12]

1 ii. 23.
2 i. 9 and iii.
3 lxii. 11.
4 33; PU. i. 10; Muṇḍ. i. 2. 11.
5 BAU. ii. 4; iv. 1 ff.
6 CU. v. 11. 7.
7 ii. 8.
8 vi. 14. ÇU. vi. 23 demands devotion to the teacher as to god.
9 x. 81. 1; cf. 129. 7; even the lord may not know the origin of creation.
10 i. 6. 3; ii. 1. 20; ii. 4. 7–9.
11 vi. 1–3; cf. vii. 1, 2; viii. 3. 1, 2.
12 BAU. iv. 4. 3, 4; ÇU. v. 1.

The Kaṭha [1] illustrates this theme: ordinary knowledge aims at pleasure, real knowledge at salvation, and it must be accorded through a teacher,[2] and by the favour of the Ātman,[3] a doctrine which develops into the express declaration that the favour of the creator is essential. The Çvetāçvatara [4] carries us to the logical result and offers prayers to the gods for assistance, inculcating devotion, Bhakti, to god and to the teacher.

On the other hand, there arises in the doctrine of Yājñavalkya a distinct and different element: the self in this view cannot be known at all.[5] There is no consciousness after death, he explains to Maitreyī, and the grounds of his explanation are that duality is essential for consciousness. The absolute self is unknowable, for there is no duality between it and anything else: the individual self is also unknowable because it must be the activity in knowing, and cannot be the object. The doctrine has echoes in other Upaniṣads,[6] and it results in fierce attacks on knowledge, which is ranked as worse than ignorance by the Īçā.[7] The Kaṭha [8] lays stress on the necessity of turning the eye inwards in contrast to the mere use of the senses to grasp what is external, and insists that the only assertion that can be made of the self is the mere declaration of existence pure and simple. The way is, therefore, clearly open to the development of the doctrine alluded to in the earlier Upaniṣads, but not developed until later,[9] which seeks by means of processes of physical and psychical disposition to produce the trance condition in which unity with the absolute, the only possible form of knowledge, is arrived at.

§ 5. *The Nature of the Absolute*

The Upaniṣads are essentially concerned with the endeavour to describe the nature of the absolute, and the rich abundance of attempts to succeed in this end, proved by the references to conflicting theories in the Upaniṣads, is clear proof of the busy mental activity of the period. From the earliest Upaniṣad we have, the view is clear that there is a unity, that it is necessary further to grasp the nature of that unity, and that the proper names of the unity are either the Brahman or the Ātman. The two ideas whose history we have seen in the Brāhmaṇas are used constantly in alternation with each other. It is clear that they must have been felt to be practically akin.

Many of these attempts were, it is clear, of little worth: Bālāki Gārgya in

[1] KU. ii. 1–6; Muṇḍ. i. 2. 8–10; Maitr. vii. 9; the later verses in BAU. iv. 4. 11, 12.

[2] KU. ii. 7–9.

[3] KU. ii. 23 and 20; ÇU. iii. 20; Mahānār. x. 1 (viii. 3); Muṇḍ. iii. 2. 3.

[4] ii. 1–5; iii. 1–6; iv. 1.

[5] ii. 4. 12; iii. 4. 2; 7. 23; 8. 11; iv. 3. 10; 4. 2. Similarly the Dharma of the Buddhists, which replaces the Brahman (W. Geiger, *Dharma und Brahman*, pp. 1 ff.), is ultimately unknowable (Stcherbatsky, *The Central Conception of Buddhism*, p. 75).

[6] CU. vi. 9, 10; 15. 1, 2; vii. 24. 1; TU. ii; Kena 3, 11.

[7] 9–11.

[8] iv. 1; vi. 12, 13; the later verse in BAU. iv. 4. 10.

[9] The Abhidharmakoça (i. 40) formally insists against older Buddhism that sensuous consciousness and material elements can be suppressed only by ecstasy, not knowledge.

his interview with Ajātaçatru puts forward twelve [1] or sixteen views of the nature of the absolute. They are all of the same type, the soul in the sun, the moon, lightning, ether, fire, water, the person in a mirror, the sound that follows one as he goes, the person in the quarters, the shadow, the person in the body, &c., to which the king opposes in reply the conception of that whence the breaths proceed, and on which the worlds, gods, and men depend. Other suggestions made by Çākalya [2] which treat breath, love, forms, ether, &c., as the basis of the absolute are refuted by Yājñavalkya, who also rejects the suggestions of speech, the breath, the eye, the ear, mind, and the heart laid before him by Janaka as doctrines enunciated on this head.[3] Yājñavalkya shows that these things are only the basis of the attributes of the divine unity, and that it is necessary to go behind the mere attributes or their manifestation, which can only be done by recognizing the essential identity of the absolute and our own spirit. The Brahmans who with Uddālaka are instructed by Açvapati Kaikeya [4] are supporters of the claims of heaven, sun, wind, ether, water, and earth as the absolute unity, there conceived as the Ātman Vaiçvānara, an idea borrowed from the Agni Vaiçvānara which forms the subject of discussion in the secret doctrine of the fire in the Çatapatha Brāhmaṇa.[5] The king, on his part, insists that the Ātman must be within, not an external object. A much longer and more elaborate series of imperfect views is represented in the instruction of Nārada by Sanatkumāra,[6] where from name the advance is made through speech, mind, conception or judgement (*saṁkalpa*), thought, intuition (*dhyāna*), knowledge (*vijñāna*), force, food (i.e. earth), water, heat, ether, memory, and longing (*āçā*), to the breath which is the individual soul, and finally to the great one, Bhūman, which comprehends all, fills space, and is identical with the principle of egoism, Ahaṁkāra, and the self, Ātman, in man. The transition from the individual to the great one is made thus: truth depends on knowledge, this on thought (*mati*), this on faith, this on concentration (*niḥṣṭhā*), this on productive power, this on pleasure, which exists in the unlimited.

More important than these theories are others: Indra [7] and the demon Virocana went to Prajāpati for instruction: he first describes the Ātman as the body, a view thought adequate by Virocana, who is the prototype of all men who merely see in the body the hope of immortality, and, therefore, deck it out on death with gay raiment. Prajāpati then explains the self as the spirit in dreams, but Indra is not satisfied, since the spirit is still in this condition opposed to a world beyond itself. Prajāpati then propounds the self in dreamless sleep, where there is no distinction of subject and object, which he explains as not the annihilation of the self, but its entry upon the fullest

[1] BAU. ii. 1; KU. iv. For the person in the eye, superior person (*atipuruṣa*) in the sun, and the supreme person in the lightning, see JUB. i. 27. The person in the eye is Prajāpati, Indra, the universe, i. 43. 10 ff.; iv. 24. 13.

[2] BAU. iii. 9. 10–17, 26. For ether a the universe, see JUB. i. 27 f.

[3] BAU. iv. 1.

[4] CU. v. 11.

[5] x. 6. 1.

[6] CU. vii.

[7] CU. viii. 7–12.

light in identification with the absolute. With this view must be compared a more developed one expressed in the Taittirīya Upaniṣad,[1] where there are distinguished five Ātmans; the first is the *annamaya*, which corresponds to the body; then the *prāṇamaya*, which corresponds to the life of the breaths or vital airs; the *manomaya*, the self of the mind, which here clearly means the activity of the self as conscious will in such actions as sacrifice and study; the *vijñānamaya*, in which for sacrifice is substituted knowledge and worship of the deity in that manner; and finally the *ānandamaya*, that of joy before whom words and thought recoil, not finding him. This last self is not an object of knowledge, and hence it is described as not real—empirically—, as unconscious and unutterable. In it is bliss, which is broken by the belief in any difference between the self and it.

Other efforts are made to realize the Ātman by a process of examination of the merits of the different claimants. Thus we have the account of the rivalry of the senses foreshadowed in the Brāhmaṇas carried out in detail. The breath is the victor over speech, the eye, the ear, and mind, because when all the others go from the body still it is left animated,[2] and from another point of view breath alone is able in the conflict of the gods, the senses, and the demons to overthrow the demons.[3] Another version [4] adds to the other powers the cosmical equivalents, and ranges speech, eye, ear and breath against one another, and fire, sun, moon, and wind against one another; in each case the result is the victory of breath and wind. In the Kauṣītaki Upaniṣad,[5] following the Aitareya Brāhmaṇa,[6] the cosmic divinities fire, sun, moon, lightning, and the psychic divinities, speech, eye, ear, mind, enter into the wind and the breath respectively. The same idea occurs in an earlier version of the Çatapatha Brāhmaṇa: [7] in sleep speech enters the breath, and so with eye, mind, ear, and correspondingly with fire, sun, moon, and the quarters in their relation to the wind. Hence we frequently find that the breath is set up as an idea of the Brahman,[8] but merely to be rejected as inadequate.

Still more clearly inadequate are the identifications of Brahman with mind,[9] which as in the Brāhmaṇas never achieves a decisive place of importance, and with more material concepts, such as the sun and as the ether. The sun is interesting, as it is clear that efforts were made—as in Egypt in the reform of Akhenaten—to penetrate beyond the mere physical sun to the man in the sun, with whom the dying man declares his identity.[10] The real

[1] ii. It has also the doctrine of the Brahman as *satyaṁ jñānam anantam* (or *ānandam*); see below. The first three cover *satyam*.

[2] CU. v. 1. 6–12; BAU. vi. 1. 7–13; AA. ii. 1. 4; Kauṣ. ii. 14; iii. 3; ÇA. ix; PU. ii. 2–4.

[3] BAU. i. 3; CU. i. 2; JUB. i. 60, &c.

[4] BAU. i. 5. 21–3.

[5] ii. 12, 13.

[6] viii. 28.

[7] x. 3. 3. 5–8. In JUB. iii. 2 breath swallows up speech, mind, sight, and hearing; Ka (Prajāpati) swallows fire, moon, sun, and the quarters.

[8] BAU. iv. 1. 3; v. 13; Kauṣ. ii. 1 and 2; CU. iv. 10. 5; TU. iii. 3. 1; JUB. i. 33. 2.

[9] CU. iii. 18; vii. 3; BAU. iv. 1. 6.

[10] BAU. v. 15; CU. iv. 11–13; i. 6, 7; TU. ii. 8; Īçā 15–18.

relation to the sun is, however, declared to be something above that,[1] and similarly against the conception of the absolute as there is set the view that the absolute is in the ether, and is the controller of the ether.[2]

Another set of conceptions is rather different : they are not so much real efforts to explain the absolute as merely to bring it into contact with the sacrifice : it was clearly the most natural thing in the world for the various schools, which were contemporary with the development of the Brahman, to apply to the chief concepts of their special branch of Vedic literature the idea of identification with the absolute. Thus the schools of the Rigveda fixed upon the Uktha,[3] the litany, especially that of the Mahāvrata ceremony as the absolute, the Sāmaveda schools chose the Sāman and in special the Udgītha,[4] and the schools of the Yajurveda the horse [5] offered at the sacrifice. Much more common is the view that by the mystic syllable, Om, originally no more perhaps than a formal word of assent, the Brahman is denoted.[6]

A more advanced conception is to be found in the Aitareya Āraṇyaka [7] which uses the old conception of breath, but identifies with it Prajñā, ' intellect '. On intellect the whole world is based, it is guided by intellect, and knowledge is the absolute. The same view is expressed in the Kauṣītaki Upaniṣad [8] where the identity of breath and intellect is asserted absolutely, but also later on is more precisely investigated : it shows that the objects of sense depend on the organs of sense, and the latter are dependent in turn on intellect, but it still adheres to the identification of the two. The Chāndogya itself identifies breath, ether, and bliss. The breath, therefore, still here and there appears with its claim to be the Ātman, but it is also now and then made dependent on it, or even the shadow of it.

But the nature of the Brahman is not intellect alone : it is also bliss and reality, and these ideas are here and there already united as in the later Upaniṣads, though the enumeration of the triad as the actual character of the Brahman is not actually found in the early Upaniṣads. In its place the Taittirīya [9] once presents the Brahman as being (*sat*), thought (*cit*), and eternity, where *ananta*, ' eternity ', stands probably in error for the Ānanda, ' bliss ', of the later triad. As being the Brahman, it is at once being and not-being : the old duplication of the Rigveda,[10] which asserts that at first there was neither being nor not-being is recognized here and there, but in the definite sense that, as not-being, the absolute is not empirical being, and that as being it is also not empirical being, so that the question is one of terminology

[1] CU. iv. 13.

[2] BAU. iii. 7. 12.

[3] AA. ii. 1–3.

[4] CU. ii. and passim in JUB.

[5] BAU. i. 1, 2.

[6] Keith, ERE. *s.v.*

[7] ii. 6=AU. iii. 1–3. Cf. *prājña ātman*, BAU. iv. 3. 21.

[8] iii. Oldenberg (*Die Lehre der Upanishaden*, pp. 350 f.) minimizes the value of these passages, but unjustly; cf. below, § 9, as to the influence of speculations as to deep sleep on the conception of the absolute.

[9] ii. 1. Deussen (*Sechzig Upanishad's*², p. 225) reads *ānandam*, followed by Jacobi, *Die Entwicklung der Gottesidee bei den Indern*, p. 16.

[10] x. 129.

alone and is decided in favour of the appellation being.[1] Much more important is the attribute of thought, which is asserted repeatedly in the doctrine of Yājñavalkya.[2] He there asserts that the hearer, the seer, the understander, the knower, are all unknown : they are the soul within, which again is in essence the divine, for all else than it is liable to suffering. In this subject of knowledge ether or space is interwoven : it is the meeting-place of all sounds, smells, sights, and other experiences. The different organs—and their functions—are only names for the one subject. In his conversation with Janaka,[3] the philosopher traces the Ātman as the knowing subject, which persists without change through the stages of waking, dreaming, deep sleep, death, transmigration, and final deliverance of the soul. The spirit in the waking state beholds the good and the evil of the world, but it is not moved by it, since as subject it is really incapable of affection : in the state of dreaming it builds up its own world, and in deep dreamless sleep, wrapped round by the intellectual self, it has no consciousness of objects, and yet is not unconscious. The self is compared to a lump of salt which has no inner or outer aspects : it is simply a single unit, and so consciousness has no inner and outer side, and is one unity alone. The Brahman is also the light of lights, and through it alone is there any light in the universe. For the wise man there is perpetual and abiding light, and this idea in the later Upaniṣads appears in a variety of metaphors such as the day of Brahman which is eternal.

The conception of the self as essentially consciousness is not, however, confined to Yājñavalkya : the same view is expressed, in words which may be dependent on the Bṛhadāraṇyaka, in the Chāndogya,[4] and the Aitareya[5] and the Kauṣītaki[6] texts as we have seen emphasize the same conception under the view that the self is intellect. In neither case, however, need we assume dependence on Yājñavalkya, for unlike the case of the Chāndogya the line of argument differs, and is, in the later case directly, and in the former indirectly, linked with the conception of the self as breath, which does not appear in the development of the ideas of Yājñavalkya.

The nature of the absolute as bliss is also asserted by Yājñavalkya,[7] who brings the conception into the closest relation with his idea of its nature. The bliss which he contemplates is that of the man in dreamless sleep, when the consciousness of individuality is lost, and when the self, therefore, is above

[1] BAU. i. 6. 3 ; ii. 1. 20.

[2] ii. 4. 11 ; iii. 4 ; 8. 11 ; *vijñānam ānandam brahma*, iii. 9. 28 ; *vijñānaghana*, ii. 4. 12 ; *prajñānaghana*, iv. 5. 13 ; *prājña ātman*, iv. 3. 21.

[3] iv. 3, 4 ; 5. 13.

[4] CU. iii. 11 ; viii. 3. 4 ; 12. 3, 4.

[5] iii.

[6] iii and iv.

[7] The unit of bliss is that of a happy man in this world ; that in the Fathers' world is ten times greater ; that of the Gandharvas 100 times; that of the gods by merit 1,000 times ; that of the gods by birth 10,000 times ; that in Prajāpati's world 100,000 times ; and that in the Brahmaloka 1,000,000 times, and this is attributed to the Brahman ; BAU. iv. 3. 33. For a later version, see TU. ii. For another series of worlds, BAU. iii. 6. 1 (atmosphere, Gandharvas, sun, moon, stars, Indra, Prajāpati, Brahman) ; KU. i. 3.

all pain and grief and enjoys pure bliss, whence it is a simple step to the equation of the absolute and bliss. Nor is there much doubt that here again the Chāndogya[1] depends on the Bṛhadāraṇyaka,[2] when it enunciates the doctrine of the absolute as ether, breath, and joy under the mystic name of Kha. The Kauṣītaki[3] also seems to borrow from the Bṛhadāraṇyaka, and the whole idea is further developed in the Taittirīya,[4] in the Ānandavallī. There special stress is laid on the error of seeking to find any division of subject and object in bliss: that would create division and would admit the idea of fear, which can arise only from division. The dependence on the Bṛhadāraṇyaka of this doctrine is borne out by the relation of the *ānandamaya* self to the *vijñānamaya*: in the former text they are the same idea, and, therefore, the conscious self is the highest, there being no difference of subject and object in it: the Taittirīya refines by making the *vijñānamaya* still have the distinction of subject and object, and then erecting the *ānandamaya* above it in rank. It is characteristic of the growth of these distinctions that, later on,[5] the *ānandamaya* itself became regarded as a mere sheath (*koça*) in which the self or the Brahman resided.

The other side of this exaltation of the bliss of the absolute is of course the view that all the world is misery,[6] but the pessimism of the Upaniṣads is moderate: we hear of the miseries of old age and death or disease, and trouble which the knowledge of the absolute removes, but the growth of the spirit of pessimism is only to be traced in Upaniṣads of the quite late class.

But, despite the giving to the absolute of these three attributes or characteristics, Yājñavalkya returns constantly to the fact that they are not to be taken in the empirical sense, and that, therefore, our knowledge of the absolute is non-existent. The most drastic expression for this view is the formula[7] *neti neti*, 'not so, not so', which denies to the absolute any and every attempt to define it in terms of ordinary knowledge. Its existence is a transcendental reality, which is essentially from the empirical point of view a nonentity: its consciousness involves the essential fusion of subject and object, and the transcendence of their diversity, although the phraseology of the Upaniṣads always treats the Ātman as subject,[8] and, therefore, is not ordinary consciousness at all, and the bliss arises from this state of non-distinction. Hence we have two different conceptions which are repeated times without number: on the one hand every empirical attribute is attributed to the absolute and also denied of it: in the second place the most contradictory

[1] iv. 10. 5.
[2] iv. 3. 19–33.
[3] iii. 8.
[4] ii; cf. iii.
[5] Maitr. vi. 27; Mahānār. lxiii. 16.
[6] BAU. iv. 2. 4; iii. 8. 8.
[7] BAU. iv. 2. 4; 4. 22; 5. 15; iii. 9. 26. Hillebrandt's theory (DLZ. 1897, p. 1929; ZDMG. lxix. 105 f.) that *na* is an affirmative particle here is clearly erroneous. Oltramare (*L'histoire des idées théosophiques*, i. 74) thinks it merely denies (*iti* signalling out *na*) every effort to define; so Jacobi, *Die Entwicklung der Gottesidee bei den Indern*, p. 15.
[8] Oldenberg, *Die Lehre der Upanishaden*, p. 101, n. 1, against Simmel, *Hauptprobleme der Philosophie*, p. 95.

observations are made regarding it. The ideas thus enunciated are clear : the absolute is not in space [1] which is expressed by the assertion that it is infinitely large and infinitely small, that space is interwoven in it, and that it is all pervading. The absolute is not in time : [2] hence it appears as above the three times, independent of the past and the future, at its feet time rolls on its course : on the one hand it is of infinite duration, but at the same time it is of the instantaneous character of the flash of the lightning, or the swift rush of thought. The absolute is also free from causal connexion : [3] it is said to be absolutely without diversity, and this point is variously developed : the Kaṭha [4] is emphatic that the absolute is independent of becoming and not becoming, of good and evil, of past and future, the knowing seer is not born, does not die, abides from everlasting. The Īçā [5] insists that it is unmoving, yet swifter than mind ; far, yet near ; within, yet without the universe ; above knowledge and ignorance ; that it differs essentially from coming into being and not coming into being. The final answer to the question of the nature of the Ātman is that recorded for us in a legend by Çañkara : Vāṣkali asked Bāhva as to the nature of the Brahman : the latter remained silent, and on being pressed for an answer replied, ' I teach you, indeed, but you understand not : silence is the Ātman.' [6]

§ 6. *The Absolute and the Universe*

The theory of Yājñavalkya asserts, as we have seen, that the absolute is unknowable and not definable by any empirical predicates. It, therefore, becomes obviously a pressing question to connect the empirical and the real universes : the gulf between the two is only accentuated by asserting, in so determined a manner, that there is a deep division between the one and the many. The relation of the universe as known to the one is, however, the problem which all philosophies find insoluble in greater or less degree, and the efforts of the Upaniṣads to bridge the difference are not at all satisfactory. The answer given in fact is merely that the absolute is the same as the world, or that the world is the product of the Brahman. The difficulty, however, arises, in considering these passages of the Upaniṣads, which present the doctrines of cosmogonism and pantheism in close and inextricable union, to know whether we have here efforts to explain the Brahman understood in the

[1] BAU. iii. 8. 7 ; CU. iii. 14. 3 ; KU. ii. 20 ; iv. 10, 11 ; ÇU. iii. 20 ; Mahānār. x. 1. How far the idea was clearly felt must be left undecided ; cf. Oldenberg, *Die Lehre der Upanishaden*, p. 73.

[2] BAU. iv. 4. 16, 17 ; KU. ii. 14 ; iii. 15 ; v. 6 ; ÇU. v. 13, &c.

[3] BAU. iii. 8 ; iv. 4. 20 ; CU. vi. 1. 3.

[4] ii. 14, 18.

[5] 4, 5, 9, 10, 12–14.

[6] Brahma Sūtra, iii. 2. 17. It is clear that such an absolute cannot be regarded either as conscious or unconscious ; Oldenberg, *Die Lehre der Upanishaden*, pp. 100–5. Hertel's view (*Die Weisheit der Upanischaden*, p. 32), that in Kena we have a polemic against the doctrine of the Brahman, is untenable. The polemic is rather against knowledge as the one way of salvation, but a reply to the Muṇḍaka specifically need not be assumed.

sense of Yājñavalkya, or merely the natural continuation of the doctrines of the Brāhmaṇas. It is on this point that it is necessary to part company with Deussen, who in his aim at system assumes that the doctrine of the absolute, as expounded in the Bṛhadāraṇyaka, underlies the whole thought of the Upaniṣads. We can only say that the deeper view of Yājñavalkya may, though not very probably, have been held now and then by those who express the more crude views of the identity of the absolute and the universe.

In the Aitareya Āraṇyaka, an early text, we find a simple and clear assertion of the presence of the self, Ātman, in living things, but in different degrees, without here, as yet, any implication of the absolute character of the self or its identity with the universe. He who knows more and more clearly the self attains fuller being; the self is revealed in an ascending order or revelation in plants and trees, animals, and man. In plants and trees sap only is found, in animals consciousness is present, but man excels since he is highly endowed with intelligence, saying what he has known, seeing what he has known, knowing to-morrow, the world and its opposite; by the mortal he desires the immortal, being thus endowed. As for the others, hunger and thirst comprise the power of knowledge of animals; they say not and see not what they have known. Man also is likened to the sea, for the insatiable nature of his desires; whatever he attains he desires to go beyond it; if he gains the sky, yet is he not content.[1]

The pantheistic view is undoubtedly present in the many passages in which the development of the world from the absolute is expressed in metaphors: thus in the metaphor of the spider from which the thread proceeds, or the fire whence come forth the sparks.[2] Often too the Ātman is declared to pervade the whole of the universe, it is likened to the lump of salt which in water disappears, indeed, but leaves all pervaded by it,[3] a view which must be older than the more refined conception, which, as we have seen, is applied to the Ātman when the object of comparison is a lump of salt, which has no inner or outer aspect, but is but one in itself. The Kaṭha Upaniṣad [4] compares the self to the light which penetrates everywhere, and adapts itself to every form. This view is found also in another form, in the laying down of the view of the self as the inward controller, as the greatest of powers, in which the heaven and the earth alike are contained. This view sets the self over against the world, and in doing so it adopts the old view that the seat of the self is the

[1] Aitareya Āraṇyaka, ii. 3. 2 f. Barua (*Prebuddh. Ind. Phil.*, pp. 51 ff.) has an elaborate account of Mahidāsa's views, but they are normally unphilosophical. His statements as to his cosmological doctrines (p. 69) are unwarranted by the text, and to style him the 'incipient Aristotle', 'who compares favourably in a great number of points with Aristotle', is inadmissible. The effort to make personalities out of the Upaniṣad teachers is vain, while to treat Aghamarṣaṇa as the first philosopher of India is absurd.

[2] Muṇḍ. i. 1. 7; ii. 1. 1.

[3] BAU. ii. 4. 12 as against iv. 15. 3.

[4] v. 9–11.

heart,[1] in which accordingly the lord of the universe resides, infinitely small, yet greater than the earth, the atmosphere, and the heaven. He is the protector of the universe, the guardian of mankind, the bond which holds the worlds together and prevents them coming into conflict. It is in this connexion that the terms [2] *tat tvam asi*, ' that thou art ', and *etad vai tat*,[3] ' that is this ', must be understood : they assert the essential identity of the self and the universe, but they do not necessarily or originally depend on the adoption of the view of Yājñavalkya, though they may later be regarded as a natural adaptation of it to meet the question of the relation of the universe and the final reality.

The impossibility of ascribing these views of the absolute and the world to attempts to solve the problem suggested by the transcendental view of the absolute is seen in the many cases where the realism is material and gross : thus the old doctrine of the creator, the primeval substance created by him, and his entry into it, which appears in the Aitareya Upaniṣad,[4] cannot be treated as a later development of a primitive identification of the universe and the absolute : it derives directly from the Brāhmaṇas, and shows the early, not the later, date of the Upaniṣad, as compared with the doctrine of Yājñavalkya. The same primitive ideas must be seen in the view that the Puruṣa dwells in the body as a span in height, as flame without smoke.

From this cosmogonism or pantheism it is not a difficult step to arrive at atheism : the attitude of the Brāhmaṇas, as we have seen, is not theistic, for they tend undoubtedly to depart from the primitive conception of Prajāpati as a creator god in favour of the idea of the more impersonal Brahman or the Ātman. But the tendency to abstraction was always, doubtless, confronted with the realism and clinging to personality of the average intellect, and that realism results in the growing tendency [5] to separate the individual and the supreme self, which is a perfectly natural development from the hasty unity of pantheisms. The Kaṭha Upaniṣad [6] undoubtedly shows this tendency in its distinction of the supreme and the individual self as light and shadow, and in the doctrine of the grace of the creator which gives man saving knowledge : the idea is, however, far more effectively brought out in the Çvetāçvatara,[7] where the identity of the supreme and the individual souls is not indeed denied, but can only be realized by the favour of the supreme lord, the Īçvara, who thus appears as in some measure distinct from the individual soul. The Īçvara is also a maker of magic, and the universe is the product, the illusion. The Upaniṣad shows no trace of the presupposition of the doctrine of Yājñavalkya : it is adequately explained as the mere development of primitive pantheism, or cosmogonism.

In this Upaniṣad it is of importance that the conception of theism is allied

[1] CU. iii. 14. 2 ; 13. 7 ; viii. 1. 3 ; BAU. iii. 7. 3. For a possible reference to the head see RV. ii. 16. 2 ; viii. 96. 3.
[2] CU. vi. 8. 16.
[3] BAU. v. 4 ; KU. iv. 3–vi. 1.
[4] i. 11, 12 ; cf. CU. vi. 3. 3 ; TU. ii. 6 ; Maitr. ii. 6.
[5] See also below, § 7.
[6] iii. 1 ; ii. 20.
[7] iv. 6, 7.

to the name of Rudra : the Vedic gods in the Upaniṣads exist as much as men,[1] but they are nothing more important than men, and need the knowledge of the Brahman as much as men; Indra and Prajāpati himself are, though the keepers of the door of heaven, unable to turn back the man who knows the Brahman. The Vedic gods are in themselves not enough to account for the prominence of the theistic aspect: it is essentially connected with Çiva or later with Viṣṇu, new great gods of the popular side of Brahmanism. The new relation is seen in the use of the term Īçvara, Īça, or synonyms, of the god, and in the use of these terms later of the supreme god in Indian philosophy: these are names obviously in harmony with the chief name of Rudra as the Īçāna, the lord, among the gods and the world in general.

The nature of the process by which the universe comes into being is considered under many different aspects, but they all rest on the old hypothesis of the mode of creation of the universe. They adopt just the same sort of language: there was according to one version first not-being, which was being: it arose : an egg was evolved : it lay for a year : it split open into two halves, one of silver which is the earth, and one of gold which is the heaven. The material of the world as it exists is in the most primitive view the waters, an idea already found in the Rigveda [2] and this conception is adhered to in the Aitareya Upaniṣad. A more developed, and probably later, view is that of the Chāndogya Upaniṣad,[3] which makes the Brahman resolve to create the world, and therefore to create [4] heat, whence arose, as sweat arises in man, the waters, and from the waters came food, after which the supreme self enters into the three as the individual self, the Jīvātman. Thereafter a further step is taken: the Jīvātman having entered, the three elements are mixed together so that existing things are composed of the three separate elements, an idea which is the source of the distinction of the subtle and the gross elements, which occurs as such first in the Praçna Upaniṣad,[5] where the earth, water, heat, wind, and ether elements are distinguished from the earth, water, heat, wind, and ether. A further and very important development of this theory is that of the Taittirīya Upaniṣad [6] which derives from the Ātman the ether, wind, fire, water, and earth. This five-fold division may be regarded as the established order in the philosophy of India, and the fact that the Aitareya [7]

[1] There are gods by meritorious action (*karman*) or by birth, BAU. iv. 3. 33; TU. ii. 9. The latter are the happier. Indra and Prajāpati have distinct heavens, BAU. iii. 6. 1.

[2] x. 121; TS. v. 6. 4; AV. iv. 2. 8; Oltramare (*L'histoire des idées théosophiques*, i. 7) compares *Genesis* i. 2; *Psalm* cvi. 4.

[3] vi. 2.

[4] A primitive materialism, seen here by Jacobi (*Festschrift Kuhn*, pp. 37 ff.) is quite improbable. See Oldenberg, GN. 1917, pp. 248 ff., and Jacobi's later view, *Die Entwicklung der Gottesidee bei den Indern*, pp. 11 ff.

[5] iv. 8.

[6] ii. 1. For the meaning of ether see below, § 10. If it is space, then a faint similarity to the *Timaios* may be recognized.

[7] AA. ii. 3. 1 (earth, wind, ether, water, light); AU. iii. 3 (these as *mahābhūtāni*); cf. ÇA. vii. 21, where small *mahābhūtāni*, of uncertain nature, appear. For its development in Buddhism, cf. Stcherbatsky, *The Central Conception of Buddhism*, pp. 12 f.

has not it in definite form shows that it is earlier than the Taittirīya. With the five elements correspond the five senses.

The absolute, after the production of the elements, must enter into the world, and many texts refer to this entry. Hence the world is penetrated throughout organic nature by the self of the absolute, which exists in the plant world, in insect life, in animal life, and in man, in things born of the egg, born alive, and sprout-born [1] or born from sweat, a category including insects.[2] The tree and the plant alike are regarded as animated by a spirit. The idea is seen frequently in the doctrine of transmigration where animals, insects, vegetables and gods appear as subject to transmigration. The Bṛhadāraṇyaka Upaniṣad [3] has, in a legend which may be compared with the famous observations of Plato in the *Symposion*,[4] a theory of the Ātman as neither male nor female which is cleft asunder and attains fresh unity in the creation of new life, human and animal alike.

It was inevitable that, in the view of the universe which regarded it as a creation, and distinguished between the soul of man and his body, there should arise the conception of the soul of the universe related to it as the soul in man to his body: this conception is made material in the person of Hiraṇyagarbha, who in the Rigveda [5] is the golden germ which enters into creation after the first action of the creator, or of Brahman as masculine. The position of either of these deities is first quite distinctly asserted in the Kauṣītaki Upaniṣad,[6] and the idea appears in prominence only in the theistic Çvetāçvatara Upaniṣad,[7] where a third name occurs, the red seer, Kapilarṣi, a term often,[8] but certainly wrongly, assumed to refer to the founder—who is a very legendary figure and may owe his name to this passage—of the Sāṁkhya system. But the idea is found in a less theoretic form in the Kaṭha Upaniṣad,[9] where in the development of principles the 'great self' stands after the undeveloped and the primeval spirit, and later in the Buddhi of the Sāṁkhya.

The absolute is not merely the creator of the universe: through it the universe after creation continues to live and move and have its being: in its bliss the universe tastes of bliss itself. Yājñavalkya expresses this thought in his conversation with Gārgī, in which [10] he points out that at the bidding of the imperishable one heaven and earth, the minutes, hours, days and nights, half-months, and months, the seasons, and the years are kept asunder, and the streams run from the mountains east and west, men praise the generous givers, the gods favour the sacrificer, and the Fathers desire the offerings to the dead. By another Upaniṣad [11] the comparison is made between the

[1] CU. vi. 3. 1.
[2] AU. iii. 3.
[3] i. 4. 3, 4. Cf. below, Appendix B.
[4] 189 C ff.
[5] x. 121. 1.
[6] i. 7. Possibly Brahman occurs also in BAU. iv. 4. 4, and in the term 'world of Brahman', but not in AA. ii. 6. 1.
[7] iii. 4; iv. 12.
[8] e.g. Garbe, *Sāṁkhya und Yoga*, p. 2; Hopkins, JAOS. xxii. 386, 387; Oldenberg, *Die Lehre der Upanishaden*, pp. 208 f.
[9] iii. 10, 11; vi. 7, 8.
[10] BAU. iii. 8. 9.
[11] KU. vi. 1.

absolute and the Açvattha tree, which sends its shoots downwards. He is the dike which holds apart the worlds to keep them asunder,[1] but the same metaphor, by another turn, is made to yield the idea that he is the bridge which secures continuity between the past and the future.[2] From another point of view [3] the absolute is the ruler, the Antaryāmin of the universe, who is the controlling power in the earth, water, fire, atmosphere, wind, sky, sun, the heavenly regions, moon and stars, ether, darkness, and light, of all living creatures, and of the eight organs, the whole complex forming his body, being distinct from him and not knowing him, but yet being ruled by him. In this way again we come to the idea of the world soul, but the difference between this and the view of the Çvetāçvatara Upaniṣad is that the internal ruler is still merely the absolute.

But an important conclusion follows inevitably from the view that the inner power in all is the absolute: he causes the man whom he will lead on high from these worlds to do good works, and he causes the man whom he will lead downwards to do evil works.[4] The gods are also determined by him: the grass cannot be burned by Agni, nor swept away by Vāyu, apart from the will of the Brahman. This idea is found repeatedly in the Upaniṣads, and is contrasted with the position of the spirit, which leaves the world after having known the soul and the true desires, and whose part then in all worlds is the life of freedom: he who departs without knowing the soul has in all worlds a life of constraint. The recognition of the freedom of the self is due to the recognition of the fact that the self is the real actor, and that, therefore, the constraint, to which it seems to be subject, is the constraint which it itself exercises on itself: as the Maitrāyaṇīya Upaniṣad [5] has it, 'He fetters himself by himself, as a bird by its nest.'

An interesting development of the doctrine occurs in the Jaiminīya Upaniṣad Brāhmaṇa;[6] the picture is drawn of a deity, described probably as 'the good deity', and therefore indicating Agni-Rudra, who bars the passage to the sun or beyond to the soul, on the score of the evil he has done, declaring that only the doer of good deeds may pass. The soul replies, 'Thou didst see whatever I used to do; thou wouldst not have made me do it (i.e. had it been evil); thou thyself art the doer.' The answer satisfies the deity, who, therefore, lets him pass. The dangerous implications of the doctrine are obvious and undeniable.

If the will is thus empirically completely subject to determination, it is inevitable that, with the growing tendency to view the relation of the soul to the absolute from the point of view of theism, there should arise the position

[1] BAU. iv. 4. 22.
[2] CU. viii. 4. 2.
[3] BAU. iii. 7. 3; cf. ii. 5.
[4] Kauṣ. iii. 8.
[5] iii. 2; cf. the Sāṁkhya and Stoic views; Dahlmann, *Die Sāṁkhya-Philosophie*, pp. 265-92.
[6] i. 5. We must doubtless read *akhalā* with Caland, *Over en uit het Jaiminīya-brāhmaṇa*, p. 47, n. 69. The god must be Agni, with whom Rudra is identified in JB. iii. 261.

that the absolute assumes the appearance of a personal providence. This is clearly the case in the Çvetāçvatara Upaniṣad,[1] where the Ātman is the overseer of actions, who apportions his qualities to each person, who executes justice, who restrains the evil, allots good fortune, and brings to maturity the actions of the soul. The Kaṭha Upaniṣad [2] faintly adumbrates the same idea in the view that the wise self-existent one has assigned ends for all time, an idea which an interpolator has made more precise by adding, to the destruction of the metre, the word *yāthātathyatas*, according to the quality of the works of the individual souls.

In detail we learn very little indeed of the creation of the earth and the world : the old Vedic ideas coexist, according to which there are three worlds, earth, air, and heaven, but the primeval waters are regarded in the Aitareya Upaniṣad [3] as lying above and below these regions. They are also said to be interwoven in the ether, by which space may be meant, as the latter is in the Brahman. From the practice of equating the regions with the worlds of the sacrifice, Bhūḥ, Bhuvaḥ, and Svar, a fourth region is added as Mahas, in the Taittirīya Upaniṣad [4] denoting the Brahman: the Muṇḍaka [5] adds three more, Janas, Tapas, and Satya are given as their names in the Mahānārāyaṇa : [6] still later, seven lower worlds are invented to correspond with them. A different conception is, however, found in the Bṛhadāraṇyaka Upaniṣad,[7] where on the basis of the old cosmic egg there is devised the view that the inhabited world is surrounded by the earth, and this again by the ocean, the world being 32 days' journey of the chariot of the sun in breadth, the earth 64, and the sea 128. Where the heaven and the earth as the two layers of the egg of the universe meet, there is the space of a razor edge or the wing of a fly, by which access is attained to the place of the offerers of the horse sacrifice, no doubt the back of heaven. A divergent view [8] is found shortly after, in which there are ten layers over the universe, the worlds of the wind, the atmosphere, the Gandharvas, the sun, moon, stars, the gods, Indra, Prajāpati, and Brahman. The only importance of these questions attaches to the case of the sun and the moon, which become associated with the doctrine of transmigration : the sun, indeed, is actually apparently deemed nearer [9] the earth than the moon.

[1] vi. 11, 12, 4 ; v. 5, &c.

[2] v. 13 ; Içā 8.

[3] i. 1. 2. The waters are not, of course, the region of fiery ether, suggested by Barua, *Prebuddh. Ind. Phil.*, p. 69.

[4] TU. i. 5.

[5] i. 2. 3.

[6] TA. x. 27, 28 ; Kirfel, *Kosmographie*, p. 24.

[7] iii. 3. There is no trace in the Upaniṣads of the view of heaven as a stone building, in which the sun, moon, and stars are doors, as held by Hertel (*Die Himmelstore im Veda und im Avesta*) ; see below, Appendix C.

[8] BAU. iii. 6 ; cf. Kauṣ. i. 3 (fire, wind, Varuṇa, Indra, Prajāpati, and Brahman) ; cf. BAU. iv. 3. 33 ; TU. ii. 8.

[9] CU. iv. 15. 5 ; v. 10. 2. The planets are unknown before Maitr. vi. 16, and a Kāṭhaka fragment of late character has in Graheṣṭi Mantras the older sun, Venus, Jupiter, Mercury, Mars, Saturn, the moon, Rāhu, Ketu (Caland, *Brāhmaṇa en Sūtra-Aanwinsten*, pp. 8, 29), which differs from the order later usual under Greek influence.

In the later systems of India it is an essential principle that, in accordance with the doctrine of transmigration, there can never be an origin of the world in time, and, since, on the other hand, the origination of the world was an accepted doctrine, the difficulty was overcome by the theory of the periodic destruction and regeneration of the world. This doctrine, which has been wrongly seen in the Atharvaveda, is certainly not to be found in any older Upaniṣad, and must be regarded as a definite sign of late date. It is found in the Çvetāçvatara Upaniṣad [1] when the god, who puts forth many times one net after another in space, is compared to a spider. It is also made clear that it is the actions of the soul which result in the activity of the creator in apportioning to each person all their attributes. The later Upaniṣads [2] recognize frankly the destruction of the universe by periodic fire. The only idea in the older texts [3] which affords the slightest analogy is the mere mention of the fact that into the Brahman the individual must fall on death, an idea which has no logical connexion with the developed theory. The latter may have arisen as a mere desire to apply to all the worlds what applied to the individual: more probably perhaps it is due to the needs of the doctrine of transmigration.

§ 7. *Māyā and Prakṛti—Illusion and Nature*

(*a*) Illusion

In the doctrine of Yājñavalkya we have seen the tendency of the Upaniṣads to assert over again, and in still more emphatic terms, the unity of the world, which the poets of the Rigveda already foreshadowed, and to deduce from it the conclusion that the world is nothing that is real in the full sense of the word, since everything in it is not ultimately to be regarded as having a truth of its own. In what sense, then, can the empiric world be said to exist? This Yājñavalkya leaves vague, but in his exposition to Maitreyī of the doctrine that after death there is no consciousness he uses terms to which later at least great weight was attached. A duality is necessary, he argued, for one to see another, smell another, hear another, and so forth, and in death no such duality is present; the phrase,[4] however, which he uses in this contention is 'where there is a duality as it were (*iva*)', and it may be deduced, not unfairly, from the addition of the qualification that he was not prepared to admit as absolutely certain the existence of the duality. Later in the Upaniṣad [5] we have similar wording, 'when there seems to be another', the same

[1] vi. 3, 4; v. 3; iv. 11 (adapting VS. xxxii. 8). Cf. Maitr. vi. 17; Atharvaçiras 6.

[2] Atharvaçikhā 1; Nṛsiṅhap. ii. 1.

[3] CU. i. 9. 1; TU. iii. 1; Muṇḍ. i. 1. 7; ii. 1. 1; Māṇḍ. 6; Cūlikā 17 f. The theory that AV. x. 8. 39, 40 refers to this is a mere speculation of no plausibility of Jacobi (GGA. 1895, p. 210), unfortunately adopted by Garbe, *Sāṁkhya und Yoga*, p. 16. The scheme, in fact, is a necessary accommodation to the fact of transmigration of the recognized doctrine of a beginning of the world; cf. Speyer, *Indische Theosophie*, pp. 132 ff.

[4] ii. 4. 14.

[5] iv. 3. 31. Oldenberg (*Die Lehre der Upanishaden*, p. 344) unduly minimizes the essence of *iva*.

particle being used. Here again we cannot simply ignore the qualification; to do so is as one-sided as to ascribe to it the value of a definite assertion of the unreality or illusory character of the universe. What we have is the germ of the illusion theory.

A further passage which has been adduced in this connexion is the declaration of the Chāndogya Upaniṣad [1] regarding the modifications of the three fundamental constituents of being, fire, water, food; just as all that is made of clay, copper, or iron, is only a modification, a verbal expression (*vācāram-bhaṇa*), a mere name, the reality being clay, copper, or iron, so all things can be reduced to the three primary forms of reality. Further, all reality, it is clearly indicated, is reducible to reality only, all things being mere modifications, &c. In Deussen's view [2] we have here the first open assertion of the unreality of the universe, a doctrine which shortly afterwards was to be realized by Parmenides in the famous declaration:

τῷ πάντ' ὄνομ' ἔσται
ὅσσα βροτοὶ κατέθεντο πεποιθότες εἶναι ἀληθῆ
γίγνεσθαί τε καὶ ὄλλυσθαι,

and later by Spinoza in his doctrine of modes of the one substance, God. The alternative view [3] is to regard the whole as frankly realistic; the name is not a mere name in the sense of disguising a reality; on the contrary it serves to mark out a reality, just as the phrase *nāma-rūpa* can be used to designate a concrete individual made up of intellectual and other faculties and matter. In this case we have a doctrine frankly pantheistic, but not of illusion. The difficulty of deciding is increased by the uncertainty of the correct rendering of the text, which Deussen interprets as directly asserting that 'change is a mere matter of words, a simple name', treating the words *vācārambhaṇaṁ vikāro nāmadheyam* as a distinct sentence, instead—as is possible—of taking it as a predicate description, 'a matter of words, a change, a simple name', and it would be unwise to draw any far-reaching conclusion from the passage.

We find also in the Bṛhadāraṇyaka Upaniṣad [4] in a verse which occurs with slight variation in the Kaṭha,[5] a distinct assertion that there is no diversity and that a failure to realize this fact is the source of repeated death. The Īçā emphatically demands that the universe be merged in God, and, moreover, denies becoming and passing away, thus condemning the doctrine of the reality of change; this at least is Deussen's interpretation,[6] though it is open to argue that the real sense is merely that the absolute stands above becoming and passing away, which it transcends. In the late Maitrāyaṇīya Upaniṣad [7] we find the comparison of the absolute with the spark which, made

[1] vi. 1. 3 ff.

[2] *Sechzig Upanishad's*², p. 156.

[3] S. Schayer, *Mahāyānistische Erlösungslehre*, p. 14. The sense of *vācārambhaṇa* (of dubious formation) is uncertain; cf. Oldenberg, p. 343.

[4] iv. 4. 19.

[5] iv. 10 f.

[6] 1, 12–14; *Sechzig Upanishad's*², p. 527; cf. Māṇḍūkya Kārikā, iii. 25.

[7] vi. 24; Kārikā, iv. 47–52.

to revolve, creates apparently a fiery circle, an idea which is taken up and expanded by Gauḍapāda in the Māṇḍūkya Kārikā, and which undoubtedly is consistent with the conception of the illusory nature of empirical reality. In other cases adduced by Deussen [1] there is no need to suspect any idea of the world as unreal, the frequent assertion,[2] that with the knowledge of the self all is known, does not exclude the reality of what is derived from the self; the reality of the absolute may be contrasted [3] with empirical reality, which is styled real by man, without making the latter an illusion; when the Aitareya [4] asserts that the universe is founded in consciousness and guided by it, it assumes its reality, not its merely apparent existence, and, if the elements of being rest on the consciousness and it on the Prāṇa,[5] we need not suspect any lack of reality in them.

Far more importance attaches to a late Upaniṣad.[6] The precise character of the nature of the external world is summed up finally in the doctrine of the Çvetāçvatara Upaniṣad,[7] which sees in the world other than the absolute—which it conceives in a theistic way—an illusion, Māyā, a term thus first introduced into the philosophy of the Upaniṣads, to become, through the adoption of this theory of the universe by Gauḍapāda and Çañkara, the basis of the orthodox Vedānta system. It would, however, it is clear, be a mistake to regard the new term as being a mere individual innovation of the Çvetāçvatara school without previous preparation in the literary tradition. The idea of the concealment of the divine nature by illusion is seen in the Atharvaveda,[8] where it is said that the flower of the water, who is Hiraṇyagarbha, the personal Brahman, in whom are fixed gods and men as spokes in a nave, is concealed by illusion, and the illusions of Indra in his many shapes are mentioned in the Rigveda.[9] It may, therefore, be assumed that the term had obtained considerable favour in philosophic circles,[10] before it appears in the Upaniṣad as a definite doctrine of importance. Still more important is the fact that the term was by no means ill adapted to express the nature of the relation of the empirical world to the real absolute, as it was conceived by Yājñavalkya. It is, of course, impossible to say that the actual term and its precise connotation would have approved themselves to that sage, or to those who evolved the doctrines which passed current under his name: on the other hand, the doctrine is a legitimate and natural development from the principles which he enunciated. They are clearly not to be derived in any reasonable way from a system, which was pantheistic or cosmogonic, and in which, therefore, the assumption that the world was illusory would have been ridiculous. A pantheism and still more a cosmogonism are under the danger of falling to the level of materialism, but not of evoking an illusionism.

[1] *Phil. of Up.*, pp. 234 ff.

[2] BAU. ii. 4. 5, 7–9; CU. vi. 1. 2; Muṇḍ. i. 1. 3.

[3] TU. ii. 6. [4] iii. 3. [5] Kauṣ. iii. 8.

[6] Oldenberg (*Die Philosophie der Upanishaden*, p. 280) denies the force of this passage, but his doubt seems hypercritical.

[7] iv. 10. [8] x. 8. 34.

[9] vi. 47. 18; BAU. ii. 5. 19; ÇB. xi. 1. 6. 10.

[10] *Contra*, Hopkins, JAOS. xxii. 385, 386. Cf. Speyer, *Indische Theosophie*, pp. 123.

A very different suggestion as to the development of ideas is put forward by Schayer.[1] On this theory the Māyā doctrine comes in as the expression of a conception wholly alien to the normal Brahmanical idea of the regular working of the world, in which nature and the ritual stand in constant parallelism. The Brahman signifies the regular and orderly procedure of the universe ; Māyā, on the other hand, introduces the conception of the unregulated, self-determined, intervention of a god ; Indra's Māyā in the Rigveda [2] is the expression of his might, revealed in his great deeds. When, naturally, opposition came into being directed against the Brahmanical conception of the Übermensch whose knowledge makes him ruler of the universe, we find the idea of the necessity of divine intervention as in the Kaṭha Upaniṣad,[3] and the condemnation by the Īçā [4] of knowledge as even more unsatisfactory than ignorance, and finally in the Çvetāçvatara [5] the natural step is taken of ascribing to god the epithet *māyāvin*. The suggestion is ingenious but unconvincing. The Çvetāçvatara certainly does not mean that god is a real creator and that matter is his real creation ; the sense of delusion or illusion [6] is paramount.

(*b*) Nature

While, however, one side of the teaching of the Upaniṣads develops in this brilliant manner, and in the hands of Gauḍapāda and Çañkara emerges as the *chef d'œuvre* of the Indian philosophical intellect, another and important scheme of philosophy was growing up, and was destined to exhibit itself, at a period not far distant from the close of the great Upaniṣads, in a living and effective form. The existence of this system as the definite Sāṁkhya of the classical period is not attested until comparatively late: the oldest text-book, the Sāṁkhya Kārikā, may be assigned to about the fourth century A. D.,[7] and for the earlier form of the system we are reduced to conjectures built on that text, the history of the parallel system of Yoga, and the indications of the epic, which knows well the Sāṁkhya and Yoga systems, but which in regard to its date is so uncertain, that it does not necessarily afford us any information older than that contained in, and to be inferred from, the

[1] *Mahāyānistische Erlösungslehre*, pp. 22 ff.

[2] x. 54. 2 ; vi. 47. 18. In iv. 16. 9 Schayer treats *ábrahmā* as 'dem *brahman* feindliche Dasyu', which is impossible.

[3] ii. 23.

[4] 9.

[5] iv. 10.

[6] Schayer's effort (cf. also pp. 42 f.) to establish the doctrine that Māyā is a free creation, not an illusion, is as ingenious as it is unconvincing. There is no evidence that the idea of illusion was unknown to India in connexion with a juggler's work (contrast the stories given *ibid.* pp. 53), and the synonyms of Māyā include such as Gandharvanagara. The idea of Māyā is akin to the product of the juggler in the Ratnāvalī who conjures up the appearance of a fire, into which the king rushes, whereas none exists. Cf. Asañga's account in the Sūtrālaṁkāra, as given by Schayer himself (ZII. ii. 103–5), which is perfectly clear as to the unreality of Māyā.

[7] A later date is usually given (cf. Garbe, *Sāṁkhya und Yoga*, p. 7), but the earlier date is now the most probable ; see Winternitz, *Gesch. d. ind. Lit.* ii. 256 ; iii. 452 f.

Sāṁkhya Kārikā itself. Very briefly put,[1] the classical Sāṁkhya system discards entirely the idea of an absolute : it reduces the universe to a multitude of individual subjects, which have nothing true about them save their subjectivity, a subjectivity which has no creative power and is not properly realized at all by having an objective content. On the contrary, it is only by error in any way connected with the existing world, through its fancied connexion with Prakṛti, 'nature'. Through the development of Prakṛti there arises the principle called the great one or intellect, Mahān or Buddhi : the Prakṛti is, therefore, to be regarded as purely unconscious, a conception vaguely analogous to the Aristotelian Hyle, and connected, directly as it would seem, with the older views of the Rigveda and the Brāhmaṇas as to the primitive condition of the universe as a chaos. The development of consciousness must therefore, it would appear, be cosmic, and the Mahān or Buddhi would thus correspond to the Hiraṇyagarbha of the later Upaniṣads and the Vedānta, the spirit which, in the earlier view, appeared on the waters after the creation of the waters by Prajāpati or the Brahman. But at the same time the Buddhi is the first element of the subtle body, the Liñga, which is the essence of the individual spirit, and which passes through transmigration. The Buddhi serves as the basis for the development of the principle of individualism, Ahaṁkāra, from which are derived on the one hand the mind and the ten organs—or rather potentialities or faculties—of sense, five of perception, and five of action, and on the other hand the subtle elements, from which in their turn come the gross elements, though an epic variant gives in lieu the elements and the objects of sense, sound, &c.[2] The Liñga, which is perhaps most appropriately called the 'psychic apparatus', contains in itself all the elements down to the subtle elements, and even of the gross elements it has the fine parts,[3] and it is through it that the individual subject experiences —or rather seems to experience—the facts of this world. The experience is painful and unhappy, even though alleviated by the joys of earth, and the real aim of life is to be rid of the connexion with nature. But that connexion does not really exist : it is only thought to exist by an error and, when this error of ignorance is removed, then the connexion is seen not to exist and ceases to exist, the subject being freed from any connexion with an object, and on the other hand, the Prakṛti is freed from any pain or trouble, since being absolutely unconscious in the absence of subject there is no possibility of its suffering or enjoying anything. Strictly speaking, therefore, the spirit is never troubled

[1] In the main I agree with Deussen (*Gesch. der Phil.* I. iii) when he departs from the views of Garbe (*Sâṃkhya-Philosophie* and *Sāṁkhya und Yoga*). The account of Deussen in the *Phil. of Up.* is slightly inaccurate. Cf. my *Sāṁkhya System* (1918, 2nd ed. 1924). Berndl's reconstruction (*Über das Sāṃkhya*) is clearly unhistorical ; see below.

[2] Cf. O. Strauss, VOJ. xxvii. 257 ff.

[3] Deussen, *Gesch. der Phil.* I. iii. 497. This is the only possible or at least natural sense of Sāṁkhya Kārikā 38–41, though this fact is often ignored, and normally the fine parts are treated as if the subtle elements included them. Maitr. vi. 10 may be thus explained instead of being amended. For an attempt to regard *sūkṣma* as *tanmātra*, see Strauss, p. 262.

or suffers anything or enjoys anything: it merely illumines nature, which accordingly suffers, but is set free by the cessation of illumination. But the difference of the result in the two cases is enormous: the subject by ceasing to have an object is emancipated for all time, the Prakṛti in that one case is delivered, but that is a matter of indifference since the infinite number of other souls means that Prakṛti is ever being unrolled for the gaze of the subject and ever is suffering.

The whole theory is one mass of difficult paradoxes, despite its seeming elegance and simplicity of structure. The main basis of the conception, that there is suffering through the connexion of the soul with nature, is contradicted by the fact that there is really no connexion: the suffering is produced by a connexion which does not exist, and is only imagined to exist, but an imagined connexion is no ground for results which a real connexion alone could produce. The relation of the one Prakṛti with the psychical apparatuses which are not conscious except under the illumination of the subject is never clearly explained, or perhaps understood.[1] At best we may endeavour to conceive the position that the connexion—which, however, as we have seen, is not really existent—of the spirit with Prakṛti, as a single undifferentiated unit, produces a primal consciousness (Buddhi), which develops under the influence of the individuation (Ahaṁkāra) of the spirit an individual form or psychic apparatus, on which is based the life of the individual. In that case the conception of a cosmic development of individuation and the other things would be in the main a mistaken complement of the system which is not essential to it. But there is the grave objection to this theory that already in the Sāṁkhya Kārikā the paternal and maternal portions of the gross elements are supposed by the author to fall back into and be picked up out of Prakṛti by the psychic apparatus in the case of death and rebirth, and not as would be logical and proper, if the development of Prakṛti were individual from the point of Buddhi onwards, recalled into and evolved from the subtle elements, while the Prabhūtas, which represent the material world, are made to stand over against the selves as an independent real world.

It is, however, unnecessary to consider further the contradictions of the Sāṁkhya, and it is only requisite to note that in the nature of Prakṛti there is supposed to be contained a triad of constituent factors, Guṇas, literally 'threads' rather than 'determinant qualities', which in the passive condition of Prakṛti are in a quiescent state of equilibrium, but which in the process of evolution develop differently in the several psychic apparatuses, producing, therefore, the very varied characters of men and of life. These factors are Sattva, the light, the intellectual principle, Rajas, the active and emotional principle, and Tamas, the dark and gloomy principle. The terms are wholly indefinite and unphilosophical, and the use made of them in practice is mainly

[1] Cf. Oltramare, *L'histoire des idées théosophiques*, i. 261 ff. Jacobi's account (*Die Entwicklung der Gottesidee bei den Indern*, pp. 30 f.) leaves the obscurity unaffected.

psychical, whereas, as constituents of Prakṛti, they ought to have received some different cosmic sense, such as that of conditional being, energy, and inertia, suggested by Hopkins.[1] Their importance in the system, however, cannot be underestimated, and it is significant that, while Çañkara rejects definitely the validity of these principles, they are accepted by the later school of Vedānta and interwoven with the Vedānta philosophy.[2]

(c) The Origin of the Sāṁkhya and Buddhism

The question inevitably arises in what manner these views are to be connected with those of the Upaniṣads,[3] and the further problem must be mentioned of the origin of Buddhism, which has been traced to the Sāṁkhya. The Buddhist system differs in one essential from the Sāṁkhya : it abolishes, as does that system, the principle of an absolute, with which the individual souls are identified, and it goes further than that system in seeking to deny the existence of soul. The latter aberration need not, however, be taken very seriously : the Buddhists, being determined believers in transmigration, had to produce an entity [4] which would transmigrate ; the entity provided does not differ, in any very essential way, from the ordinary view in India of a transmigrating soul, and certainly is philosophically inferior to the ordinary conception, unsatisfactory as that in itself is.

No Upaniṣad attains the point of view of the Sāṁkhya system, and it is therefore only possible to indicate the mode in which the conception of the absolute tended to fade away and to leave the individual spirits confronted with nature. The essential feature of the Sāṁkhya is the evolutionary series, and the name Sāṁkhya, ' examination ', ' calculation ', or ' description by enumeration of constituents ',[5] rather than a mere counting, suggests that the philosophy owed its importance to its insistence on the principle of careful examination of the elements of the process of development from the absolute. Now in the Upaniṣads the first case in which the order of evolution from the absolute is stated with precision—even then incomplete—is in the Kaṭha Upaniṣad,[6] where we find that in the carrying out of meditation, Yoga, in order to reach the absolute, the objects are merged in the senses, the senses in the mind, the mind in the intellect, Buddhi, the intellect in the great self,

[1] *Great Epic of India*, p. 113, n. 1. See also Garbe, *Sâṁkhya-Philosophie*², pp. 274 ff.

[2] E.g. in the Vedāntasāra, as pointed out by Col. Jacobs in his edition, and by Deussen in his translation (*Gesch. der Phil.* I. iii) ; Keith, *Sāṁkhya System*, chap. viii.

[3] Cf. Oldenberg, *Die Lehre der Upanishaden*, pp. 202 ff. ; GN. 1917, pp. 218 ff. ; Keith, *Buddhist Philosophy*, chap. vii.

[4] Walleser, *Die philosophische Grundlage des älteren Buddhismus*, pp. 77 ff. ; Keith, *Buddhist Philosophy*, chap. ix.

[5] Accepted by Oldenberg, *Die Lehre der Upanishaden*, p. 351, n. 129.

[6] iii. 10–13 ; vi. 7–11. The alternative view that the Sāṁkhya is of independent origin, based on an independent analysis of consciousness, and that the Kaṭha represents a compromise may be mentioned (cf. Oltramare, *L'histoire des idées théosophiques*, i. 221 ff., for a critique of Garbe's view on this point). But it is not possible to ignore the obvious fact that the Puruṣa of the Sāṁkhya is merely the Ātman made many.

which is also then merged in the undiscriminated, Avyakta, described as the calm self, and that again in the spirit, Puruṣa, which is the absolute. The similitude of these views to the series of development of the Sāṁkhya is obvious : the separation of the Mahān Ātmā, the great self, and Buddhi is a distinction which it is difficult to appreciate in the Kaṭha and would naturally disappear on further reflection, with the abandonment of a cosmic Ātman, while the interposition of the undiscriminated, which corresponds to the position of the old primitive material or waters of the Brāhmaṇas, between the spirit and the intellect, corresponds also precisely to the position of Prakṛti in the Sāṁkhya system, except for the fact that the Kaṭha is still monistic, and still regards the spirit as an absolute, whence nature is derived, the individual spirit being identified more or less clearly with the highest spirit. But it must have been an obvious, if no less a very important, step when it was decided by some thinker that there was no necessity to imagine the unity of all the spirits in one. *Ex hypothesi* the spirits were all identical with the one spirit, and, therefore, each must have the same creative power to produce the undiscriminated as the supreme spirit. To what end then to feign a supreme spirit ? Moreover, from another point of view the postulating of a supreme spirit would appear unsound : the enormous variety of individual experience of life, the plain facts of every-day existence, show that there is not one spirit merely but many.[1] The theory of unity of all spirits is difficult and confusing, and the obvious refuge from these difficulties is to admit that each spirit is a separate entity. The relation of the spirits and Prakṛti would follow at once, when this was accepted : the doctrine of Yājñavalkya was clear that the self was merely the knowing subject : clearly, therefore, as the self was the subject only, Prakṛti cannot be produced from the spirit in any material sense : it is the independent object merely of spirit.[2]

It is important to note the real similarity between the self in the view of the Yājñavalkya of the Bṛhadāraṇyaka Upaniṣad and that of the Sāṁkhya ; both are absolutely without quality or activity, completely inactive, the capacity of knowing without content ; both, we may fairly say, represent bare abstractions which could never as such be real. If the self of Yājñavalkya is wholly apart from empirical existence and knowledge, the same thing really applies to the spirit of the Sāṁkhya, for it is not really in contact with matter. In the Buddhism of the Sarvāstivādins [3] we find the same view of Vijñāna, which remains wholly apart from real connexion with the object, being, like it, merely a momentary flashing wholly transitory and uncaused. Naturally in all three cases some effort must be made to explain the connexion of this

[1] Cf. Sāṁkhya Kārikā 18.

[2] The Ātman in KU. iii. 3 f. is the lord of the chariot, who is essentially a mere spectator, for intellect is the driver, mind the reins, and the senses the horses. The absence of the Ahaṁkāra in KU. can hardly be accidental as Oldenberg (*op. cit.*, p. 231) suggests. For its frequent omission in the epic, see Hopkins, *Great Epic of India*, p. 133.

[3] Cf. Stcherbatsky, *The Central Conception of Buddhism*, pp. 63 f. ; Garbe, *Sâṁkhya-Philosophie*[2], pp. 358 ff.

subjectivity and the object which makes its potentiality concrete knowledge, and equally naturally at this point in all three systems we have a lacuna, which is filled up by unintelligible assertions, the Buddhists resorting to a relation of Sārūpya, ‘ co-ordination ’ or ‘ co-relation ’, which is found also in the Yogabhāṣya [1] of Vyāsa as the mode of bridging over the gulf between knower and knowledge.

If we seek to find in the older Upaniṣads a more direct connexion with the doctrines of the Sāṁkhya than the conception of the self in Yājñavalkya, then the most obvious parallel, in addition to the scheme of evolution in the Kaṭha, is the passage in the Kauṣītaki Upaniṣad [2] in which a list of ten senses is opposed to a corresponding number of objects, and the presence of intellect, Prajñā, is said to be essential for every kind of sense-knowledge, including the activity of mind in respect of thought and desire. We have here the prototype of the curious feature in the Sāṁkhya of the senses and mind as alike only potential until reflected in some manner in Puruṣa. The more common idea of the senses being powerless without mind lies doubtless at the back of this more advanced conception, a fact which illustrates the remarkable dependence of the Sāṁkhya on older ideas.

A certain degree of parallelism to the Kaṭha evolution series is present in doctrine of the mode in which on death according to the Chāndogya Upaniṣad speech (the eye, the ear, and the other organs are presumably here typified by speech) enters the mind, the mind the breath, the breath the brilliance of fire (the other two elements of the Chāndogya, water and earth, may be included), and that the supreme deity. In deep sleep, again, we have a series in the Praçna Upaniṣad [3] where we may understand that the five gross, the five subtle, elements, the organs of sense, all enter the mind, it the intellect, it individuation,[4] it thought, it brilliance, it breath, and it the self, but this latter passage is too vague to be of much importance save as showing how prevalent were these efforts to find the order of evolution.

In the Muṇḍaka Upaniṣad [5] we find an expression of the order of development commencing from the absolute, as all-knowing, the second element being food, an expression perhaps for the undiscriminated, the coming breath, which may correspond with Hiraṇyagarbha, mind, truth, the worlds, and actions. The more precise similarity of the doctrine of the Muṇḍaka [6] to that of the Kaṭha is maintained by Hertel,[7] who has endeavoured to reconstruct an original text of this Upaniṣad by conjecture from that which, as he holds, based on a single manuscript which was far from correct, has been preserved

[1] i. 4 ; ii. 23.

[2] iii. 5 ff. See below, § 8.

[3] iv. 7.

[4] According to Oldenberg (*Die Lehre der Upanishaden*, p. 226, n. 1) it means ‘ “ das Ichmachen,” d. h. das Ichsagen und Betätigen der Ichheit,’ rather than ‘ der Ichmacher ’. The genesis of this entity may be connected with the speculations of the Upaniṣads on deep sleep, in which individuality disappears; Heimann, *Die Tiefschlafspekulation der alten Upaniṣaden* (1922), pp. 13 f.

[5] i. 1. 8, 9 ; ii. 1. 2, 3.

[6] vi. 10.

[7] *Muṇḍaka-Upaniṣad* (1924).

to us by Çaṅkara. Reconstructions of this kind seldom permit of any satisfactory result to others than their author, and there is always the fundamental difficulty, apart from minor points, whether the incoherence of thought which gives rise to the reconstruction is not, as most probably in the case of the Bhagavadgītā, due to the author, and not the result of interpolation. If, however, we omit the whole of ii. 2, and iii. 1. 4–10 and 2. 3 and 9, we obtain the doctrine that, as in the Skambha hymn of the Atharvaveda,[1] which affords part of the material of the Upaniṣad, the highest thing in the world is regarded as personal, from which there emanates the Brahman and whatever else exists. On this view the ultimate fate of the soul on its return is not absorption in the Brahman but union with Puruṣa, the world of Brahman serving merely as the place of those who fully perform the sacrificial ritual in the mode approved by the Muṇḍaka. The other portions, however, of the text, which cannot with any assurance be ascribed to working over, definitely identify the highest principle with the Brahman, adopting the regular identification of the Brahman and the Ātman, and treating the final result to be aimed at as the recognition of the identity of the Brahman and the Ātman. Moreover, even in the verses which are spared by Hertel, we find hints contradicting his theory of a simple doctrine; thus in i. 1. 7 all is stated to arise from the imperishable (*akṣara*), while in ii. 1. 2 we find the personal highest being declared to be above the imperishable, and in ii. 1. 10 the Brahman and Puruṣa are directly identified, unless we hold with Hertel that there is a lacuna in the text for which we have no other ground. It is significant also that the interpolator has to be credited with iii. 2. 3, which adopts the Kaṭha[2] doctrine of salvation by the favour of the lord, so that we have to assume that, on the one hand, he altered the personal aspect of the Upaniṣad by insisting on the primacy of the impersonal Brahman, while, on the other, he deliberately added one of the most personal touches in the shape of the doctrine of grace. This is plainly incredible, and we may safely assume that, while the author worked on an older idea of a personal *prius* as in the Atharvaveda, and accepted the doctrine of grace from the Kaṭha, he himself adopted the Brahman standpoint.[3]

The resemblance of the Maitrāyaṇīya Upaniṣad[4] to the Sāṁkhya is of a

[1] x. 7.

[2] ii. 23.

[3] To certain of Hertel's metrical views the strongest exception must be taken. To carry out his rule that the first syllable of a dissyllabic, and the second of a trisyllabic, middle part of the Triṣṭubh is short he has to argue for *oṣădhyaḥ*, *purăstād*, *paramaṁ* (*sāmyam*) as two shorts, *sŭriasya*, *kavayŏ yānti*, and *agrăhyam*; he turns *-āni* and *-eṣu* into single final syllables, and postulates a great number of quite impossible elisions of short vowels. These, added to text alterations, enable him to reform the metre, but they do not justify his severe censure of Deussen for his perfectly just strictures on the metre of the text as we have it. Every metrical irregularity could thus be removed from any text, and Hertel's procedure is specially inconsistent, since he objects to alteration of Prākritic irregularities in grammar, which might equally well be changed, if the Upaniṣad is to be rewritten. But metre may be excused in a philosopher.

[4] Cf. E. A. Welden, AJP. xxxv. 32 ff.

different character from that of the Kaṭha ; it is due in all likelihood to direct Sāṁkhya influence at a much later date. In this Upaniṣad we find an answer attempted to the question why and how the absolute self enters the world and appears in individual form. Prajāpati, existing alone, had no joy ; therefore he created offspring as inanimate, and to enjoy them he enters with the breaths into them, thus animating them, and then by means of the organs of sense and action and the mind he has joy of them. But the absolute self, Prajāpati, remains wholly unaffected, though an apparent actor ; action actually belongs to the Bhūtātman, or elemental soul, which overcome by the fruits of action passes to a good or evil birth, and is merged in existence, while the true self remains unaffected like the drop of water on a lotus leaf. The elemental soul is overcome by the qualities or factors of nature, Prakṛti, and thus conceives the erroneous impression of individuality ; thinking 'This is I' and 'That is mine' he binds himself as a bird with a snare.[1] But the pure self is not without responsibility for this evil state, for a definite though obscure statement attributes it to the fact that the elemental self is overpowered by the inner Puruṣa.[2] The composite character of the text reveals itself in the further conception of the self as the enjoyer, while the elemental soul is made out to be the body, which it enjoys.[3] We find also the three factors named and described at length, essentially as psychic, and Prajāpati as affected by Sattva, goodness, as a factor is equated with Viṣṇu, as affected by Rajas, activity, with Brahman, and as affected with Tamas, dullness, with Rudra. It is characteristic that the Upaniṣad shows equally knowledge of the development of Yoga doctrine, though its scheme of stages of exercises has six in lieu of the classical eight.[4] Further, it is markedly pessimistic, the evils of empirical existence being set out with an elaboration of comparison and detail such as is only to be paralleled in the Buddhist texts, which it doubtless knew in some early form. It shows an advanced psychology, for it recognizes the function of individuation, though not as in the Sāṁkhya in its classical form, as placed between intellect and mind and as the source of the latter, but as following on mind and intellect, without any assertion of derivation, and it conceives of the existence of the subtle body, or Liṅga, though it is not clear whether it actually asserts that the Liṅga possesses not merely the fine elements but also the gross elements as part of its composition.[5] Moreover, the question is actually posed whether it is merely the factors that are really subject to bondage, or the self; the classical Sāṁkhya asserts definitely, though not always consistently, that the self is not really bound, but this is not the view accepted by the Upaniṣad, which insists on the bondage of the self, exhibited in the actions of intellect, mind, and individuation, and promises release when the sense organs, mind, and intellect have ceased to function.[6]

[1] ii. 3 ff. ; iii. 1 f.

[2] iii. 3.

[3] vi. 10.

[4] vi. 18.

[5] Cf. above, p. 533, n. 3. Deussen (*Sechzig Upanishad's*[2], p. 337, n. 2) amends ; Oldenberg (*op. cit.*, p. 355) prefers to see in Viçeṣa in Maitr. vi. 10 a designation of the subtle elements, not as in the epic (Strauss, VOJ. xxvii. 265), where it applies to the effects of the gross elements.

[6] vi. 30.

For the doctrine of the Guṇas or factors there is obvious a parallel in the Çvetāçvatara Upaniṣad,[1] which has on the ground of its content often been needlessly supposed to postdate the Sāṁkhya system, a view which cannot be supported on any cogent ground.[2] In it, we are told, that one she-goat, red, white, and black in hue, produces many young like herself: one he-goat leaps on her in love, the other abandons her, after associating with her. The idea of the relation of nature to the many spirits seems obviously expressed in this metaphor. But it is clear that the red, white, and black colours carry us beyond doubt to the Chāndogya Upaniṣad,[3] where everything in the universe is declared to be connected with the three elements, the red of fire, the white of water, and the black of food, probably an allusion to earth, this being the order of creation when the absolute first produced heat, thence water, then earth, in the shape of food. It is not necessary to suppose that in the Çvetāçvatara there is anything more meant than the three elements: the transformation of these to psychic forces, which is prominent in the Sāṁkhya, though the other conception is implied in the ascription of the three to Prakṛti, would then be a later development, which in the Upaniṣads occurs first in the Maitrāyaṇīya.[4]

It is clear, therefore, that the seeds of the Sāṁkhya lie in the philosophy of the Upaniṣads: the conception of the deliverance from the round of rebirth and misery is wholly absurd on the Sāṁkhya theory of the universe, which denies any real connexion of spirit and nature,[5] and, therefore, makes any suffering impossible, since without connexion there is no illumination, and without illumination of nature by spirit no suffering of any kind. In the doctrine of Māyā there is an illusion which is perfectly real though an illusion, and knowledge can dispel it and its products. But the ignorance which must be dispelled in the Sāṁkhya is the belief in a connexion which does not exist, and the Sāṁkhya philosophy never suggests that the misery of the universe is due to the belief: it is only possible because of the connexion: ignorance does not produce the connexion: therefore logically there is no misery. The mere fact of this illogicality alone and the marked pessimism of the system would testify to its derivative character.

A somewhat divergent view of the development of the Sāṁkhya is suggested by Dahlmann, who in several works[6] has insisted on the view that

[1] iv. 5.

[2] Hopkins (JAOS. xxii. 380–7) insists that *sāṁkhyayogādhigamyam* in vi. 13 must refer to the system of the epic Sāṁkhya-Yoga, but this is not in the least proved; see Deussen, *Gesch. der Phil.* I. iii. 15. Moreover it is difficult to reconcile Hopkins' view with his date of the 4th cent. (*ibid.* p. 336) for this Upaniṣad. Kapila in v. 2 is clearly mythical (cf. iv. 12), not the teacher.

[3] vi. 4.

[4] iii. 5; v. 2.

[5] This leads Speyer (*Indische Theosophie*, p. 113) to the conjecture that an originally materialistic system has been transformed in an external method idealistically. But this theory rests on no solid basis and ignores the essential link of connexion with the Upaniṣads. So with Jacobi, *Festschrift Kuhn*, pp. 37 ff., and Berndl, *Über das Sāṃkhya*. For a later view of Jacobi, see below.

[6] *Das Mahābhārata als Epos und Rechtsbuch*;

the epic reveals to us the oldest stage of the Sāṁkhya philosophy and not as maintained by Hopkins,[1] and in some degree [2] Deussen among others, an eclectic philosophical view. Dahlmann's position is obscured by its connexion with his ingenious but unsuccessful effort to prove that the epic is in itself a unity consciously produced at a period before Pāṇini, a thesis which rests on absolutely no cogent or even plausible evidence.[3] Nor have we any tolerable ground for the view that the system of Sāṁkhya as first evolved under that name was other than atheistic, in the sense not merely of denying an Īçvara which in a degree Dahlmann would admit, but also of denying an absolute. Further, it is most natural to hold that the Sāṁkhya-Yoga of the epic is a definite theistic modification of the Sāṁkhya, which is more really theistic and absolutist than the later Yoga, in which as a system attention is directed towards the Yoga practices and not so largely to the theistic aspect.[4] But the rejection of Dahlmann's theories in these respects does not deprive of value his theory of the development of Indian philosophy. He argues that the first stage must be looked for in a view which is in close touch with the expressions of the Brāhmaṇas as to the process of creation, in which there is more or less consciously assumed to be some material beyond the actual creator, and he points out that in the early speculations of the Upaniṣads we learn of the Ātman on the one hand, but also of what is not the Ātman, which is full of misery. In more philosophic form this appears as the doctrine of the Brahman, beside which stands Prakṛti, into which is emptied the whole of the ordinary world of thought and action, while the Brahman remains outside all contact with thought, affording the end, Nirvāṇa, which is to be attained by the extinguishing of all kinds of feeling, by the negation of everything empirical. From this dualistic basis he deduces on the one hand the Sāṁkhya and on the other the Vedānta of the illusionist school. The former view is arrived at by a determined effort to make logical the process of development in final release : it became intolerable to contemplate that there was really only one Ātman, which, by connexion in some unexplained way with Prakṛti, produced the innumerable separate spirits through the action of Buddhi and of Ahaṁkāra, since release became meaningless, and it, therefore, assumed that there were innumerable Ātmans, whose derivation from the primitive Ātman was proved by the fact that they retained the characteristics of omnipresence and infinity, which belong properly only to the one Ātman and which, applied to all, lead to absurdity. On the other hand, the Vedāntins laid such stress on the unity of the universe that they denied the existence as real of Prakṛti, contenting themselves with the idle doctrine of illusion, which was clearly inconsistent with their own principle of unity. Moreover, he argues, materialism was a natural product of the early view, since it really emptied

Nirvāṇa; *Genesis des Mahābhārata*; *Die Sāṁkhya-Philosophie* (1895–1902).

[1] *Great Epic of India*, pp. 97 ff.

[2] *Gesch. der Phil.* I. iii. 21 ff. ; cf. Jacobi, SBA. 1911, p. 738 ; Winternitz, *Gesch. d. ind. Lit.* i. 376, n. 1.

[3] See references in Winternitz, *Gesch. d. ind. Lit.* i. 263.

[4] Tuxen, *Yoga*, pp. 56 ff.

the Ātman of all empirical reality, and gave such reality to Prakṛti, and thus encouraged the view that matter by itself was able to produce the universe, while on the other hand by its subjectivism in the doctrine of the Ātman encouragement was given to scepticism, and finally to the philosophic indifference of early Buddhism.

Apart from the fact that there is really no good ground for calling the first stage Sāṁkhya,[1] and that the denial of illusionism cannot be accepted as absolutely true of the Upaniṣads, Dahlmann's theory has the merit of directing attention to a real aspect of the philosophy of the Upaniṣads and the epic: there is a real affinity between the process by which Buddhi and Ahaṁkāra are deemed to produce the world of experience and the older myths of Prajāpati and his desire, Kāma, as playing their parts in the creation of the world, while still further back we have the picture of Puruṣa as at once the material and the spiritual source of the world. But it would be a mistake to accept the view that the aspect insisted upon by Dahlmann was really either the sole aspect or the chief aspect of philosophy in the period of the later Upaniṣads. In particular Dahlman goes clearly too far in stressing the independent character of the evolution of Prakṛti, and in his insistence on the nature of Īçvara as the world soul arising from Prakṛti alone, thus placing Prakṛti beside the Ātman as in itself accounting for the whole of the empirical world. It must never be forgotten, as Dahlmann himself elsewhere [2] recognizes, that the spiritual side of existence is essentially conditioned by the fact that in Prakṛti the Ātman is present as the observer, a fact which in the Sāṁkhya is preserved and emphasized in the insistence on the doctrine that but for the connexion of Puruṣa and Prakṛti there would be no cognition or feeling of any kind. When due weight is accorded to this fact, we reach fairly closely to a conception which is not far different from that of Bādarāyaṇa as the normal, not unique, doctrine of the Upaniṣads: there is an absolute on which matter is dependent indeed, but not illusory, and individual souls which in the Upaniṣads, but not in the Brahma Sūtra, at the end are resolved into the absolute, but which are not in themselves illusory, being, we may assume, the necessary result of the coexistence of the absolute and matter, and therefore endowed, until united with the absolute through knowledge, with a certain relative but real independence.[3]

The real question is in a sense whether we can legitimately call Sāṁkhya a system which accepts an absolute, and differs from the normal Upaniṣad doctrine essentially in the attention given to derivation from the absolute of Prakṛti and individuals. The best defence of this suggestion is that of Oldenberg,[4] who faces the fundamental difficulty that a system with an absolute in

[1] Oldenberg (*Die Kultur der Gegenwart*[2], I. v. 34) does not deny the possibility of this view; cf. *Buddha*[5], p. 68, n. 1.

[2] *Die Sāṁkhya-Philosophie*, pp. 80 ff., where he tends to exaggerate, as usual, the Prakṛti side of the compound Jīva.

[3] Cf. also Deussen, *Gesch. der Phil.* I. iii. 259 ff.

[4] Oldenberg, *Die Lehre der Upanishaden*, pp. 206–58, who accepts an epic Sāṁkhya with an absolute as explaining Buddhism (GN. 1917, pp. 218 ff.).

the epic is not normally Sāṁkhya, and that the twenty-five principles of the Sāṁkhya of the epic seem in their correspondence with the classical school to negate the presence among them of the absolute. Oldenberg's suggestion, that the twenty-fifth principle includes both the absolute and its manifestations as individual, is ingenious, but hardly convincing, and as a matter of terminology and historic fact it seems unwise to employ the term Sāṁkhya as applicable to any system which acknowledges an absolute. The facts of the derivation of the Sāṁkhya above accepted are, of course, not affected by the question of terminology, and in view of the extremely composite nature of epic philosophy we need not be in the least surprised to find a conglomerate of this side of Aupaniṣada views with genuine Sāṁkhya, and the blend which the epic knows as Sāṁkhya-Yoga, and which has the somewhat unfortunate appearance of an effort to reconcile the Upaniṣads and the Sāṁkhya.

An interesting and ingenious effort, however, has been made by Professor Edgerton[1] to establish the doctrine that the epic knows nothing of a Sāṁkhya which denies the world soul or an Īçvara, and that in it Sāṁkhya and Yoga do not denote philosophical systems but means of realizing that unity with the world soul, which is the aim of all philosophy in this period which is not materialistic. Sāṁkhya denotes simply reflection—doubtless its primary meaning—and Yoga practical exercises tending to produce the unity desired, the details in the Mokṣadharma showing that a sort of self-hypnosis is aimed at, while in the Gītā the method is that of unselfish normal activity in the position of life in which fate has placed a man. Ingenious as this effort is, the denial of a specific Sāṁkhya doctrine appears, on the whole, untenable. It compels us in the passage xii. 11037 ff. to render the words *anīçvaraḥ katham mucyet* as 'how the soul may be saved', and to hold that in this passage no distinction is being drawn between the views of Sāṁkhya and Yoga, which is to put an intolerable strain upon the language.[2] Nor does it seem possible in xii. 11408 to render *anīçvaram* applied to the twenty-fifth principle merely as 'supreme'; the term *īçvara* in the preceding verse makes it clear that a contrast is intended.[3] Another reference to the distinctive Sāṁkhya insistence on a multitude of spirits must be seen in xii. 11483,[4] and the whole matter appears clearly from xii. 13713 ff. In this passage we find two very distinct views set out: the Sāṁkhya and the Yoga accept a multiplicity of souls, while Vyāsa insists that all the souls at bottom rest on the world soul. To endeavour[5] to explain away this obvious distinction by the theory that the real distinction is between a full and a brief exposition, and not between the views of Kapila and others and of Vyāsa, is as unsatisfactory as the suggestion that *adhyātma* in the description of Kapila's activities means that he took thought on the supreme soul; the reference is clearly to the soul only. Nor is there anything

[1] AJP. xlv. 1 ff. Contrast Hopkins, *Great Epic of India*, pp. 104 ff.
[2] The meaning must be 'how can one be saved without a creator?'
[3] Hopkins, *op. cit.*, p. 126.
[4] The rendering in AJP. xlv. 24 is certainly impossible.
[5] AJP. xlv. 27, n. 29.

out of place[1] in the allusion to the Yoga, for on the score of the multiplicity of souls Sāṁkhya and Yoga in their classical forms agree. The effort also to remove the significance of the addition of a twenty-sixth principle in the Yoga on the score that, as Oldenberg[2] suggested, the new head serves merely to distinguish the souls as released, is clearly a *tour de force* ; the twenty-sixth is Īçvara, with whom, indeed, the enlightened soul may be identified.[3]

In the very different view of Berndl[4] the Sāṁkhya system, as we have it in the Kārikā of Īçvarakṛṣṇa and later, is a serious deviation from the true views of Kapila, who may have been the first teacher to express his views in prose. The original doctrine which denied any soul has been recast to meet Brahman prejudices, and has thus lost its definite character. Traces of the older view may be found in the assertion of the Mahābhārata[5] which gives number and matter, Prakṛti, and twenty-four principles as the essence of the Sāṁkhya. Originally the doctrine recognized only three Guṇas, 'Charactere', whose interactions, themselves uncaused, since cause does not affect these things in themselves, produce the whole empirical world, which is ruled by absolute necessity. The Guṇas are not material, but are capable of mutual attraction, repulsion, and experience, and their interaction results in the formation of complexes (Empfindungszentren), which are selves, but which true knowledge shows are not distinct, eternal, metaphysical entities. But each is conscious of its essential relation to the Guṇas, and this is expressed, subjectively, in the consciousness of transcendence, and, objectively, in the will to live and to maintain one's individuality. Space is an abstraction made by the subject from the relations of things *inter se* and to itself, to which there corresponds only a manifold of heterogeneous sensations of quality, which the subject, by reason of the difference from its own homogeneity, experiences as something without. Time is also an abstraction made by the subject, to which alterations of external and internal conditions correspond, the ground for distinguishing them being their different characters, those without being many and cutting across one another, while those which are internal are individualized and unified. The suggestion is ingenious, but it is perfectly clear that it is unhistorical. To eliminate Puruṣas as an essential feature opposed to Prakṛti is to contradict everything we know of the Sāṁkhya, and it is difficult to appreciate why the system should thus have been transformed, nor do the changes in the system of Empedokles made by Anaxagoras[6] provide

[1] AJP. xlv. 29, n. 31.

[2] GN. 1917, p. 237.

[3] Hopkins, *op. cit.*, pp. 134 ff.

[4] *Über das Sāṃkhya. Versuch einer Wiederherstellung und Deutung der Sāṃkhya-Prinzipien.*

[5] xii. l. 409. He notes also the disappearance of the Ṣaṣṭitantra as supporting his view as well as the legend of Vindhyakavāsa's changes in the Sāṁkhya (see Garbe, *Sāṁkhya-Philosophie*², pp. 79 ff.).

[6] The latter invented nous because the fact that the elements of Empedokles were conscious was forgotten, in Berndl's view. The view of Kapila was similarly altered, but illogically many selves were admitted, to avoid adopting the Vedānta view. But, while Anaxagoras was a pioneer as to nous, Kapila was a rebel against the Brahman soul doctrine, which ruins the alleged parallel.

an adequate parallel. It is necessary also in Berndl's view to deny the doctrine of necessary periodical destruction of the universe, since all that is requisite is that, since things have originated, they cannot be permanent, and to question the early character of the marked pessimism of the Kārikā as inconsistent with the date of 700 or 800 B.C. ascribed to Kapila.

A different view of the relation of the Upaniṣads and the Sāṁkhya is presented by Professor Jacobi,[1] whose latest view is that a distinct gulf lies between the older Upaniṣads, and the middle and younger groups, terms which denote the Kaṭha, Īçā, Çvetāçvatara, Muṇḍaka and Mahānārāyaṇa, and the Praçna, Maitrāyaṇīya, and Māṇḍūkya respectively. The middle group is marked out from the oldest group by the absence of Āraṇyaka characteristics, the fact that the thought of the Upaniṣads is no longer in the making but already expresses itself in characteristic verses and turns of phrase, and the metrical form, while, as Jacobi points out, there appears in the middle and younger groups a large number of technical terms of philosophical interest which are unknown to the earlier texts. In Jacobi's view there is also a vital philosophical difference between the two strata ; the middle and younger Upaniṣads are composed under the direct influence of the Sāṁkhya system which had come into being after the oldest Upaniṣads. The vital element in the new point of view is the manifestation of the belief in the doctrine of the personal immortality of the souls of men and other creatures conceived as monads or as a multiplicity of immaterial substances, this view being accompanied by the clear distinction of what was material and what was immaterial. The souls of the Sāṁkhya are derived, in his view, from the aspect of the self as composed of intelligence or consciousness (*vijñānamaya*) in the older Upaniṣads, but with the essential difference that the soul is no longer regarded as being derived from and merging on death into the Brahman. At the same time the being (*sat*) of the Chāndogya Upaniṣad [2] with its three constituents, which in the Upaniṣad are regarded as living, is distinguished as purely material, and its constituents figure as the Guṇas of the Sāṁkhya, while the Buddhi of the Sāṁkhya is a transformation of the *vijñānaghana ātmā* of Yājñavalkya, the whole somewhat bizarre conception being due to an effort at an early date to make a coherent system out of the confused thoughts of the oldest Upaniṣads. This system was of influence, though it did not prove generally acceptable. The middle and younger Upaniṣad groups represent efforts to compromise between the Sāṁkhya with its kindred Yoga, and the pantheistic spirit of the Upaniṣads, an effort continued in the Bhagavadgītā and the philosophical parts of the Mahābhārata, and finally resulting in the compromise of the Purāṇas. One doctrine, however, that of the personal immortality of the soul, became generally accepted, figuring in the Nyāya and Vaiçeṣika schools,[3] the Vedānta of Bādarāyaṇa, and even the Pūrva Mīmāṅsā,[4] as well

[1] *Die Entwicklung der Gottesidee bei den Indern* (1923), pp. 19 ff.

[2] vi.

[3] Keith, *Indian Logic and Atomism*, pp. 239 ff.

[4] Keith, *Karma-Mīmāṁsā*, pp. 64 ff.

as in Jainism. In the latter case the conception both of soul and matter seems to have been developed contemporaneously with the Sāṁkhya views, though it is probable that the idea of the soul as essentially pure intelligence and immortal was taken over by the Jains from some other doctrine, much of primitive hylozoism clinging to their view of the soul.

This view has been accepted as regards the origin of the theory of soul by Prof. Stcherbatsky,[1] who holds that the fact that the theory was new was the ground why it was so bitterly assailed by the Buddhists. He admits that the idea of a surviving personality is not unknown in the Veda, and that its essence and its relation to the Brahman are the main topic of discussion in the Upaniṣads. 'But this self is a psychological entity, different explanations of its nature are proposed, and materialistic views are not excluded.[2] The idea of an immortal soul in our sense, a spiritual monad, a simple, uncomposite, eternal, immaterial substance is quite unknown in the Veda inclusive of the older Upaniṣads.' Most regrettably neither Prof. Jacobi nor Prof. Stcherbatsky has pointed out the passages in the middle or younger Upaniṣads in which this new idea of an immortal soul is to be found, as contrasted with those in the older Upaniṣads ; and it appears to me wholly impossible to find any such distinction as real. The idea that at this period in the history of Indian thought the conception of an immortal soul was first introduced appears wholly without warrant, and to misunderstand entirely the course of development of Indian philosophy.

The fact, of course, is that the primitive Vedic belief clung to the doctrine of the survival of something after death, and that, therefore, immortality was no new idea. The view as to what survived was as hazy as it is to-day in popular and philosophic thought alike, for then, as now, it was practically impossible to form any intelligible conception of what a soul is, for such a description of the modern view as that given by Prof. Stcherbatsky cannot be said to have any intelligible meaning. But superinduced on this simple view we have the philosophic doctrine passed off under the name of Yājñavalkya, which asserts that the soul is not, as the ordinary man thinks, independent ; it is only a part of a greater whole or more accurately an aspect of that whole, so that at death there is no separate existence in the sense of personal immortality. That this view was ever generally accepted in philosophic circles is not suggested in the older Upaniṣads, and the middle and younger Upaniṣads show that it was not attractive and that the tendency was to consider the matter more theistically, the absolute taking on a definitely personal appearance and less stress being laid on merger in it, though it is essential to note that merger remains as a doctrine alongside with the contemplation of continued existence. But there is not the slightest trace of the advent of

[1] *The Central Conception of Buddhism* (1923), pp. 69 ff.

[2] That such views are allowed in the older Upaniṣads seems an error, perhaps based on Jacobi's older suggestion of materialism in CU. vi, which seems tacitly revised in *op. cit.*, pp. 11 f.

personal immortality or the spiritual nature of the soul as new ideas in the period of the middle Upaniṣads; the soul there remains a psychological entity exactly to the same extent as it was such an entity in the older Upaniṣads.

Prof. Stcherbatsky, however, maintains that the old and the new soul theories were clearly distinguished; thus all Buddhists rejected the doctrine of a self corresponding to the psycho-physical individual, Ātmavāda, but the Vātsīputrīyas and Sammitīyas accepted the theory of the doctrine of permanent soul, Pudgalavāda. This basis of distinction, however, is clearly illegitimate, and is not given by the Buddhist texts; instead the Pudgala is clearly a self corresponding to the psycho-physical individual, since it is maintained that it assumes new elements at birth and throws them off at death,[1] and the other Buddhist schools justly rejected either doctrine, seeing through the subterfuge by which these two schools endeavoured, while evading direct contradiction of the master's insistence on Anattā, negation of a self, to preserve the existence of something which could transmigrate, thus preserving the reality of the doctrine of moral retribution, which utterly disappears in the ordinary conception of Buddhism.[2] Nor is there any plausibility in the view that the Kaṭha Upaniṣad already recognizes what Prof. Stcherbatsky—on dubious grounds—claims to be the fundamental doctrine of Buddhism, the existence of Dharmas conceived as a plurality of subtle, ultimate, not further analysable elements of matter, mind, and force. The theory is based on the fact that in that Upaniṣad (iv. 14) we find a condemnation of him who sees Dharmas separately (*pṛthag dharmān paçyati*), which is a very different thing from Stcherbatsky's rendering 'maintains the existence of separate elements'. The idea that Dharmas in this passage are 'elements' is as implausible as that the term Dharma in i. 21 has this sense; the word seems to mean in both instances something like 'thing' as taken by Geiger,[3] and this use harmonizes with *dharmya* as opposed to what is subtle (*aṇu*) in ii. 13, a passage ignored by Stcherbatsky. With this rendering disappears wholly the idea that the author of the Kaṭha is directing a polemic against a doctrine which denies both the old and the new theories of the soul, or that Dharma is 'a catchword referring to a new and foreign doctrine, some *anātma-dharma* theory'. Nor is there the slightest justification for the view that Pāṇini [4] is aware of Buddhist and Sāṁkhya views of causation, for his explanation of the use

[1] See Vasubandhu's account in Stcherbatsky's *Soul Theory*, p. 851.

[2] Cf. Keith, *Buddhist Philosophy*, pp. 81 ff.

[3] *Pāli Dhamma*, p. 9.

[4] ii. 3. 53; iv. 2. 16, 4. 3; vi. 1. 139. The Paribhāṣās referred to neither prove the thesis nor have validity for Pāṇini. They do not appear in the Mahābhāṣya, but in the Kāçikā (7th cent. A.D.). The absurdity of the suggestion of Pāṇini's knowledge would be increased if we accepted Charpentier's claim (ZII. ii. 140 ff.) that he lived not later than 550 B.C., since he knew the title of Kamboja King, which was extinct after the death of Kambyses (= Kamboja King, title of older Achaimenidai). But this rests on a number of conjectures, all unproved and all most implausible.

of *saṁskṛta* and *upakṛta* or *upaskṛta* corresponds very poorly with this suggestion.

Stcherbatsky [1] suggests further that from the Sāṁkhya the Buddhists derived the incentive to the doctrine of the world as consisting of momentary elements of mind, matter, and force. The Guṇas of the Sāṁkhya on this view are interpreted as fundamental principles, matter, mind-stuff, and energy-stuff, acting as interdependent moments in every real and substantial existence ; 'the infinitesimals of energy, present everywhere, are semi-material ; although different from the inertia of matter and the luminosity of mind, they are separate and substantial'. The Buddhist elements are a reply to the Sāṁkhya by an architect of greater skill. Ingenious as this theory is, it depends, even if we accept the suggested view of the Buddhist Dharmas as primitive—which seems impossible—on the belief that the interpretation of the Guṇas adopted is really that of the early Sāṁkhya. This seems frankly impossible in view of the silence of the Sāṁkhya texts and of the epic alike. The interpretation is based on the Yogabhāṣya of Vyāsa,[2] who is a comparatively late author,[3] and who shows every sign of influence by the Buddhist schools.[4] To substitute his views for those of the origin of the Sāṁkhya is as unwise as to adopt the doctrines of the Sarvāstivādins, as expounded by Vasubandhu, as representing the early doctrines of Buddhism from a philosophical point of view. The same error marks the suggestion [5] that the name of Sāṁkhya is borrowed from Sāṁkhya in the sense of Prajñā, that intellectual insight which destroys the infections (*kleças*), through which the spirit is bound to continued existence. There can be no question that the epic [6] explanation of the term as Parisaṁkhyāna, 'enumeration (of principles)', is to be preferred to this suggestion, though it is still more probable that in its earliest stage the term simply referred to reasoning.

The Upaniṣads themselves contain traces of the doctrine of Yoga, regarded

[1] *Op. cit.*, p. 22.

[2] Cf. Dasgupta, *The Study of Patañjali* ; *Ind. Phil.* i. 243 ff.

[3] Cf. Woods, *Yoga-System* of *Patañjali*, pp. xx f. His reasoning (p. xxi) that the comm. is after A.D. 650 because it is cited by Māgha is clearly a slip ; Māgha knew it apparently and so it dates before A. D. 700. Dasgupta's (*Ind. Phil.* i. 230 ff.) early date for Patañjali as identical with the grammarian is implausible in the extreme.

[4] See Stcherbatsky, *op. cit.*, pp. 46, 47, n. 3. The idea that the Sāṁkhya did not recognize substance and quality in a relation of inherence (*ibid.*, p. 27, n. 2) is clearly impossible, and is not even Vyāsa's view.

[5] *Op. cit.*, p. 51, n. 1. Berndl (*op. cit.*, p. 13 *n.*) seeks to show that the name refers to number, not of principles, but of the Guṇas as transcendent realities.

[6] See Hopkins, *Great Epic of India*, pp. 126 f. Thus Sāṁkhya indicates a stage of definition prior to the Vaiçeṣika, which defines by special difference (*viçeṣa*). In lieu it gives a description with enumeration of contents. The term Yoga, however, when used with Sāṁkhya indicates the wider sense. It itself denotes the exertion which results in hypnosis, praxis as opposed to theory, but it assumes other shades of meaning, including the restraint of the senses (cf. Güntert, *Der arische Weltkönig*, p. 225) and the joining of the spirit to that of Içvara or an absolute. Cf. Keith, *Sāṁkhya System*, chap. iv.

as a discipline by which the mind can be withdrawn from the things of this world and unity with the absolute can be attained, although it is only in the Kaṭha, the Çvetāçvatara, and the much later Maitrāyaṇīya that these traces are of importance. The Çvetāçvatara, however, contributes an element which in the classical Yoga distinguishes it from the Sāṁkhya, the presence of a personal deity, though the figure of the god in the Upaniṣad is infinitely more vivid and important than that of the Īçvara of the Yoga. This Upaniṣad, however, is distinctly marked by lack of clearness of conception, and attempts at harmonization of contrasting views. Recognizing the strength of the popular religion which craved for aid from the gods, and in no wise satisfied with mere Yoga methods of securing the end desired, the Çvetāçvatara introduces into its system the conception of god. But in this introduction we find a repeated confusion between god as an addition to the empiric universe beside matter and spirits, and god as identical with the absolute. In the first sense [1] we have the conception of the absolute as comprehending the three; god, who is the knower, the inciter to enjoyment, the lord; spirit, the enjoyer, the ignorant, not the lord; and nature, which is to be enjoyed by each spirit according to its merit or demerit. Two birds there are dwelling in one tree, one eats the sweet fruit, the other merely gazes on the scene; one, spirit, is distressed in contact with nature, but when it beholds the other, the lord, is freed from its woes. In the classical Yoga this picture presents itself in the form of a god who is a special spirit untouched by the impurity of the world, by action and its fruits, and who promotes the freedom of unemancipated spirits. The objections to the later view are obvious; how can there exist a god, who is not removed from all connexion with the world as is the released spirit, and yet is untouched by the misery of the world? In the Upaniṣad, however, god has a much more real existence; he is hailed as Rudra [2] and begged to spare the votary; he is invoked with the names of Maheçvara, Hara, and Çiva, and he is identified at times with the Brahman, which, though also set above Rudra, is immediately after [3] expressly given the name of Lord, Īça, which is essentially that of Rudra. The end of man is to know, to see mystically this god, who is the magician [4] who creates the universe in which the soul by illusion (*māyā*) is bound. He is the maker of all, all-knower, self-sourced, intelligent, the author of time,[5] yet above the three times and impartite,[6] possession of qualities, omniscient, the ruler of matter (*pradhāna*), and of the spirit, lord of qualities, the cause of transmigration and of liberation, of continuance and of bondage. When men shall roll up space as if it were a piece of leather, then only will there be an end of evil apart from the knowledge of god.[7]

Knowledge of god is vouchsafed by the grace of the lord [8] to him who has the highest devotion (*bhakti*) to god, and also to his spiritual teacher even as to

[1] i. 8–16; iv. 6, 7.
[2] iii. 1–6; iv. 16, 18, 21, 22.
[3] iii. 7.
[4] iv. 9, 10.
[5] vi. 16.
[6] vi. 5.
[7] vi. 20, obviously a polemic against views similar to those of Buddhism or the later Sāṁkhya.
[8] iii. 20 (=TA. x. 10. 1; cf. KU. ii. 20). Cf. the Yoga doctrine in Vyāsabhāṣya, i. 23 f.

god,[1] a doctrine which suggests not the later Yoga, but the spirit of the Bhagavadgītā and the general adoration of the teacher, as an essential part of the way of salvation, in the sectarian religions.

The early Upaniṣads contain no clear trace of the doctrine which is later found in the Buddhism of the Sarvāstivādins,[2] and which discriminates between the power of knowledge to remove causes of existence and that of ecstasy, assigning to the latter alone the power of suppressing all material elements and all sensuous consciousness, knowledge dealing with mental elements and mental consciousness. Such a distinction has every appearance of being an excrescence on the original Buddhist doctrine, evoked by the desire to find a logical place for ecstasy as opposed to mere knowledge, but it may have been early in appearing.

Slight as is normally the recognition in the Buddhist texts of the Brahman doctrine of their rivals, Geiger [3] has shown that the term Dhamma not rarely is used as a substitute, in expressing the Buddhist ideal, for the Brahman of the Upaniṣads, while the term Brahman itself is occasionally preserved.[4] The famous phrase 'Wheel of the Law (*dhamma-cakka*)' is also paralleled by Brahma-cakka; [5] the Dhammayāna by Brahmayāna; [6] the Tathāgata is not merely an incorporation of Dhamma but also of the Brahman, he has become not only the Dhamma but also the Brahman; [7] the Dhamma even claims the worship which is the lot of the Brahman in the Upaniṣads.[8] Nor in choosing the term Dhamma for the system was Buddhism without Upaniṣad precedent; the Bṛhadāraṇyaka [9] tells that Brahman created the Dharma, than which nothing is higher, and the Mahānārāyaṇa [10] asserts that the whole universe is encircled by the Dharma, than which there is nothing harder to describe.

While it is, as has been seen, impossible to accept the derivation of the Sāṁkhya from a materialism, it is probable that its realistic elements were partly due to a contemporary tendency in this direction of which, not unnaturally, we have no direct early evidence. The Çvetāçvatara Upaniṣad, however, records [11] possible or actual theories of the absolute or final principle (*brahman*),[12] which include necessity (*niyati*), chance (*yadṛcchā*), time, inherent nature (*svabhāva*), matter (*bhūtāni*), and spirit. In the records of Buddhism [13] we have given to us as existing contemporaneously with the Buddha the doctrine of Ajita Kesakambalin, who was in effect a materialist, and who, according to the Jain tradition,[14] believed, as did the Cārvākas of the later tradition, in pleasure as the one end to be followed. The terms used of this

[1] vi. 23.
[2] Abhidharmakoça, i. 40; Stcherbatsky, *The Central Conception of Buddhism*, p. 52 (where *dhātus* 1–5 and 7–11 (not 7–10) is to be read).
[3] *Dhamma und Brahman.*
[4] DN. iii. 232.
[5] MN. i. 69.
[6] SN. v. 5.
[7] DN. iii. 80 ff.
[8] SN. i. 138 ff.; AN. ii. 20 ff.
[9] i. 4. 14.
[10] xxi. 6.
[11] i. 2.
[12] In this general sense also in BAU. ii. 1. 1; iv. i. 2; CU. v. 11. 1; Kauṣ. iv. 1, &c.
[13] Cf. Keith, *Buddhist Philosophy*, pp. 135 ff.; Barua, *Prebuddh. Ind. Phil.*, pp. 289 ff.
[14] Cf. Sūtrakṛtāṅga, ii. 1. 17 (SBE. xlv. 341).

doctrine[1] certainly suggest that it was based on some degree at least on the principle enunciated by Yājñavalkya,[2] that on dissolution of the body there exists in certain cases no consciousness, which, if the belief in the existence of the Brahman be removed, would result in a pure materialism, regarding the body as the reality of which life is a mere accompaniment, a view attributed also in Buddhist tradition[3] to the king Pāyāsi, who experimentally established that soul did not survive bodily death. The records are important, since they show that the renunciation of belief in the Brahman could produce materialism as well as the Sāṁkhya dualism and the negation of soul in Buddhism.

The other principles enumerated by the Çvetāçvatara as possible theories are less important. Necessity figures also in the system of Makkhali Gosāla, while inherent nature appears also as an aspect of that system;[4] time has Vedic authority and persisted much later;[5] chance is rather an element in a system than an actual system, while the brevity of the allusion renders it obscure what particular doctrine is referred to.

§ 8. *The Supreme and the Individual Souls*

In the philosophy of Yājñavalkya the identity of the supreme and the individual souls is carried to the extreme extent, but at the same time the term soul is deprived of any distinct meaning. The identity of the soul of man and the absolute is due to the mere fact that, by reducing the soul to nothing save what may be termed the mere abstraction of subjectivity, or of the transcendental unity of apperception, the soul becomes nothing but an aspect of a process.[6] It is perfectly legitimate then to identify the supreme and the individual souls, but we are really carried no further by this than the occasional remarks of the Bṛhadāraṇyaka Upaniṣad, which regards the universe as made up of nothing except subject and object. It is in fact perfectly true that all the world can be regarded as distinguished as subject and object, but, unless we are able to show that this is the sum total of all that we can know, it is clearly impossible for philosophy to stop there. The actual existing world of thought, emotion, and action requires explanation and investigation. In the Vedānta the matter is solved comfortably by the doctrine of the two forms of knowledge: on the upper stage the identity of the self and the absolute is recognized, on the lower there is found to be a personal deity, Hiraṇyagarbha, and personal selves, who are indeed the absolute self, but fall under the influence of conditioning facts, the Upādhis, mind, the

[1] Cf. Sarvadarçanasaṁgraha, p. 2; Çīlāñka, Sūtrakṛtāñga (ed. Dhanapati), p. 290.
[2] BAU. ii. 4. 13; iv. 5. 13.
[3] Pāyāsi Suttanta of Dīgha Nikāya.
[4] Barua, *op. cit.*, pp. 310 ff.
[5] See below, § 8.
[6] The fact of this undue abstraction explains the view of one aspect of Buddhism in its denial of any Ātman at all. But in so doing they naturally found themselves obliged to invent a substitute in the doctrine of Karman. The praise occasionally lavished on their psychology without a soul is only conclusive of the philosophical crudity of the encomiasts. Cf. de la Vallée Poussin, *Bouddhisme*, pp. 82 ff., 156 ff.; Keith, *Buddhist Philosophy*, pp. 169 ff., 207 f.

senses, the vital airs, and the body, which, while in reality no more affecting the reality of the nature of the absolute than the red colour the rock crystal, nevertheless convert it into the self or soul, Jīva,[1] of everyday humanity. In the Upaniṣads we naturally expect to find both sides of this doctrine, and we do find them in point of fact quite clearly expressed. On the one hand, we have the constant efforts to show that there is but one self, that there is no multiplicity and no change, which is pure idealism of a very intransigeant type, and on the other the reality of the individual self is constantly insisted upon. It is, however, constantly repeated that the individual and the absolute self are the same, and this is true no less in those cases where we may accept the view that idealism of the Yājñavalkya type is present, than in those, in which there is mere pantheism or cosmogonism. In the latter cases equally there is no ground to distinguish ultimately between the selves, since at the most the individual is merely the absolute in another form. But even when the Upaniṣads are theistic in spirit, like the Kaṭha and still more decidedly by far the Çvetāçvatara, they never reach the view that the supreme and the individual souls are anything really different. The Kaṭha,[2] however, is marked by its clear enunciation for the first time of the conception of the enjoyer as the union of the self with mind and the senses. It also describes the two aspects of the souls as light and shadow, while in the Çvetāçvatara [3] we find the metaphor of the two birds on a tree, one eating the sweet berries, the other merely gazing downwards, without eating. It also develops the idea of the individual soul, as endowed with the faculty of framing concepts and resolves, individualism and intellect, as enjoying the fruit of action, as small as a thumb in height, or a needle's point, or the ten-thousandth part of the tip of a hair, which is yet identical with the infinitely great supreme soul, a statement which is clearly identical in essence with the Vedānta position as seen in Çaṅkara.

The cause of the appearance in this restricted form of the supreme soul is given by Çaṅkara as the effect of ignorance, and with him that explanation ends the matter, since it is impossible to go further than this. In the Upaniṣads, apart from the many creation legends which yield no philosophic result, the actual nature of the problem is rarely expressed and very slightly explained. The view of the Praçna [4] is that breath is born from the self, and it is likened to the shadow on a man. Unhappily the rest of its explanation is obscure: if rendered according to grammar, it distinctly says that the position is involuntary (*manokṛta*) on the part of the self: the version of Sāyaṇa, which is defiant of grammar, takes it that the result is produced by the previous acts of the will of the man in question; it is possible that we must amend so as merely to say that the mind attaches itself to the breath, but this suggestion of Böhtlingk's [5] is doubtful, and the best plan seems to be

[1] Cf. A. Guha, *Jīvātman in the Brahma-Sūtras* (Calcutta, 1921).
[2] iii. 1.
[3] iv. 6, 7; v. 2–6.
[4] iii. 1–3.
[5] Hillebrandt suggests *manodūtena*, but this gives no explanation of the misreading. Böhtlingk emends to *manaḥ. tena*.

to recognize that the process is not voluntary, which is in agreement with the Vedānta view. In the Maitrāyaṇīya,[1] which is influenced by the Sāṁkhya views of the constituents of nature, the doctrine is laid down that the self is overcome by the Guṇas, and falls into an illusion in which it becomes weak, disordered, sensual, and believes in the separate existence of the self, fettering itself by its own action like a bird by its nest, while an addition [2] to that text gives the different conception, that the supreme soul becomes individual, in order to experience life in the world as well as eternal verity.

The description of the parts of the individual souls in the Upaniṣads is far from uniform or homogeneous. In the Sāṁkhya, as we have seen, it is a union of the individual spirit with the elements of intellect, individuation, mind, the five organs of intelligence and the five organs of action, and the subtle elements as well as the fine parts of the gross elements. In the Vedānta the position is not essentially different: the soul is the absolute enveloped in the Upādhis: in this case they are mind,[3] the ten senses, the five breaths, which are the organs of nutrition, and the subtle body, that is the subtle parts of the elements which form the seeds of the body. In both cases there must be added the psychic disposition which causes the kind of rebirth and secures that rebirth, the Bhāva of the Sāṁkhya, the Karman of Çaṅkara.

In the Upaniṣads the terminology centres mainly in the word Prāṇa, which every now and then, as we have seen, is treated as a synonym of the absolute, but which on the whole is more normally of less consequence. The Prāṇa often represents the senses, but the numbers of Prāṇas, into which it is divided, differ greatly: the origin of the various calculations may certainly be traced in part at least to the Atharvaveda,[4] where we are told of the head as a drinking bowl with seven seers in the apertures: the sense ascribed to the seven appears to have been the eyes, ears, nostrils, and the organ of taste, for the Bṛhadāraṇyaka Upaniṣad [5] adds to the seven an eighth in the form of speech. The Upaniṣads normally enumerate a series of five,[6] breath, eye, ear, mind, and speech, but these are sometimes reduced to four or less; thus the Jaiminīya Upaniṣad Brāhmaṇa repeatedly dwells on the series, speech, mind, sight, hearing, and the breath or breaths; the cosmic parallels are fire, moon, sun, the quarters (i.e. space), and wind. A different view is that of a passage of the Bṛhadāraṇyaka Upaniṣad,[7] where the organs

[1] iii. 2.
[2] vii. 11.
[3] Mind in this system covers all the three activities of the Sāṁkhya Buddhi, Ahaṁkāra, and Manas, and in the epic these three appear often as two (Ahaṁkāra being suppressed); cf. Dahlmann, *Die Sāṁkhya-Philosophie*, pp. 79 ff. See also Oltramare, *L'histoire des idées théosophiques*, i. 190 ff.
[4] x. 8. 9; in ver. 44 we have one of the earliest declarations of the Ātman doctrine.
[5] BAU. ii. 2. 3.
[6] Possibly the source of the *five* Buddhist Skandhas; see Stcherbatsky, *The Central Conception of Buddhism*, p. 72. See JUB. ii. 1 f.; iii. 1 f.
[7] iii. 2. 2–9, where Prāṇa seems to mean sense of smell, Apāna odour, but the text is doubtless corrupt, despite the agreement of the recensions; cf. Deussen, *Phil. of Up.*, pp. 277 f.

of smell, speech, tongue, eye, ear, mind, hands, and skin are enumerated as the eight Grahas, and the corresponding objects, odour, name, taste, form, sound, desire, action, and touch are set over against them as the Atigrahas, possibly an indication, since Graha may mean seizer, that the soul was fettered by the organs and their activities, an idea carried out in the phrase 'bands of the heart', which is first found in the Chāndogya Upaniṣad.[1] The later term Indriya is first found in the Kauṣītaki Upaniṣad,[2] when on death the father hands over to his son his speech; smell; eye; ear; tastes; actions; pleasure and pain; bliss, delight, and procreation; movements; mind; and intellect (*prajñā*), where the usual later enumeration of ten with mind is followed, with one exception. In the Bṛhadāraṇyaka Upaniṣad[3] we find the skin as the uniting-place of touch; the tongue of tastes; the nose of odours; the eye of forms; the ear of sounds; the mind of conceptions (*saṁkalpa*); the heart of knowledge; the hands of actions; the generative organ of pleasure; the anus of procreation; the feet of movements; and speech of the Vedas; but the name, Indriya, is not used. The normal later total of ten with mind, including the heart, as Indriyas is found in the Praçna,[4] in a passage which also enumerates the five subtle elements, the five gross elements, intellect, individuation, thought, brilliance, and breath.

It is of importance in the history of Indian philosophy to note the development of the sense of Manas, 'mind'. In the earliest period, and in the Brāhmaṇas, and even in the Upaniṣads, mind is a vague term[5] denoting consciousness generally, whether feeling,[6] willing, or thinking, and it can be used as a synonym for Prajāpati, when it is sought to reduce that figure to something more abstract and less mythological. From that use it is later sometimes definitely minimized to mean the power which forms ideas and decisions, but it is probably in the wider and less precise sense that it still appears in all the old lists of the breaths beside speech, eye, ear, and breath. The more limited meaning is possible in cases where mind is said to be the uniting place of conceptions, the heart of knowledge, or mind discriminates names, and intellect (*prajñā*) deals with thoughts, what is to be understood, and desires.[7] On the other hand, there clearly evolves itself, as in Epicharmos' doctrine: νοῦς ὁρῇ καὶ νοῦς ἀκούει, τἆλλα κωφὰ καὶ τυφλά the idea that the presence of the mind, attention in fact, is necessary to see, to hear, and so forth. Desire, judgement, belief, doubt, unbelief, firmness, weakness, modesty, knowledge, fear, all these depend on the mind. Mind therefore is regarded as forming into ideas the impressions of the senses, sight, hearing, taste, smell, and touch, and it then—as will motived by desire—transforms the ideas into resolves, which

[1] vii. 26. 2; KU. vi. 15.
[2] ii. 15.
[3] iv. 5. 12; ii. 4. 11.
[4] iv. 2. A late hymn (AV. xix. 9. 5) has the five Indriyas with Manas.
[5] Oldenberg, *Weltanschauung der Brāhmaṇatexie*, pp. 69 ff. The early term *kratu* denotes will (*vaça*) as directed by intellect. The word *man* specially denotes to think that a thing is so and so; *dhī* to meditate on it.
[6] e. g., JB. i. 269; BAU. iii. 2.7.
[7] BAU. ii. 4. 11; iv. 5. 12; Kauṣ. i. 7.

are carried out by the organs of action. It is the mind which drives man to beget on his wife a son,[1] the Bṛhadāraṇyaka Upaniṣad[2] also says. Similarly the mind is the cause of all action of every kind, sacred study, or the gaining of wealth. In the metaphor of the chariot and the driver, the body and the soul, in the Kaṭha[3] the intellect is the charioteer, mind the reins, and the senses are only the horses. One of the selves in the doctrine of five selves in the Taittirīya Upaniṣad[4] is expressly called the mind-made self, and its object is sacrificial activity. The Maitrāyaṇīya Upaniṣad[5] develops the chariot metaphor further; the whip is nature, the horses the organs of action, the reins the organs of intellect, and the driver is mind who with his whip stirs the steeds to action under the control of the reins.[6]

The mind is specially concerned with Saṁkalpas, a term which appears only in a late passage of the Rigveda,[7] but is later frequent. The root idea is putting in order, so that a Saṁkalpa or conception may be equally well an idea or a decision, though in fact the word is frequently used with an implication of will. Mind is the abode of all Saṁkalpas,[8] but with the usual inconsistency we have Saṁkalpa ranked above mind, the product above the function.[9] Mind is fundamental; what one desires with it is Kratu, conscious will.

Beside mind we find sometimes the term Citta, which in the Pāli Canon is often a synonym for mind.[10] The term *cit* denotes from the Rigveda on to notice something, whether by the sense organs or by mental activity; in the Chāndogya[11] we find Citta, what is noticed, placed above Saṁkalpa which in its turn is superior to mind; a contrast is drawn between the man who knows much and has no Citta, and who is accordingly little regarded, and him who has Citta and, therefore, is in high repute. In the sense of thought as an activity Citta is later in use, beside Citti and Cetas, and occasionally mind and Citta or Cetas are directly identified.[12] The term Citta becomes of special importance later in the Yoga system.

Vijñāna, discriminating knowledge, which is made a synonym of mind in the Pāli Canon, is sometimes merely a function of mind,[13] but it also occurs not rarely in the older Upaniṣads with a distinct implication of a superior form of knowledge to the mere action of mind; thus hearing, thinking, and discrimi-

1 AU. iii. 2; Kauṣ. iii. 7; BAU. i. 5. 3.

2 iv. 1. 6; see i. 5. 3; Maitr. vi. 3.

3 iii. 3.

4 ii. 3.

5 ii. 6; for the Epic view of Manas see Deussen, *Gesch. d. Phil.* I. iii. 59–63; for the Buddhist, C. Rhys Davids, *Buddhist Manual of Psychological Ethics*², pp. lxxi ff., which, however, is very speculative and unduly modernizes; Keith, *Buddhist Philosophy*, pp. 85, 89, 161, 168 f.; Stcherbatsky, *The Central Conception of Buddhism*, pp. 15, 72. See also JUB. i. 33. 4 f.; ÇB. iv. 6. 7. 5; BAU. iii. 2; KU. iii. 6; JUB. iv. 26.

6 The contrast with the Platonic metaphor in the *Phaidros* is as obvious as the parallel.

7 x. 164. 5. Often with Kāma, 'desire'; AV. iii. 25. 2; CU. viii. 1. 5; 2; BAU. i. 5. 3.

8 BAU. ii. 4. 11 (*dhyāna* in Kauṣ. iii. 3).

9 CU. vii. 4.

10 Dīgha Nikāya, i. 21. Cf. Keith, *Buddhist Philosophy*, p. 85.

11 CU. vii. 5.

12 VS. xviii. 2; CU. iii. 6. 8; VS. xxxiv. 3.

13 ÇB. xii. 9. 1. 14. It is used of mind and the four senses in JB. i. 269.

nating, or seeing, thinking, and discriminating, are enumerated, and in the final doctrine, which denies the possibility of knowing that which knows all, the term used is *vijñā*.[1] But this idea is not formally developed, in accordance with the whole spirit of the Upaniṣads.

On the side of feeling the terminology of the Upaniṣads marks a great advance in the normal employment of Sukha to denote pleasure generically and Duḥkha, based upon it, for misery. A generic term to cover both forms of feeling is not found before the Vedanā of the Pāli texts. But we have the definite statement [2] that, when a man experiences pleasure, he acts, when he experiences pain, he refrains from action, while the Kauṣītaki [3] asserts that pleasure and pain are felt by means of the body.

Of more philosophical interest are efforts made to render more precise the functions of the senses. Thus the Bṛhadāraṇyaka Upaniṣad [4] in the doctrine above cited, of eight graspers, or apprehenders (*grahas*), and eight that are beyond (*ati*) the graspers, gives as pairs Prāṇa and Apāna, the former being used to smell odours ; speech and names ; the tongue and tastes ; the eye and visible forms (*rūpa*) (i. e. coloured extension) ; the ear and sounds ; the mind and desires ; the hands and action ; and the skin and feelings of touch.[5] In the Kauṣītaki [6] we have speech and name as its external correlate ; breath (i.e. smell) and odour ; eye and visible form ; the ear and sound ; the tongue and tastes ; the two hands and action ; the body and pleasure and pain ; the organ of generation and bliss, delight, and procreation ; the two feet and movements ; and the intellect and thoughts, what is to be understood, and desires. The Jaiminīya Upaniṣad Brāhmaṇa [7] has a series of ten : mind and matters requiring examination (*parīkṣya*) ; speech (i. e. the tongue) [8] and tastes ; breath and odours ; the eye and visible forms ; the ear and sounds ;

[1] CU. vii. 13. 1 ; 15. 4 ; 25. 2 ; BAU. iii. 4. 2 ; ii. 4. 14 ; iv. 5. 15 ; it ranks above Dhyāna, CU. vii. 7. Vijñāna is in KU. iii. 9 apparently ranked with Buddhi above mind. In Buddhism it is sometimes given a higher rank ; Oldenberg, *Buddha*[6], pp. 258 f., 264. In JB. i. 269 it is used to denote the functions of eye, ear, smell, tongue, and mind.

[2] CU. vii. 22. Cf. *priyāpriye*, CU. viii. 12. 1 ; *hṛdayajña*, *ahṛdayajña*, vii. 2. 1 ; *suhārdasa*, *durhārdasa*, JB. i. 269.

[3] i. 7.

[4] iii. 2. 2–9.

[5] ii. 4. 11 ; iv. 5. 12 of the same text have further identifications ; see above, p. 554.

[6] i. 7 (breath and names and mind and names are also given according to genders) ; cf. ii. 15, where there are variants in the two texts, see Hume's notes ; in iii. 6 (see below) mind replaces intellect in one version, doubtless correctly.

[7] iv. 26.

[8] So in JB. i. 269, where Prāṇa covers smell (as in ÇB. x. 5. 2. 15 ; BAU. i. 3. 3 ; CU. i. 2. 2 ; AU. i. 3. 4 ; KU. i. 7 ; ii. 5, &c.), and beside ear, eye, smell, and tongue we find mind which discriminates *suhārdasa* and *durhārdasa*, that pleases and displeases the heart. The distinction of functions of mind into sense-perception and the functions of heart and mind (Barua, *Prebuddh. Ind. Phil.*, p. 178) attributed to Yājñavalkya and Mahidāsa is clearly not found either in the BAU. or AA. As in JB., *l. c.*, mind and heart are related as activity and organ in Buddhism ; Rhys Davids, *Buddhist Manual of Psychological Ethics*[2], pp. lxxxvi f. ; Keith, *Buddhist Philosophy*, pp. 87, 196.

the skin and contacts (*saṁsparça*); the hands and actions; the belly and hunger; the penis and joys; and the feet and roads. These ten are for man either heavens or hells, according to their operation.

Beyond these parallelisms the relation of sense and object is left undetermined. The use of the expressions Graha and Atigraha might be held to suggest the view that sense seeks out its object and masters it, and the same doctrine may be found in the Aitareya [1] and Kauṣītaki Upaniṣads.[2] In the Kaṭha Upaniṣad [3] we find that the objects are placed above the senses, which might be the sense of the first element in Atigraha, but also that the senses are the steeds and the objects their field of action. A more penetrating analysis is to be found in another passage of the Kauṣītaki Upaniṣad,[4] where a set of ten senses [5] and their objects is drawn up, similar to that above cited. In it the objects are described as the external existential elements, Bhūtamātrā, correlated to the senses. The process of knowledge is then described by the metaphor of one mounting the object by means of intellect, Prajñā—which for the Kauṣītaki is the *prius* from which both senses and objects are derived—and thus attaining it. The senses are declared in similar detail to be unconscious without the presence of intelligence; the rule is applied even to mind, which here stands in the place of an organ and has as its object thoughts, what is to be understood, and desires. The passage, however, is characteristic of the somewhat complex and late character of the Upaniṣad, for the reason given why the other senses are unable to act without intellect is the fact that mind, in the absence of intellect, is elsewhere. Stress is laid on the necessary connexion of existential elements and intellect-elements, Prajñāmātrā; if there were no existential elements, there would be no intellect-elements and *vice versa*, and without the co-operation of both, no appearance (*rūpa*) whatever would be brought about, the term appearance doubtless standing here as an example of visual cognition and applying to all the other forms of cognition enumerated. At the same time insistence is laid on the fact that there is no ultimate diversity; as the felly rests on the spokes, and the spokes in the hub, so the existential elements rest on the intellect elements, and they again are fixed in Prāṇa, which is identified by the Upaniṣad with the intellect-self, Prajñātman.[6]

This doctrine obviously is more metaphysical than psychological in interest, and goes a very little way to solve the question of the nature of perception or sensation. This is further borne out by the failure to make clear what is meant by senses as opposed to objects; later we find in the Sāṁkhya [7] a

[1] i. 3.
[2] iii. 4.
[3] iii. 10 and 4.
[4] iii. 5 ff.
[5] Viz. speech and names; breath (smell) and odours; eye and forms; ear and sounds; tongue and tastes; hands and actions; body and pleasure and pain; organ of generation and bliss, &c.; feet and movements; mind and thoughts, &c.
[6] Deussen (*Sechzig Upanishad's*², p. 42) declares that the two are the expression of will, as unconscious and conscious (citing his *Elemente der Metaphysik*, Pt. II, chap. iv).
[7] But only in the late Sāṁkhya Sūtra, ii. 23; cf. Vijñānabhikṣu on i. 62 and v.

distinct recognition of the difference between function and the material organ, the faculty of hearing, for example, and the gross ear, but such a distinction is nowhere hinted at in the Upaniṣads, and it is uncertain how the matter was regarded in them. In the later texts we find two different theories represented: on the one hand, in the Sāṁkhya philosophy [1] there is a consistent and harmonious materialism of process which, however, is made conscious only by the intervention of the Puruṣa, which is the equivalent in that system of the Ātman of the Vedānta. On the other hand, in the Vedānta, as interpreted by Gauḍapāda,[2] stress is laid on the fact that ultimately the visions of a dream and those of our waking state cannot be absolutely distinguished: if the dream apparitions are truly produced by the activity of the Ātman, so in the case of waking states the objects are equally produced by the Ātman: the thing and its representation condition each other: each separately has no existence: they exist only in the Ātman, a position which, though differentiated by Çañkara from the idealism of the Buddhist Vijñānavāda, tends indefinitely to merge into it. As against these clear theories, which recognize the problem of ideal and real or even material factors in knowledge and supply their varying solutions, we have in Buddhist texts [3] of the earlier period a theory of contact which in the Milindapañha [4] is frankly materialist and was doubtless so *ab initio*, but which at any rate seems not to have appreciated the real question involved. It is to this confused species of thought that we must in the main turn in considering the views of the Upaniṣads: the haziness of their ideas is shown conclusively by the fact that often, as later in Buddhism, organ and function seem hardly consciously to be separated in their conception of the activities of sense. Neither realism nor idealism can be said to be yet clearly held. If, as we have seen, in the Kauṣītaki Upaniṣad [5] we find all existential elements, &c., referred to and made dependent on consciousness, i. e. apparently a subjective idealism, yet in the Mādhyandina recension of the Bṛhadāraṇyaka Upaniṣad [6] we expressly hear of the Ātman that after death it is not possessed of empirical consciousness, because it is not in contact with Mātrā, which is most naturally interpreted as a realist or materialist conception, somewhat like that of the Sāṁkhya, such consciousness arising from the contact of the mind and matter, but the term Mātrā may have a wider sense of all empirical existence. Similarly there is abundant evidence of a naïve realism, which places side by side the facts of the macrocosm and the microcosm without suggestion that there is any but a real relation. The parallelism

104; Garbe, *Sâṃkhya-Philosophie*², p. 320.

[1] Oltramare, *L'histoire des idées théosophiques*, i. 271 ff.

[2] Māṇḍūkya Kārikā, ii. 1–18; iv. 67; cf. AU. i. 3. 12.

[3] C. Rhys Davids, *Buddhist Psychology*, pp. 61 ff.; the account is speculative and the conjecture (p. 60) as to the significance of BAU. iii. 9. 20 purely fanciful. See Keith, *Buddhist Philosophy*, pp. 88 ff.

[4] p. 60.

[5] iii. 8.

[6] iv. 5. 14 (Kāṇva) omits the statement; Deussen, *Sechzig Upanishad's*², p. 485, n. 1. Cf. iv. 3. 9; in dream sleep the soul is in contact with matter, Mātrā.

of the cosmic order (*adhidaivata*) with the disposition of man (*adhyātma*) is constant and wearisome; the space within the heart is parallel to cosmic space;[1] the breath of man to the wind,[2] the speech to fire, the eye to the sun, the ear to the moon, the mind to the lightning;[3] there are five cosmic spaces, five gods of nature, five classes of beings, and correspondingly we have five vital airs, five senses, five parts of the body;[4] to name, form, and action in the world correspond speech, sight, and man in the individual;[5] there is Dharma, law, and truth for the world and for the man, and the macrocosm and the microcosm are interrelated in an indissoluble union of reciprocal service and support.[6] The general attitude of the Upaniṣads must, therefore, be described as realistic, and, accordingly, not incompatible with a rejection of the subjective idealism of the Vijñānavādins. Here and there this interpretation suggests itself with special force, as when it is expressly made clear that the Ātman is the real active force in seeing, in smelling, in speaking, in hearing, in thinking, and the senses are but means,[7] or again the Ātman is pictured like the ocean as the abode of all the sense activities.[8] From the Sāṁkhya view the Upaniṣads are distinguished in an important respect, the frank recognition accorded by them of the activity of the Ātman,[9] while in the Sāṁkhya view the Puruṣa has really no activity, though paradoxically all consciousness is made to depend on the imaginary connexion of the Puruṣa with Prakṛti.

There is, naturally enough, no trace in the Upaniṣads of any clear appreciation of the distinction between mere sensation and ideas such as Dignāga made distinct in his doctrine of sensation as without operation of abstract thought (*kalpanāpoḍha*) as opposed to definite cognition (*savikalpaka*),[10] though, in a sense, this distinction might be held to be latent in the contrast noted above of the senses and the mind as sources of knowledge. This fact renders it most improbable, *a priori*, that[11] 'from the very beginning Buddhism had established this difference: *vijñāna* and its synonyms, *citta, manaḥ*, represent pure sensation, the same as the *kalpanāpoḍha pratyakṣa* of Dignāga, and *sanjñā* corresponds to definite ideas'. The realization of the possibility

1 CU. i. 8. 3.
2 CU. iv. 3. 1.
3 KU. ii. 12 ff.
4 TU. i. 7.
5 BAU. i. 6.
6 BAU. ii. 5.
7 CU. viii. 12. 4.
8 BAU. ii. 4. 11.
9 e.g. BAU. iii. 7 and *passim*. The Vaiçeṣika school accepts the real activity of the self. See also above, § 6; Keith, *Indian Logic and Atomism*, pp. 239 ff.
10 Keith, *Indian Logic and Atomism*, pp. 70 ff.
11 Stcherbatsky, *The Central Conception of Buddhism*, p. 19 (cf. p. 105). Neglect of history and philology has led the same scholar into the inaccurate view (p. 48) that Duḥkha means unrest among the elements (*dharmas*) which Buddhism alone admits to be real; Duḥkha clearly expresses the result of the instability of existence, not the instability. Both popularly and theoretically *cakṣur duḥkham* means that vision is sorrow, not that vision is unrest. The translation of *ārya-satya* as 'Āryan facts' adopted (*ibid.* p. 48, n. 3) is philologically objectionable, because we have not the slightest ground for belief that in the time when the phrase arose Ārya had any ethnic connotation at all.

thus of treating Vijñāna in the scheme of the five Skandhas must have been slow; it is emphatically not reached by the Pāli texts of the Canon,[1] and, like all refined conceptions, can be attributed to early Buddhism only at the expense of historical truth.

Naturally it might be expected that from an examination of the relation of the Ātman to the questions of time and space some light would be cast on the aspect in which the Ātman was viewed. But unfortunately the account of time in the Upaniṣads is quite valueless from the point of view of philosophy: in the Atharvaveda we have Kāla set forth as the highest principle of the universe, and the waters and even Prajāpati are derived from it.[2] In the Upaniṣads we have little more than this: an affectedly obscure passage in the later part of the Maitrāyaṇīya Upaniṣad [3] exalts time as being the Brahman, the highest principle, the source of all that is; the Çvetāçvatara [4] mentions time, nature, necessity, accident, material, and spirit as various rival theories of being, but declares time as past, present, and future to be inferior to the Brahman; and the Bṛhadāraṇyaka Upaniṣad [5] derives time from the Brahman, and declares it to be lord of the past and the future. In the view of Çaṅkara,[6] while time is absolutely non-existent in the true sense of existence, since all but the one is illusion, time, space and causality are in themselves on the standpoint of the lower knowledge truly real; but it is perfectly clear that in the case of the Upaniṣads the nature of time has not received any real investigation.

A more favourable view of the achievement of early Indian philosophy is taken by F. Otto Schrader,[7] who contends that the distinction between the ordinary or empiric and a higher or transcendental time can be traced back to the Kāla hymns of the Atharvaveda and is recognizable in the epic in such phrases [8] as 'Time leads me in time'. With this distinction he connects the declaration of the Maitrāyaṇīya Upaniṣad regarding the time that has parts, and is later than the sun and the stars, and the non-time which is without parts, and is earlier, and the distinction later made between time which cooks, or matures, all beings and him in whom time is matured. Later doubtless we do find developed the doctrine that the changing time which we observe in daily life is only time as an effect (*kāryakāla*), the cause of which is a time without sections (*akhaṇḍakāla*) and unchanging, and that there must be a sphere or

[1] Cf. C. Rhys Davids, *Buddhist Psychology*, pp. 52 ff.; Keith, *Buddhist Philosophy*, pp. 84 ff.; Oltramare, *L'histoire des idées théosophiques*, ii. 161 ff.

[2] xix. 53, 54. For epic views, cf. Barua, *Prebuddh. Ind. Phil.*, pp. 198 ff.

[3] vi. 14–16 where time begins with the sun, a piece of shallow mysticism. Before that is impartite (as in ÇU.) non-time.

[4] vi. 5, 6; i. 2.

[5] iii. 8. 9; iv. 4. 15, 16.

[6] Cf. Frazer, *Indian Thought, Past and Present*, pp. 97, 98.

[7] *Ueber den Stand der indischen Philosophie zur Zeit Mahāvīras und Buddhas*, pp. 17–30; *Introduction to the Pāñcarātra*, pp. 65 f. Oldenberg (*Weltanschauung der Brāhmaṇatexte*, p. 40) recognizes that in the AV. Kāla *may* merely mean 'the right moment'.

[8] Mahābhārata, xii. 227. 29. The phrase seems to be incapable of bearing any serious meaning.

condition which is totally unaffected by time, though time exist in it as an instrument. But there seems no real reason why we should ascribe any of these developed conceptions to the Upaniṣad period.[1]

The same remark applies even more strongly to space, the conception of which can hardly be said to be fully apprehended in the Upaniṣads. The term Ākāça, which is rendered 'ether' in accordance with the established usage, denotes in the opinion of Böhtlingk [2] the empty space, the elements Vāyu and Ākāça, representing wind and atmosphere, corresponding to the Greek ἀήρ, there being no idea to correspond with the ether of the Greek view. The Ākāça was conceived, in his view, as empty space, the atmosphere as opposed to the wind not being regarded as corporeal. Whether this view is correct cannot be determined with certainty from the evidence: it can be made compatible with whatever is said regarding Ākāça, but on the other hand it is not clear that this conception is always adequate. The term Ākāça first appears in the Brāhmaṇa style, and denotes room or space through which one can pass or into which one can thrust a finger.[3] Further, the space between the sky and the earth when they separated is the Antarikṣa or atmosphere,[4] and, in contrast to the wind, Vāyu, which as an element is normally rendered air, at the cost of some confusion of idea, the atmosphere is regarded as something empty, being compared in the Taittirīya Saṁhitā [5] to not-being. On the other hand, just as not-being is in a sense something concrete, the Ākāça is more than mere space. Man, the Kauṣītaki [6] tells us, is born from the Ākāça as from a womb; when fire heats the Ākāça, then rain falls, in the view of the Chāndogya; [7] the Taittirīya [8] makes the Ākāça born from the self, and from the Ākāça the wind is born. Yet in it are the sun and the moon, lightning, stars and fire; by means of it one calls, hears and answers; in it a man is born, and has joy; in it he meets a woman.[9] Thus the Ākāça approaches the sense of space, though a material space, but it seems that it does not denote space in the most general sense, but rather the space between the sky and the earth, which is around us.[10] The idea is evidently a considerable advance on the mythological presentation of the quarters as divinities, which tends here and there to pass over into an attempt to express space as opposed to time, symbolized by the seasons.[11] The combination of the terms, Diç and Ākāça, appears in the Maitrāyaṇīya Upaniṣad,[12] which describes Ākāça as a lotus flower whose leaves are the four quarters and the four intermediate quarters or cardinal points. We

[1] For later views on time, see Keith, *Buddhist Philosophy*, pp. 163–8, 239; *Indian Logic and Atomism*, pp. 232 ff.; *Karma-Mīmāṁsā*, pp. 53 ff.; *Sāṁkhya System*², pp. 57, 61, 99. For an unsuccessful modern attempt to restate the problem of space and time, see Alexander, *Space, Time and Deity*.

[2] BSGW. 1900, pp. 149–51. Cf. Garbe, *Sâṃkhya-Philosophie*³, pp. 268 f.

[3] AB. iii. 42. 1; ÇB. iii. 3. 2. 19; in the body, Garbha Up. 1 (cf. AA. ii. 3. 3); Majjh. Nik. iii. 242.

[4] ÇB. vii. 1. 2. 23; xiv. 7. 1. 19.

[5] v. 4. 6. 4.

[6] i. 6.

[7] vii. 11.

[8] ii. 1.

[9] CU. vii. 12; Kena 25.

[10] Oldenberg, *Weltanschauung der Brāhmaṇatexte*, pp. 38 f.

[11] ÇB. x. 2. 6. 2 f.

[12] vi. 2.

have, however, in the fact that ether is treated regularly as one of the five elements a warning against regarding it as essentially distinct in the view of the Upaniṣads from the other more obvious material elements.[1] Yet it must be noted that in Buddhism no serious advance was made in attempting to understand the nature of space; it was for some unintelligible reason excluded from non-derived Rūpa,[2] and, when the Andhakas claimed that the room between objects was perceptible, this view was rejected, a defect which has been traced to the failure of Buddhism to investigate the true function of mind.[3]

The position with regard to causality is the same. In the Sāṁkhya system and in the Buddhist the category of causality is regarded as truly existing, and the Sāṁkhya quite seriously applies the doctrine of causality as enabling it to determine the nature of its final principles: the things of empirical life are referred ultimately to one ground in nature, Prakṛti, while again the unfolding of nature is essentially relative to some principle for whose advantage it takes place, which is the Puruṣa. In the Upaniṣads a theory of causality is not to be found, and the early texts have not the term, Kāraṇa; nor is this remarkable: in effect the Brahman is essentially above all cause: when the categories of place, time, substance, and cause disappear, then the Brahman remains over, as it is said in a very late text.[4] The Chāndogya Upaniṣad [5] uses the idea of root and shoot to convey the idea of derivation.

Imperfect, however, as are the views of the Upaniṣads on these points, the defects of their theories must not be exaggerated. The amount of progress made in developing speculation on these questions for many centuries after was very slight, as can be seen from even a brief glance at the Buddhist theory of sense as developed in the Pāli Nikāyas. In that theory the chief difference is unquestionably the effort to do without a self at all, which was clearly one aspect of the Buddhist faith, though by no means the only aspect and certainly in the long run not the most important. But apart from the *odium theologicum* [6] it is impossible to grant this attempt any real validity at all: [7] it would have been easy to show that the conception of the Ātman attained by the Brahmans was inadequate, but it was merely a retrogression to solve the problem by ignoring its existence: there is nothing in the Nikāyas to suggest the most moderate competence in treating of the matter, the whole Buddhist position

[1] So also the Ākāça is the body of the Ātman like fire, wind, moon, and stars, BAU. iii. 7. 12; cf. iv. 4. 5.

[2] C. Rhys Davids, *Buddhist Manual of Psychological Ethics*[2], pp. liv, lxvi.

[3] *Buddhist Psychology* (1924), pp. 274 ff. See also Keith, *Buddhist Philosophy*, pp. 94 f., 160, 168 f., 185 f.; *Indian Logic and Atomism*, pp. 235 ff.; *Karma-Mīmāṁsā*, pp. 53 ff.; *Sāṁkhya System*[2], pp. 43, 99.

[4] Sarvasāropaniṣad.

[5] vi. 8. 4, 6.

[6] Cf. Rhys Davids, *Buddhist India*, pp. 251 ff.

[7] It may be urged that the view of the Buddhists has an analogy—imperfect indeed—in modern psychology (Walleser, *Das Problem des Ich*, p. 74). But this proves the essential point that modern psychology is, as developed, an empirical science and therefore abstracts from its data by ignoring the transcendental aspect of the 'I' element. When as in Buddhism this aspect is absolutely denied, a process legitimate in science is introduced with fatal results into philosophy.

being rendered easy by the illegitimate assumption, whenever necessary, of the subject which is denied. It is an elementary fact that a sensation is nothing if not an experience for an individual being, and, while for a definite scientific purpose we are doubtless free, if we will, to ignore the subjective factor, if we carry this ignoring into the field of philosophy, we deal with a false abstraction ; nor is it less false because it has appealed to the enthusiastic, but confused mind of William James.[1] The Upaniṣads frankly do not face the question of memory, but leave it a possibility. But even in the Abhidhamma the problem of reinstatement and the conditions of reinstatement are not raised as matters calling for definition.[2] If even we go to a far later period, a formula [3] like 'the upspringing of potential *cittas*, not empty and mutually disconnected, but each fraught with the informing *satti* of this or that among former *citta continua*', appears both clumsy and question-begging as a substitute for the conception of a real unity in multiplicity, since a *citta continuum* is clearly impossible without such a unity.

Nor is any progress made in the analysis of consciousness. It is true [4] that in place of the occasional remarks of the Upaniṣads we find in the Buddhist texts interminable repetitions of the same facts regarding all the senses which are, therefore, more definitely recognized than in some portions of the Upaniṣads, but any real progress in defining sense perception remains to be pointed out. On the contrary, we have the old view which makes no clear distinction if any at all between the organ and the sensation, and as late as the Milindapañha, as we have seen, sensation is expressed in terms of mere material contact. The position of mind, Mano, remains precisely what it was in the Upaniṣads : it is wholly erroneous [5] to compare it with the *sensus communis* of Aristotle, whose two special functions,[6] that of self-consciousness and of consciousness of the common sensibles, by no means correspond with those of Mano, which is rather in origin a power without which the senses would in effect not perceive at all, and which in a more effective psychology might have been developed into the psychical representative of sensation conveyed through the physiological apparatus.[7] Even the position of touch as in some sense the most fundamental of the senses which is claimed for the Dhammasaṁgaṇi can hardly be accepted as in any way a really scientific theory, as it is only enunciated in company with an extraordinarily unintelligible doctrine of the position of what is somewhat hypothetically interpreted as the cohesive element.[8] The primitive nature of the process of consciousness as conceived in the Nikāyas is obvious from the stereotyped account of the origin of

[1] In the various developments of his theory of pragmatism.

[2] C. Rhys Davids, *Buddhist Psychology*, p. 142 ; cf. pp. 236 ff., and for a criticism of the Bergsonian view there adopted, B. Edgell, *Theories of Memory*, pp. 114 ff.

[3] *Ibid.* p. 198.

[4] *Ibid.* p. 63.

[5] *Ibid.* p. 68.

[6] *De An.* ii. 6 ; iii. 1, 2 ; *de Somno* 2 ; *de Mem.* 1.

[7] Cf. the hint in BAU. i. 5. 3 ; Mahābhārata, xiv. 22. 16.

[8] Contrast C. Rhys Davids, *op. cit.*, pp. 163–75, with *Buddhist Manual of Psychological Ethics*², pp. lxi ff.

knowledge.[1] Through the eye and visible form arises visual consciousness: the collision of the two factors is contact: conditioned by contact arises feeling: what one feels one perceives: what one perceives one thinks about: what one thinks about one is obsessed withal. The crudeness and valuelessness of the theory is obvious at once from the very fact that it is wholly impossible to understand what precise sense was attributed to the several terms, for the explanations of the scholiast are in all likelihood nothing but the interpretations of later generations of thinkers, who had to do their best to make the most out of the tradition of the text. The Buddhists too remain with the Upaniṣads on the basis of the dwelling of the soul or its equivalent in the heart,[2] which is thus brought into the theory of sensation. What is indeed of interest is not the development of doctrine in the Nikāyas, which give us only a few changes in terminology such as the metaphor of the doors of the senses,[3] but the extraordinary persistence in Buddhism of the psychology of the Upaniṣads.

In addition to the mind and the sense organs, the soul possesses the breaths or vital airs. Prāṇa, originally 'breath', then used often as a name for the absolute, is in the Upaniṣads a constant expression for the whole sum of the organs of sense, and at the same time a special one breath, beside eye, ear, mind, and speech. It, however, in the growing development of the doctrine of mind and the organs of sense is gradually reduced to minor importance, and becomes concerned not with the intellectual aspect of the soul, but with the principle of life as opposed to intellect. The single Prāṇa in this aspect is divided into five, which, however, are also sometimes given as two,[4] Prāṇa and Apāna, as three,[5] these with Vyāna, or four,[6] these with Udāna. The Jaiminīya Upaniṣad Brāhmaṇa gives Prāṇa, Apāna, Vyāna, Samāna, Avāna, and Udāna; or seven in the head, or nine, including two below, and a tenth in the navel.[7] The precise sense of these terms has been much disputed, but it is not open to serious doubt that alone Prāṇa or Apāna may mean breath simply, whether in or out, and therefore Prāṇa may mean smell.[8] In contrast, how-

[1] Majjhima Nikāya, i. 111. It is, however, to be noted that in the Paṭiccasamuppāda series is found the order: consciousness, name and form, the six spheres, contact, feeling, desire, &c. The hopeless contradiction of view is disposed of in the *Manual* (ed. 2) in the words (p. lxxxii), 'This mysterious old rune must not further complicate our problem', and in the *Psychology* it is passed over with due contempt. But to establish doctrines by ignoring the most important part of the evidence does not further research. See also Keith, *Buddhist Philosophy*, pp. 196 ff.

[2] *Buddhist Manual of Psychological Ethics*², p. lxxxvi; Wallesser, *Die philosophische Grundlage des älteren Buddhismus*, p. 114; S. Z. Aung, *Compendium of Philosophy*, pp. 277 ff.

[3] But the CU. iii. 13. 1 has *suṣayaḥ* for the entrances into the heart of eye, ear, speech, mind, and air.

[4] KU. v. 3.

[5] BAU. iii. 1. 10.

[6] BAU. iii. 4. 1.

[7] JUB. ii. 5.

[8] Ewing, JAOS. xxii. 249–308, and *The Hindu Conception of the Functions of Breath*; Oertel, JAOS. xvi. 236; Macdonell and Keith, *Vedic Index*, ii. 48; Keith, *Aitareya Āraṇyaka*, p. 217, n. 4; Caland, ZDMG. lv. 261 ff.; lvi. 556 ff.; Oldenberg, *Weltanschauung der*

ever, they are on the one hand expiration, on the other inspiration. Apāna, however, has the definite sense of the downward wind, which presides over evacuation in not a few passages; it also often denotes smell. Vyāna is the bond of union of the two, that is either the power which maintains life when neither expiration nor inspiration takes place, or the breath connecting the upper and the lower breaths. Samāna is not clearly defined: it is said to connect expiration and inspiration, which seems needless; or to assimilate food. Udāna conducts the soul from the body on death, or leads in deep sleep to the Brahman.

But, besides these psychical and physiological elements, in the later view, the soul has, as individual, certain other permanent entities, the elements, and a mind-disposition attached to it. It is clearly [1] in one place regarded at death as being connected with earth, water, wind, ether, and fire and its opposite, and also with desire and its opposite, anger and its opposite, and justice and its opposite, as well as with the organs. The same idea seems in metaphorical form to be found in the view [2] that for rebirth the waters are five times offered in sacrifice as faith, the Soma, rain, food, and seed to become a man. The term Liñga found in a verse added here is apparently used technically to denote the entity which transmigrates as early as the Kaṭha [3] at least, and in the Maitrāyaṇīya Upaniṣad [4] it has its full technical sense. Much more often, however, we hear of the moral qualities and power of remembrance of the self which go on the journey of transmigration.

Of the gross body we learn that the seat of the breaths, of the mind, and even of the organs of sense is really in the heart, where in sleep the organs remain and where in death they gather: nay, the heart is even identified with the Brahman, and is essentially its home: the name *hṛdayam* is derived from *hṛdy ayam*, 'he here in the heart'.[5] In the golden lotus of the heart is the ether in which heaven and earth, sun, moon, and stars are enclosed, into which

Brāhmaṇatexte, pp. 64 ff. The later view of Sadānanda's Vedāntasāra, §§ 94–8, is preluded by Maitr. ii. 6.

[1] BAU. iv. 4. 5.

[2] CU. v. 3–10; BAU. vi. 2. 1–16. These passages (Deussen, *Phil. of Up.*, pp. 280–2) are inadequate to show that the corporeal element of the Liñga was as yet clearly recognized. It is so first in Maitr. vi. 10; here we, however, must recognize the full force of the Sāṁkhya, to which system its presence in the Vedānta may be due (cf. Çañkara on Brahma Sūtra, iii. 3. 1; Deussen, *System des Vedānta*, p. 399).

[3] vi. 8; ÇU. vi. 9.

[4] vi. 10; Deussen, *Sechzig Upanishad's*², p. 337.

[5] CU. viii. 3. 3. Cf. BAU. iv. 4. 22; v. 6; KU. ii. 20, &c. In BAU. iii. 9. 20 the heart knows colours, doubtless through the mind which is seated there. This is the only possible significance of the contrast between it and the eye which depends on forms while they depend on the heart; there is no distinction between primary and secondary qualities in question. From the connexion of mind with the heart is derived the Theravādin (BSOS. iii. 353) view which places a *hadaya-vatthu* as the organ of mind, evidently the older Buddhist view as opposed to the refinement of the Sarvāstivādin (contrast Stcherbatsky, *The Central Conception of Buddhism*, pp. 17 f.). Heart is placed side by side with mind as concerned with knowledge in BAU. ii. 4. 11; iv. 5. 12, i.e. it is the place of intellect.

the soul enters in sleep, and in which the immortal golden Puruṣa resides.[1] It is the cavity in which the Brahman is concealed. Round the heart are the veins 72,000 in number,[2] and these, by another turn of thought, are conceived as of five colours, uniting with the rays of the sun similarly coloured and thus connecting the sun and the heart. In deep sleep the soul glides into the veins and through them it becomes one with the heart. At death the soul is conceived as passing out by the veins, and the rays of the sun, which the wise find open to them, while the entrance is closed to the ignorant.[3] By yet another turn of thought [4] the conception is reached that only one vein leads to the sun out of 101, the vein in question leading to the head, presumably in connexion with the fact that there is the suture, the Brahmarandhra,[5] through which in the process of creation the Brahman is supposed to enter the body as spirit. Later accounts such as that of the Praçna [6] merge the two versions of 72,000 and 101 veins into one, the 101 veins having each 100 branches, each of which has 72,000 sub-branches, in all 727,210,201.

The body itself is derived from the three elements, recognized in the Chāndogya Upaniṣad [7] by the rule that the dense parts become the coarse (faeces, urine, bone), the medium the medium (flesh, blood, marrow), constituents of the body, and the finest the mind, breath, and speech, corresponding to food or earth, water, and heat. The soul is nourished by the blood massed in the heart, thus enjoying purer (*pravivikta*) food than the gross body.[8] The production of the body is traced to the seed of the father,[9] and different views of the nature of the process of generation can be traced ; in the simplest form it is said that the seed is the self of the father, which enters the woman and becomes part of herself; [10] but it is also said, in more exact accordance [11] with the doctrine of the transmigration of souls, that the seed is merely a stage on the course of the rebirth of the soul, which in the moon has exhausted its good works : it comes down through the ether, the wind, smoke, rain, plants, seed, and the mother's womb, in each of which it of course has merely a temporary habitation : from yet another point of view [12] the cause of procreation is the desire for reunion of the two halves of the same being originally united, but divided as male and female by Prajāpati. But the primitive view of the Upaniṣads is clear that the production of offspring is a religious duty, which was inculcated on the student at the close of the studentship : a chapter on how to secure certain qualities in the child is incorporated in the Bṛhadāraṇyaka Upaniṣad[13] probably for this very reason. On the other hand there

[1] CU. viii. 1. 3.
[2] BAU. ii. 1. 19 ; cf. iv. 2. 3 ; 3. 20.
[3] CU. viii. 6. 1 ; cf. BAU. iv. 4. 8, 9 ; Muṇḍ. i. 2. 11.
[4] CU. viii. 6. 6 ; KU. vi. 6.
[5] AU. i. 3. 12.
[6] iii. 6 ; Maitr. vi. 30.
[7] vi. 5. The Garbha Upaniṣad has the more usual five (cf. BAU. iv. 4. 5). Cf. Keith, *Sāṁkhya System*², p. 110.
[8] BAU. iv. 2. 3 ; cf. Māṇḍ. 3, 4, misunderstood in Vedāntasāra, § 120.
[9] BAU. iii. 9. 22 ; vi. 1. 6 ; 4. 1, &c.
[10] AU. ii. 2, 3.
[11] CU. v. 10. 5, 6 ; BAU. vi. 2. 16 ; Kauṣ. i. 2 ; Muṇḍ. ii. 1. 5.
[12] BAU. i. 4. 3, 4.
[13] BAU. vi. 4 ; TU. i. 9.

is clear proof of the gradual advance of the spirit of asceticism, in complete harmony with the fact that the knowledge of the Ātman shows that all desires for children to continue the race, to discharge the debt to the Fathers, to expiate the faults of their parents in life, are idle and foolish. The Brahmans, who have known the self, are twice declared in the Bṛhadāraṇyaka Upaniṣad [1] to have held aloof from the desire of children, 'What need have we of off-spring, whose soul is the universe ?' By a bizarre conception, found here only in the late Garbha Upaniṣad, the embryo in the ninth month is conceived as remembering all its previous births and its good and evil deeds, a remembrance which is taken from it by the pangs of birth.[2]

In addition to creatures born alive, other creatures exist born from a germ or shoot (*udbhid*), born from eggs, and born from moisture like insects and so forth. These ideas which are found only in two passages in the Upaniṣads [3] are decisive for later philosophy, but their connexion with the theories of the Upaniṣads is nowhere indicated.

§ 9. *The Four States of the Soul*

The soul, despite its close connexion with the body, which we have traced in detail, is also enabled by its nature to approach closely the absolute. The spirit is most remote from the absolute in its normal waking activities : in that case the senses and the mind are at work, but when there is sleep the senses and the mind are merged in the breath. A further distinction is then made between the condition of the soul in the sleep of dreams, and in deep dreamless sleep, in which the soul enters into the purest light, and then as a consequence of its own nature emerges again from it. These three stages alone are found in the oldest Upaniṣads, and it is not till the latest Upaniṣads that a fourth is added in accordance with the constant tendency further to subdivide.

The philosophical importance of the doctrine [4] lies in the effect which the investigation of the stages of the soul must have had on the conception of the soul itself. The early identification of the soul with Prāṇa as breath must have been suggested by the fact of the permanence of the breath despite the cessation in sleep of the activities of the mind ; death overcomes the voice, the eye, the ear, but while these are sunk in sleep the breath perishes not.[5] It is a further step, but one intelligible enough, to the conclusion [6] that, though the body perishes in death, yet the breath remains, for the breath is invisible and there is, therefore, no ground to assume that the falling to pieces of the body affects its being. We attain thus the conception of the self as

[1] iii. 5. 1 ; iv. 6. 22.

[2] Windisch, *Buddha's Geburt*, p. 90.

[3] AU. iii. 3 ; CU. vi. 3. 1 ; cf. Brahma Sūtra, iii. 1. 21 ; Keith, *Aitareya Āraṇyaka*, p. 235 ; Manu, i. 43 ff. ; Caraka, Çārīrasthāna, iii. 25 ; Windisch, *op. cit.*, p. 191 ; A. Guha, *Jīvātman in the Brahma-Sūtras*, chap. ii.

[4] B. Heimann, *Die Tiefschlafspekulation der alten Upaniṣaden* (1922).

[5] BAU. i. 5. 21.

[6] CU. vi. 11. 3.

something which does not perish, which, therefore, is without beginning and without end, and as the essential element in man we find all activities resolved ultimately into Prāṇa on their cessation. On a higher level of thought we have the concept Prajñā, intelligence, substituted for the breath, in recognition of the psychic side of man and of the fact that it is consciousness or intelligence which is aware of breath and of all man's life, and in it also all else is resolved. Advancing still further on the path of abstraction, we attain the concept of the Ātman as that which knows, without possessing any empiric object, suggested inevitably by the condition attained in deep dreamless sleep. The identity of such an Ātman with the Brahman is obviously an easy step, and this may well have been a factor in achieving the identification. Obviously also the tendency to attain the unity in question by means of artificial processes of mental suppression arises immediately from the desire to imitate artificially the condition achieved in deep sleep, but under natural conditions inevitably only for a limited period, and subject to the possibility of dreams.

In the waking state the man uses all his faculties and is confronted by a real world, but the waking state is in reality merely a dream condition, since it has not true reality, and the man who is awake is really furthest removed from the clear knowledge usually attached to the waking condition. Hence in the Aitareya Upaniṣad [1] we find three sleeps or dreams mentioned which may well be the three states, the first regarded as dreaming no less than the other two. In the case of a dream, however, the outer world is not there : [2] there are no carts, horses, roads, but he makes them for himself; there is no joy, happiness, nor desire, but he makes them for himself ; wells, pools, and streams also he fashions for himself. The spirit serves as light for itself in this condition. From another point of view [3] the primitive idea of the absence of the mind during sleep is recognized, and a warning given not lightly to waken the sleeper, lest he not easily find his way back to the body. These two views, the activity of the self in the body in sleep, and the journeying of the self from the body, are united in a third [4] which pictures the self as engaged in the process of wandering through his own body here and there. The vital spirits are then treated as being his subjects, who attend him in his movements, like a king, through the realm of his body. The nature of the dream consciousness is shown also by the Upaniṣads to be closely connected with the character of the consciousness which was enjoyed in the waking life, and which thus is the material (*mātrā*) on which the soul acts ; what a man feared might happen to him, to be slain, to be flayed, to be trampled on by an elephant, or plunged into a pit, all these ideas crowd in upon him.[5] In the Praçna [6] the whole

[1] i. 3. 12 ; cf. Keith, *Aitareya Āraṇyaka*, p. 230, n. 10.

[2] BAU. iv. 3. 9 ff.

[3] *Ibid.* 11–14. Cf. CU. viii. 12. 3.

[4] BAU. ii. 1. 18.

[5] BAU. iv. 3. 20 ; CU. viii. 10. 2. This is not a negation of the creative power of the soul in dream-sleep, for which cf. Walleser, *Der ältere Vedānta*, p. 39 ; Çañkara on Brahma Sūtra, p. 780, as against Çañkara and Dvivedagañga, followed by Max Müller, on BAU. iv. 3. 14.

[6] iv. 5.

process of dreaming is a review of what has been experienced in the waking state.

From the ordinary process of dreaming sleep a transition is made to deep sleep, when the soul advances more closely to the world to come, and from the mere consciousness of individual things, such as the concept of being a king or a god, becomes conscious of itself as the universe, in which case, however, there is no longer any possibility of contrast between subject and object, and ordinary consciousness is superseded by the union for the time being with the Prājña Ātman, the intelligent self, the absolute. In this condition, as a man in the embrace of his darling wife does not have any consciousness of outer or inner, so the spirit embraced by the self consisting of knowledge has no consciousness of outer and inner.[1] The spirit in this condition is without desire and free from all pain; it is unaffected by good, unaffected by evil, the father ceases to be father, the mother mother, the worlds worlds, the gods gods. There is no interruption of seeing, though the spirit sees not: we have in fact the condition of a pure objectless knowing subject, continuing in this condition. The soul now passes from the 72,000 veins in which it has moved during dream-sleep, and rests in the pericardium in supreme bliss, like a great king or Brahman. The Chāndogya [2] follows the same line of thought, but it lays stress on the entry of the self into the brilliance or heat, treats the soul as existing in the veins, which is possibly found also in the Bṛhadāraṇyaka, and, by a curious confusion of ideas which is already foreshadowed or perhaps rather later borrowed and interpolated in the Bṛhadāraṇyaka, the joys of free movement which belong merely to dreaming sleep are in one later passage ascribed to the deep sleep also. The Kauṣītaki [3] makes the deep sleep the union with breath, which in its scheme is identical with the intellectual self, which is the absolute.

In this condition of sleep without dreams it is clear that the older Upaniṣads find the highest bliss,[4] the complete union of the individual with the absolute,[5] which is all that can be attained by man. In the later Upaniṣads [6] there appears the effort to add a fourth condition, called by its numerical designation the Caturtha or more archaically Turīya. This state is that which is attained not in deep sleep, but in the waking condition by the effort of concentration of the mind which is Yoga. The two conditions of deep sleep and the fourth differ, not in point of their failing to recognize plurality, but in the fact that the Turīya knows no slumber: the Turīya is neither deep asleep nor dreaming:

[1] BAU. iv. 3. 19–33; cf. ii. 1. 19, and, of death, ii. 4. 12 f. Cf. Maitr. vi. 7, 35; the pure self is *nirmama*, ii. 7; *nirātman*, ii. 4; vi. 20, 21; cf. ÇU. i. 6; Tejobindu 3.

[2] vi. 8. 1; viii. 6. 3; 11. 1; 12. 3 (as in BAU. iv. 3. 15 as to movement) is different from viii. 3. 4, and is perhaps interpolated. At least it expresses a different ideal; cf. p. 570, n. 3.

[3] iii. 3; iv. 19, 20.

[4] BAU. iv. 3. 21 f.; CU. viii. 4. 1 f.; 3. 4; 6. 1 f.; 9. 1 f.; it is free from limitation and is bliss; vii. 23, 24.

[5] CU. vi. 8. 1; vii. 25. 1.

[6] See Gauḍapāda, Māṇḍūkya Kārikā, iii. 33 ff. The first three are now styled Vaiçvānara, Taijasa, and Prājña.

the dreamer has false knowledge, the sleeper has none. It is obviously impossible to make much of this refinement and still less of the four subdivisions of it which a later Upaniṣad, the Nṛsiṅhottara,[1] invents. Oltramare,[2] while recognizing the possibility that even in the period of the Upaniṣads there may have been felt the necessity of making some effort to supply an ideal which would not, like the established conception, find the only true reality in an entity [3] deprived of that consciousness which is in experience the most essential and real part of existence, admits that in this conception of the Māṇḍūkya Upaniṣad we have nothing more than a logical construction, even if in ultimate analysis the phenomena of ecstasy may have given a basis for the conception.

The Upaniṣads assume in these accounts of the states of the soul the distinction between the knowledge possessed in dreams and that which the soul enjoys in waking moments. But in what does this important distinction consist? The answer to this problem, which is much discussed in later philosophy, cannot be supplied effectively from the Upaniṣads themselves, which, as has been seen, still fall short of developing a theory of the nature of sensation and perception.

§ 10. *The Doctrine of Transmigration*

The origin of the doctrine of transmigration is one of the most difficult problems of Indian philosophy: its extraordinarily firm hold on the mind of part at least of India, which is shown by the fact that Buddhism rests on the doctrine as an essential presupposition, makes it natural to seek the view in the earliest period of Indian religion, and this desire to find metempsychosis in the beginnings of Indian belief takes two forms. On the one hand there have been seen direct references to metempsychosis in the Rigveda, and on the other there have been traced there ideas which explain the genesis of the conception.

The references to transmigration which have been seen in the Rigveda are all of the most improbable character: it is to ignore the nature of poetry to press the wish that there may be long life for man among the gods [4] into the view that it contemplates rebirth: the attempt to find references to it in two of the verses of the riddle hymn of Dīrghatamas [5] is bold, but not very plausible: the allusion,[6] in which Vasiṣṭha is made [7] to refer to his previous

[1] 2.

[2] *L'histoire des idées théosophiques*, i. 124 ff.

[3] It is clear that the self is always an entity, but in CU. viii. 11. 1 the state of deep sleep is treated as annihilation, and in lieu the self is given the attributes of motion free from the body sporting with women or friends (as illogically in BAU. iv. 3. 15). This clearly indicates an effort to give individuality and pleasure to the self in its highest form. The BAU. passage may be interpolated (Mādhyandina has it later, iv. 3. 33); see Deussen, *Sechzig Upanishad's*², p. 468, n. 2; CU. viii. 12. 3.

[4] RV. x. 14. 4; Windisch, *Buddha's Geburt*, p. 54; Boyer, JA. sér. 9, xviii. 451–99.

[5] RV. i. 164. 30, 38; Böhtlingk, BSGW. xlv. 88–92.

[6] RV. vii. 33.

[7] Geldner, *Ved. Stud.* ii. 142.

birth, is quite impossible, and the same criticism can be applied in every other case.[1] The effort to find such views is naturally not modern merely: the commentaries on the Upaniṣads themselves seek to trace the idea, and the fact that they can adduce nothing worthy of consideration is surely conclusive proof that there was nothing. In the Bṛhadāraṇyaka Upaniṣad [2] it is sought by Çaṅkara, without any good ground, and not in accord with the Upaniṣad, to show that Vāmadeva, the reputed author of a hymn [3] beginning, 'I was aforetime Manu, I the sun', refers to his former births, and in another passage of that text,[4] in the exposition of the doctrine of transmigration, a verse [5] celebrating the two ways of the Fathers and of the gods, on which everything meets which moves between father and mother, is pressed by the Upaniṣad itself into service, though the reference is merely to day and night. A third passage in the Aitareya Āraṇyaka,[6] which refers to a third birth after death, beside that from the father and by initiation, makes also use of a verse [7] of Vāmadeva, in which lying in the womb the speaker learned all the births of the gods, but it is not proved or even plausible that the Upaniṣad itself refers to transmigration at all: the third birth may most probably have been in the next world,[8] and in any case the quotation had nothing whatever to do with the subject.

The effort to find suggestions of the origin of transmigration in Vedic beliefs [9] is worthy of more consideration. The ideas that the birds are the forms of the Fathers, and that the Fathers creep about the roots of the plants, and the practice of using an insect or other animal, which alighted on a garment spread out with an invocation to the soul of the dead, when his bones cannot be found, to serve in place of his mortal relics, are points adduced by Oldenberg [10] as suggesting the groundwork on which the Indian belief developed. It is not necessary to brush [11] these ideas lightly aside, or even to point out that the evidence for them is late, and not of value as proof for the early Vedic religion. What is necessary is to point out that, while the ideas thus recorded are of some value as showing the presence in Indian religion of the belief of the incorporation of the souls of the dead now and then in animals or plants—of the latter there is even a hint in the Rigveda [12] itself—the importance

1 Keith, *Taittirīya Saṁhitā*, i. pp. cxxviii ff. RV. ix. 113 is not good evidence.

2 i. 4. 10.

3 RV. iv. 26. 1.

4 BAU. vi. 2. 2.

5 RV. x. 88. 15.

6 AA. ii. 5.

7 RV. iv. 27. 1; Çaṅkara on Brahma Sūtra, iii. 4. 51; Windisch, *Buddha's Geburt*, p. 62, n. 2.

8 This is strongly supported by ÇB. xi. 2. 1. 1 (Lévi, *La doctrine du sacrifice*, p. 107), though the other view is taken by Windisch (*Buddha's Geburt*, p. 62), who ignores the ÇB. passage. The language of the text, moreover (*itaḥ prayann eva punar jāyate*), and JUB. iii. 9 ff., seems conclusive against a second birth on earth.

9 German belief is dubious, Appian, *Hist.* i. 4. 3; Helm, *Altgerm. Rel.* i. 254 f.; for the Druids, see Caesar, *B. G.* vi. 14; below, Chap. 29.

10 *Rel. des Veda*², pp. 563, 581; cf. Bloomfield, *Rel. of Veda*, pp. 255 ff.

11 Deussen, *Phil. of Up.*, p. 316.

12 x. 16. 3. Other considerations which may have rendered easy the growth of the doctrine are the theory that the sacrifice carries the offerer to heaven and

of transmigration lies precisely in the fact that the doctrine is an ethical system, and that it has, therefore, not merely a value totally distinct from the mere belief suggested by the evidence above adduced, but is thereby referred for its real origin to something quite other than popular belief. That it should have been so fully accepted by the people in course of time was doubtless aided by such views as that mentioned: but no such view could create metempsychosis as a system of the marked character of the Indian view.

The Brāhmaṇas contain on the whole no acceptance of the doctrine of transmigration: the soul aims at the world of the Fathers as before: the mere fact [1] that as punishment for the cursing of a Brahman, the laying of violent hands on him, or the spilling of his blood, the wrong-doer is kept a hundred, a thousand years, as many years as the grains of dust moistened by his blood, from the world of the Fathers, shows that the view still prevailed that this world was the appointed place for the holy dead even as it is in the Rigveda. Nor in the main is that world distinct from heaven to which a man naturally goes but sometimes fails to reach, confused by the smoke of the fire which burned his body.[2] The conception of weighing the good and evil of a man in a balance and his following whichever is the greater,[3] and that of two fires which hold back the wicked from the way of the gods or of the Fathers,[4] do not carry us to any definite view other than that of the Rigveda, and the conception of men being discriminated as good or bad in the presence of Yama [5] is equally unimportant. But a new and important motive appears in the growing fear of death even in the world to come.

This fear seems, as we have seen, to have developed in accordance with the desire to distinguish the diverse degrees of good acquired by different modes of sacrifice; it was obviously necessary to admit that every sacrificer would receive reward by admission to the happiness of the world to come, but the Brahmans had to consider the claims of the richer of their patrons, and had to promise them more in the world to come than the poorer, who offered and gave less. Hence we find that the need of food in the next world may be severely limited, according to the mode of offering: it can be unnecessary for a spirit to feed oftener than once in fourteen days, in four, six, or twelve months, or even once only in a hundred years, or even never at all. Again it is said that sacrifice to the gods produces less than offering to the self.[6] Naciketas begs that he may be granted the privilege that his good deeds shall not decay,[7] while it is said that day and night wear out the good deeds in the

then back to earth until he dies, and that life descended from the sky as rain to produce fruits and nourish and generate life in turn; Oltramare, *L'histoire des idées théosophiques*, i. 97, 98. Cf. also Speyer, *Indische Theosophie*, pp. 90 ff. Aboriginal belief of passing of souls into plants, &c., is probable, and may explain the ready adoption of the view; cf. Oldenberg, *Die Lehre der Upanishaden*, pp. 27 ff.; Leumann, *Buddha und Mahāvīra*, p. 15.

1 TS. ii. 6. 10. 2.

2 TB. iii. 10. 11. 1.

3 ÇB. xi. 2. 7. 33.

4 ÇB. i. 9. 3. 2.

5 TA. vi. 5. 13.

6 ÇB. xi. 2. 6. 14.

7 TB. iii. 11. 8. 5.

next world of one who does not know a certain rite.[1] The fear thus forms itself that in place of the desired immortality in the next world there will be renewed death, and many rites [2] are said to save from it, the Agnihotra, the Viṣūvant, the Naciketas fire, the piling of the fire, the study of the Veda. There can be no doubt that the repeated death is in the next world, not in this: it is applied to the Fathers,[3] and from those who are born after death to immortality are distinguished those who are born to die again.[4] The idea of the death as being a birth in the next world is not at all rare, as in the passage of the Aitareya Upaniṣad above mentioned, and the conception that death might there be repeated is a very natural one. It remained only to transfer it to the present world and the effect of transmigration was reached. But though this step is taken in the Upaniṣads it is by no means universally to be found there: there is no clear reference in the Aitareya Āraṇyaka or Upaniṣad, and the Bṛhadāraṇyaka [5] has passages which quite clearly do not recognize it at all.

The earliest notice of the doctrine of transmigration preserved for us, apart from a few very dubious allusions in the Çatapatha Brāhmaṇa,[6] is to be traced in the Bṛhadāraṇyaka Upaniṣad in the section ascribed to Yājñavalkya. It is founded in an idea which is plainly expressed but merely as an incidental view in the Rigveda [7] that at death the eye of man goes to the sun, the breath to the wind, the speech to the fire, and the members are also dispersed. This conception which has no importance for the Rigveda is developed in the Çatapatha Brāhmaṇa [8] in one of the passages which approach the Upaniṣad character, and in the Bṛhadāraṇyaka,[9] after a long enumeration of the modes of disposal of the parts of man in this way, it is asked where the man then remains. On this Yājñavalkya takes the questioner Ārtabhāga apart and confers with him in secret, and what they conversed about was work, and what they commended that was work. In truth, it is added, a man becomes good by good works, evil by evil. In a subsequent passage [10] the matter is further explained by the doctrine that on death, like a caterpillar—or grass leech—proceeding from one leaf to another, the soul, having shaken off the body and freed itself from ignorance, presumably empirical life, makes a beginning on another body. As a goldsmith chisels out a newer and fairer form from a piece of carving, so the soul fashions for itself another newer, fairer form, whether it be of the Fathers, or the Gandharvas, or the gods, or Prajāpati, or Brahman, or other living beings; [11] just as man acts, just as he behaves, so will

[1] TB. iii. 10. 11. 2.

[2] ÇB. ii. 3. 3. 9; KB. xxv. 1; TB. iii. 11. 8. 6; ÇB. x. 1. 4. 14; xi. 5. 6. 9, &c.; Oltramare, *L'histoire des idées théosophiques*, i. 50 ff.

[3] ÇB. xii. 9. 3. 12.

[4] ÇB. x. 4. 3. 10.

[5] i. 4. 15; 5. 16; iii. 8. 10, &c.

[6] ÇB. i. 5. 3. 4.

[7] x. 16. 3.

[8] x. 3. 3. 8.

[9] iii. 2. 13.

[10] BAU. iv. 4. 2–6.

[11] Hence the doctrine of Karmadevas (BAU. iv. 3. 33), men who become gods by their deeds, and men Gandharvas (TU. ii. 8). An anticipation of Karman is faintly contained in the *iṣṭāpūrta* of the

he be born. He who does good will be born good, he who does evil will be born evil: he becomes holy by holy deeds, evil by evil. Hence is explained the view that man is composed of desire, in proportion to desire is his will, in proportion to his will he performs acts, and according to his acts does it happen to him. Or, as an appended verse has it, having attained the end of his deeds committed on earth, he returns from yonder world to the world of work.

That this doctrine does not teach the transmigration from one body to another is asserted by Schrader,[1] but this view can only be taken as a *tour de force*, even apart from the appended verse, which expressly makes the transmigration clear. It is also certain that, apart from the verse which is doubtful in sense,[2] it is a simple transmigration by reason of character or action. It is a change of the soul [3] from one body into another, and the instances cited are better bodies, as they are of better results from good action in the present life: the other beings who are mentioned are, therefore, to be understood of higher beings, in all likelihood, than man. It is only in the later Mādhyandina recension of this passage that the form of a man is inserted. Yājñavalkya, then, considered that transmigration was the fate of men, who had not the knowledge of the identity of the individual and the absolute, which ended the possibility of transmigration of any kind: exactly what sort of fate awaited the bad, he does not say, but clearly they would take on at best the forms of beings inferior to themselves, perhaps men of lower degree, animals, &c.

The appended verse is interpreted by Çañkara to refer to the fact that the soul is not merely rewarded by being transferred to another body, but before

Rigveda, which is an entity preceding its master to heaven; cf. Naciketas's store of good deeds. Geldner (see Lindenau, ZII. i. 49 *n.*) sees in AV. x. 7. 11 a reference to the persistence of Tapas, which is an element of Karman, but the passage is very obscure.

[1] ZDMG. lxiv. 333–5.

[2] Deussen, *Sechzig Upanishad's*[2], p. 476, n. 3; Windisch, *Buddha's Geburt*, pp. 70, 71.

[3] This is made clear by BAU. iv. 4. 3 ff., which Jacobi (*Die Entwicklung der Gottesidee bei den Indern*, p. 9) wrongly ignores in his contention that Karman was regarded as a transcendent power bringing into being a new psychic complex, no permanent self being known. It is also very dubious if we can accept his view that the origin of Karman in a philosophic sense is to be found in the Mīmāṅsā doctrine of Apūrva, a mysterious entity, which attaches itself to the soul of man when he has offered sacrifice and clings to him until such time as his action bears its fruit (cf. Keith, *Karma-Mīmāṅsā*, pp. 36, 73 ff., 89). This theory was naturally enough evoked by the fact that the sacrifice often did not reap any immediate fruit, and it was, therefore, necessary to provide something to preserve continuity. But we need not believe this bizarre speculation very old; it can hardly have been needed so long as any real belief in the Vedic gods survived; in the Mīmāṅsā that has wholly disappeared. In the Jain theory Karman is definitely material (von Glasenapp, *Die Lehre vom Karman*), but it seems very dubious if Stcherbatsky (*The Central Conception of Buddhism*, p. 34) is right in ascribing a semi-material nature to Karman in Buddhism; the Jains remained on an extremely primitive level of thought which other schools earlier outlived. The idea of Karman, however, was doubtless affected *inter alia* by the conception of sin (*enas, āgas*) as clinging in a quasi-physical way to a man.

that period undergoes reward or punishment for its deeds in the appropriate place. The question of its precise meaning is not important: it may mean [1] merely that he transmigrates after completing one life. But the important fact is that, with the doctrine of action as determining the future life of man, there comes to be combined the doctrine of reward in heaven or punishment elsewhere, which is already seen in the Rigveda and more clearly in the Atharvaveda, and which we need not doubt was a popular belief, and this combination is already found in the two main texts which are our sources for the transmigration doctrine. Of these the Bṛhadāraṇyaka [2] version is found in the sixth book which occurs in the appendix, and this fact alone indicates its later date. The other version is in the Chāndogya,[3] and here as always that Upaniṣad shows its dependence in the case of common material on the Bṛhadāraṇyaka. A somewhat corrupt version is also given in the second Pariçiṣṭa of the Nirukta.

The account is divided naturally into two parts. The first is the theory of the five fires, which is an account apparently of the mode in which the soul on death passes immediately, without intermediate reward or punishment, into the new body. The burning of the body on death is here taken by a new turn of thought as the offering of sacrifice, and the essential part of the offering, the action of man, is figured as the waters, which are offered with faith; hence the faith takes the place of the waters as the expression for the part which transmigrates. The faith, which thus ascends in the form of the sacrificial vapour to the gods, is by them offered in the heaven, the atmosphere, the earth, the man, and the woman as sacrificial fires, changing thus first to the Soma, then to rain, then to food, then to seed,[4] and then to the embryo, and then receiving existence afresh. The mythical character of the whole is obvious, and reminds us that the new doctrine of action as determining the future life was decidedly disadvantageous to the sacrificial priest, and that it was natural to reserve it as a holy mystery.

The second part of the account deals with the two ways, that of the gods and of the Fathers, and it teaches the doctrine first of punishment in the next world, and then rebirth on earth for those persons who were not to receive full enlightenment. The Devayāna, originally in the Rigveda the path by which the sacrifice of a man was borne to the gods or by which they came for it, and by which on death he joined the Fathers and the gods in heaven, is transformed into the path by which the soul goes to the gods or to the absolute. On the burning of the body the soul enters the flame, then the day, the bright half of the month, the bright half of the year, the year, the sun, the moon (in the Chāndogya version), the lightning, and finally, led by a spiritual man or,

[1] Deussen, *Phil. of Up.*, p. 332; *Sechzig Upanishad's*[2], p. 476, n. 3.

[2] vi. 2.

[3] v. 3–10.

[4] This is a point of difference from the Buddhist theory by which the counterpart of the soul enters directly *ab extra* the womb; Windisch, *Buddha's Geburt*, pp. 29, 32, 76.

as the Chāndogya has it, a superhuman man, into the world of Brahman. The terms are of course to be understood spatially, but in later India they were interpreted as temporal, and thus in the great epic the death of Bhīṣma is delayed by that warrior so that he may die in the Uttarāyaṇa, the northern course of the sun.[1] In the case of the Pitṛyāna the course is different: the moon is common to both since the moon was often regarded as the home of the dead,[2] and in the Upaniṣads its waxing and waning were brought into connexion with the movements of the souls: hence the path is the smoke, the night, the dark half of the month, the dark half of the year, the world of the Fathers in lieu of the year, the ether not the sun, the moon, which is now not a stage of transit to the world of Brahman, but the highest place attained by the souls. The arrival of the souls fills up the moon,[3] so that in the metaphorical language of the Upaniṣads they are enjoyed by the gods, a view which the Vedānta reduces to the principle that the souls and the gods together delight therein. This time of felicity ends only when the merit of the soul is finished, and then it returns to earth by the process, in its last stages very difficult, of being materialized into ether, wind, smoke, mist, cloud, rain, plants, food, seed, and entrance into the womb of the mother to be followed by rebirth. The way of the Fathers is the lot of those who are bent on sacrifice, works of piety, and asceticism (in the Chāndogya, sacrifice, gifts, and almsgiving), while that of the gods which leads to the Brahman is allotted to the wise who know the doctrine and those who in the forest worship faith (in the Chāndogya, worship faith and asceticism, unless it means 'worship, holding that faith is asceticism'). The lot of the wicked appears to have been the third place which led to birth again as animals, of the lower insect orders, worms, or flies. In the Chāndogya Upaniṣad[4] the position is differentiated by the division of the classes of souls, which go to the moon, into those of good and those of abominable conduct: the former are reborn as Kṣatriyas, Brahmans, or Vaiçyas, the latter as dogs, pigs, or Caṇḍālas, but the absurdity is retained that the third class remains, described as beings which ever return.

The Kauṣītaki Upaniṣad[5] presents an accommodation version: here the souls are all sent to the moon: their knowledge is there tested, and according to the result they proceed by the Devayāna leading through the worlds of Agni, Vāyu, Varuṇa, Indra, and Prajāpati to that of Brahman, or they return

[1] Cf. Bhagavadgītā, viii. 24; Çaṅkara on Brahma Sūtra, iv. 2. 20; Winternitz, *Gesch. d. ind. Lit.* i. 370.

[2] Kauṣ. ii. 8. Its position in the Devayāna is only thus to be explained: it is clearly out of place; cf. JUB. iii. 13. 12.

[3] Cf. Kauṣ. i. 2; BAU. vi. 2. 16; there is a clear reference to the doctrine (RV. x. 85. 5) of the Soma cup of the moon as the food of the gods, to explain its waxing and waning.

[4] v. 10.

[5] i. 2; a difficult passage; see Keith, *Çāṅkhāyana Āraṇyaka*, p. 17; Böhtlingk, BSGW. xlii. 198 ff.; xlix. 98 f.; Windisch, BSGW. lix. 111 ff.; *Buddha's Geburt*, pp. 63, 67, 71. There are quasi parallels in JB. i. 18 and 49 (Oertel, JAOS. xix. 111 ff.). The path to the moon in the latter version is through the fire, smoke, night, day, waning half of month, waxing half of month, and soul and body unite in the moon or month.

to earth in rebirth as a worm or a fly or a fish or a bird or a lion or a boar or a serpent or a tiger or a man or as something else. The later Upaniṣads add nothing of value to this doctrine: the Kaṭha [1] refers to the rebirth of men as men or plants according to their deeds and knowledge, and the Praçna [2] follows the Chāndogya with some deviation. It, with the Jaiminīya Upaniṣad Brāhmaṇa,[3] recognizes two ways from the start, one by the north course to the world of Āditya, the other by the south course to the moon, from the former there being no return. The mention of Āditya here is an archaic touch in comparison with the world of Brahman, while on the other hand it is more recent than the conception of the goal as the world of Yama, as in the Rigveda. The Jaiminīya version contains the curious assertion [4] that a man can, after attaining the world of Brahman through the earth, Agni, Vāyu, the atmosphere, the quarters, day and night, the half months, the months, the seasons, the year, the heavenly Gandharvas, the Apsarases, the sky, the gods, the sun, the moon, each of which is the world of Brahman,[5] choose at will birth in a Brahman or a Kṣatriya family, a clear proof of a doctrine independent of Karman, and a curious parallel to the Buddhist doctrine—found also in Jainism—of the choice of family made by the Buddha while in the Tuṣita heaven.[6] In the Bhagavadgītā [7] we find the process carried one degree further and above the world of Brahman, from which once no return was possible, is set that of Kṛṣṇa as all-god. The Muṇḍaka [8] makes the soul attain release by passing through the sun; Hertel's view [9] that release is attained after life in the Brahmaloka seems erroneous; attainment of the Brahmaloka is release.

In keeping with the curious vagueness of the Upaniṣads is the failure to make it clear precisely what is the ground which secures for a man union with the absolute in lieu of rebirth. In the Chāndogya [10] the matter is fairly simple; the boon falls to those who know the doctrine of the five fires and the offerings in them which explain man's descent to earth after his death, and to those who practice worship in the forest, holding that faith is their asceticism; at least this is the more natural sense of the terms employed. Return to earth is attributed to those who in the village worship, holding that their sacrifices and their gifts to the priests are their tribute. In the Bṛhadāraṇyaka,[11] on the other hand, the distinction is between those who practise faith

[1] v. 7.

[2] i. 9, 10.

[3] iii. 20–8. In i. 3 ff. the way is to the moon, then to or through the sun.

[4] iii. 28. 4.

[5] That is, the doctrine of Brahman's world is known, but only in part accepted by being identified with either the world of the sun or the moon. Cf. i. 6.

[6] Windisch, *Buddha's Geburt*, p. 66; Mahāvastu, i. 1; Jātaka, i. 48.

[7] viii. 16. On the moon cf. T. Segerstedt, *Monde Oriental*, iv. 62 ff.

[8] i. 2. 11.

[9] *Muṇḍaka Upaniṣad*, pp. 63, 66, on iii. 2. 6.

[10] v. 10. 1, 3: the phrases are *çraddhā tapa ity upāsate* and *iṣṭāpūrte dattam ity upāsate*. In both *iti* may be enumerative, and the sense be 'practise faith and asceticism', and 'practise sacrifice gifts and generosity'.

[11] vi. 2. 15, 16.

and truth, and those who devote themselves to sacrifice, alms, and asceticism. In the Muṇḍaka Upaniṣad [1] the attainment of the absolute is the reward of those who wise, calm, of holy conduct, practise faith and asceticism, which is doubtless intended to be a reproduction of the view of the Chāndogya, though its accuracy is dubious. In the Praçna [2] the sun and the absolute are assured to those who give themselves up to holy conduct (*brahmacarya*), asceticism, faith, and knowledge, while rebirth is attained by those who hold that sacrifice and gifts are their action. It may fairly be held that the earlier sources do not accept asceticism as any essential part of the equipment for attaining the absolute, while it is assumed as necessary in the later texts.[3]

The nature of the being which passes through transmigration is not specially discussed in the accounts of the paths. The curious mention of the man, variously described as spiritual (*mānasa*) or as superhuman (*amānava*), who leads the migrating soul from the lightning to the world of Brahman, is transformed by the account of the Nirukta [4] into a change effected in the soul itself, which becomes a spiritual essence, and with this conception Windisch [5] compares the fact that the Buddha emerges in spiritual (*manomaya*) form from his mother's womb, thus avoiding all injury to her, and the gods assume such a form. No certainty, however, is possible, and Deussen [6] is equally certain that the *mānasa* of the Bṛhadāraṇyaka version is merely a corruption of the *amānava* of the Chāndogya text.

The nature of the soul which is fated, unlike this class of soul, to return to earth, is not here specifically described in any way, but in another part of the Bṛhadāraṇyaka Upaniṣad [7] we find the description of the fate of the soul on death, from which it appears that all the organs accompany the departing Ātman, that it enters into the Saṁjñāna, and so becomes possessed of knowledge and consciousness, Vijñāna, while, it is added, its learning and actions hold fast to it, and its knowledge of what has been before. With this accords well enough the Buddhist view of the migrating substance which is composed of Vijñāna, and the other four Skandhas of Vedanā, 'feeling', Saṁjñā, 'perception', Rūpa, 'corporeal form', and Saṁskāras, 'dispositions', and which also bears the compendious term of Nāmarūpa, 'name and form', the former being essentially a brief designation of the four Skandhas other than form. Here, however, and in the orthodox doctrine of Çaṅkara and the Sāṁkhya,[8] we have express recognition of a factor which is not mentioned expressly at any rate in the Bṛhadāraṇyaka, that of corporeal form. It is

[1] i. 2. 11.

[2] i. 9, 10.

[3] Thus renunciation of children is recognized in Mahānārāyaṇa (lxii. 7, 11; lxiii. 8, 13), Praçna (i. 13, 15), and in the Sannyāsa Upaniṣads, and is regarded as natural in the knower of the absolute by Yājñavalkya, despite his own two wives (BAU. iii. 5. 1; iv. 4. 22; cf. i. 4. 17).

[4] Par. ii. 9.

[5] *Buddha's Geburt*, p. 73, n. 4.

[6] *Sechzig Upanishad's*², p. 508, n. 2.

[7] iv. 4. 3 Mādh.; Windisch, *op. cit.*, p. 38; cf. CU. iii. 14. 1; KU. v. 7; Īçā 15–17.

[8] Windisch, *op. cit.*, ch. v; Oltramare, *L'histoire des idées théosophiques*, i. 246 ff.

evident that this view was not absolutely necessary for the theory of the Ātman, and its development went, we may assume, hand in hand with the development of the principle of the fine elements of matter, such fine elements being obviously necessary if they were to be conceived as accompanying an invisible entity like a transmigrating soul. We find, however, in the same Upaniṣad [1] in the dialogue between Yājñavalkya and Ārtabhāga, which is preserved in one tantalizing fragment, that in the case of death a man's speech departs to the fire, his breath to the wind, his eye to the sun, his mind to the moon, his ear to the pole, his body to the earth, his Ātman to the ether, his hair to the plants and trees, his blood and seed to the waters, but there remains to transmigrate his Karman alone.[2] It is true that Çañkara proves equal to the occasion and disposes of the mention of the disappearance of the Ātman by interpreting the ether as the space in the heart wherein dwells the self, but this explanation is a mere *tour de force*. On the other hand, Windisch [3] suggests that the necessary element of personality must be deemed to be given by the persistence of the name, which in the preceding section of the Upaniṣad Yājñavalkya has declared to be the one thing which persists on the death of man, and this interpretation appears to be necessarily correct, while it suggests the origin of the use of the term 'name' in the Buddhist conception of Nāmarūpa as the factor which passes through transmigration. Jacobi,[4] again, suggests that the force of Karman produces a new complex of the elements, holding that the idea of a permanent soul was not yet known, but this is a far-fetched conception. In the vagueness of conception we have nothing to wonder at: the whole conception is seriously regarded so bizarre, that it is not surprising that to clothe it in definite language was beyond the power of the authors of the Upaniṣads.

In the later literature [5] there exist, despite the prevalence of the Karman doctrine, none the less the inconsistent ideas that on the one hand the sin of the father passes over to the child, apart from the action of the child in former births, and on the other that the saving grace of the Lord avails to break the chain of Karman. Still more naturally in the period of the Upaniṣads, when the doctrine of Karman was far from being a fixed dogma, it is not surprising that many traces of conceptions inconsistent with the Karman belief should appear. Of these the most obvious is the belief in the power of the Ātman by special grace to manifest itself, which is found in the Kaṭha, the Muṇḍaka, and still more clearly in the Çvetāçvatara Upaniṣad, but equally important is the doctrine that in the son the father is continued in being in such a manner that the son takes over all that his father has, including his Karman,[6] though

[1] iii. 2. 13.

[2] In Caraka's Çārīrasthāna, iii. 14, the transmigrating element is the Sattva, while in each man self-consciousness, mind, senses, and the breaths are derived from the non-transmigrating self.

[3] Windisch, *Buddha's Geburt*, pp. 69, 70. BAU. iv. 4. 3 ff. must be borne in mind; see above, p. 573.

[4] *Die Entwicklung der Gottesidee bei den Indern*, p. 9.

[5] Hopkins, JRAS. 1906, pp. 581 ff.

[6] Kauṣ. ii. 15.

the term in the context applies generally to all action and has no moral reference, and that for any evil done by his father the son makes atonement,[1] a view which results in the constant insistence on begetting offspring as a religious duty,[2] and which in the later period takes the more crude and vulgar form that the mere birth of a son (*putra*) saves the father from the hell named Put, a puerile verbal play in the precise manner of the Upaniṣads. This idea must clearly be reckoned along with those passages which declare that in the son the father is born again, an idea which is in itself not strictly reconcilable with the view that the soul transmigrates on death, since in the elaborate description of the Upaniṣads the tradition from father to son is of so complete a kind that it would seem that there was nothing more which could transmigrate: we have in fact three diverse ideas more or less blended, the birth of the father in the production of a son, the handing over by the father on death to the son of his whole personality, and the migration of the father's soul into some new existence.

A further breach with the theory of Karman is to be seen in the case of the Kauṣītaki Upaniṣad,[3] which tells how the man who attains the Brahman after passing by the river of immortality casts away his good and his evil deeds, which his friends and enemies duly share, while he from his lofty position gazes calmly at good and evil deeds, and the contrasts of night and day. This idea, as Hopkins[4] has shown, has a ritual origin: in the Çatapatha Brāhmaṇa[5] we are told how the man who performs the Agnihotra after sunset and before sunrise escapes the fate which normally awaits men in the world to come, where the days and the nights gradually destroy their good deeds, and doom them in due course to that renewal of death which the Brahman regards as the worst of unhappinesses. Thus early it is clear the Karman doctrine had to face the competition of conflicting and doubtless older views, which never could be brought into real coincidence with it.

Another of the many contradictions involved in the theory arises from the view that on the departure of the soul on death it is accompanied by its recognition of the past, that is, that it retains a real personality. The difficulty of disposing of the fact that in practice the soul has no such recollection in its new birth of this previous experience is met by the statement that the child in the womb in its ninth month of existence possesses this knowledge, but through the pangs of birth is deprived of it.[6] The Buddhist view admits that the Buddha enters with complete memory and intelligence into the womb,[7] but in his case his miraculous birth prevents the loss of his supreme powers.

The later literature, by no means in harmony with the principles of Karman, assumes that great importance attaches to the thought which is in

[1] BAU. i. 5. 17.
[2] CU. iii. 17. 5; v. 8, 9; BAU. vi. 2. 13; full details in vi. 4, and the Kāma Sūtra.
[3] i. 4.
[4] JRAS. 1907, pp. 666 ff.
[5] ii. 3. 3. 8–12.
[6] Garbha Upaniṣad 3, 4; Nirukta, Par. ii.
[7] Windisch, *Buddha's Geburt*, p. 88, n. 1.

the mind of man in the moment of death,[1] and we find a faint premonition of this view in the insistence laid in the Praçna Upaniṣad [2] that man's thought determines his next life. Possibly a similar conception may underlie the prayer put by the Īçā Upaniṣad [3] in the mouth of the dying man.

§ 11. *The Way of Salvation*

In the view of the Buddhist the world is misery, and the whole end of man is to remove the misery of existence from himself by the destruction of that desire, which leads ever from birth to birth. But the wholesale pessimism of the Buddhist is by no means characteristic of the Upaniṣads : to find real pessimism in them, as apart from mild expressions of the unsatisfactoriness of the finite compared with the infinite, is impossible. It is also impossible, therefore, to trace to the empirical despair of the world the growth of pessimism ; the most that in this regard can be said is that the tendency to take a pessimistic view of life may have been favoured among the upper classes of the Indians by the effect of the climate [4] and admixture with the aborigines, which was steadily taking place and was weakening the mental character of the race. Of the latter fact there can be no doubt : the genius of the Upaniṣads is different from that of the Rigveda, however many ties may connect the two periods. The emancipation theories of the Upaniṣads must, therefore, be traced to some more intellectual ground.

In the Rigveda and in the Brāhmaṇas the ideal aimed at is length of days on earth and life in the world of heaven in companionship with the gods. In the Brāhmaṇas we find that the reward of community of being, companionship, and fellowship with the gods is promised to the performers of various rites, in the case of diverse gods, Agni most of all, but also Vāyu, Indra, Varuṇa, Āditya, Bṛhaspati, Prajāpati, and finally even with the impersonal Brahman.[5] The gods are then reduced to the position of being no more than means by which entry to the Brahman can be obtained, and even Agni is placed in this position as well as Indra and Prajāpati. When the Brahman is also regarded as the Ātman, the end becomes unity with the Ātman, and this was the saving mode of emancipation, before transmigration was believed in. The knower of the wise long-emancipated youthful Ātman ceases to fear death ; [6] the finder of the Ātman ceases to be stained by action ; [7] knowledge leads to the place where desire is at rest, where no sacrificial gift reaches, nor

[1] e.g. Bhagavadgītā, viii. 6.

[2] iii. 10 ; cf. CU. iii. 14. 1 ; BAU. iv. 4. 5.

[3] 15–17 ; BAU. v. 15.

[4] The pressure of the Brahmanical system is a doubtful factor, and is denied by Deussen, *Phil. of Up.*, p. 341. He ignores the climate ; that is, however, clearly wrong, as shown by the effects on human life of the climate at the present day. Cf. Oltramare, *L'histoire des idées théosophiques*, i. 102 ff. ; Rhys Davids, *Hibbert Lectures*, 1881[4], p. 22 ; H. Güntert, *Der arische Weltkönig*, p. 227, who greatly overestimates the pessimism of the Upaniṣads.

[5] ÇB. ii. 6. 4. 8 ; xi. 4. 4. 1, 21 ; 6. 2. 2, 3 ; TB. iii. 10. 9. 11 ; 11. 6. Immortality even in life is secured by TS. vi. 6. 9. 2.

[6] AV. x. 8. 44.

[7] TB. iii. 12. 9. 8.

the penance of the ignorant.[1] It is clear that what is contemplated is attaining by knowledge union with the Brahman, but the influence of the traditional view is seen in the fact that it is still regarded as the arrival at a world of heaven as if the Ātman were without the self.[2] The same conflict appears in the view that the Ātman is the infinitely great and the infinitely small, and that on the departure of the soul, it is to go to the Ātman, and enter in. In all these passages it is necessary to recognize that the knowledge of the Ātman leads only to unity with the Ātman after death, and that the unity is conceived on the old model of community with a deity.

A further and important step is undoubtedly taken with the recognition of the fact that the emancipation desired is already achieved in this life by means of the recognition of the fact of the unity of the self and the absolute.[3] He who knows 'I am the Brahman' becomes the universe: even the gods have no power to prevent him so becoming, for he is its soul.[4] Or, in the words of the Muṇḍaka Upaniṣad,[5] 'He who knows the supreme Brahman becomes the Brahman.' The mere knowledge constitutes the deliverance: the man ceases to be affected by any desires of any kind: his deeds good or bad cease to have any effect on him:[6] like the reed stalk in the fire, his works consume themselves away:[7] as water does not stay on the lotus leaf, further works do not cling to him.[8] The discussions of Yājñavalkya with the king, Janaka,[9] reveal the truth that the absence of desire, the disappearance of every passion,[10] is the mark of the man becoming immortal and attaining to the Brahman. Similarly, in veiled language he informs the king that death will not produce any essential change in the self, and he denies in his discussion with Maitreyī that there is any consciousness after death.[11] Though later interpreted materialistically by the Cārvākas, the sense is clearly otherwise. After death the indestructible self ceases to have that division of consciousness as subject and object, which gives the empirical consciousness of the world. The wise know that there is in the universe as we have it no reality, nor is there any further reality in immortality, if understood as a prolonged individual existence after death.

The attainment of emancipation by this knowledge which gives it, and is it, results in the immediate cessation of every emotion: how can man desire any-

[1] ÇB. x. 5. 4. 15.

[2] Deussen, *op. cit.*, p. 343.

[3] Gauḍapāda, Māṇḍūkya Kārikā, iv. 98.

[4] BAU. i. 4. 10.

[5] iii. 2. 9, which Hertel (ed., pp. 49 f.) treats as a working over of an original identification with the personal Puruṣa.

[6] BAU. iv. 4. 22; TU. ii. 9; Kauṣ. i. 4; iii. 1. So analogously in the doctrine of St. Paul and Lao Tsé enlightenment frees from the law; in the Brāhmaṇas (e.g. ÇB. i. 6. 1. 21) sacrifice has a similar potency; Oltramare, *L'histoire des idées théosophiques*, i. 114.

[7] CU. v. 24. 3.

[8] CU. iv. 14. 3.

[9] BAU. iv. 2; cf. 3 and 4.

[10] This ideal is, of course, dominant in later thought; by a singular delusion, Rhys Davids (*Early Buddhism*, p. 59) persists in his denial of the obvious truth. Cf. de la Vallée Poussin, *Bouddhisme*, pp. 60, 414.

[11] *pretya saṁjñā nāsti*; BAU. ii. 4. 12; iv. 5. 13; CU. vi. 9 (deep-sleep and death are both meant).

thing who knows himself to be all? How can he fear when there is no other? There can be no sorrow for him nor pain: he is like a blind man who has gained his sight, a wounded man healed, a sick man made whole. All his works are annihilated, as they have meaning only for an individuality. Future works have no effect upon him, but evil he cannot wish to do, since he has no desires:[1] he may, if he cares, live on for the full length of life or do any action so long as he does it disinterestedly, a view which the Īçā Upaniṣad offers, despite its paradoxical appearance, doubtless as a sop to those who did not wish to be denied the position of emancipation, but preferred also to enjoy the things of life. He cannot again ever feel any doubt;[2] he has the full and abiding knowledge for all time.

The view that the emancipation is attained in the moment of the knowledge is, however, very far from being universally expressed or believed. The idea on the contrary occurs, ever and again, that the result of the enlightenment is only complete at the end of the life of the self, and that the enlightenment takes the form of an alteration in space to a new abode.[3] These ideas are, of course, merely the ideas regarding the fate of the soul, transferred to the new conception of the gaining of knowledge. The view that the attainment of knowledge brought release was one, which, we may safely assume, was not easy to grasp or to hold, for the very good reason that it is as a matter of fact unintelligible. Hence the Upaniṣads as a rule merely consider that the advantages of the acquisition of knowledge are the winning of the desired immortality: the view of the merger of the Ātman in the Ātman as a mere recognition of identity is not the conception usually found, which is rather that the reward is eternity. Thus in the Kaṭha Upaniṣad, in which has been seen the doctrine of final release by Deussen, there is no trace, as Whitney[4] has clearly pointed out, of anything more than the mere recognition of the winning of immortality as the result of knowledge, in this case philosophical knowledge, not as in the Taittirīya Brāhmaṇa,[5] from which the conception of the Upaniṣad is borrowed, ritual knowledge. So we have many other accounts, all of the same kind: the soul is supposed to go out by the veins to the rays of the sun and to the sun;[6] in the accounts in the transmigration doctrine[7] the souls even of the men who have acquired knowledge are conceived as going by a long journey to the world of Brahman and the same idea is repeated in the variant versions of the Kauṣītaki Upaniṣad[8] where from the moon such souls go by the worlds of fire, wind, Varuṇa, Indra, Prajāpati and then reach Brahman. In the Aitareya Āraṇyaka[9] we learn

[1] BAU. iv. 4. 23.

[2] CU. iii. 14. 4.

[3] The Īçā (11; Maitr. vii. 9) actually provides for a regime of works (termed Avidyā) to conquer repeated death, and of knowledge, to conquer the migration, as simultaneously to be pursued.

[4] TAPA. 1890, pp. 88 ff.; JAOS. xiii. pp. ciii ff.; KU. iii. 7–9.

[5] iii. 11. 8.

[6] CU. viii. 6. 1–5.

[7] BAU. vi. 2; CU. v. 10; Nirukta, Par. ii. 8, 9. See also CU. iv. 15. 5, 6; Muṇḍ. i. 2. 11.

[8] i. 2; cf. JB. i. 18. 4 ff.; 49. 7 ff.

[9] ii. 5; Keith, *Aitareya Āraṇyaka*, p. 234, n. 9.

that Vāmadeva, as a result of knowing the Ātman, ascended from this world, and attained immortality in yonder world of heaven. The Kauṣītaki also has an account in detail of the world of Brahman, with the Aparājita palace, which is derived from Varuṇa's Rigvedic abode, the tree Ilya, the Sālajya city, and the sea Āra, the later conception being perhaps derived from the seas, Ara and Ṇya, in the world of Brahman invented by the Chāndogya Upaniṣad.[1] Yet another version makes the emancipated man be separated from the non-emancipated by the fact that at death his soul goes out by the 101st vein,[2] whence he proceeds by the crown of the head, fire, wind, and sun up to Brahman. All these are proofs of the perfectly simple meaning given to saving knowledge by the Upaniṣads generally. The knowledge might really confer the enlightenment in the view of a few minds, but the overwhelming opinion [3] of the age was that the reward was the heaven in one form or another.[4] The later Vedānta endeavoured to bring order into these ideas, and reconcile them with the real nature of emancipation by the theory of the contrast between the Jīvanmukta, who obtains release in perfection only on death, but who is really released in life by his attainment of knowledge, and the subject of the progressive emancipation, Kramamukti, by which the passage to the world of Brahman took place before the final release by the attainment of complete insight, but these devices remain as unnatural as possible.[5]

§ 12. *The Ethics of the Upaniṣads and Yoga*

In comparison with the intellectual activity of the Brahmans the ethical content of the Upaniṣads must be said to be negligible and valueless.[6] The total impression conveyed by the Upaniṣads is that of an intellectual exercise, whose aim was the attainment partly of immediate goods, partly of the highest good, normally the happiness of heaven which was often materially enough conceived, and there is made no attempt to make the theoretical philosophy a ground of morality of any sort. There are, here and there, moral maxims enunciated, but these are of no consequence and rise in no way above popular morality. On the contrary, the essential fact is expressed by Indra in his dialogue with Pratardana :[7] the possession of knowledge makes a man independent of all morality, the slaying of an embryo, the murder of a

[1] CU. viii. 5. 3.

[2] CU. viii. 6. 6 ; KU. vi. 16 ; *suṣumṇā*, Maitr. vi. 21. Cf. PU. iii. 7.

[3] Cf. the power of motion and enjoyment of women ascribed in the CU. viii. 12. 3 ; BAU. iv. 3. 15, however illogically. So TU. iii. 10, 5 f., where motion, eating, changing form, and singing occur.

[4] This agrees precisely with the views of Açoka, whose preoccupation is with men's future heavenly bliss ; Oltramare, *L'histoire des idées théosophiques*, ii. 55.

[5] ÇU. i. 4, 11 ; v. 7 ; Muṇḍ. iii. 2. 6 ; cf. Oltramare, *L'histoire des idées théosophiques*, i. 208–210.

[6] Radhakrishnan's dictum (*Ind. Phil.* i. 243), ' Morality, according to the Upaniṣads, expresses the true nature of things ', is not consistent with other views expressed by him (p. 230), and is wholly contrary to the spirit of the Upaniṣads.

[7] Kauṣ. iii. 1.

father or of a mother. It is, of course, true that these statements are not meant seriously, and that we may console ourselves by supposing that the priest did not hold that these crimes could really be disposed of in this way, though of that we cannot be certain as the same results can be attained by ritual practices. But they must have felt an exaggerated value to attach to their speculations, and have completely failed to see that morality is the most objective and essential part of philosophy, and is something other than sacrificial activity or intellectual gymnastics.

Here and there we have views which are sound so far as they go; the allegory of life [1] as a Soma sacrifice postulates that the fee shall be asceticism, liberality, right dealing, non-injury to life, and truthfulness, and a list of a student's duties is given in the Taittirīya Upaniṣad.[2] The student is bidden by his teacher not to be negligent of truth, virtue, welfare, prosperity, study and teaching, and in due course propagation of children. Further, duties to the gods, the Fathers, and parents are inculcated, and teachers and guests are to be ranked as gods. Those acts which are irreproachable alone should be practised, and good deeds alone should be revered. Refreshments with a seat should be provided for deserving Brahmans. Giving is regulated; [3] one should give with faith, one should not give without faith, one should give with plenty, with modesty, with fear,[4] with sympathy. Further, a very useful practical rule is enjoined; if the student has doubt concerning an act or conduct, then recourse should be had to the attitude of Brahmans, competent to judge, apt, devoted, not harsh, lovers of virtue; as they behave themselves in such a case, so should the student demean himself, and similarly should he act in regard to persons who are spoken against. There is thus given as the norm of conduct the average righteous man, who embodies in himself the standard of action. In the same Upaniṣad [5] in addition to the essential study and teaching a further list is given which runs: right dealing, truthfulness, asceticism, self-restraint, tranquility, maintenance of the sacred fire, the offering of the Agnihotra, hospitality, courtesy, and duties to children, wives, and grandchildren. Another text sees in the voice of the thunder the rules 'Be restrained, liberal, merciful'.[6] So we have condemned as sinners the stealer of gold, the drinker of Surā, the murderer of a Brahman, and the defiler of his teacher's bed, and their associates,[7] while Açvapati, the prince, boasts that his kingdom has no thief, churl, or drunkard, none who neglect the sacrifice or the sacred lore, no adulterer or courtesan.[8] This is, it is clear, purely elementary: the failure to rise to the conception even of a system of ethics is a sign not so much, as Deussen [9] suggests, of the virtue of the age,

1 CU. iii. 17.
2 i. 11.
3 Cf. AA. ii. 3. 6. For Buddhism cf. Keith, *Buddhist Philosophy*, pp. 117 f., 279 ff.
4 Possibly of hard-heartedness; cf. RV. x. 117. 5. Cf. PB. xvi. 5. 6; 6. 1; 9. 2; AA. ii. 3. 6, which urges moderation in generosity.
5 i. 9.
6 BAU. v. 2.
7 CU. v. 10. 9.
8 CU. v. 11. 5.
9 *Phil. of Up.*, p. 366.

which is not proved by any other evidence, but rather of the lack of ethical sense on the part of the Brahmans. Philosophically also the doctrine of the absolute as all-pervading resulted in the negation of human responsibility: it is the deity who really acts in and through man, and the latter cannot be blamed for what he thus seemingly does.[1]

In truth the aims of the Brahmans were bent on things which are not ethical at all, immediate profit on the one hand, or, on the other, the closer realization of the absolute in which they believed, and which they desired to appreciate in full enjoyment. The ideal is embodied in the most curious forms. Knowledge in the Upaniṣads is essentially profitable,[2] and by no means for spiritual ends alone. He who knows the world as fivefold obtains it; he who knows Indra as without a rival has no rival; the possessor of knowledge cannot be injured by an enemy; neither the northern nor the southern mountains can prevail against him, and his foes die around him, an idea found in the Aitareya Brāhmaṇa.[3] It is an easy step to the result already seen; knowledge obliterates evil; one who knows may consort with even the murderer without being contaminated.[4] With a strange contrast to Sokrates who held that the wise man would necessarily be good, we are repeatedly assured that knowledge relieves man from worrying as to whether he has done wrong or right in any matter.[5] Entry into the absolute is accompanied by the casting aside of good and evil deeds, which are transferred on one view to one's relatives or foes respectively.[6] With an anticipation of modern idealism, and in the true spirit of mysticism, good and bad may be regarded as imperfect concepts for which there is no proper place in the absolute; if speech were not, neither right nor wrong, true nor false, good nor bad, pleasant nor unpleasant, could be known.[7] The absolute self is unsullied by evil to which he is external; an etymology proves it; for he is called the person, Puruṣa, since he burned (*uṣ*) up evil before (*pūrva*) all these worlds.[8] In uniting with him the individual parts utterly from good or bad.[9] We see this even in sleep, for in it neither evil nor good attaches itself effectively to the self.[10] When we are told[11] that the world is truth, there is no ethical implication, for it is plain that there is here merely an assertion of the reality of the universe, the word Satya conveying both senses, and in the theistic Çvetāçvatara[12] the description of the lord as the bringer of right and the remover of evil is due to the confusion, there constant, between the personal deity and the absolute. The emancipated self possesses autonomy, but it is not an ethical

[1] JUB. i. 5; above, § 6.

[2] BAU. i. 4. 17; 5. 12; CU. i. 2. 8; BAU. i. 3. 28; 5. 21; v. 4; TU. ii. 1; iii. 7; Kauṣ. i. 7; ii. 13; Muṇḍ. iii. 2. 9.

[3] viii. 28; cf. TU. iii. 10. 4.

[4] BAU. v. 7; 14. 8; CU. v. 10. 9 f.; 24. 3. Cf. BAU. iv. 4. 23; CU. iv. 14. 3; PU. v. 5; Maitr. iii. 2; vi. 18. Contrast KU. ii. 24; iii. 7, 8.

[5] TU. ii. 9; BAU. iv. 4. 22; Muṇḍ. iii. 1. 3.

[6] Kauṣ. i. 4.

[7] CU. vii. 2. 1.

[8] KU. v. 11; Īçā 8; BAU. i. 4. 1.

[9] BAU. iv. 3. 21 f.

[10] BAU. iv. 3. 7, 16; CU. viii. 6. 3.

[11] CU. vi. 16.

[12] vi. 6.

state ;[1] it is merely a condition of unhindered power, the ideal of a despot, the state of the man who goes up and down these worlds, eating what he desires, assuming what form he desires.[2]

Prajāpati utterly condemns[3] the doctrine, derived allegedly from his teaching by the demon Virocana, which asserts that the man who consults his own desires in this life obtains both this world and the world to come ; this view is described as devilish, naturally enough since it would have turned all against gifts to the priests or sacrifice. But we have instead the clear doctrine[4] that the self is dearer even than a son, and that whatever is dear, be it wife, sons, wealth, the Brahman class, the Kṣatriya class, the gods, worlds, anything, is dear not for itself, but for the sake of the self or soul. We have here, not the psychological theory that things are desired for their pleasure, not for themselves, nor the suggestion that all love is ultimately self-love, but the recognition of the fact of the unity of the whole, which finds its truth in the self. Plainly, however, there is no attempt to develop a positive morality[5] which would render empiric selfishness wrong on the score that it was based on a false distinction between self and not-self. On the contrary we find only emphasized throughout the necessity of caring for one's own salvation ; Yājñavalkya abandons his faithful wives to seek the welfare of his soul, just as the Buddha abandons his young bride and his child, because they are hindrances to the attainment of release.

The true ideal, therefore, of the seeker for truth is embodied in the practice of asceticism and the adoption of renunciation : by turning away from the things of this world, and by concentrating unnaturally the mind on the object, the vision beatific was to be obtained : the utter incompatibility of this with the purely intellectual view, that the recognition of the Brahman as the self was emancipation, is obvious, but contradictions *in adjecto* are the normal characteristic of the Upaniṣads. Hence was developed the scheme by which the old rule of life was complicated and a series of four Āçramas, 'places of asceticism', was devised, through which the man should pass on his way to his home in the heaven.

In the earliest Upaniṣads we find only the conception that, beside the life of the student and the householder, men might give themselves up to ascetic practices in their seeking for the truth. There was no idea that the stages of life should be successive, ending with the ascetic stage : the ascetic stage might follow the stage of household life if desired, but equally it might not.[6] But in the later Upaniṣads, such as the Jābāla[7], we find the four stages ordered

[1] CU. vii. 25. 2 ; TU. i. 6. 2.

[2] TU. iii. 10. 5.

[3] CU. viii. 7 f.

[4] BAU. ii. 4 ; iv. 5.

[5] Radhakrishnan (*Ind. Phil.* i. 228 ff., 242 ff.) ignores the fundamental moral indifference of the Upaniṣads by reinterpreting them in the light of absolute idealism.

[6] CU. viii. 15 ; ii. 23. 1 ; v. 10 ; BAU. iv. 2. 22 ; iii. 8. 10.

[7] 4. Cf. also N. Law, IA. lii. 272 ff. S. Dutt (*Early Buddhist Monachism*, chap. ii) holds that the fourth Āçrama is an addition to the Brahmanical system of the Çramaṇas, wandering teachers of semi-Aryanized eastern communities. This seems quite unproved.

as student, householder, anchorite, Vānaprastha, and finally wandering beggar, Parivrājaka, Bhikṣu. The first two stages remain much as in the Brāhmaṇa period : it is of interest that we hear of cases, where a pupil seems to have been used by his alleged teacher mainly for the purpose of tending his cattle, in return for which the teaching might be long delayed, as in the case of Satyakāma.[1] Other pupils again were deemed unworthy of the teaching they desired : Upakosala [2] tended the fires for twelve years without his teacher making up his mind to trust him with the sacred knowledge. The householder may still attain the world of Brahman by attention to his duties, if he continues to study and brings up pious sons and pupils, subduing his organs in the self and slaying no life, save at the sacrificial ground. But another view condemns such persons to life in the moon, and then to return to earth again. Sacrifice, Veda study, liberality, and the production of sons are still the chief duties, though, as we have seen, the tendency was growing to reduce the sacrifice to symbolic acts.

The late Vaikhānasa Dharmasūtra lays down that there are four categories of householder. The first (*vārttāvṛtti*) devotes himself to the duty of agriculture, cattle rearing or trade. The second (*çālīna*) performs regularly the domestic offerings, Pākayajñas, and, after establishing his fire, carries out each fortnight the new and full moon offerings, and every four months the four-month offerings, as well as twice a year the animal offering, and once the Soma offering. The third (*yāyāvara*) performs the Çrauta sacrifices, including the Soma sacrifice, for himself and also acts as priests for others, whence his name of 'Wanderer'; he studies and teaches pupils; he gives and accepts gifts; he maintains his fire and entertains guests. The fourth (*ghorācārika*) is a man of severe observances, for he offers Iṣṭis, studies and gives gifts, practising specially rigorous abstinence in the months Mārgaçīrṣa and Jyaiṣṭha, performing morning and evening the Agnihotra, and maintaining the fire with fruits of the wood. We need not suppose that this ideal scheme corresponded to any very definite practice; it is noteworthy that it recognizes that in many cases the householder was more busied in his business than in the performance of his domestic ritual.

The business of teaching [3] was doubtless carried on by many of the householders, as well as by those who had passed this stage. For the early Vedic period we have no indication of anything corresponding to the later Maṭh, where large bodies of teachers and pupils were united in a loose form of monastic life. We seem to find nothing more than individual teachers attracting a larger or smaller number of pupils; the ideal seems to have been that a true student must dwell in his teacher's house (*antevāsin*), and this fact alone would negative large bodies. The epic tradition [4] seems to suggest that five was a maximum. From this simple relationship may be explained a dominant feature of the Buddhist and later monastic system, the free right of any person

[1] CU. iv. 4. 5.
[2] CU. iv. 10. 1, 2.
[3] Cf. Weber, *Religionssoziologie*, ii. 157 ff.
[4] Mahābhārata, xii. 328. 41.

who had entered on a course of study to abandon it. The development of monastic systems which soon became common to all sects was furthered by the rise of Buddhism, though it need not be held to have been a specific Buddhist innovation, for it may easily have risen spontaneously among Buddhists Jains and Brahmans alike as the outcome of their competition for public favour.

The third stage, that of the anchorite, is not distinguished by Yājñavalkya from that of the wanderer: when he decides to give up the life of the householder he contemplates wandering about as a beggar.[1] The value of penance for the knowledge of the Brahman is not overestimated in the oldest Upaniṣads: the king Bṛhadratha,[2] after most painful mortification, is still far from attaining the desired knowledge. Asceticism, it is even said, leads only to the way of the Fathers, and has not the result of future emancipation. The man who really realizes the Brahman is above the Āçramas;[3] he has realized all that is aimed at by asceticism; he has no longer individuality or family connexion, he wanders about homeless, begging, without possessions, and bears the name Sannyāsin, the renouncer of everything. How this ideal can be logically derived from knowledge of the Ātman is nowhere explained in the Upaniṣads.

With the usual curious turns of Indian thought the Sannyāsin, who is really a person beyond the Āçramas as the Çvetāçvatara Upaniṣad calls him, becomes in the later Upaniṣads a man striving for the knowledge of the Ātman by means of asceticism. He should undertake this stage only as a rule after being a forest hermit, though he may enter into it direct from the householder's state.[4] He parts solemnly after sacrifice from all his kin, abandons all sacrifice for ever, gives up the sacred cord and the tonsure, lays aside his former garments and his staff, is clad in rags and a loincloth, and wanders about save at the period of the rains, living on what he begs and inhabiting lonely spots: some texts even demand nudity: he bears now a triple staff or a single staff, to signify perhaps the reconciliation of caste differences. Only one night may he live in a village, five in a town, but in the four months of the rains he may stay there. He is to recite Upaniṣads and the Āraṇyaka, to meditate, perform bathings, be indifferent to every human emotion, and show charity to all creatures. He must practise Yoga, that is, exercises intended to bring the mind into mystic union with the absolute. Though the system of the later Yoga,[5] which is linked to the Sāṁkhya, and which, therefore, in theory aims really primarily at the isolation of the spirit and nature, not at union with the divinity, is not found set out in the same precise detail, most

1 BAU. ii. 4. 1.

2 Maitr. i. 2.

3 ÇU. vi. 21.

4 See Jābāla, Āçrama, Sannyāsa, Kaṇṭhaçruti (or Kaṭhaçruti), Brahma, Āruṇeya, and Paramahaṅsa.

5 The sense of 'harnessing' seems to be found in *ātmānaṁ yuñjīta* in Mahānār. lxiii. 21; Maitr. vi. 3; as a union of breath and Om, Yoga is found in Maitr. vi. 25; in KU. ii. 12 it is practically equivalent to the restraint of the senses. Cf. above, § 8.

of its elements can be traced in the Upaniṣads,[1] and in the Kaṭha we are distinctly told that it is necessary to suppress speech and mind, merging the latter in the knowledge self, that in the great self, and that in the calm self, the absolute. The highest stage is attained when the five senses cease to give knowledge, when the mind and the intellect are at rest; the firm restraint of the senses is Yoga. The Çvetāçvatara devotes its second chapter to the praise of Yoga, prefacing it with prayers, adapted from the Taittirīya Saṁhitā, in which the aid of Savitṛ is invoked to secure the application of the mind to the task set before the Yogin. He should hold erect his body, and cause his senses and mind to enter into the heart, check his movements, and breathe with diminished intensity through the nose, restraining from distraction his mind. A clean level spot, free from pebbles, fire or gravel, favourable to thought by the presence of water, not offensive to the eye, protected from the wind and secluded, is recommended. Fog, smoke, sun, fire, wind, fireflies, lightning, crystal, the moon, are given as the preliminary appearances which present themselves to the Yogin; lightness, healthiness, steadiness or freedom from desire, clearness of countenance, pleasantness of voice, sweetness of odour, and scantiness of excretions are the first stage in his progress. The revelation of the absolute procures freedom from fetters and sorrow; sickness, old age, and death are overcome. The Upaniṣad, however, does not rely on Yoga alone; the one is attainable not by Yoga merely but by reflection (*sāṁkhya*) also, terms in which we need not see references to established schools, as does Oldenberg.[2] The insistence on breathing as a matter of importance is noteworthy;[3] restraint of breath not merely banishes evil influences, it tends to generate heat, thus producing Tapas, and by restraint serves to deaden the activity of the brain, thus favouring the feeling of severance from the world and union with the absolute.

The Maitrāyaṇīya repeatedly develops the theme; the state to be aimed at is reaching the fourth stage,[4] by the suppression of the living self. By pressing the tip of the tongue against the palate,[5] by suppressing voice, mind, and breath, one sees the Brahman, the self, and becomes selfless. Another device, forming the beginning of an advance by sound to the absolute without sound, consists in closing the ears with the thumbs,[6] when the sound of the ether within the heart becomes audible. By the suppression of breath the light of the ether within the heart is made manifest.[7] Or again by using the sound Om as an arrow, with mind as its point, the Yogin pierces the darkness and sees him who sparkles like a wheel of fire, the colour of the sun, the Brah-

[1] e.g. KU. iii. 13; vi. 10, 11; cf. Hopkins, JAOS. xxii. 333 ff. According to Tuxen (*Yoga*, pp. 20 ff.) the prime sense of Yoga is Samādhi; Charpentier (ZDMG. lxv. 846, 847) thinks practical effort is the root sense. Cf. Oltramare, *L'histoire des idées théosophiques*, i. 300–2.

[2] *Die Lehre der Upanishaden*, p. 280. Contrast Deussen, *Sechzig Upanishad's*[2], p. 308, n. 3, who justly insists on the parallel of *dhyānayoga* in i. 3.

[3] Oltramare, *L'histoire des idées théosophiques*, i. 322 ff.

[4] vi. 19.

[5] vi. 20 f.

[6] vi. 22.

[7] vi. 27.

man that shines beyond the darkness, in the sun, the moon, the fire, and the lightning.[1] The oneness of the breath and mind and also of the senses and the relinquishment of all conditions of existence is declared to be Yoga. A formal list of six elements of Yoga appears in the Maitrāyaṇīya Upaniṣad.[2] These are Prāṇāyāma, 'regulation of the breathing out and in', Pratyāhāra, 'suppression' of the organs of sense such as the mind, so as to prevent its activity spoiling concentration, Dhyāna, 'meditation', Dhāraṇā, 'concentration of the attention', Tarka, 'reflection', a term of doubtful sense in this context,[3] and Samādhi, 'absorption' or complete union with the object of meditation. This list differs, in the insertion of Tarka, and in the placing of Dhyāna before Dhāraṇā, from the later list, which makes up the number of eight members by inserting as the first three items Yama, 'discipline', refraining from doing injury, truthfulness, &c., Niyama, 'self-restraint' such as purity, contentment, &c., and Āsana, 'postures in sitting'. Of all these the most important is the use of Om as a symbol of Brahman to meditate upon. It is recognized by the Kaṭha,[4] but its importance belongs to the later Upaniṣads, which delight in mystery regarding it; it has three syllables or morae, or three and a half, or three morae and three echoes, three morae and four half morae, and so on; the point of the Anusvāra is given a hidden sense and the echo is also famed. It is refreshing to find that silence is called the highest point of all.[5] The view then is that man can only enter on the meditation with Om: he must at the end attain the nothingness in that which is not a word, like the sap of the flowers in the liquid honey.[6] In the condition of Samādhi the consciousness of a separate subject and object entirely disappears, and the state of selflessness is reached. This union is attained by the ascent of the soul, from the heart through the Suṣumṇā vein and the Brahmarandhra, to union with the absolute.[7] Naturally this conception is developed with the aid of the metaphor by which the heart is called a lotus, and by the use of the veins, 72,000 in number, into wild fantasies. Yet, though most of this absurdity is found in the later Upaniṣads, it should be recognized that the needs of Āsana are hinted at in the Çvetāçvatara,[8] and the virtues of Pratyāhāra are recognized by the Chāndogya.[9]

Religious suicide, which we have not seen in the Brāhmaṇa period, is mentioned in this, but only at the latest stage, long after the period of the Upaniṣads proper, when authority is given to the beggar to abstain from food, to throw himself into the water or fire,[10] to choose a hero's death. Strange folly to emerge from the comparative rationalism of the Upaniṣads, and to reach its apotheosis in the religion of the Jina.

[1] vi. 24.

[2] Maitr. vi. 18.

[3] Possibly it indicates the stage of meditation accompanied by reflexion; cf. MBh. xii. 195. 15; the first Pāli Jhāna; Oldenberg, *Die Lehre der Upanishaden*, p. 324.

[4] ii. 17; cf. CU. i. 1; TU. i. 8; ÇU. i. 14; Muṇḍ. ii. 2. 4. See also Keith, ERE., *s.v.*

[5] Dhyānabindu 4.

[6] Maitr. vi. 22.

[7] Brahmavidyā 11, 12; Kṣurikā 8, 9; Maitr. vi. 21.

[8] ii. 10.

[9] viii. 15.

[10] Jābāla 5; Kaṇṭhaçruti 4; cf. Keith, ERE., *s.v.*

§ 13. *The Significance of the Philosophy of the Upaniṣads*

What judgement are we to pass on the main thought of the Upaniṣads? Are they really the expressions at an early date of the deepest principles of philosophy, or are they merely of historical value, interesting pictures of the early thought of man, important not *per se*, but because of their dominating influence on the future philosophy and life of India? The two interpreters, who have of recent times been most impressed by the nature of that philosophy as idealism, have passed the most diametrically opposed views on the question: Gough was impressed with the necessity of explaining the defects of the subject of which he treated by the admixture of blood among the Indians, and the corrupting influences of a low order of civilization, while Deussen [1] is lost in admiration of the Upaniṣads, as was Schopenhauer before him: 'Eternal philosophical truth', he says, 'has seldom found more decisive and striking expression than in the doctrine of the emancipating knowledge of the Ātman.' He claims [2] that Yājñavalkya had anticipated the view of Schopenhauer regarding immortality as indestructibility without continued existence; he regards the view of the nature of the self as an anticipation of the doctrine of Kant; he defends the doctrine of transmigration as the best expression of the true state of matters in the terms of empirical thought, while recognizing that such an expression is misleading: nay, he argues that the Kantian argument regarding immortality, based on the realization of the moral law within us, points not to ordinary immortality, but rather to the process of transmigration, and transmigration has been solemnly upheld as philosophic doctrine at the present time by competent authorities.

The position of Deussen is, of course, coloured by his acceptance of the view that Kant has finally [3] shown that the knowledge of the ultimate reality is not possible, with which he combines the Schopenhauerian doctrine of the primacy of the will which he traces to Christianity, and his view of the Upaniṣads is, therefore, greatly determined by his double desire, to find in them the anticipation of Kant and to show that the views of Kant, as modified by Schopenhauer, are the only possible views of philosophy. To those who do not accept his theories the arguments adduced by him fall with the theories themselves, but the investigation of this question belongs to a general philosophical discussion, which is hardly here necessary or appropriate. The more important question which arises is to what extent the doctrines of the Upaniṣads do foreshadow the views of Kant.

[1] *Phil. of Up.*, pp. 38–50.

[2] *Op. cit.*, p. 350. Contrast the judgement of Lanman (*Beginnings of Hindu Pantheism*, p. 24): 'What a prospect, dark and void—this Supreme Spirit, before whom all human endeavour, all noble ambition, all hope, all love, is blighted! What a contrast, a relief, when we turn from this to the teachings of the gentle Nazarene!'

[3] A view, of course, rejected by various schools on different grounds, e. g. H. Jones, *Philosophy of Lotze*, pp. 371 ff.; E. Caird, *Critical Philosophy of Kant*; Hobhouse, *Theory of Knowledge*; Pritchard, *Kant's Theory of Knowledge*; Taylor, *Elements of Metaphysics*; J. Ward, *A Study of Kant* (1922); F. H. Bradley, *The Principles of Logic* (1922) E. Cassirer, *Das Erkenntnisproblem*.

The answer to this question must candidly admit that the conception of the Upaniṣads formed by Deussen as containing a definite doctrine of idealism, that of Yājñavalkya, which is variously broken down by realistic intrusions, and accommodations to common-sense, is one which is contrary to all probability and reason. The ideas of Yājñavalkya, that is of the men who framed and attributed to his famous name those views, are the high-water mark of the speculation of the Upaniṣads : the rest of the material is merely the natural development of the Brāhmaṇa theories. Those theories are of historic interest : as philosophy, they are unworthy of a moment's consideration. On the other hand the views of Yājñavalkya do certainly go the length of asserting the unknowableness of the subject and the fact that the Ātman, the subject matter of the philosophy of the age, was the knowing subject within the man : it is further clear that he maintained that the Ātman was the only real thing, and that plurality was illusory. It is quite true that even in the section attributed to him there are many expressions which will not harmonize with this conception, but it would be unfair not to take the doctrines at their face value, and to recognize that we cannot reasonably expect full consistency on these matters. It is, therefore, necessary to consider these doctrines in themselves in their value for thought.

The essential result appears to lie in this, that the distinction of subject and object is realized, and that, with the recognition of this distinction, it is seen that, as such, the subject cannot possibly be an object of thought or knowledge. These propositions are perfectly true, if duly confined to what they assert : consciousness essentially involves the distinction of subject and object, and clearly it is impossible to make the subjective activity an object of knowledge in exactly the same sense as the content of that activity is an object of knowledge.[1] But with this doctrine we make little progress to the understanding of the world, and the theory that it was really an anticipation of the view that the thing-in-itself is unknowable is not supported by any evidence whatever. On the contrary, the assertion of the unity of the self and the denial of plurality cannot be deduced on any legitimate manner from the doctrine so far arrived at, and these theories amount to no more than the desire to arrive at the conception of some permanent and abiding thing. But the identity of the self and the absolute is based merely on the abstraction of the self as subjectivity, and that of the absolute as subjectivity, and the identity is therefore meaningless and a mere matter of words.

Moreover the utter difference between Yājñavalkya and Kant appears clearly when we realize that Yājñavalkya, with his theory of the unity of the

[1] For the later views on this point cf. Keith, JRAS. 1916, pp. 371, 372. The real problem of individuality is, of course, merely stated, not solved by this contrast. The question is, What is the explanation of the quasi-permanence of the knowing subject ? No Indian philosophy deals with this effectively ; Buddhism, if we believe C. Rhys Davids (JRAS. 1903, pp. 587 ff.), has not even the courage to face the problem. For an attempt to restate the Buddhist view of rebirth, see her *Buddhist Psychology*, pp. 244–68.

absolute, has no theory at all of the relation of the empiric world to the absolute, i. e. that he really leaves the whole question of philosophy unsolved, and that the followers of his theory were at the last forced to fall back, as early as the Çvetāçvatara Upaniṣad, on the mere phrase of Māyā, 'illusion', which turns the supreme lord into a conjurer.[1] The Kantian doctrine, it need hardly be said, leaves us with the whole empiric world regulated under definite principles in time and space, and subject to causality, and it merely assures us that behind these relations we must not expect by intellectual means to find the meaning of existence. That meaning, however, it finds in the moral consciousness, which then becomes of infinite importance. In the doctrine of Yājñavalkya on the contrary we have nothing save denial of all real causality and multiplicity, and on the other the normal cosmogonism of the Brāhmaṇas. Of moral principles Yājñavalkya's main text is entirely innocent: the pure intellectuality of his doctrine led to the consequence that the moral acts of the person who had knowledge were indifferent, a fact which no sophistry could conceal and which was recognized at an early date: [2] it has its precise counterpart in the view, prevalent in the Middle Ages in Europe as in India, that devotion to God or an idol was enough to wipe out any infamies.

When we pass to the doctrine of Karman, the hopeless inconsistencies of the view of Yājñavalkya become painfully obvious: the doctrine of Karman is now introduced as explaining the nature of man's fate in life, without regard to the other doctrine that knowledge means emancipation at once. How on the theory of Yājñavalkya conduct could have any effect at all, or any bearing on the matter, cannot be understood, but it is really incomprehensible how Deussen can accept the view that the knowledge of the unity of the Ātman produces liberation. All the effect of the philosophy of Yājñavalkya is to declare the difference of subject and object, and then to assert that the Ātman is one, in which there is no difference of subject and object, and therefore no consciousness, and these views do not show any connexion with emancipation or transmigration by degree of merit of conduct. It is simply inconceivable why on the ground of such theoretic knowledge men should abandon the desire for children, should give up their property, and wander about like beggars, practising a foolish asceticism. Nor as a matter of fact can we imagine that any such conception normally entered the heads of the ascetics of the Vedic age: they doubtless deemed, as the texts indeed show, that what they would attain by these practices was the mystic contemplation of the

[1] Hence in Mahāyāna Buddhism we reach the logical result that all knowledge is falling away from truth and reality and its suppression is essential; cf. Schayer, *Mahāyānistische Erlösungslehre*, p. 49; Asaṅga, *Sūtrālaṁkāra* in ZII. ii. 103 ff.

[2] Hence the constant discussion in the epic of the problem of determinism (Dahlmann, *Die Sāṁkhya-Philosophie*, pp. 113 ff., 265 ff.); O. Strauss, *Ethische Probleme aus dem Mahābhārata*. For Buddhism, see Keith, *Buddhist Philosophy*, pp. 97, 113, 135 f., 175, n. 1; Stcherbatsky (*The Central Problem of Buddhism*, pp. 5, 32), who insists on the limited role of Karman.

divine which mystics of every time and clime have aimed at winning.[1] This fact, which is clearly proved by the evidence of the many passages in which union with the absolute is aimed at, and regarded as a state of abiding bliss, is not in any degree compatible with the view that what the priests and sages of the Upaniṣads believed in was the mere fact that there existed a thing in itself, which was for ever unknowable. From such premises no such conclusions as are drawn by the Upaniṣads could possibly be derived at any time. The essence of the doctrine of the Upaniṣads must be looked for in something else.

Nor indeed is there the slightest doubt as to what that belief was, apart from occasional flashes of insight which led to other conclusions. The absolute is conceived as an ideal, with which unity is as ardently desired, as it was desired in earlier times with the gods in heaven, and the unity with the absolute is conceived in the same mode as unity with the divine had been conceived. The Upaniṣads are essentially pantheistic with a strong theistic leaning, but the extent of that theism differs from passage to passage, and in the case of Yājñavalkya and others doubtless a still more intellectual view of the situation was taken, in which the chief stress was laid on the conception of the Ātman as the one and only reality, free from pollution, serene, unalterable, far above empirical being, or thought of any kind. But this cool intellectualism is not by any means the pervading doctrine of the Upaniṣads,[2] nor indeed in the record of Yājñavalkya's views are we without indication that the Ātman itself inspired devotion of a marked kind, as comes out plainly in his address to Maitreyī, on deciding to abandon his goods and his wives and wander forth into the wilderness.[3] For most of his contemporaries, who devoted themselves to the study of philosophy, it may confidently be believed that they were pantheists, who were delighted with their discovery of this as the truth of the universe, and who conceived the fate of the enlightened soul as the enjoyment of bliss in the existence to come in union with the one essence of the world.

It is these two aspects of the Upaniṣads which explain the two diverse interpretations which, as we have seen, Çañkara, following Gauḍapāda and some Aupaniṣada school on the one hand, and Bādarāyaṇa,[4] doubtless with another Aupaniṣada school, on the other, placed on the Upaniṣads. The purely negative character of the universe of experience is insisted upon by Çañkara as a result of the stress laid on the unknowability of the Ātman, and

[1] The similarity of result between the views of Plotinus and of the Vedānta is sometimes (as by Lassen, *Ind. Alt.* iii. 379 ff.; Garbe, *Phil. of Anc. India*, pp. 46 ff.) attributed to borrowing by Neo-Platonism; for a complete refutation of the view see Caird, *Evolution of Theology in the Greek Philosophers*, where it is shown that the Neo-Platonic views were in all essentials the natural, and almost inevitable, outcome of earlier Greek philosophy. In Buddhism we have the Jhānas and Iddhis and similar ridiculous states. See also T. Whittaker, *The Neo-Platonists* (1918); F. Heidemann, *Plotin* (1921); below, Chap. 29.

[2] Bloomfield, *Rel. of Veda*, p. 281.

[3] BAU. ii. 4; iv. 5.

[4] Thibaut, SBE. xxxiv. pp. c ff.

its separation from all empirical reality, while Bādarāyaṇa takes the more simple view, which sees in the absolute a divine nature, and finds a place for the world and the souls beside that nature, though still in some degree pantheistically regarded as part of the divine. The result of true knowledge as the attainment of union with the supreme deity is thus much more easily brought into concord with the utterances of the Upaniṣads themselves. Moreover, the sense of devotion to the absolute was thus brought into accord with metaphysical reality and at the same time opportunity given to adapt the Viṣṇu worship of the masses [1] to the esoteric side of the philosophy of the Upaniṣads, a task carried out by Rāmānuja in his great commentary on the Brahma Sūtra.[2]

From the point of view of ethics the demerits of the system of the Upaniṣads are even more glaring than from the point of view of the intellect. It is doubtless impossible to arrive at certainty on questions of the ultimate nature of reality, but it is an easier matter to establish some principles of moral obligation, and to bring them into harmony with a scheme of the universe which if theoretical shall none the less be at any rate plausible. The defect of the Upaniṣads is that they render morality in the ultimate issue valueless and meaningless. We may reasonably assume that any complete metaphysic must seek to explain as essential ingredients of existence, truth, goodness, and beauty, and we may safely conclude that a system, which, like that of the Upaniṣads, regards beauty and goodness as nothing but hollow mockeries, is defective and essentially unsound in its theoretic basis.

It might indeed seem at first sight that the doctrine of Yājñavalkya which ascribes results to the action of Karman, would supply us with a ground for morality, and the Buddhist system has indeed been praised [3] as an ingenious effort to establish a rigid rule of moral order in the world and to negate selfishness by maintaining the doctrines that there is no real self on the one hand, and that every action is causally determined by some previous action on the other. Even, however, in the case of Buddhism the theory is by no means satisfactory or convincing. The conception of Karman serves indeed in an excellent way to defend and protect the established order of things, but it is essentially fatalistic, and fatalism is not for a normal mind a good incentive to moral progress. If, on the one hand, the doing of an evil deed is restrained by the thought that it will be punished in another life,[4] it is equally true that reflection shows that the actor has really no option in his acts and is an absolutely predetermined person, whose former acts produce his present motives and reasonings without the possibility of intervention of any kind on his part. This fatalism haunts the Vedānta and the Sāṁkhya no less than the Buddhist system and practically every modern system of absolute idealism,[5] and it is

[1] Cf. Senart, *Album-Kern*, pp. 104 ff.

[2] Cf. Keith, ERE. *s.v.*

[3] Walleser, *Die philosophische Grundlage des älteren Buddhismus*, pp. 74, 75.

[4] Speyer, *Indische Theosophie*, p. 90, who takes a very favourable view of this doctrine.

[5] Cf. J. Ward, *The Realm of Ends* (1911),

noteworthy that in the doctrine of Rāmānuja there is a real effort to find some place for independence on the part of the individual soul, just as in Buddhism and Jainism alike free will is often tacitly assumed as existing. Again, while in the occidental systems of absolute idealism there is ever an effort to find real value for the individual by seeing in him the conscious working of the absolute which realizes itself in some degree of reality in him, in Buddhism no such satisfaction is possible. We are indeed sometimes [1] invited to see in the Buddhists of the Pāli texts lovers of empirical pyschology and hedonists who believed that life of a certain kind, the full and perfect efflorescence of mind and character on earth, was fair and lovely beyond all non-being, beyond all after-being. Unhappily in this view we have merely the ascription to Buddhism of ideals cherished by a modern sect, in flagrant defiance of the obvious fact that the *summum bonum* of the system envisaged by these writers was precisely non-being, for in death alone have unhealthy moral conditions completely passed away for ever from a sage. From such an end the only deduction bearing upon action must obviously be the rule of avoiding passion and emotion and action of every kind, and it is significant that the development of the doctrine of active compassion in the Buddhist faith is coincident with the development of the religious aspect of that belief, which in effect overthrows entirely the old ideal and which in large measure was accomplished during foreign dominion in India under the stress of spreading the Buddhist gospel beyond the narrow bounds of India proper.

In the case of the Upaniṣads, however, the position for morality is still less favourable than in the Buddhist system. It is quite impossible to make Karman the leading principle of these texts, to many of which it was clearly a sealed book. Moreover it is quite impossible to make the Karman doctrine harmonize with the doctrine of salvation by knowledge, and this doctrine is superior to all morality. Doubtless, when restricted within the narrow circles in which it first became recognized as the fundamental truth, the doctrine of salvation by knowledge alone was not likely to produce evil living, but the effect of a doctrine, which makes morality negligible, on less trained minds can easily be recognized, and is admirably illustrated by the effect of the doctrine of faith when divorced from works. But more directly and fundamentally the system failed wholly to provide, just as the Buddhist failed to provide, a criterion for morality, since for it also the *summum bonum* had no intelligible relation to moral activity of any sort. On the contrary it declared the world of reality to be a delusion or at least not true reality and to be

pp. 270 ff.; J. Royce, *Lectures on Modern Idealism* (1919); W. R. Sorley, *Hibbert Journal*, ii. 703 ff.; *Moral Values and the Idea of God* (1918) against Bosanquet, *Principle of Individuality and Value* (1912); *The Meeting of Extremes in Contemporary Philosophy* (1921); Bradley, *Appearance and Reality*; Inge, *Plotinus*, ii. 181 ff.

[1] C. Rhys Davids, *Buddhist Manual of Psychological Ethics*², pp. xciv ff. Contrast Stcherbatsky, *The Central Conception of Buddhism*, pp. 49 ff. In her *Buddhist Psychology*, pp. 278 ff., Mrs. Rhys Davids shows a clearer appreciation of the defects of Buddhism.

miserable; it encouraged the declaration of one Upaniṣad[1] that devotion to children, wife, or parents is a means of keeping back the self from its saving knowledge: it drove Yājñavalkya to abandon his dear wife for ever, and not, as in the more sympathetic version of the Buddha legend, subject to the possibility of relations of friendship at a later period. The essence of its doctrine is that of the saving of the individual soul, which must resolutely refuse to allow itself to be blinded by the ordinary desires and sympathies of mankind. This is a logical conclusion of the metaphysic of the system. When Yājñavalkya[2] declares that the husband is dear to the wife not for his own sake but for the sake of the self, and applies the same principle to the other relations of human life, to the wife, to children, to riches, to other men, to the gods, and the universe, he is doubtless concerned mainly with a metaphysical doctrine; but not only is the selfish conclusion obvious to ordinary minds,[3] but it is essentially connected with the teaching itself, for on ultimate analysis the aim of the self turns out to be the annihilation of every human desire and activity, an ideal which renders all active philanthropy idle, and which has caused the chief virtues of India to take the form of resignation, passive compassion, and charity.[4]

On the other hand, the attainment of the ideal of union with the absolute led to the addiction to the practise of meditation, and above all in ever increasing measure in later times to the seeking of mystic states of absorption in the absolute. It is right to recognize that of this tendency on its worst side the Upaniṣads have very little to show. It is an exception when the Chāndogya Upaniṣad[5] solemnly assures us that the possession of saving knowledge enables a man to have at pleasure the presence of the Fathers, the Mothers, brothers, sisters, friends, garlands, perfumes, music, and women: doubtless in some degree concession had to be made to the desires of those who, unlike Naciketas, preferred material joys and the houris of paradise[6] to the knowledge of the truth of the fate of man after death. But it was inevitable that a doctrine, which regarded morality as not really existent, and preached the attainment of union with the absolute by means of mystic abstraction, should be productive of means of attaining the desired end which were grossly immoral: the Tantras of the later Hinduism, which in Bengal[7] have ousted the Veda, which in a very real sense are the most important books of a large section of Hindus, and which are certainly by no means without occidental and American admirers, are in ultimate analysis descendants of one side of the mysticism of which a higher form appears in the Upaniṣads. The same tendencies were from the first marked in Buddhism, as in the earliest texts we find the possession of certain supernatural powers admitted as real.

The final judgement passed on the Upaniṣads cannot, therefore, be in

[1] Maitr. vi. 28.

[2] BAU. ii. 4. 5.

[3] Oltramare, *L'histoire des idées théosophiques*, i. 137.

[4] Cf. Oldenberg, *Aus dem alten Indien*, pp. 1 ff., on the difference of Maitrī and Christian love.

[5] viii. 2; 12. 3.

[6] KU. i. 25. Cf. Kauṣ. i. 4.

[7] Ewing, JAOS. xxiii. 65; Weber, *Religionssoziologie*, ii. 322 ff.

doubt:[1] they are the products of the indigenous philosophy of India, most interesting expositions of early and acute efforts to grasp the nature of the universe and man's place in the cosmos, of vital importance for the understanding of Indian philosophy and religious life in later times, since the conceptions which they enunciate have for the rest of Indian intellectual progress preponderant weight and influence. In comparison with the rest of Indian philosophy they excel in interest no less than in literary form and in freedom of thought: the deadly defect of the Buddhist dialogues, interminable repetition and dullness accentuated by the heaping up of synonyms or quasi-synonyms, is only nascent in the Upaniṣads, which again are happily exempt from the painful duty imposed on Çañkara of expounding his idealism in the form of commentaries on texts which he must take as binding upon him and expressing one consistent doctrine, in face of the fact that obviously they do nothing of the sort. On the other hand, regarded as serious contributions to the solution of the fundamental problems of philosophy, the value of the Upaniṣads must be considered to be comparatively small: moreover they became known to the western world at a time when the development of philosophy had reached a point at which it could acquire little or nothing of great value from the Upaniṣads: to measure the exact effect of their influence on Schopenhauer would be extremely difficult,[2] especially having regard to the fact that he knew them only in a version which often completely misrepresented their sense; but in the long run Schopenhauer himself represents merely a back current in the course of the stream of philosophy to its unattainable goal.

A stronger claim,[3] however, has been made for the value of the doctrine of the Upaniṣads as a school of mysticism, 'an attempt to gain personal experience of God found within the heart as a result of self-purification', or 'as a constant process of self-purification to the intent that God may be found within', definitions in which as applied to the Upaniṣads God must be understood as the Brahman. It is claimed from this point of view that the Upaniṣads have the superiority over Christian mysticism in originality, since that depends vitally on Plotinus, while it is admitted that the mysticism of the Upaniṣads is too purely metaphysical, and lacks the ethical and social content of Christian mysticism. Much of Christian mysticism, however, seems defective in this regard equally with the Upaniṣads, though it may be conceded that, unlike the Upaniṣads, the Christian mystics

[1] Cf. Oldenberg, *Die Kultur der Gegenwart*², I. v. 56, whose judgement of Indian philosophy concludes: Für den westlichen Geist—'welch Schauspiel! aber ach! ein Schauspiel nur!' Contrast S. Radhakrishnan, *The Reign of Religion in Contemporary Philosophy*, p. 451.

[2] M. F. Hecker, *Schopenhauer und die indische Philosophie* (1897); Oldenberg, *Die Kultur der Gegenwart*², I. v. 53–5; Speyer, *Indische Theosophie*, pp. 306 ff. Oldenberg (*Die Lehre der Upanishaden*, pp. 195 ff.) rightly emphasizes the fact that mystics like Meister Eckhardt are far more akin than Kant to the spirit of the Upaniṣads.

[3] Cf. R. Gordon Milburn, *The Religious Mysticism of the Upanishads*, pp. 26 ff.

professed a faith in which essential stress was laid on morality. Christian mysticism,[1] however, is undoubtedly differentiated from that of the Upaniṣads by reason of the difference between the conception of God and that of the Brahman, even though in certain mystics the personal character of the divinity tends to be merged, while in the later Upaniṣads a personal deity appears in lieu of an impersonal absolute. In harmony with this distinction is the normally greater personal character of the mysticism of Christian seers, men and women alike. From this point of view the Upaniṣads may justly be accorded greater value and importance than from that of philosophy proper, and it is significant that it is in Christian mystics that we find utterances which the seers of the Upaniṣads would have found far easier to interpret than the Kantian system, such as that of St. Catherine, 'My being is God, not by simple participation, but by a true transformation of being', or Eckhardt's, 'When the soul has lost itself and everything in God, it finds itself again in God when it attains to the knowledge of Him, and it finds also everything which it had abandoned in God', or his emphatic denial that God has any definite character of his own.[2]

It is this fact of universalism that gives the mysticism of the Upaniṣads in its purest form its chief appeal to many minds, which find in the cult of a personal deity too narrow an outlook and too selfish a destiny for man. To such spirits as these the ideal of merger in the absolute presents an effective antidote to the narrowness of traditional religion, and thus the philosophy of the Upaniṣads has for them the same attraction as systems of absolute idealism have had for many types of western mind. The chief distinction, however, between the standpoint of the Upaniṣads in this regard and that of western theories of the absolute is that the Upaniṣads do not feel any serious necessity for finding a place for morality and political life, while in the west from Hegel onwards heroic, if unsuccessful, efforts have been made by the followers of this ideal [3] to establish morality and civil life as an essential element in the absolute. The contrast admits of explanation on many grounds, but one of the most obvious is the fact that the system of caste provided ready-made an ethical framework which no philosopher cared to attack, while political organization remained almost stationary.

[1] See, e.g., C. A. Bennett, *A Philosophical Study of Mysticism*; R. Otto, *The Idea of the Holy*; James, *Varieties of Religious Reference*; von Hügel, *Mystic Element in Religion*; Underhill, *Mysticism*, and *The Mystic Way*; cf. Keith, *Buddhist Philosophy*, p. 127. For Egyptian parallels, cf. Weinreich, *Archiv für Rel.* xix. 165 ff.

[2] Cf. John Scotus: Deus propter excellentiam non immerito nihil vocatur; Angelus Silesius: Gott ist ein lauter nichts. (James, *op. cit.*, pp. 416 f.)

[3] e.g. Bosanquet, *Philosophical Theory of the State*. Cf. Hobhouse, *Metaphysical Theory of the State*.

CHAPTER 29

GREECE AND THE PHILOSOPHY OF INDIA

It is not to be thought that the early philosophy of Greece exercised any influence on the philosophy of India. Apart from every other consideration, it is clear that the rise of philosophy in Greece was long subsequent to the beginnings of Indian philosophy in the hymns of the Rigveda, and from those hymns the history of that philosophy presents itself in the light of an ordered development. The same reason, which makes it inconceivable that the philosophy of the Upaniṣads should have been the product of external influences, such as the introduction of extraneous ideas from the warrior class, makes it inconceivable that the development of that philosophy should have been affected by influences from Greece.

The only question, therefore, which can arise is whether the early schools of Greek philosophy were affected by the tenets of the schools of the Brahmans. This question, first handled with naïve enthusiasm by Sir William Jones, has been dealt with at length by Garbe,[1] who is quite prepared to derive early Greek philosophy in large measure from India, and the merit of his work on Indian philosophy renders it necessary to consider carefully the arguments which he has adduced. The possibility of such influence must be admitted, though its probability is a very different question. Still we cannot assert that there was any insuperable barrier between early India and early Greece: the proof of such intercourse is not large in quantity or quality, but the mere fact that the two countries were not separated by uncrossed deserts or seas is so far in favour of there having been exchange of ideas. Positive evidence is sometimes alleged in the shape of the quaint legend of the wooers of Agariste in Herodotos,[2] which is traced to a Buddhist Jātaka, and even for the famous passage of the *Antigone*,[3] in which the heroine weighs the respective claims of brother and husband to consideration as regards the duty of self-sacrifice, an Indian original has been claimed. In neither instance is the case at all made out and the easy credulity with which the claims of the proof of the wandering of fables and folk-tales at an early date have been accepted [4] is scarcely creditable to the historic acumen of the critics.

1 *Philosophy of Ancient India*, pp. 32–56; *Sāṃkhya-Philosophie*², pp. 114 ff. Cf. W. Jones, *Works* (1799), i. 360 f.; von Eckstein, *Ind. Stud.* ii. 369–88.

2 vi. 130. For an uncritical account of the relationship, see Macan, *Herodotos*, III–VI. ii. 304–11; cf. Winternitz, *Gesch. d. ind. Lit.* ii. 102; Tawney, JP. xii. 131; Güntert, *Buddha*, pp. 50 ff.

3 904–20; Herodotos, iii. 119; Pischel, *Hermes*, xxviii. 465 ff.; Nöldeke, xxix. 155 ff.; Tawney, IA. x. 370; Winternitz, ii. 111.

4 e. g. by Macan, *l. c.* Cf. v. Schroeder, *Indiens Literatur und Kultur*, pp. 518ff.; Oldenberg, *Die Lit. des alten Indien*, pp. 110 ff.; Forke, *Indische Märchen*, pp. 26 ff.; Winternitz, iii. 307 ff.;

A more serious attempt to prove connexions of a literary and religious nature is made by A. Götze, who compares [1] the doctrine of correspondence of macrocosm and microcosm as enunciated in the Bundahišn [2] with the pseudo-Hippokratean treatise περὶ ἑβδομάδων. The latter work appears to have been known to Plato, and therefore goes back to the fourth century B.C., while W. H. Roscher has endeavoured to assign the short treatise to the seventh century and to regard it as the earliest work extant of Greek science and cosmology. The Bundahišn, of course, is late, and this particular portion cannot even for certain be attributed to the Sassanian recension. On the other hand we have in the Upaniṣads and even in the Brāhmaṇas [3] the idea of the parallelism of macrocosm and microcosm, so that the possibility that oriental influence lies at the basis of the Greek composition cannot be excluded. It may be conjectured also that oriental influence is to be seen in the doctrine of the pseudo-Hippokratean treatise περὶ φυσῶν, where the breath is a ground of illness, and even in the doctrine of the humours, for Pāṇini already knows in the fourth century B.C. of wind, bile, and phlegm as affecting health.[4] But, even if we grant that there was influence in these matters, the date is late; the doctrines suggested by Persia were, it is believed, introduced into Greece not before 480 B.C. by the Knidian school of medicine. We know in fact of three Greek physicians at the Persian court, Demokedes under Dareios I, Ktesias under Artaxerxes II, and Apollonides, whom Ktesias mentions. It must, however, be borne in mind that we have no evidence that the doctrines alleged to have influenced Greece were actually known in Persia in the fifth century B.C., and that a case can quite fairly be made out for Greek independence in these regards.

Still less can we deduce Indian influence on Greece from the famous Orphic hymn,[5] which celebrates the greatness of Zeus, and was in some form or other known to Plato,[6] Aischylos,[7] and Xenophanes.[8] The parallelism which has been seen between the cosmic doctrine of this hymn and that of the Puruṣasūkta [9] is interesting, but it is not claimed [10] that it is due to borrowing from India. Rather it is suggested that the Orphic movement owed much to Iranian religious conceptions of the people, which play little part in the reformed religion of Zoroaster. Nor need we doubt Iranian influence on this comparatively late movement. But, so far as ascertained facts go, the evidence of any intellectual [11] connexion of a serious character between

Garbe, *Indien und das Christentum*, p. 24; Hertel, ZDMS. lxii. 113 ff., corrected by Jacobi, 358 ff.; Cosquin, *Les contes indiens et l'occident*.

[1] ZII. ii (1923), 60 ff.

[2] c. xxviii.

[3] CU. ii. 19; ÇB. x. 1. 3. 34.

[4] B. Liebich, *Zur Einführung in die ind. einheimische Sprachwissenschaft*, iv. 22.

[5] Kern, fragm. 168.

[6] *Laws*, iv. 715 E.

[7] Frag. 70 (ed. Nauck).

[8] Frag. 24 (ed. Diels).

[9] RV. x. 90.

[10] See Götze, *op. cit.*, pp. 167 ff.

[11] To cite the presence of Greek gems of the seventh century B.C. in the Punjab (Furtwängler in *Sâṃkhya-Philosophie*², p. 119) as proof of intellectual influence of India on Greece is decidedly odd.

Greece and India in the period before the extension of the empire of Persia to the north-west of India is still to seek.

The actual proof of influence must, therefore, be derived from internal evidence, the comparison of the two systems. Garbe lays stress on the fact that Xenophanes teaches that the universe is one (εἷς θεὸς ἔν τε θεοῖσι καὶ ἀνθρώποισι μέγιστος), eternal and without change, and that Parmenides writes in verse, and holds that reality is due alone to this universal being, neither created nor to be destroyed, and omnipresent, that everything which is subject to change is unreal, and that thinking and being are identical.[1] He admits that the identity of thinking and being, and the insistence on the unreality of the universe, can be proved as a definite doctrine in India only from texts later than Parmenides; but he insists that the doctrines are implicit in the Upaniṣads, and that they, therefore, may justly be deemed to have been the sources of the Eleatic philosophy. It might be added that the two philosophies are alike in the fact that they both realize that the nature of the absolute must be deemed in some way to be intellectual, however little either is able to make the nature of that intellectual character intelligible.

When these resemblances are pointed out, however, all that can be said for the theory is said: there is no ground to assume borrowing: the clearness of the position of Parmenides regarding the nature of the one is much more pronounced than the view of the Upaniṣads, and the identification of thought and the object is carried beyond the views of the Upaniṣads, while by his view of truth and opinion as distinct Parmenides anticipates Indian thought. It is, therefore, far more probable that the Greek and the Indian views were of independent origin: the Greek bears already the mark of definiteness which is only evolved centuries later in the Indian thought, and it is also aided by its freedom from the mythological connexions, which weigh so heavily on the thought of the Upaniṣads. The fact that the Brahman is identified with thought is by no means the same thing as the idea that thought and its object are identical, a doctrine of Parmenides[2] which duly modified is brought to its most complete form in the theory of Aristotle.[3] Nor is it of any value to cite the fact that Thales's view of the origin in water of everything is much later than the Vedic conception of the waters as the primeval form of existence. The idea is not only Babylonian but is a singularly simple one, as found in primitive religion, and must have been natural to primitive man: it is even possible to trace in theory the mode in which he arrived at this result. Similarly it is idle to compare the primitive matter (ἄπειρον) of Anaximander, which is indefinite and into which things pass again as they have emerged from it, new worlds arising and passing away, with the matter of the Sāṁkhya school: apart from the fact that the nature of the Sāṁkhya is not shown to

[1] ταὐτὸν δ' ἐστὶ νοεῖν τε καὶ οὕνεκέν ἐστι νόημα. Cf. also Xenophanes: οὖλος ὁρᾷ, οὖλος δὲ νοεῖ, οὖλος δέ τ' ἀκούει.

[2] ver. 94; cf. Windelband, *Hist. of Phil.*, pp. 57 ff., where the implications of the doctrine are made clear.

[3] *de An.* i. 3. 13; cf. also Wallace, *Aristotle's Psych.*, pp. c ff.

be as old a conception as Anaximander, and that it is essentially possessed of three constituents, and even rectifying the theory by placing in the position of Prakṛti the vague conception of the Brāhmaṇas as to the primitive nature of the universe, the parallelism is far too weak to be of any value as proof. In the case of Herakleitos the argument is even more unsatisfactory: the doctrine of the constant flux of things (πάντα ῥεῖ) is certainly comparable with the movement of nature in the Sāṁkhya system and to some degree in Buddhism, and his belief in the innumerable annihilations and re-creations of the universe may be compared with the view of the Sāṁkhya of the destruction and re-creation of the world.[1] But, apart from the fact that the comparison of the doctrine of constant movement with the Sāṁkhya system of the development of Prakṛti is far from important, in view of the complete distinction between the two ideas of development, it must be pointed out once more that the Sāṁkhya system is not proved to be, and most probably was not by any means, as early as the system of Herakleitos, and the doctrine of the periodic destruction of the universe, which is probably caused in India by the doctrine of transmigration, is not recorded in one of the older Upaniṣads, and is clearly a late development; Garbe himself rejects the theory that it is known to the Atharvaveda.[2] It is hardly necessary to add that it is quite out of the question to regard Empedokles as borrowing from India his view that nothing can arise from nothing: the same view is undoubtedly held by the Sāṁkhya, but is as emphatically not normally held by the Upaniṣads. Nor is it of any importance that the character of that teacher as a prophet, a magician, a believer in purification, and a mystic is comparable with certain types of Indian sage. The view that the world is incapable of producing similar figures under similar or even different circumstances is one which must be proved first before mere similarities prove anything, and Empedokles' claim to be a god, degraded to earth, is un-Indian, being derived from the Orphic doctrine of man's defilement. The fact that a dislike to flesh as food sprung up among the believers in transmigration like Empedokles is perfectly true:[3] it is, however, striking that in India itself the belief was of more tardy appearance as at all general than the date of Empedokles,[4] and was not so far as we can see caused by the doctrine of transmigration. The great sage, Yājñavalkya, with whose name the doctrines of the Upaniṣads are mainly connected, was a beef-eater with decided views as to the condition in which he ate it. It is also argued that the position of the gods in the view of Demokritos, who holds with Empedokles that nothing arises from nothing, is precisely the position of the gods in Indian thought, as seen in the Upaniṣads, where they

[1] L. Berndl (*Über das Sâṃkhya*, p. 14) argues strongly that this element in the Sāṁkhya is late. In his novel, but untenable, theory of the Sāṁkhya, he sees parallelism with Anaxagoras, but not influence on either side.

[2] *Sâṃkhya-Philosophie*[2], p. 286; AV. x. 8. 39 f.

[3] Speyer (*Indische Theosophie*, p. 299) lays stress on this point.

[4] For many exceptions in Buddhism, cf. Hopkins, JAOS. xxvii. 455–64; cf. Macdonell and Keith, *Vedic Index*, ii. 145–7.

cease to be anything more considerable than a number of superior beings, not very essentially different from men. But this argument is clearly of no weight.

Though Garbe is in favour of the view that these comparisons are proofs of borrowing, he confines his assurance of dependence to the case of Pythagoras, which has been accepted by von Schroeder [1] and Hopkins [2] with others [3] as a clear case of the influence of Greek philosophy on Indian speculation. The question cannot be ignored nor easily disposed of. The theory of Pythagoras clearly included the belief in transmigration, the idea that a series of births serves to purify the souls, and the view that the contemplative life is the highest form of existence and that man by living it most effectively strives to rid himself of the fetters of nature. It is, therefore, argued that he must have borrowed his conception from India, as there is no earlier trace of metempsychosis in Greece, and the principle must therefore have come from an external source. Further arguments are based on detailed coincidences, which must at once be admitted to be of great value in such a question, if only they could be established. The prohibition to eat beans, the rule of ceremonial purity regarding the sun (πρὸς ἥλιον τετραμμένον μὴ ὀμιχεῖν), the vow of silence like that taken by an Indian Muni, the Pythagorean theorem, the irrational root 2, the character of the religious philosophical brotherhood treated as similar to the Indian philosophical schools, and the mystic character of the doctrine are all regarded by Hopkins as valid evidence of the connexion. Other arguments have also been adduced by von Schroeder, but have been abandoned by his own supporters : thus the theory that the Pythagorean numbers are borrowed from the Sāṁkhya system is given up even by Garbe, in face of the fact that in that system number plays no part save in so far that three Guṇas and twenty-five principles are enumerated, and the Pythagorean conception of number is something totally different.[4] The further argument adduced by Garbe that the five elements are borrowed by Pythagoras from India is open to the grave objection that the five elements are not certainly known in India early enough for this, but to the still more grave objection that the

[1] *Pythagoras und die Inder* (1884) ; *Indiens Lit. und Kultur*, pp. 717 ff. Cf. Colebrooke, *Essays*[2], i. 436 ff.

[2] *Rel. of India*, pp. 559, 560.

[3] Macdonell, *Sanskrit Literature*, p. 422 ; Gomperz, *Greek Thinkers*, i. 127, 146 ; Speyer, *op. cit.*, pp. 299 ff. C. Rhys Davids (*Buddhist Psychology*, p. 143) actually suggests that the doctrine that like is known by like in Hellenic philosophy (Aristotle, *de An.* i. 2. 5 ; Plotinus, *Enn.* i. 6. 9) may be due to Eastern sources, although a conscious statement of the doctrine appears first in Buddhaghoṣa in the fifth century A.D., and asserts that Empedokles, Plato, and Plotinus were all influenced by Eastern thought. Classical scholars naturally ignore such bare assertions, or repeat them uncritically.

[4] So also Dahlmann, *Die Sāṁkhya-Philosophie*, pp. 256, 257. Berndl (*op. cit.*, p. 4) insists on MBh. xii. 11409 as proving that number was essential for the early Sāṁkhya. One may justly dismiss as ludicrous Garbe's suggestion that Pythagoras invented his system as a result of misunderstanding information given to him as to the Sāṁkhya.

system of five elements cannot be traced back to Pythagoras himself, and further that the five by no means precisely correspond with the five of India in the concepts attached to them ; the efforts [1] to show that the word ὁλκάς as used by Philolaos of the ether is the imperfect transcript of the Ākāça of the Indian tradition must be deemed to be methodologically completely mistaken.

The detailed evidence of the arguments adduced is quite insufficient to prove the propositions contended for.[2] The origin of transmigration in Greece is probably to be traced to Thrace, and it seems to have been spread by the Orphics, whose views in part at least appear to have been brought forward in a rational form by Pythagoras : it cannot be traced, as so often urged, to the personal activity of Pythagoras : it was known by Empedokles and by Pherekydes, and was recognized by Pindar : [3] it is most probable that in Thrace it developed itself in connexion with the belief in the temporary embodiment of the divinity in animal form revealed in the Dionysiac rites : the Mainads, the Bakchai, with their close communion with nature, their adoption of animal garb, their tearing of the animal who represented the god, their efforts to produce states of ecstasy, portrayed for us by the master hand of Euripides, suggest the source from which the belief could grow.[4] The story of the Thracian Zamolxis is clear proof of the belief as existing in Thrace.[5] There was also no such spirit in Greek religion, as would prevent the ready acceptance of the view. On the contrary, it may be noted that the idea of the transfer of one soul into another body was familiar from such tales as that of Kirke and the comrades of Odysseus, and the daimons of Hesiod suggest a mode of transition. The fact that transmigration appears also among the Druids, and has independently grown up with other peoples is of importance.[6] The case of Egypt where Herodotos [7] held that transmigration prevailed is difficult : the view may have been held by a sect there, though its existence is not yet established, but this possibility does not appear to be of fundamental

[1] Von Schroeder, *op. cit.*, p. 65, n. 2 ; Garbe, VOJ. xiii. 303 ff. Cf. Böhtlingk, VOJ. xiv. 85 ; BSGW. 1900, p. 150 ; Gundermann, RM. 1904, pp. 145 ff. ; Winternitz, *Gesch. d. ind. Lit.* iii. 478.

[2] Keith, JRAS. 1909, pp. 569 ff., where full details will be found. Oldenberg (*Die Kultur der Gegenwart*[2], I. v. 52) does not accept the theory, nor Weber, *Ind. Stud.* xviii. 463 ff. ; SBA. 1890, pp. 923 ff.

[3] In Greece, it should be noted, transmigration is optimistic, not a source of pessimism ; Oltramare, *L'histoire des idées théosophiques*, i. 102 ff. For the early date of the Orphic views, see Diels, *Archiv für Gesch. der Phil.* ii. 91 ff.

[4] Burnet, *Early Greek Philosophy*[2], pp. 86 ff.

[5] Herodotos, iv. 94, 95.

[6] Among the Druids, Caesar, vi. 14. 5 ; cf. Dieterich, *Nekyia*, pp. 90 ff. ; *Archiv f. Religionswissenschaft*, viii. 29 ff. ; MacCulloch, *Rel. of Anc. Celts*, pp. 334 ff., 348 ff. The interpretation of Caesar, which sees in the belief no real transmigration, but the adoption of a new body by the soul in the land of happiness, is less probable. For Germany cf. Appian, *Hist.* i. 4. 3 ; Helm, *Altgerm. Rel.* i. 254 f.

[7] ii. 123 ; cf. Bertholet, *Seelenwanderung* (Halle a. S., 1904). Rhys Davids (*Hibbert Lectures* 1881[4], p. 75) traces Pythagoras' views to this source. Cf. J. H. Breasted, *Dev. of Rel. in Egypt*, p. 277, with Hopkins, *Origin of Rel.*, p. 234 ; Jevons, *Hist. of Rel.*, p. 317.

importance. The doctrine much more probably originated in Thrace than at any other point in the Greek area, and its development beyond crude outlines was the work of the Greek religious and philosophical genius, as will be shown below.

The effort to show that the Pythagorean theorem and the problem of the square root of the number two are older in India than in Pythagoras, is based on a mistake : the error was certainly in great measure favoured by Cantor, who declared that the Indian versions of these matters must be based on those of Greece, and it was, therefore, easy for von Schroeder to argue that the relation must be the other way, that the Indian versions occurred in works which were much older than the versions recorded in Greece. The fact is that the Çulba Sūtras which contain the earliest mentions of these matters are of uncertain date : they are nominally parts of the ritual Sūtras, in the sense that they bear the name of the school, and it is urged that further they are so essentially connected with the structure of the sacred altars that they must be held to be early. The arguments for their age cannot be taken as at all conclusive :[1] the Sūtras of the schools were works without internal connexion of such a kind as to render it in the slightest degree difficult to interpolate, and that the Çulba Sūtras may not have been added long after the Çrauta Sūtras were composed it would be absurd to contend. The existing Sūtras have no appearance of great antiquity in any way : they have new technical terms, but little or none of the irregularities of construction and the archaic phraseology which justify us in placing some of the Çrauta Sūtras about the fourth century B.C., and even then of course the date assigned to them would be too late to prove borrowing by Pythagoras. We may legitimately assume that they were composed at the close of the Sūtra period, when interest in their subject-matter had developed. What is more important, and what, it may be added, tells against borrowing by India in this regard from Greece, is that examination of the Sūtras [2] has shown that complete generality of the theorem of Pythagoras was never attained and was not even striven after. The practical form of the problem was known to the Egyptians and Babylonians, long before it was known to the Sūtras.[3] The same remark applies to the alleged knowledge of the theorem of the irrational—the mere approximate calculation of the root of two, which is all the Sūtras attained, is far from

[1] See Keith, JRAS. 1910, pp. 518–20, a passage which Garbe has unfortunately forgotten in his polemic (*Sâṃkhya-Philosophie*², p. 126), though informed of it in 1910. His second argument, that Pischel has completely proved the dependence of Buddhism on the Sāṁkhya, is without serious value for any one who prefers argument to assertion ; cf. above, Chap. 28, § 7.

[2] Kaye, JRAS. 1910, pp. 752 ff. His views confirm those expressed by me in 1909. See also his *Indian Mathematics* (Calcutta, 1915), pp. 3 ff. Cf. also Vogt, *Bibl. Math.* 1906, pp. 6 ff., and the judgement of Oldenberg, GN. 1917, p. 253, n. 1 ; *Weltanschauung der Brāhmaṇatexte*, p. 233. See also T. Heath, *Hist. of Greek Mathematics* (1921).

[3] Garbe's assertion that the theorem occurs in the TS. is due to his confusing empirical knowledge with theoretical, an error made by Bürk.

being equivalent to the discovery of the solution of an irrational. The real period when these questions came to be discussed in India was doubtless at a date considerably later than Pythagoras—not before the third century B.C. in all likelihood, when the ingenuity of the Brahmans began to deal with the questions of the signification of the exact details of the measurements of the sacrificial ground. The Brāhmaṇas themselves are guiltless of any knowledge of the discussions of numbers, and this is proof positive that the speculations found in the Çulba Sūtras are of later origin.

The other resemblances in detail are negligible: the prohibition of the eating of beans, and the rule regarding the respect due to the sun, are examples of taboos of a common sort which are ethnic, and are not subjects of borrowing: the latter being found in Hesiod,[1] it is hardly intelligible how it should have been considered by Hopkins to be valid as an argument for Indian borrowing.[2] The vow of silence taken by the Muni is, on the one hand, not a common idea in the Upaniṣads, and it cannot be shown to be as early there as the date of Pythagoras: on the other hand, silence as an observance for all sorts of religious and magic purposes is ethnic.[3] The character of the Pythagorean brotherhood bears no real similarity to the Indian, save such as is inherent in every case where any men agree together in any belief. The evidence of early Greece points to the existence of such societies for two centuries before Pythagoras, and his own society seems to have developed a political activity of a truly Greek kind:[4] in the India of the Upaniṣads we have nothing recorded precisely similar to these societies: we have instead the phenomena of individual teachers with pupils wandering here and there in disputations, of a closed or mystic brotherhood not one trace. Nor is it reasonable to lay any stress on the comparison of the speculations of the Brāhmaṇas as being fantastic with those of Pythagoras on the theory of number; that every fantastic system is derived from another is an absurd proposition, and the kinds of fantasy are quite different.

Moreover it is right to note that the spirit of Pythagoras is different in essentials from the spirit of the Upaniṣads. Plato in the *Phaidon*[5] gives as older than Philolaos, and perhaps as already held by Pythagoras, the view that the soul of man is a stranger in the world, that the body is the tomb of the soul, and that yet we may not seek to escape from it, for we are the chattels of God, and he is our herdsman, and we may not leave it without his command. This religious attitude is clearly, as will have been seen from the account of the Upaniṣads, wholly at variance with the thought of those texts. In the

[1] *Works and Days*, 727; cf. Pliny, *Nat. Hist.* xxviii. 6; AV. xiii. 1. 56.

[2] Hopkins would doubtless reject Brunnhofer's view that Hesiod's is not genuine Greek belief. Von Schroeder (VOJ. xv. 187–212) himself explains the taboo against beans as Aryan and due to their use in offerings to the dead.

[3] Cf. Deussen, *Phil. of Up.*, p. 11. For silence as a sign of the highest wisdom, cf. BAU. iii. 5. 1; CU. viii. 5. 2; Kaṭhaçruti Up. 3.

[4] Cf. A. Delatte, *Essai sur la politique pythagoricienne* (1922).

[5] 62 B; cf. *Gorg.* 493 A; *Kratyl.* 400 B; Zeller, *Presocratic Phil.*, i. 481 ff.

second place, there is a real point of difference between the form of the belief in transmigration of Pythagoras and that of the Upaniṣads : it is expressly and sarcastically recorded of Pythagoras that he recognized in the howling of a dog the voice of a friend, and that he claimed to remember his former births.[1] These characteristics are not to be found in the doctrine of the older Upaniṣads : the doctrine of the recollection of former births is only recorded later,[2] and the recognition of the voice of a friend is a peculiarity of the Greek imagination, displaying a humour which in India the doctrine of transmigration does not excite in the times of the Upaniṣads. Further the Indian doctrine of knowledge resulting in emancipation is not to be found in Pythagoras, who was a believer in the essential character of purification, probably in origin a physical purification,[3] but soon transformed into one of moral character.

It is in fact hopeless to seek any real derivation of Greek philosophy from India : the alleged travels of Pythagoras and others to India are foolish and late inventions, of no real value whatever. The efforts made, and often most uncritically accepted, to find the influence of Pythagorean views derived from India on Plato is hopeless : the fact that Plato believes in the bondage of the soul in matter and in its immortality and transmigration is made the ground for the belief that he is indebted to the Sāṁkhya philosophy by Barthélemy St. Hilaire,[4] a view which would be comic if it were not endorsed by the authority of Hopkins. The broad fact which should be recognized

[1] Xenophanes *ap*. Diog. Laert. viii. 36.

[2] The view that this is meant in BAU. i. 4. 10 ; AU. ii. 4 (Deussen, *Phil. of Up*., pp. 317, 318), is clearly speculative; it is not stated in either text and is a bad guess of the commentators who read their own views into the Upaniṣads wholesale, which unfortunately has misled Deussen. According to Deussen in the former passage Vāmadeva is stated to have recognized his identity with the Brahman, 'and as a proof of his knowledge of Brahman alleged his acquaintance with his former births as Manu and Sūrya '. But the Upaniṣad has nothing whatever as to former births, and the argument is quite different. By knowledge of the Brahman one becomes the Brahman, as it did itself, and as may the gods and seers; in substantiation of this doctrine is cited the fact that Vāmadeva became (*not* ' once was ') Manu and Sūrya by recognizing his identity with them (a complete misunderstanding, of course, of the hymn which is not spoken by Vāmadeva : cf., last, Charpentier, *Die Suparṇasage*, pp. 135 ff.). In AU., on the other hand, the citation is merely to establish the fact that Vāmadeva knew the three forms of birth ; not a word is said of his having passed through any series of births at all.

[3] Cf. Farnell, *Evolution of Religion*, pp. 88 ff. The eschatology of Pindar, as we gather it from the second Olympian and the Threnoi, is vitally different from that of the Upaniṣads. On death the souls are judged ; the good then dwell in bliss with Pluto and Persephone ; the evil must undergo anguish to punish and purify them. Then they are sent back again to earth, and on death are judged once more. Those who in three different stages of life live uprightly, and abstain from evil, are permitted eternal life in the Tower of Kronos (cf. Christ, *Pindar*, pp. 21 f.).

[4] *Premier mémoire sur le Sāṅkhya*, pp. 512, 513, 521, 522. Röer's comparison of the chariot metaphor in the Kaṭha Upaniṣad and the *Phaidros* (p. 246) is no proof of borrowing.

is that, the nature of the problem of existence being the same everywhere, and the mind of man not being essentially different in the India of the Upaniṣads and the Greece of the Pythagoreans and Plato, the results of the philosophy tend to resemble each other in diverse points.[1] But in philosophy it is not the results which matter : the solution of the riddle of the universe is, we may feel assured, reserved for no mortal, and the comparative value of two philosophies, even when the results in the mere sphere of theory as opposed to practical philosophy are similar, depends in the main on the methods adopted. In this respect the discrepancy between the Upaniṣads and Plato is sufficient to make us realize from what different foundations the structures of the two edifices of thought were raised.

One further point of suggested contact between Indian and Greek thought should be noted, as it has the support of the authority of Garbe.[2] Weber [3] suggested that there might possibly be some degree of dependence on India through Alexandria of the philosophy of Neo-Platonism in its doctrine of the Logos, as compared with the position of Vāc, speech, in the Brāhmaṇas. In that literature, as we have seen, Vāc now and then appears as the instrument by which the creator god carries out the process of the creation of the universe. Moreover, in a few passages there is a suggestion that Vāc is even higher than her normal lord, Prajāpati : thus at the Vājapeya offering we learn that some offered to her the last of the seventeen oblations in the hope to win her,[4] and she is credited with the creation of the whole universe and identified with Viçvakarman.[5] The conception of speech as the final power in the universe, which thus grows up naturally in the Brāhmaṇas, is contrasted by Weber with the sudden and unexpected appearance of the Logos in Greek philosophy. Garbe, accepting this view, presses it further : the Logos in Greek philosophy came to Neo-Platonism through Philo, and he borrowed it from the Stoics,[6] who in their turn inherited it from Herakleitos whose dependence on India for his philosophy is thus triumphantly proved.[7] The whole theory is clearly without any solid foundation of truth : the essence of the view that the sporadic doctrine of the importance of Vāc should have given rise to the very definite and clear conception of the Logos [8] is in itself wholly incredible, seeing that at the most it is reasonable to assume that a

[1] Cf. E. Leumann, *Buddha und Mahāvīra*, pp. 55–70.

[2] *Philosophy of Ancient India*, pp. 55 ff.

[3] *Ind. Stud.* ix. 473–80.

[4] ÇB. v. 1. 3. 11, which disapproves.

[5] ÇB. viii. 1. 2. 9 ; cf. xi. 1. 6. 8.

[6] Dahlmann (*Die Sāṁkhya-Philosophie*, pp. 255–81) suggests that the Stoic doctrine of logic, physics, and ethics owes much to India, but his parallelisms—often just and forcible—prove nothing save the similarity of the mind of man.

[7] If Hertel's doctrine of Brahman as fire were accepted (see above, Chap. 27, § 2) the case for borrowing would be far stronger. But, as we have seen, this is most implausible.

[8] Burnet, *Greek Philosophy*, Part I, pp. 57–63 ; cf. Mills, JRAS. 1902, pp. 897 ff. ; Aall, *Die Lehre vom Logos*. S. Langdon (JRAS. 1918, pp. 443 ff.) argues for a Babylonian origin of the Logos as cosmic, connected with the primeval waters, suggesting that Thales derived his doctrine of water as the origin of things from Babylonian thought.

view which was widely spread and normal in the philosophy of India might be conveyed by chance to Greece: to assume this of an idea which plays comparatively speaking no part in the Brāhmaṇas and which in the Upaniṣads, i.e. in the early philosophy of India, has no part at all, is contrary to all plausibility.[1]

The true relation between Greek and Indian philosophy can be seen clearly from the parallel which, quite legitimately, has been drawn [2] between the view of Empedokles and of Pakudha Kaccāyana, whose opinions are recorded for us by Buddhist texts. The date of the views of the latter teacher is such that it is absurd to assume that his opinions, which were obviously never widely held, could have reached Greece and influenced Empedokles. Kaccāyana asserted the existence of seven distinct elements whose interaction gave rise to the world of experience, namely earth, air, fire, water, pleasure and pain as sources of attraction and repulsion, and the soul, Jīva. The first six of these factors clearly correspond closely with the four elements of Empedokles, to which he added love and strife as sources of motion. Both agree in regarding their elements as unchanging, both recognize pores in organized bodies,[3] both deny the existence of a void. Yet the fact that Pakudha Kaccāyana accepted the existence of soul reminds us that he derives from a philosophic tradition to which the conception of souls was familiar, while Empedokles' opinions are based on a naturalistic philosophy, although, like Kaccāyana, he believes in the doctrine of transmigration.

When in Anaxagoras we find Nous introduced as an element, comparison with the Sāṁkhya is far from convincing, for nor merely is Nous one, not many, but it clearly bore no resemblance in nature or function to the Puruṣa of the Sāṁkhya.

Parallelism again is the cause of most of the similarities which have often been traced between Indian thought and post-Aristotelian philosophy. Garbe has, very wisely, discounted much of the borrowing assumed by the pioneer researches of Lassen,[4] but his own efforts to trace borrowings from the Sāṁkhya in the case of Plotinus are far from happy. The doctrine that the soul is in reality free from sorrow, which, on the contrary is essentially involved in the world of matter, is the development of a Platonic conception, and farther back is Orphic in origin. The conception of the soul as light is Aristotelian, and, as it is an essential doctrine of the Upaniṣads, derivation from the Sāṁkhya in any event would be wholly unnecessary. The metaphor of the mirror applied to the explanation of consciousness of knowledge is traced by Garbe to the Sāṁkhya, though we have not a scrap of proof that the school knew the doctrine for centuries after his date, since the Kārikā is

[1] Cf. Oldenberg, *Weltanschauung der Brāhmaṇatexte*, p. 81; Hopkins, *Rel. of India*, p. 558. For the doctrine in the Hermetic writings in Egypt see Flinders Petrie, *Trans. Third Internat. Congress of Rel.* i. 196 ff.

[2] Barua, *Prebuddh. Ind. Phil.*, pp. 281 ff.; DN. i. 48; MN. i. 198, 250; ii. 2, &c.

[3] Aristotle, *de Gen. et Corr.* i. 8.

[4] *Ind. Alt.* iii. 379 ff., 384 ff. (Gnostics), 417 ff. (Plotinus), 430 ff. (Porphyry), 438 (Abammon).

absolutely silent regarding it. The fact that the system of Plotinus is directed to freeing man from misery follows from his own doctrine, nor in any case could it be made specially Sāṁkhyan in derivation, and the same observation applies to the view of Plotinus that even in sleep happiness is possible since the soul does not sleep. His reduction [1] of all souls to one (εἰ πᾶσαι αἱ ψυχαὶ μία) is, of course, opposed to the Sāṁkhya, and can be explained perfectly well without the introduction of derivation from the Vedānta. His belief in the turning away of the mind from things of the sense and the achievement of a condition of union with the divine in ecstasy is parallel with the Pratibhā, intuitive knowledge,[2] of the Yoga doctrine, but it also follows inevitably from the foundations of his philosophy.

It is remarkable also that, though in the case of Porphyry (A. D. 232–304) we know that he used Bardesanes and actually reproduces remarks of his regarding the Brahmans, we find nothing conclusive of borrowing from the Sāṁkhya. The distinction which he makes between spirit and matter is merely in keeping with the views of Plotinus; equally so are the doctrines of the superiority of spirit to matter, of the omnipresence of the soul when freed from matter, and of the fact that the world has no beginning. His objection to sacrifice and the slaying of animals might be traced with Lassen to Buddhism with far greater likelihood than to the Sāṁkhya, but it has historical antecedents in Greece. Abammon's doctrine of the remarkable magic powers possessed by persons in ecstasy agrees perfectly with Buddhist views as well as those of the Brahmans, but we cannot forget the delusions attributed by Euripides to the Bakchai and in special to Pentheus. We may see an echo of the Sāṁkhya Guṇas in the Gnostic divisions of men as πνευματικοί, ψυχικοί, and ὑλικοί, and in the according of personal existence to such mental states as the intellect, will, &c., in the manner in which existence is assigned to Buddhi, Ahaṁkāra, Manas, &c. But the case for real borrowing is far from certain; in the later case Iranian influence is probably at work; in other instances, as in the system of Basilides, Buddhist influence is clear.[3]

On the other hand the efforts which have been made by Satis Chandra Vidyabhusana [4] to establish the gradual reception in India of Greek logic, while ingenious and interesting, are equally without assured ground. It is, indeed, far more probable, if borrowing really took place, that India obtained the impulse to logical investigation from Greece in a general way and proceeded *more suo* to develop her doctrines without detailed intervention of Greek ideas. At least this would suit the history of Indian logic far more satisfactorily than the suggestions of Vidyabhusana, whose readiness to recognize Greek influence is, however, admirable testimony to the scientific spirit in which his valuable researches were conducted. Nor in any case is there any doubt that he is perfectly in the right in distinguishing, as against

[1] *Enn.* iv. 9; Deussen, *Allgem. Gesch. der Phil.* II. i. 497; Inge, i. 205 ff.; ii. 82 ff.

[2] Yoga Sūtra, iii. 33.

[3] Kennedy, JRAS. 1902, pp. 376 ff. See also T. Whittaker, *The Neo-Platonists* (1918); Reitzenstein, *Die hellenistischen Mysterienreligionen* (1910); *Das iranische Erlösungsmysterium* (1921); Keith, JHS. xli. 280 f.

[4] *History of Indian Logic*, pp. 497 ff.

the contentions of Barua and others, the use of syllogism from the theoretical exposition. A similar error, as has been seen, has led Bürk and Garbe to hold that at the time of the Taittirīya Saṁhitā the Pythagorean problem was known, when in truth all that is recorded is the correct measurement of the sides of a right-angled triangle.

We have in fact to admit that the human spirit, in virtue of its character, is able to produce in different parts of the world systems which agree in large measure, without borrowing by one side from the other. The stress laid in the cave metaphor in the *Republic* by Plato, as by Parmenides, on the relative unreality of the world of sense and experience bears a certain similarity to the conception of the Brahman as alone real, but Plato was the inheritor of the Sophists and Sokrates, and as a result his philosophy is something vitally distinct from any known to India. The metaphor of the chariot and its steeds in the *Phaidros* has, as we have seen, an interesting parallel in the Kaṭha, but the details of the two are perfectly distinct, for Plato uses the conception to illustrate the struggle between the rational and the irrational elements in the soul, and his distinction of θυμός and ἐπιθυμία has no real parallel in the Upaniṣads. In the Bṛhadāraṇyaka Upaniṣad [1] we hear of procreation as the result of the desire for reunion of the two halves of the primitive being, divided by Prajāpati into man and woman. The brilliant myth in the *Symposion* of Plato has been compared by Deussen,[2] who argues that the view departs from truth merely in that it places in the past what lies in the future, for the being that brings together man and woman is the child that is to be born. The two passages must certainly be independent, and afford an excellent instance of what parallelisms can be adduced.

Yet another instance is that of the five elements. As Deussen [3] points out there are characteristic differences between the two lists which show a divergence of origin; the Greeks place fire between ether and air, the Indians air—which is really for them wind, Vāyu—between ether and fire. Moreover there is a perfectly simple natural fact to which the series corresponds, the division of states of matter into the solid, the fluid, the fiery or gaseous, the elastic, and the imponderable, which could not fail to win early attention. In point of fact we can trace in Greek philosophy the gradual emergence of the doctrine of the five elements in a perfectly characteristic manner. Thales claimed water as the primary source of reality, Anaximenes air, Herakleitos fire, Parmenides, in the part of his work dealing with opinion as opposed to true knowledge, admitted the hot and the cold, fire and earth, and Empedokles, accepting four, set fire off against the other three, and, in a wholly un-Indian manner, experimentally proved air to be different from space. The fifth element was added, whether under the title 'ether' or not, by the school of Pythagoras, not himself, and is derived from a conception of a πνεῦμα surrounding the world, which is also regarded as space.[4]

[1] i. 4.

[2] *Phil. of Up.*, p. 293. His comparison of Maitr. vi. 15 as to the beginning of time with *Tim.* 37 D seems decidedly far-fetched (*op. cit.*, p. 153).

[3] *Op. cit.*, p. 189.

[4] See Keith, JRAS. 1909, pp. 595 f. with references: Appendix H.

APPENDIX

A. THE AGE OF THE AVESTA AND THE RIGVEDA

An effort definitely to establish the date of the reform of Iranian religion by Zoroaster has been made by J. Hertel,[1] who seeks to trace the activity of the prophet from 559–522 B.C., a result of much importance in view of the probability that no very great interval of time can intervene between the Rigveda and the Gāthās of the Avesta.

Stress is naturally laid by Hertel on the fact that the religion of the Persians as described by Herodotos contains nothing specifically Zoroastrian, while it accepts much that Zoroaster rejected, especially the direct veneration of nature gods, and the animal sacrifice; moreover Herodotos records the drunkenness of the Persians, which may be connected with the Haoma offering, the fear of defiling fire or water, and the practice of the Magoi of permitting the bodies of the dead to be torn by birds or beasts, matters which are not recognized in the Gāthās. Hence it may be concluded that Zoroaster's activity fell at no great date before the reign of Xerxes I. Nor can we form any reasoned judgement to the contrary on the strength of the view of Xanthos of Lydia, a contemporary of Artaxerxes I (465–424 B.C.), who places Zoroaster 6,000 years [2] before the expedition of Xerxes, or the slightly variant account of Aristotle which makes him 6,000 years before the death of Plato.[3]

The Persian inscriptions show Dareios I as a believer in Auramazdā, who is clearly the god of Zoroaster, not the sky god of the nature worship of the Persians, whose name Herodotos heard under a form akin to the Indian Dyaus. The devotion of Dareios to this god can be accounted for only by the view that he was the deity of his branch of the family of the Achaimenidai. Dareios had to struggle against the hostility of the Magoi, representing the traditional faith, and it was his earnestness under the influence of the prophet's teaching, which secured the sudden predominance of the Zoroastrian view, despite its abstract character and lack of popular elements. But this means that Zoroaster had lived just before Dareios or was still alive, for if he had lived some centuries before, and his religion had still at the time of Dareios been of so small account, it could never have suddenly expanded to important dimensions. This view, in Hertel's opinion, is strengthened by the terms used by Dareios himself, when he asserts that the earlier kings had failed to accomplish what in one year he had wrought by the aid of Auramazdā, and when he advises his successors to punish the adherents of the lie. His successors omit this warning, which was only in place when a new god was being first proclaimed. Under Artaxerxes II (404–359 B.C.) we find Auramazdā worshipped along with Mithra and Anāhita, showing the contamination of Zoroastrianism with the older nature worship under the influence of the Magoi, who had accepted the duty of preaching the new faith, but naturally permeated it with ideas of the older belief.

[1] *Die Zeit Zoroasters* (1924).

[2] There is a variant 600; Moulton, *Early Zoroastrianism*, p. 412 (a work unknown to Hertel). It is preferred by Rapp, ZDMG. xix. 25; Maspero, *Passing of the Empires*, p. 572, n. 8.

[3] Pliny, *N.H.* xxx. 2. 1; see Jackson, *Zoroaster*, pp. 152 ff.

Ingenious as are the arguments of Hertel, it is clearly impossible to accept them as adequate to prove his thesis that Zoroaster was an earlier contemporary of Dareios I. The attitude of the king is certainly that of the adherent of a faith who believes strongly in his god; it does not prove that the faith was a new one; it might well have existed for some centuries in comparative obscurity, to be brought into prominence by the moral earnestness of a king who shared the spirit of the founder of the reformed faith and of his successors. The evidence *a priori* is simply negative in direction, and the conclusion drawn by Hertel is wholly uncertain, unless it can be supported by other evidence.

Such evidence Hertel finds in the Parsi tradition which gives something like 595–594 B.C. as the opening of Zoroaster's ministry and makes him live about 660–583 B.C. The date is earlier than his own, but in view of the deplorable nature of the Parsi tradition generally, he deems this of no importance, and refers to the fact that Anquetil du Perron [1] arrives at the date 559 B.C. for the beginning of Zoroaster's work, on the strength of the fact that a religious sect, which immigrated into China about A.D. 600 and which is evidently of Zoroastrian origin, had an era dating approximately from that time, which Anquetil interpreted as fixed by the prophet's leaving his home and entering on his mission. For the accuracy of the tradition the best argument to be adduced is that, if Zoroaster had not lived at a comparatively later epoch, the Parsis would not have brought his date down, since no sect willingly depreciates the age of its founder. Here, however, we are left to mere guess-work, and we have a very formidable argument to confront in the fact that tradition does not make the patron of Zoroaster, Vīštāspa, identical with the father of Dareios until as late as Ammianus Marcellinus (5th cent. A.D.), whose evidence in this regard, Hertel very frankly admits, is worthless.

The later Avesta in fact and the Parsi tradition ascribe the patron of Zoroaster to a Kavi dynasty, founded by a certain Kavāta; moreover it is silent regarding the great Persian kings who favoured the faith. It also, like the Greek tradition, gives Zoroaster the position of one of the Magoi. In Hertel's view the dynasty of Kavi is a pure invention, Kavi Vīštāspa in the Avesta really denoting merely the king [2] Vīštāspa; the omission to mention the Achaimenidai is due to the opposition of Dareios to the Magoi, and the connexion of Zoroaster with that body is mythical.[3] On the contrary, in vv. 8 and 9 of the Gāthā (Yasna, liii.) Hertel finds a direct encitement to Vīštāspa to overthrow the usurper Gaumāta and the Magoi, the passage dating shortly before Dareios acted on the hint in lieu of his father, and brought about by treachery the destruction of the Magoi. This suggestion, however, seems wholly implausible. The verses form part of the utterance of the prophet at the marriage of his daughter Pourucistā; what he says naturally applies generally to evil-doers and to their punishment by the Lord, and it is illegitimate to read into them an admonition, carefully disguised from motives of prudence under a double entendre in the later Indian style.

Hertel naturally rejects the argument [4] in favour of an earlier date of Zoroaster derived from the occurrence of Mazdaku as a royal name in Media

[1] Jackson, *op. cit.*, p. 165.

[2] But Vīštāspa does not appear as a king in the inscriptions; Herodotos (iii. 70) makes him only ὕπαρχος in Persia.

[3] So, for very different reasons, Moulton, *op. cit.*, pp. 116, 197.

[4] Meyer, KZ. xlii. 16. See Moulton, *op. cit.*, pp. 30 f., 422 ff. Hertel ignores C. Clemen's important work, *Die griechischen und lateinischen Nachrichten über die persische Religion* (Giessen, 1920), where the date, not later than 1000 B.C., is contended for, and where (pp. 54–77) a fair case is made out for the view that Cyrus was a Zoroastrian; cf. Keith, JHS. xl. 232.

about 715 B.C., on the ground, also adopted by Jackson, that the name need not be derived from Mazdāh as a divine name, but merely from the word in its signification of wisdom, parallel to Sanskrit *medhā.* The occurrence of Assara Mazāš as a divine name in an inscription of the seventh century B.C. probably, in view of its form, carries back the existence of Ahura Mazdāh to a period before the life of Zoroaster, so that, even if the royal name were theophoric, it would prove nothing for the date of Zoroaster.[1]

It remains, therefore, impossible to establish with any certainty Zoroaster's date. The views of Hertel rest on *a priori* reasoning so far as they have any validity; the tradition which supports them as regards date contradicts them on the vital point of ancestry, and there are certain considerations of high importance to be set against his contentions. In the first place, we find Greek reports as early as the fifth century B.C. placing Zoroaster in the very remote past; in the second place, the younger Avesta already treats Zoroaster as a mythical figure. It is very difficult to reconcile these facts with the theory that Zoroaster was alive as late as 522 B.C., and it must be recognized that even the Parsi tradition declines to place him as late as that, for it is out of the question to take seriously the suggestion of Anquetil, on which Hertel relies for his upper date of 559 B.C. as the beginning of the work of the prophet.

It seems, therefore, that the date of the Gāthās of the Avesta must remain unascertained; it remains, however, to consider the value of the evidence adduced by Hertel regarding the position of the Rigveda. He finds in that text evidence of hostility to the tenets of Zoroaster openly expressed, in the condemnation of the *brahmadviṣ*[2] and the *devanid.*[3] The doctrine of the Brahman was held by persons who insisted on negating the pre-existence and future existence of each individual; the believers in the Daēnā of Zoroaster, for which the younger Avesta has Fravaši, held opposing views, and thus can be censured as *brahmadviṣ.* Similarly the Zoroastrians were the only persons known to us who degraded the gods of the Aryans to demons. The answer in either case seems irresistible; the *devanid* of the Rigveda is most naturally and normally applied to the non-Aryan foes of the Vedic Indians, and the *brahmadviṣ* is even more obviously not to be interpreted in the strange way suggested by Hertel, whose assertion that the believers in the doctrine of Brahman did not accept an individual pre-existence and future existence of the soul is a pure hypothesis, quite unsupported by anything which we know of any historical Brahman doctrine as opposed to that invented by Hertel,[4] in which, doubtless, the individual is to be regarded as the result of the streaming out of the cosmic fire, into which he is reabsorbed. Hertel does not state how he connects this view with the obvious belief in transmigration of the Upaniṣads. Even more remarkable is his assertion that in Rigveda vii. 104. 2 the term *brahmadviṣ* is applied to a Piçāca, the Piçācas being a cannibalistic race found in the Indus valley and in the Hindu Kush. Apart from any dubiety as to the correctness of Grierson's views on Piçācas,[5] there is the uncontrovertible fact that Piçāca does not appear in the passage cited at all, which clearly and obviously applies to a Rakṣas, the hymn being directed against these demons. Even on Hertel's own theory it is obvious that it is

[1] Maspero (*op. cit.*, pp. 455, 572) argues that the name Phraortes denotes Fravartiš, 'confessor' of the Zoroastrian faith, which, of course, would give an early date as Deiokes' father bore the name (Herodotos, i. 96), but the etymology is dubious (Moulton, *Early Zoroastrianism*, pp. 269 ff.).

[2] *Die Zeit Zoroasters*, p. 62.

[3] IF. xli. 200. The term occurs only in RV. i. 152. 2; vi. 61. 3.

[4] *Ibid.* 185 ff. Cf. above, Chap. 27, § 2.

[5] Cf. above, p. 73.

unlucky that the Rigveda should apply the same term *brahmadviṣ* to the Zoroastrians and to a race of eaters of dead bodies, who are severely censured and denounced in the Avesta.[1] Nor does he adduce any reason why, even on his own theory, the term should not always apply to Piçācas, if it actually once does so.

It appears impossible also to derive any results as to the age of the Rigveda or the Avesta from the discovery of Aryan elements in the speeches of Asia used in the Hittite Empire, Sumerian, Babylonian or Akkadian, Kanisian (Hittite), Luvian, Balāian, Charrian, Proto-Hittite, and that of the Manda.[2] That Indo-European elements of *centum* type may be traced in Kanisian and Luvian is quite natural in view of the obvious activity of the Indo-European tribes. More immediate value attaches to the evidence of the Aryan speech of the Manda tribes on the borders near Mitanni, to whose speech Forrer ascribes the names of Mitanni gods, which as pronounced he holds to have been Midrassil, Ur(u)vanassil, Nasattiyana, and Indar. The first three names are preceded by the determinative An (-Meš) which marks them as denoting groups of gods, which may as regards Mitra and Varuṇa serve as an indication of their being closely united. The variant Arunassil is regarded as due to influence by the Kanisian word *arunas*, ocean, a view interesting if it may be taken as indicating a connexion between Varuṇa and the ocean in the minds of the Manda tribes. As Manda also he classes the terms of horse-breeding and training found in a text emanating from a man of Mitanni ; they include in his view, *aika-vartanna*, ' one round ', *tēravartanna* or *tērōrtanna*, ' three rounds ', *panzavartanna, sattavartanna, satvartanna, navartanni vasannasaya*, ' in nine rounds of the stadium ', and *auzomēwa*, ' run ', in which he sees the *-wa* of an infinitive termination comparable to Vedic *-mane* and *-vane*, drawing the further conclusion that in a period prior to the period of Indo-European speech unity there existed a spirant which in Kanisian became a *v* sound, in Greek and Luvian an *m* sound. This is much too speculative ; what is clear is that the numerals are by no means Vedic and that they can be set down as Aryan with equal plausibility. We are, therefore, still left without any definite evidence to aid us in dating the distinction of Aryan into Iranian and Indian, and we should probably revise our conception of this division. In an area of considerable extent over which Aryan was spoken we may assume dialectical differences sprang up, accelerated in development by contact with different racial elements, and the fragments of Mitanni speech akin to Aryan found of late represent developments of what may conveniently be called Aryan, not either Iranian or Indian. This natural hypothesis removes the need of imagining movements back from India to the west, while the possession of some gods in common well accords with the Aryan character of the speech.

Hertel [3] accepts as proved Ipsen's effort [4] to establish the theory that the period of Indo-European unity lasted until the period 2000 B.C. The evidence, however, for this thesis is inadequate ; it rests merely on the view that the prototype of the Indo-European variants of the word star [5] could only have been borrowed then. It is, however, obvious that, even if we assume that the word was borrowed, the evidence is quite insufficient to establish either the date or the unity of the Indo-Europeans at the time of the borrowing. What

[1] Vend. vii. 23 f. ; viii. 73 f.
[2] E. Forrer, ZDMG. lxxvi. 174–269 ; cf. J. Friedrich, *ibid.* 153–73 ; IF. xli. 369–76 ; Bloomfield, JAOS. xli. 195–209 ; Prince, *ibid.* 210–24 ; Sayce, JRAS. 1922, pp. 563 ff. ; cf. A. Ungnad, *Die ältesten Völkerwanderungen Vorderasiens* (1923) ; ZDMG. lxxvii. 87 ff. ; A. E. Cowley, *The Hittites* (1918).
[3] IIQF. ii. 7.
[4] IF. xli. 174 ff.
[5] Greek ἀστήρ, Latin *stella*, OE. *steorra*.

is fairly well established is only the existence in the latter part of the first half of the second millennium B.C. of dialects which may generically be styled Aryan, and which have developed beyond the hypothetical language, which may be regarded as Indo-European.

Peake,[1] who argues for the Indo-Europeans, or Wiros, as of Nordic race, with heads rather narrow than broad, transparent skin, light hair, and grey eyes, settled in the steppes east of Dnieper about 3000 B.C., holds that drought about 2200 B.C. sent some of them to the Iranian plateau where they appear as the Kassites,[2] while the Aryas proper, speaking Indo-Iranian dialects, were still living together in Russian Turkestan in 2000 B.C. He places about 1760 B.C., contemporaneously with the Kassite occupation of Mesopotamia, the separation of the Indians and the Iranians. The Mitanni barons he regards as a group of Aryas who spoke a language with Iranian affinities and separated themselves from the main body somewhat after 2000 B.C., rejecting Sayce's suggestion that they were Phrygians, who entered their territory from Thracian homes in the west. Yet other Wiros established their power in the Hittite Empire,[3] which they reached *via* Gallipoli. This reconstruction is interesting, but it lacks decisive proof of any kind. The Hungarian home of the Wiros claimed by Dr. Giles [4] he rejects, save in so far as he admits that many of the Wiros may have been descendants of the late Aurignacian and Solutrean horse-hunters, and that they may have developed the rudiments of their language in some post-Solutrean time within the Carpathian ring. The Germanic origin of the Wiros is also wholly rejected, nor despite the arguments of Kossinna [5] and others does it seem tenable.[6]

Some would fix the Vedic period by first establishing the probable date of the Bhāratan war, and then by reckoning of generations on the basis of epic or Purāṇa genealogies dating certain kings who figure in the Rigveda. Thus the war is placed by various modern critics, contrary to tradition, about 950 B.C. or 850 B.C., whence it is deduced that some at least of the personages of the Rigveda flourished no more than a couple of centuries earlier.[7] There is nothing impossible in such a result, but it must be confessed that it is difficult to put any faith on the epic or Purāṇa genealogies, and that the probative value of such reasonings must be admitted to be minimal.[8] Least of all is it

[1] *The Bronze Age and the Celtic World*, chaps. xii. and xiv. Cf. CAH. i. 82–5, where attention is called to their invention of wheeled transport and domestication of the horse.

[2] This view, followed in CAH. i. 553, depends on the equations Buriaš = Boreas; Šuriaš = Sūrya; Maruttaš = Marut; *bugaš* = Slav *bogu*, Phrygian *bagaios*, 'god'. But this is all very dubious; Keith, IHQ. i. 15 f.

[3] *Op. cit.*, p. 158, where erroneously Wiro gods are ascribed as adopted by the Hittites, among whom Wiros were merely military adventurers (Sayce, JHS. xliii. 48 f.).

[4] CHI. i. 67 ff.; CAH. ii. 28 f.

[5] *Die Herkunft der Germanen* (1911). Cf. C. Schuchhardt, *Alteuropa* (Berlin, 1919). An effort is made by C. Antran (*Phéniciens*, 1920) to assign Minoan culture to the Caro-Lelegians of Caucasian origin.

[6] That Indo-European is a composite trade-route language of Baltic-Mesopotamian origin is a mere guess, of an improbable character. That it was an easy language is equally implausible; all extant Indo-European speeches are vastly more simple than the original (see, e.g., Jespersen, *Progress in Language*).

[7] Cf. Hemchandra Raychaudhuri, *Calcutta Review*, xiii. (1924), 67–77, who places Parikṣit in the ninth century B.C.

[8] When legendary accounts can be checked, their extraordinary inaccuracy is seen; cf., e.g., the 'pseudo-Kallisthenes' version of the history of Alexander the Great; the Charlemagne cycle with its colossal exaggeration of the reverse at Roncesvalles in the *Roman de Roland* (a case which should give pause to all arguments of a great Bhāratan war); the utter confusion of the legend of Dietrich of Bern (Theodoric of Verona) —see Chadwick, *The Heroic Age*, pp. 23 f.; the amazing development of

possible to find any support for the proposed date of the war in Jain tradition, which places Ariṣṭanemi, the second predecessor of Mahāvīra, contemporary with Kṛṣṇa. This can be made to support the date only by assuming a period of two hundred years between each Tīrthaṁkara. For this idle assumption we have not the slightest evidence of any kind. The Jain tradition gives Pārçvanātha a semblance of reality by placing him 250 years before Mahāvīra, Ariṣṭanemi it banishes to the remotest antiquity, and we have not the slightest evidence of any kind that any Tīrthaṁkara of that or any other name existed *c.* 950 B.C. Even the historical existence of Pārçvanātha is totally unproved. But at any rate, since the Jains themselves did not believe that Ariṣṭanemi was a figure of comparatively recent history, it is really otiose for us to rewrite their scriptures.

B. THE SACRIFICE OF PURUṢA AND THE ORIGIN OF THE WORLD

H. Güntert[1] has traced the common possession over an area extending from Germany, through the Thraco-Phrygian area, to the Indo-Iranians of a number of mythological elements, which are preserved for us in complex and contaminated forms in the religious records of these peoples. The first of these ideas is that of the origin of mankind and the world from the sacrifice of a primeval being, an idea suggested by the great potency which primitive religious thought ascribes to the bloody sacrifice.[2] This is preserved for us in the legend of the sacrifice of Puruṣa and of Ymir, whose original character he strongly defends against suggestion of Christian influence ; it is reflected also in the strange, though late, legend of Odin who records how for nine nights he hung on a tree, wounded by the spear, dedicated to Odin, himself to himself. The action of the god in permitting himself to be sacrificed is one of free will, motived by the desire to create the world and establish the race of men. Yama, he holds, is such a god ; the difficult passage of the Rigveda, x. 13. 4, he explains as a reference to a deliberate decision by Yama to sacrifice himself for the sake of mankind ; it is as a sacrificer of himself that Yama performs the feat of finding the hidden Agni,[3] who is the mediator in the sacrifice between the offerer and the gods. Later we find in Iran the conception of some sin in the primitive being, as in Yima, and, when the human sacrifice became antiquated, the creator as in the legend of Mithra slays a bull, not a human being.[4]

The second motif is the belief that men are sprung from a primeval

the Vergilian tradition (Comparetti, *Virgilio in medio evo*). To treat as historical the Indian traditions, which confuse hopelessly recent history, when they deal with events 900–1000 B.C., is explicable only on the theory that those who do so are ignorant of any history save that of India, and are wholly unversed in the principles of historical evidences. The various accounts of the basis of the Bhāratan war are all vitiated by this naïve lack of criticism. The Homeric controversy is peculiarly instructive as to the difficulty of securing results of historic value ; thus Leaf (*Homer and History*) surrenders the Catalogue of Ships (*Iliad*, ii.) as an invention (contrast T. W. Allen, *The Homeric Catalogue of Ships*, 1921 ; *Homer*, 1924). See also U. v. Wilamowitz-Moellendorff, *Die Ilias und Homer* ; E. Schwartz, *Zur Entstehung der Ilias* (1918) ; Cauer, GGA. 1917, pp. 201 ff. ; Bethe, GGA. 1919, pp. 141–9 ; J. A. Scott, *The Unity of Homer* (1921).

1 *Der arische Weltkönig*, pp. 315 ff.

2 Bousset, *Hauptprobleme d. Gnosis*, p. 211.

3 RV. x. 51. 3. All metres rest on Yama, x. 14. 16.

4 Cf. perhaps the bull sacrificed by the gods in AV. ix. 4.

creature of bi-sexual character. This idea can be traced in Teutonic mythology in legends of Tuisto, Ymir, Tveggi, in the Doias of Phrygia, in Prajāpati and Puruṣa [1] in India, and in Zrvān in Iran, while the Yama legend shows the variant by which a twin sister is given to the primeval man, in order to explain the origin of man, a conception found also in Iran in the legends of Yimak, Manušak, and Mašyānīk.

The third motif is the view that the first to die becomes, like Yama and Yima, the lord of the blessed dead, and, like Yama, the judge of the dead. Further, he may be regarded as the ancestor of men, and in virtue of his paternal power a great king when on earth, and one whence royal families are fain to claim descent, ideas found in the legends of Yima, Jamšed, Yama, and the Teutonic Mannus. The first mortal is also deemed the first sacrificer, like Manu and Yama, from whom as in the case of Manuš in Iran priests claim their origin.

Güntert, while admitting the possibility of Asianic origin for the myth of an androgynous primeval creator of mankind, does not claim that the motifs discussed are Indo-European, but rather takes them as evidence of a long-continued contact between the special peoples among whom they occur. A similar contact he finds [2] suggested by the partial parallelisms of Odin-Wodan with Varuṇa and Ahura Mazdāh, the root idea in all these cases being, in this view, that of a lord and creator of the world, a cosmic magician, one of whose aspects is that of him who binds the sinner, whence the name Varuṇa from *ver*, bind, while Mitra, whose name has a similar force,[3] binds men together in bonds of social obligation. A connecting link between the Aryans and the Teutons may be seen in the Thracian deity Darzales, whose name denotes him as the binder, and who may be the source of the Egyptian Sarapis,[4] while the Thracians and the Phrygians had a goddess Bendis with similar functions. Savitṛ again is merely a hypostasis of Varuṇa,[5] the aspect in which the world lord stretches aloft his mighty hands, the beams of the sun, and his figure accords with the delineations of a god with mighty hands uplifted which are found freely in the German and Thraco-Phrygian areas, while a remnant of the idea is to be seen in the epithet 'long-handed' applied to the Iranian demon Būšyasta.

The ingenuity of these suggestions deserves recognition, but it must be regarded as very dubious whether they really serve to establish the closer religious connexions between certain of the Indo-European peoples which are postulated. The case of Savitṛ is clearly unconvincing; the parallel is too general to be of value; the idea of representing the sun as of human form with uplifted hands is one which might easily occur independently; there is nothing specially distinctive in the resemblance of Odin and Varuṇa as magicians, and the evidence for the origin of the world from a primitive sacrifice is too slight to enable us to feel any assurance of a common origin. It must be added that the evidence for Yama as originally the primeval being from whose sacrifice the world springs is inconclusive, for the Rigvedic passage cited naturally denotes a sacrifice of Bṛhaspati, not of Yama, and says no more than that Yama died. The finding of Agni by Yama does not absolutely

[1] RV. x. 90. 5; Virāj, a feminine principle born from Puruṣa, and he from her. So with Aditi and Dakṣa. Cf. also Ziegler, *Neue Jahrb.* xxxi (1913), 529 ff. on Plato's *Symposion* and Empedokles.

[2] *Op. cit.*, pp. 150 ff.

[3] *Op. cit.*, pp. 147 f. For Mitra cf. μίτρη.

[4] Weinreich, *Neue Urkunden zur Sarapis-Religion* (1919), p. 7.

[5] Güntert, p. 161. The further effort (p. 168) to find a Swedish rock delineation of the parallel of Varuṇa with his noose (15 cent. B.C.) is as speculative as that in respect of the Dioskouroi (pp. 272 f.).

prove his divinity, and in any case has no necessary connexion with his sacrificing himself. Moreover the contention that the idea of the origin of the world in sacrifice must be old because it rests on the belief in the peculiar efficacy of human sacrifice, and that form of sacrifice is essentially primitive, is wholly speculative, and by no means probable. At least as good a case can be made out for the belief that the high value attached to the human offering is a product of religious development. This is so whether we take [1] the cause of human offerings to be the desire to propitiate a god who naturally menaces human life, such as a god of death, of war, or of the sea, or whether the sacrifice is one of a man to represent the god; [2] in the latter case the offering of a man is associated with anthropomorphic conceptions of deity, and, while we need not believe that animal conceptions are older, we certainly cannot think anthropomorphic the oldest.[3] Substitution legends are aetiological and mark a refined speculation, not primitive ideas.

Güntert [4] contends that in the case of Yama a distinction must be made between the ideas of 'dead', 'human', and 'immortal'; Yama was a god who permitted himself to be sacrificed, and therefore died, but he is not a man (*mānuṣa, mānava*). Thus the Atharvaveda [5] describes him as the first of mortals (*mártya*) to die, but not as a man, while the Rigveda [6] refers to his innate immortality (*Yamásya jātám amṛ́tam*). But despite his relation to Vivasvant it is impossible to deny his mortality by these distinctions; whatever his origin, to the Vedic poet he was the first of men to die.

C. THE ARYAN CONCEPTION OF THE HEAVEN

J. Hertel [7] claims that in India and Iran alike we find the conception of the heaven as a great stone building, filled with light, through whose doors, the sun and the stars, the light of heaven shines upon men. For this view is adduced the reference in the Rigveda to the palace of Varuṇa with a thousand doors, which is asserted to be none other than the heaven with its stars. For Iran there is the narrative in Vendīdād ii, which has long passed as the Iranian version of the legend of the flood, but in which we should rather see the account of Yama's reign in the golden age and of the way in which he conveyed the first to die through the opening of the heaven, i.e. the sun, into the heaven of light. It is, however, true that this original legend of the Magian faith has been altered in the form in which we have it, since it could not, as it stood, be made consistent with the Zoroastrian doctrine of the fate of the dead. The Vara mentioned in the Vendīdād is to be compared with the Vedic Vala,[8] which is none other than the closed firmament which the lord of the heaven of light, Bṛhaspati, or sometimes Indra, cleaves in order to set free the ruddy kine, i.e. the stars. Yet a further confirmation of the new interpretation of the Vendīdād is seen in an obscure verse of the Rigveda,[9] which is made to yield the sense that Manu adorned with flames the door of the heaven of Indra. By yet another conjecture we are to see in Rigveda x. 14. 2 ('Yama as the

[1] E. Mogk (*Die Menschenopfer der Germanen*, Leipzig, 1909) thus explains the origin of German human sacrifices. See also F. Schwenn, *Die Menschenopfer bei den Griechen und Römern*; Reid, JHS. ii. 34 ff.

[2] Cf. Preuss, *Globus*, lxxxvi. 108 ff.; Frazer, *The Dying God*; Farnell, *Cults of the Greek States*, v. 167 ff.; W. Weber, *Archiv f. Religionswissenschaft*, xix. 333 ff.; Wissowa, xxii. 201 ff. (expulsion of evil).

[3] Cf. Helm, *Altgerm. Rel.* i. 51.

[4] *Op. cit.*, pp. 388 f.

[5] xviii. 3. 13.

[6] i. 83. 5.

[7] *Die Himmelstore im Veda und im Avesta* (1924).

[8] Contrast above, Chap. 9, § 1.

[9] viii. 63. 1.

first hath found this way to the heaven for us, and this pastureland none can take from us ') the sole allusion to a legend of the gradual failure of the earth to support the number of those alive and the departure of Yama with the superfluous population, involving the introduction of death into the world.

It is clearly impossible to accept this evidence as establishing the doctrine enunciated. That in one passage [1] Varuṇa's palace with a thousand doors should be spoken of, is not the slightest proof that the Vedic Indian normally regarded the firmament as a building filled with light, whose doors were the sun and the stars, and the rendering of Rigveda viii. 63. 1, which ascribes to Manu the making of flames in the heaven of Indra, is clearly impossible; [2] even on Hertel's hypothesis, all that Manu could naturally be said to do would be to enter by a flaming door, not to create it, and in fact the term *dhiyaḥ* here used refers clearly to devotion and not to flames. The version of Vala is wholly implausible, while the interpretation of the Vendīdād passage is accomplished merely by the process of inventing a meaning and explaining away everything which contradicts it by the theory of adaption to Zoroastrian ideas. Peculiarly gratuitous is the interpretation of Rigveda x. 14. 2, which has not the slightest reference to an overburdened earth, but merely to the winning of an abode which knows no ending in the sky. The whole doctrine that Yama removed the surplus population to the heaven because the earth was overcrowded is un-Vedic, and even the epic [3] knows it not. For the Veda we have merely the aetiological legends of the expansion of the earth from a small nucleus, often by the action of a cosmic boar,[4] and the wholly unconnected and late legend of the sinking of the earth in the ocean because the evil-minded Viçvakarman, son of Bhuvana, sought to bestow it upon the priest Kaçyapa, though no mortal had the right to do so.[5]

There is, therefore, no ground to hold that the term açmānam svaryam in Rigveda, v. 56. 4, with the derivative v. 30. 8, refers to the firmament of stone which the Maruts cause to move. Quite different is vii. 86. 1, which ascribes to Varuṇa the motion of the lofty vault of heaven, that is the starry firmament, for that passage says nothing of the firmament as a building of stone. Wholly irrelevant also are passages in the Upaniṣads and later [6] which treat of the sun as a stage on the way to the highest place; this is not the view of the Rigveda [7] which expressly prays that those who despise Vedic practices (*apavrata*) may be debarred from the sun itself, doubtless as the abode of the holy, not as the way to it; Hertel himself recognizes that in ix. 113. 8 the pious man desires to win immortality in the place where is the closure of the sky, i.e. the sun. When in the Upaniṣads [8] the moon appears as the door of the world of heaven, nothing whatever is said to suggest that this refers to an opening through which the waters of heaven are poured forth; clearly the reference is to the old idea that the souls of the dead go to the moon to dwell there, as the text in question expressly lays down. When the Aitareya Brāhmaṇa [9] says that the rain springs from the moon and enters back into it, it says nothing of water from the heaven. Varuṇa's connexion with rain is sufficiently natural without deriving it from the fact that the firmament is his

[1] vii. 88. 5. Cf. Sraoša's palace in Yasna, lvii. 21.

[2] RV. x. 68. 11, cited as parallel, deals with the souls of the dead as stars, not as making holes in the sky; cf. AV. xviii. 2. 47.

[3] MBh. iii. 142. 35 ff.; xii. 255. 15 ff.

[4] MS. i. 6. 3; KS. viii. 2; TB. i. 1. 3. 5–7; ÇB. xiv. 1. 2. 11. For other legends of the expansion of the earth (*pṛthivī*, the broad), see PB. xx. 14. 5; TS. ii. 1. 2. 3.

[5] AB. viii. 21; ÇB. iii. 7. 1. 14 ff.

[6] BAU. v. 10. 1; CU. viii. 6. 2; Muṇḍ. i. 2. 5, &c.

[7] v. 42. 9.

[8] KU. i. 2.

[9] viii. 28.

palace, and that the ocean of the heaven is connected with the fire of heaven. Still less plausible is the treatment of Bṛhaspati as merely lord of the fire-heaven, who, therefore, can send down rain, or the assertion that the ruddy kine which he sets free are the stars who send rain, and that this conception of them is only explicable on the theory that they are doors to the fiery heaven.

Final arguments for the view of Hertel are based on a new interpretation of the Tištrya legend [1] as revealing the production of rain through the overflowing of the celestial ocean Vourukaša through the stars as the openings in the firmament, and on the view that the divine doors invoked in the Āprī hymns are really the sun, moon, and stars ; it is sufficient to note his admission that this view was already unknown to the author of Rigveda x. 70. 5, and to add that this ignorance was fully justified by the incredible nature of the theory.[2]

D. THE DRINK OF IMMORTALITY

G. Dumézil in his *Le Festin d'Immortalité* [3] seeks to establish, despite the silence of the Veda, the existence of an Indo-European myth of the winning of the drink of immortality. From the epic legend of the churning of the ocean he derives a myth which tells how, in fear of death, the gods took counsel as to procuring a drink to preserve them from it. Viṣṇu advises them to churn the ocean for it, and, after coming to terms with the demons, and obtaining the assent of the god of the ocean, they accomplish their end, producing the Amṛta, and other good things, including Lakṣmī ; a poison engendered in the churning is drunk by Çiva, whose neck thus becomes blue. The Asuras, however, steal the Amṛta, and demand Lakṣmī ; Viṣṇu-Nārāyaṇa, in female guise, accompanied by Nara, in similar costume, goes to them, and wins them over to give him the Amṛta, which then he bears back to the gods. They proceed to drink the nectar ; the demon, Rāhu, found among them is decapitated by Viṣṇu, and the fall of his body produces much commotion of the earth. A fight follows, in which the Asuras, defeated by the gods, are banished to the earth and the waters, and the gods remain in definitive possession of the drink.[4]

Dumézil seeks to show [5] that on principle the silence of the Vedic texts is not fatal to the early character of the legend, considering that these texts show no disinterested narratives of legends, and that the philosophical thought of the Vedic age was not concerned with this special theme. Similarly, he insists that the Avesta represents most imperfectly the true Iranian nature beliefs. The arguments *a priori* have weight, but it seems impossible to accept his reconstructed primitive legend [6] as established by the legends he recounts, including the Scandinavian legend of the beer of the Ases, the Greek legends of the war of the gods and the giants and of Prometheus and the Pithos of Immortality, the Latin tale of Anna Perenna or its Christian version as Anna Petronilla, a Celtic Grail legend and the Slav legend of Mikhailo Potyk and Maria, the white swan. Here and there in these tales common ideas can be seen, often doubtless much transformed, but there is far too little evidence

[1] Yašt, viii. Contrast Moulton, *Early Zoroastrianism*, pp. 22 ff., 436 f.

[2] Hertel rejects the view of Grassmann and Oldenberg (*Prolegomena*, pp. 28, n. 1, 194 f.) that the Āprī hymn in ix. is a mere imitation of those for Agni in the other books, holding that it is due to the fire nature of Soma, shown by its effect on man and its identification with the moon. But the older theory is clearly the more plausible.

[3] *Annales du Musée Guimet*, xxxiv (Paris, 1924).

[4] MBh. i. 1095 ff.

[5] pp. viii ff.

[6] pp. 24 ff.

to enable us to claim Indo-European antiquity for the complex myth which Dumézil evolves from the scanty evidence. The conclusion to be drawn is rather against than for the epic as a source of early myths; in truth what is in origin mythical is there often so transformed by imagination as to be barely recognizable, and a good deal more can be said for Hertel's contention that the Brāhmaṇas present a much superior field for the discovery, in thin disguises, of true nature myths.

Dumézil further [1] deduces as the basis of the legends the existence of an Indo-European festival in the spring, at which was drunk in communion the sacred drink, originally a kind of beer derived from barley, which was replaced by wine in Greece, and by Soma among the Indo-Iranians. With this drink the Indo-Europeans associated the idea of life without end, and the success of the gods over the demons their rivals; but in the rites of which we have historical information many other elements of vegetation ritual have intruded themselves. He negatives [2] the idea that the mead was primitively the ambrosia; nothing in the legends recalls either the special characteristics nor the mode of preparation of the hydromel. If in Greece the ideas of ἀμβροσία and μέθυ were confused, it was because both lost their precise sense, and similarly in India the distinction between Amṛta and Madhu was obliterated by reason of the attraction of the idea of Soma. A trace of the old pre-eminence of beer is to be seen in a legend of the Çatapatha Brāhmaṇa,[3] where the barley is declared to have alone remained faithful to the gods in their demon contests, while the episode in the epic of the poison which arose in the churning of the ocean is held to be a distant echo of the process of fermentation of the beer which is apt to go too far, as in the narrative of the Kalevala.[4] In these details again it is clearly impossible to find any cogent proof of the existence of an Indo-European rite.

Geldner [5] has suggested that references to the legend of the churning of the ocean are to be found in the Rigveda. Thus in v. 2. 3 he interprets the *amṛtaṁ vipṛkvat*, which the Purohita throws on the fire, as denoting the ghee which separates itself out, as did the Amṛta at the churning of the ocean. Again in i. 163 he holds that the poet is dealing, not with the sun-horse, but with the coming into being of the 'Urross', whether from the sun (verse 2) or, along with the Soma, from the ocean (*asi somena samayā vipṛktaḥ*). The whole stress of the argument rests on the artificial sense ascribed to *viprc* in both passages, and it is quite impossible to accept Geldner's suggestion, which is not repeated by Dumézil.

Another and very different view of Amṛta is put forward by Slater [6] as part of the quite implausible hypothesis of the predominance in India of a Dravidian civilization based on reaction to Egyptian influence. He suggests that Amṛta was either Egyptian beer or the fermented juice of the date palm, palmyra, or coconut palm, the great intoxicating beverage of India, the art of making toddy of this kind having reached India from Mesopotamia, the home of the date palm cultivation. It is sufficient to observe that the maker of the conjecture appears to be ignorant of the patent fact that Amṛta in the Rigveda denotes beyond doubt the Soma drink, and there is no conceivable possibility of reconciling the description of the Soma plant as contained in Vedic references and the date palm.

[1] pp. 265 ff.
[2] pp. 279 ff.
[3] iii. 6. 1. 8, 9.
[4] xx; Dumézil, pp. 284 f.
[5] *Festgruss an Roth*, p. 192, but cf. *Der Rigveda*, i. 203.
[6] *The Dravidian Element in Indian Culture*, pp. 78 ff. See below, Appendix G.

E. THE INDO-EUROPEAN FIRE CULT

That fire should be regarded in its own right as a divine power, worthy of worship, appears so natural that it is only reasonable to recognize such worship as Indo-European. The sanctity of Agni in the Rigveda is, of course, especially that of the fire regarded as the recipient of sacrifice and the bearer of oblations, but it seems wholly unjustifiable to suggest [1] that his sanctity arose from his nature as the sacrificial fire; rather he was the recipient of offerings as sacred in his own right.

In Greece, in addition to Hephaistos, Hestia must, it seems, be accorded an origin as fire, especially the fire on the hearth, not the hearth with its fire as Farnell [2] suggests. He bases this view on the identity of the words for hearth and for the goddess, but there seems no reason whatever for accepting this suggestion, which derives Hestia from *vas*, dwell, when it is at least as natural to assume that the name of the fire on the hearth was used to denote the hearth, and connexion with *vas* or possibly some other root with the signification of shining or burning is easy.[3] Moreover the earliest literary references point singularly clearly to a conception like that of Agni; the Homeric Hymns [4] tell of Hestia as the goddess who haunts the house of Apollo in Pytho and from whose locks sweet unguents trickle down, and of her sitting in the middle of the house, taking the fat of sacrifice. Euripides [5] definitely calls her the lady of fire and associates her with Hephaistos. At Delphi we find her associated with the deathless fire in the Amphictyonic oath. Moreover the maintenance of a sacred fire in the Prytaneion at Athens, and the fact that it was regarded as in a sense the source of the Ionic colonies, because they carried thence the sacred fire, show clearly enough that the essential element in the idea is the fire, not the hearth. Nor is there any evidence for the suggestion [6] that the hearth in Mediterranean lands was built of sacred stones or that its sanctity is a reflex of the pillar cult of pre-Hellenic times. The parallelism of the expressions 'Hephaistos is laughing' and 'Hestia is laughing', used of the crackling of the fire, suggests essential identity of both deities with fire.

The rules in India which urge the householder to maintain a sacred fire, a duty especially incumbent on the king, is paralleled by the Greek evidence as to the fires of the Prytaneia and the Roman cult of Vesta, which bears adequate evidence of independence to render derivation from Greece unnatural. The fire of the Sabhā clearly approaches the conception of these public fires in Greece and Rome. For the practice in Greece and Rome various explanations have been offered. That of Frazer [7] stresses the importance of preserving one fire at least in a village which would never be extinguished, while Farnell [8] contends that the rite was religious in origin, depending on the belief that the fire on the hearth was the external thing in which the soul of the chief resided, so that the whole tribe had an interest in keeping it up; when kingship passed away the idea was transferred to the fire of the state in the Prytaneion, with which the fortune of the state might be held to be inextricably connected. It may be granted that the purpose of maintaining the fire was religious from the start, but the motive had, it seems probable, nothing to do with any idea of the connexion of the chief's soul with the fire; rather the fire as a most

[1] *Cults of the Greek States*, v. 358.
[2] *Ibid.*, 359.
[3] Brugmann, *Griech. Gramm.*[4], p. 52; Ehrlich, KZ. xli. 289 f.
[4] xxiv. and xxix.
[5] *Phaeth.* frag. 781, l. 55.
[6] Farnell, *ibid.*, 360.
[7] JP. xiv. 167 ff.
[8] *Ibid.*, 353 f.

important [1] and ever valuable deity was to be preserved alight if possible by every sacrificer, an idea which naturally enough with civic organization results in the fires of the Prytaneia and the cult of Vesta at Rome.

The nature of such deities as Hestia and Vesta is often misunderstood by students of Greek and Roman religion, who are accustomed to reckon personality in terms of clear anthropomorphism, and who fail to appreciate that the conception of fire as living and active is in essence a personal conception. This error, fostered by the fact that what we know of old Roman religion is only on its formal side, has led to the view [2] that early Roman religion could not be nature worship of the type usually attributed to Indo-Europeans. The conclusion obviously rests on the wholly erroneous view that Indo-European worship was that of personifications of nature forces ; it was the worship of nature as animate, and what is animate is not impersonal. The theory that Roman or any other religion developed from the indeterminate conception of an impersonal force ascribes to early man the power of framing a complex conception which is wholly implausible. It is absurd to suppose that the daily reverence paid in the household to the flame of Vesta into which a morsel of salted cake was thrown was not paid to a personal deity, although she was not represented by an image. The reason for this paucity of representation in Rome as in Greece was precisely the same as in Greece ; the living flame is the present deity, and to a people to whom this was a living belief the idea of making an image would have appeared idle. The formalism of the Indigitamenta is the result of priestly ingenuity,[3] not primitive belief, and all our knowledge of Roman religion is obscured by the lateness of our records and the effect of Greek ideas. It is characteristic of the tendency to treat Roman religion as more abstract than it really was that efforts are made to explain away the facts recorded of the connexion of the wolf and the woodpecker with Mars as representing a late development, and to deny the paternity of Jupiter [4] and the maternity of Earth, and to make even sun worship a borrowing.[5]

F. CREMATION AND BURIAL

The view that cremation was a distinctively Indo-European form of disposal of the dead cannot be supported by any evidence of value. There is abundant proof that burial is at least as ancient a method, and, indeed, it is possible to hold that it was Indo-European, while burning was introduced after that period among the different peoples either independently or by borrowing. The Vedic evidence, as has been shown, proves that burial was early ; Herodotos [6] ascribes the usage to the Persians, while the Magoi, possibly by religious conservatism, preserved the method of exposure ; burial he also

[1] Learned Brahmans, village headmen, and Kṣatriyas are enumerated as called upon so to act, and the ritual still rarely survives ; Hillebrandt, *Ved. Myth.*, pp. 54 f.

[2] W. R. Halliday, *Roman Religion*, pp. 89 ff.

[3] This is recognized by Halliday, *op. cit.*, pp. 114 ff.

[4] Warde Fowler (*Roman Ideas of Deity*, pp. 30 ff.) exalts Jupiter into a primitive monotheistic deity, a result of his treatment of the religion as abstract. Grierson's theory (*Trans. Third Int. Cong. Hist. Rel.* ii. 44 f.) of an early Indian monotheism developed from Indo-Iranian sun worship is incapable of serious demonstration.

[5] Cumont (*Théologie solaire*, pp. 3 ff.) has induced Fowler (pp. 56 f.) to believe sun worship an invention of astronomers, and to disbelieve the evidence of Varro, *L.L.* v. 68, 74, and the existence of Sol Indiges. The effort of L. Malten (*Arch. Jahrb.* xxvii (1912), 232 ff.) to prove Hephaistos Lycian, not Greek, is clearly unconvincing.

[6] i. 140. Cf. C. Clemen, *Die griechischen und lateinischen Nachrichten über die persische Religion*, pp. 201 ff.

assigns to the Iranian Scythians.[1] In the case of Greece the existence of a pre-Hellenic population which practised burial renders the evidence [2] specially obscure, but it is important that in the earliest Athenian cemeteries in the 'dipylon' graves of the geometric period of art cremation is very rare. The evidence from Italy shows burials preceding cremations in the oldest cemeteries, and even if the people of the terremare, perhaps in part the ancestors of the Latins, were addicted to burning,[3] it is impossible to assume that burial was in Italy derived from the non-Indo-European population. The laws of the Ten Tables [4] forbade the burial or burning of a dead man within the city, and there is a remarkable provision in an old law of the regal period which provides for the saving of the embryo in the case of the burial of a pregnant woman.[5] That burial was the more ancient custom is suggested strongly by the fact that conservative families like the Cornelii persisted in burying their dead until the time of the Dictator Sulla, whose cremation was dictated by political reasons. Archaeological evidence in the lands held by the Slavs, Teutons, and Celts establishes the priority of burial, and it is not plausible to suppose that the appearance of burning there meant the advent of a new race. Cremation is recorded for the Celts by Caesar [6] and the Hallstatt cemetery; for the Teutons by Tacitus,[7] and later evidence establishes it for the Slavs and Lithuanians. All the evidence, therefore, is compatible with the view that burning was a rite introduced, comparatively late in some cases, in the separate life of the Indo-European peoples.

It is, however, extremely difficult to arrive at any theory establishing the period when or the place whence the new practice came to be disseminated. The theory of Ridgeway [8] which makes the Celts protagonists in the matter is most implausible in the form in which he has stated it, and there is no conclusive reason to assume that the use must have been started by one only of the Indo-European peoples. Whether the motive of burning was due to a change in the aspect in which men regarded the dead, or arose from practical considerations, such as those affecting the advance of a people who could not continue to bury their dead and to cherish them in their ancestral homes, there is no special reason to suppose that only one Indo-European people invented it. The Greeks invading Hellas, and the Indians invading India, may have been moved by similar motives independently, or again in one case one, in another yet a different, motive may have been operative, and it is not necessary to seek any theory which will explain all cases. Borrowing from any non-Indo-European source is implausible, in the absence of any clear evidence of the prevalence of the rite among peoples by whom the Indo-Europeans could have been influenced.

[1] iv. 71.

[2] See e.g. Zehetmaier, *Leichenverbrennung und Leichenbestattung im alten Hellas*. The lake dwellers of Europe first buried, then burned their dead, and it has been suggested that cremation is a specific usage of broad-headed peoples (CAH. i. 73).

[3] Peet, *Stone and Bronze Ages in Italy*, p. 370; von Duhn, *Rückblick auf die Gräberforschung* (Heidelberg, 1911), p. 18; Modestov, *Introduction à l'histoire romaine* (Paris, 1907), p. 107; cf. Peake, *The Bronze Age and the Celtic World*, pp. 122, 131, 163; CAH. i. 74, 108, 110, where they are taken as Alpine in race; Indo-European, CAH. ii. 569.

[4] x. 1. Cf. x. 8 f.; Cicero, *Leg.* ii. 22; Pliny, *N. H.* vii. 187.

[5] *Dig.* xi. 8. 2 (Bruns, *Fontes Iuris Romani*[6], p. 11). Similar instructions are given in India before cremation; Baudhāyana Pitṛmedha Sūtra, ii. 15; Vaikhānasa Gṛhya Sūtra, vii. 4.

[6] *B.G.* vi. 19; Pomponius Mela, iii. 19. Cf. MacBain, *Celtic Mythology and Religion*, pp. 235 ff.; CAH. ii. 592 ff.

[7] *Germ.* 27.

[8] *Early Age of Greece*, i. chap. vii. Peake (*The Bronze Age and the Celtic World*, pp. 101 ff.) does not adopt this theory. Cf. CAH. ii. 473 ff.

The motives which may have influenced burning are many, apart from the necessities or convenience of invaders. The removal of a dangerous object is obviously one possibility ; the view that it was intended to facilitate the celestial existence of the soul by ridding it of the encumbrance of the body has been strongly supported,[1] but, as we have seen, is not borne out by any Vedic evidence. Paton [2] adopts the suggestion of E. Meyer [3] that cremation existed in Indo-European times alongside with burial, but that it was performed originally only in the case of heroes, chiefs or kings, who were believed to partake of the divine nature and, therefore, were returned by fire to the celestial regions. In support of this is adduced the fact that in Egypt [4] the ideas of the future of the king gradually became applied to the ordinary people, as did cremation in Greece. But the evidence for this distinction is inadequate ; in India there is nothing of the kind, the fact that children under two years of age were not cremated, adduced by Paton, is irrelevant, for ascetics shared the same fate, and there is no trace of the caste differentiation in this regard which would be necessary on the theory of a distinction based on an aristocratic practice. It is not the case that the distinction can be seen in Homer,[5] and the evidence of Caesar and Tacitus regarding the Celts and the Teutons says nothing of a distinction between the treatment of the great and the mere clansmen.

Definite proof of the Indo-European character of burial of the dead would be afforded if it were possible to accept as proved Peake's [6] identification of them with the Kurgan people of the steppes east of the Dnieper, who certainly buried their dead in a contracted position, the skeletons found being thickly covered with red ochre, a custom which is attested as early as Aurignacian times. The evidence, as has been mentioned, for this theory is

[1] Cf. Sophus Müller, *Nord. Altertumskunde*, i. 363 ff. ; Scheftelowitz, *Archiv f. Religionswissenschaft*, xix. 219 f., who connects it with the belief in a star destiny for the soul. His argument that, if the use is apotropaeic, the burning of utensils, &c., is meaningless, is clearly mistaken. A banned soul might return for his own, and his connexion with them has rendered their retention unwise.

[2] *Spiritism*, p. 129.

[3] *Gesch. des Alt.*[2] ii. 771.

[4] See e.g. J. H. Breasted, *Development of Religion and Thought in Ancient Egypt*, pp. 103, 256 ; *Cambridge Ancient History*, i. 350 f.

[5] Cf. Lang, *Homer and his Age*, p. 99 ; Keith, JRAS. 1912, p. 473, n. The ethnic question discussed by me there still remains unsolved. Leaf (*Homer and History*, p. 37) adopts the impossible view that the Greek mainland was occupied by neolithic peoples speaking a Greek dialect of which Arcadian may be a descendant, who were first dominated over by Minoan and next by Hellenic Achaeans ; Peake (*The Bronze Age and the Celtic World*, chap. ix) makes the mainland population of eastern Alpine, the Cretan of Mediterranean (pp. 28 ff.) stock, while the Minoan overlords are ' Prospectors ', of a blend of Mediterranean and eastern Alpine stocks, who may be of Sumerian origin and akin to the Etruscans. The Achaeans are a small body of intrusive Nordics, while no place is left for an earlier Greek-speaking population. Evans again (JHS. xxxii. 281 ff.), by insisting on the continuity of Minoan and Mycenaean culture, brings down any real influence of the Hellenic influx to the period of dipylon culture, which is clearly too late, and has provoked the equally impossible suggestion (T. W. Allen, JHS. xxxiii. 115) that the Minoans must have been Achaeans. It is much more probable that early Greeks took a substantial part in developing Mycenaean civilization under Minoan influence, and that the epic reflects this Greek civilization, not memories of the Minoan epic. See against G. Murray's traditionalist theory of the *Iliad*, J. T. Sheppard's able analysis, *The Pattern of the Iliad* (1922); Bury, CAH. ii. 502 ff.

[6] *The Bronze Age and the Celtic World*, pp. 67 ff. ; cf. Minns, *Scythians and Greeks*, pp. 142 ff. ; Rostovtzeff, *Journal des Savants*, 1920, pp. 60, 109 ff.

[7] Cf. the blood-offerings for the dead, to strengthen their life ; Paton, *Spiritism*, pp. 72 f., 140 f.

inadequate to establish it, but it may be noted that the Vedic Indians appear to have agreed with these people in their tendency to simplicity and economy in regard to the offerings deposited with the dead, for the Vedic offerings are, as we have seen, strictly limited in quantity and quality. The contracted position of the dead may have been induced by the desire to reproduce the character of a foetus, awaiting new birth in the world to come, and the idea of rebirth as an embryo is conspicuous in the Vedic Dīkṣā ceremonial. The barrow may be compared with the Vedic memorial mound.[1] It might further be conjectured that the use of burning was influenced by the practice of the neighbouring peoples of Tripolye culture [2] who regularly, if not invariably burned their dead. But we have no real means of arriving at any valid conclusion.

G. THE DRAVIDIAN ELEMENT IN INDIAN THOUGHT

The desire to prove that Dravidian or pre-Dravidian peoples affected deeply Vedic thought and life is natural, and is supported by the generally accepted view that the population of India is predominantly Dravidian or at least of non-Indo-European origin. It is true, however, that in the absence of any real certainty of the physical characteristics of the Indo-Europeans this belief cannot be made the subject of strict proof. Assuming, however, the validity of the doctrine, there remains the question whether the invaders were essentially responsible for the Vedic religion and philosophy, imposing a superior culture on inferior races, or whether the process as regards culture was reversed; instances of analogical cases can be easily adduced.[3] Here again, however, we must remember that we have no satisfactory evidence of the relative numbers of the invaders and the earlier settlers; we are left in this matter wholly to conjecture.

The best case that can be made out for the Indo-European character of Vedic religion or philosophy depends on comparison with the achievements of other Indo-European peoples, and, of course, in this case we are met with the problem to what extent these religions and philosophies were Indo-European in character, or on the contrary represent elements borrowed by the invaders from the countries they occupied. Thus, for instance, we have Sir A. Evans' suggestion [4] that the Homeric epic embodies largely traditions of the pre-Hellenic Minoans, though the language is Indo-European, and, even if we dismiss the suggestion as not very plausible, we are not in a position to disprove it definitely by the evidence available. More important is the close similarity of many Indian and Iranian ideas, as developed by Julius von Negelein in his *Weltanschauung des indogermanischen Asiens*, but it may be noted even here that, as that work shows, many of the important ideas of Aryan belief can be paralleled among other races.

On the other hand, we must admit that when we come to definite attempts to prove Dravidian influence on Vedic religion or philosophy we are in the region of conjecture. The absence of any really early Dravidian evidence as to

[1] This is not to be high nor too large, according to the ritual texts (cf. Megasthenes in Strabo, xv. 54), negativing any idea of a great chamber (cf. Bloch and Hillebrandt's view of RV. x. 18. 13); see Caland, *Versl. en Meded. der Kon. Akad. v. Wet. te Amsterdam*, 4e R., dl. xi. 378 ff.; *Archiv f. Religionswissenschaft*, xviii. 482.

[2] Minns, *op. cit.*, pp. 133 ff.; Peake, *op. cit.*, pp. 64 f.; CAH. i. 80 ff.

[3] See, e.g., Leaf, *Homer and History*, pp. 44 ff., following E. Meyer, *Gesch. des Alt.*[2] ii. 52.

[4] JHS. xxxii. 281 ff., 293; on Minoan religion, in correction of Evans' views, see R. Dussaud, *Les civilisations préhelléniques*[2] (Paris, 1914), pp. 327–413.

culture deprives us of any assured knowledge of pre-Indo-European conditions such as would enable us effectively to gauge Dravidian influences in Vedic religion or philosophy. This leads to the necessity of relying on conjectures, of which many may be easily shown to have no sound foundation, or at most to be mere possibilities. We may, of course, accept such possibilities if we like, but in doing so we cease to be judicial and arrive merely at subjective judgements which have no lasting value.

It must be noted that the Dravidians are not allowed the credit of originality by such writers as Elliot Smith,[1] and Fleure, who insist instead on oversea and overland influences from Mesopotamia and Egypt as settling the course of Dravidian culture, though the evidence for this influence in the third millennium B. C. and much later is entirely speculative, depending on the existence of megaliths alleged to be connected with metallic deposits, and on the certainly unproved theory of the dissemination of this mode of building by a particular race, moved by peculiar religious views, who sought life-giving substances. The structures raised on this basis by Elliot Smith and Perry seems to me entirely unfounded and in every respect implausible, nor is there much probability of their receiving general endorsement by competent critics. It is, however, needless here to discuss their views, and Slater,[2] quite justly, lays more stress than his authorities on the independent power of the Dravidians to develop their culture. Moreover he rejects,[3] very plausibly, the doctrine that the Dravidians represent the admixture of Mediterranean bearers of heliolithic culture with pre-Dravidians to form the Dravidian race, and his position treats the Dravidians as immigrants from the north-west who passed through Babylonia before the Sumerians were practising agriculture there.

Slater[4] contends that there is evidence to prove the superiority of the Dravidians in culture, ascribing to them the possession of castles, cities, wealth, luxury, the use of magic, superior architectural skill, and ability to restore the dead to life. He holds that they possessed a priest-magician clan or caste such as did not exist among the Aryans. Unfortunately he adduces no evidence for these assertions beyond the unscientific opinions of Mr. C. F. Oldham,[5] and a couple of even less plausible conjectures, and it is sufficient to observe that there is nothing whatever to induce us to believe in the superiority of the culture of the Dravidians or the Muṇḍā-speaking tribes, and that on the contrary the evidence points rather in the opposite direction.

It is further held[6] that caste is Dravidian, the Brahmans being the product of the mingling of the bringers of the heliolithic culture from Egypt with the Dravidians. They achieved domination over the Dravidians, and, when the Aryans entered India, showing superior prowess, as users of horses, the Brahmans saw the wisdom of adopting the allegedly easier language which the masters spoke, and became the guardians and exponents of the Vedas, until finally they succeeded in imposing themselves as leaders of the Aryans who were Dravidized in culture. It is important to note that on this theory the Rigveda is left to the Aryans during the period when they were in the full flush of their conquests. It is difficult to reconcile this with the assertion that Viṣṇu is certainly not an Aryan god, since he most unmistakably

[1] *Migrations of Early Culture*; cf. Perry, *Children of the Sun*; Fleure in Slater, *The Dravidian Element in Indian Culture*, pp. 35 ff.; Peake, *The Bronze Age and the Celtic World*, chap. iv. But see CAH. i. 94 ff. On alleged Dravidian remains (Mohen-jo-Daro, Harappa), see IHQ. i. 176 ff.

[2] *Op. cit.*, pp. 8, 22 ff.

[3] *Op. cit.*, p. 158.

[4] *Op. cit.*, chap. ii.

[5] *The Sun and the Serpent.*

[6] Slater, pp. 48 ff., 157 ff. But see Macdonell and Keith, *Vedic Index*, ii. 247 ff.

exists in the Rigveda, which also knows Rudra, who is in part the prototype of Çiva, also asserted to be not Aryan.

The doctrine of the Egypto-Dravidian origin of caste is supported by the following arguments. (1) It is admitted that the Brahmans of the south claim Aryan descent and that they are differentiated from the bulk of the Dravidian population in facial appearance, complexion, and intellectual habit; but the justice of the claim to Aryan connexion is discounted on the score that it may be explained on the Egyptian hypothesis. This contention proves nothing, and leaves the traditional view unaffected. (2) It is alleged that the bearers of the heliolithic culture claimed divinity and established in Indonesia and elsewhere ruling classes claiming divine descent, while the traditional Brahman theory is that every Brahman is a god. The alleged facts are wholly problematical; the divinity of rulers when it exists can be traced to various ethnic causes, and the claims of the Brahmans are easily explicable without going beyond the Aryans.[1] (3) The carriers of the heliolithic culture are asserted to have been worshippers of the sun and the serpent; the Nambudiris, who are specially conservative, worship the cobras in Nayar households, and Brahman was a solar deity. The Brahmans of the Rigveda, however, do not worship cobras, and do not know a god Brahman. (4) The sacred cord of the Brahman is of cotton[2] which indicates an original association of the caste with cotton spinning, which certainly was no art of the Vedic Aryans. This, it is held, is a clear indication of the descent of Brahmans from foreigners who earned the gratitude and homage of the people of India by teaching them to spin and weave. The argument is clearly without value, and Slater himself admits that India itself was the home of the art of spinning and weaving cotton—primarily tree cotton, so that it is wholly needless to look to Egyptians of problematic reality. Moreover, it will be seen that the account of the origin of caste accepted by Slater is in effect merely a transfer to an Egyptian element of the tendency to stress racial distinctions, which together with occupation he believes to explain caste. A final complication introduced by Slater is his view that when they achieved supremacy the Brahmans became largely Aryanized in blood, because they aimed at securing the fairest wives.

Finally may be noted the argument which ascribes special potency in magic to the Dravidians, including the power of raising the dead, on the strength of 'the Vedas'.[3] No such statement, of course, has any Vedic authority.[4]

Nothing more substantial is adduced by Mr. G. W. Brown in his examination of the sources of Indian philosophy.[5] He claims that animism is Dravidian, and that in it Jainism and Buddhism show closer adherence to Dravidian ideas, rejecting the new Aryan gods. The Aryans must have learned in India to worship new trees like the peepal and banyan, the peafowl, the serpent, the monkey, various species of grass, and sacred places innumerable, from their predecessors, to whom also is due the doctrine of transmigration with its corollary of release. But here again we have nothing of substantial importance; we have no right to hold that animistic or animatistic ideas were un-Aryan; Roman religion for instance is permeated by them, and Greek has relics of

[1] Cf. Frazer, *The Magic Art and the Evolution of Kings*; Warde Fowler, *Roman Ideas of Deity*, chap. iv; von Negelein, *Weltanschauung des indogermanischen Asiens*, pp. 127 ff.

[2] Cotton is unknown from early texts; cf. on the thread, BDS. i. 5. 5; GDS. i. 36; VDS. xii. 14; ApDS. ii. 4. 22; Manu, ii. 44.

[3] Slater, p. 117.

[4] A passage like TS. ii. 1. 1. 3 neither refers to revival as real nor to Dravidians.

[5] *Studies in honor of Bloomfield*, pp. 75 ff.

them.[1] Transmigration again is recorded as a Druid belief,[2] and was adopted in Greece, apparently from Thrace, and independently of India. The more concrete suggestion that the terms Sāṁkhya and Yoga, and even Upaniṣad are really derived from Dravidian names is clearly illegitimate in the absence of any difficulty of explaining satisfactorily the terms as Aryan contributions. For asceticism and caste as Dravidian no proof is even attempted.[3]

An effort to render probable pre-Dravidian influence on Vedic civilization and religion has recently been made by Professor S. Lévi,[4] who revives the hint of Barth [5] that the Atharvan *tābuva* may really be derived from the taboo of the Australians and Polynesians, and refers also to Mr. J. Hornell's conclusions,[6] from the facts regarding Indian boats, of Polynesian influence, and even of a Polynesian invasion, the latter in Dravidian times, which introduced the coco-nut palm into India. Lévi's evidence is based on the existence of pairs—or triads—of ethnic names, applied to neighbouring peoples, which are differentiated by an initial preformant, a usage neither Indo-European nor Dravidian. Thus the Atharvaveda Pariçiṣṭa knows of Tosala as well as Kosala, a union found later in the Purāṇas and textbooks of rhetoric, while Açoka records Tosalī, the name of which Lévi would even identify with Dhauli. Aṅga is found in the Atharvaveda, while with Vaṅga it appears from the epic onwards, usually in close association with Kaliṅga. For the latter again we have a parallel in the quite late [7] name of the Telegu country Tiliṅga, Triliṅga, Tailiṅga, &c., whose antiquity, however, may be supported by Trilingon or Triglypton in Ptolemy's geography.[8] Lévi compares also the Bhuliṅgas, known to Pliny and Ptolemy and the Gaṇapāṭha, who appear to have been a part of the Sālvas,[9] though the epic ignores them. Both epics, however, have the combination Utkala with Mekala (with the variant Melaka). We have also Uḍradeça, Orissa, which goes back to an Uḍa to be recognized in Manu,[10] for which Uṇḍa is a variant; comparable are the Puṇḍras, and even the Muṇḍas. The Pulindas are known from the Aitareya Brāhmaṇa onwards; the Bṛhatkathāçlokasaṁgraha [11] represents them in terms which suggest that they were small and black, like the pre-Dravidians,[12] and practised totemism. The epic mentions with them the Kulindas who may more properly have been Kalindas, as the name, Kālindī, of the Yamunā suggests, and another variant is Kuṇindas.[13] The Muṇḍā languages permit the use of consonants as prefixes and the infixation of a nasal in certain cases between the prefix and the root, facts which would explain these variants, and which suggest that in the ultimate issue Utkala is Uḍra, differentiated by the infixation of a *k*, and Mekala Muṇḍa. There

[1] See, e.g., Farnell, *Cults of the Greek States*, iii. 2 ff.; iv. 302 f.; v. 361 ff.

[2] See also Dieterich, *Mutter Erde*, pp. 33, 56; von Negelein, *op. cit.*, pp. 54 f.

[3] On Sanskrit and Dravidian cf. J. Bloch, *Bull. Soc. Ling.* xxv. 1 ff.; J. Przyluski (*ibid.* pp. 66 f.; xxiv. 118 f., 255 f.) finds Austro-Asiatic words borrowed (including the term *karpāsa*, cotton), and strengthens the argument for borrowing of the phallic cult by the Aryans from the aborigines by the fact that this worship is prominent in Indo-China. It may be noted that here the paucity of phallic worship in the case of other Indo-European peoples strengthens the argument for borrowing. None of the instances alluded to by Farnell, *op. cit.* v. 8, is clearly or probably Indo-European.

[4] *JA.* cciii. 1–56.

[5] *Œuvres*, ii. 254.

[6] *Memoirs of the Asiatic Society of Bengal*, VII. iii (1920).

[7] Mārkaṇḍeya Purāṇa, lviii. 28, &c.

[8] vii. 2. 23.

[9] Kāçikā Vṛtti, iv. 1. 173.

[10] x. 44.

[11] viii. 31 ff.; cf. for colour, Nāṭyaçāstra, xxi. 89.

[12] Thurston, *The Madras Presidency*, p. 124; above, p. 11.

[13] Varāhamihira, Bṛhatsaṁhitā, iv. 24; xiv. 30, 33.

may be noted also the parallelism of Takkola as a place-name and the plant-name Kakkola, and of *kṣumā* (*kṣauma*) and *umā* (*aumīna*, *umya*) as the name of linen. The element *-liṅga* in some of these names suggests comparison with Laṅkā as denoting 'island', applied in both the Mahanadi and Godavari regions,[1] though P. Schmidt[2] has suggested for Kaliṅga comparison with the Nicobar word *kalāṅ*, sea-eagle, which would suggest that the ethnic names were of totemic origin. In the Indian archipelago names such as Karmaraṅga, Kāmaraṅga, Tāmraliṅga, suggest that in Kāmarūpa and Tāmralipti in its varied forms we have variants of a pre-Dravidian word. Kam again reappears probably in Kamboja, which is in its turn equated with Kapiça, both imperfect representations of an old form. Without a prefix we have Bhoja, the aspirate of which is due to contamination with the root *bhuj* of Sanskrit. The pairs of names suggest certain conclusions as to the social and political importance of a people who must have created political unities of considerable extent, so firmly connected with the real life of the country that they have persisted through thousands of years to the present day.

This evidence, unfortunately, hardly carries us any farther towards ascertaining the amount of pre-Dravidian influence on Vedic civilization, and it must be added that much of it seems of very dubious value. The evidence that Tiliṅga was an early form is negligible; Ptolemy has already Triliṅga before him and he localizes the place in Arakan. Utkala may be Uḍra, but obviously, if we can operate with such names, we can establish anything we like; similarly with Kāmarūpa and Tāmralipti. The attempt to deduce from Yāska[3] that he classed the Bhojas, of whom the Kambojas were a branch, as different from the Āryas appears hardly justifiable, *bhoja* in the passage cited having probably the sense 'enjoying', and not an ethnic significance, and the one thing certain about that people is that they were reckoned by Yāska as using a language closely akin to that of the Āryas. Clearly a very necessary proof of the thesis is still lacking, plausible etymologies from Austric languages, and these are clearly by no means easy to find, for Lévi rejects the one suggested, *prima facie* with plausibility, for Kaliṅga. If it were true that *tābuva* was taboo, it would seem natural to expect that even the modern languages which are our chief means of investigating Austric language construction should show in other words similar conservatism of form. But in point of form nothing very satisfactory can be made out of the comparisons already, very ingeniously, made by Przyluski.[4] The conditions under which the investigation has to be conducted perhaps fatally preclude the adduction of really convincing cases, at any rate where Vedic words are concerned. We may readily believe in pre-Dravidian language and religion or even political organization as affecting the same phenomena among the Vedic peoples, but we still lack strict proof.

An effort to determine the characteristics of the pre-Dravidians has been made by Professor Giuffrida Ruggeri,[5] who holds that India was successively

[1] Tibetan *gliṅ*; Pliny, *N.H.* vi. 18, has Modogalinga in the Ganges. Cf. the Laṅkā of the Rāmāyaṇa, which is not Ceylon (Jacobi, pp. 90 ff.).

[2] BEFEO. vii. 261.

[3] Nirukta, ii. 2. Cf. E. Kuhn, *Avesta, Pahlavi, and Ancient Persian Studies* (1904), pp. 213 ff.; Nariman, JRAS. 1912, pp. 255 ff.; L. Sarup (trs., p. 22, n. 5) misunderstands Roth's view on this point; Yāska himself uses *çu* as 'go' (iii. 18; iv. 13), which contradicts his assertion that the Kambojas used *çavati*, the Aryans *çavas* only. Roth does not deny the Āryan use of *çavas*, which Yāska doubtless connected (as *bala*) with *gatikarman*. Yāska is either inconsistent or there is an old interpolation (known to Patañjali, Mahābhāṣya, i. 1. 1).

[4] MSL. xxii. 205 ff.; BSL. xxiv. 118 ff.

[5] *Outlines of a Systematic Anthropology of Asia* (1921), pp. 43 ff.

occupied by Negritos apparently platyrrhine; pre-Dravidians (Australo-Veddaic); Dravidians (akin to Homo Indo-Africanus Aethiopicus); tall dolichocephalic (Mesopotamaic ?) elements seen in the Todas; dolichocephalic Aryans; and brachycephalic Leukoderms—presumably of the Alpine type. The pre-Dravidians, on his view, were numerically preponderant, as held by Chanda, but the Dravidians imposed their language on large bodies of them, though the Muṇḍā languages persisted. The Dravidians were mesorrhine as opposed to the pre-Dravidian platyrrhines, the Niṣādas of Vedic texts, the 'noseless' enemies of the Rigveda. Similarly he assumes that the pre-Dravidians imposed their language on the Negritos, thus accounting for the fact that the speeches kindred to the Muṇḍā are spoken by tribes of Negrito as well as of pre-Dravidian type.[1] It must be admitted, however, that despite the ingenuity of this reconstruction evidence for it of any decisive character is wholly lacking, as it is based on recent anthropometrical data, whence conjectures are made for events of some four thousand years ago.[2]

H.—PYTHAGORAS AND PARMENIDES

U. von Wilamowitz-Moellendorff [3] holds that in the doctrine of Philolaos the five bodies in the sphaira are the four elements, which compose it, with as fifth ὁ τᾶς σφαίρας ὁλκός in the sense of that which gives the sphaira its form, the nature of that something being only vaguely felt; in the *Timaios* Plato makes the world-soul perform an analogous function. He insists [4] that it is to Aristotle we must look for the conception of the ether as a fifth element, for he evidently deliberately claims this as his own invention. The assertion of Xenokrates [5] which ascribes the doctrine to Plato he explains either as referring to a casual adoption of the idea by Plato, which he did not carry farther, or to his accepting an innovation of Aristotle's. Doubtless ascription to Plato or Aristotle of the precise form of the doctrine is legitimate, but there is force in the view of Rostagni [6] that already in the early Pythagorean view, if we accept the traditional accounts, the basis of the doctrine existed. The fifth element is the περιέχον which is described also as the other as well as the ἄπειρον πνεῦμα, while on the immaterial side we have the world spirit as the power which binds together the mass. In any event there is no close

[1] W. Schmidt, *Die Mon-Khmer-Völker* (1906); *Die Gliederung der australischen Sprachen* (1919).

[2] Cf. the divergent views of Myres, CAH. i. chap. i; Haddon, *The Races of Man* (new ed., 1924). It is natural to regard the Dravidians as ultimately not essentially different from the pre-Dravidians or even the Negritos, but all these views rest on insufficient grounds. Giuffrida-Ruggeri adopts the idea of the Aryan 'Midland' as excluding the Punjab and Rajputana with the United Provinces, but this view is not in harmony with any ancient authority on the Midland. Chanda (*The Indo-Aryan Races*, i. 74 ff.) regards the men of the Alpine race as Tocharians, a branch of the Indo-Europeans of *centum* speech, and ascribes to their influence the difference between 'Outer' and 'Inner' languages. But we have no proof of the early existence of these Tocharians in East Turkestan, and the 'Outer' languages show no *centum* features. His view of Yadus, Turvaças, &c., as immigrants — partially Semitized— from Mesopotamia, is quite implausible, as is his denial of the aboriginal character of the Çūdras; though that class may, of course, have included Aryan slaves, this is implausible on the evidence (Macdonell and Keith, *Vedic Index*, ii. 380 ff.). Cf. JRAS. 1917, pp. 167 ff.

[3] *Platon*[2], ii. 91 f.

[4] *Ibid.* i. 718. For Plato's claim, see Frank, *Plato und die sogenannten Pythagoreer* (1923), pp. 233, 319 f.

[5] Simplikios, *Phys.* 1165; Eva Sachs, *Die fünf platonischen Körper*, pp. 9 ff., 41 ff.

[6] *Il Verbo di Pitagora* (1924), pp. 56 ff.

similarity between the Greek and the Indian conception of ether, whether as regards the final doctrine as seen in Aristotle or the material whence it was developed.

Frank,[1] as against Wilamowitz-Moellendorff, insists that in the fragment of Philolaos there is a reference to the twofold doctrine of the five regular bodies and their correspondence with the five elements, but he holds that this is merely one of many proofs that the ascription of the fragment to Philolaos is a mere error. He points out [2] that the natural deduction to be made from Plato's writings is that both the doctrine of the irrational and the discovery of the five figures were invented shortly before the time when he accepted them, apparently by Theaitetos. He denies to the real Pythagoras the mathematical achievements claimed for him, but ignored by Xenophanes, Herakleitos, Empedokles, and Herodotos,[3] placing them in the Platonic age, while he traces the mathematical philosophy of the Pythagoreans to an effort to reconcile the doctrines of Anaxagoras and Demokritos, pointing out that their views are inconceivable before Anaxagoras (*c.* 460–430 B.C.) had clearly distinguished the ideas of quality and quantity, and first Protagoras and then Demokritos (*c.* 430 B.C.) had established the doctrine of the subjectivity of sense qualities. The Pythagorean view was thus one of points as monads, related to the dynamic conception of matter in Anaxagoras and the materialistic atomism of Demokritos as was the Monadologia physica of Kant's youth to the dynamic conception of matter in Leibnitz and the atomism of Huyghens and Newton. Without necessarily accepting the whole of Frank's contentions, and in particular the view that Speusippos is the real author of the Philolaos fragments, it is clear that we cannot safely accord to Pythagoras himself credit for his mathematical discoveries, and thus one important ground for the alleged derivation of his views from India disappears.

Frank, who candidly recognizes [4] the influence of Egypt on the beginnings of Greek mathematics and derives [5] thence the Greek knowledge of the planets—which, of course, were certainly not borrowed from India—insists [6] that the essential turning point in Greek thought came with the Persian war, after which Greece broke free from connexion with the general oriental tendency of thought, and Anaxagoras formulated the fundamental principle of the distinction between our subjective world and reality, as it appears to an ideal spectator, in his doctrine of optics. In the Chāndogya Upaniṣad [7] we find the assertion that all things can be resolved into one or other of three elements, but no proof is attempted, and the difference is indicative of the distance which separates Greek and Indian trends of thought. Others again tend to argue that Iranian ideas, partly themselves of Babylonian origin, were influential [8] on early Greek thought as well as later,[9] but, whatever the value of these views, they do not support any direct, nor probably any indirect, influence of India on Greece.

The probability of parallelism as regards the development of the doctrine

[1] *Op. cit.*, pp. 318 ff.

[2] *Ibid.*, pp. 227 ff. Cf. Vogt, *Bibl. Math.* x. 97 ff.; Heath, *Greek Math.* i. 157.

[3] *Ibid.*, pp. 219–22.

[4] *Ibid.*, p. 79; Heath, i. 121.

[5] *Ibid.*, pp. 197, 201 f. Cf. K. Kerényi, *Archiv f. Religionswissenschaft*, xxii. 245–56.

[6] *Ibid.*, pp. 143 ff.

[7] vi. 2 ff.

[8] Thus Eudoxos is credited with being the intermediary for the introduction of oriental ideas by Norden, *Geburt des Kindes* (1924), pp. 29 ff. Cf. Kerényi, *Archiv*, xxii. 256; Jäger, *Aristoteles*, p. 133.

[9] The effort to find the influence of the Brāhmaṇa conception of Prajāpati as the year on the Aion doctrine made by Reitzenstein, *Das iranische Erlösungsmysterium* (cf. L. Troje, *Archiv*, xxii. 87 ff.) and others is not at all convincing.

of transmigration is shown by the fact that Plato in the *Laws* [1] treats the idea as pre-Pythagorean and illustrates one motive creating it in the view that the murderer of a father or mother must be reborn to endure in his own person the punishment of a similar fate. It is no more surprising that such an idea should be found independently in two countries than that the Jaiminīya Brāhmaṇa [2] should record as a symptom of divinely induced madness the action of a priest in cutting off the heads of his father's cattle, even as Aias shows his dementia by his onslaught on his kine. The tale of Aias was known to the *Little Iliad*,[3] and was probably current by 700 B. C., far too early to permit of borrowing. For Greece Wilamowitz-Moellendorff [4] finds the cause of the doctrine in the succession of generations, the grandson bearing the grandfather's name and reproducing him, while Rostagni [5] insists on the fact that the early mind, when it reflects, is unable to conceive of anything utterly perishing or coming into being from nothing, and thus is induced to accept transmigration. It is surprising that Gomperz,[6] who recognizes this fact, should insist on deriving the Greek view from India. His view is evidently based in part on inaccurate information, as in the case of his contention that 'the formulae which summarize the whole of the "circle and wheel" of birth are likewise the same in both' Pythagorean and Indian belief. Similarly he finds [7] a curious parallel between the appearance of the doctrine of transmigration shortly before the belief of Parmenides in the one reality, as compared with the first records of transmigration in India as occurring not long before the doctrine of the eternal one; this suggestion of Oldenberg [8] is not supported by the facts, which suggest that the order in time of the doctrines was rather the reverse. Gomperz admits, however, the radical difference between the Greek outlook as scientific as well as religious, and the Indian as mainly religious. A most striking illustration of the divergence is furnished by the doctrine of the Pythagoreans recorded by Aristotle [9] explaining how souls were always available to enter new bodies when these came into being. They found the explanation in the existence of particles of dust in the sunlight, which they conceived to be living souls, not immaterial but formed of fine matter, a conception which maintained itself as late as the Neo-Platonists [10] in one aspect of the doctrine of πνεῦμα.

The parallel drawn by Garbe between the doctrine of the Upaniṣads and that of Parmenides is, of course, largely discounted, if we accept the view that Parmenides was essentially not the father of idealism but of materialism, as claimed by Burnet,[11] who with Zeller [12] denies to Parmenides the assertion of the identity of thought and being which is attributed to him by Garbe. Burnet [13] also further differentiates Parmenides from the doctrine of the Upaniṣads by denying that the second part of his poem is intended as an exposition of appearances as opposed to reality in the sense that Parmenides admitted in some degree that appearances existed. On his view, as on that of Diels, this part of the poem merely deals with opinions of others, which are necessarily false, those others being, as he thinks, Pythagoreans, not, as in Diels's view, followers of Herakleitos. But this latter view is opposed

[1] 870 ff.
[2] ii. 269–72 (Yavakrī's story).
[3] Jebb, *Ajax*, pp. xvi f.
[4] *Platon*,[2] i. 251. Cf. Tylor, *Primitive Culture*, ii. 14. For the Orphic belief, see Rohde, *Psyche*, ii[4]. 109, 121, and for the close relations of Pythagorean and Orphic views, Frank, *op. cit.*, pp. 356 f.
[5] *Op. cit.*, p. 150.
[6] *Greek Thinkers*, i. 124.
[7] *Op. cit.* i. 552.
[8] *Buddha*[2], p. 45.
[9] *de An.* i. 2. The doctrine may be from Demokritos (cf. Frank, pp. 101 ff.).
[10] Inge, *Plotinus*, i. 219 f.
[11] *Early Greek Philosophy*[2], pp. 198, n. 1, 208.
[12] *Pre-Socratic Phil.* i. 584, n. 1 (*Phil. d. Griech.* i[5]. 588, n. 1).
[13] *Op. cit.*, pp. 210 ff.

both by Gomperz [1] and Wilamowitz,[2] and it must be regarded as far from satisfactorily made out,[3] while the treatment by Plato of Parmenides is inconsistent with the view that he was really a mere materialist. The analogy of Spinoza cited by Gomperz is perhaps the most enlightening; the one is material but also it is spiritual; 'It is universal matter and universal spirit at once, but the matter is sterile because capable of no expansion and the spirit powerless because capable of no action.' Gomperz, however, is clearly erroneous in comparing the Vedānta philosophy, which in no form develops this precise doctrine.

K. Reinhardt,[4] again, insists that Parmenides admits no distinction between thinking and being,[5] but in his doctrine of opinion he aims, not at describing any merely apparent reality, but at the world as it necessarily presents itself to man, a world in which being and not-being stand side by side commingled, although he has no means of explaining their union, whence arises this empirical universe, save by hinting (μορφὰς γὰρ κατέθεντο δύο γνώμας ὀνομάζειν) that it is conventional as opposed to the one reality. Parmenides, on this view, in lieu of being essentially a materialist, was rather a logician, who, however, had not reached the stage when thought could be held to be other than reality. Like Frank, Reinhardt [6] rejects the idea of any connexion between Parmenides and the Pythagoreans; nor indeed is there any real ground for this suggestion, least of all for the conception of Burnet that Parmenides was a Pythagorean who was renouncing the false doctrines of his youth.

The views of Parmenides, therefore, must be deemed a parallel of interest to Indian thought, but not derived from India. In this regard interest also attaches to his treatment of the ideas of being, not-being, and being and not-being, which is reiterated in Gorgias,[7] and presents a certain similarity, but also in its dialectic an instructive contrast, to the treatment of the issue in the Chāndogya Upaniṣad.[8]

[1] *Op. cit.* i. 179. Cf. Diels, *Parmenides*, pp. 63, 100.

[2] *Platon*², i. 75 f., 562 f.; *Hermes*, xxxiv. 203 ff. Cf. Reinhardt, *Parmenides* (1916), pp. 5 ff.; Arnim, *Kultur der Gegenwart*, I. v. 106.

[3] Despite Rostagni, *op. cit.*, pp. 22 ff.; A. Covetti, *Ann. delle Univ. Toscane*, xxiii. 40 ff.

[4] *Parmenides*, pp. 30 ff., 69 ff. His view that Herakleitos is later than Parmenides (pp. 64, 155 ff.) is plausible, but not certain; cf. Rostagni, *Il Verbo di Pitagora*, pp. 12 ff. That frag. 6 and 8 of Parmenides refer to Herakleitos is equally dubious.

[5] In the famous passage τὸ γὰρ αὐτὸ νοεῖν ἔστιν τε καὶ εἶναι Burnet insists (*Greek Philosophy*, i. 67, n. 1) that the infinitives cannot be regarded as subjects, and that the meaning must be that it is the same thing that can be thought and that can be. He leaves unexplained what Parmenides conceived to be the relation between being and thought, and his dictum is not valid. That the infinitive was not originally a subject is no proof that it could not become one, i. e. be felt as one. Cf. Gildersleeve, *Syntax of Classical Greek*, i. 132; Goodwin, *Greek Moods and Tenses*, p. 300; Herakleitos, frag. 112 τὸ φρονεῖν ἀρετὴ μεγίστη, καὶ σοφία ἀληθέα λέγειν; *Iliad*, i. 274; x. 174; Stahl, *Syntax d. griech. Verbums*, pp. 601 ff.

[6] *Op. cit.*, pp. 231 ff.

[7] Reinhardt, pp. 36 f.; Gorgias, frag. 3. If Reinhardt is right in the effort (pp. 89 ff.) to place Xenophanes's theistic interpretation of the unity of the universe after Parmenides's philosophical discoveries, the parallel (p. 153, n. 1) with the development in India to the Çvetāçvatara Upaniṣad's theism is noteworthy. But the view is uncertain.

[8] vi. 2. 1, 2; *contra*, v. 19. 1; TU. ii. 7; the absolute includes both being and not-being in the Muṇḍaka (ii. 2. 1) and Praçna (ii. 5). The fourfold treatment of being, not-being, being and not-being, neither being nor not-being is first developed in Buddhist texts. For dialectic comparable in quality with that of Gorgias we must wait until such texts as the Māṇḍūkya Kārikā (e. g. iv. 3 f., 83) or Nāgārjuna (Keith, *Buddhist Philosophy*, pp. 237 ff.). Cf. for Gorgias, Reinhardt, pp. 37 ff.; Gomperz, *Greek Thinkers*, i. 482 ff.; Plato's *Sophist*.

GENERAL INDEX

Bādarāyaṇa, author of Brahma Sūtra, 507, 545, 595, 596.
Bagaios, Phrygian god, 37, 116, 618.
Bagha, Iranian, 100.
Bāhīkas, people, 92, 147.
Bahiṣpavamāna Stotra. 329.
Bahram Yašt, 63.
Bāhva, on nature of the Brahman, 522.
Baka, spirit, 242.
Bakchai, 606.
Balāian or Balaic, language, 617.
Balance, ordeal for soul, 393, n. 3, 572.
Bali, offerings, 55, 175, 210, nn. 1, 4, 213, 287, n. 3, 359, 360.
Bamboo seeds, offered, 323.
Barber, rewarded, 369.
Bardesanes, Gnostic (2nd cent. A.D.), 612.
Barley, in ritual, 167, 323, 359, 366.
Barrier between dead and living, 422.
Basilides, Gnostic (2nd cent. A.D.), 612.
Bath, in ritual, 304, 321, 322, 345, 372.
Battle, to foresee result of a, 391.
Baudhāyana Dharma Sūtra, 29, 200, 415.
Baudhāyana Gṛhya Sūtra, 28.
Baudhāyana Çrauta Sūtra, 28.
Bdellion, used to drive away demons, 384.
Beans, taboo against use of, 608.
Beating of King, to expel evil, 342.
Beer, Indo-European drink, 624; of the Ases, Scandinavian legend of, 623.
Beginnings of Vedic philosophy, 433–9.
Being, 483, 485, 507, 519, 525 ; Parmenides' identification of thought and, 636, 637.
Bendis, Phrygian deity, 620.
Berndl, L., theory of Sāṁkhya, 544, 604, n. 1, 605, n. 5.
Bhadrakālī, deity, 212.
Bhadra Sāman, 249, 352.
Bhaga, god, 34, 86, 99, 100, 105, 106, 120, 191, 206.
Bhagavadgītā, 538, 550, 577, *and see* Gītā.
Bhāng, Soma supposed to be, 172, n. 1.
Bharadvāja, Bharadvājas, 1, 91, 92, 127, n. 2, 152, 176, 227, 291, 459.
Bhāradvāja Gṛhya Sūtra, 28.
Bhāratan war, 618, 619, n.
Bharatas, people, 12, n. 1, 64, n. 5, 79, 80, 80, n. 1, 173, n. 3, 200.
Bhāratī, goddess, 193, 200, 328.
Bhārgavas, priests, 226.
Bhauma, spirit, 362 ; *see also* Bhūmi.
Bhava, name of Rudra, 92, 144, 150, 193, 399.
Bhavānī, wife of Bhava, 364.
Bheda, defeated by Sudās, 131.
Bhīru, spirit, 242.
Bhojas, alleged to be pre-Dravidian, 633.
Bhujyu, son of Tugra, rescued by the Açvins, 115.
Bhuliñgas, a people, 632.
Bhūmi, earth, 174, 197, 212, 366 ; *see also* Bhauma.
Bhūt, modern use of term, 214.
Bhūtapati, deity, 153, 214.
Bhūtas, spirits, 73.
Bhūti, goddess, 186, 212, 366.
Bhṛgu, seer, 38, 71, 138, 158, 162, n. 1.
Bhṛgus, seers, 223, 225, 226, 228, 313, 317, 410, 413, 440, n. 4, 474, 475.
Bhṛgvañgiras, 225.
Binding of self in matter, 534, 539.
Bird form of altar, 466.
Birds, 63, 71, 87, 105, 119, 133, n. 6, 150, 153, 155, 169, 190, 193, 197, 209, 237, 391; as dead, 571 ; of omen, 392 ; taboos on eating, 318.
Birth, different kinds of, 526 ; *see also* Rebirth *and* Transmigration.
Birth ceremonies, 366–9.
Birthday offerings, 368.
Bisexual being, world sprung from, 462, n. 10, 620.
Bithynians, religion of, 39.
Black birds, 392.
Black dog, offered to Rakṣases, 324.
Black garments, in rain spell, 309, 324, 339.
Black magic, 396.
Black offerings, 212, 363, 389.
Black Yajurveda, 17.
Bliss (*ānanda*), 507, 518, 519, 520, 521, 556, 557, 569.
Blood (for Egyptian religion, see Wiedemann, *Archiv f. Religionswissenschaft*, xxii. 58 ff.), 56, 194, 241, 273, 281, 284, n. 2.
Blood suckers, demons as, 237.
Blue-black, connected with the dead, 143, n. 1.
Blue colour of demons, 237.
Boar, theriomorphic form of deities or demons, 111, 143, 157, 192, 208 ; cosmic, 81, n. 3, 208, 622.
Bodily presence of gods among men, 83.
Body (*çarīra*), 556, 557, 565, 566.
Boghaz-Köi, gods invoked in inscriptions found at, 5, 617.
Boiling oil ordeal, 393.
Bonds, of Varuṇa, 97, 246.
Bones of dead, burial of, 415, 420, 421.

the three brothers of Agni, 157, 160; taboos arising from, 308, 309.
Debts, three, owed by man, 480.
Deduction, logical, 485.
Deep sleep, 537, 566, 567–70.
Definition, 484, 548, n. 6.
Deformed shapes of demons, 237.
Deified States or Conditions, 211–15.
Deiokes, father of, 616, n. 1.
Demokedes, Greek physician at the Persian court, 602.
Demokritos, Greek philosopher (5th cent. B.C.), 604, 635, 636, n. 9.
Demons, or spirits, Wundt's classification of, 44, 45.
Demons, 72, 76, 427, 517, 518; and Maruts, 153; killed by Agni, 158; by Soma, 168; mixed form of, 225, 237.
Descent from animals or plants, 196.
Desertion of Indra by the gods, 127.
Desire, 436, 442, 480, 523, 554, 556, 574, 582.
Deṣṭrī, 'disposing' deity, 206.
Destruction of the universe by fire, periodic, 529.
Destructive character of Rudra, 143.
Determinism, 527, 586, 594, *and see* Will.
Deussen, P., theory of meaning of Upaniṣads, 509–12, 592.
Devabhāga Çrautarṣa or Çrautarṣi, sacrificer, 320, n. 1, 482.
Devalakas, colporteurs of idols, 30.
Devāpi, Purohita, 261, 292, 293.
Devavāta, Agni of, 158.
Devayajana, Vināyaka, 242.
Deviations from the Karman doctrine, 579, 580.
Dhammasaṁgaṇi, 563.
Dhanapati, offering to, 360.
Dhanvantari, 175, 214, 224, n. 4, 227, n. 8.
Dhanvantari Bharadvāja, 360; offerings to, 358, 361.
Dharma Sūtra, 27, n. 1, 29.
Dhartṛ, supporter god, 206.
Dhātṛ, god, 65, 86, n. 3, 104, 205, 206, 214.
Dhauli, perhaps Tosalī, 632.
Dhiṣaṇā, deity, 211.
Dhruva, pole-star, 4, 22, 79, n. 6, 164.
Dhuni, chief or demon, 130, 236.
Dhūrta, epithet of Rudra, 150, n. 2.
Dialectic, 506.
Dialogue form in Upaniṣads, 505.
Diarrhoea, means of curing, 386; *see also* Apvā.
Dice, and Apsarases, 182.
Dicing, 87, 258, 317.
Diction of Upaniṣads, 500.
Dietrich of Bern, 618, n. 9.
Dignāga, 559, 560.
Dione, goddess, 61.
Dionysos, Thracian and Greek god (CAH. ii. 615, 619 ff.), 47, 48, 250, 284, n. 2.
Dioskouroi, Greek deities, 38, 117, 119, 620, n. 5.
Dīrghajihvī, Asura woman, relations of, with Indra, 126.
Dīrghamukhī, bird of omen, 392.
Dīrghatamas, seer, 434.
Dīrghatamas Aucathya, Āprī hymn of, 165.
Dirt, as sign of asceticism, 401.
Disease, demons, 72, 147, 240, 381, 382.
Disguise, adopted by gods, 125; *see also* Transformation of gods.
Disinterested action, 583.
Dislike of flesh, 604.
Disposal of the dead, 415–24.
Distinction, not denoted by *vyaṣṭi*, 506, n. 11.
Distinction between offerings to the dead and those to the gods, 429, 430.
Distributive aggregate, alleged sense of *vyaṣṭi*, 506, n. 11.
Diti, goddess, 217, 218.
Divākara, the sun, 104.
Diversity denied, 507.
Divination, 390–2.
Divine animals, 189–95.
Divine implements, 188, 189.
Divine judgement of the dead, 464.
Divine ladies, connected with Tvaṣṭṛ, 205.
Divodāsa Atithigva, King, 91, 158, 228, 496.
Divyāvadāna, 414.
Do ut des principle of Vedic sacrifices (for an idealistic interpretation, see van der Leeuen, *Archiv f. Religionswissenschaft*, xx. 241 ff.), 259.
Dog, 62, 128, 144, 150, 192, 237; not usually sacrificed, 324; offered, 279, 324, 406, n. 9; skin, 267.
Dogs of death, 406, 424, n. 6.
Dogs of Rudra, 144.
Doias, Phrygian god, 620.
Dolphin form of Apollo, 123.
Domestic fire, 158, 159, 287–9, 358.
Domestic ritual, 55, 175, 201, n. 2, 358–78, (*see Contents*).
Domestication of the horse, 618, n. 1.
Donar, Teutonic god, 37.
Doors of the heaven, 621–3.
Doors of the place of sacrifice, as divine, 189.
Double of Indra, 125.

Five-headed snake, 363.
Five regular figures, discovered by Theaitetos, 635.
Fjörgynn and Fjörgyn, 61, n. 5, 141.
Flamen, Roman, 39 ; Dialis, sanctity of, 276.
Flames, as deciding fate of the dead, 410, n. 8.
Flesh, restrictions on eating (cf. Hopkins, *Ethics of India*, pp. 160 ff.), 307.
Flesh offering, at Aṣṭakās, 429.
Flies, Greek offering to the, 194.
Flight of Agni, 153, 154.
Flood, 25, 111, 229, 621.
Food, as designation of earth in CU., 525 ; left over from meals, offered to Rudra, 145 ; of the gods, 87.
Footprints, man can be injured through, 381 ; veneration of, 108, n. 4, 389.
Forecasting the weather, 392.
Forest cattle, Vāyu as lord of, 144, n. 13.
Forest fires, wind as producing, 138.
Forgiveness of sin, 246, 247.
Form, 486, 487, 554, 556, and see *rūpa*.
Four ages, 82, n. 9.
Four-eyed dog, 344, 346, 406.
Four-month sacrifices (*cāturmāsya*), 155, 160, 178, 298, 305, 321–3.
Four states of the soul, 567–70.
Frank, E., views cited, 635.
Frankish kings, long hair of, 343.
Fravartiš, Phaortes, 616, n. 1.
Fravaši, in Iranian religion, 616.
Frazer, Sir J. G., theory of sacrifices, 262.
Freedom, as opposed to Determination of the will, 469, 503, 527, 586, 594.
Freyr and Freyja, 61, n. 5.
Friction, lighting of fire by, 155, n. 1.
Friends, duties to, 480.
Frogs, in myth and ritual, 141, 294, 302, 381, 386, 390, 420, 434.
Full moon, offerings to, 213.
Funeral hymn, 256, 282, 418–20 ; *see also* Disposal of the dead.
Furrow, *see* Sītā.

Gambling, *see* Dicing.
Gaṇapati, epithet of Bṛhaspati, 162.
Gaṇas, troupes, 242.
Gānas, of Sāmaveda, 16.
Gandarewa, 34, 180.
Gandhabba, in Buddhist belief, 180.
Gandhāra, 385, 496.
Gandharva, Gandharvas, 8, 24, 34, 72, 76, 82, n. 9, 83, 91, 92, 104, n. 1, 142, 179–84, 199, 213, 214, 218, 327, 375, 376, 402, 456, 470, 482, 520, n. 7, 577 ; Kali, 478, n. 8 ; men as, 573.
Gāndharva marriage, 373.
Gandharvaloka, 179, n. 7, 301.
Gandharvanagara, 532, n. 6.
Gaṇeça, a deity, 242.
Ganges, descent from heaven of the, 173 ; oath by water of the, 395.
Ganymede legend, Indian parallel to, 131, n. 4.
Gaotema, in Avesta, 35.
Garbe, R., doctrine of Indian origin of Greek philosophy, 601–13.
Garbha Upaniṣad, 476, n. 2, 501, 567.
Gārgya Bālāki, teacher, 493, 496, 498, 516.
Garuḍa, the sun-bird, 109, 190, 381.
Garutmant, the sun as, 193.
Gate of the heaven, 397, n. 6.
Gauḍapāda, author of Māṇḍūkya Kārikā, 501, 503, 505, 512, n. 1, 531, 532, 558, 637, n. 8.
Gaulish religion, 39, 233, n. 2 ; *see also* Celtic religion.
Gaumāta, usurper of Persian throne, 615.
Gaurī, goddess, 17, n. 3.
Gauṣūkti, teacher, 22.
Gautama, Gotama, 1, 132, 221, n. 1.
Gautama Dharma Sūtra, 29.
Gāyatra Sāman, 352.
Gazelle form of Uṣas, 208.
General character of the Brāhmaṇa philosophy, 440–2.
General conceptions, 484.
Generality, not denoted by *samaṣṭi*, 506, n. 11.
Generalization of activity of Rudra, 145.
Generation, as connected with Tvaṣṭṛ, 205.
Generative organ (*upastha*), 554, 556, 557, n. 5.
Generosity, 250, 477, n. 10, 480, *and see* Gifts.
Germanic religion, 35, 36, 37, 38, 39, 59, 117, n. 3, 121, n. 1, 136, n. 11, 172, n. 2, 178, 193, 258, n. 2, 283, n. 2, 286, n. 2, 287, n. 3, 303, n. 1, 318, n. 4, 322, n. 4, 360, 361, 376, 397, 407, n. 2, 422, n. 5, 448, 571, n. 9, 620, 621, n. 1.
Geryoneus, Greek legend of, 38, 127, 235.
Ghee, as food of Agni, 154.
Ghoṣiṇī, guardian of cattle at pasture, 214.
Ghosts, 413, 414, 427.
Ghouls of the burial places, 237.
Giant, 81 ; Gandharva as a, 181.
Gift theory of sacrifice, 48, 256–60.

Jainism, views of, 20, 56, 459, 503, n. 7, 504, 514, 546, 577, 591, 631.
Jamadagni, Āprī hymn of, 165.
Jambhaka, spirit, 242.
Jamšed, in Persian legend, 620.
Janaka, King of Videha, 64, 459, 493, 495, 496, 505, 517, 520.
Jātavedas, epithet of Agni, 160, 316.
Jaundice, transferred to birds by magic rite, 385, 386.
Jayanta, deity (cf. Arthaçāstra, ii. 4), 197, 365.
Jealousy of heaven, Herodotos' doctrine of the, 243–4.
Jevons, H. B., theory of sacrifice, 278.
Jewish week, 41.
Joint-curses, 395, 396.
Journey, mode of predicting, 390.
Jumbaka, as Varuṇa, 304.
Juno, Roman goddess, 117, n. 3.
Jupiter, Roman deity, 37, 45, 51, 96, 117, n. 3, 448, 626, n. 4.
Jus trium noctium, 376.
Jyeṣṭha Sāman, 309, 371.
Jyotiṣmant, a Marut, 153, n. 6.

Ka, god, 207, 321, 518, n. 7.
Kabeiroi, alleged connexion with Kubera, 38.
Kai Kāōs, Iranian hero, 227, 232.
Kakkola, parallel to Takkola, 633.
Kāla, deity, 24, 209.
Kalaha, spirit, 242.
Kālakañjas, Asuras, 234.
Kālī, goddess, 212.
Kali, legend of Açvins' aid to, 116.
Kali, age of the world, 82.
Kali Gandharvas, 82, n. 9, 179, n. 7, 478, n. 8.
Kalindas, people, 632.
Kaliñga country, 633.
Kalyāṇī, spirit, 400, n. 5.
Kāma, desire, 24, 210, 352 (Agnias), 359, 374, 542, 555, n. 7.
Kāmaduh, wish-cow, 191.
Kamadyū, wife of Purumitra, 116.
Kāmarañga, country, 633.
Kāmarūpa, country, 633.
Kāma Sūtra, 476, n. 2, 488, n. 4, 491, n. 5.
Kamboja, people, 547, n. 4, 633.
Kanisian or Kanesian (i.e. late Hittite, containing Indo-European elements, CAH. ii. 253 f., 428, n. 1 ; Friedrich, *Streitberg-Festschrift*, pp. 307 ff.), 617.
Kaṅsa, legend of, 262.
Kant, E., German philosopher (A.D. 1724–1804), 480, 551, 554, 563, 564, 592, 635.
Kaṇṭhaçruti Upaniṣad, 589, n. 4.
Kaṇva, disease demon, 381, n. 7.
Kaṇvas, family, 2, 227, 228, 330, 400, n. 12, 426.
Kapila Ṛṣi, 526, 543, 544, n. 6.
Kapiṣṭhala Saṁhitā, 17.
Karañja, enemy of Indra, 129.
Karapans, in Avesta, 232.
Karāṭa, 17, n. 3.
Kāravapacava, place, 352.
Kārotī, river, 354.
Kāçi, place and people, 496.
Kaçyapa, cosmic tortoise, 196, 214, *and see* Akūpāra.
Kaçyapa, a priest, 193, 622 ; *see also* Udalākāçyapa.
Kaṣaka (Kṛçana, Karçana), 213.
Kassites, 6, 618.
Kaṭha Upaniṣad, 499, 500, 502, 503, 506, 510, 511, 513, 514, 515, 516, 518, 519, 522, 523, 526, 531, 535, 536, 537, 538, 539, 545, 547, 549, 552, 555, 557, 577, 579, 583, 591, 617.
Kāṭhaka Saṁhitā, 17, 21, 157.
Kaṭhaçruti Upaniṣad, 589, n. 4.
Kaṭhas, ritual school, 323.
Kathenotheism, 88, 89.
Kātyāyana Çrauta Sūtra, 28.
Kaurama, King of Ruçamas, 250, 400, n. 11.
Kauçika, as epithet of Indra, 132.
Kauçikas, Vedic clan, 196.
Kauçika Sūtra, 28, 29, 194, 205, 214, 356, 361, 382, 388, 393, 396, 397, 400, 421.
Kauṣītaki Brāhmaṇa, 17, 19, 144, 148, 209, 333, 410, 464, 474.
Kauṣītaki Upaniṣad, 493, 496, 498, 501, 520, 521, 537, 554, 556, 557, 558, 561, 567, 576, 577, 580, 583, 584.
Kauṭilīya Arthaçāstra, 481, n. 12, 491, n. 5, 505.
Kavaṣa Ailūṣa, sage, 459.
Kavāta, of Kavi dynasty, 615.
Kavi, dynasty, 615.
Kavis, 315.
Kāvya Uçanā, mythical priest, 159, 227, 232.
Kāvyas, Fathers as, 329.
Kena Upaniṣad, 19, 499, 500, 502, 522, n. 6.
Kentauros, alleged connexion with Gandharva, 104, n. 1, 180.
Kerberos, dog of Hades, 38, 192, 407.
Keresāni, Iranian hero, 34.
Keresāspa, 180.
Keçava, Viṣṇu as, 17, n. 3.

Passions, 581 ; *see also* Desire.
Paths, Pūṣan's connexion with, 106, 107.
Pātrapāṇi, demon, 240.
Patricide, of Indra, 125.
Paurṇamāsī, offerings to, 201.
Pāyāsi, King, 551.
Pedu, recipient of a steed from the Açvins, 116.
Pehrkon, Lettish deity, 140, n. 4.
Pelops, death of, 119, n. 5.
Penance, *see* Asceticism.
Penis, as organ, 557.
Pentheus, origin of legend of, 48, 612.
People, plundered by the king, 151, n. 1.
Perception (*pratyakṣa*), 453, n. 5, 482, 559, 560, 564.
Performers of the sacrifice, 289–99.
Perfumes, offered to Brahmans for the dead, 427.
Periodic destruction of universe by fire, 529.
Perjury, *see* Truth.
Perkunas, Lithuanian deity, 37, 140, n. 4, 141.
Persian influence on court of Candragupta, 306, n. 3 ; *see also* Iranian religion.
Persian religion, 39, 626, *and see* Iranian religion.
Personal deity, 509, 511, 626.
Personality of deities, development of, 45 ; of the absolute, 522, n. 6.
Perun, Slav god, 140, n. 4, 141.
Pessimism, not early Vedic, 581.
Pestle and mortar, used in pressing Soma, 167.
Petavatthu, 29, 74.
Phaidros, of Plato, chariot metaphor in, 609, n. 4, 613.
Phallic worship, 10, 56, 129, 148, 632, n. 3.
Pharmakoi, scapegoats (cf. Wissowa, *Archiv f. Religionswissenschaft*, xxii. 21), 263.
Pherekydes, Greek poet (*c.* 540 B.C.), 606.
Philo, Jewish philosopher (*c.* 30 B.C.–A.D. 50 ; cf. on his Logos, Inge, *Plotinus*, i. 98), 610.
Philolaos, Pythagorean philosopher (5th cent. B.C.), 608, 634, 635.
Philosophical hymns, in the Rigveda, 2, 14.
Philosophical myths, 60.
Philosophy of the Veda, *see Contents*, Part V.
Phlegyai, 38, 226.
Phraortes, sense of name, 616, n. 1.
Phrygian religion, 620.
Physical paternity, sense of *pater* in Roman religion, 96, 626.
Physicians of the gods, Açvins as, 115.
Piercing of skin of cow, as rain spell, 351.
Pig, not offered in sacrifice, 279.
Pigeon, as bird of omen, 193, 383, 392.
Pigmy size of mind, 404.
Piling of the fire, 271, 282, 352, 354–6, 364, 397, 440, n. 1, 465–7.
Pindar, Greek lyric poet, eschatology of, 609, n. 3.
Pipru, Asura, 130, 231, 236.
Piçācas, demons, 73, 74, 76, 91, 180, n. 9, 181, 238, 239, 384, 386, 414, 478, n. 8, 616.
Pits, and dead, 411.
Pity, *see* Compassion.
Places of the dead, 406–15.
Plakṣa Prāsravaṇa, offering at the, 352.
Planets (cf. v. Negelein, *Weltanschauung*, p. 126), 79, 108, n. 4, 200, 201, 416, n. 2, 528, n. 9, 635.
Plant demons, 239, 240.
Plant life, influenced by the moon (for epic, cf. Meyer, *Das Weib im altind. Epos*, p. 353 ; v. Glasenapp, *Hinduismus*, p. 49), 170.
Plants (*oṣadhayaḥ*), 34, 64, 184, 225, 523, 526, 631 ; and souls of the dead, 415.
Plato, Greek philosopher (B.C. 427–347), 526, 602, 605, n. 4, 613, 620, n. 1, 635, 636, 637.
Pleasure (*sukha*), 520, n. 7, 521, n. 5, 550, 556, 557.
Pleiades, 202, 416, n. 2.
Plotinus, Neo-Platonist (A.D. 204–70), 599, 611.
Plough festival, 390.
Ploughshare, deity, 64, 188.
Plurality of selves, 536.
Poison, 150 ; sent by Rudra, 144 ; to produce ecstasy, 402.
Poison ordeal, 393.
Polar dawn, theory of a, 122, n. 1.
Pole star, in marriage ritual, 4, 375 ; worship of, 202.
Political theory, 480, 481, 600.
Polyandry, apparent in case of marriage of Sūryā, 119, n. 5.
Polydaemonism, 204, n. 1.
Polynesian influence on India, 634.
Pool of youth, 116.
Popular and hieratic religion, 55–7.
Porcupine quill, used by bride, 367, 374.
Porphyry, Neo-Platonist (A.D. 232–301), 612.
Porridge, as cosmic principle, 275, 445.
Portents, 392.
Poseidon, Greek god (on derivation Ποτει Δᾶς; Kretschmer, Ποτι-Δᾶ (Δαον) ; Hoffmann, see R. Loewe, KZ. li. 219 f.), 469, n. 4.

Possession by evil spirit, modes to remove, 385.
Post, sacrificial (*yūpa*), 254, 264, 324, 325, 334.
Potṛ, priest, 252, 294, 296, 297, 298, 328.
Pourucistā, daughter of Zoroaster, 615.
Power, holy, *see* Brahman.
Pṛthi Vainya, King, 355.
Pṛthivī, goddess, 86, 87, 95, 145, 197, 622, n. 4 ; *see also* Earth.
Pṛçni, goddess, 151, 198.
Pṛṣātaka, offering and deity, 362.
Prabhus, class of Ṛbhus, 176.
Prahrāda Kāyādhava, an Asura, 232.
Prajāpati, god, 24, 65, 68, 84, n. 3, 86, 88, 96, n. 5, 101, 105, 111, 122, 125, 146, 192, 196, 213, 218, 233, 324, 345, 346, 347, 350, 359, 363, 376, 393, 396, 428, 437, 442–4, 449, 450, 454, 455, 456, 464, 465, 466, 467, 469, 470, 471, 473, 479, 480, n. 6, 481, 482, 486, 506, 510, 517, 524, 525, 539, 554, 560, 573, 581, 583, 610, 613, 635, n. 9.
Prākritic languages, origin of, 52.
Prākrits, 233, 238.
Pramṛçant, demon, 240, n. 6.
Praçāstṛ, priest, 252, 253, 294, 296.
Praçna Upaniṣad, 500, 501, 525, 537, 545, 552, 568, 577, 578, 581.
Prāsahā, wife of Indra, 125, 219.
Prastotṛ, priest, 297, 298, 314.
Pratardana, King, 584.
Pratīdarça Çvaikna, sacrificer, 320, n. 1.
Pratihartṛ, priest, 297, 298, 314.
Pratiprasthātṛ, priest, 294, 295, 321, 326, 330, 336, 371.
Prātiçākhyas, 488.
Praüga Çastra, of the Hotṛ, 255, 315, 329.
Pravāhaṇa Jaivali, philosopher, 493.
Prayer (for an implausible critique of RV. vii. 86, see v. Negelein, *Weltanschauung*, pp. 44–6), 65, 162–4, 310–12, 479, 480 ; and spell, 390.
Predestination, 511 ; *see also* Determinism.
Pre-Dravidians, 11, 632–4 ; *see also* Niṣādas.
Pregnant woman, funeral rite of a, 424, 627.
Preparation of Soma, 166–8.
Pressing stones (*grāvan*), 66, 167, 254.
Priest, 223–7, 289–99 ; power to injure his patron or enemy, 312 ; *see also* Brahmans.
Priesthood, 39, 40, 55–7, 58, n. 1, 72.
Primitive matter, 438, 483, 510, 532–5 ; see also *prakṛti*.
Primitive savages, alleged, 42.
Prince in exile, magic rite to restore, 387.
Principles, Sāṁkhya system of, 532–4.
Priyamedha, seer, 227.
Probe, used in medicine, 398.
Problem and Conditions of Knowledge, 513–16.
Procreation, 566, 567.
Prodigies, 392.
'Projection' theory of religion, 49.
Prometheus, Greek hero, 138, 158, 162, n. 1, 226, n. 5, 289, n. 2.
Prostitution, disapproved, 585.
Proto-Hittite, language (Sayce, JRAS. 1924, pp. 245 ff.), 617.
Prussian religion, 39.
Prytaneia, sacred fires of the, 625.
Pseudo-Hippokratean treatises, 602.
Pseudo-Kallisthenes, 618, n. 9.
Psychic apparatus, 405, and see *liṅga*.
Public sacrifices, paucity of, 159, 258, 625.
Pulindas, people, 632.
Puloman, father of Çacī, 125.
Punishment of crime, as a sacrifice, 348, n. 2.
Punjab, 3, 91, 121, 127, 337, n. 3, 634, n. 2.
Puraṁdhi, goddess, 211.
Purāṇas, 111, 112.
Purification, 141, 142, 383 ; *see also* Expulsion of evil.
Purohita, domestic priest, 159, 162, 227, 253, 292, 293, 319, 341, 342, 363, 394, 481.
Pūru, Asura, 234.
Purukutsa, wife of, 90.
Purūravas, and Urvaçī, 84, n. 3, 183, 200.
Pūrus, people, 9 ; and Vaiçvānara, 164, n. 5.
Pūrva Mīmāṅsā, 260, 505, 545, 574.
Pūṣan, god, 63, 70, 81, 87, 92, 93, 105–8, 110, 115, 125, 126, 142, 150, 166, 169, 170, 188, 192, 205, 211, 219, 221, 264, 274, 280, 328, 360, 364, 365, 374, 376, 400.
Puṣyamitra, King, 495.
Put, hell, 580.
Putting crop into the barn, Anaghā worshipped on occasion of, 186.
Pythagoras, Greek philosopher (6th cent. B.C.), and his school, 605–10, 634–7.
Pythagorean theorem, 607, 635.

Quail, saved from a wolf by the Açvins, 116, 117.
Quantity and quality, ideas of, distinguished by Anaxagoras, 635.
Quarters, 213, 483, 486, 518, n. 7, 553, 561.
Queen at Rājasūya (for a quasi-parallel, see v. Negelein, *Weltanschauung*, p. 93), 190, n. 7.

Ṛbhukṣan, leader of the Ṛbhus, 176.
Ṛbhus, elves, 38, 93, 168, 176–8, 255, 315, 461.
Ṛgvidhāna, 382.
Ṛjiçvan, son of Vidathin, protégé of Indra, 130.
Ṛjrāçva, saved by the Açvins, 116.
Ṛkṣa, father of Saṁvaraṇa, 196.
Ṛtu, seasons, 93, 178.
Race at wedding of Soma and Sūryā, 114, 139.
Races, mingling of, as religious factor, 51–5.
Racing, in ritual, 339, 340.
Rahasyu Devamalimluc, slayer of the Vaikhānasas, 129, n. 4, 458.
Rāhu, demon of eclipse, 235, 623.
Raikva, sage, 496, n. 5, 505.
Rain, 622, 623 ; *see also* Clouds ; and Soma, 151, 169, 172, 176, 178.
Rainbow, Gandharva as the, 181.
Rain spells, 309, 310, 331, 351, 389.
Rain water, as impure, 383.
Raivata Sāman, 350.
Rājana Sāman, 352.
Rājanyas, 92, 326, 341, 342, 481.
Rākā, goddess, 199, 201, 355.
Rākṣasa, form of marriage, 373.
Rakṣases, demons, 56, 73, 75, 76, 111, n. 1, 158, 213, 237, 238, 241, 272, 281, 285, 301, 320, 324, 360, 382, 383, 384, 386, 414, 427, n. 1, 430, 457, 470, 472, 478, n. 8, 616.
Rākṣasī, as house deity, 76.
Ram, 359 ; of Medhātithi, Indra invoked as, 131, n. 4.
Rāma, epic hero, 64, 92.
Rāmānuja, philosopher, 501, 508, 509, 512, 596.
Rāmāyaṇa, 30.
Ramman, Semitic deity, 222, n. 8.
Rāṣṭrabhṛt, Apsaras, 184.
Rathakāras, caste, 298, 299, 316, 317.
Rathakṛt, 178.
Rathantara Sāman, 253, 335, 350, 351, 461, 486.
Rātri, night, 198.
Real, 507, 519.
Realism, 558, 559.
Reasoning, 482, 484, 485 ; *see also* Knowledge.
Rebha, saved by the Açvins, 116.
Rebirth in the consecration, 302 ; *see also* Transmigration.
Recollection of previous births, 580, 609.
Red, colour of Rudra, 145 ; connected with the dead, 143, n. 1 ; ochre, used in Kurgan burials, 628.
Redemption of self in sacrifice, *see* Sacrifice.
Reed arrow points in magic, 387, 395.
Re-establishment of the fires (*punarādheya*), 317, 318.
Reinhardt, views cited, 635.
Relations of magic to religion, 379 ; *see also* Magic *and* Sacrifice.
Release, *see* Salvation.
Remains of offerings, 275.
Remedies, of Rudra, 143.
Remembrance of former births, 580, 609.
Removal of hostile influences by magic, 382–6.
Renewed death (cf. v. Negelein, *Weltanschauung*, p. 96), 573, 583, n. 3.
Renunciation, 515.
Repeated death, *see* Renewed death.
Repeating a formula backwards, 394.
Repentance of sin, 244, 471.
Replacing of offering by butter, 334.
Resignation, 598.
Restoration of dead to life by Indra, 125, n. 7, 458.
Restriction on nature of offerings, 258.
Retribution, see *karman*.
Ribaldry, in ritual, 258 ; at horse sacrifice, 345, 346 ; at Mahāvrata, 351.
Rice, 323, 359, 366 ; not known to Rigveda, 23.
Riddles, 258 ; in Upaniṣads, 505, 506, 507.
Right, see *ṛta* and *dharma*.
Rigveda, 1–15, 16, 17, 23, 24, 33, 48–52, 53, 58, 59, 60, 61, 63, 64, 68, 74, 77, 87, 88, 89, 90, 91, 92, 97, 98, 111, 115, 119, 131, 134, 135, 136, 137, 138, 140, 142, 143, 147, 150, 155, 158, 159, 164, 166, 167, 169, 170, 171, 176, 180, 181, 187, 188, 191, 192, 193, 199, 210, 213, 227, 229, 230, 231, 237, 243, 245, 249, 250, 252, 253, 254, 259, 260, 261, 272, n. 10, 275, 282, 283, 286, 290, 291, 294, 295, 296, 297, 300, 301, 303, 316, 331, 332, 347, 351, 354, 371, 375, 391, 393, 402, 403, 404, 405, 406, 409, 417, 420, 422, 423, 426, 427, 428, 438, 443, 445, 446, 449, 451, 454, 468, 479, 480, 483, 486, 490, 491, 515, 519, 555, 570, 571, 575, 581, 616–19, 621, 622.
Rinsing of the mouth by the sacrificer, 325, n. 1.
Rites ancillary to the sacrifice : the consecration, 300–3 ; the Avabhṛtha, 303, 304 ; taboo, 304–10 ; form of prayer, 310, 311.
Ritual in the Rigveda, 252–6 ; in the later texts, 257–402 ; *see Contents*.
Rivalry in sacrifice, 251.

River, crossed by dead, 406, n. 9, 412 n.
Rivers, as divine, 176, 213.
Robbers, &c., Rudra as patron of, 144, 150.
Robbery, marriage by, 375, n. 3.
Robigus, dog offered to, 324, n. 4.
Rock, cloud as, 157, 169.
Rodasī, goddess, 151, 220.
Rohiṇī, constellation, 146, 170, 179.
Rohita, deity, 209, 444, 467, n. 3.
Roman de Roland, 618, n. 9.
Roman religion, 36, 39, 45, 48, n. 3, 51, 53, 57, 117, 121, 188, 258, 259, 260, n. 5, 262, n. 2, 269, 270, n. 2, 273, n. 4, 274, 276, 279, n. 5, 280, 281, n. 1, 283, 284, n. 2, 286, n. 4, 289, 291, 318, n. 4, 325, n. 4, 329, n. 3, 346, 361, 376, 378, n. 1, 385, 418, 419, n. 5, 421, n. 2, 422, n. 5, 455, 626, 627, 631.
Royal consecration, see *rājasūya*.
Royal hair washing, 306.
Rubbing, in ritual, 271, 272, 343, 367.
Rudhikrā, demon or enemy, 236.
Rudra, god, 24, 46, 56, 57, 61, 69, 71, 81, 91, 92, 105, 106, 110, 112, 137, 142–50, 153, 156, 159, 188, 191, 192, 194, 199, 200, 208, 214, 215, 221, 222, 229, 241, 242, 244, 257, 272, 273, 287, 322, 331, 338, 355, 359, 364, 383, 399, 410, n. 8, 497, 501, 510, 511, 525, 527, 539, 549.
Rudrāṇī, wife of Rudra, 218, 364.
Rudras, 81, 86, 143, 150–3, 222, 223, 270, 455 ; *see also* Maruts.
Rudriyas, 143.
Ruçamas, people, 250 ; Kaurama, king of, 400, n. 11.

Çabala, Çabara, dog of Yama, 192, 406.
Çabalī, deity, 191, n. 6, 456, n. 1 ; offering, 456, n. 1.
Çabara, 38 ; *and see* Çabala.
Çabarasvāmin, on Mīmāṅsā Darçana, 508, n. 5.
Çacī, 81, 125, 219 ; Paulomnī, wife of Indra, 470.
Çāka, uncertain sense of, 201, n. 1.
Çaka invasions of India, 54.
Çakadhūma, weather prophet, 201, n. 1, 392.
Çākalya, author of Pada Pāṭha of Rigveda, 20.
Çākalya, sage, 506, 517.
Çākapūṇi, author, 164.
Çakuntalā, Apsaras, mother of Bharata, 184.
Çākvara Sāman, 253, 350.
Çakvarī, verses, 253, 309.
Çākya, line, 21 ; alleged connexion with non-Aryan Scyths, 36.
Çālakaṭañkaṭa, spirit, 242.
Çamā, goddess, 186, 212, 366.
Çambara, son of Kulitara, demon, 129, 131, 236.
Çāmbavya Gṛhya Sūtra, 28, n. 3.
Çamitṛ, priest, 253, 325.
Çanaiçcara, planet, 200.
Çaṇḍa, Asura, 232, 329.
Çāṇḍilya, sage, 354, 467, 576.
Çañkara, philosopher, 367, 501, 503, n. 6, 504, 507, 508, 509, 512, 522, 531, 532, 551, 552, 553, 558, 560, 571, 574, 578, 579, 595, 596, 599.
Çañkara, name of Rudra, 144, n. 8, 146.
Çāñkhāyana Āranyaka, 490.
Çāñkhāyana Gṛhya Sūtra, 413.
Çāñkhāyana Çrauta Sūtra, 347, 354, 476.
Çaṅstṛ, priest, 252.
Çarkara Çiṅçumāra, dolphin, 129, 201, n. 11.
Çarva, god, 35, n. 4, 92, 144, 147, 399.
Çarvāṇī, wife of Çarva, 364.
Çaçin, as name of the moon, 122.
Çatānīka, King, 394.
Çatapatha Brāhmaṇa, 17, 19, 22, 23, 25, 29, 36, 86, 92, 96, 106, 110, 113, 116, 117, 144, 148, 182, 188, 192, 193, 208, 226, 229, 242, 298, 304, 333, 347, 354, 403, 404, 409, 410, 414, 416, 417, 421, 443, 450, 451, 452, 453, 457, 464, 466, 474, 479, 483, 495, 499, 517, 573, 624.
Çatarudriya litany, 144, 150, 215.
Çatru, demon, 240.
Çatruṁjaya, spirit, 214.
Çāṭyāyana Brāhmaṇa, 18, n. 2.
Çaunaka, on Çrāddhas, 427.
Çauṇḍikeya, demon, 240.
Çavasī, mother of Indra, 81, 125, 217.
Çigrus, people, 196.
Çiçu Āñgirasa, a seer, 458.
Çitibāhu, *see* Aiṣakṛta.
Çiva, god, 30, 76, 137, 144, 148, 149, 150, 209, 362, 399, 525, 549, 623.
Çiva, as style of the jackal, 150, n. 4.
Çivasaṁkalpa section of Vājasaneyi Saṁhitā, 452.
Çrāddhas, offerings to dead, 427–32.
Çramaṇas, ascetics, 587, n. 7.
Çrauta ritual, 55, 93, 149, 177, 287–9, 289–99, 313–57 (*see* Contents), 429–32, 607.
Çrautarṣi Devabhāga, sage, 482.
Çrauta Sūtras, 27, 28, 29.
Çrāvaṇa, snake offering in, 362.

SANSKRIT INDEX

aṅçu, cup, 328, 339.
akhaṇḍakāla, impartite time, 560.
akhala, epithet of Rudra, 144, n. 4 ; *akhalā devatā*, 145, 327, n. 6.
agnicayana, 352, 354–6, 364, 397, 440, n. 1, 465–7, *and see* Piling of the fire.
agnihotra, fire-offering, 161, 261, 289, 297, 317, 318, 319, 321, 323, 514, 580, 585, 588.
agniṣṭoma, sacrifice, 155, 255, 272, 310, 313, 326–32.
Agnīṣomīya, victim, 324.
agnyādhāna, *agnyādheya*, 297, 316, 317, *and see* Establishment of the fires.
aghnyā, applied to the cow, 191.
aṇu, subtle, 547.
at, move, 466.
atigraha, objects of sense, 554, 556, 557.
atigrāhya, cup, 330.
atirātra, sacrifice, 119, n. 1, 256, n. 3, 327, 335, 336, 348, 350, 351.
ἀτμός, ἀϋτμήν, 466.
atyagniṣṭoma, sacrifice, 335, 350.
adābhya, cup, 328, 339.
adri, pressing stone, 167.
adhidevatam, *adhidaivatam*, 486, 559.
adhyāṇḍā, plant, 376.
adhyātmam, psychologically, 486, 559.
an, breathe, 466.
anattā, doctrine of, 547.
ananta, or *ānanda*, of absolute, 519.
anindrāḥ, people who do not believe in Indra, 433.
anucara, in Çastras, 315.
anubandhyā, cow, 334.
anumāna, inference, 482.
anuyājas, afterofferings, 320.
anurūpa, verses in Çastras, 315, 316.
anu-vaṣaṭkāra, secondary *vaṣaṭ* call, 295.
anuvākyā, verse of invitation, 255.
anṛta, untruth, 473, 479.
anṛtadeva, sense of, 247, n. 4.
antarikṣa, 486, 520, n. 7, 561, *and see* Atmosphere.
antaryāma, cup, 329.
antaryāmin, internal controller, 527.
andhas, used of Soma, 167.
annaprāçana, *see* Solid food, feeding of child with.
annamaya, epithet of self, 518.
anvaṣṭakya, rite, 428, 429.
anvārambhaṇīyā iṣṭi, 320, 321.
anvāhārya, mess, 320.
anvāhāryapacana, fire, 288.
apaciti, offerings, 338.
apavrata, despisers of Vedic rites, 622.
apāna, inspiration, 453, 553, n. 7, 556, 564, 565.
apāpa, epithet of slayer at animal sacrifice, 274, n. 7.
apāmārga, plant, 265, 384, 404.
apāvya, libations, 325.
apiçarvara, Indra as, 335.
apūrva, Mīmāṅsā doctrine of, 574, n. 3.
aptoryāma (*āptoryāma*), form of sacrifice, 334, 336.
apsaras, meaning of, 182.
apsujit, sense of, 81, n. 2.
abhipitva, sense of, 255.
abhiplava ṣaḍaha, form of sacrifice, 348, 351.
abhiṣecanīya, aspersion of the king, 340, n. 6.
amānava, superhuman, used of psychopomp, 578.
amṛta, drink of immortality, 623, 624.
amedhya, impure, 470.
ayas, meaning of, 22, n. 5.
argha, gift for Snātaka, 372, 374.
arghya, ceremony, 363 ; water, 427.
arta, *urta*, Iranian counterpart of *ṛta*, 35.
avakā, plant, 142, n. 3, 355, 363, 381, 390.
avamas, Fathers as, 329.
avabhṛtha, final bath, 286, 303, 304, 330.
avāna, a form of breath, 564.
avāntaradīkṣā, intermediate consecration, 327, 328.
avidyā, ignorance, 515.
avivākya, tenth day in main part of *dvādaçāha*, 350.
açlīlā vāc, haunts the evil doer, 477.
açva, origin of, from Prajāpati's swollen eye, 208.
açvattha, 339, 341, 363, 398, 527 ; as home of Apsarases, 184.
açvatva, horse-nature, 484.
açvamedha, horse sacrifice, 40, 63, 105, 114, 118, 119, 175, 195, 198, 199, 200, 202, 213, 218, 227, 254, 260, 262, 263, 279, 285, 304, 311, 343–7, 389, 476.
aša (*urta*), right, 35, 83.
aṣāḍha, brick, 354.
aṣṭakās, offerings on the, 93, 177, 197, 201, 280, 300, 372, 428, 429.
asādhu, evil, 479, n. 7.
asu, breath, spirit, 233, 403, 404, 405, 447, 453.
asunīti, spirit-leading, 405.
asura (on etym. cf. Güntert, *Der arische Weltkönig*, pp. 97 ff.), 232.

jyotis, form of *agniṣṭoma*, 351.

jhānas, forms of trance, Buddhist, 595, n. 1.

takṣ, fashion, 205.
takṣan, carpenter, 298.
tat tvam asi, that thou art, 506, 524.
tadvanam, epithet of absolute, 491, 506.
tanū, body, 380, n. 4, 486.
tanūhavis, offering to three forms of Agni, 317.
tapas, heat, asceticism, 210, 300, 303, 306, 307, 436, 437, 514, n. 11, 590.
tapas (*tapoloka*), 528.
tamas, darkness, as a *guṇa*, 535, 539.
tarakṣu, offered to Rakṣases, 324.
tarka, reflection, 591.
tarpaṇa, ceremony, 213.
tānūnaptra, ceremonial, 166, 309, 385, 399, 473.
tāpasa, Indian as contrasted with Christian, 447.
tābuva, alleged identity with taboo, 632, 633.
titaū, Iranian form, 8.
tithi, lunar day, not early Vedic, 28, n. 2.
taijasa, as soul state, 569, n. 6.
taimāta, dubious sense of, 26, n. 4, 81, n. 2.
turāyaṇa iṣṭi, sacrifice, 324.
tūṣṇīṁjapa, in morning litany, 315.
triṣṭubh, metre, 255.
tvakṣ, fashion, 205.
tvac, *see* Skin.

tha, imperative termination, 500, n. 9.

dakṣa, effective desire, 484.
dakṣiṇa, fire, 157, 159, 254, 268, 288, 316, 317, 318, 320, 321, 322, 344, 473.
dakṣiṇā, as epithet of Dawn, 121.
dakṣiṇās, fees, 299, 352, 495.
datta, give, *dāna*, gift, 480.
dadhikrā, sense of, 190.
dayadhvam, be compassionate, *dayā*, pity, 480.
darbha, grass, 70, 89, 142, n. 3, 329, 364, 366, 367, 372, 397, 430, 445, 472.
darvī, ladle, 254, 359.
daçapeya, offering, 342.
daçarātra, ten-day rite, 335.
daçahotṛ, formula, 356, 394.
dasra, wonder workers, 114.
Dākṣāyaṇa, form of new and full-moon sacrifice, 320.
dānastutis, praises of gifts, 250, 400.
dāman, in Avesta, 487, n. 6.
dāmyata, be subdued, 480.
dīkṣā, consecration, 182, n. 10, 276, 285, 300–3, 306, 336, 341, 377, n. 2, 401, 629 ; etymology of, 302.
duḥkha, pain, 556, 559, n. 11.
durvarāha, not sacrificed, 324.
durhārdasa, unpleasant, 556, nn. 2, 8.
dūrvā, plant, 142, n. 3.
deva, sense of term, 75, 76, 231, 232.
devajana, kind of deity, 76.
devanid, sense of, 616.
devayajña, in domestic ritual, 215, 359, 361.
devayāna, way of the gods, 14, 15, 160, 575, 576.
daiva, form of marriage, 330.
druj, hostile spirit, 34, 38, 239, 469.
droṇakalaça, wooden vessel, 255.
dvādaça, year, 4, n. 6.
dvādaçāha, twelve-day offering, 177, 178, 314, 335, 350.

dhammayāna, Buddhist term, 550.
dharma, law, 361, 479, 481, 516, n. 5, 517, 518.
dharman, law, 84, n. 4, 249, 479.
dharmya, 547.
dhāman, form or abode, 487.
dhāyyās, verses in Çastras, 315, 316.
dhāraṇā, fixing in memory, 372, 591.
dhārāgrahas, cups, 329.
dhiṣaṇā, might, 401 ; *see also* Dhiṣaṇā.
dhiṣṇyas, of priests, 328.
dhī, meditation, 251, 448, 556, 622.
dhīti, 448.
dhṛtavrata, of firm ordinances, 479, n. 5.
dhṛti, libations, 344.
dhyāna, meditation, 391, 517, 555, n. 8, 556, n. 1.
dhruva, cup, 329.

nakra, offered to Varuṇa, 175.
naraka loka, hell, 409.
na (or *nā*) *vartanna* (apparently *nava* and *vṛt*), in Mitanni, 617.
nānātva, difference, 483.
nāndīmukha, Fathers as, 427.
nāman, name, 455, 486, 554.
nāmarūpa, name and form, 530, 578, 579.
nārakāḥ, of hell, 410, nn. 6, 8.
nārāçaṅsa, cups, 329, 330.
niḥṣṭhā, concentration, 517.
nigadas, not used in domestic ritual, 359, 459.
nidhana, finale of Sāman, 314.
niyati, as final principle, 550.
niyama, self-restraint, 591.
nirūḍhapaçubandha, offering, 324.
nirvaruṇatvāya, to evade Varuṇa, 97, n. 3.
nirveda, indifference, 504.
nivid, inserted verses, 253, 295, 315, 316.
nivṛtti, refraining from activity, 483.
niṣad, form of literature, 492, n. 1.

nīlagrīva, epithet of Rudra, 142.
neti, negative of absolute, 491, 506, 521.
nyagrodha, tree, 23, 341, 363; as home of Apsarases, 184.
nyāsa, renunciation, 515.

panzavartanna (probably connected with *pañca*, and possibly with *vṛt*), Mitanni, 617.
pañcahotṛ, formula, 356,
pañcāvattins, those who make five portions, 313.
paṭiccasamuppāda, formula of causation of misery, 564, n. 1.
patnīsaṁyājas, offerings to the gods with their wives, 320.
parijman, epithet of various gods, 114.
paridhānīyās, concluding verses, 256.
pariplavā, vessel, 329.
parivartinī, form of arrangement of verses, 314.
pariṣad, assembly, 492.
parisaṁkhyāna, enumeration, 548.
parīkṣya, matters requiring investigation, 556.
parokṣa, beyond perception, 482.
parokṣakāma, loving the recondite, 456, n. 8.
parokṣapriya, 456, n. 8.
paropta, of dead, 417.
parṇa, tree, purifying influence of, 420.
palāça, wood, 319, 341, 363, 365.
pavamāna, epithet of Soma, 167; form of Agni, 317.
pavāka (i. e. *pāvaka*), form of Agni, 317.
pāka, offerings, 359, 588.
pāṭā, plant, 402, n. 5.
pāṇi, *see* Hands.
pātnīvata, cup, 330, 334.
pāda, *see* Feet.
pāpa, evil, 249, 479, n. 7.
pāpa-kṛtyā, 479, n. 5.
pāpman, evil, 381.
pāyu, *see* Anus.
pārtha, libations, at *rājasūya*, 341.
pārvaṇa çrāddha, fortnightly offerings, to the dead, 428.
pāvīravī, daughter of the lightning, 173.
piṇḍapitṛyajña, offering to the Fathers, 429, 430.
pitu, used of Soma, 167.
pitṛyajña, in domestic ritual, 360, 361, 430, 431; in *sākamedhas*, 322.
pitṛyāṇa (° *yāna*), way of the Fathers, 14, 160, 575, 576.
puṁsavana, ceremony, 366, 367.
puṇya, good, merit, 479, n. 7.
putra, derivation of, 580.
pudgala, person, 547.
pudgalavāda, in Buddhism, 547.
punarādheya, 289, 317, 318, *and see* Re-establishment of the fires.
punarmṛtyu, *see* Renewed death.
puruṣa, spirit (cosmic and individual), 104, 208, 220, 261, 282, 352, 355, 405, 437, 438, 444, 452, 453, 454, 469, 503, 511, 524, 535, 536, 537, 542, 544, 558, 559, 562, 582, n. 5, 586, 619–21.
puruṣasūkta, 8, 104, 125, 189, 352, 405, 438, 480, 486, 602.
puronuvākyā, verse, 294, 295.
puroruc, verses in Çastras, 253, 315.
pūtabhṛt, vessel, 255, 329.
pūrta çrāddha, form of offerings to the dead, 427.
pṛṣatī, steeds of the Maruts, 151.
pṛṣṭhya ṣaḍaha, form of sacrifice, 323, 330, 348, 350, 351.
prakṛti, base form of sacrifice, 313.
prakṛti, nature, 483, 510, 532–5, 559, 562, 604.
pragātha, form of verse, 253, 314, 315.
prajñā, consciousness, intellect, 513, 548, 554, 556, 557, 568.
prajñātman, conscious or intelligent self, 557.
prajñānaghana, made up of intelligence, 520, n. 2.
prajñāmātrā, intellect-elements, 557.
pratipad, in Çastras, 315.
pratihāra, part of Sāman, 314.
pratyakṣa, perception, 482; in Dignāga, 559, 560.
pratyāhāra, suppression of the organs of sense, 591.
pradhāna, matter, 549.
prapitva, sense of, 255.
prabhūtas, represent material world, 534.
pramantha, alleged connexion with Prometheus, 38, 289, n. 2.
pravat, sense of, 411.
pravara, enumeration of seer ancestors of sacrificer, 319.
pravargya, sacrifice, 68, 213, 255, 309, 327, 332, 333, 435, 490.
pravṛtti, activity, 483.
prastara, bundles of grass as representing the sacrificer, 320.
prastāva, part of Sāman, 314.
prājña, as soul state, 569, n. 6.
prājña ātman, 520, n. 2, 569.
prāṇa, breath collectively, or specifically expiration, 209, 403, 404, 531, 553, 554, 556, 564, 565.
prāṇas, breaths, 352, 452, 454, 531, 553, 556, 564, 565, 589.
prāṇamaya, epithet of self, 518.
prāṇāyāma, regulation of the breath, 591.